EVE CURIE
ALEXANDER WOOLLCOTT
LUDWIG BEMELMANS
THOMAS MANN
GEORGE R. LEIGHTON
VINCENT McHUGH
JOHN DOS PASSOS
W. SOMERSET MAUGHAM
GEORGE SANTAYANA
H. W. FOWLER
C. K. OGDEN
FRANK MOORE COLBY
JAMES THURBER
R. B. CUNNINGHAME GRAHAM
VIRGINIA WOOLF
HON. JOHN M. WOOLSEY
E. M. FORSTER
SARAH ORNE JEWETT
RING LARDNER
ERNEST HEMINGWAY
JOHN STEINBECK
M. F. K. FISHER
CHRISTINA STEAD
JULES ROMAINS
ROGER MARTIN DU GARD
A. E. COPPARD
W. F. HARVEY
MAX BEERBOHM
CONRAD AIKEN
E. B. WHITE
S. J. PERELMAN
BERTRAND RUSSELL
KATHERINE ANNE PORTER
KIN HUBBARD
DONALD CULROSS PEATTIE
JUSTICE OLIVER WENDELL HOLMES

Reading I've Liked

A PERSONAL SELECTION
DRAWN FROM TWO DECADES
OF READING AND REVIEWING
PRESENTED WITH AN
INFORMAL PROLOGUE AND
VARIOUS COMMENTARIES

BY

Clifton Fadiman

SIMON AND SCHUSTER
NEW YORK
1941

MANUFACTURED IN THE UNITED STATES OF AMERICA
AMERICAN BOOK—STRATFORD PRESS, INC., NEW YORK

PRESENTING

My thanks are due to:

D. Appleton-Century Co., Inc., for their permission to quote from The Salzburg Tales by Christina Stead, copyright, 1934, by D. Appleton-Century Co., Inc. The Bobbs-Merrill Company for their permission to quote from Abe Martin's Pump by Kin Hubbard, copyright, 1929. Mrs. Kin Hubbard for selection of excerpts from her husband's writings. Harcourt, Brace and Company, Inc., for permission to reprint Noon Wine by Katherine Anne Porter, copyright, 1939, by Katherine Anne Porter; and to reprint two essays from Abinger Harvest by E. M. Forster, copyright, 1936, by E. M. Forster. Brandt & Brandt for the selection from Seven Men by Max Beerbohm, copyright, 1920, by Max Beerbohm and published by Alfred A. Knopf, Inc.; and for selections from Adam and Eve and Pinch Me by A. E. Coppard, copyright, 1922, by A. E. Coppard and published by Alfred A. Knopf, Inc. The Clarendon Press, Oxford, England, for permission to quote from Fowler's Modern English Usage. J. M. Dent & Sons, Ltd., London, for permission to include W. F. Harvey's "August Heat" from The Midnight House. John Dos Passos and his publishers, Harcourt, Brace and Company, Inc., for permission to reprint excerpts from U.S.A. by John Dos Passos, copyright, 1937, by John Dos Passos. Doubleday, Doran and Company, Inc., for permission to reprint three stories from The Mixture as Before by W. Somerset Maugham, copyright, 1940, by W. Somerset Maugham; to reprint one chapter from Madame Curie by Eve Curie, copyright, 1937, by Doubleday, Doran & Co., Inc.; to reprint an essay from Rodeo by R. B. Cunninghame Graham, copyright, 1936, by Doubleday, Doran & Co., Inc.; to reprint an essay from The Hogarth Essays, copyright, 1928, by Doubleday, Doran & Co., Inc. Harper & Brothers for permission to reprint in its entirety My Life and Hard Times by James Thurber, copyright, 1933, by James Thurber; to reprint a selection from America's Growing Pains by George R. Leighton, copyright, 1939, by Harper & Brothers; to reprint two chapters from Serve It Forth by M. F. K. Fisher, copy-

copyright, 1939, by John Steinbeck; The Thibaults by Roger Martin du Gard, copyright, 1939, by The Viking Press, Inc.; and The Grapes of Wrath by John Steinbeck, copyright, 1939, by John Steinbeck.

To the editors of The New Yorker I am indebted for kind permission to reprint, in modified form, many passages from reviews that originally appeared in its pages. I am similarly obliged to the editors of The Nation for abetting me in one or two petty larcenies from myself.

Franklin P. Adams, Henry Seidel Canby, J. A. Goodman, M. Lincoln Schuster, Judge Sidney St. F. Thaxter of Portland, Maine, and Jerome Weidman gave much-appreciated help.

This compilation, whatever its merits or demerits, could never have been completed without the unfailing co-operation, relentless prodding, and stern good sense of my friend and assistant, Miss Bert Hunt, to whom I owe an unrepayable debt of gratitude.

C. F.

MY LIFE IS AN OPEN BOOK:
CONFESSIONS AND DIGRESSIONS
OF AN INCURABLE

Is it some constant nervous need for reassurance that makes human beings so alert to point out the capacities that separate them from the lower animals? Thus, we have rationality (I am hastily wiping that silly grin off my face), and the beasts do not. We use tools; they don't. Man, some solemn ass once pointed out, is an animal that laughs; animals do not laugh. We have long memories; beasts, save for the proverbial elephants, do not. We make war on each other and have at last, after much trial and error, learned how to exterminate our species, whereas the animals have to depend for their own destruction largely on the mere accidents of nature.

These are some of the criteria which man has set up to demonstrate his superiority. Criteria being cheap, I should like to add another. Man, modern man, is a word-making and word-reading animal. Both of us, I who compile this book, you who read it, are engaged in specifically human acts. Writing, and more especially reading, represent habits that we engage in constantly almost from the cradle to the grave. Civilized man is a reader. Irrevocably he would appear to be committed to the scanning of small black marks on plane surfaces. It is, when you come to think it over, an odd gesture, like the movement the camera catches of the heads of a tennis audience. But there it is—we are readers, and it's too late to change.

Some are more delivered over to the habit than others. With them reading has become as closely interwoven with life in general as, let us say, the killing of defenseless animals has become interwoven with the life of the (former) British hunting aristocracy. In both cases a hobby has developed into a passion, and this passion colors all others. There is no doubt, for instance, that a fox-slaughtering man makes love in a manner subtly different from the way a non-fox-slaughtering man does. The same must be true of an omnivorous reader and a more desultory one. In some cases the impulse to read (and reflect on what one has read) dominates completely. Then you get queer but interesting specimens like Robert Burton, who wrote The Anatomy of Melancholy. In such a case reading has become a kind of disease, a fascinating, proliferating cancer of the mind.

Between Robert Burton and the Nazi who said, "When I hear the word culture I draw my revolver," stand the great majority of us, ranging all the way from the casual reader who can take his book or let it alone, to the reading enthusiast who knows that books are but a part of life but would feel a serious void if deprived of that part.

This collection is compiled by a reading enthusiast and will probably be read by others whose inclinations are somewhat similar. It might, then, be mildly appropriate to arrange this casual commentary in the form of some confessions—and digressions—of an incurable reader. I guarantee this as my first, last, and only venture into autobiography.

Those to whom reading is fated to become important generally shake hands with books early. But this is not always true. Many distinguished writers were blockheads at their letters until a comparatively advanced age. I think, however, of an undistinguished one who was a busy reader at four: me. My first book was entitled The Overall Boys. The Overall Boys was and doubtless still is a rousing tale of two devoted brothers, aged five and seven, and their monosyllabic adventures on a farm. The style was of transparent lucidity. I found The Overall Boys a perfect job then, and, looking back, I haven't yet been able to detect any flaws in it. I remember it in greater detail and certainly with greater pleasure than I do the 576-page novel I finished yesterday. At four I was convinced that The Overall Boys represented the peak of the art of narrative and sternly rejected all attempts to make me continue my reading adventures. This resistance endured for a lengthy period—about a week, I should say. Then I broke down, tried another book, and have been doing the same sort of thing ever since. But all devout readers will agree that my first literary judgment was correct. Everything after The Overall Boys has been anticlimax. The same new world can never be discovered twice. One's first book, kiss, home run, is always the best.

Between the ages of four and ten I read but moderately and with absolute catholicity. We had in our household the usual meaningless miscellany that accumulates if the parents are not specifically literary. Thus I read whatever lay behind the glassed-in shelves of two dreary-looking black-walnut bookcases. I devoured the standard "boys' books" scornfully discarded by my elder brother. I bored my way through at least ten volumes of an unreadable set of historical novels by some worthy named Mühlbach, I think, and got absolutely nothing from them; the same result would be achieved were I to read them now. I read an adventure story about the Belgian Congo that made an anti-imperialist out of me when I was eight; I have seen no reason to change my views since then. Something called Buck Jones at Annapolis similarly made me permanently skeptical of the warrior virtues.

I read an odd collection of "daring" books that many families of the period kept around the house, often hidden under lock and key: Reginald Wright Kaufman's The House of Bondage; something called The Yoke, which was on the same order; Maupassant complete, though this may not have been until I had reached the mature estate of twelve or thirteen; and similar luridnesses. These had no effect of any sort on me, as far I can recollect, though I suppose a psychoanalyst could, at a price, make me tell a different story.

The child reader is an automatic selecting mechanism. What he is not emotionally ready to absorb, his mental system quietly rejects. When in later years I became a teacher of literature I could never see the point in censoring my young charges' extracurricular reading. Very often the mothers (never the fathers) of my high-school students would ask me to explain my refusal to forbid Mary or John to read James Joyce's Ulysses. I never offered any satisfactory explanation except to say that if John or Mary were ready to understand Ulysses then they were ready to understand Ulysses, which was a Good Thing. If they were not ready to understand it, which was apt to be the case, then Ulysses would at most waste their time, on which

I was not prepared to set any exaggerated value. Often an anxious mother would inquire whether I didn't agree that the last chapter (Mrs. Leopold Bloom's uncorseted memories of an exuberant life) was shocking. My reply may have been frivolous, but it seems to me it contained the germ of the truth: that she found it shocking mainly because she had not had the chance to read Ulysses when she was seventeen, wherein Mary or John had an advantage over her. This generally closed, without settling, the controversy.

As you can see, part of my four-to-ten reading was unorthodox for a small child (I forgot to tell you that I also toddled through a volume of Ibsen, and found him impenetrable) but the unorthodoxies had no effect whatsoever. What I really liked was what any small boy or girl would like—what I was ready for. This included, of course, a moderate amount of what is called trash—the Rover Boys, Horatio Alger, Wild West yarns, Jack Harkaway, the whole conventional canon of those days.

I say trash. Actually such books are "trash" only by standards which should not be applied to children's reading. They have the incalculable value that listening to perfectly inane adult conversation holds for children: they increase the child's general awareness. They provide admittedly rough paradigms of character, motivation, life experiences. That is why it seems to me that the trash of my generation was superior to the trash of today. I submit that The Rover Boys in the Everglades and Frank on a Gunboat are preferable to Superman and his kind on two counts: they were cleanly and clearly written, and their characters were credible and not entirely unrelated to the child's experience. When I was nine I could learn something interesting about life from even such highly colored affairs as the Frank Merriwell series, but I know that my son can learn nothing whatsoever of genuine interest (that is, which he can check against the expanding universe within himself) from the comics. I believe firmly that the current juvenile literature of the impossible is meretricious compared with the honest hackwork my own generation enjoyed. I also think that the kids are about ready to kick over this thriller fare in favor of something saner and more natural.

During my younger years, mainly between the ages of eight and ten, I, like my contemporaries, read a few "good" books, though they were not recommended to me as good. Such recommendations are hardly necessary. The child, if reasonably intelligent, has almost infallible good taste. Probably his good taste reaches its peak at that time. We all felt, when we encountered Tom Sawyer or, to hit a lower lever, Thomas Bailey Aldrich's Story of a Bad Boy or, on a still lower level, that fine New England classic Lem (is it still read?) that these books had something not possessed by The Pony Rider Boys in the Ozarks. It wasn't that they were more exciting, for sometimes they weren't, but that they were more "real." The other books were read eagerly and with joy, and then forgotten—indeed, they were read to be forgotten, to be "finished." But Tom Sawyer was something you caught yourself remembering a week later, and a year later. I know now, of course, the reason the child feels these books is that the authors felt them. It is as simple as that. That is why the so-called "better" juveniles that flood the bookdealers' shelves every year—the skillfully constructed, highly educational, carefully suited-to-age, morally sanitary, psychologically impeccable children's books—don't really make much of a dent on the child's consciousness. They are constructed for "the market." I don't mean the commercial market, but the market that is supposed to be the child's brain, as if that brain were a kind of transaction center in which each transaction was expressible in definite educational quanta.

The trouble with these juveniles is that their authors are greatly interested in children and not at all interested in themselves. Now, when Mark Twain wrote Tom Sawyer and Huckleberry Finn he never stopped to figure out whether his "boy psychology" was correct, or whether his story was properly adapted to a given age level. He wrote because he was passionately interested in himself, and the Mississippi River in himself, and the boy still alive in himself. Children ever since have unconsciously felt this intense reality, and that's what they've loved.

They've loved Huckleberry Finn even though it is over their heads, or written in old-fashioned English or dialect, or concerned with events that happened a long time ago. The machine-turned juveniles of our own day are "carefully adapted to the child's understanding," and that isn't what the child really wants. The child wants to be puzzled—not too much, but just enough. He doesn't want the characters' motivations to be automatically clear to him. He wants the satisfaction of figuring them out. As a matter of fact, the child delights as much in ambiguity as he does in clarity. Alice in Wonderland is still an overwhelming favorite, not because it's so funny but because it's so strange; it's a wonderful, gorgeous puzzle.

In this connection I always think of a comment my great and good friend Hendrik van Loon made to me one day. Going over, for editorial purposes, one of his manuscripts intended primarily for children, I pointed out to him the large number of long, difficult words which, as I thought, youngsters would never understand. He merely said, "I put them in on purpose." I learned later what he meant: that long words tickle the fancy of children, that they like the slight atmosphere of mystery distilled by a really bang-up polysyllable.

I think also that children—just ordinary, wholesome children, not bookworms—are more sensitive to beautiful writing than is generally supposed. They'll read reams of careless prose with great enjoyment, but when they come across the real thing, they know it. I don't know how they know it, but they do. My own son is not overfond of books. Rather than forgo an airplane flight he would willingly see the Forty-second Street library vanish in flames. Two years ago I tried the young barbarian—he was about seven—on The Wind in the Willows, and he could make nothing of it. I tried him again some few months ago. He finished it with absorbed calm, clapped the book to, and said with finality, "Now, that's what I call well written!" He has never said this about any other book he's read, many of which he has "enjoyed" more. The fact is that The Wind in the Willows is the best-written book he has read so far, and he somehow knew it, though he had never been given any hint to affect his judgment.

The smooth confections the publishers turn out today are not well written in the sense that The Wind in the Willows is. They are merely correctly written. The authors in most cases have unconsciously curbed any impulse toward style, because style would express

themselves, whereas they are supposed to be writing for the sake of
the children. If they would forget all about the children and set down
freely and lovingly the child in themselves, they might by some
glorious accident produce masterpieces. Little Women was not written for little women or little men or little anybodies; it was the
expression of a passionate memory. When Louisa May Alcott set
herself to produce "juveniles," the result was often unsatisfactory,
except when her native genius outwitted her conscious resolutions.

I am a firm believer in the newer methods of understanding and
handling children. But it is arguable that they have made difficult
the creation of a twentieth-century Little Women or Alice in Wonderland. Such books are the product not of knowledge, or even of
wisdom, but of a kind of dream life, a dreaming-back to childhood
on the part of the writer. That dream life and "child psychology" do
not mix. That perhaps is why the modern child classics are not to
be found in books at all, but in the cartoons of Walt Disney, master
of an art newer, naïver, less touched by "science" than is the art of
literature.

This has been a long and prosy digression, and while I'm at it, I'd
like to make it a trifle longer. One of the games bibliomaniacs play
in their weaker moments is the game of Century-Hencery, or literary
prophecy. It's a harmless sport, the best part of it being that there
can never be a loser. Here's how it works. You list the ten books you
believe will be most widely read and generally admired a hundred or
five hundred or a thousand years from now. Then you defend your
choices. Making the unwarrantable assumption that in 2441 our civilization will still be recognizably related to that of 1941, I will now
set down the ten works of literary imagination produced by the
English-speaking race that I believe will be most universally alive (not
merely admired in the schoolroom) five hundred years from now.
Here they are, in no special order:

> The Plays of William Shakespeare
> Moby Dick
> Gulliver's Travels
> Robinson Crusoe

Alice in Wonderland
Huckleberry Finn
Little Women
*Some novel of Charles Dickens, probably
David Copperfield or Pickwick Papers*
Treasure Island
The Mother Goose Rhymes

It is possible that in constructing this list I have been ingenious rather than ingenuous. Whether by accident or design it reflects one of my favorite theories—that the gods tend to grant immortality to those books which, in addition to being great, are loved by children. For mark well that only two books out of the ten—Shakespeare and Moby Dick—cannot, generally speaking, be enjoyed by youngsters. Of the remaining eight, seven are usually ranked as children's favorites. My point is simple: as the generations pass, children's tastes change more slowly than do those of grownups. They are not affected by the ukases of critics or the whims of literary fashion. Thus Shakespeare was not universally admired by the eighteenth century and again may not be (though I'd place a small bet against that possibility) by the twenty-third. But the rhymes of Mother Goose—to my mind literature, even if of a simple order—have suffered no diminution of popularity and, being unmoved by the winds of literary doctrine, are not likely to suffer any.

This is what happens. All children who read at all are introduced at a fairly early age to, let us say, Robinson Crusoe. Most of them like it. Later on they meet it again in school. They are told it is literature, and its hold on their minds is re-enforced. Still later, in adult life, they may encounter it again, when they are ripe to see in it qualities not apparent to them as children. Any possible resistance to accepting Robinson Crusoe as a great book had been broken down years ago during their childhood. Thus Robinson Crusoe's prestige remains undimmed. But a classic of greater artistic weight, such as Paradise Lost, does not enjoy the advantage of having been liked by readers as children. It is read by a small, select group of adults (college students) and so never passes into the consciousness of the generality. I do not mean that Milton will not be read five hundred years from now. I mean he will not be a casually accepted, generally enjoyed classic as I think Little Women or even Treasure Island (the most uncertain item, by the way, on my list) is apt to be. But remember, the book must be literature to begin with. Defoe's Robinson Crusoe will live, but A. R. Wyss' The Swiss Family Robinson is already dying.

We talk a great deal about the Greek classics. Yet what Greek classic has really penetrated among us? Not Plato surely, or any of the dramatists, but Homer and more particularly the simple, beautiful Greek myths that are read with pleasure by each generation of children. Similarly, I think Perrault and The Three Musketeers will outlast Proust and Stendhal, and Grimm's fairy tales still be widely read when Goethe is forgotten. If you wish to live long in the memory of men, perhaps you should not write for them at all. You should write what their children will enjoy. Or, to put it in another way and use a phrase that I think belongs to Lewis Mumford, a book already has one leg on immortality's trophy when "the words are for children and the meanings are for men."

May I make one or two further random comments on this list? Note that three titles—Moby Dick, Robinson Crusoe, and Treasure Island—have no women characters to speak of, and several of the others depend hardly at all on romantic interest. I do not believe that love, commonly considered one of the great staples of literature, tends as a subject to have any supreme preservative value. It is Dickens' sentiment and humor, not his lovers, that attract us. It is hardly the most romantic of Shakespeare's plays that stand highest in popular esteem. And Melville, in providing his masterpiece with an all-male cast, knew what he was doing.

Finally, if I were asked to make a wild stab at the one book likely to outlast the nine others, I would name Alice in Wonderland. This does not mean it is the "best" book on the list, for obviously it is not. In the end the best survives but the best of the best does not necessarily survive longest. Mankind will cling to what it admires, but even more fiercely will it cling to what it loves. And what we love perhaps above all else (as Dr. Freud pointed out in other and more dismaying connections) is ourselves as children. That is why I think it quite conceivable that Lewis Carroll will be read at some remote future time when Shakespeare is no more remembered than, let us say, Plautus and Terence are today. Twenty centuries from now Shakespeare may be entirely owned and operated by scholars. But I do not see why people should not still be laughing and exclaiming over Alice in Wonderland. Among the few things resistant to the tooth of time, great fantasy is one, and great fantasy is always the special possession of children.

I seem to have abandoned myself some pages back. I had just reached the age of ten. Between ten and seventeen I did the major bulk of my reading. I have never read as many books (I don't mean manuscripts) per year since, nor do I expect to in the future. Those were the splendid years, and it is my notion that they are the splendid years of most devoted readers. After seventeen (in some cases a year or two later) the books choose you, not you the books. You read within limits. Reading becomes a program. You read as part of your college curriculum, or to gain knowledge in a specific field, or to be able to bore your neighbor at dinner-table conversation. Adult reading is usually purposive. In my own case—I shall speak of this later on— it is more than purposive. I make a living by it.

Even the reading done during one's college years lacks the spontaneity, the high waywardness of one's pre-adolescent and adolescent reading. It circles around the classroom. It consists of authors recommended by authority or who you feel should be "covered." Or it has to do with books you know a good deal about in advance, one of the most effective ways to spoil one's reading pleasure. Such reading may be mentally stimulating or socially useful. It may benefit you in a dozen ways. But it is not an adventure in quite the same sense that reading in your second decade so often is.

I am not, in this random biblio-autobiography, proposing to list the books I have read. Nothing could be duller or less useful, except when he who does the listing owns a mind whose operations are really of interest to mankind, as was the case, for example, with John Stuart Mill. All I am here endeavoring to do is to outline some of the processes whereby an average person became an above-the-average reader, which is what I immodestly claim to be. To understand these processes a mere catalogue of titles is of no avail.

Yet I would like to list a few names, mainly to indicate the kind of writer that, as I recall, influenced the more bookish boys and girls of my generation. Shaw, Galsworthy, Bennett, Conrad, Merrick, Barrie, Moore, Dunsany, Yeats, Synge, Swinnerton, Chesterton, Meredith, Wilde, Hewlett, Gissing, Zangwill, and above all H. G. Wells— these, to confine the list to Englishmen only, are a few of the authors I remember devouring from my tenth to my eighteenth year, miscomprehending many, overprizing some, but getting from all an exultant sense of discovery, a peak-in-Darien thrill rarely enjoyed since.

The secret of second-decade reading, of course, is that you are not really finding out what Shaw thinks or Conrad feels, but what you think and you feel. Shaw and Conrad and the rest are but handy compasses to guide you through the fascinating jungle of your young self. When I read Wells' Tono-Bungay at fourteen or fifteen, I found myself saying in delight, "But that's just the way I feel!" When I now read Thomas Mann's Joseph story I find myself thinking how true it is to the experience of men in general. There is a difference in the quality of the emotion. The grown-up emotion may be larger and wiser (and probably more pompous), but the boyish one is unique just because it is so utterly, innocently self-centered.

During this adolescent period of my reading life I had a lucky break. My brother, five years my senior and a student at Columbia College, was at the time taking a conventional survey course that used a sound standard anthology known, I think, as Century Readings in English Literature, edited by Cunliffe, Pyre, and Young. For some reason, possibly a mild fraternal sadism, he made me take the course along with him—he at college, I at home. The whole thing was over my head—I was fourteen—but when I had finished my Century Readings, which took a year, I had at least a hazy notion of the course and development, from Beowulf to Stevenson, of the most magnificent, after the Greek, of all literatures. I remember writing essays, perhaps no more interminable than my subjects, on Hakluyt and Spenser. I am still unable to dislodge from my memory—which is not a good one—odd lines of verse from subminor poets like Drayton. That is all of no account. The important thing is that I got through my head at an early age a few simple truths: that the proper reading of a good writer requires energy and application; that reading is not mere "diversion"; that it is impossible to admire writing you do not understand; that understanding it does not destroy but rather enhances its beauty; that unless a writer's mind is superior to, more complicated than, your own, it is a bore to read him. (That is why I never recommend a book to a person if it is on his own mental level.)

I learned also that daydreaming and intelligent reading do not go together. There is a story told by Dr. Sandor Ferenczi, the psychoanalyst, about a Hungarian aristocrat who, while devouring a quick lunch between trains, was recognized by a boorish acquaintance.

"My dear Count! How are you?"

"Umph."

"And how is the Countess?"

"Dead."

"How shocking! It must be terrible for your daughter."

"She's dead."

"But your son—"

"Dead! Everybody's dead when I'm eating!"

During my all-out period everybody was dead when I was reading. Most children and adolescents know this magical secret of concentration, though it is not till they are older and duller that they realize it was magical.

I remember that, when I was fourteen, we lived about two miles from the nearest library. I had a choice. I could cycle there, borrow my books, and cycle back in a very few minutes—but those few minutes were lost to reading. Or, if I wished, I could walk to the library, reading the last fifty or seventy-five pages of my calculatedly unfinished book en route, make my borrowings, and walk back, reading a new volume on the way. I usually preferred the latter procedure. It is no trick at all to read while walking, to step off and onto curbs with unconscious skill, to avoid other pedestrians while your eyes are riveted to the page. There was a special pleasure in it: I had outwitted Father Time. I think Providence meant me to be an ambulant reader, for I never once even stumbled. But one afternoon when I was cycling home from the library with my wire basket full of books, I was hit from behind by a car and sent sprawling.

This absorption, this "losing yourself" in a book, though clearly quite remote from "practical life" (for children "practical life" is simply what grownups want them to do), is not daydreaming. The child does not interpose a continuous, fuzzy, wavering screen of personal desires and wishful visions between himself and the page. On the contrary, he and the page are one. The Victorian female, with whom novel reading was a disease, was the real daydreamer. For her, reading became a drug, a kind of literary marijuana, an instrumentality for the production of needed visions. The child's hearty relation to his book is devoid of this sick quality.

Well, the course my brother gave me, via that blessed trinity Cunliffe, Pyre, and Young, was calculated to make me understand that literature, beyond helping one to discover oneself, has a higher, more impersonal function. It is a challenge issued by a higher mind, the author's, to a lower mind, the reader's. Even if the challenge is not met, much pleasure may still result. But if it is met, or if a sincere attempt to meet it is made, a finer, rarer pleasure is experienced. If you read for pure diversion, well and good, but if you read for any other purpose, always read above yourself. One of the reasons for the general mental fuzziness of most "cultivated" people we know is that publishers have become too shrewd. They have learned, the cunning little fellows, just how to temper their books to the lamb-like mental innocence of their readers. The result is that every week we are deluged with books which, the publishers assure us, we can understand. It is quite true. We can understand them, all too easily. It would be much better for us if now and then we read a book just a few rungs beyond our mental capacities in their most relaxed state.

My second-decade reading—and I think this is sadly true of most of us—was in this sense educationally more valuable than any I have done since, with certain notable (and I shall note them later) exceptions. During adolescence our feeling of bewilderment and insecurity tends to be greater than at any other time. Hence the need to know, to learn, is greater. Therefore whatever reading is done is intense. It is utterly assimilated. We pay absorbed attention to it, as we would to the instructions of an expert before venturing into a trackless forest.

It seems to me that in my late teens I did more "heavy" reading and digested it more thoroughly than at any succeeding period. In this connection I recall two antithetical experiments I made extending over an interval of six months. The first was an experiment in difficult reading. The other was an experiment in nonreading.

One summer I decided to spend my evenings reading only "hard" books. I went at it with the humorless obstinacy of a sixteen-year-old—and I was more humorless and more obstinate than most. I staggered wildly through stuff like Ueberweg's History of Philosophy, Winwood Reade's Martyrdom of Man, Saintsbury's History of English Prosody, Taine's History of English Literature, Gibbon's Decline and Fall of the Roman Empire. It was enough for a book to seem important and forbidding—I read it at once. No novels, no light literature of any sort, no magazines for three solid months—hot months, too. Now, as I look back on this extravagant experiment, it seems like the disagreeable behavior of a young prig. Yet I was not really priggish; I didn't read for show-off purposes. I read my Ueberweg as a challenge to myself, as a test, as a deliberate gesture, if you will, of self-punishment. The boy of sixteen by overexercise will punish his body deliberately just to see how much it can take. That same boy may punish his mind in the same way. It is a kind of initiation ceremony that he performs upon himself, a queer, grotesque test of approaching manhood. Sometimes he will decide to go right through The Encyclopaedia Britannica.

The notable part of the experience is that just because that summer's reading came out of a powerful emotional impulse it has stuck with me, as more formal reading, particularly that done as part of my school work, has not. Also, it left me with a taste for a certain kind of "difficult" reading, a taste which, because I am a book reviewer, I rarely have an opportunity to indulge. This does not mean that I read heavy books with ease. On the contrary, I have to go through painful mental struggles to understand them, but the struggle still gives me an odd satisfaction, which I know has something to do with that lunatic summer I spent perusing nothing but huge volumes several miles above my head.

Today, for example, the books I look forward with most pleasure to reading and reviewing are books of popular science, of the Hogben-Julian Huxley-Eddington type. I am not really competent to judge them, but I like to read them, perhaps primarily because for me—I am a scientific illiterate—they present challenging difficulties. It may be an illusion, but I always feel, when I have finished a book of this sort, that I have "got" something out of it. I hardly ever get this feeling from a novel or a conventional biography.

Well, that was Experiment Number One. The second was its polar opposite. I decided to spend three months reading nothing at all, not even a daily newspaper. (The three months coincided with a long absence from school, so the conditions for the experiment were at their optimum.) Now, why did I want to do this? It was again a matter of self-testing. I felt I had grown too dependent upon other people's ideas. The only way I could perceive to cure myself of this dependence was to abjure other people's ideas completely. The mental life of the adolescent is frequently characterized by this oscillatory quality. He can find out what his real nature is only by leaping from one extreme to the other.

And so for three months I read, as nearly as I can recall, virtually nothing. It was by no means a fruitless experiment, and to those held too tightly in the grip of the reading habit I heartily recommend it. The effect is purgative. The mind disgorges a good deal of waste and clutter, it slows down, for a time it seems vacant. Then gradually it fills again, this time not with the myriad, secondhand impressions induced by nonstop reading, but with the few clear ideas and desires that reflect more accurately your true self. The experience, in addition to being cleansing, is humbling; you realize how sparse is the net content of your mind.

I have known men and women who read so voraciously and continuously that they never have the time or opportunity to discover who they really are. Indeed, I suspect it is precisely because they prefer not to make that discovery that they cling so limpetlike to books. I suppose this is better for them than alcohol or hasheesh, but it is not very different. All of us, I am sure, have noticed people who suffer from reader's fidgets. If there is a book, a magazine, any piece of print within easy reach, they will at once take it up, idly, without real intent to peruse it, but out of a kind of mechanical compulsion. They will do this while they are talking to you, while you are talking to them, while engaged in some other activity. They are victims of print. Perhaps some dim premonition that unless I watched out I too would become afflicted with reader's fidgets made me carry through with entire success my three months' literary fast.

Some years ago I helped to manage a bookstore featuring a circulating library. The main body of customers consisted of commuters. Every evening, a few minutes after five, the commuters would dash in.

"Give me a novel!"

"Any special title?"

"No, any novel will do: it's for my wife"—as if that somehow made everything clear.

These commuters' wives—there are tens of thousands of them— were not really in any active sense doing any reading at all. They were taking their daily novel in a numbed or somnambulistic state. They were using books not for purposes of entertainment, but as an anodyne, a time-killer, a life-killer. Many "great readers" are of this class. Truth to tell, they have never read a book in their lives.

Akin to these novel-addicts are the newspaper fiends who read three, four, or five papers a day and supplement them with radio news reports. There is only one Keeley cure I can recommend for this weakness, and that is for these people to save their papers for a week, and go back and read the news of seven days before. They will then see, even in the short perspective thus provided, how contradictory, foolish, ineptly stated most "spot news" is. They will perceive that, if taken in overfrequent doses, its main effect is to bewilder or even to frighten, rather than to inform. A ration of one newspaper a day ought to be enough for anyone who still prefers to retain a little mental balance.

Serious reading is an art. An art is something you have to learn. To learn an art requires a teacher. There are too few such teachers of reading in the United States, and that is one of the reasons why we are still only a semieducated people. I, like my fellow Americans, was never taught, in elementary and high school, how to read properly. Thus, when I reached college, I was but ill-equipped to understand any really original book that was handed to me, though I found no particular difficulty in getting through the required textbooks, manuals, and other predigested matter. I do not think I would ever have learned how to read had it not been for one man and one college course.

The man was John Erskine and the course was, rather absurdly, called Honors. Erskine himself was largely responsible for the conception underlying Honors, which in turn was the only begetter of Robert Hutchins' Chicago Plan, of the St. John's College classics curriculum, and in fact of the whole return in modern education to the great tradition of Western thought. John Erskine is a man of such varied talents that his original contribution to American education is often forgotten.

It is very hard to explain why Erskine was a great teacher. He was not a character as Copeland of Harvard was. Although always genial and fair, he never attempted to make the students like him. He did not act as if he were a perennial contestant in a popularity contest. (I am convinced, by the way, that those teachers who year after year are voted Most Popular by the undergraduates are rarely educators of great value.) In his literature courses Erskine never swooned over beauty or tried to make you "feel" the lines or the paragraph.

There were two things about Erskine that may help to explain the influence he wielded over his students, even over those who didn't care greatly about literature. One was his enormous respect (not merely liking) for his subject matter. This may seem a commonplace, but it is not. Many teachers—no more surprisingly than other frustrated human beings—have a silent, gnawing contempt for what they teach. Unaware of this contempt, they often find it subtly translated into a resentment of their students. The result is vitiated teaching, teaching of a purely formal sort.

Erskine not only loved his subject but reverenced it and respected himself for teaching it. There was thus a good moral relationship between himself and his work. It may seem high-flown to say that this moral relationship was a vital aid in the production of good teaching. Yet I'm sure this was the case. He could teach his students to read because he had a large and lofty attitude toward what we were reading.

At the same time, if Erskine had been able to communicate only this attitude, he would not have been the great teacher he was. He went beyond this. To put it simply, he challenged us to understand what we were reading. He called upon us for a kind of mental exercise that is ordinarily devoted to mastering such "hard" subjects as philosophy and the sciences. (Actually, there are no "hard" or "easy" subjects. Donne is as difficult and as rewarding as Euclid.) Erskine made us work and the odd thing about it was that the more we understood, the more we liked the particular book we were reading.

The Honors Course was but a systematic extension of the Erskine educational program. For two years, under the guidance of a group of selected instructors, we read and talked about one great book a week, beginning with Homer and concluding, as I recollect, with William James. That was all there was to the course, and it was by far the most valuable one I took at college. You will find a good account of it and its influence in How to Read a Book. (Mortimer Adler was also one of my teachers, and a first-rate one, too.)

This course in the classics has had a somewhat souring effect on my work as a reviewer. Just because I was forced to spend a week on Fielding's Tom Jones, I could not possibly, let us say, hail Anthony Adverse as a great novel. I have been compulsorily provided with a standard of comparison that proves a handicap to me. I may seem curmudgeonly and grudging when really my whole trouble is that I cannot forget my Honors class.

Well, Erskine and a few other teachers (particularly the poet Mark Van Doren) plus the two years I spent in the excellent company of fifty or sixty of the great writers of all time taught me, I hope and believe, how to read. Later on, a year or so after I was graduated, I myself helped in a fumbling way to teach this same course to others. They weren't college students. They were laborers, clerks, recently naturalized Americans—just men and women of imperfect education but reasonable intelligence and great willingness to think. The group of which I was one taught Plato and Gibbon and Montaigne and Thomas Aquinas to small classes all over the city, in public libraries, Y.M.C.A. classrooms, and at Cooper Union. We taught them to anybody who cared to learn how to read the best. I, of course, learned more than my students, but the most valuable part of what I learned was that the abundant wealth of great literature lies open to anyone with a functioning brain. The great books have no particular home. They do not belong only behind college walls. But fifteen years ago the notion that they were anybody's property was a novel one. Today that is all changing. Today the universal appeal of our Western tradition is readily acknowledged. You can turn your radio dial (at the moment, at least) and listen to a discussion of these same books by three competent readers and talkers, one of whom, Mark Van Doren, originally taught this same Honors group in Columbia way back in the early twenties, when all the world was young, lad, and all the trees were green.

I had the good luck, as I say, to be a member of this college Honors group. But, as it happens, during those same college years, I engaged in a number of extracurricular activities, some of which by accident re-enforced my interest in reading, writing, and talking about books. Two of these jobs I particularly remember.

For the better part of a year I acted as reader to a charming and generous lady who had once been a fairly well-known actress. Her eyesight was impaired and it was my job not only to read to her but to select the reading matter. I chose whatever book happened to interest me at the moment, and this high-handed procedure seemed to work out quite smoothly. One learns a great deal about literature in general from reading even one good book aloud slowly. Our forefathers, for whom such reading was a usual thing, read fewer books than we do, but probably also had a finer feeling for literary values than we have. It is regrettable that modern living makes impossible the practice of reading aloud. Perhaps the radio can do something about it. My hunch is that if it can develop a group of really first-class narrators (not actors, which is a different thing entirely) their efforts would in time attract a good-sized audience. Experiments in this direction have already been made, but with insufficient backing.

Another odd job I had during my college years resulted in a closer acquaintance with the works of William Shakespeare than I would ordinarily have secured. One afternoon the college job-placement bureau (to whom I really owe my college education, for without the bureau I would never have been able to pay for it) sent me to see a prospective employer. Let us call him Mr. Jones.

I was informed that Mr. Jones wanted a reader. (It turned out that this was not precisely the case.) He was about seventy-five. He looked like a slightly insane old wolf. In fact, in his more vigorous years, he had been a wolf, a wolf of the Wall Street variety, a terrific, ruthless plunger the legend of whose feats was yet green in the memories of the Wall Street Hot Stove League. Though he still visited his office regularly, Mr. Jones' interest in the market had gradually attenuated, and its place, so far as I could judge, was now taken up by a miscellaneous assortment of activities, including an extraordinary kind of golf (see below), the making and imbibing of Martinis, furious running quarrels with his household—and the study of Shakespeare. I was the Shakespeare boy. I learned later that I was merely the latest of a long line.

I visited Mr. Jones three afternoons a week, from 3:30 to 6. Our routine never varied. I would knock on the door of his study on the fourth floor of a decaying but luxurious old house fit only to be the setting for a murder mystery. Mr. Jones would scream something —he never talked. I would yell out my name (which he never remembered) and then shout, "It's the young man!" Mr. Jones would admit the young man, violently lock the door of his study, and begin to pile chairs, a table, any easily movable furniture, against it. This barricade completed, he would shriek, "Now, you can't come in, you prowling apes!" or some similar phrase. Who these prowling apes were I never found out, though I got to know Mr. Jones fairly well.

Then, with his own hands, and very much as if he were an alchemist transmuting a base metal into gold, he would prepare a shakerful of Martinis (this was during prohibition). They were very good Martinis and I always wanted more than the one he allowed me. Mr. Jones would drink about six during the afternoon, always to the accompaniment of violent, self-accusatory exclamations: "This will be the death of me, I know it will, I'm killing myself, I'm my own murderer."

Mr. Jones was, as I have indicated, a Shakespeare addict, but of a highly specialized sort. He was really familiar, in an unintelligent way, with all of Shakespeare, but his particular interest lay in those passages of an inflammatory, lickerish, and erotic nature. He had, for example, memorized the whole of Venus and Adonis, a rather long poem. It was my duty, book in hand, to listen to him recite. It was mildly fantastic: the locked door with its furniture barricade, Mr. Jones hopping about, Martini in hand, quoting, in a voice that mingled a shriek, a snarl, and a whine, some torrid passage, and myself, crowded into a corner, doing my best to handle the old gentleman tactfully. Naturally, he would stumble from time to time, but woe to me if I prompted him! His emendations of Shakespeare were extraordinary but I soon found it expedient to let them stand.

On Saturdays we would repair to the golf links. I had two duties there. One was to keep shouting, as he addressed the ball, "Keep your head down!" The other was to listen to him recite his favorite passages of Shakespeare between strokes. The caddy, had he possessed any Elizabethan vocabulary, would surely have been shocked.

My association with Mr. Jones must have been satisfactory to him, or else his love of the bard gradually deepened, for one day he proposed to me an additional duty: that I accompany him downtown in his car every morning, attended by good old Shakespeare. As I got five dollars an hour for these services (ten on Saturdays, for some reason) and as I was receiving a free education in a great classic, I made no objection.

Now, this part of the story is somewhat indelicate. I must warn you that Mr. Jones, like many elderly people, was troubled with an inconvenient weakness of the bladder. In the morning we would start out in the car, Shakespeare going full blast. The drive took

about forty minutes. But forty minutes just about represented the
limit of Mr. Jones' endurance. The last five minutes of the drive may
have sounded something like this:

"Now quick desire—O God!—hath caught the yielding prey—how
much longer is it?—and glutton-like she feeds, yet never filleth—God
almighty, you're driving like a damned turtle—where was I?—Her lips
—her lips are conquerors, his lips obey—Lord, how everybody makes
me suffer!—his lips obey—Ow!—Paying what ransom the insulter
willeth—hurry, hurry, you confounded slow-coach!—O Lord!"

Shakespeare was never intoned in stranger circumstances. Sometimes art won and sometimes nature.

But Mr. Jones was the means whereby the works of Shakespeare,
or, at any rate, certain parts of them, became as familiar to me as
my own name. Mr. Jones died owing me twenty dollars, but I hold
no rancor. Take him all in all, he was a good boss. I shall not look
upon his like again.

In 1927, a couple of years after college had finished with me, I began
a new and entirely different course of reading, a course that lasted
almost a decade. I became an editorial assistant in what was then
an up-and-coming publishing house and is now a staid, highly respectable establishment. During a period of almost ten years I read millions upon millions of words, of which only the tiniest fraction were
the right ones in the right order. I have not read as much good literature as thousands of others have, but I think I have read as much
bad literature as any man or woman of my age. This is a boast that,
on the whole, I would prefer not to be able to make, for, except as
a means of making a living, I don't think the experience was particularly valuable.

It revealed to me one thing, however—the profound, unconscious
egotism of the human race. Our universal capacity for self-esteem has,
I am told, been remarked by other observers. Each of us makes the
discovery in his own way. My way involved the reading of twenty-
five hundred hopeless manuscripts each year for ten years.

It is a fact that no man will set out to knock together a bookcase
or repair a leak in the plumbing unless he knows how to handle the

tools required and has a fair notion of the problems involved. A
woman who has never boiled an egg in her life will not volunteer to
prepare a five-course dinner. Yet this same man, this same woman
will cheerfully write you a book, though he or she may not have the
remotest idea of how books are written.

There are no "born" writers. Writing can be an art. On its lower
levels it is certainly at least a craft, which means that it must be
learned. Yet I should say that not fifty out of the twenty-five hundred
would-be authors whose works I annually considered had even a
remote glimpse of this simple truth.

Most of the manuscripts were really disguised confessions—novels,
plays, poems, essays, each in one way or another an outlet for the
author's sense of his own personal tragedy or dilemma. They were not
books. They were diaries. They were merely a mechanism whereby the
author "expressed" himself. They were a circuitous and therapeutically
valueless substitute for the Catholic confessional, the psychoanalyst's
couch, or the ear of a friend. Particularly the last, for most of these
manuscripts supplied pathetic testimony to the spiritual loneliness of
so many of us Americans. They were voices crying in the dark.

But the voices—this was the unsettling part of it—had a note of
strident self-confidence. The authors of these manuscripts had no inkling that they were not writers but just people in trouble. They acted
like writers, they demanded criticism, and they were often sore when
they got it. It was all very odd.

And each hopeless manuscript represented at least a year or more
of its author's life. I used to reflect sadly on this enormous wastage,
on all the man-hours of energy that go annually into the useless production of unpublishable words. There should be some small central
editorial board (not one in each of sixty publishing houses) which
would act as a gentle discourager to all these well-meaning amateurs.
For a very small sum—say fifty cents—it would pass judgment on
manuscripts. But not on finished ones. Just the first chapter would
be enough—indeed, I may say in confidence, just the first paragraph.
No geniuses, I assure you, would be overlooked, no lives ruined, but
many perfectly amiable people would be saved from wasted effort and
eventual disillusionment.

My job as a publisher's reader, then, gave me a wholesome respect for the mere craft of writing. This respect I have never since lost. It is only after you have read a few million bad sentences that you realize what thought goes into the construction of a single good one.

This realization has probably saved the American public from at least one bad book. Had it not been for my editorial labors, had I not been driven to understand how the English language must not be misused, I would beyond the shadow of a doubt have written a novel. With publishing standards as generous, shall we say, as they are, it would have achieved publication. It is even possible that some of my present audience might have been seduced into reading it. But this did not happen and will never happen, a happy circumstance that you and I owe to my melancholy experience with twenty-five thousand examples of organized literary mediocrity.

I suppose, like any nasty old frustrated writer, I have had to secure my revenge somehow. Perhaps that accounts for the persistent, monotonous reiteration of my belief that most young American novelists (the ones who do get published) simply do not know their trade. I don't care what the richness or depth of their experience may be; they do not know the rules of rhetoric. The English language is a magnificently flexible instrument, but it asks of every writer that he use it with a certain regard for its possibilities and its limitations. The savage, spontaneous young people who rush their novels into print every year are superior to these possibilities and these limitations. It is true that they get by for a while on a certain childish freshness, a certain apparent originality. Then they are forgotten. But in the meantime they have cluttered up the book market, wasted the time of readers, and certainly contributed nothing to the clarification or development of sound literary standards. I hope this does not sound too righteous; it's so sore a point with me that I find it hard to be gently humorous. Every man, in addition to his formal religion, has a private religion, consisting of a set of ideas, or a hobby or perhaps, like Dubedat in The Doctor's Dilemma, a group of heroes. I have that feeling about the English language. I don't mean its great masters, but the tongue itself. I am myself a most indifferent wielder of English, but a sinner is not debarred from worship. And I think that, in our own strange, wild, headlong period, reverence for the language is growing rarer and rarer. When it is not present in professional writers, in those who owe their very being to it, I get depressed, and so, I think, do all those who really love the tongue they speak.

The plain fact of the matter is—every publisher knows it but which one will dare confess it?—that about twenty per cent of the new books issued are actually worth publishing, from a literary and, I daresay, even from a commercial point of view. I do not propose to discuss the conditions that account for the other eighty per cent. They are complex and somewhat technical. But every honest reviewer, when he goes back over the books of the preceding year (not at the time he reads each book) admits in his heart that the great majority of them were hardly worth the attention he gave them. It isn't that they are definitely bad, it's that they just aren't good enough, don't move enough people, don't contribute enough to the general sum of things to make their publication, involving the labor of thousands of men and women, worth while.

Since about 1915 the American publishing business has been over-producing beyond reason. Perhaps publishers are unconsciously realizing this, which would explain the emergence of so many excellent cheap reprint series, the new emphasis on the classics, and even such modest ventures as this volume itself.

I referred above to reviewers. Perhaps, in this prologue which so far consists almost entirely of digressions, here is as good a place as any to talk for a while about the reviewing business. For more than fifteen years I have been a reviewer of new books. That means that most of my reading during this period has been confined to ephemera, to books certainly better than those I read in manuscript form as a publisher's assistant, but not so much better (with the usual exceptions) that the world could not have wagged along quite well without them. I propose to talk for a few pages about this business of mine, for it has certainly played its part in the autobiography of this particular reader.

Note that in using the word "business," I employ it as a wedge with which to separate book reviewing from literary criticism. Literary criticism is an art, like the writing of tragedies or the making of love, and, similarly, does not pay. Book reviewing is a device for earning a living, one of the many weird results of Gutenberg's invention. Movable type made books too easy to publish. Some sort of sieve had to be interposed between printer and public. The reviewer is that sieve, a generally honest, usually uninspired, and mildly useful sieve.

To use an example conveniently near at hand, the compiler of this volume is such a sieve. To the best of my knowledge and belief I have never written a sentence of literary criticism in my life. Unless I become a vastly different person from what I now am, I never will. My colleagues and myself are often called critics, a consequence of the amiable national trait that turns Kentuckians into colonels and the corner druggist into Doc. But, no matter what my publishers may say, I am a mere book reviewer.

True literary criticism is a subtle and venerable art, going back to the ancient Hindoos, who doubtless wrote sanskriticism. Aristotle was the first great literary Poo-Bah. He had no more charm than an old knothole, but the things he said about narrative and drama are so sensible that they're still useful today. Aristotle had a first-rate mind, which is what most really good literary critics have, or something pretty near it. You can number the top-notchers on your fingers and toes—that's the way I taught my small son to count: Aristotle, Horace, Coleridge, Lessing, Sainte-Beuve, Taine, Goethe, Arnold, Shaw (one of the greatest), and a few others. In our own time and nation, literary criticism is almost a lost art, partly because no one except a few other literary critics cares to read it.

What follows, then, is not a discussion of literary criticism but merely shop talk about my trade. I justify its inclusion on the somewhat boggy ground that this book is largely a by-product of that trade. I offer herein the selections not of a reader but of a particular kind of reader, specialized like a retriever or an aphid: in short, a reviewer. A literary critic (just this once and then we're through with him) is a whole man exercising his wholeness through the accidental medium of books and authors. A reviewer is not a whole man. He is that partial man, an expert. Many of his human qualities are vestigial, others hypertrophied. All experts are monsters. I shall now briefly demonstrate the reviewer's monstrosity.

We must first of all remember that reading maketh not a full man. Any reviewer who has been in harness for twenty years or so will be eager to tell you that Bacon was just dreaming up sentences. I suppose I have read five or ten thousand books—it doesn't matter which —in the last couple of decades. Every so often I catch myself wondering whether I wouldn't be a sight wiser if I had read only fifteen, and they the right ones. You see, a reviewer does not read to instruct himself. If he remembered even a moderate quantum of what he read, he would soon be unfit for his job. Forced to comment on book Z, he would at once recollect everything that books A to Y, previously reviewed, contained that might throw light on Z. This is not the mental attitude that makes for useful book reviewing. As a matter of fact, what the reviewer should have above all things is a kind of mental virginity, a continual capacity to react freshly. I said that he was an expert. He is. He is an expert in surprisability. The poor fool is always looking forward to the next book.

This does not mean the reviewer has the memory of a moron. He doubtless remembers something of what he has read, but not enough to handicap him. His mind is not so much well stocked as well indexed. If challenged, I think I could tell you the authors and titles of the three or four best books of the last ten years dealing with the ancient Maya civilization. I can even make a fair fist at grading the books in the order of their completeness, authority, and readability. But what I don't know about the Mayans in the way of real information would fill several volumes and no doubt has done so.

The reviewer, then, granting him any mind at all, has a fresh one. Frank Moore Colby, whom I greatly admire (you will find some of his work starting on pages 275 and 287), held a different point of view. In 1921 he wrote a little piece from which I quote:

Beans Again

IF a man had for one day a purée of beans, and the next day haricots verts, and then in daily succession bean soup, bean salad, butter beans, lima, black, navy, Boston baked, and kidney beans, and then back to purée and all over again, he would not be in the relation of the gen-

eral eater to food. Nor would he be in the relation of a general reader
to books. But he would be in the relation of a reviewer toward novels.
He would soon perceive that the relation was neither normal nor
desirable, and he would take measures, violent if need be, to change
it. He would not say on his navy-bean day that they were as brisk
and stirring little beans of the sea as he could recall in his recent
eating. He would say grimly, "Beans again," and he would take prompt
steps to intermit this abominable procession of bean dishes.

If change for any reason were impossible he would either conceive
a personal hatred toward all beans that would make him unjust to any
bean however meritorious, or he would acquire a mad indiscrimi-
nateness of acquiescence and any bean might please. And his judgment would be in either case an unsafe guide for general eaters.

This, I believe, is what happens to almost all reviewers of fiction
after a certain time, and it accounts satisfactorily for various phenomena that are often attributed to a baser cause. It is the custom at
certain intervals to denounce reviewers for their motives. They are
called venal and they are called cowardly by turns. They are blamed
for having low standards or no standards at all. I think their defects
are due chiefly to the nature of their calling; that they suffer from
an occupational disease.

Now, I can understand why Colby felt this way. He could afford
to be superior. He was an encyclopedia editor, which is several cuts
above a reviewer. But his beans-again notion, though plausible, is not
cogent. The truth is, that a competent reviewer's stomach does not
summon up remembrance of beans past. Though there are exceptions
(I shall mention some of my own weaknesses in a moment), he does
not hail or damn novels out of a kind of hysteria of surfeit. If he
makes a stupid judgment it is simply because his judgment is stupid.
It may be stupid for a variety of reasons, no one of which will have
anything to do with the fact that he reads half a dozen novels a week.
In other words, a jaded reviewer sooner or later realizes that he is not
a good reviewer, and tries to get another job. A good reviewer is a
perennially fresh hack.

But, as I say, this doesn't work out one hundred per cent of the time. For example, I confess that I no longer look forward to next week's American historical novel with any bridegroom eagerness. I have read too many such. I am positive that they (not I, you see) have slipped into a groove, are standardized products, and therefore there is nothing helpful I can say about them. (Yet my fatuousness is such that I do not honestly believe I would muff another Red Badge of Courage if by some miracle one were published tomorrow.)

Never to be bored is merely an active form of imbecility. Do not trust the man who is "interested in everything." He is covering up some fearful abyss of spiritual vacancy. Ennui, felt on the proper occasions, is a sign of intelligence. All this is by way of saying that, of course, no reviewer is interested in every book he reads. He should have the ability to be bored, even if this ability is much feebler than his ability not to be bored. A competent reviewer knows his blind spots, tries to counteract them, and, if he can't, never drives himself into phony enthusiasm. Indiscriminate love of books is a disease, like satyriasis, and stern measures should be applied to it.

I, for example, do not react eagerly to books on the delights of gardening; to novels about very young men lengthily and discursively in love; to amateur anthropologists who hide a pogrom-mania under learned demonstrations of the superiority of Nordic man; to books by bright children Who Don't Know How Funny They're Being; to diplomatic reminiscences by splendid gaffers with long memories and brief understandings; to autobiographies by writers who feel that to have reached the age of thirty-five is an achievement of pivotal significance; to thorough jobs on Chester A. Arthur; to all tomes that aim to make me a better or a more successful man than I would be comfortable being; to young, virile novelists who would rather be found dead than grammatical; to most anthologies of humor; to books about Buchmanism, astrology, Yogi, and internal baths, all of which seem to me to deal with the same subject matter as does the last of the four subjects named; to the prospect of further "country" books, such as Country Mortician, Country Dog-Catcher, and Country Old Ladies' Home Attendant.

It is books like these that make a successful appeal to my apathy. Every reviewer has his own list. He does his best to keep it a small one, for he knows that his responsibility is to his public, not himself. He knows that he cannot afford to any great extent the luxury of indulging his own prejudices. A reviewer is not in the self-expression business. If he were he would run the risk of becoming an artist. He is, by the nature of his trade, uncreative, or, if his creative impulses are too strong, he sooner or later finds himself a dud at his job, and turns into a writer. But if he is a good reviewer and keeps in the groove fifteen or twenty years, he has no more chance of becoming a writer than a pig has of flying. There is nothing tragic about this and no reviewer who has any respect for his trade wastes any sentimentality over it. One decent hack, to my mind, is worth a stable of would-be Pegasuses.

Reviewers interest the public. I cannot fathom the reason, for we are among the mildest and most conventional of citizens, pure Gluyas Williams types. A life spent among ephemeral best sellers and publishers' announcements is not apt to produce characters of unusual contour. But the fact remains that people are curious about us and are likely to ask more questions of a reviewer than they would of a successful truss manufacturer, though probably the trussman leads the more abundant life.

To satisfy this curiosity I list herewith a few of the queries most commonly directed at my tribe, together with one man's answers:

Do you really read all those books? This question is generally put with an odd inflection, combining cynical disbelief with man-of-the-world willingness to overlook any slight dishonesty. There is no need for this hard-boiled attitude. A reviewer reads the books he reviews, exactly as an accountant examines his cost sheets, with the same routine conscientiousness. It's his job, that's all.

Back of this question, however, lies a peculiar condition, which baffles me and I think many others who are forced to read a great deal. The reason people think we bluff is that they themselves read so slowly they cannot believe we read as "fast" as we actually do. Now, I do not believe dogmatically either in fast or slow reading. I believe tripe should be read practically with the speed of light and, let us say, Toynbee's A Study of History with tortoise deliberation. And most books are nearer to tripe than to Toynbee. But the trouble with practically all of us is that we suffer from chronic reverence. We make the unwarranted assumption that because a man is in print he has something to say, and, acting on this assumption, we read his every word with scrupulous care. This may be good manners, but it's a confounded waste of time.

If I am at all partial, it is to the man who reads rapidly. One of the silliest couplets ever composed is to be found in The Art of Reading, by one William Walker, a seventeenth-century hollow-head who wrote:

> Learn to read slow; all other graces
> Will follow in their proper places.

This is unmitigated balderdash and if taken seriously can easily result in the wasting of ten or fifteen per cent of the few waking hours God has put at our disposal.

For example, I am simply unable to understand those—and there must be millions of them—who spend hours over the daily paper. Why, if you add up those hours, you will find that some people pass more time with the Herald Tribune than they do with their wives or husbands. I do not draw from this any conclusions about the state of either American journalism or American matrimony. I merely infer that such paper-maniacs simply do not know how to skip, to take in a paragraph at a time, to use the headlines, one of mankind's most blessed inventions.

No, reviewers do their job, but they know how to read quickly, in large units, to seize a point and be off to the next one while the author is still worrying the first one to death. Anybody can learn to do this; the reviewer simply is forced to learn it. I happen to be an exceptionally rapid reader, which is no more to my credit than would be the possession of exceptionally bushy eyebrows. Of the average novel (a description that covers virtually all novels) I can read one hundred pages an hour. Of the average historical novel I can read two hundred pages an hour, but that is because I am so familiar with the plot and characters. It took me two weeks, about five hours a day, to read Thomas Mann's Joseph in Egypt. I submit that in all three cases I did my reading with the proper speed and with conscientious attention to the value of what was being said.

How do you select books for review? Well, each reviewer has his own system. Here's mine. I try to juggle five factors, whose relative importance varies with each book.

First, I ask myself whether the book is apt to interest me. This is only fair. I am apt to write better, more usefully, about something that naturally engages my attention. I don't have to like the book, necessarily. It may interest me because its author happens to represent a great many things I dislike, as is the case with Gertrude Stein, Mabel Dodge Luhan, Charles Morgan, and William Faulkner.

Second, does the book have news value? A book reviewer is partly a purveyor of news. Any book by Ernest Hemingway would have to be reviewed whether it be a good one, like For Whom the Bell Tolls, or a poor one, like Green Hills of Africa, for Hemingway is news. This does not make him a better or a worse writer, of course. It has nothing to do with his literary value, but it has a great deal to do with whether or not the public expects information about his new book.

Let me give you another example. A few years ago everybody was all worked up over the Edward-Simpson affair (remember?). I said then and I say now (nobody listened then and nobody's listening now) that the whole mess was of very little political importance and that the persons involved were not sufficiently interesting even for the thing to have much scandal value. I was in a chilly minority of one. One week, with public interest at fever heat, three or four books bearing on the case appeared. Not one of them would have been worth a line of comment had it not possessed at the moment an inflated news value. To my mind they weren't worth a line of comment anyway, but I would have been an incompetent reviewer had I not given them considerable space. A reviewer is a journalist.

The third factor is allied to the second: Is the book apt to be of interest to the reviewer's particular audience? At the present time I have a job with The New Yorker, a humorous and satirical family magazine. There is no such animal as a typical New Yorker reader, but we know that most of this magazine's readers do not enjoy Temple Bailey, and no doubt vice versa. Miss Bailey has her virtues (indeed she is all virtue), but they are not the virtues that happen to interest the people who read my small screeds. Hence Miss Bailey does not get a look-in in my column. I cannot notice that her sales suffer in consequence.

The fourth factor is the only one that might not occur to a non-professional. A reviewer, in selecting books, takes into careful account the opinion of the publisher with respect to his own publications. If a publisher writes me that Hyacinthe Doakes' novel is terrific, that it is his fall leader, that he is going to lay $10,000 worth of advertising money on the line—why, I make a note to read Hyacinthe's book with care. I may not like it, and in that case will say so. (I have not once, in more than fifteen years in the trade, received a letter of protest from any publisher whose offering I had panned, except in a few cases when I had made misstatements of fact.) But the truth is that I am more apt to like it than I am to like some little yarn that this same publisher is so ashamed of he hides it away in the back of his catalogue. Publishers have their faults (a profound remark that I have often heard them apply to reviewers), but they know a good deal about books and their judgment of the relative values of their productions is hearkened to by any sensible reviewer.

Finally, a book may not be of great personal interest, it may possess no news value, my audience may not care deeply about it, and the publisher will not be in a position to give it any special publicizing. Nevertheless, I will review it in some detail. Why? Because I feel it to be important. That is to say, it is a book of literary or instructive value by a criterion (a cloudy one, I admit) that has nothing to do with the four factors already mentioned. A short time ago, as these words were written, there appeared a long, scholarly, rather solemn work of literary criticism, American Renaissance, by F. O. Matthiessen. Factor 1 applied moderately; factors 2, 3, 4 hardly applied at all. But I gave it a column and a half. I did so because the book is clearly an important work of creative scholarship and in years to come is bound to take a considerable place in its restricted field. It is my duty (to whom I don't know; I suppose to Literature itself) to comment on such a book to the best of my ability. Every reviewer feels the same way and does the same thing.

How reliable are reviewers' estimates? There's no exact answer to that one. If his estimates weren't appreciably more reliable than those of your dinner-table companion, he wouldn't hold his job long. But he is several light-years distant from infallibility. He works under pressure, he's human, he's been out too late the night before, his eyes bother him—for one reason or another, the result may be a stupid verdict. I've rendered many. At the end of each year I give myself something life itself, less generous than I am, doesn't allow us: a second chance. I go over the books I've reviewed and correct my first estimates. I try to be honest, but it's not easy.

This annual donning of sackcloth and ashes, by the way, began some years back. At the end of the book season, one cold December, the lull was terrific. I had no books to review and a column to deliver. To fill the gap I decided to assume the winter garment of repentance. A column resulted. Readers liked it, I have kept it up ever since, and at present enjoy a somewhat unmerited reputation for extreme conscientiousness.

As to this question of reliability, I would say that on the whole we reviewers err in the direction of overamiability, though not so noticeably as was the case fifteen years ago, when the Great American Novel was being hailed about as regularly as a Fifth Avenue bus. What has happened, roughly, is that the old type of book reviewer, to whom the job was a game, has gradually been replaced by a new type, to whom the job is a job. In the days of Laurence Stallings and Heywood Broun you would on occasion get superb pieces of enthusiastic journalism, but more frequently sickening examples of hullabalunacy. Today book reviewing is staider, duller, but unquestionably juster and more serious. It has a professional touch. It is growing up.

Nevertheless, I should hazard a guess that its standards of judgment are still too relaxed. Just what my tribe has to be mellow about I can't figure out, but we are mellow, and the result is a certain lack of acerbity. There's too much good-nature-faking among us, a continuous observance of Be-Kind-To-Dumb-Novelists Week. Literature does not grow only on praise. It needs the savage and tartarly note, even the astringence of insult.

In order to keep his sword sharp, the reviewer should see to it that he does not make too many close friends among writers. A decade or so ago, during the heyday of the literary tea and the publisher's cocktail party, this was a difficult assignment. Today, now that book publishers have finally put on long pants, the problem is easier. A reviewer may go from one end of the year to the other without flushing a single novelist, and I have known some reviewers, now quite grown men, who have never met a literary agent in the flesh. This alienation from what used to be known laughingly as the Literary Life is a good thing for us. It makes possible a cool inhumanity toward authors, which in turn results in more detached comment. The road to a reviewer's disintegration is marked by many milestones, each one a statue erected to commemorate a beautiful friendship. I am sure of this even though I would not go so far as to agree with the man who thought the proper relationship between reviewer and author should be that between a knife and a throat.

What, then, is a reviewer to do when unavoidably confronted with a book written by a close friend? I have had to face this situation perhaps a dozen times in the course of my daily work, and it is not an easy one to handle if one wishes to be scrupulously honest. In my case the difficulty was never disastrous, for it is my policy, when choosing friends who write, to choose of course only those who write well, thus making it a matter of inexorable duty for me to praise their work. So far this policy has worked pretty successfully. I do not know what would happen in the event that I should get to conceive a warm personal affection for, let us say, Miss Gertrude Stein. However, careful planning should enable me to head off this possibility.

The fact is that no reviewer is really objective when dealing with a friend's book, for if the book has anything to it at all, he is really dealing with the friend himself. He does the best he can, trying not to crack his spine in an attempt to lean over backward. But I doubt the final accuracy of his judgment. For example, I have praised rather

heatedly two books by close friends of mine: Mortimer Adler's How
to Read a Book and Oscar Levant's A Smattering of Ignorance. I still
do not know whether these books are as good as I made them out to
be. On rereading my admittedly amiable pieces, I detect no conscious
dishonesty. Of course, as one of my most sympathetic readers, I may
be giving myself the benefit of the doubt. There are some Alexanders
among us who cut the Gordian knot, such as the famous literary com-
mentator who is reported to have said with dulcet candor, "Any
reviewer who won't praise a friend's book is a louse."

How influential are reviewers? This is a hard one to answer. All the
publishers' questionnaires, scientifically designed to discover just why
a given book is bought, throw but a dim light on the subject, though
they provide any desired quantity of statistics. Reader A buys a book
because his friend B has mentioned it; that is apparently the strongest
single definable factor. But this means nothing unless you know why
B happened to mention it. You ask B. B replies, let us suppose, that
he himself bought, read and recommended the book as the result of
reading an advertisement. Now you have to find out what in that
particular advertisement caused the positive reaction to the book.
Was it the publisher's statement of the book's merits? Was it a quotation from a reviewer? If the latter, B bought the book because the
reviewer liked it—and therefore A indirectly did the same. The whole
matter is very complex.

With a great best seller, a large number of factors operate simultaneously or follow rapidly on each other, causing an irresistible, constantly mounting wave of popularity. If we take the case of For Whom
the Bell Tolls, we might list these factors somewhat as follows, in the
order of their conceivable importance:

(1) Author's reputation (but that didn't make a best seller of his
previous book).

(2) Timeliness and importance of the subject matter.

(3) Literary excellence.

(4) It was a Book-of-the-Month Club selection, which automatically set in motion a wave of bookish conversation, for the club
members form a mighty army of talkers.

(5) *Almost unanimously favorable reviews.*

(6) *Erotic and "shocking" passages.*

(7) *Book-store recommendation.* (A factor very difficult to judge—perhaps it should be placed much higher in the list.)

(8) *Publisher's advertising and general promotion*—in this case, I should say, a minor factor.

( ) *Talkability.* I don't give this a number because any of the factors (1) to (8) might have contributed to the book's talkability, and no one can determine the relative importance of any of them.

Now, this casual analysis (whose arrangement would probably be sharply questioned by my colleagues, the publisher, and Mr. Hemingway) would not apply identically to any other great best seller. In some cases (8) might be very near the head of the list. Anthony Adverse, for example, benefited by one of the most skillful advertising campaigns in recent publishing history; Jurgen was made mainly by (6), or rather by a Vice Society's alert appreciation of (6); and so it goes. Mrs. Lindbergh's sublime example of the prophetic fallacy, The Wave of the Future, succeeded through a combination of (1) and (2) plus certain other less savory factors.

The reviewer alone cannot make a book popular. A superb novel such as Elizabeth Bowen's Death of the Heart may be praised by every reviewer who knows his job and still sell but a few thousand copies. Only factors (3) and (5) applied to this book; other factors would have been necessary to push it over into solid popularity.

Occasionally a book may be "made" or set in motion by one man's recommendation. William Lyon Phelps did a great deal for The Bridge of San Luis Rey. Will Rogers' admiration for The Good Earth helped that book. A book of some years back called Recovery, by Sir Arthur Salter, owed its success almost entirely to Walter Lippmann. More recently Alexander Woollcott tickled the lachrymatory glands of all America to the considerable advantage of Mr. James Hilton. It's interesting to observe that none of these four commentators is or was a regular day-in-day-out book reviewer. They're Gentlemen rather than Players. We professionals do not in the nature of things wield any such power. I have never heard of Lewis Gannett or Harry Hansen or Sterling North or Joseph Henry Jackson or Donald

Adams or Clifton Fadiman "making" a book singlehanded. As a matter of fact, a few of the authors included in this volume are present because all my tumult and shouting, when their books first appeared, resulted in nothing but a nation-wide lack of demand.

A minor trait in the American character makes us pay less attention to the literary judgments of professionals than to those of distinguished nonprofessionals. A striking instance, to go back almost a generation, is the instant popularity into which J. S. Fletcher, the English detective-story writer, sprang when Woodrow Wilson, then President, happened to praise his work, which was no better or worse than that of fifty other thriller manufacturers. A parallel instance in England was Stanley Baldwin's endorsement some years ago of the novels of Mary Webb. They were at once gobbled up by the thousand, unfortunately a little too late to do the author any good, for she had died some time before in utter poverty.

If Franklin D. Roosevelt should happen to go all out for some novel tomorrow it would at once become a best seller, irrespective of its real merits, but if he should issue a weekly verdict on new books, his opinion within a few months would cease to have any great influence.

Columnists, radio commentators, editorial writers, lecturers, even big businessmen will on occasion influence the sale of books more sharply than reviewers can. On the other hand, preachers, whose literary influence a generation or so ago was marked, have now sunk to a minor role as book recommenders.

One of the paradoxes of bookselling, observable only during the last few years, is that a book may be helped by one or more of the so-called competitive media. A book's sale will be increased by its translation into a moving picture. Alice Duer Miller's The White Cliffs became a best seller largely because it was so successfully broadcast. And, to take a more striking example, the condensations of popular books to be found in the Reader's Digest frequently tend to accelerate the sale of these publications in their original form. There is no such thing as bad publicity for books.

I am inclined to think that one thing that does not sell them is the publisher's jacket blurb. This is generally written after much brow furrowing and is almost completely ineffective. Sometimes blurbs help the reviewer, but not much; more often they aid the harried book-seller. Yet I have never seen a potential book buyer influenced by them. My own practice is to be wary of them. Their extravagance is often so absurd that the reviewer loses his detachment and is unduly severe with the innocent book. "One of the outstanding biographers of our time," said the blurbist a year or two ago—about whom? About a journalist named Hector Bolitho, who has devoted himself to the extremely dull task of composing official slop about the English royal family. "The greatest of living historians" is the blurb characteriza-tion of Philip Guedalla, a writer of quality, but no more the greatest of living historians than I am. A tedious Scandinavian named Trygve Gulbranssen was tagged by his publishers as "One of the great writers of the day," which may have been literally true, the day being un-specified. This jacket racket alienates reviewers.

One comment I must add about my life as a reviewer. It is directly responsible for the making of this book. This is a book of rereadings. In fact, I had originally intended to call it A Reviewer's Rereader. It is the result of a re-examination or reconsideration of a great many of the thousands of books I have read and reviewed or just read. I wanted for my own satisfaction to discover how much of what I had read (or characteristic excerpts from it) would stand the entirely per-sonal acid test of at least three reperusals.

In this business of reperusal I spent many interesting months. I got a great deal of fun out of it, and many disappointments, too. As I read I thought of some of my friends who never reread and of others who don't like any book unless, like game, it is just a trifle moldy. I must admit that I could never exercise any Christian charity on that old gander who said with lardy self-satisfaction that whenever a new book appeared he reread an old one. What did he do in 1849 when David Copperfield was a new book? I don't suppose he paid any attention in 1605 when a grizzled Spanish veteran came out with a tale called Don Quixote de la Mancha. And the first time Homer smote 'is bloomin' lyre I imagine our friend was busy scrutinizing the cave drawings of Altamira.

That most of the best books were written some time ago we may freely admit. But when you consider how much more Was than Now there has always been (with every passing moment busily increasing the odds in Was' favor) the circumstance is not surprising. But what of it? Can we May-fly mortals afford to spend all our brief allotment reading only the best? So much is missed that way. Transients and second-raters ourselves, why should we deny ourselves the warm and homely feeling of kinship that comes of reading the pages of other transients and second-raters?

"Old wine, old friends, old books are best," said Hug-the-Hearth, wrapping the mantle of conservatism about the trembling bones of his timidity. This may be so, in a measure, but that is no reason for not testing our palate against new wine, our personality against new friends, our mental pliancy against new books. How many males in full possession of their faculties have been put off the quest of novelty by the reflection that to know one woman is to know all? The rut of "the best that has been thought and said in the world" is nonetheless a rut, if a noble one.

How often have you not fled the biblio-hobbyists who sport a favorite author as they would a favorite flower? The whimsical bores who "know their Alice"—and little else. The Jane-ites, so proud and prejudiced, for whom nothing has happened to the English novel since Miss Austen turned up her genteel toes. The Thackerayans, for whom rereading The Newcomes semiannually is a religious rite. The W. S. Gilbert-quoters, the Moby Dickensians—but why go on? Somerset Maugham puts it mildly but well: "I know people who read the same book over and over again. It can only be that they read with their eyes and not with their sensibility. It is a mechanical exercise like the Tibetan turning of a prayer wheel. It is doubtless a harmless occupation but they are wrong if they think it is an intelligent one."

On the other hand—these matters are always conveniently ambidextrous—he is no less tiresome who "keeps up with the new books" as though current literature were a motor-paced bicycle race. I should say they are well worth shunning, those earnest souls to whom reading is a form of competition, who, on finishing a new publication, feel they have beaten someone or something. Such worship of the book-of-the-day is infantile.

My venerated Columbia professor, Raymond Weaver, whose knowledge and personality are alike classical, is credited with an apposite legend. At a dinner party one evening a bright young thing queried, in her most buffed and polished finishing-school voice, "Mr. Weaver, have you read So-and-so's book?" (naming a modish best seller of the moment).

Mr. Weaver confessed he had not.

"Oh, you'd better hurry up—it's been out over three months!"

Mr. Weaver, an impressive gentleman with a voice like a Greek herald, turned to her, and said, "My dear young lady, have you read Dante's Divine Comedy?"

"No."

"Then you'd better hurry up—it's been out over six hundred years."

To the average male there is something a little ridiculous in the aspect of a woman wearing a hat which he has just seen advertised as the very latest thing. More, to him she is provincial. Lacking the independence that would permit her to choose a hat of yesterday, of tomorrow, or even a timeless hat, if timeless hats there be, she is, in his eyes, the prisoner of the moment, her hat-horizon bounded by the confines of a split second. The stylish (repulsive word) hat has no true style.

As with millinery, so with literature. There is no reader so parochial as the one who reads none but this morning's books. Books are not rolls, to be devoured only when they are hot and fresh. A good book retains its interior heat and will warm a generation yet unborn. He who confines himself only to today's books is more narrowly circumscribed by time than he who reads only yesteryear's. You can be inexorably old-fashioned or perennially up to the minute. In either case you are dated.

We are driven, then, to the dull, sane conclusion that the proper diet is a mixed one. No special magic virtue inheres in either old or new books.

But let us return to our muttonhead who, whenever a new book appeared, reread an old one. He must have owned one of Mr. Lindbergh's mechanical hearts, incapable of mutation, for rereading is one of the barometers by which we note the changes in our mental and emotional climate. Rarely do we reread a book once greatly loved and receive from it exactly our original pleasure. Note that I say receive; this is not to assert that we cannot recall our original pleasure, but that is not the same thing.

Of this recall value William Hazlitt says: "In reading a book which is an old favourite with me (say the first novel I ever read) I not only have the pleasure of imagination and of a critical relish of the work, but the pleasures of memory added to it. It recalls the same feelings and associations which I had in first reading it, and which I can never have again in any other way. Standard productions of this kind are links in the chain of our conscious being. They bind together the different scattered divisions of our personal identity. They are landmarks and guides in our journey through life. They are pegs and loops on which we can hang up, or from which we can take down, at pleasure, the wardrobe of a moral imagination, the relics of our best affections, the tokens and records of our happiest hours. They are 'for thoughts and for remembrance!' They are like Fortunatus's Wishing-Cap—they give us the best riches—those of Fancy; and transport us, not over half the globe, but (which is better) over half our lives, at a word's notice!"

There you have the sunny side of rereading. In the course of preparing this collection, however, I have constantly been confronted with a shady side also. For the "pleasures of memory" are not all Hazlitt cracked them up to be. Most of the time rereading is a melancholy experience. Turning pages out of which a decade or two ago surprise and excitement fairly leaped at us, we find surprise and excitement no longer summonable. A breath of autumn invades the heart—vacancy, almost a kind of paralysis. Surely this is not the book we once read, but a faded photograph of it, with all its original lights and shadows smoked over into a dim, pathetic grayness. We close the book ruefully. It is, we say, dated.

Dated? But perhaps it is we who are dated. The book may have died, but just as frequently we have died ourselves, or changed our temperament just as the physiologists tell us we replace our bodies completely every seven years or so. The other day, for example, I reread Knut Hamsun's Pan. A score of years ago it moved me greatly; today I cannot stomach it. Who has changed, Hamsun or I? Like the unfortunate little old woman in the rhyme, the one whose petticoats were half shot from under her, I found myself wondering if this could be I.

And it was not I, or not the same I. I tried to figure it out. Perhaps my taste had decayed. Or perhaps the book had been bad all along, and my original judgment was faulty. My pride (one of the elements of the human personality which apparently remains constant) prevented me from accepting either solution with pleasure. I introspected busily for a half-hour or so, and came up with an odd tangle of theoretical explanations.

Pan deals in part with romantic love, a subject in which I had a more burning interest at seventeen than I now have at thirty-seven. There is a kind of emotional mistiness about Pan which corresponded, it may be, to the Schwärmerei of youth. Today, quite possibly overvaluing it, I look for clarity above all in what I read. Finally, today I dislike Hamsun because he is a Nazi. Who am I to say that my subconscious (never a sound literary critic) does not rise up to prevent me from enjoying anything at all by a man whose political opinions I now detest?

What I am struggling to indicate is that a book may be a "good" book at one stage of your life and a "bad" book at another—and to tell absolutely how "bad" or "good" it is is impossible. The factors that make it good or bad may be nonliterary, matters of accident.

There is the whole question of "mood"—a question so involved that neither psychologists nor literary critics can say anything about it at all convincing. You just "happen" to pick up a book on Wednesday evening, and it reads well. On Tuesday evening it might have seemed a bore. What factors enter here? Who knows—metabolic rate, what you did at the office during the day, the presence or absence of fatigue, worry. . . . The fact is that a book, if it has blood in it and is not merely some standard confection, is a vital thing. To read a book is to enter into contact with something alive. It is more like talking to a friend than like driving a car. Reading is not an operation performed on something inert but a relationship entered into with another being.

At certain times you just "can't stand" anybody—your best friend, your wife or husband; it makes no difference. You don't really know why your mind refuses to touch that of another person, but you know that it does refuse. So is it with books—and that is one reason rereading even the best of books is often a disillusioning procedure.

Are there any books that the "intelligent reader" (a phrase invented by critics to circumvent immodesty) can always profitably reread? People like Mortimer Adler are certain that there are. He calls them classics, and would base education on them. To a degree he is right. There is a quality of inexhaustibility about some of the great Greeks, for example, that makes them always rereadable in that there are always new insights to be drawn from them. They have also the quality of difficulty (not to be confused with obscurity)—a quality which often helps to keep alive a book that would perish were it simpler. But even these great classics can on occasion be unrereadable. I do not contest the greatness of Plato, and yet there are certain moods in which I cannot read him, moods in which he (or his mouthpiece Socrates) seems to me to be a clever, self-satisfied, quibbling, hair-splitting, intellectual snob. And when I feel this way, the page of Plato turns to dust and ashes, and even the Phaedo (which I know to be one of the greatest things ever written) seems contrived. No matter how superior the author may be to the reader, there must be a certain harmony between them, or they cannot mate. This harmony is elusive, unattainable by mere wishing, a function of mood, whim, perhaps even temperature. I should not be surprised if our reading reactions were in part influenced by the sunspots.

There are certain books that you attempt again and again, and which continue to resist you because you are not ripe for them. During the last twenty years, for instance, I have tried perhaps ten times to read The Brothers Karamazov and each time given up in a rage directed equally at Dostoevsky and myself. Only recently I tried it once more and found its reputation thoroughly deserved. Reading it now with the greatest absorption, I am convinced it is the sort of book that requires the reader (that is, most readers) to be of a certain age. Until now I was simply too young for it, and that's why it seemed to me dull and farfetched. It is a book you (I mean myself) have to grow up to. One of these days I am going to reread Turgenev's Fathers and Sons, which I raced through at fifteen, getting, I am sure, precisely nothing from it. I have the feeling that I am now about ready for it. But I may be mistaken; I may still be too young for it.

I often think of that quiet story of the Franciscan monk who was found reading Willa Cather's Death Comes for the Archbishop. Asked his opinion of it, he replied, "Well, I have read it five times, but, you see, I have not finished it yet." All of us have read books that we have not finished yet, books perhaps unfinishable, books so subtle and multileveled as to reveal themselves newly with each re-reading. I have, for example, reread Thomas Mann's The Magic Mountain five times (there is an extract from it in this book) and I know I have still to give it a final reading. Such books do not sur-render themselves at once but are like the most desirable of women, difficult in the beginning but, once won, durable in their appeal.

What makes a book rereadable? The answer depends on the reader as well as on the book. To Mr. Adler a rereadable book is an "origi-nal communication," one marking a milestone in the history of West-ern thought and imagination. To the sentimentalist (that takes in a lot of us) it may be a book read in childhood; he rereads and reloves not only the book, but himself as a child. (This explains why so many people to whom their childhood is an obsession cannot bear to throw away their nursery classics.) To another a book may be rereadable if it echoes his own unalterable prejudices. It is a gauge by which he may complacently measure his lack of mental progress. People who believe in The Truth often read one book or group of books all their lives. For them the last word has been uttered by, say, Thomas Aquinas or Adolf Hitler or Friedrich Nietzsche. Hence they stick to their particular Bible and wear it to shreds. Such readers are almost always psychopaths. A one-book man is a dangerous man and should be taken in hand and taught how to diversify his literary investments.

I have been trying for some time to determine what kind of book
I myself reread with pleasure. This is an exercise of no particular
importance to anyone. Still, inasmuch as this entire volume consists of
material that I have enjoyed, its purchaser is perhaps entitled to some
explanation of my choices.

All of us are familiar with the dismaying fact that an attractive
personality often has little to do with a person's moral qualities or
even his physical appearance. It is quite possible to be extremely fond
of a man who neglects his mother. Even his mother is often fond of
him. Similarly, what I call the "magical" quality of a book—the
quality which for me makes it rereadable—is not necessarily dependent on the book's importance, its intellectual weight, its position
in the critics' hierarchy of values.

For example, serious students of literature would doubtless rank
Madame Bovary as a more significant work of fiction than Great
Expectations. Probably it is. There is no question but that it has
influenced the course of literature, whereas Great Expectations happens to be merely a Dickens novel that millions of plain readers have
enjoyed. But for me Madame Bovary has no virtues except those of
perfection. It is without magic, without personality, it is not rereadable. It is about as interesting as Sir Galahad. Great Expectations, on
the other hand, is magical, and its magic works every time. For me the
scene on the deserted moor in which Pip meets the convict beats anything in Madame Bovary. I don't quite understand why this should
be so, but so it is. A lycée-trained Frenchman might have the opposite
reaction and be equally unable to defend it.

Now this magic is a very elusive thing. It may have any of a
hundred shapes and forms. It may be a comic magic, as in the
"swarry" scene from Pickwick. It may be a fearsome magic, as in
the cave episode from Tom Sawyer. It may be deeply tragical—
Lear on the heath. In all these cases the writing has a penumbra, a
"thickness" which the most intellectually precise notation of a Flau-
bert does not have. This penumbra does not necessarily have anything to do with remoteness from reality, with "romanticism." Nothing could be more "romantic" than the tales of Poe. Yet, to my taste,
admirable as they are, they lack magic. They are mathematical, their

romance is calculated. Indeed, most tales of the supernatural have this planned quality and that is why so few of them are great literature. It is when the supernatural is accepted by the author as related to the human that literature results. There is nothing artificial about the Iliad or the Odyssey, though they are full of miracles and divinities.

Penumbral literature, to use a horrible phrase, is not necessarily fanciful, then. Cabell is full of fancy but he has no magic. His words cast no shadow. Huck Finn and Jim on the river are about as unfanciful as you can imagine. But what they say has nonterminating reverberations.

Magic is not confined to "imaginative" literature. For me there is magic in Russell's "A Free Man's Worship," which you will find in this book. There is magic in Gibbon's explanation of how he came to write the Decline and Fall. There is magic in the scientific popularizations of Sir Arthur Eddington. All of these works set a bell ringing in the brain. They do not become merely additions to your mental store but inhabitants of your mind. There are certain clear and precise ideas that are as haunting as Heathcliff. Descartes' system of analytical geometry can be as stimulating to the imagination as the soliloquies of Ahab, though on a different level.

A few pages back I said that everything in this book has been read by the compiler at least three times with pleasure. By this I do not mean that everything in this book is forever rereadable or that all of it is great literature. Some of it I am sure is, but many things are included that are not of permanent value. For example, the included stories of Somerset Maugham have no immortal qualities. They set no bells ringing in the mind. But they are so admirably composed, they do so perfectly the minor thing the author set out to do, they are so exact an expression of a particular attitude toward life, that they give me a rare and special pleasure. I have found this pleasure, I say, repeatable three times. Three times should be enough for any man.

In making up the contents of this book I worked within no limitations except my own taste, a certain size, in excess of which the volume would not have been commercially feasible, and the usual restrictions of copyright. With respect to the last, however, I may say that everything I originally wanted to include is here, with one exception—Lee Strout White's ineffably touching "Farewell to Model T," which was gently denied me for reasons I found perfectly satisfactory. Please manage to read it anyway.

I have made no attempt to "balance" the reading ration, to have equal proportions of "light" and "heavy" material, or of English and American productions. I included what I liked of the work I had read and reviewed, or in some cases only read, during the last two decades or so.

It happens that you will find in this book biographies, anecdotes, brief fiction, semilong fiction, excerpts from novels, sketches, essays (both familiar and formal), a book review, humorous pieces (including one complete book of humor), excerpts from a dictionary, a judicial decision, reflections on nature, a long letter, an excerpt from a speech, and a collection of epigrams. You will find work by Americans, Englishmen, Frenchmen, Germans, a Spanish-American, and an Australian. You will find lengthy pieces and brief pieces, trivial work and weighty work, work that I believe permanent and work that I know is transient, work by established writers and by newcomers, by the radical and the reactionary, the traditionalist and the experimentalist, the old and the young, the living and the dead. Variety is not a major virtue, but this book has it.

It may be objected that the taste which governed the selection is so catholic as to be in effect no taste at all. How can a man be so barren of the salt of preference that he can at the same time like a gentle old lady such as Sarah Orne Jewett and a tough mug such as Ernest Hemingway? How can he at once admire the elegant frippery of Alexander Woollcott and the profound seriousness of Thomas Mann? What is there in common between the homely Indiana cracker-box philosophy of Kin Hubbard and the jeweled suavity of Santayana's sinuous thought?

I must unmask and declare myself at once. My friends, I am that most despised of literary animals, an eclectic. I am so disunified, such a miserable polymorph of a man, that my nature responds to other natures that are wildly disparate. I suppose the humanists of a decade ago would say that I have no standards. Moralists of any decade would say that I have no convictions. Logicians will point out that my taste is contradictory. And my colleagues will simply say that I could have made better choices, which is quite possible.

I plead guilty to the charge of being able to enjoy more than one kind of writing, which is far from equivalent to enjoying all kinds. (Someday I should like to compile an anthology of work that I detest, with reasons.) My personality, like that of most people I meet, is full of splits; and the variations in temper and mood that you will find in this book correspond, I dimly feel, to those lines of cleavage. Something in me is satisfied by the lunacies of S. J. Perelman and something else by the lucidities of Bertrand Russell. Yet I feel it is somehow the same fellow that is satisfied, that I am not a ragbag but a man.

A keen critic—perhaps it was Edmund Wilson—once pointed out that the major characters in a great novel were often unconscious projections of unreconciled factors in the author's own character. I believe this to be profoundly true. I suppose that on an inconceivably lower level this book is a projection of unreconciled factors in the character of the compiler. No doubt a good analyst (he must also be a man of literary perception) could, by a careful examination of the contents, make a shrewd guess at the personality of the compiler. For just as all actions imply a choice, so all choices are actions, and actions are the man.

But these are refinements that have little to do with whether or not you will enjoy this book. I can only say that I have not consciously included anything insincere or false, or anything careless in craftsmanship. I believe everything you will read here, if the product of hands other than my own, is of its kind extremely well written. I believe nothing here is dead, inert, but that these words, whether major or minor, are vascular.

As to the commentaries that accompany them, I would say only that they are intended not to be criticism but rather the most informal kind of personal annotation. Most of them are examples of what Swinburne called "the noble pleasure of praising," for this is a book

of enthusiasms. The commentaries need not be read at all, if the
reader so wishes, for each selection is perfectly comprehensible without their aid. I guess I just enjoyed writing them.

One last word. It is in a way a fatuous gesture, some might think,
to produce a book of this character at a time when mankind is
engaged in a life-and-death struggle with itself. Why should we concern ourselves with these stories and essays, however pleasing they
may be, when in another decade the very conditions that produced
them may have vanished from the tormented face of the earth? I
say, for that very reason.

I have lately been reading a disturbing book called The Managerial
Revolution, by a professor of philosophy named James Burnham.
(One should never underestimate professors of philosophy; Socrates
was one.) Mr. Burnham's thesis is at the moment being widely discussed, I am told, by businessmen, a circumstance I happen to find
almost humorous, for among the groups who will have no place in
Mr. Burnham's projected society of the future will assuredly be those
accustomed to thinking in terms of buying and selling, profit and
loss.

Briefly, here is what Mr. Burnham expounds, with a chilly logic
that is perhaps too symmetrical to be completely convincing. The
whole world is now in the grip of an irreversible revolutionary process. This revolution has nothing to do with traditional socialist or
communist conceptions. On the contrary, socialism has already failed
irretrievably, and capitalism has either abdicated or is abdicating. The
world of the immediate future (we are already partially living in that
future) is a world of superstates, probably three in number, in which
the master class will be a group of "managers" and their bureaucratic,
technical, and military assistants. This class will dominate completely
a servile mass of workers and common fodder. The objective of the
superstate, within its own confines, will be not profit but order. This
order is largely definable in terms of efficient production. The final
objective of each of the three superstates (the European, dominated
by Germany; the Asiatic, dominated by Japan; the American, dominated by the United States) is world mastery, obtainable by war.

This war has already begun. We are in its first phase. This is the first managerial war. It will be won (temporarily) by that state which most efficiently substitutes managerial techniques for the outmoded democratic-capitalist ones.

Mr. Burnham, by the way, does not like the world whose blueprints he so firmly draws. But he is quite convinced of its imminence. Any fair-minded reader will have to admit that much of what he says seems at the moment to make sense of a horrible kind.

It may be that he is right. It may be that mankind's next stage is the managerial state—possibly, as Mr. Burnham hopes, a managerial state in which will be incorporated some of the humane and democratic values in which you and I believe. But these values, if Mr. Burnham is right, will be subordinated, at least in the near future, to the military and economic necessities of the state, and to high conceptions of efficiency and order.

That means the death of the individual, for the masters, if they are to remain masters, will have to abandon their unique personalities just as surely as will the serfs. They, too, will become the slaves of the state they head, even if all the emoluments—mainly power—revert to them.

And with the death of the individual comes the death of the arts, literature among them. After all, what is art? It is the mode by which the solitary heart of any one man bridges the gap which separates him from all of his brothers, mankind in general. All literature is but a message, strong or feeble, sent out by an individual and addressed to the human race. "Only connect," says E. M. Forster; literature is such a means of connection.

But if the future is to abolish the individual, it must also abolish the notion of humanity in general, in favor of the state. When the individual and humanity have both vanished, who shall send a message to whom? Thus literature perishes, and art and architecture and music, and all the great and little outcries of man.

I do not admit that there is no alternative to this Spenglerian world view, but I am not so naïve as not to see that already the system of the superstate obtains over large portions of our planet. The new Dark Age has begun. Already the man of words, the man of sounds, the man of patterns, the man of symbols, is losing face, for he does not seem necessary if wars are to be won, trade routes guarded, bombs dropped, and bodies smashed. He is not at all the bringer of order but rather of that divine disorder which expresses man's painful desire to communicate without coalescing. He is, it may be, already out of date.

But, as it seems to me, if he is out of date, it is because he is dateless. He may, perhaps he will, disappear for a time, a long time. But disappear forever he cannot, for he is man himself, just as truly as the bomb dropper and the sword wielder are man himself. This is a great civil war in which we are engaged, greater, I think, than even Mr. Burnham conceives. Man is struggling with himself. A certain part of him is now paramount—the blind impulse to mass unity, the blind impulse to obedience, and the blind impulse, most powerful of all, to death. Yet these impulses war with others, now submerged and overcast—the impulse to communicate, the impulse to free one's self and one's neighbor, the impulse to live. Sooner or later, and it may be very much later, that part of man which sings and writes, paints and prays, laughs and cries will rise like Excalibur from the deep lake into which it has been thrown.

In the meantime we can and must, by a crazy paradox, shed blood in order that the shedding of blood may once again become a detestable rather than an habitual thing. And in the meantime, whether we enter a Dark Age or overcome it, it is our duty to keep alive in our own memories, confused and shaken as they be, the tones of men who believe in each other, who talk to each other, using words, simple or profound, but words, living speech, the signature of civilization.

CLIFTON FADIMAN

New York City
July 10, 1941

Reading
I've Liked

EVE CURIE

COMMENTARY

It is hard to think of many first-rate scientists in whom some major flaw of character does not show itself, confounding our natural desire for wholehearted hero worship. Descartes was ignoble, Leibnitz a fawning courtier, Willard Gibbs a recluse, Gauss cold and secretive. For all his nobility, Pasteur was stained with chauvinism and race hatred. An infantile religiosity clouded to the end the magnificent minds of Newton and Pascal. But the lives of Marie and Pierre Curie, two of the most beautiful lives, I suppose, that have ever been lived, provide exceptions. It was theatrically apt that these characters of shining purity should have built their careers around a physical element recognizable by its inner radiance.

Eve Curie's life of her mother, published in English in 1937, already has the ring of a classic. The chapter following, one of the finest, describes the climax of a life that might have been conceived by the patterning brain of a tragic dramatist. Before you read it, I suggest that you look at a photograph of Madame Curie. I have one before me now, taken when she was sixty-two. The face is lined. From underneath the white and casually arranged hair arcs an abnormally spacious brow. She is dressed in a simple black dress that looks like a laboratory smock. The face is that of a truly beautiful woman, the beauty lying in the bones and in the brain that sends its clear signals through the deep, penetrating eyes.

The story of Marie Curie is not merely that of a poor Polish governess who struggled triumphantly against adversity. The story of Marie Curie lies in the fact that she was happiest during her struggles and least happy when a vulgar world acclaimed her. Hers is a success story à rebours. Einstein has said, "Marie Curie is, of all celebrated beings, the only one whom fame has not corrupted." "She did not know how to be famous," says Eve Curie. In one deliberate sentence she strikes to the heart of the secret: "I hope that the reader may constantly feel, across the ephemeral movement of one existence,

1

what in Marie Curie was even more rare than her work or her life: the immovable structure of a character; the stubborn effort of an intelligence; the free immolation of a human being that could give all and take nothing, could even receive nothing; and above all the quality of a soul in which neither fame nor adversity could change the exceptional purity."

Recall that unbelievable dramatic life. She is born Marya Sklodovska, youngest child of a Warsaw physicist and a sensitive, tubercular mother. The childhood is unhappy, torn by the death of mother and eldest sister, grayed by poverty, given a certain tenseness by the fact that she is a member of a subject race, the Poles. She grows up, becomes the conventional intellectual rebel of her time, like "all the little Polish girls who had gone mad for culture." She is intelligent, but nothing yet reveals that "immovable structure" of which her daughter speaks. She becomes a governess, a bit of a bluestocking touched with Tolstoyan sentimentality. Now "the eternal student" begins to rise in her. The little child who at five stood in rapt awe before her father's case containing the "phys-ics ap-pa-ra-tus" reawakens in the girl of eighteen. Her duties as a governess do not prevent her from studying. She has no money, not even for stamps so that she may write to her brother. But "I am learning chemistry from a book." Back in Warsaw, she is allowed to perform elementary chemical experiments in a real laboratory, and, at last, after inconceivable setbacks and economies, after years of weary waiting, she goes to Paris to study at the Sorbonne.

In 1894 she meets Pierre Curie, already a physicist of note, a mind "both powerful and noble." In an atmosphere of garrets and laboratories, these two, very grave and serious, conduct their love affair. They marry. On her wedding day, to the generous friend who wishes to give her a bridal dress, she writes, "I have no dress except the one I wear every day. If you are going to be kind enough to give me one, please let it be practical and dark so that I can put it on afterwards to go to the laboratory."

It is a perfect marriage, the marriage not merely of two people who love each other but, what is incomparably more important, of two great physicists who can help each other. It is Marie, attracted by the uranium researches of Becquerel, who starts herself and her husband on the long, tedious, glorious path at the end of which glows radium. They know that radium and polonium (named by Marie to commemorate her beloved native land) exist, but they must prove it. From 1898 to 1902, in a dilapidated, leaking, freezing shed, with primitive apparatus, with little or no help, unaided by the scientific bureaucracy or by the State, these two gentle fanatics work in an absorption that is like a dream. The government is too busy spending money on armament to buy them the few tons of pitchblende they need. Somehow they get their pitchblende, paying for its transportation themselves out of their insufficient salaries. With "her terrible patience," Marie, doing the work of four strong men, pounds away at her chemical masses, boils, separates, refines, stirs, strains. Somewhere in this inert brown stuff lies radium. During these five years Marie loses fifteen pounds. At last they isolate the element.

All this time they have been bringing up a family. They have had sorrows, family illnesses. Pierre's mother has died of the very disease against which radium is soon to prove a beneficent weapon. All this time no provision is made for these selfless geniuses. The State, as always, cares nothing. Recognition comes first from other countries, from Switzerland, England. "With great merit and even greater modesty," says Montaigne, "one can remain unknown for a long time."

Now the full implications of their work begin to appear. The immovable atom moves; matter is touched with a mysterious life; physics revises its nineteenth-century conceptions of the indestructibility of matter and the conservation of energy. The Curies are triumphant; and their first major decision is to refrain from patenting their radium-extraction process. Says Pierre: "Radium is not to enrich anyone. It is an element; it is for all the people." They offer it freely to the world. This gesture alone, the inevitable expression of their characters, is enough to give their lives a depth that can never attach to a commercial career like that of Edison. The difference between a Curie and an Edison is not merely one of scientific genius, it is a difference of order. The Curies are one kind of human being, Edison was another.

In 1903 the Curies, with Becquerel, receive the Nobel Prize for Physics. The world pursues them. They must flee the world. "In science we must be interested in things, not in persons," says Marie, who was never to be interested in herself. One evening, at the height of their fame, as they are about to leave for a banquet, Pierre looks at his wife, with her ash-gray eyes, her ash-blond hair, her exquisite wrists and ankles, and he murmurs, "It's a pity. Evening dress becomes you." Then, with a sigh, he adds, "But there it is, we haven't got time."

They are offered the slimy vulgarity of decorations, ribbons, rosettes. But no laboratory. (Pierre eventually died without getting his laboratory, without being allowed to work properly.) The life of the Curies will remain, forever terrible, as a somber reminder of the stupidity, the greed, even the sadism of the French ruling class of the period, the class which, biding its time, was at last to betray its country thoroughly and forever.

Then on April 19, 1906, Aeschylean tragedy, cutting Marie's life in two, giving it at the same time a new emotional dimension. Pierre's head is crushed by a van in a street accident, and Marie becomes "a pitiful and incurably lonely woman." She refuses a pension (always the State makes its generous offers too late); she proceeds with the education of her daughters; she takes over Pierre's teaching post and, in a dry, monotonous voice, without making any reference to her predecessor, resumes the lectures at the exact point at which Pierre had left off.

The rest of her life is the story of her marriage with radium. For her laboratory, for science, she will do anything, even try to be "famous." In 1911 she receives the Nobel Prize for Chemistry. During the war she equips, with superhuman energy, a fleet of radiological cars so that the wounded may be helped by X rays. She is no rotogravure ministering angel, no Queen Marie of Rumania. She actually works—works for the State which had done its best in those dark years to prevent her from working. Later, again for the sake of science, she comes to America to receive a gram of radium from the hand of an amiable poker player who could not possibly have understood even the most trivial of the thoughts in Marie Curie's mind.

Then, applauded by all America, she goes back to France, and all America turns to the next celebrity, Carpentier, to lavish an identical adulation upon him. Almost blind, her hands and arms scarred, pitted, and burned by thirty years of radium emanations, she continues her work almost to the day of her death, caused in part by that very element which she had released for the use of mankind.

Four Years in a Shed

FROM "MADAME CURIE" BY

EVE CURIE

A MAN CHOSEN at random from a crowd to read an account of the discovery of radium would not have doubted for one moment that radium existed: beings whose critical sense has not been sharpened and simultaneously deformed by specialized culture keep their imaginations fresh. They are ready to accept an unexpected fact, however extraordinary it may appear, and to wonder at it.

The physicist colleagues of the Curies received the news in slightly different fashion. The special properties of polonium and radium upset fundamental theories in which scientists had believed for centuries. How was one to explain the spontaneous radiation of the radioactive bodies? The discovery upset a world of acquired knowledge and contradicted the most firmly established ideas on the composition of matter. Thus the physicist kept on the reserve. He was violently interested in Pierre and Marie's work, he could perceive its infinite developments, but before being convinced he awaited the acquisition of decisive results.

The attitude of the chemist was even more downright. By definition, a chemist only believes in the existence of a new substance when he has seen the substance, touched it, weighed and examined it, confronted it with acids, bottled it, and when he has determined its "atomic weight."

Now, up to the present, nobody had "seen" radium. Nobody knew the atomic weight of radium. And the chemists, faithful to their principles, concluded: "No atomic weight, no radium. Show us some radium and we will believe you."

To show polonium and radium to the incredulous, to prove to the

world the existence of their "children," and to complete their own conviction, M. and Mme Curie were now to labor for four years.

The aim was to obtain pure radium and polonium. In the most
strongly radioactive products the scientists had prepared, these substances figured only in imperceptible traces. Pierre and Marie already
knew the method by which they could hope to isolate the new metals,
but the separation could not be made except by treating very large
quantities of crude material.

Here arose three agonizing questions:

How were they to get a sufficient quantity of ore? What premises
could they use to effect their treatment? What money was there to
pay the inevitable cost of the work?

Pitchblende, in which polonium and radium were hidden, was a
costly ore, treated at the St Joachimsthal mines in Bohemia for the
extraction of uranium salts used in the manufacture of glass. Tons of
pitchblende would cost a great deal: a great deal too much for the
Curie household.

Ingenuity was to make up for wealth. According to the expectation
of the two scientists, the extraction of uranium should leave, intact
in the ore, such traces of polonium and radium as the ore contains.
There was no reason why these traces should not be found in the
residue. And, whereas crude pitchblende was costly, its residue after
treatment had very slight value. By asking an Austrian colleague for
a recommendation to the directors of the mine of St Joachimsthal
would it not be possible to obtain a considerable quantity of such
residue for a reasonable price?

It was simple enough: but somebody had to think of it.

It was necessary, of course, to buy this crude material and pay for
its transportation to Paris. Pierre and Marie appropriated the required
sum from their very slight savings. They were not so foolish as to
ask for official credits. . . . If two physicists on the scent of an immense discovery had asked the University of Paris or the French government for a grant to buy pitchblende residue they would have been
laughed at. In any case their letter would have been lost in the files
of some office, and they would have had to wait months for a reply,

probably unfavorable in the end. Out of the traditions and principles of the French Revolution, which had created the metric system, founded the Normal School, and encouraged science in many circumstances, the State seemed to have retained, after more than a century, only the deplorable words pronounced by Fouquier-Tinville at the trial in which Lavoisier was condemned to the guillotine: "The Republic has no need for scientists."

But at least could there not be found, in the numerous buildings attached to the Sorbonne, some kind of suitable workroom to lend to the Curie couple? Apparently not. After vain attempts, Pierre and Marie staggered back to their point of departure, which is to say to the School of Physics where Pierre taught, to the little room where Marie had done her first experiments. The room gave on a courtyard, and on the other side of the yard there was a wooden shack, an abandoned shed, with a skylight roof in such bad condition that it admitted the rain. The Faculty of Medicine had formerly used the place as a dissecting room, but for a long time now it had not even been considered fit to house the cadavers. No floor: an uncertain layer of bitumen covered the earth. It was furnished with some worn kitchen tables, a blackboard which had landed there for no known reason, and an old cast-iron stove with a rusty pipe.

A workman would not willingly have worked in such a place: Marie and Pierre, nevertheless, resigned themselves to it. The shed had one advantage: it was so untempting, so miserable, that nobody thought of refusing them the use of it. Schutzenberger, the director of the school, had always been very kind to Pierre Curie and no doubt regretted that he had nothing better to offer. However that may be, he offered nothing else; and the couple, very pleased at not being put out into the street with their material, thanked him, saying that "this would do" and that they would "make the best of it."

As they were taking possession of the shed, a reply arrived from Austria. Good news! By extraordinary luck, the residue of recent extractions of uranium had not been scattered. The useless material had been piled up in a no-man's-land planted with pine trees, near the mine of St Joachimsthal. Thanks to the intercession of Professor

Suess and the Academy of Science of Vienna, the Austrian government, which was the proprietor of the State factory there, decided to
present a ton of residue to the two French lunatics who thought they
needed it. If, later on, they wished to be sent a greater quantity of
the material, they could obtain it at the mine on the best terms. For
the moment the Curies had to pay only the transportation charges
on a ton of ore.

One morning a heavy wagon, like those which deliver coal, drew
up in the Rue Lhomond before the School of Physics. Pierre and
Marie were notified. They hurried bareheaded into the street in their
laboratory gowns. Pierre, who was never agitated, kept his calm; but
the more exuberant Marie could not contain her joy at the sight of the
sacks that were being unloaded. It was pitchblende, *her* pitchblende,
for which she had received a notice some days before from the freight
station. Full of curiosity and impatience, she wanted to open one of
the sacks and contemplate her treasure without further waiting. She
cut the strings, undid the coarse sackcloth and plunged her two hands
into the dull brown ore, still mixed with pine needles from Bohemia.

There was where radium was hidden. It was from there that Marie
must extract it, even if she had to treat a mountain of this inert stuff
like dust on the road.

Marya Sklodovska had lived through the most intoxicating moments
of her student life in a garret; Marie Curie was to know wonderful
joys again in a dilapidated shed. It was a strange sort of beginning
over again, in which a sharp subtle happiness (which probably no
woman before Marie had ever experienced) twice elected the most
miserable setting.

The shed in the Rue Lhomond surpassed the most pessimistic expectations of discomfort. In summer, because of its skylights, it was
as stifling as a hothouse. In winter one did not know whether to
wish for rain or frost; if it rained, the water fell drop by drop, with
a soft, nerve-racking noise, on the ground or on the worktables, in
places which the physicists had to mark in order to avoid putting
apparatus there. If it froze, one froze. There was no recourse. The

stove, even when it was stoked white, was a complete disappointment. If one went near enough to touch it one received a little heat, but two steps away and one was back in the zone of ice.

It was almost better for Marie and Pierre to get used to the cruelty of the outside temperature, since their technical installation—hardly existent—possessed no chimneys to carry off noxious gases, and the greater part of their treatment had to be made in the open air, in the courtyard. When a shower came the physicists hastily moved their apparatus inside: to keep on working without being suffocated they set up draughts between the opened door and windows.

Marie probably did not boast to Dr Vauthier of this very peculiar cure for attacks of tuberculosis.

We had no money, no laboratory and no help in the conduct of this important and difficult task [she was to write later]. It was like creating something out of nothing, and if Casimir Dluski once called my student years "the heroic years of my sister-in-law's life," I may say without exaggeration that this period was, for my husband and myself, the heroic period of our common existence.

. . . And yet it was in this miserable old shed that the best and happiest years of our life were spent, entirely consecrated to work. I sometimes passed the whole day stirring a mass in ebullition, with an iron rod nearly as big as myself. In the evening I was broken with fatigue.

In such conditions M. and Mme Curie worked for four years from 1898 to 1902.

During the first year they busied themselves with the chemical separation of radium and polonium and they studied the radiation of the products (more and more active) thus obtained. Before long they considered it more practical to separate their efforts. Pierre Curie tried to determine the properties of radium, and to know the new metal better. Marie continued those chemical treatments which would permit her to obtain salts of pure radium.

In this division of labor Marie had chosen the "man's job." She accomplished the toil of a day laborer. Inside the shed her husband was absorbed by delicate experiments. In the courtyard, dressed in her old dust-covered and acid-stained smock, her hair blown by the wind, surrounded by smoke which stung her eyes and throat, Marie was a sort of factory all by herself.

I came to treat as many as twenty kilograms of matter at a time [she writes], which had the effect of filling the shed with great jars full of precipitates and liquids. It was killing work to carry the receivers, to pour off the liquids and to stir, for hours at a stretch, the boiling matter in a smelting basin.

Radium showed no intention of allowing itself to be known by human creatures. Where were the days when Marie naïvely expected the radium content of pitchblende to be *one per cent?* The radiation of the new substance was so powerful that a tiny quantity of radium, disseminated through the ore, was the source of striking phenomena which could be easily observed and measured. The difficult, the impossible thing, was to isolate this minute quantity, to separate it from the gangue in which it was so intimately mixed.

The days of work became months and years: Pierre and Marie were not discouraged. This material which resisted them, which defended its secrets, fascinated them. United by their tenderness, united by their intellectual passions, they had, in a wooden shack, the "antinatural" existence for which they had both been made, she as well as he.

At this period we were entirely absorbed by the new realm that was, thanks to an unhoped-for discovery, opening before us [Marie was to write]. In spite of the difficulties of our working conditions, we felt very happy. Our days were spent at the laboratory. In our poor shed there reigned a great tranquillity: sometimes, as we watched over some operation, we would walk up and down, talking about work in the present and in the future; when we were cold a cup of hot tea taken near the stove comforted us. We lived in our single preoccupation as if in a dream.

. . . We saw only very few persons at the laboratory; among the physicists and chemists there were a few who came from time to time, either to see our experiments or to ask for advice from Pierre Curie, whose competence in several branches of physics was well-known. Then took place some conversations before the blackboard—the sort of conversation one remembers well because it acts as a stimulant for scientific interest and the ardor for work without interrupting the course of reflection and without troubling that atmosphere of peace and meditation which is the true atmosphere of a laboratory.

Whenever Pierre and Marie, alone in this poor place, left their apparatus for a moment and quietly let their tongues run on, their talk about their beloved radium passed from the transcendent to the childish.

"I wonder what *It* will be like, what *It* will look like," Marie said one day with the feverish curiosity of a child who has been promised a toy. "Pierre, what form do you imagine *It* will take?"

"I don't know," the physicist answered gently. "I should like it to have a very beautiful color. . . ."

It is odd to observe that in Marie Curie's correspondence we find, upon this prodigious effort, none of the sensitive comments, decked out with imagery, which used to flash suddenly amid the familiarity of her letters. Was it because the years of exile had somewhat relaxed the young woman's intimacy with her people? Was she too pressed by work to find time?

The essential reason for this reserve is perhaps to be sought elsewhere. It was not by chance that Mme Curie's letters ceased to be original at the exact moment when the story of her life became exceptional. As student, teacher or young wife, Marie could tell her story. . . . But now she was isolated by all that was secret and inexpressible in her scientific vocation. Among those she loved there was no longer anybody able to understand, to realize her worries and her difficult design. She could share her obsessions with only one person, Pierre Curie, companion. To him alone could she confide rare thoughts and dreams. Marie, from now on, was to present to all others, however near they might be to her heart, an almost commonplace picture of herself. She was to paint for them only the bourgeois side of her life. She was to find sometimes accents full of contained emotion to express her happiness as a woman. But of her work she was to speak only in laconic, inexpressive little phrases: news in three lines, without even attempting to suggest the wonders that work meant to her.

Here we feel an absolute determination not to illustrate the singular profession she had chosen by literature. Through subtle modesty, and also through horror of vain talk and everything superfluous, Marie, concealed herself, dug herself in; or rather, she offered only one of her profiles. Shyness, boredom, or reason, whatever it may have been, the scientist of genius effaced and dissimulated herself behind "a woman like all others."

Marie to Bronya, 1899:

Our life is always the same. We work a lot but we sleep well, so our health does not suffer. The evenings are taken up by caring for the child. In the morning I dress her and give her her food, then I can generally go out at about nine. During the whole of this year we have not been either to the theater or a concert, and we have not paid one visit. For that matter, we feel very well. . . . I miss my family enormously, above all you, my dears, and Father. I often think of my isolation with grief. I cannot complain of anything else, for our health is not bad, the child is growing well, and I have the best husband one could dream of; I could never have imagined finding one like him. He is a true gift of heaven, and the more we live together the more we love each other.

Our work is progressing. I shall soon have a lecture to deliver on the subject. It should have been last Saturday but I was prevented from giving it, so it will no doubt be this Saturday, or else in a fortnight.

This work, which is so dryly mentioned in passing, was in fact progressing magnificently. In the course of the years 1899 and 1900 Pierre and Marie Curie published a report on the discovery of "induced radioactivity" due to radium, another on the effects of radioactivity, and another on the electric charge carried by the rays. And at last they drew up, for the Congress of Physics of 1900, a general report on the radioactive substances, which aroused immense interest among the scientists of Europe.

The development of the new science of radioactivity was rapid, overwhelming—the Curies needed fellow workers. Up to now they had had only the intermittent help of a laboratory assistant named Petit, an honest man who came to work for them outside his hours of service—working out of personal enthusiasm, almost in secret. But they now required technicians of the first order. Their discovery had important extensions in the domain of chemistry, which demanded attentive study. They wished to associate competent research workers ,with them.

Our work on radioactivity began in solitude [Marie was to write]. But before the breadth of the task it became more and more evident that collaboration would be useful. Already in 1898 one of the laboratory chiefs of the school, G. Bémont, had given us some passing help. Toward 1900 Pierre Curie entered into relations with a young chemist, André Debierne, assistant in the laboratory of Professor Friedel, who esteemed him highly. André Debierne willingly accepted work on radioactivity. He undertook especially the research of a new radio element, the existence of which was suspected in the group of iron and rare clays. He discovered this element, named "actinium." Even though he worked in the physico-chemical laboratory at the Sorbonne directed by Jean Perrin, he frequently came to see us in our shed and soon' became a very close friend to us, to Dr Curie and later on to our children.

Thus, even before radium and polonium were isolated, a French scientist, André Debierne, had discovered a "brother," *actinium.*

At about the same period [Marie tells us], a young physicist, Georges Sagnac, engaged in studying X rays, came frequently to talk to Pierre Curie about the analogies that might exist between these rays, their secondary rays, and the radiation of radioactive bodies. Together they performed a work on the electric charge carried by these secondary rays.

Marie continued to treat, kilogram by kilogram, the tons of pitchblende residue which were sent her on several occasions from St Joachimsthal. With her terrible patience, she was able to be, every day for four years, a physicist, a chemist, a specialized worker, an engineer and a laboring man all at once. Thanks to her brain and muscle, the old tables in the shed held more and more concentrated products—products more and more rich in radium. Mme Curie was approaching the end: she no longer stood in the courtyard, enveloped in bitter smoke, to watch the heavy basins of material in fusion. She was now at the stage of purification and of the "fractional crystallization" of strongly radioactive solutions. But the poverty of her haphazard equipment hindered her work more than ever. It was now that she needed a spotlessly clean workroom and apparatus perfectly protected against cold, heat and dirt. In this shed, open to every wind, iron and coal dust was afloat which, to Marie's despair, mixed itself into the products purified with so much care. Her heart sometimes constricted before these little daily accidents, which took so much of her time and her strength.

Pierre was so tired of the interminable struggle that he would have been quite ready to abandon it. Of course, he did not dream of dropping the study of radium and of radioactivity. But he would willingly have renounced, for the time being, the special operation of preparing pure radium. The obstacles seemed insurmountable. Could they not resume this work later on, under better conditions? More attached to the meaning of natural phenomena than to their material reality, Pierre Curie was exasperated to see the paltry results to which Marie's exhausting effort had led. He advised an armistice.

He counted without his wife's character. Marie wanted to isolate radium and she would isolate it. She scorned fatigue and difficulties, and even the gaps in her own knowledge which complicated her task. After all, she was only a very young scientist: she still had not the certainty and great culture Pierre had acquired by twenty years' work, and sometimes she stumbled across phenomena or methods of calculation which she knew very little, and for which she had to make hasty studies.

So much the worse! With stubborn eyes under her great brow, she clung to her apparatus and her test tubes.

In 1902, forty-five months after the day on which the Curies announced the probable existence of radium, Marie finally carried off the victory in this war of attrition: she succeeded in preparing a decigram of pure radium, and made a first determination of the atomic weight of the new substance, which was 225.

The incredulous chemists—of whom there were still a few—could only bow before the facts, before the superhuman obstinacy of a woman.

Radium officially existed.

It was nine o'clock at night. Pierre and Marie Curie were in their little house at 108 Boulevard Kellermann, where they had been living since 1900. The house suited them well. From the boulevard, where three rows of trees half hid the fortifications, could be seen only a dull wall and a tiny door. But behind the one-story house, hidden from all eyes, there was a narrow provincial garden, rather pretty and very quiet. And from the "barrier" of Gentilly they could escape on their bicycles toward the suburbs and the woods. . . .

Old Dr Curie, who lived with the couple, had retired to his room. Marie had bathed her child and put it to bed, and had stayed for a long time beside the cot. This was a rite. When Irène did not feel her mother near her at night she would call out for her incessantly, with that "Mé!" which was to be our substitute for "Mamma" always. And Marie, yielding to the implacability of the four-year-old baby, climbed the stairs, seated herself beside the child and stayed there in the darkness until the young voice gave way to light, regular breathing. Only then would she go down again to Pierre, who was growing impatient. In spite of his kindness, he was the most possessive and jealous of husbands. He was so used to the constant presence of his wife that her least eclipse kept him from thinking freely. If Marie delayed too long near her daughter, he received her on her return with a reproach so unjust as to be comic:

"You never think of anything but that child!"

Pierre walked slowly about the room. Marie sat down and made some stitches on the hem of Irène's new apron. One of her principles was never to buy ready-made clothes for the child: she thought them too fancy and impractical. In the days when Bronya was in Paris the two sisters cut out their children's dresses together, according to patterns of their own invention. These patterns still served for Marie.

But this evening she could not fix her attention. Nervous, she got up; then, suddenly:

"Suppose we go down there for a moment?"

There was a note of supplication in her voice—altogether superfluous, for Pierre, like herself, longed to go back to the shed they had left two hours before. Radium, fanciful as a living creature, endearing as a love, called them back to its dwelling, to the wretched laboratory.

The day's work had been hard, and it would have been more reasonable for the couple to rest. But Pierre and Marie were not always reasonable. As soon as they had put on their coats and told Dr Curie of their flight, they were in the street. They went on foot, arm in arm, exchanging few words. After the crowded streets of this queer district, with its factory buildings, wastelands and poor tenements, they arrived in the Rue Lhomond and crossed the little courtyard. Pierre put the key in the lock. The door squeaked, as it had squeaked thousands of times, and admitted them to their realm, to their dream.

"Don't light the lamps!" Marie said in the darkness. Then she added with a little laugh:

"Do you remember the day when you said to me 'I should like radium to have a beautiful color'?"

The reality was more entrancing than the simple wish of long ago. Radium had something better than "a beautiful color": it was spontaneously luminous. And in the somber shed where, in the absence of cupboards, the precious particles in their tiny glass receivers were placed on tables or on shelves nailed to the walls, their phosphorescent bluish outlines gleamed, suspended in the night.

"Look . . . Look!" the young woman murmured.

She went forward cautiously, looked for and found a straw-bottomed chair. She sat down in the darkness and silence. Their two faces turned toward the pale glimmering, the mysterious sources of radiation, toward radium—their radium. Her body leaning forward, her head eager, Marie took up again the attitude which had been hers an hour earlier at the bedside of her sleeping child.

ALEXANDER WOOLLCOTT

COMMENTARY

The story which follows shows us how a first-rate raconteur can make literature, if of puff-paste lightness, out of a simple anecdote. Mr. Woollcott did not invent "Entrance Fee." It had been floating about the world like thistledown for many years, no doubt often in ruder forms, and no one had had the wit to reduce it, or inflate it, to writing. Mr. Woollcott has worked out the perfect tone: elegant, wistful, and, of course, aseptic.

"Entrance Fee" persuades one to reflect sadly on the taboos which make impossible in our as-yet-primitive moral era the publication in artistic form of a thousand other contes drolatiques, many of them, it may be, slightly more earthy. It is an open secret that some of the wisest, some of the funniest, some of the most searching tales the fancy of man (and woman, if the truth were known) has devised must be circulated orally. Many such stories would be offensive only to a minority, but so far this minority has established a successful censorship. Occasionally it has suffered a setback (see Judge Woolsey's decision on page 382 of this book).

Do not put this comment down as a plea for erotica, an inferior form of literature suitable only to very young men and women and very old men and women. It is merely a melancholy rumination on the curious herd morality that prevents the artistic development of one of the forms of narration most natural to the human animal: the gallant tale revolving around the incredible grotesqueness and high splendor of the fact that the world is permanently divided into two main sexes.

18

Entrance Fee

BY

ALEXANDER WOOLLCOTT

THIS, THEN, is the story of Cosette and the Saint-Cyrien, much as they tell it (and these many years have been telling it) in the smoky *popotes* of the French army.

In the nineties, when one heard less ugly babel of alien tongues in the sidewalk cafés, the talk at the *apéritif* hour was sure to turn sooner or later on Cosette—Mlle. Cosette of the *Variétés,* who was regarded by common consent as the most desirable woman in France. She was no hedged-in royal courtesan, as her possessive fellow-citizens would point out with satisfaction, but a distributed du Barry, the *chère amie* of a republic.

Her origins were misty. Some said she had been born of fisher folk at Plonbazlanec on the Brittany coast. Others preferred the tale that she was the love-child of a famous actress by a very well-known king. In any case, she was now a national legend, and in her pre-eminence the still-bruised French people found in some curious way a balm for their wounded self-esteem. Her photographs, which usually showed her sitting piquantly on a café table, were cut from *L'Illustration* and pinned up in every barracks. Every French lad dreamed of her, and every right-minded French girl quite understood that her sweetheart was saying in effect, "Since I cannot hope to have Cosette, will you come to the river's edge at sundown?" Quite understood, and did not blame him.

Everyone had seen the pictures of Cosette's tiny, vine-hung villa at Saint-Cloud, with its high garden wall and its twittering aviary. And even those for whom that wall was hopelessly high took morbid pride in a persistent detail of the legend which said that no man was ever a guest there for the night who could not bring five thousand francs with him. This was in the nineties, mind you, when francs were francs, and men—by a coincidence then more dependable—were men.

The peasant blend of charm and thrift in Cosette filled the cadets at Saint-Cyr with a gentle melancholy. In their twilight hours of relaxation they talked it over, and all thought it a sorrowful thing that, so wretched is the soldier's pittance, not one of those who must some day direct the great *Revanche* would ever carry into battle a memory of the fairest woman in France. For what cadet could hope to raise five thousand francs? It was very sad. But, cried one of their number, his voice shaking, his eyes alight, there were a thousand students at Saint-Cyr, and not one among them so lacking in resource that he could not, if given time, manage to raise at least five francs.

That was how the Cosette Sweepstakes were started. There followed then all the anxious distraction of ways and means, with such Spartan exploits in self-denial, such Damon-and-Pythias borrowings, such flagrant letters of perjured appeal to unsuspecting aunts and godmothers, as Saint-Cyr had never known. But by the appointed time the last man had his, or somebody's, five francs.

The drawing of numbers was well under way when a perplexed instructor stumbled on the proceedings and reported his discovery to the Commandant. When the old General heard the story he was so profoundly moved that it was some time before he spoke.

"The lad who wins the lottery," he said at last, "will be the envy of his generation. But the lad who conceived the idea—ah, he, my friend, will some day be a Marshal of France!"

Then he fell to laughing at the thought of the starry-eyed youngster arriving at the stage door of the *Variétés* with nothing but his youth and his entrance fee. The innocent budget had made no provision for the trip to Paris, none for a carriage, a bouquet, perhaps a supper party. The Commandant said that he would wish to meet this margin of contingency from his own fatherly pocket.

"There will be extras," he said. "Let the young rascal who wins be sent to me before he leaves for Paris."

It was a cadet from the Vendée who reported to the Commandant next afternoon—very trim in his red breeches and blue tunic, his white gloves spotless, his white cockade jaunty, his heart in his mouth. The Commandant said no word to him, but put a little purse of gold *louis* in his hand, kissed him on both cheeks in benediction, and stood at his window, moist-eyed and chuckling, to watch until the white cockade disappeared down the avenue of trees.

The sunlight, latticed by the *jalousies,* was making a gay pattern on Cosette's carpet the next morning when she sat up and meditated on the day which stretched ahead of her. Her little cadet was cradled in a sweet, dreamless sleep, and it touched her rather to see how preposterously young he was. Indeed, it quite set her thinking of her early days, and how she had come up in the world. Then she began speculating on *his* early days, realized with a pang that he was still in the midst of them, and suddenly grew puzzled. Being a woman of action, she prodded him.

"Listen, my old one," she said, "how did a cadet at Saint-Cyr ever get hold of five thousand francs?"

Thus abruptly questioned, he lost his head and blurted out the tale of the sweepstakes. Perhaps he felt it could do no harm now, and anyway she listened so avidly, with such flattering little gasps of surprise and such sunny ripples of laughter, that he quite warmed to his story. When he came to the part about the Commandant, she rose and strode up and down, the lace of her peignoir fluttering behind her, tears in her violet eyes.

"Saint-Cyr has paid me the prettiest compliment I have ever known," she said, "and I am the proudest woman in France this day. But surely I must do my part. You shall go back and tell them all that Cosette is a woman of sentiment. When you are an old, old man in the Vendée you shall tell your grandchildren that once in your youth you knew the dearest favors in France, and they cost you not a sou. Not a sou."

At that she hauled open the little drawer where he had seen her lock up the lottery receipts the night before.

"Here," she said, with a lovely gesture. "I give you back your money."

And she handed him his five francs.

LUDWIG BEMELMANS

"Putzi" is, I wager, the only successful story ever written about an embryo. Certainly it is the only humorous one. And just as certainly it could have been devised by none but Ludwig Bemelmans. His sympathies are so catholic, his fancy is so flexible, that he sees nothing impossible or even incongruous in combining an anecdote about the weather with an account of a miscarriage. Across the years this South German ex-waiter receives a smile of understanding from another poetical prankster, the one who put an ass' head in fairyland.

I wish we could reproduce in this book some of the absurd pen-and-inks and colored drawings of Bemelmans. They will never influence the course of the history of art, but on the other hand the course of the history of art will never influence Bemelmans, a comforting reflection. His vision is his own. It is inaccurate to say that his simple hues, droll perspectives, and gnomelike figures have the charm of children's drawings. They may remind you of kindergarten art, but no child could command the gemütlich irony informing them. No child, I say, could draw them, but the child hidden in the chuckling man could, and does. The singularity of Bemelmans, whether he draws or writes, is his double capacity to see freshly like a child and comment shrewdly like a grownup. The product is an awry wisdom, the wisdom of a reflective innocent who is surprised at nothing and delighted with everything.

I am not a pro-whimsey man, because the whimsey masters seem to me generally such fools about everything else. But the Bemelmans whimsey is of a different order; it is the wisdom of a volatile but not irresponsible mind. For proof I refer you to his books, notably My War with the United States, Life Class, and The Donkey Inside.

Bemelmans' humor is national; that is, it is South German. Its drollery is (or was, for I suppose drollery too can be gleichschaltet) the kind you find in the people of Austria and Bavaria and the Tirol. It can be at once slightly delicate and slightly gross; it is always eccentric, yet firmly founded in its own folk wisdom; it is gently philosophical; it is leisurely; above all, it is harmless. As a good brief example of it I repeat here the classic Bemelmans story of the elephant cutlet. The story is probably not his, but the manner is pure Bemelmans. I give you

THE ELEPHANT CUTLET

Once upon a time there were two men in Vienna who wanted to open a restaurant. One was a Dentist who was tired of fixing teeth and always wanted to own a restaurant, and the other a famous cook by the same of Souphans.

The Dentist was, however, a little afraid. "There are," he said, "already too many restaurants in Vienna, restaurants of every kind, Viennese, French, Italian, Chinese, American, American-Chinese, Portuguese, Armenian, Dietary, Vegetarian, Jewish, Wine and Beer Restaurants, in short all sorts of restaurants."

But the Chef had an Idea. "There is one kind of restaurant that Vienna has not," he said.

"What kind?" said the Dentist.

"A restaurant such as has never existed before, a restaurant for cutlets from every animal in the world."

The Dentist was afraid, but finally he agreed, and the famous Chef went out to buy a house, tables, and chairs, and engaged help, pots and pans and had a sign painted with big red letters ten feet high saying:

"Cutlets from Every Animal in the World."

The first customer that entered the door was a distinguished lady, a Countess. She sat down and asked for an Elephant Cutlet.

"How would Madame like this Elephant Cutlet cooked?" said the waiter.

"Oh, Milanaise, sauté in butter, with a little spaghetti over it, on that a filet of anchovy, and an olive on top," she said.

"That is very nice," said the waiter and went out to order it.

"Jessas Maria and Joseph!" said the Dentist when he heard the order, and he turned to the Chef and cried: "What did I tell you? Now what are we going to do?"

The Chef said nothing, he put on a clean apron and walked into the dining room to the table of the Lady. There he bowed, bent down to her and said: "Madame has ordered an Elephant Cutlet?"

"Yes," said the Countess.

"With spaghetti and a filet of anchovy and an olive?"

"Yes."

"Madame is all alone?"

"Yes, yes."

"Madame expects no one else?"

"No."

"And Madame wants only one cutlet?"

"Yes," said the Lady, "but why all these questions?"

"Because," said the Chef, "because, Madame, I am very sorry, but for one Cutlet we cannot cut up our Elephant."

Putzi

BY

LUDWIG BEMELMANS

They thought he had asked for more volume, but Nekisch, the conductor, had caught a raindrop on the end of his baton and another in the palm of his hand.

He stopped the orchestra, glared up into the sky and then at Ferdinand Loeffler, the Konzertmeister.

Loeffler reached out for a flying-away page of *Finlandia,* and the audience opened umbrellas and left. The musicians ran into the shelter of the concert hall carrying their instruments, and Herr Loeffler walked sadly to the back of the wide stage and took off his long black coat and shook the rain out of it.

There Nekisch arrested him with his baton. He stuck it into Herr Loeffler, between the two upper buttons of his waistcoat, and held him there against the tall platform. Ganghofer, the percussionist, could hear him say, "You're an ass, Herr Loeffler, not a Konzertmeister, an ass; it's the last time, Herr Loeffler; you can't do the simplest things right; we have a deficit, Herr Loeffler, these are not the good old days, Herr Loeffler—I am telling you for the last and last time: *Inside! Here* in this hall we play when it rains, and *outside* when the sun shines."

Herr Loeffler silently took his blue plush hat and his first violin and went out and waited for a street car to take him to that part of the city where his wife's brother Rudolf had a small café, The Three Ravens.

Frau Loeffler sat in a corner of the little café reading the *Neue Freie Presse* out of a bamboo holder. She stirred her coffee.

"Ah, Ferderl," she said, and squeezed his hand, "but you are early

25

today." She could read his face . . . and she looked with him through the plate glass windows into the dripping street.

"Outside again," she said, and turned to the front page of the *Freie Presse,* and, pointing to the weather report, read, *"Slight disturbances over Vienna but lovely and bright in the Salzkammergut.*

"Inside, outside," she said, over and over again. These two words had taken on the terror that the words death, fire, police, and bankruptcy have for other people.

Behind a counter, next to the cash register, sat Frau Loeffler's sister Frieda. Frau Loeffler pointed at her with the thumb of her right hand. "Look, Ferderl. Look at Frieda. Since I am waiting for you she has eaten three ice creams, four slices of nut tart, two cream puffs, and two portions of chocolate, and now she's looking at the petits fours."

"Yes," said Herr Loeffler.

"Ah, why, Ferderl, haven't we a little restaurant like this, with guests and magazines and newspapers, instead of worrying about that conductor Nekisch and inside and outside?"

"He called me an ass, Nekisch did," said Herr Loeffler. " 'It's the last time,' he said."

"Who does he think you are? The Pope? Why doesn't he decide himself, if he's so smart! I go mad, Ferderl—I can't sleep for two days when you play, reading about the weather, calling up, looking at the mountains, even watching if dogs eat grass. I tried to ask farmers—they don't know either. You can never be sure, they come from nowhere—these clouds—when you don't want them, and when you play inside and hope that it rains outside, the sun shines, just like in spite, and they blame you!"

They put their four hands together in silent communion, one on top of another, as high as a waterglass. Frau Loeffler looked into her coffee cup and she mumbled tenderly, "Ferderl, I have to tell you something." With this she looked shy, like a small girl, then she told him into his ear. . . .

"No!" said Loeffler, with unbelieving eyes.

"Yes! Yes, Ferderl!" she said.

"When?" asked Herr Loeffler.

"In January. About the middle of January . . . Dr. Grausbirn said. . . ."

Loeffler guessed right about the weather for the next two concerts. The sun shone. Outside, it was. Nekisch was talking to him again and Loeffler walked to the concerts with light steps, whistling.

One day at a rehearsal of *Till Eulenspiegel,* he could hold it in no longer; he had to tell them. They patted his shoulder and shook his hand. Even Nekisch stepped down from his stand and put both hands on Loeffler's arms. "Herr Loeffler," he said, just "Herr Loeffler."

And then one day, after the "Liebestod," Loeffler coming home, found in front of his house the horse and carriage of Dr. Grausbirn.

Loeffler ran upstairs and into the living-room, just as Dr. Grausbirn came out of the other door, from his wife's room.

"My wife?" asked Herr Loeffler.

"No," said Dr. Grausbirn. "No, Herr Loeffler, not your wife." Dr. Grausbirn washed his hands. Herr Loeffler went to kiss his poor wife and came back again.

"Herr Doktor," he said, "we won't—I am not going to——"

Dr. Grausbirn closed his bag and slipped on his cuffs.

"Pull yourself together, Loeffler. Be a man," he said, "but you won't be a father——"

"Never?" asked Herr Loeffler.

"Never," said Dr. Grausbirn.

Herr Loeffler sat down on the edge of his chair. "We are simple people," he addressed the table in front of him. "We ask so little of life. We have always wanted him. We have even named him—Putzi, we call him—why, Annie has burned candles to St. Joseph, the patron saint of fathers." He sighed again.

"Why does this happen to me?" he said. "And how could it happen? We ask so little."

Dr. Grausbirn pointed out of the window. "There, Herr Loeffler," he said. "It's like this. Do you see that lovely little late-blooming apple tree? It has many blossoms. . . .

"Then comes the wind." Dr. Grausbirn reached into the air and swept down. *"Schrumm*—like this—and some of the blossoms fall— and the rain—takes more"—with his short fat fingers the doctor imitated the rain—"and brr r r, the frosts—more blossoms fall—they are not strong enough. Do you understand, Herr Loeffler, what I mean?"

They looked out at the little tree: it was rich with blossoms, so rich that the earth below it was white.

"That blossom, our little Putzi—" said Herr Loeffler.

"Yes," said the doctor. "Where is my hat?"

The doctor looked for his hat and Herr Loeffler walked down the stairs with him.

"If you are going into town—" said Dr. Grausbirn, opening the door of his landau. Loeffler nodded and stepped in.

At the end of the street a lamp post was being painted. The carriage turned into the tree-lined avenue; a column of young soldiers passed them. After the lamp post, Herr Loeffler talked earnestly to Dr. Grausbirn, but the doctor shook his head—"No no no, no no, Herr Loeffler. Impossible—cannot be done." Herr Loeffler mumbled on, "We ask so little." He underlined his words, *the only one*—never again—my poor wife—love—family"—and all this time he tried to tie a knot in the thick leather strap that hung down the door of the wagon.

"No," said Dr. Grausbirn.

The driver pulled in his reins and the horse stopped to let a street car and two motor cars pass. Herr Loeffler was red in the face. Under the protection of the noises of starting motors, horns, and the bell of the trolley, he shouted, "Putzi belongs to us!" and he banged with his umbrella three times on the extra seat that was folded up in front of him. The driver looked around.

"Putzi?" asked Dr. Grausbirn.

"Our little blossom," said Herr Loeffler, pointing to the doctor's bag.

Dr. Grausbirn followed the flight of a pigeon with his eyes. The pigeon flew to a fountain and drank. Under the fountain was a dog; he ate grass and then ran to the curb. From there the doctor's eyes turned to the back of the driver and across to Herr Loeffler—a tear ran down the Konzertmeister's face. The doctor put his hand on Loeffler's knee.

"Loeffler, I'll do it. There's no law—every museum has one. Properly prepared, of course . . . in a bottle . . . next Monday . . . *Servus*, Herr Loeffler."

"Auf Wiedersehen, Herr Doktor."

And so Putzi was delivered to Herr Loeffler. Herr Loeffler, who wrote a fine hand, designed a lovely label for the bottle. "Our dear Putzi," he wrote, and under the name he printed the date.

The next week Herr Loeffler guessed wrong again—rain for Beethoven outside—and sunshine for Brahms inside—and conductor Nekisch broke his baton.

"Go away, Herr Loeffler," he said. "I am a man of patience, but you've done this once too often. Get out of my sight, far away—where I never see you again, ass of a Konzertmeister!"

Herr Loeffler walked home. . . .

For a year Putzi had stood on the mantelpiece. He was presented with flowers on his birthday, and on Christmas he had a little tree with one candle on it. Now Herr Loeffler sat for hours in his chair, looking out the window and at little Putzi in his bottle, and thought about the weather, about the orchestra—about inside and outside.

The *Neue Freie Presse* was mostly wrong; the government reports were seldom right. Nekisch was always wrong—more often than when Loeffler had given the word—but Putzi in his little bottle, Putzi was always right, well in advance. . . .

It was not until months had passed, though, that Herr Loeffler noticed it. He watched closely for a few more days and then he told his wife. He took a pad and a pencil and he drew a line across the middle of the pad. On the lower half he wrote "Inside," on the upper half "Outside"—then he rubbed his hands and waited. . . .

Long, long ere the tiniest blue cloud showed over the rim of any of the tall mountains that surrounded the beautiful valley of Salzburg, Putzi could tell: he sank to the bottom of his bottle, a trace of two wrinkles appeared on his little forehead, and the few tiny hairs which were growing over his left ear curled into tight spirals.

On the other hand, when tomorrow's sun promised to rise into the clear mountain air to shine all day, Putzi swam on top of his bottle with a Lilliputian smile and rosy cheeks.

"Come, Putzi," said Herr Loeffler, when the pad was filled—and he took him and the chart to Nekisch. . . .

Herr Loeffler now is back again—Inside when it rains—Outside when the sun shines.

THOMAS MANN

COMMENTARY

Where live Thomas Mann and those of his temper, however scattered or broken they be, there lives Germany.

The career of Thomas Mann offers the rare spectacle of a youthful prodigy who has never stopped developing. It is a career which opens in the flush of genius and continues to progress with almost symphonic logic, harmony, and beauty. At twenty-five he had written Buddenbrooks, a novel of the first order. In his late forties he had gone far beyond Buddenbrooks to the heights of The Magic Mountain, a long selection from which I include in this book. Now, in his full maturity, he is completing his profoundest work, his great Biblical tetralogy of Joseph and his brothers.

It is appalling to reflect that in his mid-twenties he had completed not merely Buddenbrooks but two long short stories of genius— "Tonio Kröger" and "Tristan." One already feels here something far more imposing than the lushly lauded prodigies of a youthful Keats or Shelley. But Mann, calmly, surely, with the unremitting serenity of a Goethe, was to go on to "Death in Venice," written in his thirty-sixth year. I say "written," but in fact "Death in Venice" seems rather to be played on a cello. The tone, in its mingling of melancholy, gravity, and controlled power, is equivalent to that of Casals. "Death in Venice" is a sort of culmination, for in it Mann gathered up all the themes upon which he had touched during the first fifteen years of his writing career—the anomalous position of the artist in bourgeois society, the sinister attraction of decadence and disease, the fusion of Northern and pagan modes of feeling, the troubling and even evil effects of beauty upon those well past their youth.

Thomas Mann, though he has never since written anything as purely beautiful as "Death in Venice," was to go beyond it in other ways. In 1925 came "Disorder and Early Sorrow," in which the terrible pulse of the German inflation beats through a narrative that is on the surface a tender, muted story about a child's ephemeral grief. The finest of all his short stories, however, is "Mario and the Magician" (1929), which I have chosen because it seems to me to dig even deeper than does "Death in Venice."

Here is the tale of a stage hypnotist and the fate he meets at the hands of one of his puppets. But to call this the story of Mario and the magician is to say that Moby Dick is about a mad sea captain who revengefully pursues a white whale and is at last destroyed by his quarry. "Mario" is brief, simple, a small fragment of life, and Moby Dick is vast as the Pacific. Yet they are written on the same emotional level. Mann and Melville are identically obsessed. Both are tortured by the metaphysical problem of evil, though Mann, writing in a psychoanalytic age, sees evil as illness, as a multiform malady. Confronted by a riotously rotting society, he has sought the cancerous spots, particularly in their subtler manifestations. From the diseases of its parts he deduces the nature of the whole. The ground theme of Buddenbrooks—what is it but the sickness of an acquisitive society, considered as a sickness? To the same problem, more grandly treated, the pages of The Magic Mountain are devoted. And this little tale of Mario and the magician emerges from the identical preoccupation. It is a study of malevolence, of the power the will attains when it is distorted and willing to crucify itself that it may dominate other, healthier wills. "Shall we go away," muses the author, "whenever life looks like turning the slightest uncanny, or not quite normal, or even rather painful and mortifying?" As ever, his answer is "No, surely not."

Had Mann been content merely to pose and examine the problem of the will to evil in terms of the magician Cipolla and the youth Mario, his story would have been interesting, but possibly rather thin, as this sort of symbolism is apt to be. With weird skill, however, he thickens his narrative, carefully blurs its implications, so that the idea skeleton does not affright us with its bare and pallid bones. By insensible degrees we are led along a pathway of conflict and unwholesomeness, beginning with the petty irritations offered by an overbearing hotel management and closing with a horrible psychic struggle ended only by death. When we reach the last page we realize that it is the honor of the human race which has been resisting the evil

Cipolla. Thus the tone of the story preserves a deepening unity of atmosphere which mesmerizes us apart from the incidents. Again, the macabre quality of these incidents is touched with its own special irony in that we are bidden to view them through the gleefully uncomprehending eyes of little children. To the children, of course, Cipolla's entire performance is a sort of glorified romp. Who, indeed, can tell how far Mann's irony extends? Cipolla, with his strident and theatrical patriotism, seems a deep thrust at the domination ideal of the Fascisti, a prophecy of the pit they are digging for themselves. Also, and perhaps more obviously, this Cipolla is a type figure out of Freud: his hump is a symbol of his organ inferiority, he is destroyed by the very Eros he thinks to mock.

Finally, the chiaroscuro attains an added density and terror through the circumstance that the chief character is both trickster and miracle worker. To that misty mid-region of phenomena which seems to partake both of charlatanry and the supernatural, Thomas Mann has always been attracted—witness the manifestation scene in The Magic Mountain and his interest in Schrenck-Notzing. What attracts the psychologist in him is the ambiguity of the human will, which, even when it seeks merely to exercise itself playfully or out of the mere pride of technique, finds itself involved in the darkest of human relationships and at times with powers we cannot or dare not name. Cipolla becomes more than a super-Svengali. The theatrical atmosphere with which he surrounds himself is more than theatrical. It is agonized and broken and disturbing. It haunts us, not like the elegiac strains of "Death in Venice" but like a nightmare which is also a parable.

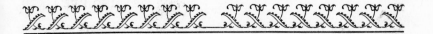

Mario and the Magician

BY

THOMAS MANN

THE ATMOSPHERE of Torre di Venere remains unpleasant in the memory. From the first moment the air of the place made us uneasy, we
felt irritable, on edge; then at the end came the shocking business of
Cipolla, that dreadful being who seemed to incorporate, in so fateful
and so humanly impressive a way, all the peculiar evilness of the situation as a whole. Looking back, we had the feeling that the horrible
end of the affair had been preordained and lay in the nature of things;
that the children had to be present at it was an added impropriety,
due to the false colours in which the weird creature presented himself.
Luckily for them, they did not know where the comedy left off and
the tragedy began; and we let them remain in their happy belief that
the whole thing had been a play up till the end.

Torre di Venere lies some fifteen kilometres from Portoclemente,
one of the most popular summer resorts on the Tyrrhenian Sea. Portoclemente is urban and elegant and full to overflowing for months on
end. Its gay and busy main street of shops and hotels runs down to
a wide sandy beach covered with tents and pennanted sand-castles and
sunburnt humanity, where at all times a lively social bustle reigns, and
much noise. But this same spacious and inviting fine-sanded beach,
this same border of pine grove and near, presiding mountains, continues all the way along the coast. No wonder then that some competition of a quiet kind should have sprung up further on. Torre di
Venere—the tower that gave the town its name is gone long since, one
looks for it in vain—is an offshoot of the larger resort, and for some
years remained an idyll for the few, a refuge for more unworldly
spirits. But the usual history of such places repeated itself: peace has

33

had to retire further along the coast, to Marina Petriera and dear knows where else. We all know how the world at once seeks peace and puts her to flight—rushing upon her in the fond idea that they two will wed, and where she is, there it can be at home. It will even set up its Vanity Fair in a spot and be capable of thinking that peace is still by its side. Thus Torre—though its atmosphere so far is more modest and contemplative than that of Portoclemente—has been quite taken up, by both Italians and foreigners. It is no longer the thing to go to Portoclemente—though still so much the thing that it is as noisy and crowded as ever. One goes next door, so to speak: to Torre. So much more refined, even, and cheaper to boot. And the attractiveness of these qualities persists, though the qualities themselves long ago ceased to be evident. Torre has got a Grand Hotel. Numerous pensions have sprung up, some modest, some pretentious. The people who own or rent the villas and pinetas overlooking the sea no longer have it all their own way on the beach. In July and August it looks just like the beach at Portoclemente: it swarms with a screaming, squabbling, merrymaking crowd, and the sun, blazing down like mad, peels the skin off their necks. Garish little flat-bottomed boats rock on the glittering blue, manned by children, whose mothers hover afar and fill the air with anxious cries of Nino! and Sandro! and Bice! and Maria! Pedlars step across the legs of recumbent sun-bathers, selling flowers and corals, oysters, lemonade, and *cornetti al burro,* and crying their wares in the breathy, full-throated southern voice.

Such was the scene that greeted our arrival in Torre: pleasant enough, but after all, we thought, we had come too soon. It was the middle of August, the Italian season was still at its height, scarcely the moment for strangers to learn to love the special charms of the place. What an afternoon crowd in the cafés on the front! For instance, in the Esquisito, where we sometimes sat and were served by Mario, that very Mario of whom I shall have presently to tell. It is well-nigh impossible to find a table; and the various orchestras contend together in the midst of one's conversation with bewildering effect. Of course, it is in the afternoon that people come over from Portoclemente. The excursion is a favourite one for the restless denizens of that pleasure resort, and a Fiat motor-bus plies to and fro, coating inch-thick with dust the oleander and laurel hedges along the highroad—a notable if repulsive sight.

Yes, decidedly one should go to Torre in September, when the great public has left. Or else in May, before the water is warm enough to tempt the Southerner to bathe. Even in the before and after seasons Torre is not empty, but life is less national and more subdued. English, French, and German prevail under the tent-awnings and in the pension dining-rooms; whereas in August—in the Grand Hotel, at least, where, in default of private addresses, we had engaged rooms—the stranger finds the field so occupied by Florentine and Roman society that he feels quite isolated and even temporarily *déclassé*.

We had, rather to our annoyance, this experience on the evening we arrived, when we went in to dinner and were shown to our table by the waiter in charge. As a table, it had nothing against it, save that we had already fixed our eyes upon those on the veranda beyond, built out over the water, where little red-shaded lamps glowed—and there were still some tables empty, though it was as full as the dining-room within. The children went into raptures at the festive sight, and without more ado we announced our intention to take our meals by preference in the veranda. Our words, it appeared, were prompted by ignorance; for we were informed, with somewhat embarrassed politeness, that the cosy nook outside was reserved for the clients of the hotel: *ai nostri clienti*. Their clients? But we were their clients. We were not tourists or trippers, but boarders for a stay of some three or four weeks. However, we forbore to press for an explanation of the difference between the likes of us and that clientèle to whom it was vouchsafed to eat out there in the glow of the red lamps, and took our dinner by the prosaic common light of the dining-room chandelier—a thoroughly ordinary and monotonous hotel bill of fare, be it said. In Pensione Eleonora, a few steps landward, the table, as we were to discover, was much better.

And thither it was that we moved, three or four days later, before we had had time to settle in properly at the Grand Hotel. Not on account of the veranda and the lamps. The children, straightway on the best of terms with waiters and pages, absorbed in the joys of life on the beach, promptly forgot those colourful seductions. But now there arose, between ourselves and the veranda clientèle—or perhaps more correctly with the compliant management—one of those little unpleasantnesses which can quite spoil the pleasure of a holiday. Among the guests were some high Roman aristocracy, a Principe X and his family. These grand folk occupied rooms close to our own, and the Principessa, a great and a passionately maternal lady, was thrown into a panic by the vestiges of a whooping-cough which our little ones had lately got over, but which now and then still faintly troubled the unshatterable slumbers of our youngest-born. The nature of this illness is not clear, leaving some play for the imagination. So we took no offence at our elegant neighbour for clinging to the widely held view that whooping-cough is acoustically contagious and quite simply fearing lest her children yield to the bad example set by ours. In the fullness of her feminine self-confidence she protested to the management, which then, in the person of the proverbial frock-coated manager, hastened to represent to us, with many expressions of regret, that under the circumstances they were obliged to transfer us to the annexe. We did our best to assure him that the disease was in its very last stages, that it was actually over, and presented no danger of infection to anybody. All that we gained was permission to bring the case before the hotel physician—not one chosen by us—by whose verdict we must then abide. We agreed, convinced that thus we should at once pacify the Princess and escape the trouble of moving. The doctor appeared, and behaved like a faithful and honest servant of science. He examined the child and gave his opinion: the disease was quite over, no danger of contagion was present. We drew a long breath and considered the incident closed—until the manager announced that despite the doctor's verdict it would still be necessary for us to give up our rooms and retire to the *dépendance*. Byzantinism like this outraged us. It is not likely that the Principessa was responsible for the wilful breach of faith. Very likely the fawning management had not even dared to tell her what the physician said. Anyhow, we made it clear to his understanding that we preferred to leave the hotel altogether and at once—and packed our trunks. We could do so with a light heart, having already set up casual friendly relations with Casa Eleonora. We had noticed its pleasant exterior and formed the acquaintance of its proprietor, Signora Angiolieri, and her husband: she slender and black-haired, Tuscan in type, probably at the beginning of the thirties, with the dead ivory complexion of the southern woman, he quiet and bald and carefully dressed. They owned a larger establishment in Florence and presided only in summer and early autumn over the branch in Torre di Venere. But earlier, before her marriage, our new landlady had been companion, fellow-traveller, wardrobe mistress, yes, friend, of Eleonora Duse and manifestly regarded that period as the crown of her career. Even at our first visit she spoke of it with animation. Numerous photographs of the great actress, with affectionate inscriptions, were displayed about the drawing-room, and other souvenirs of their life together adorned the little tables and étagères. This cult of a so interesting past was calculated, of course, to heighten the advantages of the signora's present business. Nevertheless our pleasure and interest were quite genuine as we were conducted through the house by its owner and listened to her sonorous and staccato Tuscan voice relating anecdotes of that immortal mistress, depicting her suffering saintliness, her genius, her profound delicacy of feeling.

Thither, then, we moved our effects, to the dismay of the staff of the Grand Hotel, who, like all Italians, were very good to children. Our new quarters were retired and pleasant, we were within easy reach of the sea through the avenue of young plane trees that ran down to the esplanade. In the clean, cool dining-room Signora Angiolieri daily served the soup with her own hands, the service was attentive and good, the table capital. We even discovered some Viennese acquaintances, and enjoyed chatting with them after luncheon, in front of the house. They, in their turn, were the means of our finding others —in short, all seemed for the best, and we were heartily glad of the change we had made. Nothing was now wanting to a holiday of the most gratifying kind.

And yet no proper gratification ensued. Perhaps the stupid occasion of our change of quarters pursued us to the new ones we had found. Personally, I admit that I do not easily forget these collisions with ordinary humanity, the naïve misuse of power, the injustice, the sycophantic corruption. I dwelt upon the incident too much, it irri-

tated me in retrospect—quite futilely, of course, since such phenomena
are only all too natural and all too much the rule. And we had not
broken off relations with the Grand Hotel. The children were as
friendly as ever there, the porter mended their toys, and we sometimes
took tea in the garden. We even saw the Principessa. She would come
out, with her firm and delicate tread, her lips emphatically corallined,
to look after her children, playing under the supervision of their
English governess. She did not dream that we were anywhere near, for
so soon as she appeared in the offing we sternly forbade our little one
even to clear his throat.

The heat—if I may bring it in evidence—was extreme. It was African. The power of the sun, directly one left the border of the indigo-
blue wave, was so frightful, so relentless, that the mere thought of
the few steps between the beach and luncheon was a burden, clad
though one might be only in pyjamas. Do you care for that sort of
thing? Weeks on end? Yes, of course, it is proper to the south, it is
classic weather, the sun of Homer, the climate wherein human culture
came to flower—and all the rest of it. But after a while it is too much
for me, I reach a point where I begin to find it dull. The burning void
of the sky, day after day, weighs one down; the high coloration, the
enormous naïveté of the unrefracted light—they do, I dare say, induce light-heartedness, a carefree mood born of immunity from down-
pours and other meteorological caprices. But slowly, slowly, there makes
itself felt a lack: the deeper, more complex needs of the northern soul
remain unsatisfied. You are left barren—even, it may be, in time, a little
contemptuous. True, without that stupid business of the whooping-
cough I might not have been feeling these things. I was annoyed,
very likely I wanted to feel them and so half-unconsciously seized
upon an idea lying ready to hand to induce, or if not to induce, at
least to justify and strengthen, my attitude. Up to this point, then, if
you like, let us grant some ill will on our part. But the sea; and the
mornings spent extended upon the fine sand in face of its eternal
splendours—no, the sea could not conceivably induce such feelings.
Yet it was none the less true that, despite all previous experience, we
were not at home on the beach, we were not happy.

It was too soon, too soon. The beach, as I have said, was still in the hands of the middle-class native. It is a pleasing breed to look at, and among the young we saw much shapeliness and charm. Still, we were necessarily surrounded by a great deal of very average humanity— a middle-class mob, which, you will admit, is not more charming under this sun than under one's own native sky. The voices these women have! It was sometimes hard to believe that we were in the land which is the western cradle of the art of song. *"Fuggièro!"* I can still hear that cry, as for twenty mornings long I heard it close behind me, breathy, full-throated, hideously stressed, with a harsh open *e,* uttered in accents of mechanical despair. *"Fuggièro! Rispondi almeno!"* Answer when I call you! The *sp* in *rispondi* was pronounced like *shp,* as Germans pronounce it; and this, on top of what I felt already, vexed my sensitive soul. The cry was addressed to a repulsive youngster whose sunburn had made disgusting raw sores on his shoulders. He outdid anything I have ever seen for ill-breeding, refractoriness, and temper and was a great coward to boot, putting the whole beach in an uproar, one day, because of his outrageous sensitiveness to the slightest pain. A sand-crab had pinched his toe in the water, and the minute injury made him set up a cry of heroic proportions—the shout of an antique hero in his agony—that pierced one to the marrow and called up visions of some frightful tragedy. Evidently he considered himself not only wounded, but poisoned as well; he crawled out on the sand and lay in apparently intolerable anguish, groaning *"Ohi!"* and *"Ohimè!"* and threshing about with arms and legs to ward off his mother's tragic appeals and the questions of the bystanders. An audience gathered round. A doctor was fetched—the same who had pronounced objective judgment on our whooping-cough—and here again acquitted himself like a man of science. Good-naturedly he reassured the boy, telling him that he was not hurt at all, he should simply go into the water again to relieve the smart. Instead of which, Fuggièro was borne off the beach, followed by a concourse of people. But he did not fail to appear next morning, nor did he leave off spoiling our children's sand-castles. Of course, always by accident. In short, a perfect terror.

And this twelve-year-old lad was prominent among the influences that, imperceptibly at first, combined to spoil our holiday and render it unwholesome. Somehow or other, there was a stiffness, a lack of innocent enjoyment. These people stood on their dignity—just why, and in what spirit, it was not easy at first to tell. They displayed much self-respectingness; towards each other and towards the foreigner their bearing was that of a person newly conscious of a sense of honour. And wherefore? Gradually we realized the political implications and understood that we were in the presence of a national ideal. The beach, in fact, was alive with patriotic children—a phenomenon as unnatural as it was depressing. Children are a human species and a society apart, a nation of their own, so to speak. On the basis of their common form of life, they find each other out with the greatest ease, no matter how different their small vocabularies. Ours soon played with natives and foreigners alike. Yet they were plainly both puzzled and disappointed at times. There were wounded sensibilities, displays of assertiveness—or rather hardly assertiveness, for it was too self-conscious and too didactic to deserve the name. There were quarrels over flags, disputes about authority and precedence. Grown-ups joined in, not so much to pacify as to render judgment and enunciate principles. Phrases were dropped about the greatness and dignity of Italy, solemn phrases that spoilt the fun. We saw our two little ones retreat, puzzled and hurt, and were put to it to explain the situation. These people, we told them, were just passing through a certain stage, something rather like an illness, perhaps; not very pleasant, but probably unavoidable.

We had only our own carelessness to thank that we came to blows in the end with this "stage"—which, after all, we had seen and sized up long before now. Yes, it came to another "cross-purposes," so evidently the earlier ones had not been sheer accident. In a word, we became an offence to the public morals. Our small daughter—eight years old, but in physical development a good year younger and thin as a chicken—had had a good long bathe and gone playing in the warm sun in her wet costume. We told her that she might take off her bathing-suit, which was stiff with sand, rinse it in the sea, and put it on again, after which she must take care to keep it cleaner. Off goes the costume and she runs down naked to the sea, rinses her little jersey, and comes back. Ought we to have foreseen the outburst of anger and resentment which her conduct, and thus our conduct, called forth? Without delivering a homily on the subject, I may say that in the last decade our attitude towards the nude body and our feelings regarding it have undergone, all over the world, a fundamental change. There are things we "never think about" any more, and among them is the freedom we had permitted to this by no means provocative little childish body. But in these parts it was taken as a challenge. The patriotic children hooted. Fuggièro whistled on his fingers. The sudden buzz of conversation among the grown people in our neighbourhood boded no good. A gentleman in city togs, with a not very apropos bowler hat on the back of his head, was assuring his outraged womenfolk that he proposed to take punitive measures; he stepped up to us, and a philippic descended on our unworthy heads, in which all the emotionalism of the sense-loving south spoke in the service of morality and discipline. The offence against decency of which we had been guilty was, he said, the more to be condemned because it was also a gross ingratitude and an insulting breach of his country's hospitality. We had criminally injured not only the letter and spirit of the public bathing regulations, but also the honour of Italy; he, the gentleman in the city togs, knew how to defend that honour and proposed to see to it that our offence against the national dignity should not go unpunished.

We did our best, bowing respectfully, to give ear to this eloquence. To contradict the man, overheated as he was, would probably be to fall from one error into another. On the tips of our tongues we had various answers: as, that the word "hospitality," in its strictest sense, was not quite the right one, taking all the circumstances into consideration. We were not literally the guests of Italy, but of Signora Angiolieri, who had assumed the rôle of dispenser of hospitality some years ago on laying down that of familiar friend to Eleonora Duse. We longed to say that surely this beautiful country had not sunk so low as to be reduced to a state of hypersensitive prudishness. But we confined ourselves to assuring the gentleman that any lack of respect, any provocation on our parts, had been the furthest from our thoughts. And as a mitigating circumstance we pointed out the tender age and physical slightness of the little culprit. In vain. Our protests were

waved away, he did not believe in them; our defence would not hold
water. We must be made an example of. The authorities were notified,
by telephone, I believe, and their representative appeared on the beach.
He said the case was *"molto grave."* We had to go with him to the
Municipio up in the Piazza, where a higher official confirmed the
previous verdict of *"molto grave,"* launched into a stream of the usual
didactic phrases—the selfsame tune and words as the man in the
bowler hat—and levied a fine and ransom of fifty lire. We felt that
the adventure must willy-nilly be worth to us this much of a contribution to the economy of the Italian government; paid, and left. Ought
we not at this point to have left Torre as well?

If we only had! We should thus have escaped that fatal Cipolla.
But circumstances combined to prevent us from making up our minds
to a change. A certain poet says that it is indolence that makes us
endure uncomfortable situations. The *aperçu* may serve as an explanation for our inaction. Anyhow, one dislikes voiding the field immediately upon such an event. Especially if sympathy from other quarters
encourages one to defy it. And in the Villa Eleonora they pronounced
as with one voice upon the injustice of our punishment. Some Italian
after-dinner acquaintances found that the episode put their country
in a very bad light, and proposed taking the man in the bowler hat
to task, as one fellow-citizen to another. But the next day he and his
party had vanished from the beach. Not on our account, of course.
Though it might be that the consciousness of his impending departure
had added energy to his rebuke; in any case his going was a relief.
And, furthermore, we stayed because our stay had by now become
remarkable in our own eyes, which is worth something in itself, quite
apart from the comfort or discomfort involved. Shall we strike sail,
avoid a certain experience so soon as it seems not expressly calculated
to increase our enjoyment or our self-esteem? Shall we go away whenever life looks like turning in the slightest uncanny, or not quite
normal, or even rather painful and mortifying? No, surely not. Rather
stay and look matters in the face, brave them out; perhaps precisely in
so doing lies a lesson for us to learn. We stayed on and reaped as
the awful reward of our constancy the unholy and staggering experience with Cipolla.

I have not mentioned that the after season had begun, almost on the very day we were disciplined by the city authorities. The worship-ful gentleman in the bowler hat, our denouncer, was not the only person to leave the resort. There was a regular exodus, on every hand you saw luggage-carts on their way to the station. The beach de-nationalized itself. Life in Torre, in the cafés and the pinetas, became more homelike and more European. Very likely we might even have eaten at a table in the glass veranda, but we refrained, being content at Signora Angiolieri's—as content, that is, as our evil star would let us be. But at the same time with this turn for the better came a change in the weather: almost to an hour it showed itself in harmony with the holiday calendar of the general public. The sky was overcast; not that it grew any cooler, but the unclouded heat of the entire eighteen days since our arrival, and probably long before that, gave place to a stifling sirocco air, while from time to time a little ineffectual rain sprinkled the velvety surface of the beach. Add to which, that two-thirds of our intended stay at Torre had passed. The colourless, lazy sea, with sluggish jellyfish floating in its shallows, was at least a change. And it would have been silly to feel retrospective longings after a sun that had caused us so many sighs when it burned down in all its arrogant power.

At this juncture, then, it was that Cipolla announced himself. Cavaliere Cipolla he was called on the posters that appeared one day stuck up everywhere, even in the dining-room of Pensione Eleonora. A travelling virtuoso, an entertainer, *"forzatore, illusionista, prestidiga-tore,"* as he called himself, who proposed to wait upon the highly re-spectable population of Torre di Venere with a display of extraordinary phenomena of a mysterious and staggering kind. A conjuror! The bare announcement was enough to turn our children's heads. They had never seen anything of the sort, and now our present holiday was to afford them this new excitement. From that moment on they besieged us with prayers to take tickets for the performance. We had doubts, from the first, on the score of the lateness of the hour, nine o'clock; but gave way, in the idea that we might see a little of what Cipolla had to offer, probably no great matter, and then go home. Besides, of course, the children could sleep late next day. We bought four

tickets of Signora Angiolieri herself, she having taken a number of
the stalls on commission to sell them to her guests. She could not
vouch for the man's performance, and we had no great expectations.
But we were conscious of a need for diversion, and the children's
violent curiosity proved catching.

The Cavaliere's performance was to take place in a hall where during
the season there had been a cinema with a weekly programme. We had
never been there. You reached it by following the main street under
the wall of the *"palazzo,"* a ruin with a "For sale" sign, that suggested a castle and had obviously been built in lordlier days. In the
same street were the chemist, the hairdresser, and all the better shops;
it led, so to speak, from the feudal past the bourgeois into the proletarian, for it ended off between two rows of poor fishing-huts, where
old women sat mending nets before the doors. And here, among the
proletariat, was the hall, not much more, actually, than a wooden
shed, though a large one, with a turreted entrance, plastered on either
side with layers of gay placards. Some while after dinner, then, on
the appointed evening, we wended our way thither in the dark, the
children dressed in their best and blissful with the sense of so much
irregularity. It was sultry, as it had been for days; there was heat
lightning now and then, and a little rain; we proceeded under umbrellas. It took us a quarter of an hour.

Our tickets were collected at the entrance, our places we had to find
ourselves. They were in the third row left, and as we sat down we saw
that, late though the hour was for the performance, it was to be interpreted with even more laxity. Only very slowly did an audience—
who seemed to be relied upon to come late—begin to fill the stalls.
These comprised the whole auditorium; there were no boxes. This
tardiness gave us some concern. The children's cheeks were already
flushed as much with fatigue as with excitement. But even when we
entered, the standing-room at the back and in the side aisles was
already well occupied. There stood the manhood of Torre di Venere,
all and sundry, fisherfolk, rough-and-ready youths with bare forearms
crossed over their striped jerseys. We were well pleased with the
presence of this native assemblage, which always adds colour and
animation to occasions like the present; and the children were frankly

delighted. For they had friends among these people—acquaintances picked up on afternoon strolls to the further ends of the beach. We would be turning homeward, at the hour when the sun dropped into the sea, spent with the huge effort it had made and gilding with reddish gold the oncoming surf; and we would come upon bare-legged fisherfolk standing in rows, bracing and hauling with long-drawn cries as they drew in the nets and harvested in dripping baskets their catch, often so scanty, of *frutta di mare*. The children looked on, helped to pull, brought out their little stock of Italian words, made friends. So now they exchanged nods with the "standing-room" clientèle; there was Guiscardo, there Antonio, they knew them by name and waved and called across in half-whispers, getting answering nods and smiles that displayed rows of healthy white teeth. Look, there is even Mario, Mario from the Esquisito, who brings us the chocolate. He wants to see the conjuror, too, and he must have come early, for he is almost in front; but he does not see us, he is not paying attention; that is a way he has, even though he is a waiter. So we wave instead to the man who lets out the little boats on the beach; he is there too, standing at the back.

It had got to a quarter past nine, it got to almost half past. It was natural that we should be nervous. When would the children get to bed? It had been a mistake to bring them, for now it would be very hard to suggest breaking off their enjoyment before it had got well under way. The stalls had filled in time; all Torre, apparently, was there: the guests of the Grand Hotel, the guests of Villa Eleonora, familiar faces from the beach. We heard English and German and the sort of French that Rumanians speak with Italians. Madame Angiolieri herself sat two rows behind us, with her quiet, bald-headed spouse, who kept stroking his moustache with the two middle fingers of his right hand. Everybody had come late, but nobody too late. Cipolla made us wait for him.

He made us wait. That is probably the way to put it. He heightened the suspense by his delay in appearing. And we could see the point of this, too—only not when it was carried to extremes. Towards half past nine the audience began to clap—an amiable way of expressing justi-fiable impatience, evincing as it does an eagerness to applaud. For the

little ones, this was a joy in itself—all children love to clap. From the
popular sphere came loud cries of *"Pronti!" "Cominciamo!"* And lo,
it seemed now as easy to begin as before it had been hard. A gong
sounded, greeted by the standing rows with a many-voiced "Ah-h!"
and the curtains parted. They revealed a platform furnished more
like a schoolroom than like the theatre of a conjuring performance—
largely because of the blackboard in the left foreground. There was a
common yellow hat-stand, a few ordinary straw-bottomed chairs, and
further back a little round table holding a water carafe and glass, also
a tray with a liqueur glass and a flask of pale yellow liquid. We had
still a few seconds of time to let these things sink in. Then, with no
darkening of the house, Cavaliere Cipolla made his entry.

He came forward with a rapid step that expressed his eagerness
to appear before his public and gave rise to the illusion that he had
already come a long way to put himself at their service—whereas, of
course, he had only been standing in the wings. His costume supported
the fiction. A man of an age hard to determine, but by no means
young; with a sharp, ravaged face, piercing eyes, compressed lips,
small black waxed moustache, and a so-called imperial in the curve
between mouth and chin. He was dressed for the street with a sort of
complicated evening elegance, in a wide black pelerine with velvet
collar and satin lining; which, in the hampered state of his arms, he
held together in front with his white-gloved hands. He had a white
scarf round his neck; a top hat with a curving brim sat far back on
his head. Perhaps more than anywhere else the eighteenth century
is still alive in Italy, and with it the charlatan and mountebank type
so characteristic of the period. Only there, at any rate, does one still
encounter really well-preserved specimens. Cipolla had in his whole
appearance much of the historic type; his very clothes helped to con-
jure up the traditional figure with its blatantly, fantastically foppish
air. His pretentious costume sat upon him, or rather hung upon him,
most curiously, being in one place drawn too tight, in another a mass
of awkward folds. There was something not quite in order about his
figure, both front and back—that was plain later on. But I must
emphasize the fact that there was not a trace of personal jocularity or
clownishness in his pose, manner, or behaviour. On the contrary, there

was complete seriousness, an absence of any humorous appeal; occasionally even a cross-grained pride, along with that curious, self-satisfied air so characteristic of the deformed. None of all this, however, prevented his appearance from being greeted with laughter from more than one quarter of the hall.

All the eagerness had left his manner. The swift entry had been merely an expression of energy, not of zeal. Standing at the footlights he negligently drew off his gloves, to display long yellow hands, one of them adorned with a seal ring with a lapis-lazuli in a high setting. As he stood there, his small hard eyes, with flabby pouches beneath them, roved appraisingly about the hall, not quickly, rather in a considered examination, pausing here and there upon a face with his lips clipped together, not speaking a word. Then with a display of skill as surprising as it was casual, he rolled his gloves into a ball and tossed them across a considerable distance into the glass on the table. Next from an inner pocket he drew forth a packet of cigarettes; you could see by the wrapper that they were the cheapest sort the government sells. With his fingertips he pulled out a cigarette and lighted it, without looking, from a quick-firing benzine lighter. He drew the smoke deep into his lungs and let it out again, tapping his foot, with both lips drawn in an arrogant grimace and the grey smoke streaming out between broken and saw-edged teeth.

With a keenness equal to his own his audience eyed him. The youths at the rear scowled as they peered at this cocksure creature to search out his secret weaknesses. He betrayed none. In fetching out and putting back the cigarettes his clothes got in his way. He had to turn back his pelerine, and in so doing revealed a riding-whip with a silver claw-handle that hung by a leather thong from his left forearm and looked decidedly out of place. You could see that he had on not evening clothes but a frock-coat, and under this, as he lifted it to get at his pocket, could be seen a striped sash worn about the body. Somebody behind me whispered that this sash went with his title of Cavaliere. I give the information for what it may be worth—personally, I never heard that the title carried such insignia with it. Perhaps the sash was sheer pose, like the way he stood there, without a word, casually and arrogantly puffing smoke into his audience's face.

People laughed, as I said. The merriment had become almost general when somebody in the "standing seats," in a loud, dry voice, remarked: *"Buona sera."*

Cipolla cocked his head. "Who was that?" asked he, as though he had been dared. "Who was that just spoke? Well? First so bold and now so modest? *Paura,* eh?" He spoke with a rather high, asthmatic voice, which yet had a metallic quality. He waited.

"That was me," a youth at the rear broke into the stillness, seeing himself thus challenged. He was not far from us, a handsome fellow in a woollen shirt, with his coat hanging over one shoulder. He wore his curly, wiry hair in a high, dishevelled mop, the style affected by the youth of the awakened Fatherland; it gave him an African appearance that rather spoiled his looks. *"Bè!* That was me. It was your business to say it first, but I was trying to be friendly."

More laughter. The chap had a tongue in his head. *"Ha sciolto la scilinguágnolo,"* I heard near me. After all, the retort was deserved.

"Ah, bravo!" answered Cipolla. "I like you, *giovanotto.* Trust me, I've had my eye on you for some time. People like you are just in my line. I can use them. And you are the pick of the lot, that's plain to see. You do what you like. Or is it possible you have ever not done what you liked—or even, maybe, what you didn't like? What somebody else liked, in short? Hark ye, my friend, that might be a pleasant change for you, to divide up the willing and the doing and stop tackling both jobs at once. Division of labour, *sistema americano, sa'!* For instance, suppose you were to show your tongue to this select and honourable audience here—your whole tongue, right down to the roots?"

"No, I won't," said the youth, hostilely. "Sticking out your tongue shows a bad bringing-up."

"Nothing of the sort," retorted Cipolla. "You would only be *doing* it. With all due respect to your bringing-up, I suggest that before I count ten, you will perform a right turn and stick out your tongue at the company here further than you knew yourself that you could stick it out."

He gazed at the youth, and his piercing eyes seemed to sink deeper into their sockets. *"Uno!"* said he. He had let his riding-whip slide down his arm and made it whistle once through the air. The boy faced

about and put out his tongue, so long, so extendedly, that you could
see it was the very uttermost in tongue which he had to offer. Then
turned back, stony-faced, to his former position.

"That was me," mocked Cipolla, with a jerk of his head towards
the youth. *"Bè!* That was me." Leaving the audience to enjoy its sensations, he turned towards the little round table, lifted the bottle,
poured out a small glass of what was obviously cognac, and tipped it
up with a practised hand.

The children laughed with all their hearts. They had understood
practically nothing of what had been said, but it pleased them hugely
that something so funny should happen, straightaway, between that
queer man up there and somebody out of the audience. They had no
preconception of what an "evening" would be like and were quite
ready to find this a priceless beginning. As for us, we exchanged a
glance and I remember that involuntarily I made with my lips the
sound that Cipolla's whip had made when it cut the air. For the rest,
it was plain that people did not know what to make of a preposterous
beginning like this to a sleight-of-hand performance. They could not
see why the *giovanotto*, who after all in a way had been their spokes-
man, should suddenly have turned on them to vent his incivility. They
felt that he had behaved like a silly ass and withdrew their counte-
nances from him in favour of the artist, who now came back from his
refreshment table and addressed them as follows:

"Ladies and gentlemen," said he, in his wheezing, metallic voice,
"you saw just now that I was rather sensitive on the score of the rebuke this hopeful young linguist saw fit to give me"—*"questo lin-
guista di belle speranze"* was what he said, and we all laughed at the
pun. "I am a man who sets some store by himself, you may take it
from me. And I see no point in being wished a good-evening unless it
is done courteously and in all seriousness. For anything else there is no
occasion. When a man wishes me a good-evening he wishes himself
one, for the audience will have one only if I do. So this lady-killer of
Torre di Venere" (another thrust) "did well to testify that I have one
tonight and that I can dispense with any wishes of his in the matter. I
can boast of having good evenings almost without exception. One not
so good does come my way now and again, but very seldom. My call-

ing is hard and my health not of the best. I have a little physical defect which prevented me from doing my bit in the war for the greater
glory of the Fatherland. It is perforce with my mental and spiritual
parts that I conquer life—which after all only means conquering oneself. And I flatter myself that my achievements have aroused interest
and respect among the educated public. The leading newspapers have
lauded me, the *Corriere della Sera* did me the courtesy of calling me a
phenomenon, and in Rome the brother of the *Duce* honoured me by
his presence at one of my evenings. I should not have thought that in a
relatively less important place" (laughter here, at the expense of poor
little Torre) "I should have to give up the small personal habits which
brilliant and elevated audiences had been ready to overlook. Nor did I
think I had to stand being heckled by a person who seems to have
been rather spoilt by the favours of the fair sex." All this of course at
the expense of the youth whom Cipolla never tired of presenting in
the guise of *donnaiuolo* and rustic Don Juan. His persistent thin-
skinnedness and animosity were in striking contrast to the self-confidence and the worldly success he boasted of. One might have assumed
that the *giovanotto* was merely the chosen butt of Cipolla's customary
professional sallies, had not the very pointed witticisms betrayed a genuine antagonism. No one looking at the physical parts of the two men
need have been at a loss for the explanation, even if the deformed man
had not constantly played on the other's supposed success with the fair
sex. "Well," Cipolla went on, "before beginning our entertainment this
evening, perhaps you will permit me to make myself comfortable."

And he went towards the hat-stand to take off his things.

"*Parla benissimo*," asserted somebody in our neighbourhood. So far,
the man had done nothing; but what he had said was accepted as an
achievement, by means of that he had made an impression. Among
southern peoples speech is a constituent part of the pleasure of living, it
enjoys far livelier social esteem than in the north. That national cement, the mother tongue, is paid symbolic honours down here, and
there is something blithely symbolical in the pleasure people take in
their respect for its forms and phonetics. They enjoy speaking, they
enjoy listening; and they listen with discrimination. For the way a
man speaks serves as a measure of his personal rank; carelessness and

clumsiness are greeted with scorn, elegance and mastery are rewarded
with social éclat. Wherefore the small man too, where it is a question
of getting his effect, chooses his phrase nicely and turns it with care.
On this count, then, at least, Cipolla had won his audience; though he
by no means belonged to the class of men which the Italian, in a singular mixture of moral and æsthetic judgments, labels *"simpatico."*

After removing his hat, scarf, and mantle he came to the front of
the stage, settling his coat, pulling down his cuffs with their large cuff-
buttons, adjusting his absurd sash. He had very ugly hair; the top of
his head, that is, was almost bald, while a narrow, black-varnished frizz
of curls ran from front to back as though stuck on; the side hair, likewise blackened, was brushed forward to the corners of the eyes—it
was, in short, the hairdressing of an old-fashioned circus-director, fantastic, but entirely suited to his outmoded personal type and worn with
so much assurance as to take the edge off the public's sense of humour.
The little physical defect of which he had warned us was now all too
visible, though the nature of it was even now not very clear: the chest
was too high, as is usual in such cases; but the corresponding malfor-
mation of the back did not sit between the shoulders, it took the form
of a sort of hips or buttocks hump, which did not indeed hinder his
movements but gave him a grotesque and dipping stride at every step
he took. However, by mentioning his deformity beforehand he had
broken the shock of it, and a delicate propriety of feeling appeared to
reign throughout the hall.

"At your service," said Cipolla. "With your kind permission, we will
begin the evening with some arithmetical tests."

Arithmetic? That did not sound much like sleight-of-hand. We
began to have our suspicions that the man was sailing under a false
flag, only we did not yet know which was the right one. I felt sorry
on the children's account; but for the moment they were content
simply to be there.

The numerical test which Cipolla now introduced was as simple as it
was baffling. He began by fastening a piece of paper to the upper
right-hand corner of the blackboard; then lifting it up, he wrote something underneath. He talked all the while, relieving the dryness of his
offering by a constant flow of words, and showed himself a practised

speaker, never at a loss for conversational turns of phrase. It was in
keeping with the nature of his performance, and at the same time
vastly entertained the children, that he went on to eliminate the gap
between stage and audience, which had already been bridged over by
the curious skirmish with the fisher lad: he had representatives from
the audience mount the stage, and himself descended the wooden steps
to seek personal contact with his public. And again, with individuals,
he fell into his former taunting tone. I do not know how far that was
a deliberate feature of his system; he preserved a serious, even a peevish air, but his audience, at least the more popular section, seemed convinced that that was all part of the game. So then, after he had written
something and covered the writing by the paper, he desired that two
persons should come up on the platform and help to perform the calculations. They would not be difficult, even for people not clever at figures. As usual, nobody volunteered, and Cipolla took care not to molest
the more select portion of his audience. He kept to the populace. Turning to two sturdy young louts standing behind us, he beckoned them
to the front, encouraging and scolding by turns. They should not stand
there gaping, he said, unwilling to oblige the company. Actually, he
got them in motion; with clumsy tread they came down the middle
aisle, climbed the steps, and stood in front of the blackboard, grinning
sheepishly at their comrades' shouts and applause. Cipolla joked with
them for a few minutes, praised their heroic firmness of limb and the
size of their hands, so well calculated to do this service for the public.
Then he handed one of them the chalk and told him to write down
the numbers as they were called out. But now the creature declared
that he could not write! *"Non so scrivere,"* said he in his gruff voice,
and his companion added that neither did he.

God knows whether they told the truth or whether they wanted to
make game of Cipolla. Anyhow, the latter was far from sharing the
general merriment which their confession aroused. He was insulted
and disgusted. He sat there on a straw-bottomed chair in the centre of
the stage with his legs crossed, smoking a fresh cigarette out of his
cheap packet; obviously it tasted the better for the cognac he had indulged in while the yokels were stumping up the steps. Again he inhaled the smoke and let it stream out between curling lips. Swinging

his leg, with his gaze sternly averted from the two shamelessly chuckling creatures and from the audience as well, he stared into space as
one who withdraws himself and his dignity from the contemplation of
an utterly despicable phenomenon.

"Scandalous," said he, in a sort of icy snarl. "Go back to your places!
In Italy everybody can write—in all her greatness there is no room for
ignorance and unenlightenment. To accuse her of them, in the hearing of this international company, is a cheap joke, in which you yourselves cut a very poor figure and humiliate the government and the
whole country as well. If it is true that Torre di Venere is indeed the
last refuge of such ignorance, then I must blush to have visited the
place—being, as I already was, aware of its inferiority to Rome in more
than one respect——"

Here Cipolla was interrupted by the youth with the Nubian coiffure
and his jacket across his shoulder. His fighting spirit, as we now saw,
had only abdicated temporarily, and he now flung himself into the
breach in defence of his native heath. "That will do," said he loudly.
"That's enough jokes about Torre. We all come from the place and we
won't stand strangers making fun of it. These two chaps are our
friends. Maybe they are no scholars, but even so they may be straighter
than some folks in the room who are so free with their boasts about
Rome, though they did not build it either."

That was capital. The young man had certainly cut his eye-teeth.
And this sort of spectacle was good fun, even though it still further
delayed the regular performance. It is always fascinating to listen to
an altercation. Some people it simply amuses, they take a sort of kill-
joy pleasure in not being principals. Others feel upset and uneasy, and
my sympathies are with these latter, although on the present occasion
I was under the impression that all this was part of the show—the
analphabetic yokels no less than the *giovanotto* with the jacket. The
children listened well pleased. They understood not at all, but the
sound of the voices made them hold their breath. So this was a "magic
evening"—at least it was the kind they have in Italy. They expressly
found it "lovely."

Cipolla had stood up and with two of his scooping strides was at
the footlights.

"Well, well, see who's here!" said he with grim cordiality. "An old acquaintance! A young man with his heart at the end of his tongue" (he used the word *linguaccia,* which means a coated tongue, and gave rise to much hilarity). "That will do, my friends," he turned to the yokels. "I do not need you now, I have business with this deserving young man here, *con questo torregiano di Venere,* this tower of Venus, who no doubt expects the gratitude of the fair as a reward for his prowess——"

"*Ah, non scherziamo!* We're talking earnest," cried out the youth. His eyes flashed, and he actually made as though to pull off his jacket and proceed to direct methods of settlement.

Cipolla did not take him too seriously. We had exchanged apprehensive glances; but he was dealing with a fellow-countryman and had his native soil beneath his feet. He kept quite cool and showed complete mastery of the situation. He looked at his audience, smiled, and made a sideways motion of the head towards the young cockerel as though calling the public to witness how the man's bumptiousness only served to betray the simplicity of his mind. And then, for the second time, something strange happened, which set Cipolla's calm superiority in an uncanny light, and in some mysterious and irritating way turned all the explosiveness latent in the air into matter for laughter.

Cipolla drew still nearer to the fellow, looking him in the eye with a peculiar gaze. He even came half-way down the steps that led into the auditorium on our left, so that he stood directly in front of the trouble-maker, on slightly higher ground. The riding-whip hung from his arm.

"My son, you do not feel much like joking," he said. "It is only too natural, for anyone can see that you are not feeling too well. Even your tongue, which leaves something to be desired on the score of cleanliness, indicates acute disorder of the gastric system. An evening entertainment is no place for people in your state; you yourself, I can tell, were of several minds whether you would not do better to put on a flannel bandage and go to bed. It was not good judgment to drink so much of that very sour white wine this afternoon. Now you have such a colic you would like to double up with the pain. Go ahead, don't be embarrased. There is a distinct relief that comes from bending over, in cases of intestinal cramp."

He spoke thus, word for word, with quiet impressiveness and a kind of stern sympathy, and his eyes, plunged the while deep in the young man's, seemed to grow very tired and at the same time burning above their enlarged tear-ducts—they were the strangest eyes, you could tell that not manly pride alone was preventing the young adversary from withdrawing his gaze. And presently, indeed, all trace of its former arrogance was gone from the bronzed young face. He looked open-mouthed at the Cavaliere and the open mouth was drawn in a rueful smile.

"Double over," repeated Cipolla. "What else can you do? With a colic like that you *must* bend. Surely you will not struggle against the performance of a perfectly natural action just because somebody suggests it to you?"

Slowly the youth lifted his forearms, folded and squeezed them across his body; it turned a little sideways, then bent, lower and lower, the feet shifted, the knees turned inward, until he had become a picture of writhing pain, until he all but grovelled upon the ground. Cipolla let him stand for some seconds thus, then made a short cut through the air with his whip and went with his scooping stride back to the little table, where he poured himself out a cognac.

"*Il boit beaucoup,*" asserted a lady behind us. Was that the only thing that struck her? We could not tell how far the audience grasped the situation. The fellow was standing upright again, with a sheepish grin—he looked as though he scarcely knew how it had all happened. The scene had been followed with tense interest and applauded at the end; there were shouts of "*Bravo, Cipolla!*" and "*Bravo, giovanotto!*" Apparently the issue of the duel was not looked upon as a personal defeat for the young man. Rather the audience encouraged him as one does an actor who succeeds in an unsympathetic rôle. Certainly his way of screwing himself up with cramp had been highly picturesque, its appeal was directly calculated to impress the gallery—in short, a fine dramatic performance. But I am not sure how far the audience were moved by that natural tactfulness in which the south excels, or how far it penetrated into the nature of what was going on.

The Cavaliere, refreshed, had lighted another cigarette. The numerical tests might now proceed. A young man was easily found in the back row who was willing to write down on the blackboard the numbers as they were dictated to him. Him too we knew; the whole entertainment had taken on an intimate character through our acquaintance with so many of the actors. This was the man who worked at the greengrocer's in the main street; he had served us several times, with neatness and dispatch. He wielded the chalk with clerkly confidence, while Cipolla descended to our level and walked with his deformed gait through the audience, collecting numbers as they were given, in two, three, and four places, and calling them out to the grocer's assistant, who wrote them down in a column. In all this, everything on both sides was calculated to amuse, with its jokes and its oratorical asides. The artist could not fail to hit on foreigners, who were not ready with their figures, and with them he was elaborately patient and chivalrous, to the great amusement of the natives, whom he reduced to confusion in their turn, by making them translate numbers that were given in English or French. Some people gave dates concerned with great events in Italian history. Cipolla took them up at once and made patriotic comments. Somebody shouted "Number one!" The Cavaliere, incensed at this as at every attempt to make game of him, retorted over his shoulder that he could not take less than two-place figures. Whereupon another joker cried out "Number two!" and was greeted with the applause and laughter which every reference to natural functions is sure to win among southerners.

When fifteen numbers stood in a long straggling row on the board, Cipolla called for a general adding-match. Ready reckoners might add in their heads, but pencil and paper were not forbidden. Cipolla, while the work went on, sat on his chair near the blackboard, smoked and grimaced, with the complacent, pompous air cripples so often have. The five-place addition was soon done. Somebody announced the answer, somebody else confirmed it, a third had arrived at a slightly different result, but the fourth agreed with the first and second. Cipolla got up, tapped some ash from his coat, and lifted the paper at the upper right-hand corner of the board to display the writing. The cor-

rect answer, a sum close on a million, stood there; he had written it
down beforehand.

Astonishment, and loud applause. The children were overwhelmed.
How had he done that, they wanted to know. We told them it was a
trick, not easily explainable offhand. In short, the man was a conjuror. This was what a sleight-of-hand evening was like, so now they
knew. First the fisherman had cramp, and then the right answer was
written down beforehand—it was all simply glorious, and we saw
with dismay that despite the hot eyes and the hand of the clock at
almost half past ten, it would be very hard to get them away. There
would be tears. And yet it was plain that this magician did not
"magick"—at least not in the accepted sense, of manual dexterity—
and that the entertainment was not at all suitable for children. Again,
I do not know, either, what the audience really thought. Obviously
there was grave doubt whether its answers had been given of "free
choice"; here and there an individual might have answered of his own
motion, but on the whole Cipolla certainly selected his people and
thus kept the whole procedure in his own hands and directed it towards the given result. Even so, one had to admire the quickness of
his calculations, however much one felt disinclined to admire anything
else about the performance. Then his patriotism, his irritable sense of
dignity—the Cavaliere's own countrymen might feel in their element
with all that and continue in a laughing mood; but the combination
certainly gave us outsiders food for thought.

Cipolla himself saw to it—though without giving them a name—
that the nature of his powers should be clear beyond a doubt to even
the least-instructed person. He alluded to them, of course, in his talk—
and he talked without stopping—but only in vague, boastful, self-
advertising phrases. He went on awhile with experiments on the same
lines as the first, merely making them more complicated by introducing operations in multiplying, subtracting, and dividing; then he sim-
plified them to the last degree in order to bring out the method. He
simply had numbers "guessed" which were previously written under
the paper; and the guess was nearly always right. One guesser admitted that he had had in mind to give a certain number, when Ci-

polla's whip went whistling through the air, and a quite different one slipped out, which proved to be the "right" one. Cipolla's shoulders shook. He pretended admiration for the powers of the people he questioned. But in all his compliments there was something fleering and derogatory; the victims could scarcely have relished them much, although they smiled, and although they might easily have set down some part of the applause to their own credit. Moreover, I had not the impression that the artist was popular with his public. A certain ill will and reluctance were in the air, but courtesy kept such feelings in check, as did Cipolla's competency and his stern self-confidence. Even the riding-whip, I think, did much to keep rebellion from becoming overt.

From tricks with numbers he passed to tricks with cards. There were two packs, which he drew out of his pockets, and so much I still remember, that the basis of the tricks he played with them was as follows: from the first pack he drew three cards and thrust them without looking at them inside his coat. Another person then drew three out of the second pack, and these turned out to be the same as the first three—not invariably all the three, for it did happen that only two were the same. But in the majority of cases Cipolla triumphed, showing his three cards with a little bow in acknowledgment of the applause with which his audience conceded his possession of strange powers—strange whether for good or evil. A young man in the front row, to our right, an Italian, with proud, finely chiselled features, rose up and said that he intended to assert his own will in his choice and consciously to resist any influence, of whatever sort. Under these circumstances, what did Cipolla think would be the result? "You will," answered the Cavaliere, "make my task somewhat more difficult thereby. As for the result, your resistance will not alter it in the least. Freedom exists, and also the will exists; but freedom of the will does not exist, for a will that aims at its own freedom aims at the unknown. You are free to draw or not to draw. But if you draw, you will draw the right cards— the more certainly, the more wilfully obstinate your behaviour."

One must admit that he could not have chosen his words better, to trouble the waters and confuse the mind. The refractory youth hesitated before drawing. Then he pulled out a card and at once de-

manded to see if it was among the chosen three. "But why?" queried
Cipolla. "Why do things by halves?" Then, as the other defiantly insisted, *"E servito,"* said the juggler, with a gesture of exaggerated
servility; and held out the three cards fanwise, without looking at
them himself. The left-hand card was the one drawn.

Amid general applause, the apostle of freedom sat down. How far
Cipolla employed small tricks and manual dexterity to help out his
natural talents, the deuce only knew. But even without them the result
would have been the same: the curiosity of the entire audience was
unbounded and universal, everybody both enjoyed the amazing character of the entertainment and unanimously conceded the professional
skill of the performer. *"Lavora bene,"* we heard, here and there in our
neighbourhood; it signified the triumph of objective judgment over
antipathy and repressed resentment.

After his last, incomplete, yet so much the more telling success, Cipolla had at once fortified himself with another cognac. Truly he did
"drink a lot," and the fact made a bad impression. But obviously he
needed the liquor and the cigarettes for the replenishment of his energy, upon which, as he himself said, heavy demands were made in all
directions. Certainly in the intervals he looked very ill, exhausted and
hollow-eyed. Then the little glassful would redress the balance, and the
flow of lively, self-confident chatter run on, while the smoke he inhaled
gushed out grey from his lungs. I clearly recall that he passed from
the card-tricks to parlour games—the kind based on certain powers
which in human nature are higher or else lower than human reason:
on intuition and "magnetic" transmission; in short, upon a low type
of manifestation. What I do not remember is the precise order things
came in. And I will not bore you with a description of these experiments; everybody knows them, everybody has at one time or another
taken part in this finding of hidden articles, this blind carrying out of
a series of acts, directed by a force that proceeds from organism to
organism by unexplored paths. Everybody has had his little glimpse
into the equivocal, impure, inexplicable nature of the occult, has been
conscious of both curiosity and contempt, has shaken his head over
the human tendency of those who deal in it to help themselves out
with humbuggery, though, after all, the humbuggery is no disproof

whatever of the genuineness of the other elements in the dubious amalgam. I can only say here that each single circumstance gains in weight and the whole greatly in impressiveness when it is a man like Cipolla who is the chief actor and guiding spirit in the sinister business. He sat smoking at the rear of the stage, his back to the audience while they conferred. The object passed from hand to hand which it was his task to find, with which he was to perform some action agreed upon beforehand. Then he would start to move zigzag through the hall, with his head thrown back and one hand outstretched, the other clasped in that of a guide who was in the secret but enjoined to keep himself perfectly passive, with his thoughts directed upon the agreed goal. Cipolla moved with the bearing typical in these experiments: now groping upon a false start, now with a quick forward thrust, now pausing as though to listen and by sudden inspiration correcting his course. The rôles seemed reversed, the stream of influence was moving in the contrary direction, as the artist himself pointed out, in his ceaseless flow of discourse. The suffering, receptive, performing part was now his, the will he had before imposed on others was shut out, he acted in obedience to a voiceless common will which was in the air. But he made it perfectly clear that it all came to the same thing. The capacity for self-surrender, he said, for becoming a tool, for the most unconditional and utter self-abnegation, was but the reverse side of that other power to will and to command. Commanding and obeying formed together one single principle, one indissoluble unity; he who knew how to obey knew also how to command, and conversely; the one idea was comprehended in the other, as people and leader were comprehended in one another. But that which was *done,* the highly exacting and exhausting performance, was in every case his, the leader's and mover's, in whom the will became obedience, the obedience will, whose person was the cradle and womb of both, and who thus suffered enormous hardship. Repeatedly he emphasized the fact that his lot was a hard one—presumably to account for his need of stimulant and his frequent recourse to the little glass.

Thus he groped his way forward, like a blind seer, led and sustained by the mysterious common will. He drew a pin set with a stone out of its hiding-place in an Englishwoman's shoe, carried it, halting and pressing on by turns, to another lady—Signora Angiolieri—and handed it to her on bended knee, with the words it had been agreed he was to utter. "I present you with this in token of my respect," was the sentence. Their sense was obvious, but the words themselves not easy to hit upon, for the reason that they had been agreed on in French; the language complication seemed to us a little malicious, implying as it did a conflict between the audience's natural interest in the success of the miracle, and their desire to witness the humiliation of this presumptuous man. It was a strange sight: Cipolla on his knees before the signora, wrestling, amid efforts at speech, after knowledge of the preordained words. "I must say something," he said, "and I feel clearly what it is I must say. But I also feel that if it passed my lips it would be wrong. Be careful not to help me unintentionally!" he cried out, though very likely that was precisely what he was hoping for. "Pensez très fort," he cried all at once, in bad French, and then burst out with the required words—in Italian, indeed, but with the final substantive pronounced in the sister tongue, in which he was probably far from fluent: he said *vénération* instead of *venerazione,* with an impossible nasal. And this partial success, after the complete success before it, the finding of the pin, the presentation of it on his knees to the right person—was almost more impressive than if he had got the sentence exactly right, and evoked bursts of admiring applause.

Cipolla got up from his knees and wiped the perspiration from his brow. You understand that this experiment with the pin was a single case, which I describe because it sticks in my memory. But he changed his method several times and improvised a number of variations suggested by his contact with his audience; a good deal of time thus went by. He seemed to get particular inspiration from the person of our landlady; she drew him on to the most extraordinary displays of clairvoyance. "It does not escape me, madame," he said to her, "that there is something unusual about you, some special and honourable distinction. He who has eyes to see descries about your lovely brow an aureola —if I mistake not, it once was stronger than now—a slowly paling radiance . . . hush, not a word! Don't help me. Beside you sits your husband—yes?" He turned towards the silent Signor Angiolieri. "You are the husband of this lady, and your happiness is complete. But in

the midst of this happiness memories rise . . . the past, signora, so it
seems to me, plays an important part in your present. You knew a
king . . . has not a king crossed your path in bygone days?"

"No," breathed the dispenser of our midday soup, her golden-brown
eyes gleaming in the noble pallor of her face.

"No? No, not a king; I meant that generally, I did not mean literally
a king. Not a king, not a prince, and a prince after all, a king of a
loftier realm; it was a great artist, at whose side you once—you would
contradict me, and yet I am not wholly wrong. Well, then! It was a
woman, a great, a world-renowned woman artist, whose friendship
you enjoyed in your tender years, whose sacred memory overshadows
and transfigures your whole existence. Her name? Need I utter it,
whose fame has long been bound up with the Fatherland's, immortal
as its own? Eleonora Duse," he finished, softly and with much solemnity.

The little woman bowed her head, overcome. The applause was like
a patriotic demonstration. Nearly everyone there knew about Signora
Angiolieri's wonderful past; they were all able to confirm the Cavaliere's intuition—not least the present guests of Casa Eleonora. But we
wondered how much of the truth he had learned as the result of professional inquiries made on his arrival. Yet I see no reason at all to
cast doubt, on rational grounds, upon powers which, before our very
eyes, became fatal to their possessor.

At this point there was an intermission. Our lord and master withdrew. Now I confess that almost ever since the beginning of my tale
I have looked forward with dread to this moment in it. The thoughts
of men are mostly not hard to read; in this case they are very easy.
You are sure to ask why we did not choose this moment to go away—
and I must continue to owe you an answer. I do not know why. I cannot defend myself. By this time it was certainly eleven, probably later.
The children were asleep. The last series of tests had been too long,
nature had had her way. They were sleeping in our laps, the little one
on mine, the boy on his mother's. That was, in a way, a consolation;
but at the same time it was also ground for compassion and a clear
leading to take them home to bed. And I give you my word that we
wanted to obey this touching admonition, we seriously wanted to. We

roused the poor things and told them it was now high time to go. But they were no sooner conscious than they began to resist and implore— you know how horrified children are at the thought of leaving before the end of a thing. No cajoling has any effect, you have to use force. It was so lovely, they wailed. How did we know what was coming next? Surely we could not leave until after the intermission; they liked a little nap now and again—only not go home, only not go to bed, while the beautiful evening was still going on!

We yielded, but only for the moment, of course—so far as we knew —only for a little while, just a few minutes longer. I cannot excuse our staying, scarcely can I even understand it. Did we think, having once said A, we had to say B—having once brought the children hither we had to let them stay? No, it is not good enough. Were we ourselves so highly entertained? Yes, and no. Our feelings for Cavaliere Cipolla were of a very mixed kind, but so were the feelings of the whole audience, if I mistake not, and nobody left. Were we under the sway of a fascination which emanated from this man who took so strange a way to earn his bread; a fascination which he gave out independently of the programme and even between the tricks and which paralysed our resolve? Again, sheer curiosity may account for something. One was curious to know how such an evening turned out; Cipolla in his remarks having all along hinted that he had tricks in his bag stranger than any he had yet produced.

But all that is not it—or at least it is not all of it. More correct it would be to answer the first question with another. Why had we not left Torre di Venere itself before now? To me the two questions are one and the same, and in order to get out of the impasse I might simply say that I had answered it already. For, as things had been in Torre in general: queer, uncomfortable, troublesome, tense, oppressive, so precisely they were here in this hall tonight. Yes, more than precisely. For it seemed to be the fountain-head of all the uncanniness and all the strained feelings which had oppressed the atmosphere of our holiday. This man whose return to the stage we were awaiting was the personification of all that; and, as we had not gone away in general, so to speak, it would have been inconsistent to do it in the particular case. You may call this an explanation, you may call it inertia,

as you see fit. Any argument more to the purpose I simply do not
know how to adduce.

Well, there was an interval of ten minutes, which grew into nearly
twenty. The children remained awake. They were enchanted by our
compliance, and filled the break to their own satisfaction by renewing
relations with the popular sphere, with Antonio, Guiscardo, and the
canoe man. They put their hands to their mouths and called messages
across, appealing to us for the Italian words. "Hope you have a good
catch tomorrow, a whole netful!" They called to Mario, Esquisito
Mario: *"Mario, una cioccolata e biscotti!"* And this time he heeded and
answered with a smile: *"Subito, signorini!"* Later we had reason to recall this kindly, if rather absent and pensive smile.

Thus the interval passed, the gong sounded. The audience, which
had scattered in conversation, took their places again, the children sat
up straight in their chairs with their hands in their laps. The curtain
had not been dropped. Cipolla came forward again, with his dipping
stride, and began to introduce the second half of the programme with
a lecture.

Let me state once for all that this self-confident cripple was the most
powerful hypnotist I have ever seen in my life. It was pretty plain now
that he threw dust in the public eye and advertised himself as a presti-
digitator on account of police regulations which would have prevented
him from making his living by the exercise of his powers. Perhaps this
eye-wash is the usual thing in Italy; it may be permitted or even con-
nived at by the authorities. Certainly the man had from the beginning
made little concealment of the actual nature of his operations; and this
second half of the programme was quite frankly and exclusively devoted to one sort of experiment. While he still practised some rhetorical
circumlocutions, the tests themselves were one long series of attacks
upon the will-power, the loss or compulsion of volition. Comic, exciting, amazing by turns, by midnight they were still in full swing; we
ran the gamut of all the phenomena this natural-unnatural field has to
show, from the unimpressive at one end of the scale to the monstrous
at the other. The audience laughed and applauded as they followed
the grotesque details; shook their heads, clapped their knees, fell very
frankly under the spell of this stern, self-assured personality. At the

same time I saw signs that they were not quite complacent, not quite unconscious of the peculiar ignominy which lay, for the individual and for the general, in Cipolla's triumphs.

Two main features were constant in all the experiments: the liquor glass and the claw-handled riding-whip. The first was always invoked to add fuel to his demoniac fires; without it, apparently, they might have burned out. On this score we might even have felt pity for the man; but the whistle of his scourge, the insulting symbol of his domination, before which we all cowered, drowned out every sensation save a dazed and outbraved submission to his power. Did he then lay claim to our sympathy to boot? I was struck by a remark he made—it suggested no less. At the climax of his experiments, by stroking and breathing upon a certain young man who had offered himself as a subject and already proved himself a particularly susceptible one, he had not only put him into the condition known as deep trance and extended his insensible body by neck and feet across the backs of two chairs, but had actually sat down on the rigid form as on a bench, without making it yield. The sight of this unholy figure in a frock-coat squatted on the stiff body was horrible and incredible; the audience, convinced that the victim of this scientific diversion must be suffering, expressed its sympathy: *"Ah, poveretto!"* Poor soul, poor soul! *"Poor soul!"* Cipolla mocked them, with some bitterness. "Ladies and gentlemen, you are barking up the wrong tree. *Sono io il poveretto.* I am the person who is suffering, I am the one to be pitied." We pocketed the information. Very good. Maybe the experiment was at his expense, maybe it was he who had suffered the cramp when the *giovanotto* over there had made the faces. But appearances were all against it; and one does not feel like saying *poveretto* to a man who is suffering to bring about the humiliation of others.

I have got ahead of my story and lost sight of the sequence of events. To this day my mind is full of the Cavaliere's feats of endurance; only I do not recall them in their order—which does not matter. So much I do know: that the longer and more circumstantial tests, which got the most applause, impressed me less than some of the small ones which passed quickly over. I remember the young man whose body Cipolla converted into a board, only because of the accompanying remarks

which I have quoted. An elderly lady in a cane-seated chair was lulled
by Cipolla in the delusion that she was on a voyage to India and gave
a voluble account of her adventures by land and sea. But I found this
phenomenon less impressive than one which followed immediately
after the intermission. A tall, well-built, soldierly man was unable to
lift his arm, after the hunchback had told him that he could not and
given a cut through the air with his whip. I can still see the face of that
stately, mustachioed colonel smiling and clenching his teeth as he
struggled to regain his lost freedom of action. A staggering performance! He seemed to be exerting his will, and in vain; the trouble,
however, was probably simply that he could not will. There was involved here that recoil of the will upon itself which paralyses choice—
as our tyrant had previously explained to the Roman gentleman.

Still less can I forget the touching scene, at once comic and horrible,
with Signora Angiolieri. The Cavaliere, probably in his first bold survey of the room, had spied out her ethereal lack of resistance to his
power. For actually he bewitched her, literally drew her out of her
seat, out of her row, and away with him whither he willed. And in
order to enhance his effect, he bade Signor Angiolieri call upon his
wife by her name, to throw, as it were, all the weight of his existence
and his rights in her into the scale, to rouse by the voice of her husband
everything in his spouse's soul which could shield her virtue against
the evil assaults of magic. And how vain it all was! Cipolla was standing at some distance from the couple, when he made a single cut with
his whip through the air. It caused our landlady to shudder violently
and turn her face towards him. "Sofronia!" cried Signor Angiolieri—
we had not known that Signora Angiolieri's name was Sofronia. And he
did well to call, everybody saw that there was no time to lose. His wife
kept her face turned in the direction of the diabolical Cavaliere, who
with his ten long yellow fingers was making passes at his victim, moving backwards as he did so, step by step. Then Signora Angiolieri, her
pale face gleaming, rose up from her seat, turned right round, and
began to glide after him. Fatal and forbidding sight! Her face as
though moonstruck, stiff-armed, her lovely hands lifted a little at the
wrists, the feet as it were together, she seemed to float slowly out of
her row and after the tempter. "Call her, sir, keep on calling,"

prompted the redoubtable man. And Signor Angiolieri, in a weak voice, called: "Sofronia!" Ah, again and again he called; as his wife went further off he even curved one hand round his lips and beckoned with the other as he called. But the poor voice of love and duty echoed unheard, in vain, behind the lost one's back; the signora swayed along, moonstruck, deaf, enslaved; she glided into the middle aisle and down it towards the fingering hunchback, towards the door. We were convinced, we were driven to the conviction, that she would have followed her master, had he so willed it, to the ends of the earth.

"*Accidente!*" cried out Signor Angiolieri, in genuine affright, springing up as the exit was reached. But at the same moment the Cavaliere put aside, as it were, the triumphal crown and broke off. "Enough, signora, I thank you," he said, and offered his arm to lead her back to her husband. "Signor," he greeted the latter, "here is your wife. Unharmed, with my compliments, I give her into your hands. Cherish with all the strength of your manhood a treasure which is so wholly yours, and let your zeal be quickened by knowing that there are powers stronger than reason or virtue, and not always so magnanimously ready to relinquish their prey!"

Poor Signor Angiolieri, so quiet, so bald! He did not look as though he would know how to defend his happiness, even against powers much less demoniac than these which were now adding mockery to frightfulness. Solemnly and pompously the Cavaliere retired to the stage, amid applause to which his eloquence gave double strength. It was this particular episode, I feel sure, that set the seal upon his ascendancy. For now he made them dance, yes, literally; and the dancing lent a dissolute, abandoned, topsy-turvy air to the scene, a drunken abdication of the critical spirit which had so long resisted the spell of this man. Yes, he had had to fight to get the upper hand—for instance against the animosity of the young Roman gentleman, whose rebellious spirit threatened to serve others as a rallying-point. But it was precisely upon the importance of example that the Cavaliere was so strong. He had the wit to make his attack at the weakest point and to choose as his first victim that feeble, ecstatic youth whom he had previously made into a board. The master had but to look at him, when this young man would fling himself back as though struck by lightning, place his hands rigidly at his sides, and fall into a state of military somnambulism, in which it was plain to any eye that he was open to the most absurd suggestion that might be made to him. He seemed quite content in his abject state, quite pleased to be relieved of the burden of voluntary choice. Again and again he offered himself as a subject and gloried in the model facility he had in losing consciousness. So now he mounted the platform, and a single cut of the whip was enough to make him dance to the Cavaliere's orders, in a kind of complacent ecstasy, eyes closed, head nodding, lank limbs flying in all directions.

It looked unmistakably like enjoyment, and other recruits were not long in coming forward: two other young men, one humbly and one well dressed, were soon jigging alongside the first. But now the gentleman from Rome bobbed up again, asking defiantly if the Cavaliere would engage to make him dance too, even against his will.

"Even against your will," answered Cipolla, in unforgettable accents. That frightful *"anche se non vuole"* still rings in my ears. The struggle began. After Cipolla had taken another little glass and lighted a fresh cigarette he stationed the Roman at a point in the middle aisle and himself took up a position some distance behind him, making his whip whistle through the air as he gave the order: *"Balla!"* His opponent did not stir. *"Balla!"* repeated the Cavaliere incisively, and snapped his whip. You saw the young man move his neck round in his collar; at the same time one hand lifted slightly at the wrist, one ankle turned outward. But that was all, for the time at least; merely a tendency to twitch, now sternly repressed, now seeming about to get the upper hand. It escaped nobody that here a heroic obstinacy, a fixed resolve to resist, must needs be conquered; we were beholding a gallant effort to strike out and save the honour of the human race. He twitched but danced not; and the struggle was so prolonged that the Cavaliere had to divide his attention between it and the stage, turning now and then to make his riding-whip whistle in the direction of the dancers, as it were to keep them in leash. At the same time he advised the audience that no fatigue was involved in such activities, however long they went on, since it was not the automatons up there who danced, but himself. Then once more his eye would bore itself into the back of the Roman's neck and lay siege to the strength of purpose which defied him.

One saw it waver, that strength of purpose, beneath the repeated summons and whip-crackings. Saw with an objective interest which yet was not quite free from traces of sympathetic emotion—from pity, even from a cruel kind of pleasure. If I understand what was going on, it was the negative character of the young man's fighting position which was his undoing. It is likely that *not* willing is not a practicable state of mind; *not* to want to do something may be in the long run a mental content impossible to subsist on. Between not willing a certain thing and not willing at all—in other words, yielding to another person's will—there may lie too small a space for the idea of freedom to squeeze into. Again, there were the Cavaliere's persuasive words, woven in among the whip-crackings and commands, as he mingled effects that were his own secret with others of a bewilderingly psychological kind. *"Balla!"* said he. "Who wants to torture himself like that? Is forcing yourself your idea of freedom? *Una ballatina!* Why, your arms and legs are aching for it. What a relief to give way to them— there, you are dancing already! That is no struggle any more, it is a pleasure!" And so it was. The jerking and twitching of the refractory youth's limbs had at last got the upper hand; he lifted his arms, then his knees, his joints quite suddenly relaxed, he flung his legs and danced, and amid bursts of applause the Cavaliere led him to join the row of puppets on the stage. Up there we could see his face as he "enjoyed" himself; it was clothed in a broad grin and the eyes were halfshut. In a way, it was consoling to see that he was having a better time than he had had in the hour of his pride.

His "fall" was, I may say, an epoch. The ice was completely broken, Cipolla's triumph had reached its height. The Circe's wand, that whistling leather whip with the claw handle, held absolute sway. At one time —it must have been well after midnight—not only were there eight or ten persons dancing on the little stage, but in the hall below a varied animation reigned, and a long-toothed Anglo-Saxoness in a pince-nez left her seat of her own motion to perform a tarantella in the centre aisle. Cipolla was lounging in a cane-seated chair at the left of the stage, gulping down the smoke of a cigarette and breathing it impudently out through his bad teeth. He tapped his foot and shrugged his shoulders, looking down upon the abandoned scene in the hall; now and then he snapped his whip backwards at a laggard upon the stage. The children were awake at the moment. With shame I speak of them. For it was not good to be here, least of all for them; that we had not taken them away can only be explained by saying that we had caught the general devil-may-careness of the hour. By that time it was all one. Anyhow, thank goodness, they lacked understanding for the disreputable side of the entertainment, and in their innocence were perpetually charmed by the unheard-of indulgence which permitted them to be present at such a thing as a magician's "evening." Whole quarter-hours at a time they drowsed on our laps, waking refreshed and rosy-cheeked, with sleep-drunken eyes, to laugh to bursting at the leaps and jumps the magician made those people up there make. They had not thought it would be so jolly; they joined with their clumsy little hands in every round of applause. And jumped for joy upon their chairs, as was their wont, when Cipolla beckoned to their friend Mario from the Esquisito, beckoned to him just like a picture in a book, holding his hand in front of his nose and bending and straightening the forefinger by turns.

Mario obeyed. I can see him now going up the stairs to Cipolla, who continued to beckon him, in that droll, picture-book sort of way. He hesitated for a moment at first; that, too, I recall quite clearly. During the whole evening he had lounged against a wooden pillar at the side entrance, with his arms folded, or else with his hands thrust into his jacket pockets. He was on our left, near the youth with the militant hair, and had followed the performance attentively, so far as we had seen, if with no particular animation and God knows how much comprehension. He could not much relish being summoned thus, at the end of the evening. But it was only too easy to see why he obeyed. After all, obedience was his calling in life; and then, how should a simple lad like him find it within his human capacity to refuse compliance to a man so throned and crowned as Cipolla at that hour? Willy-nilly he left his column and with a word of thanks to those making way for him he mounted the steps with a doubtful smile on his full lips.

Picture a thickset youth of twenty years, with clipt hair, a low forehead, and heavy-lidded eyes of an indefinite grey, shot with green and yellow. These things I knew from having spoken with him, as we often had. There was a saddle of freckles on the flat nose, the whole upper half of the face retreated behind the lower, and that again was dominated by thick lips that parted to show the salivated teeth. These thick lips and the veiled look of the eyes lent the whole face a primitive melancholy—it was that which had drawn us to him from the first. In it was not the faintest trace of brutality—indeed, his hands would have given the lie to such an idea, being unusually slender and delicate even for a southerner. They were hands by which one liked being served.

We knew him humanly without knowing him personally, if I may make that distinction. We saw him nearly every day, and felt a certain kindness for his dreamy ways, which might at times be actual inattentiveness, suddenly transformed into a redeeming zeal to serve. His mien was serious, only the children could bring a smile to his face. It was not sulky, but uningratiating, without intentional effort to please —or, rather, it seemed to give up being pleasant in the conviction that it could not succeed. We should have remembered Mario in any case, as one of those homely recollections of travel which often stick in the mind better than more important ones. But of his circumstances we knew no more than that his father was a petty clerk in the Municipio and his mother took in washing.

His white waiter's-coat became him better than the faded striped suit he wore, with a gay coloured scarf instead of a collar, the ends tucked into his jacket. He neared Cipolla, who however did not leave off that motion of his finger before his nose, so that Mario had to come still closer, right up to the chair-seat and the master's legs. Whereupon the latter spread out his elbows and seized the lad, turning him so that we had a view of his face. Then gazed him briskly up and down, with a careless, commanding eye.

"Well, *ragazzo mio,* how comes it we make acquaintance so late in the day? But believe me, I made yours long ago. Yes, yes, I've had you in my eye this long while and known what good stuff you were made of. How could I go and forget you again? Well, I've had a good deal to think about. . . . Now tell me, what is your name? The first name, that's all I want."

"My name is Mario," the young man answered, in a low voice.

"Ah, Mario. Very good. Yes, yes, there is such a name, quite a common name, a classic name too, one of those which preserve the heroic traditions of the Fatherland. *Bravo! Salve!*" And he flung up his arm slantingly above his crooked shoulder, palm outward, in the Roman salute. He may have been slightly tipsy by now, and no wonder; but he spoke as before, clearly, fluently, and with emphasis. Though about this time there had crept into his voice a gross, autocratic note, and a kind of arrogance was in his sprawl.

"Well, now, Mario *mio*," he went on, "it's a good thing you came this evening, and that's a pretty scarf you've got on; it is becoming to your style of beauty. It must stand you in good stead with the girls, the pretty pretty girls of Torre——"

From the row of youths, close by the place where Mario had been standing, sounded a laugh. It came from the youth with the militant hair. He stood there, his jacket over his shoulder, and laughed outright, rudely and scornfully.

Mario gave a start. I think it was a shrug, but he may have started and then hastened to cover the movement by shrugging his shoulders, as much as to say that the neckerchief and the fair sex were matters of equal indifference to him.

The Cavaliere gave a downward glance.

"We needn't trouble about him," he said. "He is jealous, because your scarf is so popular with the girls, maybe partly because you and I are so friendly up here. Perhaps he'd like me to put him in mind of his colic—I could do it free of charge. Tell me, Mario. You've come here this evening for a bit of fun—and in the daytime you work in an ironmonger's shop?"

"In a café," corrected the youth.

"Oh, in a café. That's where Cipolla nearly came a cropper! What you are is a cup-bearer, a Ganymede—I like that, it is another classical allusion—*Salvietta!*" Again the Cavaliere saluted, to the huge gratification of his audience.

Mario smiled too. "But before that," he interpolated, in the interest of accuracy, "I worked for a while in a shop in Portoclemente." He seemed visited by a natural desire to assist the prophecy by dredging out its essential features.

"There, didn't I say so? In an ironmonger's shop?"

"They kept combs and brushes," Mario got round it.

"Didn't I say that you were not always a Ganymede? Not always at the sign of the serviette? Even when Cipolla makes a mistake, it is a kind that makes you believe in him. Now tell me: Do you believe in me?"

An indefinite gesture.

"A half-way answer," commented the Cavaliere. "Probably it is not easy to win your confidence. Even for me, I can see, it is not so easy. I see in your features a reserve, a sadness, *un tratto di malinconia* . . . tell me" (he seized Mario's hand persuasively) "have you troubles?"

"Nossignore," answered Mario, promptly and decidedly.

"You *have* troubles," insisted the Cavaliere, bearing down the denial by the weight of his authority. "Can't I see? Trying to pull the wool over Cipolla's eyes, are you? Of course, about the girls—it is a girl, isn't it? You have love troubles?"

Mario gave a vigorous head-shake. And again the *giovanotto's* brutal laugh rang out. The Cavaliere gave heed. His eyes were roving about somewhere in the air; but he cocked an ear to the sound, then swung his whip backwards, as he had once or twice before in his conversation with Mario, that none of his puppets might flag in their zeal. The gesture had nearly cost him his new prey: Mario gave a sudden start in the direction of the steps. But Cipolla had him in his clutch.

"Not so fast," said he. "That would be fine, wouldn't it? So you want to skip, do you, Ganymede, right in the middle of the fun, or, rather, when it is just beginning? Stay with me, I'll show you something nice. I'll convince you. You have no reason to worry, I promise you. This girl—you know her and others know her too—what's her name? Wait! I read the name in your eyes, it is on the tip of my tongue and yours too——"

"Silvestra!" shouted the *giovanotto* from below.

The Cavaliere's face did not change.

"Aren't there the forward people?" he asked, not looking down, more as in undisturbed converse with Mario. "Aren't there the young fighting-cocks that crow in season and out? Takes the word out of your mouth, the conceited fool, and seems to think he has some special right to it. Let him be. But Silvestra, your Silvestra—ah, what a girl that is! What a prize! Brings your heart into your mouth to see her walk or laugh or breathe, she is so lovely. And her round arms when she washes, and tosses her head back to get the hair out of her eyes! An angel from paradise!"

Mario stared at him, his head thrust forward. He seemed to have forgotten the audience, forgotten where he was. The red rings round his eyes had got larger, they looked as though they were painted on. His thick lips parted.

"And she makes you suffer, this angel," went on Cipolla, "or, rather, you make yourself suffer for her—there is a difference, my lad, a most important difference, let me tell you. There are misunderstandings in love, maybe nowhere else in the world are there so many. I know what you are thinking: what does this Cipolla, with his little physical defect, know about love? Wrong, all wrong, he knows a lot. He has a wide and powerful understanding of its workings, and it pays to listen to his advice. But let's leave Cipolla out, cut him out altogether and think only of Silvestra, your peerless Silvestra! What! Is she to give any young gamecock the preference, so that he can laugh while you cry? To prefer him to a chap like you, so full of feeling and so sympathetic? Not very likely, is it? It is impossible—we know better, Cipolla and she. If I were to put myself in her place and choose between the two of you, a tarry lout like that—a codfish, a sea-urchin—and a Mario, a knight of the serviette, who moves among gentlefolk and hands round refreshments with an air—my word, but my heart would speak in no uncertain tones—it knows to whom I gave it long ago. It is time that he should see and understand, my chosen one! It is time that you see me and recognize me, Mario, my beloved! Tell me, who am I?"

It was grisly, the way the betrayer made himself irresistible, wreathed and coquetted with his crooked shoulder, languished with the puffy eyes, and showed his splintered teeth in a sickly smile. And alas, at his beguiling words, what was come of our Mario? It is hard for me to tell, hard as it was for me to see; for here was nothing less than an utter abandonment of the inmost soul, a public exposure of timid and deluded passion and rapture. He put his hands across his mouth, his shoulders rose and fell with his pantings. He could not, it was plain, trust his eyes and ears for joy, and the one thing he forgot was precisely that he could not trust them. "Silvestra!" he breathed, from the very depths of his vanquished heart.

"Kiss me!" said the hunchback. "Trust me, I love thee. Kiss me here." And with the tip of his index finger, hand, arm, and little finger outspread, he pointed to his cheek, near the mouth. And Mario bent and kissed him.

It had grown very still in the room. That was a monstrous moment, grotesque and thrilling, the moment of Mario's bliss. In that evil span of time, crowded with a sense of the illusiveness of all joy, one sound became audible, and that not quite at once, but on the instant of the melancholy and ribald meeting between Mario's lips and the repulsive flesh which thrust itself forward for his caress. It was the sound of a laugh, from the *giovanotto* on our left. It broke into the dramatic suspense of the moment, coarse, mocking, and yet—or I must have been grossly mistaken—with an undertone of compassion for the poor bewildered, victimized creature. It had a faint ring of that *"Poveretto"* which Cipolla had declared was wasted on the wrong person, when he claimed the pity for his own.

The laugh still rang in the air when the recipient of the caress gave his whip a little swish, low down, close to his chair-leg, and Mario started up and flung himself back. He stood in that posture staring, his hands one over the other on those desecrated lips. Then he beat his temples with his clenched fists, over and over; turned and staggered down the steps, while the audience applauded, and Cipolla sat there with his hands in his lap, his shoulders shaking. Once below, and even while in full retreat, Mario hurled himself round with legs flung wide apart; one arm flew up, and two flat shattering detonations crashed through applause and laughter.

There was instant silence. Even the dancers came to a full stop and stared about, struck dumb. Cipolla bounded from his seat. He stood with his arms spread out, slanting as though to ward everybody off, as though next moment he would cry out: "Stop! Keep back! Silence!

What was that?" Then, in that instant, he sank back in his seat, his
head rolling on his chest; in the next he had fallen sideways to the floor,
where he lay motionless, a huddled heap of clothing, with limbs awry.

The commotion was indescribable. Ladies hid their faces, shudder-
ing, on the breasts of their escorts. There were shouts for a doctor, for
the police. People flung themselves on Mario in a mob, to disarm him,
to take away the weapon that hung from his fingers—that small, dull-
metal, scarcely pistol-shaped tool with hardly any barrel—in how
strange and unexpected a direction had fate levelled it!

And now—now finally, at last—we took the children and led them
towards the exit, past the pair of *carabinieri* just entering. Was that the
end, they wanted to know, that they might go in peace? Yes, we assured them, that was the end. An end of horror, a fatal end. And yet a
liberation—for I could not, and I cannot, but find it so!

THOMAS MANN

I have often reflected, as doubtless many have before me, that supreme works of literary art generally combine clarity and ambiguity. By ambiguity I do not mean obscurity. I mean they can be understood in more than one sense. A great book is never unclear but it is rarely clear in only one way. It is not a reflecting mirror but that far more fascinating object, a kaleidoscope, capable of a variety of images.

To take a simple example, Gulliver's Travels may be read by children for its fanciful story and by men for its satire on themselves. Swift never bothered to point out this plain fact. Dante, a much more solemn and portentous fellow, stated explicitly that his Divine Comedy was "polysemous"—comprehensible in any of four ways: literally, allegorically (or mystically), morally, or anagogically. This pronouncement has been for centuries the cornerstone of the fortunes of Dante commentators.

Most great works of the imagination have this quality of ambiguity. It is a quality of which the creator may be blandly unaware. Take Charles Dickens. When this twenty-four-year-old shorthand reporter undertook the job of providing serial letterpress to accompany the drawings of a popular illustrator, he had not the remotest idea that he was about to create a story that will probably live as long as men know how to laugh. (Right now, that doesn't seem so very long.) Dickens sat down to write a rollicking narrative of comic incident. He succeeded. But so, to take the first example that comes to mind, is Lover's Handy Andy a rollicking narrative of comic incident. Handy Andy is a curio, Pickwick a masterpiece. Why? Pickwick is better written? Granted. Its characters are better drawn? Agreed. Its episodes are funnier? Admitted, though Andy's trouble with the "soda wather" is as funny as most things in Pickwick. I think we must go deeper.

Here is where our old friend ambiguity raises his Janus head, or even his Hydra head. Pickwick exists on two levels, like Grand Cen-

tral station. Grand Central's lower level is suburban, serving useful
but unromantic places like Yonkers and Scarsdale. But from the
upper level depart the gleaming chariots of the streamliners, bound
for the remotest names on a broad continent. Similarly, on its lower,
mundane level, Pickwick is a loose-jointed yarn about readily recognizable comic personages, careering through a perfectly real and solid
England. But on its upper level Pickwick is a great comic myth. It is
nearer to the Odyssey than it is to Handy Andy. Sam Weller tells
tales of the street, but they are mythical tales. Sam Weller issues
moral quips, but they are odds and ends from a gigantic underground
system of folk wisdom. Sam Weller is a miracle worker, his great
talent lying in his possession of that most uncommon of qualities,
the common touch. Because of the Fat Boy, the entire magnificent
conception of gormandizing will mean something to us a thousand
years hence, even if we should happen to be living on dark-brown
vitamin tablets. The medical students, Jack Hopkins and Bob Sawyer,
cannot be tied down to the time, place, and profession they are supposed to satirize. They are buoyant with a helium life of their own
and escape at once to those upper airs where they soar and curvet
forever with Falstaff and Uncle Toby. Pickwick lasts because it is a
branch on one of the evergreens of literature, the fairy tale.

   I have spoken of Pickwick at perhaps tedious length precisely because at first blush it seems so remote from Thomas Mann's The
Magic Mountain, a selection from which you may read at once by
skipping the next thousand words or so. My point is simple: The
Magic Mountain and Pickwick are alike in that both are works of
double-entendre. Mann and Dickens are both symbolists, the difference being that Mann is a conscious symbolist and Dickens an unconscious one. It is an odd fact that symbols, so vague and evasive,
last. We are so constituted as to be fascinated forever by the idea of
a thing that stands for something else. Our greatest works of art have
about them this atmosphere of indirection. That is what binds all
great books together. That is why Pickwick and The Magic Mountain
are brothers under their skin. For all masterful creative stories are
nourished by the same amniotic fluid circulating in the womb of the
great mother of myths.

Pickwick deals with cockneys and comic mishaps. The Magic Mountain deals with the profoundest problems of life and death. Mann may be more intelligent than Dickens but I do not believe he is one whit the greater artist. Both are myth makers. Both books have a value beyond that of mere narrative. With both books you find yourself interested in something more than "how the story comes out." This something more is what makes both of them works of art. One of the ways by which a supreme literary character is identified is our lack of interest in his fate. The least important thing about Hamlet is his death. Who, save the Baker Street Irregulars, remembers how Sherlock Holmes perished, locked in the arms of Moriarty?

Now let me recall for you the simple outlines of The Magic Mountain. It is a long, leisurely novel. Mae West once remarked, "I like a man who takes his time." Thomas Mann has put it in another way: "Only the exhaustive is truly interesting." The setting is a Swiss tuberculosis sanitarium during the years immediately preceding the outbreak of the First (or Rehearsal) World War. The characters comprise the patients, their visitors, and the hospital staff. The hero is Hans Castorp, an intelligent, amiable, naïve young German. On the surface the book concerns itself with the "education" of Hans: his education by the disease insidiously inhabiting him, his education by other characters—the rationalist Settembrini; the Jesuit-Jew Naphta, that terrifying prefiguring of certain Nazi doctrines; the enigmatic Clavdia Chauchat, with whom Hans falls so fatally in love; "Rhadamanthus" the doctor; and others. The Magic Mountain is about the adventures of Hans' mind. It is a picaresque novel of the intellect as Pickwick is a picaresque novel of the body.

But just as there is an underside to Pickwick, so there are many undersides to The Magic Mountain. Not incidentally but essentially, Mann's book is the following: an imaginative discourse on the nature of time; a study of the interrelationship of life, disease, and death; a Faustian novel about the soul of man (see whether you can sense this in the extract here presented); a dramatic illumination of the sickness of an acquisitive society (for remember that the Berghof Sanitarium is also another name for bourgeois Europe); an interpre-

tation of European history, past, present, and future. We say glibly
that The Magic Mountain is a philosophical novel. This does not
mean that the characters sit around and talk "philosophy." Philosophy
means the love of wisdom. A philosophical novel therefore is one
informed with wisdom. Wisdom has to do with unalterable truths;
hence a philosophical novel is always about something more permanent than the time and place that make up its setting.

Novelists and poets have their own way of expressing wisdom.
Their tool is the symbol, their form the myth. The richer the symbolism and the more complex the myth, the more enduring is the
work of art. The myth of Oedipus is a lode—one might even say a
mother lode—still yielding gold. The sad fact is that an author, if
he desires immortality, should never say exactly what he means. It
is even better if, like Dostoevsky, he doesn't even always know what
he means. For example, The Grapes of Wrath, which I happen to
admire greatly, will not, I imagine, be read a hundred years from
now. Its trouble is that Mr. Steinbeck is too clear a writer. He is too
explicit a writer. He keeps his eye on the object. The object happens
to interest us a great deal now. But when the object—the plight of
the Dust Bowl farmers—disappears or changes its form, The Grapes
of Wrath will no longer be read. Parts of it, which have very little to
do with the object, will still be moving. I have included two of those
parts in this book. If I've chosen the wrong ones I'll feel a perfect
fool a hundred years from now.

Let's get back to The Magic Mountain. Perhaps it is foolhardy of ·
me to scissor out a chapter from it and offer it to you with any hope
of having you enjoy it. The Magic Mountain is really a mountain;
more, it is a monolith. It does not break up well into purple patches
or set pieces.

I chose the chapter "Snow" because it may be read, I hope, without much knowledge or recollection of the plot and characters. Although devoid of action, conflict, intrigue, it is the nearest thing in
the book to a self-contained short story. It moves me for a number
of reasons.

It moves me first because it bares certain fundamental and permanent sensations of man—the sensation of solitude, for example, the sensation of lostness, spiritual as well as physical.

Second, I have chosen this chapter because it is an excellent projection of one of the main themes of the book, Hans' thought that "all interest in death and disease is only another expression of interest in life."

Finally, Hans' vision of the smiling pagan world, with its heart of horror, is an example of that masterful ambiguity we have been discussing—for it is at once the sort of delirious fantasy that might logically invade such a mind as that of Hans Castorp, and at the same time a perfect expression of the Teutonic Sehnsucht after the South, the land of beauty, the country of the classic. Here we have perfect proof that a great writer always writes better than he knows. Hans' phantasmagoria was moving when I first read it, but now that Hitler has compelled Germany (perhaps forever) to kill that element in her which longs for harmony and reason, the phantasmagoria suddenly assumes added significance. That is the way with great works of art. The events of history in some mysterious manner enhance rather than obscure them.

Snow

FROM "THE MAGIC MOUNTAIN" BY

THOMAS MANN

DAILY, FIVE TIMES A DAY, the guests expressed unanimous dissatisfaction with the kind of winter they were having. They felt it was not what they had a right to expect of these altitudes. It failed to deliver the renowned meteorological specific in anything like the quantity indicated by the prospectus, quoted by old inhabitants, or anticipated by new. There was a very great failure in the supply of sunshine, an element so important in the cures achieved up here that without it they were distinctly retarded. And whatever Herr Settembrini might think of the sincerity of the patients' desire to finish their cure, leave "home" and return to the flat-land, at any rate they insisted on their just dues. They wanted what they were entitled to, what their parents or husbands had paid for, and they grumbled unceasingly, at table, in lift, and in hall. The management showed a consciousness of what it owed them by installing a new apparatus for heliotherapy. They had two already, but these did not suffice for the demands of those who wished to get sunburnt by electricity—it was so becoming to the ladies, young and old, and made all the men, though confirmed horizontallers, look irresistibly athletic. And the ladies, even though aware of the mechanico-cosmetical origin of this conquering-hero air, were foolish enough to be carried away by it. There was Frau Schönfeld, a red-haired, red-eyed patient from Berlin. In the salon she looked thirstily at a long-legged, sunken-chested gallant, who described himself on his visiting-card as *"Aviateur diplomé et Enseigne de la Marine allemande."* He was fitted out with the pneumothorax and wore "smoking" at the mid-day meal but not in the evening, saying this was their custom in the navy. "My God," breathed Frau Schönfeld at him, "what a tan this demon has—he gets it from the helio—it makes him look like a hunter of eagles!" "Just wait, nixie!" he whispered in her ear, in the lift, "I'll make you pay for looking at me like that!" It made goose-flesh and shivers run over her. And along the balconies, past the glass partitions, the demon eagle-hunter found his way to the nixie.

But the artificial sun was far from making up for the lack of the real one. Two or three days of full sunshine in the month—it was not good enough, gorgeous though these were, with deep, deep velvety blue sky behind the white mountain summits, a glitter as of diamonds and a fine hot glow on the face and the back of the neck, when they dawned resplendent from the prevailing thick mantle of grey mist. Two or three such days in the course of weeks could not satisfy people whose lot might be said to justify extraordinary demands from the external world. They had made an inward compact, by the terms of which they resigned the common joys and sorrows proper to flat-land humanity, and in exchange were made free of a life that was, to be sure, inactive, but on the other hand very lively and diverting, and care-free to the point of making one forget altogether the flight of time. Thus it was not much good for the Hofrat to tell them how favourably the Berghof compared with a Siberian mine or a penal settlement, nor to sing the praises of the atmosphere, so thin and light, well-nigh as rare as the empty universal ether, free of earthly admixture whether good or bad, and even without actual sunshine to be preferred to the rank vapours of the plain. Despite all he could say, the gloomy disaffection gained ground, threats of unlicensed departure were the order of the day, were even put into execution, without regard for the warning afforded by the melancholy return of Frau Salomon to the fold, now a "life member," her tedious but not serious case having taken that turn by reason of her self-willed visit to her wet and windy Amsterdam.

But if they had no sun, they had snow. Such masses of snow as Hans Castorp had never till now in all his life beheld. The previous winter had done fairly well in this respect, but it had been as nothing compared to this. The snow-fall was monstrous and immeasurable, it made one realize the extravagant, outlandish nature of the place. It snowed day in, day out, and all through the night. The few roads kept open

were like tunnels, with towering walls of snow on either side, crystal
and alabaster surfaces that were pleasant to look at, and on which the
guests scribbled all sorts of messages, jokes and personalities. But even
this path between walls was above the level of the pavement, and made
of hard-packed snow, as one could tell by certain places where it gave
way, and let one suddenly sink in up to the knee. One might, unless
one were careful, break a leg. The benches had disappeared, except
for the high back of one emerging here and there. In the town, the
street level was so raised that the shops had become cellars, into which
one descended by steps cut in the snow.

And on all these lying masses more snow fell, day in, day out. It fell
silently, through air that was moderately cold, perhaps twenty to thirty
degrees of frost. One did not feel the cold, it might have been much
less, for the dryness and absence of wind deprived it of sting. The
mornings were very dark, breakfast was taken by the light of the
artificial moon that hung from the vaulted ceiling of the dining-room,
above the gay stencilled border. Outside was the reeking void, the
world enwrapped in grey-white cotton-wool, packed to the window-
panes in snow and mist. No sight of the mountains; of the nearest
evergreens now and again a glimpse through the fog, standing laden,
and from time to time shaking free a bough of its heavy load, that flew
into the air, and sent a cloud of white against the grey. At ten o'clock
the sun, a wan wisp of light, came up behind its mountain, and gave
the indistinguishable scene some shadowy hint of life, some sallow
glimmer of reality; yet even so, it retained its delicate ghostliness, its
lack of any definite line for the eye to follow. The contours of the
peaks dissolved, disappeared, were dissipated in the mist, while the
vision, led on from one pallidly gleaming slope of snow to another,
lost itself in the void. Then a single cloud, like smoke, lighted up by
the sun, might spread out before a wall of rock and hang there for
long, motionless.

At midday the sun would half break through, and show signs of
banishing the mist. In vain—yet a shred of blue would be visible, and
suffice to make the scene, in its strangely falsified contours, sparkle
marvellously far and wide. Usually, at this hour, the snow-fall stopped,
as though to have a look at what it had done; a like effect was pro-

duced by the rare days when the storm ceased, and the uninterrupted power of the sun sought to thaw away the pure and lovely surface from the new-fallen masses. The sight was at once fairylike and comic, an infantine fantasy. The thick light cushions plumped up on the boughs of trees, the humps and mounds of snow-covered rock-cropping or undergrowth, the droll, dwarfish, crouching disguise all ordinary objects wore, made of the scene a landscape in gnome-land, an illustration for a fairy-tale. Such was the immediate view—wearisome to move in, quaintly, roguishly stimulating to the fancy. But when one looked across the intervening space, at the towering marble statuary of the high Alps in full snow, one felt a quite different emotion, and that was awe of their majestic sublimity.

Afternoons between three and four, Hans Castorp lay in his balcony box, well wrapped, his head against the cushion, not too high or too low, of his excellent chair, and looked out at forest and mountain over his thick-upholstered balustrade. The snow-laden firs, dark-green to blackness, went marching up the sides of the valley, and beneath them the snow lay soft like down pillows. Above the tree line, the mountain walls reared themselves into the grey-white air: huge surfaces of snow, with softly veiled crests, and here and there a black jut of rock. The snow came silently down. The scene blurred more and more, it inclined the eye, gazing thus into woolly vacuity, to slumber. At the moment of slipping off one might give a start—yet what sleep could be purer than this in the icy air? It was dreamless. It was as free from the burden—even the unconscious burden—of organic life, as little aware of an effort to breathe this contentless, weightless, imperceptible air as is the breathless sleep of the dead. When Hans Castorp stirred again, the mountains would be wholly lost in a cloud of snow; only a pinnacle, a jutting rock, might show one instant, to be rapt away the next. It was absorbing to watch these ghostly pranks; one needed to keep alert to follow the transmutations, the veiling and unveiling. One moment a great space of snow-covered rock would reveal itself, standing out bold and free, though of base or peak naught was to be seen. But if one ceased to fix one's gaze upon it, it was gone, in a breath.

Then there were storms so violent as to prevent one's sitting on the balcony for the driven snow which blew in, in such quantity as to cover floor and chair with a thick mantle. Yes, even in this sheltered valley it knew how to storm. The thin air would be in a hurly-burly, so whirling full of snow one could not see a hand's breadth before one's face. Gusts strong enough to take one's breath away flung the snow about, drew it up cyclone-fashion from the valley floor to the upper air, whisked it about in the maddest dance; no longer a snow-storm, it was a blinding chaos, a white dark, a monstrous dereliction on the part of this inordinate and violent region; no living creature save the snow-bunting—which suddenly appeared in troops—could flourish in it.

And yet Hans Castorp loved this snowy world. He found it not un-like life at the sea-shore. The monotony of the scene was in both cases profound. The snow, so deep, so light, so dry and spotless, was the sand of down below. One was as clean as the other: you could shake the snow from boots and clothing, just as you could the fine-ground, dustless stone and shell, product of the sea's depth—neither left trace behind. And walking in the snow was as toilsome as on the dunes; unless, indeed, a crust had come upon it, by dint of thawing and freez-ing, when the going became easy and pleasant, like marching along the smooth, hard, wet, and resilient strip of sand close to the edge of the sea.

But the storms and high-piled drifts of this year gave pedestrians small chance. They were favourable only for skiing. The snow-plough, labouring its best, barely kept free the main street of the settlement and the most indispensable paths. Thus the few short feasible stretches were always crowded with other walkers, ill and well: the native, the permanent guest, and the hotel population; and these in their turn were bumped by the sleds as they swung and swerved down the slopes, steered by men and women who leaned far back as they came on, and shouted importunately, being obsessed by the importance of their occu-pation. Once at the bottom they would turn and trundle their toy sledges uphill again.

Hans Castorp was thoroughly sick of all the walks. He had two desires: one of them, the stronger, was to be alone with his thoughts and his stock-taking projects; and this his balcony assured to him. But the other, allied unto it, was a lively craving to come into close and freer touch with the mountains, the mountains in their snowy desolation; toward them he was irresistibly drawn. Yet how could he, all unprovided and footbound as he was, hope to gratify such a desire? He had only to step beyond the end of the shovelled paths—an end soon reached upon any of them—to plunge breast-high in the snowy element.

Thus it was Hans Castorp, on a day in his second winter with those up here, resolved to buy himself skis and learn to walk on them, enough, that is, for his purposes. He was no sportsman, had never been physically inclined to sport; and did not behave as though he were, as did many guests of the cure, dressing up to suit the mode and the spirit of the place. Hermine Kleefeld, for instance, among other females, though she was constantly blue in the face from lack of breath, loved to appear at luncheon in tweed knickers, and loll about after the meal in a basket-chair in the hall, with her legs sprawled out. Hans Castorp knew that he would meet with a refusal were he to ask the Hofrat to countenance his plan. Sports activities were unconditionally forbidden at the Berghof as in all other establishments of the kind. This atmosphere, which one seemed to breathe in so effortlessly, was a severe strain on the heart, and as for Hans Castorp personally, his lively comment on his own state, that "getting used to being up here consisted in getting used to not getting used," had continued in force. His fever, which Rhadamanthus ascribed to a moist spot, remained obstinate. Why else indeed should he be here? His desire, his present purpose was then clearly inconsistent and inadmissible. Yet we must be at the pains to understand him aright. He had no wish to imitate the fresh-air faddists and smart pseudo-sportsmen, who would have been equally eager to sit all day and play cards in a stuffy room, if only that had been interdicted by authority. He felt himself a member of another and closer community than this small tourist world; a new and a broader point of view, a dignity and restraint set him apart and made him conscious that it would be unfitting for him to emulate their rough-and-tumbling in the snow. He had no escapade in view, his plans were so moderate that Rhadamanthus himself, had he known, might well have approved them. But the rules stood in the way, and Hans Castorp resolved to act behind his back.

He took occasion to speak to Herr Settembrini of his plan—who for sheer joy could have embraced him. "*Si, si, si!* Do so, do so, Engineer, do so with the blessing of God! Ask after nobody's leave, but simply do it! Ah, your good angel must have whispered you the thought! Do it straightway, before the impulse leaves you. I'll go along, I'll go to the shop with you, and together we will acquire the instruments of this happy inspiration. I would go with you even into the mountains, I would be by your side, on winged feet, like Mercury's—but that I may not. May not! If that were all, how soon would I do it! That I cannot is the truth, I am a broken man.—But you—it will do you no harm, none at all, if you are sensible and do nothing rash. Even—even if it did you harm—just a little harm—it will still have been your good angel roused you to it. I say no more. Ah, what an unsurpassable plan! Two years up here, and still capable of such projects—ah, yes, your heart is sound, no need to despair of you. Bravo, bravo! By all means pull the wool over the eyes of your Prince of Shadows! Buy the snow-shoes, have them sent to me or Lukaçek, or the chandler below-stairs. You fetch them from here to go and practise, you go off on them——"

So it befell. Under Herr Settembrini's critical eye—he played the connoisseur, though innocent of sports—Hans Castorp acquired a pair of oaken skis, finished a light-brown, with tapering, pointed ends and the best quality of straps. He bought the iron-shod staff with the little wheel, as well, and was not content to have his purchases sent, but carried them on his shoulder to Settembrini's quarters, where he arranged with the grocer to take care of them for him. He had looked on enough at the sport to know the use of his tools; and choosing for his practice-ground an almost treeless slope not far behind the sanatorium, remote from the hubbub of the spot where other beginners learned the art, he began daily to make his first blundering attempts, watched by Herr Settembrini, who would stand at a little distance, leaning on his cane, with legs gracefully crossed, and greet his nursling's progress with applause. One day Hans Castorp, steering down the cleared drive toward the Dorf, in act to take the skis back to the grocer's, ran into the Hofrat. Behrens never recognized him, though it was broad day, and our beginner had well-nigh collided with him. Shrouded in a haze of tobacco-smoke, he stalked past regardless.

Hans Castorp found that one quickly gets readiness in an art where strong desire comes in play. He was not ambitious for expert skill, and all he needed he acquired in a few days, without undue strain on wind or muscles. He learned to keep his feet tidily together and make parallel tracks; to avail himself of his stick in getting off; he learned how to take obstacles, such as small elevations of the ground, with a slight soaring motion, arms outspread, rising and falling like a ship on a billowy sea; learned, after the twentieth trial, not to trip and roll over when he braked at full speed, with the right Telemark turn, one leg forward, the other bent at the knee. Gradually he widened the sphere of his activities. One day it came to pass that Herr Settembrini saw him vanish in the far white mist; the Italian shouted a warning through cupped hands, and turned homewards, his pedagogic soul well-pleased.

It was beautiful here in these wintry heights: not mildly and ingratiatingly beautiful, more as the North Sea is beautiful in a westerly gale. There was no thunder of surf, a deathly stillness reigned, but roused similar feelings of awe. Hans Castorp's long, pliant soles carried him in all directions: along the left slope to Clavadel, on the right to Frauenkirch and Glaris, whence he could see the shadowy massif of the Amselfluh, ghostlike in the mist; into the Dischma valley, or up behind the Berghof in the direction of the wooded Seehorn, only the top of which, snow-covered, rose above the tree line, or the Drusatscha forest, with the pale outline of the Rhätikon looming behind it, smothered in snow. He took his skis and went up on the funicular to the Schatzalp; there, rapt six thousand feet above the sea, he revelled at will on the gleaming slopes of powdery snow—whence, in good weather, there was a view of majestic extent over all the surrounding territory.

He rejoiced in his new resource, before which all difficulties and hindrances to movement fell away. It gave him the utter solitude he craved, and filled his soul with impressions of the wild inhumanity, the precariousness of this region into which he had ventured. On his one hand he might have a precipitous, pine-clad declivity, falling away into the mists; on the other sheer rock might rise, with masses of snow, in monstrous, Cyclopean forms, all domed and vaulted, swelling or cavernous. He would halt for a moment, to quench the sound of his own movement, when the silence about him would be absolute, complete, a wadded soundlessness, as it were, elsewhere all unknown. There was no stir of air, not so much as might even lightly sway the tree-boughs; there was not a rustle, nor the voice of a bird. It was primeval silence to which Hans Castorp hearkened, when he leaned thus on his staff, his head on one side, his mouth open. And always it snowed, snowed without pause, endlessly, gently, soundlessly falling.

No, this world of limitless silences had nothing hospitable; it received the visitor at his own risk, or rather it scarcely even received him, it tolerated his penetration into its fastnesses, in a manner that boded no good; it made him aware of the menace of the elemental, a menace not even hostile, but impersonally deadly. The child of civilization, remote from birth from wild nature and all her ways, is more susceptible to her grandeur than is her untutored son who has looked at her and lived close to her from childhood up, on terms of prosaic familiarity. The latter scarcely knows the religious awe with which the other regards her, that awe which conditions all his feeling for her, and is present, a constant, solemn thrill, in the profoundest depth of his soul. Hans Castorp, standing there in his puttees and long-sleeved camel's-hair waistcoat, on his skis *de luxe,* suddenly seemed to himself exceedingly presumptuous, to be thus listening to the primeval hush, the deathlike silence of these wintry fastnesses. He felt his breast lightened when, on his way home, the first chalets, the first abodes of human beings, loomed visible through the fog. Only then did he become aware that he had been for hours possessed by a secret awe and terror. On the island of Sylt he had stood by the edge of the thundering surf. In his white flannels, elegant, self-assured, but most respectful, he had stood there as one stands before a lion's cage and looks deep into the yawning maw of the beast, lined with murderous fangs. He had bathed in the surf, and heeded the blast of the coastguard's horn, warning all and sundry not to venture rashly beyond the first line of billows, not to approach too nearly the oncoming tempest—the very last impulse of whose cataract, indeed, struck upon him like a blow from a lion's paw. From that experience our young man had learned the fearful pleasure of toying with forces so great that to approach them nearly is destruction. What he had not then felt was the temptation to come closer, to carry the thrilling contact with these deadly natural forces up to a point where the full embrace was imminent. Weak human being that he was—though tolerably well equipped with the weapons of civilization—what he at this moment knew was the fascination of venturing just so far into the monstrous unknown, or at least abstaining just so long from flight before it, that the adventure grazed the perilous, that it was just barely possible to put limits to it, before it became no longer a matter of toying with the foam and playfully dodging the ruthless paw—but the ultimate adventure, the billow, the lion's maw, and the sea.

In a word, Hans Castorp was valorous up here—if by valor we mean not mere dull matter-of-factness in the face of nature, but conscious submission to her, the fear of death cast out by irresistible oneness. Yes, in his narrow, hypercivilized breast, Hans Castorp cherished a feeling of kinship with the elements, connected with the new sense of superiority he had lately felt at sight of the silly people on their little sleds; it had made him feel that a profounder, more spacious, less luxuriant solitude than that afforded by his balcony chair would be beyond all price. He had sat there and looked abroad, at those mist-wreathed summits, at the carnival of snow, and blushed to be gaping thus from the breastwork of material well-being. This motive, and no momentary fad—no, nor yet any native love of bodily exertion—was what impelled him to learn the use of skis. If it was uncanny up there in the magnificence of the mountains, in the deathly silence of the snows—and uncanny it assuredly was, to our son of civilization— this was equally true, that in these months and years he had already drunk deep of the uncanny, in spirit and in sense. Even a colloquy with Naphta and Settembrini was not precisely the canniest thing in the world, it too led one on into uncharted and perilous regions. So if we can speak of Hans Castorp's feeling of kinship with the wild powers of the winter heights, it is in this sense, that despite his pious awe he felt these scenes to be a fitting theatre for the issue of his involved thoughts, a fitting stage for one to make who, scarcely knowing how, found it had devolved upon him to take stock of himself, in reference to the rank and status of the *Homo Dei.*

No one was here to blow a warning to the rash one—unless, indeed, Herr Settembrini, with his farewell shout at Hans Castorp's disappearing back, had been that man. But possessed by valorous desire, our youth had given the call no heed—as little as he had the steps behind him on a certain carnival night. *"Eh, Ingegnere, un po' di ragione, sa!"* "Yes, yes, pedagogic Satana, with your *ragione* and your *ribellione,"* he thought. "But I'm rather fond of you. You are a windbag and a hand-organ man, to be sure. But you mean well, you mean much better, and more to my mind, than that knife-edged little Jesuit and Terrorist, apologist of the Inquisition and the knout, with his round eye-glasses—though he is nearly always right when you and he come to grips over my paltry soul, like God and the Devil in the mediæval legends."

He struggled, one day, powdered in snow to the waist, up a succession of snow-shrouded terraces, up and up, he knew not whither. Nowhither, perhaps; these upper regions blended with a sky no less misty-white than they, and where the two came together, it was hard to tell. No summit, no ridge was visible, it was a haze and a nothing, toward which Hans Castorp strove; while behind him the world, the inhabited valley, fell away swiftly from view, and no sound mounted to his ears. In a twinkling he was as solitary, he was as lost, as heart could wish, his loneliness was profound enough to awake the fear which is the first stage of valour. *"Præterit figura huius mundi,"* he said to himself, quoting Naphta, in a Latin hardly humanistic in spirit. He stopped and looked about. On all sides there was nothing to see, beyond small single flakes of snow, which came out of a white sky and sank to rest on the white earth. The silence about him refused to say aught to his spirit. His gaze was lost in the blind white void, he felt his heart pulse from the effort of the climb—that muscular organ whose animal-like shape and contracting motion he had watched, with a feeling of sacrilege, in the x-ray laboratory. A naïve reverence filled him for that organ of his, for the pulsating human heart, up here alone in the icy void, alone with its question and its riddle.

On he pressed; higher and higher toward the sky. Walking, he thrust the end of his stick in the snow and watched the blue light follow it out of the hole it made. That he liked; and stood for long at a time to test the little optical phenomenon. It was a strange, a subtle colour, this greenish-blue; colour of the heights and deeps, ice-clear, yet holding shadow in its depths, mysteriously exquisite. It reminded him of the colour of certain eyes, whose shape and glance had spelled his destiny; eyes to which Herr Settembrini, from his humanistic height, had referred with contempt as "Tartar slits" and "wolf's eyes"—eyes seen long ago and then found again, the eyes of Pribislav Hippe and Clavdia Chauchat. "With pleasure," he said aloud, in the profound stillness. "But don't break it—*c'est à visser, tu sais.*" And his spirit heard behind him words of warning in a mellifluous tongue.

A wood loomed, misty, far off to the right. He turned that way, to the end of having some goal before his eyes, instead of sheer white transcendence; and made toward it with a dash, not remarking an intervening depression of the ground. He could not have seen it, in fact; everything swam before his eyes in the white mist, obliterating all contours. When he perceived it, he gave himself to the decline, unable to measure its steepness with his eye.

The grove that had attracted him lay the other side of the gully into which he had unintentionally steered. The trough, covered with fluffy snow, fell away on the side next the mountains, as he observed when he pursued it a little distance. It went downhill, the steep sides grew higher, this fold of the earth's surface seemed like a narrow passage leading into the mountain. Then the points of his skis turned up again, there began an incline, soon there were no more side walls; Hans Castorp's trackless course ran once more uphill along the mountain-side.

He saw the pine grove behind and below him, on his right, turned again toward it, and with a quick descent reached the laden trees; they stood in a wedge-shaped group, a vanguard thrust out from the mist-screened forests above. He rested beneath their boughs, and smoked a cigarette. The unnatural stillness, the monstrous solitude, still oppressed his spirit; yet he felt proud to have conquered them, brave in the pride of having measured to the height of surroundings such as these.

It was three in the afternoon. He had set out soon after luncheon, with the idea of cutting part of the long rest-cure, and tea as well, in order to be back before dark. He had brought some chocolate in his breeches pocket, and a small flask of wine; and told himself exultantly that he had still several hours to revel in all this grandeur.

The position of the sun was hard to recognize, veiled as it was in haze. Behind him, at the mouth of the valley, above that part of the mountains that was shut off from view, the clouds and mist seemed to thicken and move forward. They looked like snow—more snow— as though there were pressing demand for it! Like a good hard storm. Indeed, the little soundless flakes were coming down more quickly as he stood.

Hans Castorp put out his arm and let some of them come to rest on his sleeve; he viewed them with the knowing eye of the nature-lover. They looked mere shapeless morsels; but he had more than once had their like under his good lens, and was aware of the exquisite precision of form displayed by these little jewels, insignia, orders, agraffes—no jeweller, however skilled, could do finer, more minute work. Yes, he thought, here was a difference, after all, between this light, soft, white powder he trod with his skis, that weighed down the trees, and covered the open spaces, a difference between it and the sand on the beaches at home, to which he had likened it. For this powder was not made of tiny grains of stone; but of myriads of tiniest drops of water, which in freezing had darted together in symmetrical variation—parts, then, of the same anorganic substance which was the source of protoplasm, of plant life, of the human body. And among these myriads of enchanting little stars, in their hidden splendour that was too small for man's naked eye to see, there was not one like unto another; an endless inventiveness governed the development and unthinkable differentiation of one and the same basic scheme, the equilateral, equiangled hexagon. Yet each, in itself—this was the uncanny, the anti-organic, the life-denying character of them all—each of them was absolutely symmetrical, icily regular in form. They were too regular, as substance adapted to life never was to this degree—

the living principle shuddered at this perfect precision, found it deathly, the very marrow of death—Hans Castorp felt he understood now the reason why the builders of antiquity purposely and secretly introduced minute variation from absolute symmetry in their columnar structures.

He pushed off again, shuffling through the deep snow on his flexible runners, along the edge of the wood, down the slope, up again, at random, to his heart's content, about and into this lifeless land. Its empty, rolling spaces, its dried vegetation of single dwarf firs sticking up through the snow, bore a striking resemblance to a scene on the dunes. Hans Castorp nodded as he stood and fixed the likeness in his mind. Even his burning face, his trembling limbs, the peculiar and half-intoxicated mingled sensations of excitement and fatigue were pleasurable, reminding him as they did of that familiar feeling induced by the sea air, which could sting one like whips, and yet was so laden with sleepy essences. He rejoiced in his freedom of motion, his feet were like wings. He was bound to no path, none lay behind him to take him back whence he had come. At first there had been posts, staves set up as guides through the snow—but he had soon cut free from their tutelage, which recalled the coastguard with his horn, and seemed inconsistent with the attitude he had taken up toward the wild.

He pressed on, turning right and left among rocky, snow-clad elevations, and came behind them on an incline, then a level spot, then on the mountains themselves—how alluring and accessible seemed their softly covered gorges and defiles! His blood leaped at the strong allurement of the distance and the height, the ever profounder solitude. At risk of a late return he pressed on, deeper into the wild silence, the monstrous and the menacing, despite that gathering darkness was sinking down over the region like a veil, and heightening his inner apprehension until it presently passed into actual fear. It was this fear which first made him conscious that he had deliberately set out to lose his way and the direction in which valley and settlement lay—and had been as successful as heart could wish. Yet he knew that if he were to turn in his tracks and go downhill, he would reach the valley bottom—even if at some distance from the Berghof—and that

sooner than he had planned. He would come home too early, not
have made full use of his time. On the other hand, if he were overtaken unawares by the storm, he would probably in any case not find
his way home. But however genuine his fear of the elements, he
refused to take premature flight; his being scarcely the sportsman's
attitude, who only meddles with the elements so long as he knows
himself their master, takes all precautions, and prudently yields when
he must—whereas what went on in Hans Castorp's soul can only be
described by the one word challenge. It was perhaps a blameworthy,
presumptuous attitude, even united to such genuine awe. Yet this much
is clear, to any human understanding: that when a young man has
lived years long in the way this one had, something may gather—may
accumulate, as our engineer might put it—in the depths of his soul,
until one day it suddenly discharges itself, with a primitive exclamation of disgust, a mental "Oh, go to the devil!" a repudiation of all
caution whatsoever, in short with a challenge. So on he went, in his
seven-league slippers, glided down this slope too and pressed up the
incline beyond, where stood a wooden hut that might be a hayrick
or shepherd's shelter, its roof weighted with flat stones. On past this
to the nearest mountain ridge, bristling with forest, behind whose
back the giant peaks towered upward in the mist. The wall before
him, studded with single groups of trees, was steep, but looked as
though one might wind to the right and get round it by climbing a
little way up the slope. Once on the other side, he could see what lay
beyond. Accordingly Hans Castorp set out on this tour of investigation, which began by descending from the meadow with the hut into
another and rather deep gully that dropped off from right to left.

He had just begun to mount again when the expected happened,
and the storm burst, the storm that had threatened so long. Or may
one say "threatened" of the action of blind, nonsentient forces, which
have no purpose to destroy us—that would be comforting by comparison—but are merely horribly indifferent to our fate should we become
involved with them? "Hullo!" Hans Castorp thought, and stood still,
as the first blast whirled through the densely falling snow and caught
him. "That's a gentle zephyr—tells you what's coming." And truly
this wind was savage. The air was in reality frightfully cold, probably

some degrees below zero; but so long as it remained dry and still one
almost found it balmy. It was when a wind came up that the cold
began to cut into the flesh; and in a wind like the one that blew now,
of which that first gust had been a forerunner, the furs were not
bought that could protect the limbs from its icy rigours. And Hans
Castorp wore no fur, only a woollen waistcoat, which he had found
quite enough, or even, with the faintest gleam of sunshine, a burden.
But the wind was at his back, a little sidewise; there was small inducement to turn and receive it in the face; so the mad youth, letting that
fact reinforce the fundamental challenge of his attitude, pressed on
among the single tree-trunks, and tried to outflank the mountain he
had attacked.

It was no joke. There was almost nothing to be seen for swimming
snow-flakes, that seemed without falling to fill the air to suffocation
by their whirling dance. The icy gusts made his ears burn painfully, his
limbs felt half paralysed, his hands were so numb he hardly knew if
they held the staff. The snow blew inside his collar and melted down
his back. It drifted on his shoulders and right side; he thought he
should freeze as he stood into a snow-man, with his staff stiff in his
hands. And all this under relatively favouring circumstances; for let
him turn his face to the storm and his situation would be still worse.
Getting home would be no easy task—the harder, the longer he put
it off.

At last he stopped, gave an angry shrug, and turned his skis the
other way. Then the wind he faced took his breath on the spot, so
that he was forced to go through the awkward process of turning
round again to get it back, and collect his resolution to advance in
the teeth of his ruthless foe. With bent head and cautious breathing
he managed to get under way; but even thus forewarned, the slowness
of his progress and the difficulty of seeing and breathing dismayed
him. Every few minutes he had to stop, first to get his breath in the
lee of the wind, and then because he saw next to nothing in the blinding whiteness, and moving as he did with head down, had to take
care not to run against trees, or be flung headlong by unevenness in
the ground. Hosts of flakes flew into his face, melted there, and he
anguished with the cold of them. They flew into his mouth, and died

away with a weak, watery taste; flew against his eyelids so that he winked, overflowed his eyes and made seeing as difficult as it was now almost impossible for other reasons: namely, the dazzling effect of all that whiteness, and the veiling of his field of vision, so that his sense of sight was almost put out of action. It was nothingness, white, whirling nothingness, into which he looked when he forced himself to do so. Only at intervals did ghostly-seeming forms from the world of reality loom up before him: a stunted fir, a group of pines, even the pale silhouette of the hay-hut he had lately passed.

He left it behind, and sought his way back over the slope on which it stood. But there was no path. To keep direction, relatively speaking, into his own valley would be a question far more of luck than management; for while he could see his hand before his face, he could not see the ends of his skis. And even with better visibility, the host of difficulties must have combined to hinder his progress: the snow in his face, his adversary the storm, which hampered his breathing, made him fight both to take a breath and to exhale it, and constantly forced him to turn his head away to gasp. How could anyone—either Hans Castorp or another and much stronger than he—make head? He stopped, he blinked his lashes free of water drops, knocked off the snow that like a coat of mail was sheathing his body in front—and it struck him that progress, under the circumstances, was more than anyone could expect.

And yet Hans Castorp did progress. That is to say, he moved on. But whether in the right direction, whether it might not have been better to stand still, remained to be seen. Theoretically the chances were against it; and in practice he soon began to suspect something was wrong. This was not familiar ground beneath his feet, not the easy slope he had gained on mounting with such difficulty from the ravine, which had of course to be retraversed. The level distance was too short, he was already mounting again. It was plain that the storm, which came from the south-west, from the mouth of the valley, had with its violence driven him from his course. He had been exhausting himself, all this time, with a false start. Blindly, enveloped in white, whirling night, he laboured deeper and deeper into this grim and callous sphere.

"No, you don't," said he, suddenly, between his teeth, and halted. The words were not emotional, yet he felt for a second as though his heart had been clutched by an icy hand; it winced, and then knocked rapidly against his ribs, as it had the time Rhadamanthus found the moist cavity. Pathos in the grand manner was not in place, he knew, in one who had chosen defiance as his rôle, and was indebted to himself alone for all his present plight. "Not bad," he said, and discovered that his facial muscles were not his to command, that he could not express in his face any of his soul's emotions, for that it was stiff with cold. "What next? Down this slope; follow your nose home, I suppose, and keep your face to the wind—though that is a good deal easier said than done," he went on, panting with his efforts, yet actually speaking half aloud, as he tried to move on again: "but something has to happen, I can't sit down and wait, I should simply be buried in six-sided crystalline symmetricality, and Settembrini, when he came with his little horn to find me, would see me squatting here with a snow-cap over one ear." He realized that he was talking to himself, and not too sensibly—for which he took himself to task, and then continued on purpose, though his lips were so stiff he could not shape the labials, and so did without them, as he had on a certain other occasion that came to his mind. "Keep quiet, and get along with you out of here," he admonished himself, adding: "You seem to be wool-gathering, not quite right in your head, and that looks bad for you."

But this he only said with his reason—to some extent detached from the rest of him, though after all nearly concerned. As for his natural part, it felt only too much inclined to yield to the confusion which laid hold upon him with his growing fatigue. He even remarked this tendency and took thought to comment upon it. "Here," said he, "we have the typical reaction of a man who loses himself in the mountains in a snow-storm and never finds his way home." He gasped out other fragments of the same thought as he went, though he avoided giving it more specific expression. "Whoever hears about it afterwards, imagines it as horrible; but he forgets that disease—and the state I am in is, in a way of speaking, disease—so adjusts its man that it and he can come to terms; there are sensory appeasements, short circuits, a merciful narcosis—yes, oh yes, yes. But one must fight against them, after all, for they are two-faced, they are in the highest degree equivocal, everything depends upon the point of view. If you are not meant to get home, they are a benefaction, they are merciful; but if you mean to get home, they become sinister. I believe I still do. Certainly I don't intend—in this heart of mine so stormily beating it doesn't appeal to me in the least—to let myself be snowed under by this idiotically symmetrical crystallometry."

In truth, he was already affected, and his struggle against oncoming sensory confusion was feverish and abnormal. He should have been more alarmed on discovering that he had already declined from the level course—this time apparently on the other slope. For he had pushed off with the wind coming slantwise at him, which was ill-advised, though more convenient for the moment. "Never mind," he thought, "I'll get my direction again down below." Which he did, or thought he did—or, truth to tell, scarcely even thought so; worst of all, began to be indifferent whether he had done or no. Such was the effect of an insidious double attack, which he but weakly combated. Fatigue and excitement combined were a familiar state to our young man—whose acclimatization, as we know, still consisted in getting used to not getting used; and both fatigue and excitement were now present in such strength as to make impossible any thought of asserting his reason against them. He felt as often after a colloquy with Settembrini and Naphta, only to a far greater degree: dazed and tipsy, giddy, a-tremble with excitement. This was probably why he began to colour his lack of resistance to the stealing narcosis with half-maudlin references to the latest-aired complex of theories. Despite his scornful repudiation of the idea that he might lie down and be covered up with hexagonal symmetricality, something within him maundered on, sense or no sense: told him that the feeling of duty which bade him fight against insidious sensory appeasements was a purely ethical reaction, representing the sordid bourgeois view of life, irreligion, Philistinism; while the desire, nay, craving, to lie down and rest, whispered him in the guise of a comparison between this storm and a sand-storm on the desert, before which the Arab flings himself down and draws his burnous over his head. Only his lack of a burnous, the unfeasibility of drawing his woollen waistcoat over his head, prevented him from following suit—this although he was no longer a child, and pretty well aware of the conditions under which a man freezes to death.

There had been a rather steep declivity, then level ground, then again an ascent, a stiff one. This was not necessarily wrong; one must of course, on the way to the valley, traverse rising ground at times. The wind had turned capriciously round, for it was now at Hans Castorp's back, and that, taken by itself, was a blessing. Owing, perhaps, to the storm, or the soft whiteness of the incline before him, dim in the whirling air, drawing him toward it, he bent as he walked. Only a little further—supposing one were to give way to the temptation, and his temptation was great; it was so strong that it quite lived up to the many descriptions he had read of the "typical danger-state." It asserted itself, it refused to be classified with the general order of things, it insisted on being an exception, its very exigence challenged comparison—yet at the same time it never disguised its origin or aura, never denied that it was, so to speak, garbed in Spanish black, with snow-white, fluted ruff, and stood for ideas and fundamental conceptions that were characteristically gloomy, strongly Jesuitical and anti-human, for the rack-and-knout discipline which was the particular horror of Herr Settembrini, though he never opposed it without making himself ridiculous, like a hand-organ man for ever grinding out "*ragione*" to the same old tune.

And yet Hans Castorp did hold himself upright and resist his craving to lie down. He could see nothing, but he struggled, he came forward. Whether to the purpose or not, he could not tell; but he did his part, and moved on despite the weight the cold more and more laid upon his limbs. The present slope was too steep to ascend directly, so he slanted a little, and went on thus awhile without much heed whither. Even to lift his stiffened lids to peer before him was so great and so nearly useless an effort as to offer him small incentive. He merely caught glimpses: here clumps of pines that merged together; there a ditch or stream, a black line marked out between overhanging banks of snow. Now, for a change, he was going downhill, with the wind in his face, when, at some distance before him, and seeming to hang in the driving wind and mist, he saw the faint outline of a human habitation.

Ah, sweet and blessed sight! Verily he had done well, to march stoutly on despite all obstacles, until now human dwellings appeared, in sign that the inhabited valley was at hand. Perhaps there were even human beings, perhaps he might enter and abide the end of the storm under shelter, then get directions, or a guide if the dark should have fallen. He held toward this chimerical goal, that often quite vanished in mist, and took an exhausting climb against the wind before it was reached; finally drew near it—to discover, with what staggering astonishment and horror may be imagined, that it was only the hay-hut with the weighted roof, to which, after all his striving, by all his devious paths, he had come back.

That was the very devil. Hans Castorp gave vent to several heartfelt curses—of which his lips were too stiff to pronounce the labials. He examined the hut, to get his bearings, and came to the conclusion that he had approached it from the same direction as before—namely, from the rear; and therefore, what he had accomplished for the past hour—as he reckoned it—had been sheer waste of time and effort. But there it was, just as the books said. You went in a circle, gave yourself endless trouble under the delusion that you were accomplishing something, and all the time you were simply describing some great silly arc that would turn back to where it had its beginning, like the riddling year itself. You wandered about, without getting home. Hans Castorp recognized the traditional phenomenon with a certain grim satisfaction—and even slapped his thigh in astonishment at this punctual general law fulfilling itself in his particular case.

The lonely hut was barred, the door locked fast, no entrance possible. But Hans Castorp decided to stop for the present. The projecting roof gave the illusion of shelter, and the hut itself, on the side turned toward the mountains, afforded, he found, some little protection against the storm. He leaned his shoulder against the rough-hewn timber, since his long skis prevented him from leaning his back. And so he stood, obliquely to the wall, having thrust his staff in the snow; hands in pockets, his collar turned up as high as it would go, bracing himself on his outside leg, and leaning his dizzy head against the wood, his eyes closed, but opening them every now and then to look down his shoulder and across the gully to where the high mountain wall palely appeared and disappeared in mist.

His situation was comparatively comfortable. "I can stick it like this all night, if I have to," he thought, "if I change legs from time to time, lie on the other side, so to speak, and move about a bit between whiles, as of course I must. I'm rather stiff, naturally, but the effort I made has accumulated some inner warmth, so after all it was not quite in vain, that I have come round all this way. Come round— not coming round—that's the regular expression they use, of people drowned or frozen to death.—I suppose I used it because I am not quite so clear in the head as I might be. But it is a good thing I can stick it out here; for this frantic nuisance of a snow-storm can carry on until morning without a qualm, and if it only keeps up until dark it will be quite bad enough, for in the dark the danger of going round and round and *not* coming round is as great as in a storm. It must be toward evening already, about six o'clock, I should say, after all the time I wasted on my circular tour. Let's see, how late is it?" He felt for his watch; his numbed fingers could scarcely find and draw it from his pocket. Here it was, his gold hunting-watch, with his monogram on the lid, ticking faithfully away in this lonely waste, like Hans Castorp's own heart, that touching human heart that beat in the organic warmth of his interior man.

It was half past four. But deuce take it, it had been nearly so much before the storm burst. Was it possible his whole bewildered circuit had lasted scarcely a quarter of an hour? " 'Coming round' makes time seen long," he noted. "And when you *don't* 'come round'—does it seem longer? But the fact remains that at five or half past it will be regularly dark. Will the storm hold up in time to keep me from running in circles again? Suppose I take a sip of port—it might strengthen me."

He had brought with him a bottle of that amateurish drink, simply because it was always kept ready in flat bottles at the Berghof, for excursions—though not, of course, excursions like this unlawful escapade. It was not meant for people who went out in the snow and got lost and night-bound in the mountains. Had his senses been less befogged, he must have said to himself that if he were bent on getting home, it was almost the worst thing he could have done. He did say so, after he had drunk several swallows, for they took effect at once, and it was an effect much like that of the Kulmbacher beer on the evening of his arrival at the Berghof, when he had angered Settembrini by his ungoverned prattle anent fish-sauces and the like—Herr Ludovico, the pedagogue, the same who held madmen to their senses when they would give themselves rein. Hans Castorp heard through thin air the mellifluous sound of his horn; the orator and schoolmaster was nearing by forced marches, to rescue his troublesome nursling, life's delicate child, from his present desperate pass and lead him home.—All which was of course sheer rubbish, due to the Kulmbacher he had so foolishly drunk. For of course Herr Settembrini had no horn, how could he have? He had a hand-organ, propped by a sort of wooden leg against the pavement, and as he played a sprightly air, he flung his humanistic eyes up to the people in the houses. And furthermore he knew nothing whatever of what had happened, as he no longer lived in House Berghof, but with Lukaçek the tailor, in his little attic room with the water-bottle, above Naphta's silken cell. Moreover, he would have nor right nor reason to interfere—no more than upon that carnival night on which Hans Castorp had found himself in a position quite as mad and bad as this one, when he gave the ailing Clavdia Chauchat back *son crayon*—his, Pribislav Hippe's, pencil. What position was that? What position could it be but the horizontal, literally and not metaphorically the position of all long-termers up here? Was he himself not used to lie long hours out of doors, in snow and frost, by night as well as day? And he was making ready to sink down when the idea seized him, took him as it were by the collar and fetched him up standing, that all this nonsense he was uttering was still inspired by the Kulmbacher beer and the impersonal, quite typical and traditional longing to lie down and sleep, of which he had always heard, and which would by quibbling and sophistry now betray him.

"That was the wrong way to go to work," he acknowledged to himself. "The port was not at all the right thing; just the few sips of it have made my head so heavy I cannot hold it up, and my thoughts are all just confused, stupid quibbling with words. I can't depend on them—not only the first thought that comes into my head, but even the second one, the correction which my reason tries to make upon the first—more's the pity. *'Son crayon!'* That means her pencil, not his pencil, in this case; you only say *son* because *crayon* is masculine. The rest is just a pretty feeble play on words. Imagine stopping to talk about that when there is a much more important fact; namely, that my left leg, which I am using as a support, reminds me of the wooden leg on Settembrini's hand-organ, that he keeps jolting over the pavement with his knee, to get up close to the window and hold out his velvet hat for the girl up there to throw something into. And at the same time, I seem to be pulled, as though with hands, to lie down in the snow. The only thing to do is to move about. I must pay for the Kulmbacher, and limber up my wooden leg."

He pushed himself away from the wall with his shoulder. But one single pace forward, and the wind sliced at him like a scythe, and drove him back to the shelter of the wall. It was unquestionably the position indicated for the time; he might change it by turning his left shoulder to the wall and propping himself on the right leg, with sundry shakings of the left, to restore the circulation as much as might be. "Who leaves the house in weather like this?" he said. "Moderate activity is all right; but not too much craving for adventure, no coying with the bride of the storm. Quiet, quiet—if the head be heavy, let it droop. The wall is good, a certain warmth seems to come from the logs—probably the feeling is entirely subjective.—Ah, the trees, the trees! Oh, living climate of the living—how sweet it smells!"

It was a park. It lay beneath the terrace on which he seemed to stand—a spreading park of luxuriant green shade-trees, elms, planes, beeches, oaks, birches, all in the dappled light and shade of their fresh, full, shimmering foliage, and gently rustling tips. They breathed a deliciously moist, balsamic breath into the air. A warm shower passed over them, but the rain was sunlit. One could see high up in the sky the whole air filled with the bright ripple of raindrops. How lovely it was! Oh, breath of the homeland, oh, fragrance and abundance of the plain, so long foregone! The air was full of bird song—dainty, sweet, blithe fluting, piping, twittering, cooing, trilling, war-

bling, though not a single little creature could be seen. Hans Castorp
smiled, breathing gratitude. But still more beauties were preparing.
A rainbow flung its arc slanting across the scene, most bright and
perfect, a sheer delight, all its rich glossy, banded colours moistly
shimmering down into the thick, lustrous green. It was like music,
like the sound of harps commingled with flutes and violins. The blue
and the violet were transcendent. And they descended and magically
blended, were transmuted and reunfolded more lovely than at first.
Once, some years before, our young Hans Castorp had been privileged
to hear a world-famous Italian tenor, from whose throat had gushed
a glorious stream to witch the world with gracious art. The singer
took a high note, exquisitely; then held it, while the passionate harmony swelled, unfolded, glowed from moment to moment with new
radiance. Unsuspected veils dropped from before it one by one; the
last one sank away, revealing what must surely be the ultimate tonal
purity—yet no, for still another fell, and then a well-nigh incredible
third and last, shaking into the air such an extravagance of tear-
glistening splendour, that confused murmurs of protest rose from the
audience, as though it could bear no more; and our young friend
found that he was sobbing.—So now with the scene before him, constantly transformed and transfigured as it was before his eyes. The
bright, rainy veil fell away; behind it stretched the sea, a southern sea
of deep, deepest blue shot with silver lights, and a beautiful bay, on
one side mistily open, on the other enclosed by mountains whose
outline paled away into blue space. In the middle distance lay islands,
where palms rose tall and small white houses gleamed among cypress
groves. Ah, it was all too much, too blest for sinful mortals, that glory
of light, that deep purity of the sky, that sunny freshness on the
water! Such a scene Hans Castorp had never beheld, nor anything
like it. On his holidays he had barely sipped at the south, the sea for
him meant the colourless, tempestuous northern tides, to which he
clung with inarticulate, childish love. Of the Mediterranean, Naples,
Sicily, he knew nothing. And yet—he *remembered*. Yes, strangely
enough, that was recognition which so moved him. "Yes, yes, its very
image," he was crying out, as though in his heart he had always
cherished a picture of this spacious, sunny bliss. Always—and that

always went far, far, unthinkably far back, as far as the open sea there on the left where it ran out to the violet sky bent down to meet it.

The sky-line was high, the distance seemed to mount to Hans Castorp's view, looking down as he did from his elevation on the spreading gulf beneath. The mountains held it embraced, their tree-clad foot-hills running down to the sea; they reached in half-circle from the middle distance to the point where he sat, and beyond. This was a mountainous littoral, at one point of which he was crouching upon a sun-warmed stone terrace, while before him the ground, descending among undergrowth, by moss-covered rocky steps, ran down to a level shore, where the reedy shingle formed little blue-dyed bays, minute archipelagoes and harbours. And all the sunny region, these open coastal heights and laughing rocky basins, even the sea itself out to the islands, where boats plied to and fro, was peopled far and wide. On every hand human beings, children of sun and sea, were stirring or sitting. Beautiful young human creatures, so blithe, so good and gay, so pleasing to see—at sight of them Hans Castorp's whole heart opened in a responsive love, keen almost to pain.

Youths were at work with horses, running hand on halter alongside their whinnying, head-tossing charges; pulling the refractory ones on a long rein, or else, seated bareback, striking the flanks of their mounts with naked heels, to drive them into the sea. The muscles of the riders' backs played beneath the sun-bronzed skin, and their voices were enchanting beyond words as they shouted to each other or to their animals. A little bay ran deep into the coast line, mirroring the shore as does a mountain lake; about it girls were dancing. One of them sat with her back toward him, so that her neck, and the hair drawn to a knot above it, smote him with loveliness. She sat with her feet in a depression of the rock, and played on a shepherd's pipe, her eyes roving above the stops to her companions, as in long, wide garments, smiling, with outstretched arms, alone, or in pairs swaying gently toward each other, they moved in the paces of the dance. Behind the flute-player— she too was white-clad, and her back was long and slender, laterally rounded by the movement of her arms—other maidens were sitting, or standing entwined to watch the dance, and quietly talking. Beyond them still, young men were practising archery. Lovely and pleasant

it was to see the older ones show the younger, curly-locked novices,
how to span the bow and take aim; draw with them, and laughing
support them staggering back from the push of the arrow as it leaped
from the bow. Others were fishing, lying prone on a jut of rock,
waggling one leg in the air, holding the line out over the water,
approaching their heads in talk. Others sat straining forward to fling
the bait far out. A ship, with mast and yards, lying high out of the
tide, was being eased, shoved, and steadied into the sea. Children
played and exulted among the breaking waves. A young female, lying
outstretched, drawing with one hand her flowered robe high between
her breasts, reached with the other in the air after a twig bearing fruit
and leaves, which a second, a slender-hipped creature, erect at her
head, was playfully withholding. Young folk were sitting in nooks
of the rocks, or hesitating at the water's edge, with crossed arms
clutching either shoulder, as they tested the chill with their toes.
Pairs strolled along the beach, close and confiding, at the maiden's
ear the lips of the youth. Shaggy-haired goats leaped from ledge to
ledge of the rocks, while the young goatherd, wearing perched on his
brown curls a little hat with the brim turned up behind, stood watching them from a height, one hand on his hip, the other holding the
long staff on which he leaned.

"Oh, lovely, lovely," Hans Castorp breathed. "How joyous and
winning they are, how fresh and healthy, happy and clever they look!
It is not alone the outward form, they seem to be wise and gentle
through and through. That is what makes me in love with them, the
spirit that speaks out of them, the sense, I might almost say, in which
they live and play together." By which he meant the friendliness, the
mutual courteous regard these children of the sun showed to each
other, a calm, reciprocal reverence veiled in smiles, manifested almost
imperceptibly, and yet possessing them all by the power of sense association and ingrained idea. A dignity, even a gravity, was held, as it
were, in solution in their lightest mood, perceptible only as an inef-
fable spiritual influence, a high seriousness without austerity, a reasoned
goodness conditioning every act. All this, indeed, was not without its
ceremonial side. A young mother, in a brown robe loose at the shoulder, sat on a rounded mossy stone and suckled her child, saluted by

all who passed with a characteristic gesture which seemed to comprehend all that lay implicit in their general bearing. The young men, as
they approached, lightly and formally crossed their arms on their
breasts, and smilingly bowed; the maidens shaped the suggestion of
a curtsy, as the worshipper does when he passes the high altar, at the
same time nodding repeatedly, blithely and heartily. This mixture of
formal homage with lively friendliness, and the slow, mild mien of
the mother as well, where she sat pressing her breast with her forefinger to ease the flow of milk to her babe, glancing up from it to
acknowledge with a smile the reverence paid her—this sight thrilled
Hans Castorp's heart with something very close akin to ecstasy. He
could not get his fill of looking, yet asked himself in concern whether
he had a right, whether it was not perhaps punishable, for him, an
outsider, to. be a party to the sunshine and gracious loveliness of all
these happy folk. He felt common, clumsy-booted. It seemed unscrupu-
lous.

A lovely boy, with full hair drawn sideways across his brow and
falling on his temples, sat directly beneath him, apart from his companions, with arms folded on his breast—not sadly, not ill-naturedly,
quite tranquilly on one side. This lad looked up, turned his gaze
upward and looked at him, Hans Castorp, and his eyes went between
the watcher and the scenes upon the strand, watching his watching,
to and fro. But suddenly he looked past Hans Castorp into space, and
that smile, common to them all, of polite and brotherly regard, disappeared in a moment from his lovely, purely cut, half-childish face.
His brows did not darken, but in his gaze there came a solemnity
that looked as though carven out of stone, inexpressive, unfathomable,
a deathlike reserve, which gave the scarcely reassured Hans Castorp a
thorough fright, not unaccompanied by a vague apprehension of its
meaning.

He too looked in the same direction. Behind him rose towering
columns, built of cylindrical blocks without bases, in the joinings of
which moss had grown. They formed the façade of a temple gate, on
whose foundations he was sitting, at the top of a double flight of steps
with space between. Heavy of heart he rose, and, descending the stair
on one side, passed through the high gate below, and along a flagged

street, which soon brought him before other propylæa. He passed
through these as well, and now stood facing the temple that lay before
him, massy, weathered to a grey-green tone, on a foundation reached
by a steep flight of steps. The broad brow of the temple rested on the
capitals of powerful, almost stunted columns, tapering toward the
top—sometimes a fluted block had been shoved out of line and projected a little in profile. Painfully, helping himself on with his hands,
and sighing for the growing oppression of his heart, Hans Castorp
mounted the high steps and gained the grove of columns. It was very
deep, he moved in it as among the trunks in a forest of beeches by the
pale northern sea. He purposely avoided the centre, yet for all that
slanted back again, and presently stood before a group of statuary,
two female figures carved in stone, on a high base: mother and
daughter, it seemed; one of them sitting, older than the other, more
dignified, right goddesslike and mild, yet with mourning brows above
the lightless empty eye-sockets; clad in a flowing tunic and a mantle
of many folds, her matronly brow with its waves of hair covered with
a veil. The other figure stood in the protecting embrace of the first,
with round, youthful face, and arms and hands wound and hidden
in the folds of the mantle.

Hans Castorp stood looking at the group, and from some dark
cause his laden heart grew heavier still, and more oppressed with its
weight of dread and anguish. Scarcely daring to venture, but following an inner compulsion, he passed behind the statuary, and through
the double row of columns beyond. The bronze door of the sanctuary
stood open, and the poor soul's knees all but gave way beneath him at
the sight within. Two grey old women, witchlike, with hanging
breasts and dugs of finger-length, were busy there, between flaming
braziers, most horribly. They were dismembering a child. In dreadful
silence they tore it apart with their bare hands—Hans Castorp saw
the bright hair blood-smeared—and cracked the tender bones between
their jaws, their dreadful lips dripped blood. An icy coldness held
him. He would have covered his eyes and fled, but could not. They
at their gory business had already seen him, they shook their reeking
fists and uttered curses—soundlessly, most vilely, with the last obscenity, and in the dialect of Hans Castorp's native Hamburg. It made.

him sick, sick as never before. He tried desperately to escape; knocked into a column with his shoulder—and found himself, with the sound of that dreadful whispered brawling still in his ears, still wrapped in the cold horror of it, lying by his hut, in the snow, leaning against one arm, with his head upon it, his legs in their skis stretched out before him.

It was no true awakening. He blinked his relief at being free from those execrable hags, but was not very clear, nor even greatly concerned, whether this was a hay-hut, or the column of a temple, against which he lay; and after a fashion continued to dream, no longer in pictures, but in thoughts hardly less involved and fantastic.

"I felt it was a dream, all along," he rambled. "A lovely and horrible dream. I knew all the time that I was making it myself—the park with the trees, the delicious moisture in the air, and all the rest, both dreadful and dear. In a way, I knew it all beforehand. But how is it a man can know all that and call it up to bring him bliss and terror both at once? Where did I get the beautiful bay with the islands, where the temple precincts, whither the eyes of that charming boy pointed me, as he stood there alone? Now I know that it is not out of our single souls we dream. We dream anonymously and communally, if each after his fashion. The great soul of which we are a part may dream through us, in our manner of dreaming, its own secret dreams, of its youth, its hope, its joy and peace—and its blood-sacrifice. Here I lie at my column and still feel in my body the actual remnant of my dream—the icy horror of the human sacrifice, but also the joy that had filled my heart to its very depths, born of the happiness and brave bearing of those human creatures in white. It is meet and proper, I hereby declare that I have a prescriptive right to lie here and dream these dreams. For in my life up here I have known reason and recklessness. I have wandered lost with Settembrini and Naphta in high and mortal places. I know all of man. I have known mankind's flesh and blood. I gave back to the ailing Clavdia Chauchat Pribislav Hippe's lead-pencil. But he who knows the body, life, knows death. And that is not all; it is, pedagogically speaking, only the beginning. One must have the other half of the story, the other side. For all interest in disease and death is only another expression of interest in

life, as is proven by the humanistic faculty of medicine, that addresses
life and its ails always so politely in Latin, and is only a division of
the great and pressing concern which, in all sympathy, I now name
by its name: the human being, the delicate child of life, man, his
state and standing in the universe. I understand no little about him, I
have learned much from 'those up here,' I have been driven up from
the valley, so that the breath almost left my poor body. Yet now from
the base of my column I have no meagre view. I have dreamed of
man's state, of his courteous and enlightened social state; behind
which, in the temple, the horrible blood-sacrifice was consummated.
Were they, those children of the sun, so sweetly courteous to each
other, in silent recognition of that horror? It would be a fine and right
conclusion they drew. I will hold to them, in my soul, I will hold
with them and not with Naphta, neither with Settembrini. They are
both talkers; the one luxurious and spiteful, the other for ever blowing on his penny pipe of reason, even vainly imagining he can bring
the mad to their senses. It is all Philistinism and morality, most certainly it is irreligious. Nor am I for little Naphta either, or his religion, that is only a *guazzabuglio* of God and the Devil, good and
evil, to the end that the individual soul shall plump into it head first,
for the sake of mystic immersion in the universal. Pedagogues both!
Their quarrels and counter-positions are just a *guazzabuglio* too, and
a confused noise of battle, which need trouble nobody who keeps a
little clear in his head and pious in his heart. Their aristocratic question! Disease, health! Spirit, nature! Are those contradictions? I ask,
are they problems? No, they are no problems, neither is the problem
of their aristocracy. The recklessness of death is in life, it would not be
life without it—and in the centre is the position of the *Homo Dei,*
between recklessness and reason, as his state is between mystic community and windy individualism. I, from my column, perceive all
this. In this state he must live gallantly, associate in friendly reverence
with himself, for only he is aristocratic, and the counter-positions are
not at all. Man is the lord of counter-positions, they can be only
through him, and thus he is more aristocratic than they. More so than
death, too aristocratic for death—that is the freedom of his mind. More
aristocratic than life, too aristocratic for life, and that is the piety in

his heart. There is both rhyme and reason in what I say, I have made a dream poem of humanity. I will cling to it. I will be good. I will let death have no mastery over my thoughts. For therein lies goodness and love of humankind, and in nothing else. Death is a great power. One takes off one's hat before him, and goes weavingly on tiptoe. He wears the stately ruff of the departed and we do him honour in solemn black. Reason stands simple before him, for reason is only virtue, while death is release, immensity, abandon, desire. Desire, says my dream. Lust, not love. Death and love—no, I cannot make a poem of them, they don't go together. Love stands opposed to death. It is love, not reason, that is stronger than death. Only love, not reason, gives sweet thoughts. And from love and sweetness alone can form come: form and civilization, friendly, enlightened, beautiful human intercourse—always in silent recognition of the blood-sacrifice. Ah, yes, it is well and truly dreamed. I have taken stock. I will remember. I will keep faith with death in my heart, yet well remember that faith with death and the dead is evil, is hostile to humankind, so soon as we give it power over thought and action. *For the sake of goodness and love, man shall let death have no sovereignty over his thoughts.*—And with this—I awake. For I have dreamed it out to the end, I have come to my goal. Long, long have I sought after this word, in the place where Hippe appeared to me, in my loggia, everywhere. Deep into the snow mountains my search has led me. Now I have it fast. My dream has given it me, in utter clearness, that I may know it for ever. Yes, I am in simple raptures, my body is warm, my heart beats high and knows why. It beats not solely on physical grounds, as finger-nails grow on a corpse; but humanly, on grounds of my joyful spirits. My dream word was a draught, better than port or ale, it streams through my veins like love and life, I tear myself from my dream and sleep, knowing as I do, perfectly well, that they are highly dangerous to my young life. Up, up! Open your eyes! These are your limbs, your legs here in the snow! Pull yourself together, and up! Look—fair weather!"

The bonds held fast that kept his limbs involved. He had a hard struggle to free himself—but the inner compulsion proved stronger. With a jerk he raised himself on his elbows, briskly drew up his knees, shoved, rolled, wrestled to his feet; stamped with his skis in the snow, flung his arms about his ribs and worked his shoulders violently, all the while casting strained, alert glances about him and above, where now a pale blue sky showed itself between grey-bluish clouds, and these presently drew away to discover a thin sickle of a moon. Early twilight reigned: no snow-fall, no storm. The wall of the opposite mountain, with its shaggy, tree-clad ridge, stretched out before him, plain and peaceful. Shadow lay on half its height, but the upper half was bathed in palest rosy light. How were things in the world? Was it morning? Had he, despite what the books said, lain all night in the snow and not frozen? Not a member was frost-bitten, nothing snapped when he stamped, shook and struck himself, as he did vigorously, all the time seeking to establish the facts of his situation. Ears, toes, finger-tips, were of course numb, but not more so than they had often been at night in his loggia. He could take his watch from his pocket—it was still going, it had not stopped, as it did if he forgot to wind it. It said not yet five—was in fact considerably earlier, twelve, thirteen minutes. Preposterous! Could it be he had lain here in the snow only ten minutes or so, while all these scenes of horror and delight and those presumptuous thoughts had spun themselves in his brain, and the hexagonal hurly vanished as it came? If that were true, then he must be grateful for his good fortune; that is, from the point of view of a safe home-coming. For twice such a turn had come, in his dream and fantasy, as had made him start up—once from horror, and again for rapture. It seemed, indeed, that life meant well by her lone-wandering delicate child.

Be all that as it might, and whether it was morning or afternoon—there could in fact be no doubt that it was still late afternoon—in any case, there was nothing in the circumstances or in his own condition to prevent his going home, which he accordingly did: descending in a fine sweep, as the crow flies, to the valley, where, as he reached it, lights were showing, though his way had been well enough lighted by reflection from the snow. He came down the Brehmenbühl, along the edge of the forest, and was in the Dorf by half past five. He left his skis at the grocer's, rested a little in Herr Settembrini's attic cell, and told him how the storm had overtaken him in the mountains.

The horrified humanist scolded him roundly, and straightway lighted his spirit-kettle to brew coffee for the exhausted one—the strength of which did not prevent Hans Castorp from falling asleep as he sat.

An hour later the highly civilized atmosphere of the Berghof caressed him. He ate enormously at dinner. What he had dreamed was already fading from his mind. What he had thought—even that selfsame evening it was no longer so clear as it had been at first.

GEORGE R. LEIGHTON

COMMENTARY

Somewhere in Housman's The Name and Nature of Poetry he says something to the effect that a line may come to him while shaving, and then his beard prickles and his skin contracts, and he knows it is a good line. Each of us has some such physical reaction to what he considers a really fine job of writing. I find myself catching my breath and then uttering, in a tone combining reverence and a kind of pain, the ridiculous vocable "Wow!" The litle sketch that follows is a Wow piece.

George R. Leighton, a talented journalist, wrote a book a few years ago called America's Growing Pains. It deals searchingly with the birth, youth, maturity, and variant stages of decay of five American cities: Shenandoah, Louisville, Birmingham, Omaha, Seattle. To the book, factual, reportorial, and perishable in interest, he affixed a few prefatory pages that don't seem to have much to do with those that follow them. Almost by accident, it seems to me—much fine writing is semiaccidental—he has in this introduction written something extraordinarily moving, rhythmical, and truly American.

The point is that though Mr. Leighton is, as I have said, a talented journalist, this little piece is far more than talented journalism. I may be off my base, but to my ear it has the true Gettysburg ring, the same ring you find in Edgar Lee Masters' "Lucinda Matlock" and "Ann Rutledge." Try reading it aloud to the family.

Arminia Evans Avery

FROM "AMERICA'S GROWING PAINS" BY

GEORGE R. LEIGHTON

ON AN AFTERNOON in March, 1938, Arminia Evans Avery lay asleep in Tunkhannock, a little Pennsylvania town on the Susquehanna River, not far north of Wilkes-Barre. She was ninety-four years old and she was dying a slow, deliberate death of old age. During the preceding days her descendants had been coming by ones and twos to take their farewell. Now beside her bed were her grandson and her one great-grandson awaiting their turn.

She was intensely old. In maturity she had been a slender woman with delicate features. Now her head was barely more than a skull, all the bones showing plainly and her closed eyes sunk deep in their sockets. Her white hair was cut short, one hand little more than bone rested upon the patchwork comfortable. Her breath came in long, slow breaths, so slow that sometimes it seemed that breathing had stopped altogether. Then it would come, evidence that the machinery that had operated so faithfully all those ninety-four years was still obedient to the demands made upon it.

"Is she dead yet?" said the little boy.

"No," said his father. "She's asleep. She will wake up pretty soon."

The man and the little boy watched.

This woman's preacher father had ridden circuit through this Pennsylvania wilderness region where Indians still lived, helping the settlers build log churches. This woman's mother had told her of a day when money was scarcely seen, when a little silver was hoarded to pay taxes and buy tea. This woman's Welsh grandfather, a soldier in the British Army sent to subdue the rebellious colonists, was buried over on the other side of Miller Mountain. Nothing was known of him except

117

that he could write his name and was thought to have been a yeoman. The bones of another forebear were in the Wyoming monument, along with the others killed in the massacre. All were immigrants from the old country, settling in a wilderness.

When this woman at sixteen went to the Seminary, she went down the river road to Kingston in a stagecoach. She was at school there when the news came of the firing on Sumter and she had said good-bye to Southern boys, going home to fight. She had seen the war spirit die away and in her own village had heard the cursing against the draft. In 1864 she had married a young man who ran a grist mill down by the river and had seen him die of a mysterious "consumption." As a widow she kept a dame school in the village and so little was known of contagion that her own small daughter, ill of scarlet fever, was left in bed near the schoolroom.

Her own brother, a wilderness boy, had gone to New York in the sixties and become an iron broker. She had married again and had seen the village tannery bought by "the Trust" and closed down; she had seen her husband's foundry and machine shop slowly fade out and her sons become interested in automobiles. She had seen the old stagecoach river road turned into a concrete highway for trucks that never stopped in the village but went straight through to Buffalo. She had seen the farm families over the river die out one by one and the farms go to ruin. She had seen Polish coal miners come up from Wilkes-Barre and Pittston and buy the run-down farms and make them bloom again. She had seen almost a hundred years of America and now she was dying.

Slowly her eyelids lifted and the old woman lay quiet, looking straight up at the ceiling.

"Has the funeral been arranged?" she said, seeing no one.

Her daughter heard, looked in the door, and then went away again.

Then, with deliberation so slow that it was difficult to follow the movement, the old woman began to turn her head. Little by little it moved until, after a lapse of minutes, her eyes, gray and clear and steady, rested upon the man and the little boy. There was no recognition. But as the two watched they could see the recognition coming, just as deliberately as had been the turning of the head. At last it came. She knew.

"I am glad that you have come," she said.

She looked at the little boy for a while.

"A fine boy," she said.

She looked at the man.

"How is everything?"

"All right."

There was a considerable pause while she thought.

"Are you finding out a good deal about the country?"

"A good deal," the man said.

"You have found out some things about the people in those towns but not all. Shenandoah you tell about. They have trouble now but they do not have a lot of the trouble you tell about because the people who had those troubles are all dead and it was long ago."

The old woman closed her eyes.

"Can I go now?" the little boy asked.

"Yes," his father said.

After a while the old woman opened her eyes again and, without effort, since her head was turned, looked directly at her grandson.

"I would like to ask you a question," he said.

"All right."

"Why was it that you never gave anyone—your children, your friends, anyone—your confidence? Did you have some secret?"

The old woman's eyes were fixed upon her grandson.

"The secret is that there was never any secret . . . I didn't give anybody any confidences because there weren't any to give."

She was silent again and it was almost as though under the skull and the transparent skin the machinery of her mind could be seen at work—thinking—so slowly that one could all but see each thought being put together, every nail and screw in each thought, slowly and surely being driven home. Finally:

"For a long time when I was young it was very difficult for me to talk to people. I could not get through. It troubled me a great deal because I was fond of people, I could not live without them. I was

uneasy and could not feel at home . . . in the world. Then, one day,
I knew. I knew that in some way I could not understand, people
knew how I felt and that I did not need to worry or work over it any
more. That is all there is to the secret and that is why there were no
confidences. Confidences are made by people who are afraid, but I
was no longer afraid and so there was nothing to tell."

She stopped talking in order to think again.

"The world," she said, "is in dreadful torment now." The clock on
her dresser could be heard ticking. "I hear a great deal of criticism
of the President. Do you?"

Her grandson nodded.

"Do you know anyone," she said, "who could do any better?"

"No."

"Neither do I," she said.

The old woman's daughter came into the room.

"Are you tired from talking, Mother?" she asked.

"If I don't talk now," said the old woman, "I never will."

She looked at her grandson again.

"Do you believe—you know, Hitler, Russia, people here without
food or hope—do you believe that the world is coming to an end?"

"Almost," the man said, "but not quite."

A look of confidence, born out of some knowledge that the man
could not fathom, spread over the old woman's face. Her body was
almost done, but thought and spirit remained.

"It isn't coming to an end. It's such a little while since men got up
off the ground. So many ways are useless now. They shut down the
tannery. They don't come down the river road to market any more."

With the slowest of motions she raised her hand, so soon to be just
a member of a skeleton, and laid it against her face.

"We get so used to doing things one way . . . and you can only
change a little at a time. We have got to believe we can find new
ways because that is what we always do and until we do believe it,
people are afraid. That's what makes this awful trouble, being afraid."

She closed her eyes again and then spoke without opening them.

"All over the world there are people afraid . . . millions of people crying in the dark. They are frightened . . . they tear each other to pieces."

When she opened her eyes again her grandson could see in them complete repose.

"It will never work that way," she said. "But when the strain gets so people can't stand it any more, somehow light will come and we shall see many things that have been here all the time."

She was very tired now but from somewhere in her she found a breath of effort left.

"You have to work with what you've got and that's all there is to work with. You can't start out anywhere except from the place you come from. People can't do it any other way here in the United States either. It's all plain, but we don't see it yet. The people in all those towns, they are frightened and sometimes murderous, just because in one way or another they're crying in the dark. And that's all, I guess."

Just before suppertime she died.

VINCENT McHUGH

I advance two reasons for including in this book the piece that follows. The first is that Mr. McHugh writes brilliantly. The second is connected with the fact that in a sense Mr. McHugh didn't write it at all.

In 1938 Random House, a firm of New York publishers, issued New York Panorama, subtitled "A Comprehensive View of the Metropolis, Presented in a Series of Articles Prepared by the Federal Writers' Project of the Works Progress Administration in New York City." The book was one of the American Guide Series, which when complete will for the first time introduce all of the United States to all of its citizens.

New York Panorama is a communal project. It issued from the labor of a number of New York writers, some good, some bad, for whom our competitive system at the time had no place. It is assembly-line composition, and in its field highly meritorious. When I first read it I was struck by the fact that the introductory chapter was composed on a level of feeling and insight to which the balance of the book did not attain. A bit of minor sleuthing revealed that it had been written by a young novelist and poet named Vincent McHugh. Thus we, the citizens of the United States, through our support of the WPA, have all inadvertently become the sponsors of a piece of literature.

I remarked that in a sense Mr. McHugh didn't write this at all. His facts, in some cases, were garnered by coworkers and the whole spirit of the enterprise was communal and anonymous. The introductory chapter itself, however, bears the stamp of a powerfully individual style. It may have had a group inception but the final product is one man's job.

I do not know anyone who has written more truly about New York in as little space. Mr. McHugh develops his discussion of New York through two central concepts: the notion (true) of the city as

122

an accumulation, a mere gigantic exercise in quantification, with all the misery, waste, and ugliness that such an exercise always brings in its train; and the notion (true) that implicit in the city's development and today becoming more and more explicit is an equally powerful drive toward unity and order. These concepts he expresses and re-expresses in a dozen ways, and particularly through the use of a striking vocabulary, poetical on the one hand and twentieth-century-technical on the other.

It has often been pointed out that much of the best writing about the city is the work of nonnatives. I like to reflect that The New Yorker, a magazine which behind its casual airs and mock self-depreciation conceals a precise feeling for much of the city's life, is largely edited by men and women from the outlands, its central genius being a Coloradoan. The images that gather in our minds when we think of the city are images of approach. Dos Passos called his novel Manhattan Transfer. Thomas Wolfe wrote best about the city when telling us how it feels to enter it. New York is a place to which people come; it is hard to remember that it is also a place in which people are born. It is this which differentiates it in essence from such cities as Philadelphia and Boston, and it is this which makes New York an apt image, as Whitman felt, of the democratic process. The sense of the city as a place to approach, as a goal, as the end of a quest, informs Mr. McHugh's essay, and perhaps would not so subtly inform it were Mr. McHugh a native New Yorker. He hails from Rhode Island.

A word or two about him. He has written two novels, one of which, Sing Before Breakfast, has been highly praised by good authorities. To a not sufficiently large public he is also known as the author of Caleb Catlum's America, as successful an attempt as has yet been made to condense the history of our country into one great, jolly, sprawling comic legend. My faith in Mr. McHugh's literary future rests in the main on his capacity to feel and record the complex pulse of American life and at the same time to make use of the literary techniques and insights of Continental writing. Though he feels America as his particular province, he feels all literature as one. It is a combination not too frequently found in our young writers. I hope you will feel its force in the pages that follow.

Metropolis and Her Children

BY

VINCENT McHUGH

THE RUMOR of a great city goes out beyond its borders, to all the latitudes of the known earth. The city becomes an emblem in remote minds; apart from the tangible export of goods and men, it exerts its cultural instrumentality in a thousand phases: as an image of glittering light, as the forcing ground which creates a new prose style or a new agro-biological theory, or as the germinal point for a fresh technique in metal sculpture, biometrics or the fixation of nitrogen. Its less ponderable influence may be a complex of inextricable ideas, economic exchanges, associations, artifacts: the flask of perfume which brings Fifth Avenue to a hacienda in the Argentine, the stencil marks on a packing case dumped on the wharf at Beira or Reykjavik, a flurry of dark-goggled globe-trotters from a cruise ship, a book of verse

> Under the stone I saw them flow
> express Times Square at five o'clock
> eyes set in darkness

read in a sheepherder's hut in New South Wales, or a Harlem band playing *Young Woman's Blues* from a phonograph as the safari breaks camp in Tanganyika under a tile-blue morning sky.

The orbit of such a world city as New York also intersects the orbits of other world cities. New York, London, Tokyo, Rome exchange preferred stocks and bullion, ships' manifests and radio programs— in rivalry or well-calculated friendship. During the 1920's, for example, a jump spark crackled between New York and Paris. The art of Matisse, Derain, Picasso commanded the Fifty-Seventh Street market.

The French developed a taste for *le jazz* and *le sport;* in an atmosphere of war debts and the Young Plan, the Americanization of Europe was mentioned. Paris, capital of the *Valutaschweine,* became the bourne of good and gay New Yorkers, the implicit heroine of a comedy by Philip Barry or a novel by Ernest Hemingway. The French replied, though not always in kind. Georges Duhamel pronounced a jeremiad against the machine apocalypse in America and Paul Morand, an amateur of violence, explored the sensational diversity of New York. These were symptomatic. The comments of Jules Romains went deeper and established fixed points for contrast with a later period.

All the rays of force alive in the modern world move inward upon the city, and the burning glass of its attraction concentrates them in the flame that is New York. Historically, it has been to an exceptional degree a city of accumulation: its methods promotion and commerce, its principle aggrandizement. About a nucleus of Dutch and English —even French Huguenot—settlers it subsequently collected swarm after swarm of Irish, German, Italian, Jewish and Russian immigrants, a proportion of other nationalities, and Americans of many stocks from the seaboard and the interior. For the most part, those immigrants who remained in the city were compacted into districts especially suited to their exploitation, districts as verminous and sunless as the Cloaca Maxima. Here, in dwellings that reproduced the foetor of the slave ship in all but the promise of eventual liberty held out to the more intelligent or ruthless, they formed a crawling agglomeration. This was the frontier of New York and the grim apotheosis of the frontier in the United States, preserved almost untouched into the third decade of the 20th century.

The shawled refugees from European want and oppression, most of whom crossed the ocean in immigrant ships under conditions of the utmost squalor, were also transported by a succession of great New York trade vessels: the Black Ball and other Western Ocean packet lines, the world-ranging Donald McKay clippers, the first wood and iron steamships. These were conned through the Narrows by men off the superb Sandy Hook pilot schooners which had been worked out from the designs of Isaac Webb in the 1830's, the hollow-entrance experiments of Griffiths in the 1840's, and the later masterly work of George Steers in such craft as the *Moses H. Grinnell* and the *America,* for which the *America's* Cup was named. Great numbers of immigrants and New York ers moved inland by way of the Hudson River sloops and steamboats, the Conestoga wagons, the Erie Canal barges and the railroads. Very early, therefore, the history of New York began to be a history of the successive phases in American transportation. As its lines of influence spread out into the interior, thickened and were fixed, it became more and more the commanding American city, the maker or merchant of dress silks and pannikins and spices, wines and beds and grub hoes. Long before the paramount age of sail ended, New York had taken on its alternate character as a great two-way transfer point and classification yard for men and goods and ideas moving between the other countries of the world and the great central plain of America. It has consolidated and enlarged this character with a multiplicity of functions which help to determine its position as the first city of the Western Hemisphere.

Approach to the City

For the American traveler coming home from Cape Town or St. Moritz or the Caribbean, and for those others who converge upon the city from Chicago and El Paso and Kildeer and Tonopah, New York has a nearer meaning. It is, in whatever sense, a substitute home town —a great apartment hotel, as Glenway Wescott wrote, in which everyone lives and no one is at home. In other eyes it may be a state fair grown to magnificence, a Main Street translated into the imperial splendor of Fifth Avenue. For such travelers the city is a coat of many colors—becoming to each, but not quite his own. It is both novelty and recognition that pleases him: the novelty of its actual and amazing encompassment, the recognition of great shafts and crowds and thoroughfares remembered from a hundred motion pictures, rotogravures and advertisements.

The man from another city will perhaps be least discommoded, his sense of the familiar both intensified and expanded. But to the men and women of the small towns, the sierras, the cornlands and grasslands, the seaboard coves and Gulf bayous—farmers, automobile me-

chanics, pack-rats, schoolteachers—New York cannot help but stand
as a special order: the place which is not wilderness, the place of light
and warmth and the envelopment of the human swarm, the place in
which everyone is awake and laughing at three in the morning. These
things are not altogether true, of course—but magic does not need to
be true.

The traveler will know many things about New York and there will
be guides to tell him many more, in the particular and the large; but
he will see by looking, and find out by asking, and match the figure
to the phenomenon. He may know that New York City is made up of
five boroughs, four of which—Brooklyn, Queens, Richmond, the
Bronx—compose like crinkled lily pads about the basking trout of
Manhattan. He will not know, perhaps, that he and the other men and
women who travel with him helped to make up a total of 68,999,376
visitors to the city in 1936, an off year. If he is an agronomist, he may
find a certain perverse irony in the fact that the 198,330 acres of the
five boroughs, without any tillage worth mentioning, supported an esti-
mated population of 7,434,346 in 1937.

But it is less likely that the visitor who moves down one of those
enormous radials that converge on New York from Seattle and Gal-
veston and Los Angeles and Chicago will understand how Thomas
Campanella's vision of a City of the Sun, published in 1623, has influenced the growth of such a modern metropolis as New York. Nor will
he be aware, perhaps, that the verses of Walt Whitman and the paint-
ings of "The Eight" and the landscape architecture of Olmsted the
elder, quite as much as the Roeblings' Brooklyn Bridge and the Hoe
press and the steel converters of Kelly and Bessemer, helped to create
the social climate of the emerging city.

In the larger aspects of New York he may glimpse not only the re-
sults of the Randall Plan of 1811, but evidences of the influence of
Geddes, Norton, Wright, McClellan, Bassett, Delano, Burnham, Kep-
pel, James, the Olmsteds, Lewis, Whitten, Howard, Unwin, Wilgus,
Mumford, Adams, McAneny, Stein, Perkins, Walsh, the indefatigable
Moses, and a hundred others of the noble guild of city planners, up to
and including the work of the Regional Plan of New York and Its
Environs, the Port of New York Authority, the New York Depart-

ment of Parks and the New York City Planning Commission. He will wish to know how the city changes, the extent and character of its physical property, and something about the nature and complexity of its functions. But he will understand that plant and function are never more than indicators of a series of cultural choices and directions. Finally, he will be made aware of these choices and directions at their source, in the character, convictions and behavior of New Yorkers themselves: the faces, vivid or distracted, washed in neon light the color of mercurochrome, faces of men and women who work and eat and make love in catacombs under the enormous pylons of their city.

The traveler approaches in bare winter or rainy autumn, in keen seaboard spring or the dog days. He drives a faded sedan with a child slung in a hammock cradle in the rear; or he takes the hot bouillon and crackers of the great airlines. He walks the glassed-in promenade deck of the *Normandie* or the open boat deck of the *Nieuw Amsterdam;* or he lounges in the doorway of the *Manhattan's* radio room. In the streamlined club cars of the Yankee Clipper, the Twentieth Century, the Royal Blue, the Broadway Limited, or in the day coaches of slower trains, he turns the pages of a national or trade journal published in New York—*Women's Wear, Collier's, Life, Variety, Printers' Ink*—and watches the conglomerate backyards of Albany-Bridgeport-Trenton slide past the window. Painted with slipstream whorls, his blunt-nosed bus trundles out of the lunch stop and bores Manhattan-ward again, the whipcord back of the driver twisted as he pulls out and around a great dark pantechnicon truck with small lamps at its clearance points.

The traveler is a fuel company executive returning from a trip through the West, a copy of *Saward's Coal Annual* wedged into the briefcase beside him; an elementary school principal from Lewiston, bound for special courses at Barnard College; a Cleveland printer out of a job, a men's wear buyer from Jacksonville, a Brooklyn clergyman on his return trip from Rome, a Pittsburgh engineer coming back from a South American cruise, a San Francisco divorcee loosed in Reno and remarried to a Hollywood fashion designer commuting to New York. These make up a composite American as alive and definite as Chaucer's pilgrims or Whitman's cameradoes of democracy.

But perhaps only the industrial engineer begins to comprehend the technical changes in transportation between Chaucer's time—or even Whitman's—and the 1930's. Unless the traveler drives his own car, he must resign himself to the helmsmen of the neotechnic age—locomotive engineers, ships' quartermasters, bus drivers, transport pilots—whose responsibilities have been reapportioned into a vast complex of schedules, maintenance men, radio directional and telephone signals, cartographers, traffic lights, instrument panels and routine instructions, all centered on New York.

The helmsmen themselves are aware of their place in this network. The locomotive engineer knows it, intent on the block signals aimed at and swallowed by the rush of his train, a full minute to be made up between Poughkeepsie and Grand Central Terminal. The bus driver gunning his coach in heavy traffic over US1 from New England, or the Albany Post Road, or the Sunrise Highway, or the loop over the Pulaski Skyway into the Jersey City mouth of the Holland Tunnel feels responsibility like a small knot between his shoulder blades: the need for quick and certain decisions, the judgment of space and time and the intent of drivers and a small boy heedless on a bicycle.

The pilot of Flight 16 eastbound, crossing the Alleghenies in cloud at 7,000 feet, knows it well. When his tally of instruments—altimeter, clock, air speed, bank and turn, artificial horizon—indicates that he has passed the outer marker, he reports by radio to the company dispatcher at Newark Metropolitan Airport, chief terminus for the New York district. Passengers rub at the bleared windows. But as he nears the inner marker at Martin's Creek, the mist begins to fade apart into soft translucent islands drenched with sun and the voice from the Newark radio control tower comes in with the tone of a man speaking clearly in the same room: "WREE to Western Trip 16, Pilot Johnson. Stuff breaking up fast. You are cleared at 3,000 feet to the range station. You're Number Two airplane."

In the chart-room of a transatlantic liner inbound from Cherbourg to New York, 200 miles off Fire Island in a pea-soup fog, the blasts of the automatic ship's siren at intervals of one minute vibrate amongst the polished metal or enameled instruments: the chronometers, telephone, radio compass, loudspeaker, mercury and aneroid barometers, gyro course-indicator and other devices of the new scientific navigation. The senior watch officer checks his chronometers against time signals from Nauen, Arlington and the Eiffel Tower. A seaman at the radio directional compass slowly swivels the frame of his antenna ring until the note of the Fire Island radio beacon—plangent as a tuning fork, but crisper—is loudest in his headphones. Making a cross-check, the junior watch officer sets down fathometer depth readings on a length of tracing paper in such a way that it can be laid over the chart for comparison with course and position marks.

Immobile in the dark wheelhouse, the helmsman concentrates on the lighted compass before him. No longer must he watch for the telltale flutter of the leech, or nurse his ship in weather seas. In the 330 years between Henry Hudson's *Half Moon,* steered into the future New York Harbor with a wheel-and-whipstaff rig that resembled a four-armed capstan with elongated bars, and the great express ships of the 1930's, already obsolescent in view of operating costs, irreducible vibration and other factors, the helmsman's responsibilities have been shorn away by engineers and technicians. The automatic steering device, or "Iron Mike," has even in part replaced him.

These new helmsmen of land and sea and air are the creatures of demanding time, their senses extended in the antennules of a hundred instruments. So they must necessarily regard the city a little as the gunnery officer does his target; but they too feel its magnetism. It comes to the traveler a great way off, like the intimation of any other dense human engagement. The expectant nerves contract, the mind is sensitized in advance. A familiar visitor, a New Yorker, waits for the sense of the city's resumed envelopment; but the bus passenger coming down over the Boston Post Road from New England watches traffic slow and thicken as the environs towns become larger, draw together, give off the effect of a brisker life. There is a moment in which he asks himself: "Are we in the city yet? Is this New York?" The visitor by rail, if he approaches from the south, may get hardly a glimpse of the towers before he tunnels under the river and coasts to a stop along the platform at Pennsylvania Station. Coming in from the north, he cannot help but be struck by the infinite pueblo of the Bronx.

But to the traveler by air, especially from the north or east, the city appears with the instancy of revelation: the slowly crinkling samite of its rivers and New York Harbor vaporous beyond, the Bronx splayed out and interwoven with the tight dark Hudson Valley foliage, Brooklyn and Queens and Staten Island dispersed in their enormous encampments about the narrow seaward-thrusting rock of Manhattan. Seen thus from above, the pattern of the island suggests a weirdly shaped printer's form. It is as if the lead rules had been picked out for avenues between the solid lines of type which are buildings. The skyscrapers—those characters too pointed to be equalized by the wooden mallet of the makeup man—prickle up along the lower rim of Central Park, through the midtown section, and most densely at the foot of the island.

These last are what the homebound traveler by water sees as his vessel comes through the Narrows into the Lower Bay, a journey and journey's end which has always somehow the quality of a public triumph. There stand the inconceivable spires of Manhattan—composed, repeating the upthrust torch of Liberty, at first almost without the sense of great weight, the distraction of archaic and heterogeneous detail. The forms of "gypsum crystals," a giant's cromlech, a mass of stalagmites, "the Cathedrals and Great White Thrones of the National Parks," an Arizona mesa, a "ship of living stone," a petrified forest, "an irregular tableland intersected by shadowy cañons," a mastodon herd, "a pin-cushion," the Henry Mountains in Utah, "a vertical aggregation," dividends in the sky: such metaphors reflect its diversity of association. As Melville's *Redburn* indicates, the term *skyscraper* itself—a noun full in the homely tradition of the American vernacular —was once synonymous with *moon-sail* and *cloud-raker* as the name for a ship's topmost kites.

Le Corbusier, celebrated French architect in the International style, refers to this massed upthrust as "the winning of a game: proclamation by skyscraper." And in the third book of Jules Romains' *Psyché,* Pierre Febvre thinks of it as "a rivalry of tumefactions constructed in haste on the rock of Manhattan, a typical fragment of American unreality." Taken together, both images—a sense of the grandiose subjective exemplified in architectural terms, and the perhaps consequent suggestion of imperfectly realized forms—help to clarify a profound intimation of the familiar experienced by many travelers, even those who have no acquaintance with the city. In one of the Regional Plan volumes, this intimation is dramatized, simply enough, by photographs on facing pages: one of lower Manhattan, the other of Mont-Saint-Michel, the ancient fortress rock of France, a cluster of towers about which the tides swirl like level avalanches.

The visual analogy is striking, but it does not end there. The image of the medieval castle-town has gone deep into the consciousness of western man. Preserved in masonry at Mont-Saint-Michel and Carcassonne, stylized in the perspectives of a hundred medieval and Renaissance painters, translated into fantasy in the fairy tales of Andersen and Perrault and the towers of Cloud Cuckoo Land, popularized in the colors of Dulac and Rackham and Parrish and the mass-production lampshade, it reappears in the apparition of lower Manhattan evoked by the new technology: the medieval image of power, the infantile or schizoid fantasy of withdrawal, the supreme image of escape to the inaccessible.

The Concept of the City

Historically, as Robert L. Duffus points out in *Mastering a Metropolis,* cities "have tended to grow up *around* something—a fortification, a temple, a market-place, a landing-place." In other words, the selection of site and arrangement have usually been determined by a choice of social function, a definite cultural emphasis. Sometimes it was relatively accidental. On the principle that travelers may be customers, a market town grew up at a crossroads. The walled towns of the Middle Ages, usually grouped about a castle for efficient defense, retained to some extent the lines of a military camp; but the exigencies of space within the walls made for a certain homogeneous and charming irregularity. The radial plans of the Renaissance, of which Karlsruhe is the most striking example, probably developed from the Greek and Roman cities clustered around a central temple or forum, although they retained some of the medieval irregularities.

Parallel with the unplanned growth of cities, there has always been a tradition of planned cities, conceived either as Utopias—by Plato in his *Republic*, More in his *Utopia*, Campanella in his *City of the Sun*, Bellamy in his *Looking Backward*, Samuel Butler in his *Erewhon*, to name only a few—or by architects and city planners for actual realization in stone and mortar. The geometrical design for Alexandria, and Wren's project for the rebuilding of London after the great fire were examples of this kind. Notable among them was the plan for Washington. Challenged by the unexpectedly possible, Jefferson studied the city patterns of Europe and with Washington and L'Enfant evolved the American capital city.

But it is significant that in general the tradition of abstract design, surviving through the Renaissance, through Karlsruhe and Palladio and Wren into the era of L'Enfant's Washington and Haussmann's renovation of Paris, is basically eclectic, corresponding almost exactly to the anachronistic revivals of the classic orders or the Gothic in architecture. But the criticism is not merely negative; it implies a basic disregard of the primacy of cultural function, of the possible and fruitful coordination between plant and function and environment in a new order of the city.

In any case, for good or ill, planned cities did not by any means represent the dominant mode in urban evolution. If there was one, it can only be called agglomeration; the gathering of flies around a stain of honey. More often than not, that honey was commerce, additionally sweetened by the perquisites of a capital city. Philip II, for example, deliberately built up the municipal strength of Paris as an offset to the challenge of the nobles, thus contributing to the new nationalism and the upswing of the merchant classes. Tudor London, clamorous with trades and spiky with the masts of ships, added central cells of industry to the commercial swarming of the city. After the great fires of the next century, Wren suggested that wherever possible industries should be relocated on the outer margins of the city—a recommendation seconded by Walter Curt Behrendt and the New York Regional Plan in the 1930's.

The advent of what Sir Patrick Geddes called the paleotechnic period, early in the 19th century, with its criteria of absolute utilitarianism, gradually created the inhuman ratholes of London and Glasgow and Birmingham and New York and Berlin—that "home city of the rent barracks." Dickens described a composite of industrial cities as Coketown. "It had a black canal in it, and a river that ran purple with ill-smelling dye"; and "the piston of the steam engine worked monotonously up and down, like the head of an elephant in a state of melancholy madness. It contained several large streets all very like one another, inhabited by people exactly like one another, who all went in and out at the same hours, with the same sound upon the same pavements to do the same work, and to whom every day was the same as yesterday and tomorrow, and every year the counterpart of the last and the next."

New York City, of all the great communities in the modern world, has been most acted upon by the agencies incident to the 19th century revolution in industry and techniques, most subject to the devastating consequences of 19th century *laissez faire* and the tensions of excessively rapid growth, most influenced by the multiplication and hypertrophy of functions, most compromised by a street plan which united some of the inconvenient features of the rigidly classical and the narrowly utilitarian, most unstable in the number and distribution of its population, most opportunistic in land uses, most anarchic in the character of its building, and most dynamic in the pulse and variety of its living ways.

In a history of some 330 years, of which hardly more than a century has been taken up with major growth, New York has somehow condensed and accommodated the stresses of 20 centuries in the evolution of Rome or Paris. Such drastic foreshortening exacted a price and developed an opportunity. The price was paid and is being paid in the primary conception of the city as merely an accumulation: the largest size, the greatest number (even of units of quality), and the highest speed. It was paid in the ruthlessness—and the complementary meliorism that all this would somehow right itself—of what may be called the utilitarian imperative, which cut off waterside areas from public use, gobbled up available park sites, covered blocks with sunless tenements and no less sunless apartment houses, made night and day indistinguishable under the overhanging scarps of lower Manhattan, fostered duplication and peculation and high taxes in municipal government, and centered a terrific volume of traffic in a few sectors already overburdened by subway and elevated concentration, the lack of through highways and the density of building.

These became commonplaces, even rules of thumb. At a certain point, the practical effect was that a man could not go to the theater or visit a friend without a wholly disproportionate expenditure of time, energy, ingenuity and money. But in the deepest sense—the sense, that is, in which these processes were at once an expression and reflection of the New Yorker's cultural attitude toward his city—such factors tended to become psychological vested interests. The healthy dynamism of a developing metropolis was perpetuated as neurotic action for its own sake. The original necessity of enduring noise, dirt, conflict, confusion as symptoms of a transitional phase developed into a taste for the mindless intoxicant of sensation. Tall buildings convenient for intracommunication in such activities as finance became tall buildings for the sake of mere height and vainglory. In fine, the psychology of swift growth—its quick sense of the expedient, its prompt resource, its urgent energy, its prodigality in human waste, its impatience with deeper interrelationships and effects, by-products or details—was carried over and intensified in a period which demanded consolidation, an assay of cultural attitudes and values, planning, a new concept of the city.

By 1938 the signs of this new attitude were already sharply manifest. Long before that, in 1931, Thomas Adams could write: "There is no city in the world that has a greater influence than New York. . . . All over this continent it is imitated, even where it is said to be feared. Men say New York is a warning rather than an example, and then proceed to make it an example. Outside America, New York is America, and its skyscraper a symbol of the spirit of America. It is not only the largest city in the world, it is the greatest and most powerful city that is not a capital of a nation." There were jeremiads and panegyrics; this was a temperate statement of the fact.

All through the 1920's, New York had been not only the symbol of America but the daemonic symbol of the modern—the fortunate giant in his youth, the world city whose past weighed least heavily upon its future. Had not Paul Morand testified that the latest skyscraper was always the best? It was a city infallible in finance, torrential in pace, unlimited in resource, hard as infrangible diamonds, forever leaping upon the moment beyond. "You can get away with anything," said Ellen Thatcher in John Dos Passos' *Manhattan Transfer,* "if you do it quick enough." Speed—with its dividend, sensation—became the master formula in every human activity and technique: Wall Street, dancing, crime, the theater, construction, even death. "Don't get much time to sleep," said a Broadway soda clerk. "I have to sleep so fast I'm all tired out when I get up in the morning." This was rueful Eddington, the telescoping of time and space—a cliché of the period— in terms of the wear and tear on human metabolism. Photographers, draughtsmen, commentators all attempted to catch this loud moment or to translate it in terms of indefinite extension. An aseptic skyscraper city, an immense machine for living, was projected by such draughtsmen and writers as Hugh Ferriss, Sheldon Cheney, Raymond Hood and Norman Bel Geddes (of whom an anonymous satirist remarked in 1937 that he suffered from "an edifice complex").

In this period too New York had broken out full sail as the American capital of the arts and a world capital of major importance. This was in itself an extraordinary phenomenon. Other large, recently colonial cities—Melbourne, Rio de Janeiro, Toronto, even Mexico City—had shown no such versatile and autochthonous upsurge. It could be explained only in part by a reference to great concentration of wealth and commerce—as usual, a concentration in which artists had little share and against which, for the most part, they swung the shoulder of revolt. This cultural definition came out of the native genius of the city itself and was inseparably collateral with it. To a remarkable degree, the formulation and interpretation of that genius became the first task of the artist in New York.

Historians of another age may find the cultural rivalries of the Eastern seaboard cities in the middle of the 19th century as fruitful a source of social interpretation as their contests in trade. Philadelphia had receded, Charleston and Baltimore settled into their graceful mold. But Boston, as Van Wyck Brooks has superbly recreated it in *The Flowering of New England,* produced a culture articulated in all its parts. It is necessary to indicate more closely here the relative scale of that culture. Its perfect symbol, perhaps, was the figure of Hawthorne confronting the Marble Faun. Its faithfulness to a special Anglo-American tradition at once defined its limits and committed it to contest with the assimilative turbulence of its more democratic neighbor to the southward. Even in Emerson, perhaps, there was something of the merely benign clergyman; even in Thoreau, a little of the truant schoolboy decorating his metaphorical hut at Walden with the knick-knacks of Athens and Rome. And even in Emily Dickinson's triumph of the microcosmic, it was possible to feel the sedate child who withdraws from the world to thread in quietude the quicksilver necklaces of the imagination. The neat coherence of parts, the good scholars competing for the prizes of the intelligence, the inflexibility of ethical referents, the absence of that excess which is also the evidence of supreme vitality, the frugality and unanimity of pattern—all these were the sedate lamplight of a provincial culture, a culture comparable to that of Ghent in the late 14th century or 18th century Dublin and Stockholm.

But there were giants to the southward—men who had consorted with the buffalo and leviathan, who were privy to enormous griefs and ecstasies, who had faced the tremendous gales of the world in their most disintegrative onslaught. These men—Whitman and Melville—were of another breed, another stature; and they proclaimed themselves men of Manhattan. They came of the same Dutch-English stock, bred by that Empire State through which the commerce of the nation had begun to pour. *Moby Dick* appeared in 1851, *Leaves of Grass* in 1855. Both books were shunned or excoriated. Then and later, the culture of New York resembled the tumultuous cross-rips of Hell Gate. Museums, opera, the theater, libraries, lecture halls, schools, the superb education of street and waterfront: these were lavishly available, and Whitman in particular made good use of them. But the dominant tenor of the city was savage in its commercial excesses, ravenous in land use (though the salvaging of Central Park began a few years before the Civil War) and brutal in its disregard for health, amenities, the elementary kindness of life. The deeper significance of such personalities as Whitman and Melville is that they were archetypes of the city's character-to-be. Their decisive feeling for the supreme importance, the frequent nobility of the common man, their immersion by choice in his hopes and occupations—these were as foreign to the men of Boston, with their uneasy self-awareness in the role of scholar-gentlemen, as they would have been to that earlier New Yorker, the James Fenimore Cooper who wrote *The American Democrat.*

"He who touches the soil of Manhattan and the pavement of New York," said Lewis Mumford, "touches, whether he knows it or not, Walt Whitman." Certainly it was Whitman who conceived the city as an image of the democratic process—an historic reversal, it may be noted, of Thomas Jefferson's primary design. The city spoke out of Whitman's fiber: out of the broadest and most intimate lines of *A Broadway Pageant* and *Crossing Brooklyn Bridge,* out of

> Walt Whitman, a kosmos, of Manhattan the son,
> Turbulent, fleshy, sensual, eating, drinking
>   and breeding,

or out of

> . . . submit to no models
>   but your own O city!

But in *Democratic Vistas* he faced all the implications of his image: splendor in the amplitude and onrush, "the sparkling sea-tides" and "masses of gay color" which were New York, but confession that to the cold eye appeared "pervading flippancy and vulgarity, low cunning, infidelity" and the rest, even to a degree beyond the average of mankind. But there were poets to be called up, poets to make "a literature underlying life"; to fertilize it, to create again and again the corrective vision of the city in an order more nobly human than itself. Whitman said it and said it plain:

> A great city is that which has the greatest men and women.

Did he not help to make good his own words?

But in its essence, Whitman's concept of New York as a symbol of the democratic maelstrom was a neo-romantic one. It rejoiced in the splendor of the fact, hewed close to it, made it Homeric. But was it not, even in that society of transitional latitude, precisely a begging of the question as to *what* means were to be applied to the creation of *what* forms for *what* ends—ends, that is, which might be translated concretely from the abstract *liberty, equality, fraternity, plenty?* Affirmation of greatness to nurture greatness, exultation in diversity for the use and promise of diversity, acceptance of barbarous poverty and wrong in the name of a more humane future, faith in the destiny of the free man intermingling freely with his fellows: these demanded a confident and practical vision of the city as a whole—a vision broader than Campanella's, as instrumental as the machine lathe—formulated and canalized in terms of New York's own native function and genius.

On the contrary, Whitman's noble disorder, with its hospitality to everything human, tended to emphasize precisely those impulses toward unoriented mass, energy, diversity which came to their anarchic ultimate at the end of the 1920's. It was Whitman's dynamic, with its dramatization of the common impulse, that prevailed in the evolving folkways of New York. Even in 1937, the city was most often presented in terms of speed, energy, quantity rather than as a correlative for human use and aspiration. Nor is it enough to point out, as Marie Swabey does in *Theory of the Democratic State,* that the natural criteria of democracy are predominantly quantitative. The confusion inheres in the fact that big numbers have so often been used as if they were equivalent to definitions of quality—as if a tremendous number of housing units, even slum dwellings, somehow indicated a corresponding total of human happiness.

Side by side with the most devouring greed, it has almost always been possible to find a superb generosity of life in New York—even, in the late 1930's, signs of a nascent change of heart. If the vainglory of power began to give way a little to the order of a genuine and mature society, there were men to be thanked for it—too many names for this place. These were the men who created and recreated values; who translated those values, under one form or another, into instruments of civic welfare; and who implemented the common aspiration. Together with that aspiration, the sum of their vision and accomplishments determined the living concept of New York: that basic unity,

that prerequisite and final virtue of persons, which must be vital to
the coherence of any human organization.

There were engineers—the Roeblings of Brooklyn Bridge, Clifford
M. Holland of the Holland Tunnel, Nelson P. Lewis of the Board of
Estimate and Apportionment, Singstad and Amman of the Port
Authority—whose probity blossomed in highways and tunnels, or in
the piers and cables of a bridge: such a bridge as Hart Crane had
envisaged, a figure of the flight of time and the passage of mankind
across the gulf. Stubborn bands and lone fighters—John Peter Zenger
of the New York *Weekly Journal,* whose trial in 1735 vindicated free
expression in the press; Nast and Parkhurst and the Lexow Committee; Seabury and the City Affairs Committee of the 1920's—these and
a hundred others struck for the integrity of a free commonwealth.
Scientists and research technicians, who worked with sludge digestion
tanks and chlorination and polyphase alternators, created a fresh environment available to the social imagination of an ampler culture.
A John Dewey reground the tools of the mind; a Thorstein Veblen
challenged the directions of American civilization, especially those
directions which New York had long controlled.

"A very little boy stood upon a heap of gravel for the honor of
Rum Alley" in Stephen Crane's exact nightmare of the slum; John
Dos Passos' Ellen Thatcher murmured: "I think that this city is full of
people wanting inconceivable things"; and Thomas Wolfe's Eugene
Gant cried: "Proud, cruel, everchanging and ephemeral city, to whom
we came once when our hearts were high . . ." These were novelists
answerable to the truth of the living. There were men who created
vivid museums, set up liberal schools, fought to establish capable
hospitals. Even politicians who hoped for nothing but their own
advantage sometimes inadvertently contributed to the civic total, as
Tweed did in setting out the pleasant boulevard along Broadway
north of Sixty-Fifth Street, later routed by the subway.

Painters and photographers—Albert Ryder and Thomas Eakins, the
ancestors; Stieglitz and Paul Strand and Berenice Abbott; the genre
work of Sloan, Glenn Coleman, Reginald Marsh, Lawson, Glackens,
Kenneth Hayes Miller; John Marin's vision of the skyscrapers in a
vibrating rondure of forms; Demuth's *My Egypt* and Billings' and

Sheeler's stylization of industrial masses—these and others literally created the human face of the city for the endowment of its citizens. The work of Hardenbergh and R. M. Hunt, among the older men, and of McKim and Stanford White in the 1890's; Goodhue's churches and Snyder's neo-Gothic schools; the loft buildings of Ely Jacques Kahn; the skyscraper designs of Harvey Wiley Corbett and Raymond Hood; the model apartment groups laid out by Clarence Stein and Henry Wright, which helped to anticipate the Federal Government's plans for housing developments in the 1930's: these were among the factors that made New York architecture the most exciting and various, if not always the soundest, in the world. Too, Whitman had his poets—not often prophets, but men and women who struck a dark accusatory music from the city's agonism: Edna St. Vincent Millay, Hart Crane, Louise Bogan, Archibald MacLeish, Horace Gregory.

Forecast by such lively wine salesmen of the arts as James Huneker, a more thorough school of cultural commentators whose origins were mainly literary set out in the early 1920's to reexamine the pattern of New York as a prefiguration of the new America. Randolph Bourne's voice, and such books as Harold Stearns' *Civilization in the United States,* Waldo Frank's *Our America,* Paul Rosenfeld's *Port of New York,* Van Wyck Brooks' *America's Coming of Age* and William Carlos Williams' *In the American Grain* managed to make themselves heard above the noise of traffic. Lewis Mumford's broad and precise imagination, the warmth and vitality of his interpenetrating sense of the whole distinguished half a dozen volumes that culminated in the definitive *Technics and Civilization* and *The Culture of Cities.* There were, finally, the innumerable common heroes in the patient and immense body of the city: the workers in laboratories and hospitals who died of X-ray burns or a finger pricked at an autopsy; the riveter tumbled from his hawk's perch, falling voiceless and alone; orange-helmeted sandhogs coughing with silicosis or twisted with the bends; and the men who could work no more, the unremembered ones Stephen Crane found in the city's scratch houses in *An Experiment in Misery,* whose successors were still there when Joseph Mitchell published his sketch, *A Cold Night Downtown,* in 1938.

Together these engineers and artists and milk-wagon drivers forged a concept of the city, a unity for the city, out of the collective character and history of its inhabitants, just as the individuality of Paris was defined by Villon's reckless verses, the gardens of Marie Antoinette, Julian the Apostate's addresses to "my dear Lutetia," Victor Hugo, the engineer Eiffel, Marie Curie's dedication and Jules Romains' great antiphonal hymn. This unity, in fact, is at the root of the caricature visualized by outsiders as "a real New Yorker"—a certain large and shrewd liberality of thought and behavior, easy wit, compulsive energy, a liking for risk and the new, curiosity, restlessness.

There are those who consider that it is impossible to find any unity in the chaotic pattern of New York; or that, romantically enough, the emergence of unity would cancel its major charm. But the uneconomic and anti-social nature of many of the city's living ways demands a clear reorientation. The potential unity necessary to such reorientation already exists in the New Yorker's own concept of his city. In this shared consciousness—generated by a look, a grin, an anecdote as cabalistic to outsiders as the shop talk of mathematicians—the complex of the metropolis finds its organizing principle, deeper than civic pride and more basic than the domination of mass or power. To the degree that this principle, this wise geolatry, can be instrumented by the forms and processes appropriate to it, New York will emerge in greatness from the paradox of its confusion.

JOHN DOS PASSOS

COMMENTARY

What the French are at this writing no one, perhaps least of all the French, knows. They used to be a race who carefully and profitably cultivated a reputation for frivolity and were at bottom extremely grave. They had a commercial phrase that was illuminating: maison sérieuse. A maison sérieuse means one that is solidly established and keeps its responsibilities constantly in mind. We would say "it really means business."

In this sense there are certain writers, not necessarily the best, who are sérieux. Others, often talented, are not. Miss Margaret Mitchell, for example, is not serious. (This does not mean that she is frivolous.) If we were to list the truly serious American novelists, John Dos Passos would be near the top. He is not, for me, a great writer or even a brilliant one. But he means business. He is less interested in striking attitudes, however memorable, of his own than in noting the far more memorable attitudes of whole classes and generations. He is not, like that gloomy Robinson Crusoe, William Faulkner, marooned on the island of his own sensibility. When he grasps American life it is always at the center. He works with cross sections, but the cross sections are of maximum density. When he fails, as he does on occasion, it is still with major material. If you lean to the exquisite and prefer small things done perfectly, Dos Passos is not your man, nor are you his.

His solidest work to date consists of the trilogy U.S.A., composed of The 42nd Parallel, Nineteen Nineteen, and The Big Money. This triptych attempts to do on a relatively small scale what Jules Romains does on a larger one. Romains gives you France from 1908 to—well, name your own date. Dos Passos traces the crosscurrents of American life in the post-First World War years.

To do this at all intelligently requires the invention of some kind of shorthand, otherwise the material would overwhelm one. Dos Passos works out four sets of symbols. The first and most conventional

143

consists of the biographies of a few crucially representative imaginative Americans. The second is the life histories of a few equally representative actual ones. The third is the Newsreel, made up of scraps of popular songs, newspaper headlines, advertisements, speeches—a recall device to bring back the time from your unconscious memory, a kind of mood music, as the Hollywood composer would call it. The fourth symbol is the Camera Eye, consisting of lyric flashbacks which derive from the author's own experience. By manipulating, intertwining, and counterpointing this quartet of devices Dos Passos establishes a hundred and one lines of relation and so maps the general pattern of the life of the era.

The Camera Eye is pretty arty at its worst, the Newsreel has its tedious moments, the fictional biographies are sound, interesting, and packed with meaning. Yet for me the straightaway narratives of the careers of real Americans show Dos Passos at his best. Read casually, they do not seem extraordinary, merely clean, journalistic, biographical rewrites. But analyze them carefully and, best of all, read them aloud, and you will see how powerful they can be.

In the first place they have rhythm. It is not mere typographical whimsicality that makes Dos Passos break up his long sentences and paragraph clauses as he does.

In the second place, they have meaning. Each man is cunningly chosen for a specific purpose, to bear a dense weight of social interpretation. For example, in The Big Money, dealing with the "boom decade," Dos Passos tells the life stories of ten Americans. Four of them—Frederick Winslow Taylor, Henry Ford, and the Wright brothers—provided the technical framework of ideas and inventions that made possible the lunatic industrial expansion of the decade. Two—Samuel Insull and William Randolph Hearst—represent the kind of success the decade most valued. The arts yield a shrewdly selected trio: Rudolph Valentino, whose own life was not of great importance, but who, by the adoration in which he was held, revealed as in a mirror the emotional anemia of the lives of millions of others; Isadora Duncan, the bohemian rebel; and the architect, Frank Lloyd Wright, the real rebel who had all to give but few takers. The final exhibit is Thorstein Veblen, who understood the whole "big money" period in terms of its basic economic weaknesses. I submit that when you have studied carefully Dos Passos' account of the lives of these ten men and women, you already know a good deal about the spiritual contour of the twenties.

But these narratives do more than convey significant information. They do more than put across, often with subtle irony, a moral judgment. They are more than swift, direct pieces of American prose, making unobtrusive use of our vernacular rhythms and folk sayings. They are—and that is why I have included three of them in this book—first-rate versions of great American legends. For our legendary literature no longer consists of sweet little stories about Hiawatha. It does not even consist primarily of folk tales on the Paul Bunyan order. The point is that, owing to the outsize, fabulous character of our history, there is more mythic poetry in the true stories of certain Americans than there is in all of our fantastic fables.

Henry Ford, the Wright brothers, Wilson are not only interesting and important men. They are representative figures, almost as Prometheus is representative. They are not only part of American history but part of the American imagination. They are, whether you admire them or not, Heroes. It is this which comes through to us in Dos Passos' sharp, economical narrative. These stories have been told a hundred times in a hundred ways, and they will be told again, when you and I are forgotten and Dos Passos may be. But for our time, for the particular level of historic self-consciousness that we have reached, Dos Passos tells the stories in what seems to me a classic form. He does this quite without romanticizing his subjects. He creates his Heroes without any admixture of Hero worship. But he is all the more truly American for his cool, man-to-man democratic treatment.

At times even his unbluffable eye kindles at the sight of something truly noble, and his direct lines of prose unconsciously change character, and swell with emotion, and we get a passage like the moving conclusion to "The Campers at Kitty Hawk."

Tin Lizzie

FROM "U.S.A." BY

JOHN DOS PASSOS

"Mr. Ford *the automobileer*," the featurewriter wrote in 1900,

"*Mr. Ford the automobileer began by giving his steed three or four sharp jerks with the lever at the righthand side of the seat; that is, he pulled the lever up and down sharply in order, as he said, to mix air with gasoline and drive the charge into the exploding cylinder. . . . Mr. Ford slipped a small electric switch handle and there followed a puff, puff, puff. . . . The puffing of the machine assumed a higher key. She was flying along about eight miles an hour. The ruts in the road were deep, but the machine certainly went with a dreamlike smoothness. There was none of the bumping common even to a streetcar. . . . By this time the boulevard had been reached, and the automobileer, letting a lever fall a little, let her out. Whiz! She picked up speed with infinite rapidity. As she ran on there was a clattering behind, the new noise of the automobile.*"

For twenty years or more,

ever since he'd left his father's farm when he was sixteen to get a job in a Detroit machineshop, Henry Ford had been nuts about machinery. First it was watches, then he designed a steamtractor, then he built a horseless carriage with an engine adapted from the Otto gasengine he'd read about in *The World of Science,* then a mechanical buggy with a onecylinder fourcycle motor, that would run forward but not back;

at last, in ninetyeight, he felt he was far enough along to risk throwing up his job with the Detroit Edison Company, where he'd worked his way up from night fireman to chief engineer, to put all his time into working on a new gasoline engine, (in the late eighties he'd met Edison at a meeting of electriclight employees in Atlantic City. He'd gone up to Edison after Edison had delivered an address and asked him if he thought gasoline was practical as a motor fuel. Edison had said yes. If Edison said it, it was true. Edison was the great admiration of Henry Ford's life);

and in driving his mechanical buggy, sitting there at the lever jauntily dressed in a tightbuttoned jacket and a high collar and a derby hat, back and forth over the level illpaved streets of Detroit,

scaring the big brewery horses and the skinny trotting horses and the sleekrumped pacers with the motor's loud explosions,

looking for men scatterbrained enough to invest money in a factory for building automobiles.

He was the eldest son of an Irish immigrant who during the Civil War had married the daughter of a prosperous Pennsylvania Dutch farmer and settled down to farming near Dearborn in Wayne County, Michigan;

like plenty of other Americans, young Henry grew up hating the endless sogging through the mud about the chores, the hauling and pitching manure, the kerosene lamps to clean, the irk and sweat and solitude of the farm.

He was a slender, active youngster, a good skater, clever with his hands; what he liked was to tend the machinery and let the others do the heavy work. His mother had told him not to drink, smoke, gamble or go into debt, and he never did.

When he was in his early twenties his father tried to get him back from Detroit, where he was working as mechanic and repairman for the Drydock Engine Company that built engines for steamboats, by giving him forty acres of land.

Young Henry built himself an uptodate square white dwellinghouse with a false mansard roof and married and settled down on the farm,

but he let the hired men do the farming;

he bought himself a buzzsaw and rented a stationary engine and cut the timber off the woodlots.

He was a thrifty young man who never drank or smoked or gambled or coveted his neighbor's wife, but he couldn't stand living on the farm.

He moved to Detroit, and in the brick barn behind his house tinkered for years in his spare time with a mechanical buggy that would be light enough to run over the clayey wagonroads of Wayne County, Michigan.

By 1900 he had a practicable car to promote.

He was forty years old before the Ford Motor Company was started and production began to move.

Speed was the first thing the early automobile manufacturers went after. Races advertised the makes of cars.

Henry Ford himself hung up several records at the track at Grosse Pointe and on the ice on Lake St. Clair. In his 999 he did the mile in thirtynine and fourfifths seconds.

But it had always been his custom to hire others to do the heavy work. The speed he was busy with was speed in production, the records records in efficient output. He hired Barney Oldfield, a stunt bicyclerider from Salt Lake City, to do the racing for him.

Henry Ford had ideas about other things than the designing of motors, carburetors, magnetos, jigs and fixtures, punches and dies; he had ideas about sales,

that the big money was in economical quantity production, quick turnover, cheap interchangeable easilyreplaced standardized parts;

it wasn't until 1909, after years of arguing with his partners, that Ford put out the first Model T.

Henry Ford was right.

That season he sold more than ten thousand tin lizzies, ten years later he was selling almost a million a year.

In these years the Taylor Plan was stirring up plantmanagers and manufacturers all over the country. Efficiency was the word. The same ingenuity that went into improving the performance of a machine could go into improving the performance of the workmen producing the machine.

In 1913 they established the assemblyline at Ford's. That season the profits were something like twentyfive million dollars, but they had trouble in keeping the men on the job, machinists didn't seem to like it at Ford's.

Henry Ford had ideas about other things than production.

He was the largest automobile manufacturer in the world; he paid high wages; maybe if the steady workers thought they were getting a cut (a very small cut) in the profits, it would give trained men an inducement to stick to their jobs,

wellpaid workers might save enough money to buy a tin lizzie; the first day Ford's announced that cleancut properlymarried American workers who wanted jobs had a chance to make five bucks a day (of course it turned out that there were strings to it; always there were strings to it)

such an enormous crowd waited outside the Highland Park plant all through the zero January night

that there was a riot when the gates were opened; cops broke heads, jobhunters threw bricks; property, Henry Ford's own property, was destroyed. The company dicks had to turn on the firehose to beat back the crowd.

The American Plan; automotive prosperity seeping down from above; it turned out there were strings to it.

But that five dollars a day

paid to good, clean American workmen

who didn't drink or smoke cigarettes or read or think,

and who didn't commit adultery

and whose wives didn't take in boarders,

made America once more the Yukon of the sweated workers of the world;

made all the tin lizzies and the automotive age, and incidentally,

made Henry Ford the automobileer, the admirer of Edison, the birdlover,

the great American of his time.

But Henry Ford had ideas about other things besides assemblylines and the livinghabits of his employees. He was full of ideas. Instead of going to the city to make his fortune, here was a country boy who'd made his fortune by bringing the city out to the farm. The precepts he'd learned out of McGuffey's Reader, his mother's prejudices and preconceptions, he had preserved clean and unworn as freshprinted bills in the safe in a bank.

He wanted people to know about his ideas, so he bought the *Dearborn Independent* and started a campaign against cigarettesmoking.

When war broke out in Europe, he had ideas about that too. (Suspicion of armymen and soldiering were part of the midwest farm tradition, like thrift, stickativeness, temperance and sharp practice in money matters.) Any intelligent American mechanic could see that if the Europeans hadn't been a lot of ignorant underpaid foreigners who drank, smoked, were loose about women and wasteful in their methods of production, the war could never have happened.

When Rosika Schwimmer broke through the stockade of secretaries and servicemen who surrounded Henry Ford and suggested to him that he could stop the war,

he said sure they'd hire a ship and go over and get the boys out of the trenches by Christmas.

He hired a steamboat, the *Oscar II,* and filled it up with pacifists and socialworkers,

to go over to explain to the princelings of Europe

that what they were doing was vicious and silly.

It wasn't his fault that Poor Richard's commonsense no longer rules the world and that most of the pacifists were nuts,

goofy with headlines.

When William Jennings Bryan went over to Hoboken to see him off, somebody handed William Jennings Bryan a squirrel in a cage; William Jennings Bryan made a speech with the squirrel under his arm. Henry Ford threw American Beauty roses to the crowd. The band played *I Didn't Raise My Boy to Be a Soldier.* Practical jokers let loose more squirrels. An eloping couple was married by a platoon of ministers in the saloon, and Mr. Zero, the flophouse humanitarian, who reached the docks too late to sail,

dove into the North River and swam after the boat.

The *Oscar II* was described as a floating Chautauqua; Henry Ford said it felt like a middlewestern village, but by the time they reached Christiansand in Norway, the reporters had kidded him so that he had gotten cold feet and gone to bed. The world was too crazy outside of Wayne County, Michigan. Mrs. Ford and the management sent an Episcopal dean after him who brought him home under wraps,

and the pacifists had to speechify without him.

Two years later Ford's was manufacturing munitions, Eagle boats; Henry Ford was planning oneman tanks, and oneman submarines like the one tried out in the Revolutionary War. He announced to the press that he'd turn over his war profits to the government,

but there's no record that he ever did.

One thing he brought back from his trip
was the Protocols of the Elders of Zion.

He started a campaign to enlighten the world in the *Dearborn Independent;* the Jews were why the world wasn't like Wayne County, Michigan, in the old horse and buggy days;

the Jews had started the war, Bolshevism, Darwinism, Marxism, Nietzsche, short skirts and lipstick. They were behind Wall Street and the international bankers, and the whiteslave traffic and the movies and the Supreme Court and ragtime and the illegal liquor business.

Henry Ford denounced the Jews and ran for senator and sued the *Chicago Tribune* for libel,

and was the laughingstock of the kept metropolitan press;

but when the metropolitan bankers tried to horn in on his business he thoroughly outsmarted them.

In 1918 he had borrowed on notes to buy out his minority stockholders for the picayune sum of seventy-five million dollars.

In February, 1920, he needed cash to pay off some of these notes that were coming due. A banker is supposed to have called on him and

offered him every facility if the bankers representative could be made
a member of the board of directors. Henry Ford handed the banker
his hat,

   and went about raising the money in his own way:

   he shipped every car and part he had in his plant to his dealers and
demanded immediate cash payment. Let the other fellow do the bor-
rowing had always been a cardinal principle. He shut down production and canceled all orders from the supplyfirms. Many dealers were
ruined, many supplyfirms failed, but when he reopened his plant,

   he owned it absolutely,

   the way a man owns an unmortgaged farm with the taxes paid up.

   In 1922 there started the Ford boom for President (high wages,
waterpower, industry scattered to the small towns) that was skillfully
pricked behind the scenes

   by another crackerbarrel philosopher,

   Calvin Coolidge;

   but in 1922 Henry Ford sold one million three hundred and thirty-
two thousand two hundred and nine tin lizzies; he was the richest
man in the world.

   Good roads had followed the narrow ruts made in the mud by the
Model T. The great automotive boom was on. At Ford's production
was improving all the time; less waste, more spotters, strawbosses,
stoolpigeons (fifteen minutes for lunch, three minutes to go to the
toilet, the Taylorized speedup everywhere, reach under, adjust washer,
screw down bolt, shove in cotterpin, reachunder adjustwasher, screw-
down bolt, reachunderadjustscrewdownreachunderadjust until every
ounce of life was sucked off into production and at night the workmen
went home grey shaking husks).

   Ford owned every detail of the process from the ore in the hills until
the car rolled off the end of the assemblyline under its own power, the
plants were rationalized to the last tenthousandth of an inch as measured by the Johansen scale;

   in 1926 the production cycle was reduced to eightyone hours from
the ore in the mine to the finished salable car proceeding under its own
power,

   but the Model T was obsolete.

New Era prosperity and the American Plan
(there were strings to it, always there were strings to it)
had killed Tin Lizzie.
Ford's was just one of many automobile plants.
When the stockmarket bubble burst,
Mr. Ford the crackerbarrel philosopher said jubilantly,
"I told you so.
Serves you right for gambling and getting in debt.
The country is sound."
But when the country on cracked shoes, in frayed trousers, belts
tightened over hollow bellies,
idle hands cracked and chapped with the cold of that coldest March
day of 1932,
started marching from Detroit to Dearborn, asking for work and
the American Plan, all they could think of at Ford's was machineguns.
The country was sound, but they mowed the marchers down.
They shot four of them dead.

Henry Ford as an old man
is a passionate antiquarian,
(lives besieged on his father's farm embedded in an estate of thousands of millionaire acres, protected by an army of servicemen, secretaries, secret agents, dicks under orders of an English exprizefighter,
always afraid of the feet in broken shoes on the roads, afraid the
gangs will kidnap his grandchildren,
that a crank will shoot him,
that Change and the idle hands out of work will break through the
gates and the high fences;
protected by a private army against
the new America of starved children and hollow bellies and cracked
shoes stamping on souplines,
that has swallowed up the old thrifty farmlands
of Wayne County, Michigan,
as if they had never been).
Henry Ford as an old man
is a passionate antiquarian.

He rebuilt his father's farmhouse and put it back exactly in the state he remembered it in as a boy. He built a village of museums for buggies, sleighs, coaches, old plows, waterwheels, obsolete models of motor-cars. He scoured the country for fiddlers to play old-fashioned square-dances.

Even old taverns he bought and put back into their original shape, as well as Thomas Edison's early laboratories.

When he bought the Wayside Inn near Sudbury, Massachusetts, he had the new highway where the newmodel cars roared and slithered and hissed oilily past (*the new noise of the automobile*),

moved away from the door,
put back the old bad road,
so that everything might be
the way it used to be,
in the days of horses and buggies.

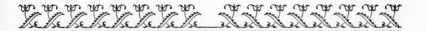

The Campers at Kitty Hawk

FROM "U.S.A." BY

JOHN DOS PASSOS

ON DECEMBER SEVENTEENTH, nineteen hundred and three, Bishop Wright of the United Brethren onetime editor of the *Religious Telescope* received in his frame house on Hawthorn Street in Dayton, Ohio, a telegram from his boys Wilbur and Orville who'd gotten it into their heads to spend their vacations in a little camp out on the dunes of the North Carolina coast tinkering with a homemade glider they'd knocked together themselves. The telegram read:

SUCCESS FOUR FLIGHTS THURSDAY MORNING ALL AGAINST TWENTYONE MILE WIND STARTED FROM LEVEL WITH ENGINEPOWER ALONE AVERAGE SPEED THROUGH AIR THIRTYONE MILES LONGEST FIFTYSEVEN SECONDS INFORM PRESS HOME CHRISTMAS

The figures were a little wrong because the telegraph operator misread Orville's hasty penciled scrawl
but the fact remains
that a couple of young bicycle mechanics from Dayton, Ohio
had designed constructed and flown
for the first time ever a practical airplane.

After running the motor a few minutes to heat it up I released the wire that held the machine to the track and the machine started forward into the wind. Wilbur ran at the side of the machine holding the wing to balance it on the track. Unlike the start on the 14th made in a calm the machine facing a 27 mile wind started very slowly.... Wilbur was able to stay with it until it lifted from the track after a forty-foot run. One of the lifesaving men snapped the camera for us taking a picture just as it reached the end of the track and the machine had risen to a height of about two feet. . . . The course of the flight up and down was extremely erratic, partly due to the irregularities of the air, partly to lack of experience in handling this machine. A sudden dart when a little over a hundred and twenty feet from the point at which it rose in the air ended the flight. . . . This flight lasted only 12 seconds but it was nevertheless the first in the history of the world in which a machine carrying a man had raised itself by its own power into the air in full flight, had sailed forward without reduction of speed and had finally landed at a point as high as that from which it started.

A little later in the day the machine was caught in a gust of wind and turned over and smashed, almost killing the coastguardsman who tried to hold it down;
   it was too bad
   but the Wright brothers were too happy to care
   they'd proved that the damn thing flew.

When these points had been definitely established we at once packed our goods and returned home knowing that the age of the flying machine had come at last.

They were home for Christmas in Dayton, Ohio, where they'd been born in the seventies of a family who had been settled west of the Alleghenies since eighteen fourteen, in Dayton, Ohio, where they'd been to grammarschool and highschool and joined their father's church and played baseball and hockey and worked out on the parallel bars and the flying swing and sold newspapers and built themselves a print-ingpress out of odds and ends from the junkheap and flown kites and tinkered with mechanical contraptions and gone around town as boys doing odd jobs to turn an honest penny.

The folks claimed it was the bishop's bringing home a helicopter, a fiftycent mechanical toy made of two fans worked by elastic bands that was supposed to hover in the air, that had got his two youngest boys hipped on the subject of flight

so that they stayed home instead of marrying the way the other boys
did, and puttered all day about the house picking up a living with
jobprinting,

bicyclerepair work,

sitting up late nights reading books on aerodynamics.

Still they were sincere churchmembers, their bicycle business was
prosperous, a man could rely on their word. They were popular in
Dayton.

In those days flyingmachines were the big laugh of all the cracker-
barrel philosophers. Langley's and Chanute's unsuccessful experiments
had been jeered down with an I-told-you-so that rang from coast to
coast. The Wrights' big problem was to find a place secluded enough
to carry on their experiments without being the horselaugh of the
countryside. Then they had no money to spend;

they were practical mechanics; when they needed anything they
built it themselves.

They hit on Kitty Hawk,

on the great dunes and sandy banks that stretch south towards Hat-
teras seaward of Albemarle Sound,

a vast stretch of seabeach

empty except for a coastguard station, a few fishermen's shacks and
the swarms of mosquitoes and the ticks and chiggers in the crabgrass
behind the dunes

and overhead the gulls and swooping terns, in the evening fishhawks
and cranes flapping across the saltmarshes, occasionally eagles

that the Wright brothers followed soaring with their eyes

as Leonardo watched them centuries before

straining his sharp eyes to apprehend

the laws of flight.

Four miles across the loose sand from the scattering of shacks, the
Wright brothers built themselves a camp and a shed for their gliders.
It was a long way to pack their groceries, their tools, anything they
happened to need; in summer it was hot as blazes, the mosquitoes
were hell;

but they were alone there

and they'd figured out that the loose sand was as soft as anything
they could find to fall in.

There with a glider made of two planes and a tail in which they
lay flat on their bellies and controlled the warp of the planes by shimmying their hips, taking off again and again all day from a big dune
named Kill Devil Hill,

they learned to fly.

Once they'd managed to hover for a few seconds
and soar ever so slightly on a rising aircurrent
they decided the time had come
to put a motor in their biplane.

Back in the shop in Dayton, Ohio, they built an airtunnel, which
is their first great contribution to the science of flying, and tried out
model planes in it.

They couldn't interest any builders of gasoline engines so they had
to build their own motor.

It worked; after that Christmas of nineteen three the Wright brothers weren't doing it for fun any more; they gave up their bicycle business, got the use of a big old cowpasture belonging to the local banker
for practice flights, spent all the time when they weren't working on
their machine in promotion, worrying about patents, infringements,
spies, trying to interest government officials, to make sense out of the
smooth involved heartbreaking remarks of lawyers.

In two years they had a plane that would cover twentyfour miles at
a stretch round and round the cowpasture.

People on the interurban car used to crane their necks out of the
windows when they passed along the edge of the field, startled by the
clattering pop pop of the old Wright motor and the sight of the white
biplane like a pair of ironingboards one on top of the other chugging
along a good fifty feet in the air. The cows soon got used to it.

As the flights got longer
the Wright brothers got backers,

engaged in lawsuits,
lay in their beds at night sleepless with the whine of phantom millions, worse than the mosquitoes at Kitty Hawk.

In nineteen seven they went to Paris,
allowed themselves to be togged out in dress suits and silk hats,
learned to tip waiters
talked with government experts, got used to gold braid and postponements and vandyke beards and the outspread palms of politicos.
For amusement
they played diabolo in the Tuileries gardens.

They gave publicized flights at Fort Myers, where they had their first fatal crackup, St. Petersburg, Paris, Berlin; at Pau they were all the rage,
such an attraction that the hotelkeeper
wouldn't charge them for their room.
Alfonso of Spain shook hands with them and was photographed sitting in the machine,
King Edward watched a flight,
the Crown Prince insisted on being taken up,
the rain of medals began.

They were congratulated by the Czar
and the King of Italy and the amateurs of sport, and the society climbers and the papal titles,
and decorated by a society for universal peace.

Aeronautics became the sport of the day.
The Wrights don't seem to have been very much impressed by the upholstery and the braid and the gold medals and the parades of plush horses,
they remained practical mechanics
and insisted on doing all their own work themselves,
even to filling the gasolinetank.

In nineteen eleven they were back on the dunes
at Kitty Hawk with a new glider.

Orville stayed up in the air for nine and a half minutes, which remained a long time the record for motorless flight.

The same year Wilbur died of typhoidfever in Dayton.

In the rush of new names: Farman, Blériot, Curtiss, Ferber, Esnault-Peltrie, Delagrange;

in the snorting impact of bombs and the whine and rattle of shrapnel and the sudden stutter of machineguns after the motor's been shut off overhead,

and we flatten into the mud

and make ourselves small cowering in the corners of ruined walls,
the Wright brothers passed out of the headlines

but not even headlines or the bitter smear of newsprint or the choke of smokescreen and gas or chatter of brokers on the stockmarket or barking of phantom millions or oratory of brasshats laying wreaths on new monuments

can blur the memory
of the chilly December day
two shivering bicycle mechanics from Dayton, Ohio,
first felt their homemade contraption
whittled out of hickory sticks,
gummed together with Arnstein's bicycle cement,
stretched with muslin they'd sewn on their sister's sewingmachine
in their own backyard on Hawthorn Street in Dayton, Ohio,
soar into the air
above the dunes and the wide beach
at Kitty Hawk.

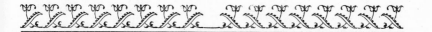

Meester Veelson

FROM "U.S.A." BY

JOHN DOS PASSOS

THE YEAR THAT Buchanan was elected president Thomas Woodrow Wilson

was born to a presbyterian minister's daughter

in the manse at Staunton in the valley of Virginia; it was the old Scotch-Irish stock; the father was a presbyterian minister too and a teacher of rhetoric in theological seminaries; the Wilsons lived in a universe of words linked into an incontrovertible firmament by two centuries of calvinist divines,

God was the Word

and the Word was God.

Dr. Wilson was a man of standing who loved his home and his children and good books and his wife and correct syntax and talked to God every day at family prayers;

he brought his sons up

between the bible and the dictionary.

The years of the Civil War

the years of fife and drum and platoonfire and proclamations

the Wilsons lived in Augusta, Georgia; Tommy was a backward child, didn't learn his letters till he was nine, but when he learned to read his favorite reading was Parson Weems'

Life of Washington.

In 1870 Dr. Wilson was called to the Theological Seminary at Columbia, South Carolina; Tommy attended Davidson college,

where he developed·a good tenor voice;

then he went to Princeton and became a debater and editor of the
Princetonian. His first published article in the Nassau Literary Magazine was an appreciation of Bismarck.

Afterwards he studied law at the University of Virginia; young Wilson wanted to be a Great Man, like Gladstone and the eighteenth century English parliamentarians; he wanted to hold the packed benches
spellbound in the cause of Truth; but lawpractice irked him; he was
more at home in the booky air of libraries, lecturerooms, college chapel,
it was a relief to leave his lawpractice at Atlanta and take a Historical
Fellowship at Johns Hopkins; there he wrote *Congressional Government*.

At twentynine he married a girl with a taste for painting (while
he was courting her he coached her in how to use the broad "a") and
got a job at Bryn Mawr teaching the girls History and Political Economy. When he got his Ph.D. from Johns Hopkins he moved to a pro-
fessorship at Wesleyan, wrote articles, started a History of the United
States,

spoke out for Truth Reform Responsible Government Democracy
from the lecture platform, climbed all the steps of a brilliant university
career; in 1901 the trustees of Princeton offered him the presidency;

he plunged into reforming the university, made violent friends and
enemies, set the campus by the ears,

and the American people began to find on the front pages
the name of Woodrow Wilson.

In 1909 he made addresses on Lincoln and Robert E. Lee
and in 1910
the democratic bosses of New Jersey, hardpressed by muckrakers
and reformers, got the bright idea of offering the nomination for governor to the stainless college president who attracted such large audiences
by publicly championing Right.

When Mr. Wilson addressed the Trenton convention that nominated
him for governor he confessed his belief in the common man, (the

smalltown bosses and the wardheelers looked at each other and scratched their heads); he went on, his voice growing firmer:

that is the man by whose judgment I for one wish to be guided, so that as the tasks multiply, and as the days come when all will feel confusion and dismay, we may lift up our eyes to the hills out of these dark valleys where the crags of special privilege overshadow and darken our path, to where the sun gleams through the great passage in the broken cliffs,   the sun of God,

the sun meant to regenerate men,

the sun meant to liberate them from their passion and despair and lift us to those uplands which are the promised land of every man who desires liberty and achievement.

The smalltown bosses and the wardheelers looked at each other and scratched their heads; then they cheered; Wilson fooled the wiseacres and doublecrossed the bosses, was elected by a huge plurality;

so he left Princeton only half reformed to be Governor of New Jersey,

and became reconciled with Bryan

at the Jackson Day dinner: when Bryan remarked, "I of course knew that you were not with me in my position on the currency," Mr. Wilson replied, "All I can say, Mr. Bryan, is that you are a great big man."

He was introduced to Colonel House,

that amateur Merlin of politics who was spinning his webs at the Hotel Gotham

and at the convention in Baltimore the next July the upshot of the puppetshow staged for sweating delegates by Hearst and House behind the scenes, and Bryan booming in the corridors with a handkerchief over his wilted collar, was that Woodrow Wilson was nominated for the presidency.

The bolt of the Progressives in Chicago from Taft to T.R. made his election sure;

so he left the State of New Jersey halfreformed

(pitiless publicity was the slogan of the Shadow Lawn Campaign) and went to the White House our twentyeighth president.

While Woodrow Wilson drove up Pennsylvania Avenue beside Taft the great buttertub, who as president had been genially undoing T.R.'s reactionary efforts to put business under the control of the government,

J. Pierpont Morgan sat playing solitaire in his back office on Wall Street, smoking twenty black cigars a day, cursing the follies of democracy.

Wilson flayed the interests and branded privilege refused to recognize Huerta and sent the militia to the Rio Grande

to assume a policy of watchful waiting. He published *The New Freedom* and delivered his messages to Congress in person, like a college president addressing the faculty and students. At Mobile he said:

I wish to take this occasion to say that the United States will never again seek one additional foot of territory by conquest;

and he landed the marines at Vera Cruz.

We are witnessing a renaissance of public spirit, a reawakening of sober public opinion, a revival of the power of the people the beginning of an age of thoughtful reconstruction . . .

but the world had started spinning round Sarajevo.

First it was *neutrality in thought and deed,* then *too proud to fight* when the *Lusitania* sinking and the danger to the Morgan loans and the stories of the British and French propagandists set all the financial centers in the East bawling for war, but the suction of the drumbeat and the guns was too strong; the best people took their fashions from Paris and their broad "a's" from London, and T.R. and the House of Morgan.

Five months after his reelection on the slogan *He kept us out of war,* Wilson pushed the Armed Ship Bill through congress and declared that a state of war existed between the United States and the Central Powers:

Force without stint or limit, force to the utmost.

Wilson became the state (war is the health of the state), Washington his Versailles, manned the socialized government with dollar a year men out of the great corporations and ran the big parade

of men munitions groceries mules and trucks to France. Five million men stood at attention outside of their tarpaper barracks every sundown while they played *The Star Spangled Banner.*

War brought the eight hour day, women's votes, prohibition, compulsory arbitration, high wages, high rates of interest, cost plus contracts and the luxury of being a Gold Star Mother.

If you objected to making the world safe for cost plus democracy you went to jail with Debs.

Almost too soon the show was over, Prince Max of Baden was pleading for the Fourteen Points, Foch was occupying the bridgeheads on the Rhine and the Kaiser out of breath ran for the train down the platform at Potsdam wearing a silk hat and some say false whiskers.

With the help of *Almighty God, Right, Truth, Justice, Freedom, Democracy, the Selfdetermination of Nations, No indemnities no annexations,*

and Cuban sugar and Caucasian manganese and Northwestern wheat and Dixie cotton, the British blockade, General Pershing, the taxicabs of Paris and the seventyfive gun

we won the war.

On December 4th, 1918, Woodrow Wilson, the first president to leave the territory of the United States during his presidency, sailed for France on board the *George Washington,*

the most powerful man in the world.

In Europe they knew what gas smelt like and the sweet sick stench of bodies buried too shallow and the grey look of the skin of starved children; they read in the papers that Meester Veelson was for peace and freedom and canned goods and butter and sugar;

he landed at Brest with his staff of experts and publicists after a rough trip on the *George Washington.*

La France héroïque was there with the speeches, the singing schoolchildren, the mayors in their red sashes. (Did Meester Veelson see the gendarmes at Brest beating back the demonstration of dockyard workers who came to meet him with red flags?)

At the station in Paris he stepped from the train onto a wide red carpet that led him, between rows of potted palms, silk hats, legions of honor, decorated busts of uniforms, frockcoats, rosettes, boutonnières, to a Rolls Royce. (Did Meester Veelson see the women in black, the cripples in their little carts, the pale anxious faces along the streets, did he hear the terrible anguish of the cheers as they hurried him and his new wife to the hôtel de Mûrat, where in rooms full of brocade, gilt clocks, Buhl cabinets and ormolu cupids the presidential suite had been prepared?)

While the experts were organizing the procedure of the peace conference, spreading green baize on the tables, arranging the protocols,

the Wilsons took a tour to see for themselves: the day after Christmas they were entertained at Buckingham Palace; at Newyears they called on the pope and on the microscopic Italian king at the Quirinal. (Did Meester Veelson know that in the peasants' wargrimed houses along the Brenta and the Piave they were burning candles in front of his picture cut out of the illustrated papers?) (Did Meester Veelson know that the people of Europe spelled a challenge to oppression out of the Fourteen Points as centuries before they had spelled a challenge to oppression out of the ninetyfive articles Martin Luther nailed to the churchdoor in Wittenberg?)

January 18, 1919, in the midst of serried uniforms, cocked hats and gold braid, decorations, epaulettes, orders of merit and knighthood, the High Contracting Parties, the allied and associated powers met in the Salon de l'Horloge at the quai d'Orsay to dictate the peace,

but the grand assembly of the peace conference was too public a place to make peace in

so the High Contracting Parties

formed the Council of Ten, went into the Gobelin Room and, surrounded by Rubens's History of Marie de Medici,

began to dictate the peace.

But the Council of Ten was too public a place to make peace in

so they formed the Council of Four.

Orlando went home in a huff

and then there were three:

Clemenceau,

Lloyd George,
Woodrow Wilson.
Three old men shuffling the pack,
dealing out the cards:
the Rhineland, Danzig, the Polish corridor, the Ruhr, self determination of small nations, the Saar, League of Nations, mandates, the
Mespot, Freedom of the Seas, Transjordania, Shantung, Fiume and
the Island of Yap: •
machine gun fire and arson
starvation, lice, cholera, typhus;
oil was trumps.

Woodrow Wilson believed in his father's God
so he told the parishioners in the little Lowther Street Congrega-
tional church where his grandfather had preached in Carlisle in Scotland, a day so chilly that the newspaper men sitting in the old pews
all had to keep their overcoats on.

On April 7th he ordered the *George Washington* to be held at
Brest with steam up ready to take the American delegation home;
but he didn't go.

On April 19 sharper Clemenceau and sharper Lloyd George got him
into their little cosy threecardgame they called the Council of Four.

On June 28th the Treaty of Versailles was ready
and Wilson had to go back home to explain to the politicians who'd
been ganging up on him meanwhile in the Senate and House and to
sober public opinion and to his father's God how he'd let himself be
trimmed and how far he'd made the world safe
for democracy and the New Freedom.
From the day he landed in Hoboken he had his back to the wall of
the White House, talking to save his faith in words, talking to save his
faith in the League of Nations, talking to save his faith in himself, in
his father's God.
He strained every nerve of his body and brain, every agency of the

government he had under his control; (if anybody disagreed he was a crook or a red; no pardon for Debs).

In Seattle the wobblies whose leaders were in jail, in Seattle the wobblies whose leaders had been lynched, who'd been shot down like dogs, in Seattle the wobblies lined four blocks as Wilson passed, stood silent with their arms folded staring at the great liberal as he was hurried past in his car, huddled in his overcoat, haggard with fatigue, one side of his face twitching. The men in overalls, the workingstiffs let him pass in silence after all the other blocks of handclapping and patriotic cheers.

In Pueblo, Colorado, he was a grey man hardly able to stand, one side of his face twitching:

Now that the mists of this great question have cleared away, I believe that men will see the Truth, eye for eye and face to face. There is one thing the American People always rise to and extend their hand to, that is, the truth of justice and of liberty and of peace. We have accepted that truth and we are going to be led by it, and it is going to lead us, and through us the world, out into pastures of quietness and peace such as the world never dreamed of before.

That was his last speech;

on the train to Wichita he had a stroke. He gave up the speaking tour that was to sweep the country for the League of Nations. After that he was a ruined paralysed man barely able to speak;

the day he gave up the presidency to Harding the joint committee of the Senate and House appointed Henry Cabot Lodge, his lifelong enemy, to make the formal call at the executive office in the Capitol and ask the formal question whether the president had any message for the congress assembled in joint session;

Wilson managed to get to his feet, lifting himself painfully by the two arms of the chair. "Senator Lodge, I have no further communication to make, thank you . . . Good morning," he said.

In 1924 on February 3rd he died.

W. SOMERSET MAUGHAM

COMMENTARY

Most writers, even those who talk glibly of his "selling out," have a genuine respect for Somerset Maugham. They respect him because, whatever his limitations as an artist, he is an honest craftsman and an honest man. Perhaps honest isn't the word. Ingenuous might be better. I don't mean that he is naïve, but rather that he is an ingenuous hawker of his wares. Every so often he will do a job obviously carpentered for the trade and with little else to recommend it. My point is that he doesn't really dissimulate. When he prepares tripe, he practically puts a label on it stating its high percentage of adulteration. I find this a virtue. It makes his work so much more agreeable than the novels, for example, of Mr. Charles Morgan, which are not only tripe but are rendered doubly unpalatable by the fact that Mr. Morgan doesn't seem to know it.

Take Mr. Maugham's recent confection, Up at the Villa. The materials are stock melodrama but Maugham's touch relieves them of their vulgarity. It's almost a pleasure to be sold so smooth and shiny a gold brick. The same thing is true of his novel Theatre, whose title is suspiciously apt. It is a clockwork job of gadgetry. It's old hat, but old hat from an old hand, deft as the devil at refurbishing the backshelf millinery, the faded flowers and dead birds of fiction. Theatre may be theatrical, but it's a good show.

No, Somerset Maugham doesn't fool himself. In The Summing Up, a book of reflections tinged with autobiography, he says, "I have a clear and logical brain, but not a very subtle nor a very powerful one." He has not tried to write subtly or powerfully, to make grand generalizations about humanity, to beat his breast in public. He knows what he can do. "Never having felt some of the fundamental emotions of normal men, it is impossible that my work should have the intimacy, the broad human touch and the animal serenity which the greatest writers alone can give." I do not believe Maugham has

169

ever struck a pose in his work. His plays are often cheap, but they have an honest and candid cheapness.

He will live mainly by one book, but it is unfair to say that he could have followed it, had he wished, with others just as good. Of Human Bondage was the product of a brief period of belief, of certain special emotional pressures in his life, pressures that never repeated themselves. At all times he wrote what he could, and that alone.

Writers respect Maugham, too, because he respects his own craft. He has actually spent years of his life studying it. How many American novelists, now in their twenties or early thirties, have considered it necessary to spend several hours a day doing what Maugham did— analyzing model prose writers, charting his limitations, working out a style that would correspond both to what he was as a person and what he wanted to be as a writer? "On taking thought it seemed to me that I must aim at lucidity, simplicity and euphony." He has attained them by diligence, patience, and the subordination of his ego to his craft.

I suppose Somerset Maugham is really the cynical, embittered man of the world that rumor makes him. Still, I cannot help feeling that he must be getting a great deal of pleasure out of these, his latter years. For one thing, his contemporaries are dying off in the most satisfactory manner. Not only his own talent but mortality itself is helping him to a commanding position in the literary hierarchy. Again, by some curious twist, while his colleagues as they age lose almost daily in reputation, he seems to gain. Even his poorer books are greated with salvos of approbation, and the fact that he has produced only one important work is an asset rather than a liability, for at least it is a novel everyone has read and none disliked. But most gratifying of all, I should imagine, is the complete mastery he has gained in late maturity over his own talents. Through study and hard work he has finally evolved a style adequate to anything he wishes to say.

It is this which accounts for the feeling we have, when we open a new Maugham, that although we will never be lifted up, we will never be let down. He is the most comforting, if not the weightiest, of modern English writers. When he is entertaining, he is so without vulgarity or pretentiousness. When he is thoughtful, he offers his undeniable cultivation of mind without pompousness or any claim upon the attention of posterity.

A good example of what I mean is to be found in "Don Fernando," a ruminative essay, which I should think many might enjoy, on the Golden Age of Spain. "Don Fernando" has no great depth— it is almost too consciously civilized for that—but it is far from superficial. Maugham does not say a single witty thing, yet he gives the constant impression of wit. He is never enthusiastic, always interesting; never learned, always easy and copious in his fund of information; never daringly original, yet a personality is quietly present in every line. He is neither Hispanophile nor Hispanophobe. He writes not to persuade us to any special view of the epoch of Cervantes or El Greco but merely to amuse himself, intelligently, without frivolity. His fatal fault is one he would gladly confess—complete lack of conviction. But opinions dressed in charm offer a palatable substitute.

In "Don Fernando" he has much to say of the art of prose. Many of his comments are self-flattering half-truths, such as his judgment that "good writing should be like the conversation of a well-bred man." Apropos the autobiography of Saint Teresa, he remarks upon "that sound of the living voice that we all, for the most part without success, aim at." He has aimed at it successfully. His books of nonfiction are causerie carried to its highest point of development.

Maugham is one of those writers, never of the highest rank, who seem to have been born civilized. He takes his own disillusion calmly, without emphasis, making no Noel Coward pose of it. He is always interesting and never absorbing, always intelligent and intelligible but quite without the passion, the frenzy, that he admires in the great Russians. His mind is made up. He observes the vagaries of humans with a sympathy that enlists the reader's eager interest but never betrays Maugham himself into anything like abandon. Thus his insights are always shrewd, rarely deep, and his stories more remarkable for their lucidity and formal perfection than for those more enduring qualities we associate with the masters.

In one of his tales he makes a character (obviously close to his own heart) say, "If to look truth in the face and not resent it when it's unpalatable, and take human nature as you find it, smiling when it's absurd and grieved without exaggeration when it's pitiful, is to be cynical, then I suppose I'm a cynic." There is a casual gravity about the statement which removes it completely from a merely literary attitude.

To read his stories is like listening to the reminiscential talk of a man who has been everywhere and seen everything but prefers not to absorb too much, not to take anything either too seriously or too frivolously. Among those authors who steer a kind of middle course between first-rate art and first-rate entertainment, Somerset Maugham emerges foremost by a generous margin. He is as good a writer as a man of the world can possibly be.

"In my twenties," he says, and he is not complaining, "the critics said I was brutal, in my thirties they said I was flippant, in my forties they said I was cynical, in my fifties they said I was competent, and now in my sixties they say I am superficial." It is an excellent summing up of the changes in public taste as well as of the curve of Maugham's own development. He has been all of these things, but one thing he has never been: careless.

Of Human Bondage, of course, is in a class by itself. Of his other novels I think only one will last: Cakes and Ale, one of the most masterly satires on the literary temperament to be found anywhere. It is minor and it is delicious. Maugham obviously enjoyed writing it, and as long as people enjoy a perfect puncturing of pretense and hypocrisy they will enjoy reading it.

Then there are the short stories. For the purposes of this book I reread them—there must be around a hundred—and discovered a fact about Maugham that he may not be aware of himself. The best stories are the most recent, the ones you will find in a collection called The Mixture as Before. In his introduction to this volume Maugham, as the title indicates, seems to assume that his latest stories are about on a level with his earlier ones. I thought this was probably so, until I went through the whole series. My judgment may be faulty, but it seems to me that these swan-song tales (the author says, "I shall not write any more" of them) have a concision, a directness, that his earlier stories, even the famous "Sadie Thompson," lack. Also, they are less mechanical. Their comments on life, though of a piece with everything Maugham has ever said about that popular institution, are no longer slick ironies, but genuine worldly wisdom, and there is a place in literature for wisdom that is worldly.

From this volume I have chosen three tales. One of them, "Lord Mountdrago," is just a trick story and has been placed, for a reason, in another part of this book. The remaining two, "The Treasure" and "The Facts of Life," show Maugham at his best. They are urbane without affectation, they are sagacious without cynicism, they have that note of perfect craftsmanship, literary conscientiousness, modest reasonableness which is pure Somerset Maugham. And they are infused with a dry-sherry humor that will, I think, keep them alive when his more famous short stories—the ones they make bad films out of— are no longer read.

The Treasure

BY

W. SOMERSET MAUGHAM

RICHARD HARENGER was a happy man. Notwithstanding what the pessimists, from Ecclesiastes onwards, have said, this is not so rare a thing to find in this unhappy world, but Richard Harenger knew it, and that is a very rare thing indeed. The golden mean which the ancients so highly prized is out of fashion, and those who follow it must put up with polite derision from those who see no merit in self-restraint and no virtue in common sense. Richard Harenger shrugged a polite and amused shoulder. Let others live dangerously, let others burn with a hard gemlike flame, let others stake their fortunes on the turn of a card, walk the tightrope that leads to glory or the grave, or hazard their lives for a cause, a passion or an adventure. He neither envied the fame their exploits brought them nor wasted his pity on them when their efforts ended in disaster.

But it must not be inferred from this that Richard Harenger was a selfish or a callous man. He was neither. He was considerate and of a generous disposition. He was always ready to oblige a friend, and he was sufficiently well off to be able to indulge himself in the pleasure of helping others. He had some money of his own, and he occupied in the Home Office a position that brought him an adequate stipend. The work suited him. It was regular, responsible and pleasant. Every day when he left the office he went to his club to play bridge for a couple of hours, and on Saturdays and Sundays he played golf. He went abroad for his holidays, staying at good hotels, and visited churches, galleries and museums. He was a regular first-nighter. He dined out a good deal. His friends liked him. He was easy to talk to. He was well read, knowledgeable and amusing. He was besides of a personable

exterior, not remarkably handsome, but tall, slim and erect
with a lean, intelligent face; his hair was growing thin,
now approaching the age of fifty, but his brown eyes re
smile and his teeth were all his own. He had from nat
constitution, and he had always taken care of himself. There was no
reason in the world why he should not be a happy man, and if there
had been in him a trace of self-complacency he might have claimed
that he deserved to be.

He had the good fortune even to sail safely through those perilous,
unquiet straits of marriage in which so many wise and good men have
made shipwreck. Married for love in the early twenties, his wife and
he, after some years of almost perfect felicity, had drifted gradually
apart. Neither of them wished to marry anyone else, so there was
no question of divorce (which indeed Richard Harenger's situation in
the government service made undesirable), but for convenience' sake,
with the help of the family lawyer, they arranged a separation which
left them free to lead their lives as each one wished without inter-
ference from the other. They parted with mutual expressions of respect
and good will. ·

Richard Harenger sold his house in St. John's Wood and took a
flat within convenient walking distance of Whitehall. It had a sitting
room which he lined with his books, a dining room into which his
Chippendale furniture just fitted, a nice-sized bedroom for himself,
and beyond the kitchen a couple of maids' rooms. He brought his
cook, whom he had had for many years, from St. John's Wood, but
needing no longer so large a staff dismissed the rest of the servants
and applied at a registry office for a house-parlourmaid. He knew
exactly what he wanted, and he explained his needs to the superintendent of the agency with precision. He wanted a maid who was
not too young, first because young women are flighty and secondly
because, though he was of mature age and a man of principle, people
would talk, the porter and the tradesmen if nobody else, and both
for the sake of his own reputation and that of the young person he
considered that the applicant should have reached years of discretion.
Besides that he wanted a maid who could clean silver well. He had
always had a fancy for old silver, and it was reasonable to demand

that the forks and spoons that had been used by a woman of quality under the reign of Queen Anne should be treated with tenderness and respect. He was of a hospitable nature and liked to give at least once a week little dinners of not less than four people and not more than eight. He could trust his cook to send in a meal that his guests would take pleasure in eating and he desired his parlourmaid to wait with neatness and dispatch. Then he needed a perfect valet. He dressed well, in a manner that suited his age and condition, and he liked his clothes to be properly looked after. The parlourmaid he was looking for must be able to press trousers and iron a tie, and he was very particular that his shoes should be well shone. He had small feet, and he took a good deal of trouble to have well-cut shoes. He had a large supply, and he insisted that they should be treed up the moment he took them off. Finally the flat must be kept clean and tidy. It was of course understood that any applicant for the post must be of irreproachable character, sober, honest, reliable and of a pleasing exterior. In return for this he was prepared to offer good wages, reasonable liberty and ample holidays. The superintendent listened without batting an eyelash, and telling him that she was quite sure she could suit him, sent him a string of candidates which proved that she had not paid the smallest attention to a word he said. He saw them all personally. Some were obviously inefficient, some looked fast, some were too old, others too young, some lacked the presence he thought essential; there was not one to whom he was inclined even to give a trial. He was a kindly, polite man, and he declined their services with a smile and a pleasant expression of regret. He did not lose patience. He was prepared to interview house-parlourmaids till he found one who was suitable.

Now it is a funny thing about life, if you refuse to accept anything but the best you very often get it: if you utterly decline to make do with what you can get, then somehow or other you are very likely to get what you want. It is as though Fate said, "This man's a perfect fool, he's asking for perfection," and then just out of her feminine wilfulness flung it in his lap. One day the porter of the flats said to Richard Harenger out of a blue sky:

"I hear you're lookin' for a house-parlourmaid, sir. There's someone I know lookin' for a situation as might do."

"Can you recommend her personally?"

Richard Harenger had the sound opinion that one servant's recommendation of another was worth much more than that of an employer.

"I can vouch for her respectability. She's been in some very good situations."

"I shall be coming in to dress about seven. If that's convenient to her I could see her then."

"Very good, sir. I'll see that she's told."

He had not been in more than five minutes when the cook, having answered a ring at the front door, came in and told him that the person the porter had spoken to him about had called.

"Show her in," he said.

He turned on some more light so that he could see what the applicant looked like, and getting up, stood with his back to the fireplace. A woman came in and stood just inside the door in a respectful attitude.

"Good evening," he said. "What is your name?"

"Pritchard, sir."

"How old are you?"

"Thirty-five, sir."

"Well, that's a reasonable age."

He gave his cigarette a puff and looked at her reflectively. She was on the tall side, nearly as tall as he, but he guessed that she wore high heels. Her black dress fitted her station. She held herself well. She had good features and a rather high colour.

"Will you take off your hat?" he asked.

She did so, and he saw that she had pale brown hair. It was neatly and becomingly dressed. She looked strong and healthy. She was neither fat nor thin. In a proper uniform she would look very presentable. She was not inconveniently handsome, but she was certainly a comely, in another class of life you might almost have said a handsome, woman. He proceeded to ask her a number of questions. Her answers were satisfactory. She had left her last place for an adequate reason. She had been trained under a butler and appeared to be well acquainted with her duties. In her last place she had been head parlour-maid of three, but she did not mind undertaking the work of the flat single-handed. She had valeted a gentleman before who had sent her to a tailor's to learn how to press clothes. She was a little shy, but neither timid nor ill at ease. Richard asked her his questions in his amiable, leisurely way, and she answered them with modest composure. He was considerably impressed. He asked her what references she could give. They seemed extremely satisfactory.

"Now look here," he said, "I'm very much inclined to engage you. But I hate changes, I've had my cook for twelve years: if you suit me and the place suits you I hope you'll stay. I mean, I don't want you to come to me in three or four months and say that you're leaving to get married."

"There's not much fear of that, sir. I'm a widow. I don't believe marriage is much catch for anyone in my position, sir. My husband never did a stroke of work from the day I married him to the day he died, and I had to keep him. What I want now is a good home."

"I'm inclined to agree with you," he smiled. "Marriage is a very good thing, but I think it's a mistake to make a habit of it."

She very properly made no reply to this, but waited for him to announce his decision. She did not seem anxious about it. He reflected that if she was as competent as she appeared she must be well aware that she would have no difficulty in finding a place. He told her what wages he was offering, and these seemed to be satisfactory to her. He gave her the necessary information about the place, but she gave him to understand that she was already apprised of this, and he received the impression, which amused rather than disconcerted him, that she had made certain enquiries about him before applying for the situation. It showed prudence on her part and good sense.

"When would you be able to come in if I engaged you? I haven't got anybody at the moment. The cook's managing as best she can with a char, but I should like to get settled as soon as possible."

"Well, sir, I was going to give myself a week's holiday, but if it's a matter of obliging a gentleman I don't mind giving that up. I could come in tomorrow if it was convenient."

Richard Harenger gave her his attractive smile.

"I shouldn't like you to do without a holiday that I daresay you've been looking forward to. I can very well go on like this for another week. Go and have your holiday and come to me when it's over."

"Thank you very much, sir. Would it do if I came in tomorrow week?"

"Quite well."

When she left, Richard Harenger felt he had done a good day's work. It looked as though he had found exactly what he was after. He rang for the cook and told her he had engaged a house-parlour-maid at last.

"I think you'll like her, sir," she said. "She came in and 'ad a talk with me this afternoon. I could see at once she knew her duties. And she's not one of them flighty ones."

"We can but try, Mrs. Jeddy. I hope you gave me a good character."

"Well, I said you was particular, sir. I said you was a gentleman as liked things just so."

"I admit that."

"She said she didn't mind that. She said she liked a gentleman as knew what was what. She said there's no satisfaction in doing things proper if nobody notices. I expect you'll find she'll take a rare lot of pride in her work."

"That's what I want her to do. I think we might go farther and fare worse."

"Well, sir, there is that to it, of course. And the proof of the pudding's the eating. But if you ask my opinion I think she's going to be a real treasure."

And that is precisely what Pritchard turned out. No man was ever better served. The way she shone shoes was marvellous, and he set out of a fine morning for his walk to the office with a more jaunty step because you could almost see yourself reflected in them. She looked after his clothes with such attention that his colleagues began to chaff him about being the best-dressed man in the Civil Service. One day, coming home unexpectedly, he found a line of socks and handkerchiefs hung up to dry in the bathroom. He called Pritchard.

"D'you wash my socks and handkerchiefs yourself, Pritchard? I should have thought you had enough to do without that."

"They do ruin them so at the laundry, sir. I prefer to do them at home if you have no objection."

She knew exactly what he should wear on every occasion, and without asking him was aware whether she should put out a dinner jacket and a black tie in the evening or a dress coat and a white one. When he was going to a party where decorations were to be worn he found his neat little row of medals automatically affixed to the lapel of his coat. He soon ceased to choose every morning from his wardrobe the tie he wanted, for he found that she put out for him without fail the one he would have himself selected. Her taste was perfect. He supposed she read his letters, for she always knew what his movements were, and if he had forgotten at what hour he had an engagement he had no need to look in his book, for Pritchard could tell him. She knew exactly what tone to use with persons with whom she conversed on the telephone. Except with tradesmen, with whom she was apt to be peremptory, she was always polite, but there was a distinct difference in her manner if she was addressing one of Mr. Harenger's literary friends or the wife of a Cabinet Minister. She knew by instinct with whom he wished to speak and with whom he didn't. From his sitting room he sometimes heard her with placid sincerity assuring a caller that he was out, and then she would come in and tell him that So-and-so had rung up, but she thought he wouldn't wish to be disturbed.

"Quite right, Pritchard," he smiled.

"I knew she only wanted to bother you about that concert," said Pritchard.

His friends made appointments with him through her, and she would tell him what she had done on his return in the evening.

"Mrs. Soames rang up, sir, and asked if you would lunch with her on Thursday, the eighth, but I said you were very sorry but you were lunching with Lady Versinder. Mr. Oakley rang up and asked if you'd go to a cocktail party at the Savoy next Tuesday at six. I said you would if you possibly could, but you might have to go to the dentist's."

"Quite right."

"I thought you could see when the time came, sir."

She kept the flat like a new pin. On one occasion soon after she entered his service, Richard, coming back from a holiday, took out a book from his shelves and at once noticed that it had been dusted. He rang the bell.

"I forgot to tell you, when I went away, under no circumstances ever to touch my books. When books are taken out to be dusted they're never put back in the right place. I don't mind my books being dirty, but I hate not being able to find them."

"I'm very sorry, sir," said Pritchard. "I know some gentlemen are very particular and I took care to put back every book exactly where I took it from."

Richard Harenger gave his books a glance. So far as he could see, every one was in its accustomed place. He smiled.

"I apologize, Pritchard."

"They were in a muck, sir. I mean, you couldn't open one without getting your hands black with dust."

She certainly kept his silver as he had never had it kept before. He felt called upon to give her a special word of praise.

"Most of it's Queen Anne and George I, you know," he explained.

"Yes, I know, sir. When you've got something good like that to look after, it's a pleasure to keep it like it should be."

"You certainly have a knack for it. I never knew a butler who kept his silver as well as you do."

"Men haven't the patience women have," she replied modestly.

As soon as he thought Pritchard had settled down in the place, he resumed the little dinners he was fond of giving once a week. He had already discovered that she knew how to wait at table, but it was with a warm sense of complacency that he realized then how competently she could manage a party. She was quick, silent and watchful. A guest had hardly felt the need of something before Pritchard was at his elbow offering him what he wanted. She soon learned the tastes of his more intimate friends and remembered that one liked water instead of soda with his whisky and that another particularly fancied the knuckle end of a leg of lamb. She knew

exactly how cold a hock should be not to ruin its taste and how long
claret should have stood in the room to bring out its bouquet. It was
a pleasure to see her pour out a bottle of burgundy in such a fashion
as not to disturb the grounds. On one occasion she did not serve the
wine Richard had ordered. He somewhat sharply pointed this out to
her.

"I opened the bottle, sir, and it was slightly corked. So I got the
Chambertin, as I thought it was safer."

"Quite right, Pritchard."

Presently he left this matter entirely in her hands, for he discovered
that she knew perfectly what wines his guests would like. Without
orders from him she would provide the best in his cellar and his
oldest brandy if she thought they were the sort of people who knew
what they were drinking. She had no belief in the palate of women,
and when they were of the party was apt to serve the champagne
which had to be drunk before it went off. She had the English servant's instinctive knowledge of social differences, and neither rank
nor money blinded her to the fact that someone was not a gentleman,
but she had favourites among his friends, and when someone she
particularly liked was dining, with the air of a cat that has swallowed
a canary she would pour out for him a bottle of a wine that Harenger
kept for very special occasions. It amused him.

"You've got on the right side of Pritchard, old boy," he exclaimed.
"There aren't many people she gives this wine to."

Pritchard became an institution. She was known very soon to be
the perfect parlourmaid. People envied Harenger the possession of her
as they envied nothing else that he had. She was worth her weight
in gold. Her price was above rubies. Richard Harenger beamed with
self-complacency when they praised her.

"Good masters make good servants," he said gaily.

One evening, when they were sitting over their port and she had
left the room, they were talking about her.

"It'll be an awful blow when she leaves you."

"Why should she leave me? One or two people have tried to get
her away from me, but she turned them down. She knows where she's
well off."

"She'll get married one of these days."

"I don't think she's that sort."

"She's a good-looking woman."

"Yes, she has quite a decent presence."

"What are you talking about? She's a very handsome creature. In another class of life she'd be a well-known society beauty with her photograph in all the papers."

At that moment Pritchard came in with the coffee. Richard Harenger looked at her. After seeing her every day, off and on, for four years it was now, my word, how time flies, he had really forgotten what she looked like. She did not seem to have changed much since he had first seen her. She was no stouter than then, she still had the high colour, and her regular features bore the same expression which was at once intent and vacuous. The black uniform suited her. She left the room.

"She's a paragon, and there's no doubt about it."

"I know she is," answered Harenger. "She's perfection. I should be lost without her. And the strange thing is that I don't very much like her."

"Why not?"

"I think she bores me a little. You see, she has no conversation. I've often tried to talk to her. She answers when I speak to her, but that's all. In four years she's never volunteered a remark of her own. I know absolutely nothing about her. I don't know if she likes me or if she's completely indifferent to me. She's an automaton. I respect her, I appreciate her, I trust her. She has every quality in the world, and I've often wondered why it is that with all that I'm so completely indifferent to her. I think it must be that she is entirely devoid of charm."

They left it at that.

Two or three days after this, since it was Pritchard's night out and he had no engagement, Richard Harenger dined by himself at his club. A page boy came to him and told him that they had just rung up from his flat to say that he had gone out without his keys and should they be brought along to him in a taxi? He put his hand to his pocket. It was a fact. By a singular chance he had forgotten to place them when he had changed into a blue serge suit before coming out to dinner. His intention had been to play bridge, but it was an off night at the club, and there seemed little chance of a decent game; it occurred to him that it would be a good opportunity to see a picture that he had heard talked about, so he sent back the message by the page that he would call for the keys himself in half an hour.

He rang at the door of his flat, and it was opened by Pritchard. She had the keys in her hand.

"What are you doing here, Pritchard?" he asked. "It's your night out, isn't it?"

"Yes, sir. But I didn't care about going, so I told Mrs. Jeddy she could go instead."

"You ought to get out when you have the chance," he said, with his usual thoughtfulness. "It's not good for you to be cooped up here all the time."

"I get out now and then on an errand, but I haven't been out in the evening for the last month."

"Why on earth not?"

"Well, it's not very cheerful going out by yourself, and somehow I don't know anyone just now that I'm particularly keen on going out with."

"You ought to have a bit of fun now and then. It's good for you."

"I've got out of the habit of it somehow."

"Look here, I'm just going to the cinema. Would you like to come along with me?"

He spoke in kindliness, on the spur of the moment, and the moment he had said the words half regretted them.

"Yes, sir, I'd like to," said Pritchard.

"Run along then and put on a hat."

"I shan't be a minute."

She disappeared, and he went into the sitting room and lit a cigarette. He was a little amused at what he was doing, and pleased, too; it was nice to be able to make someone happy with so little trouble to himself. It was characteristic of Pritchard that she had shown neither surprise nor hesitation. She kept him waiting about five minutes, and when she came back he noticed that she had changed her dress. She wore a blue frock in what he supposed was artificial silk, a small black hat with a blue brooch on it, and a silver fox round her neck. He was a trifle relieved to see that she looked neither shabby nor showy. It would never occur to anyone who happened to see them that this was a distinguished official in the Home Office taking his housemaid to the pictures.

"I'm sorry to have kept you waiting, sir."

"It doesn't matter at all," he said graciously.

He opened the front door for her, and she went out before him. He remembered the familiar anecdote of Louis XIV and the courtier and appreciated the fact that she had not hesitated to precede him. The cinema for which they were bound was at no great distance from Mr. Harenger's flat, and they walked there. He talked about the weather and the state of the roads and Adolf Hitler. Pritchard made suitable replies. They arrived just as Mickey the Mouse was starting, and this put them in a good humour. During the four years she had been in his service Richard Harenger had hardly ever seen Pritchard even smile, and now it diverted him vastly to hear her peal upon peal of joyous laughter. He enjoyed her pleasure. Then the principal attraction was thrown on the screen. It was a good picture, and they both watched it with breathless excitement. Taking his cigarette case out to help himself, he automatically offered it to Pritchard.

"Thank you, sir," she said, taking one.

He lit it for her. Her eyes were on the screen and she was almost unconscious of his action. When the picture was finished they streamed out with the crowd into the street. They walked back towards the flat. It was a fine starry night.

"Did you like it?" he said.

"Like anything, sir. It was a real treat."

A thought occurred to him.

"By the way, did you have any supper tonight?"

"No, sir. I didn't have time."

"Aren't you starving?"

"I'll have a bit of bread and cheese when I get in and I'll make meself a cup of cocoa."

"That sounds rather grim." There was a feeling of gaiety in the air, and the people who poured past them, one way and another, seemed filled with a pleasant elation. In for a penny, in for a pound, he said to himself. "Look here, would you like to come and have a bit of supper with me somewhere?"

"If you'd like to, sir."

"Come on."

He hailed a cab. He was feeling very philanthropic and it was not a feeling that he disliked at all. He told the driver to go to a restaurant in Oxford Street which was gay, but at which he was confident there was no chance of meeting anyone he knew. There was an orchestra, and people danced. It would amuse Pritchard to see them. When they sat down a waiter came up to them.

"They've got a set supper here," he said, thinking that was what she would like. "I suggest we have that. What would you like to drink? A little white wine?"

"What I really fancy is a glass of ginger beer," she said.

Richard Harenger ordered himself a whisky and soda. She ate the supper with hearty appetite, and though Harenger was not hungry, to put her at her ease he ate too. The picture they had just seen gave them something to talk about. It was quite true what they had said the other night, Pritchard was not a bad-looking woman, and even if someone had seen them together he would not have minded. It would make rather a good story for his friends when he told them how he had taken the incomparable Pritchard to the cinema and then afterwards to supper. Pritchard was looking at the dancers with a faint smile on her lips.

"Do you like dancing?" he said.

"I used to be a rare one for it when I was a girl. I never danced much after I was married. My husband was a bit shorter than me, and somehow I never think it looks well unless the gentleman's taller, if you know what I mean. I suppose I shall be getting too old for it soon."

Richard was certainly taller than his parlourmaid. They would look all right. He was fond of dancing and he danced well. But he hesitated. He did not want to embarrass Pritchard by asking her to dance with him. It was better not to go too far perhaps. And yet what did it matter? It was a drab life she led. She was so sensible, if she thought it a mistake he was pretty sure she would find a decent excuse.

"Would you like to take a turn, Pritchard?" he said, as the band struck up again.

"I'm terribly out of practice, sir."

"What does that matter?"

"If you don't mind, sir," she answered coolly, rising from her seat.

She was not in the least shy. She was only afraid that she would not be able to follow his step. They moved on to the floor. He found she danced very well.

"Why, you dance perfectly, Pritchard," he said.

"It's coming back to me."

Although she was a big woman, she was light on her feet, and she had a natural sense of rhythm. She was very pleasant to dance with. He gave a glance at the mirrors that lined the walls, and he could not help reflecting that they looked very well together. Their eyes met in the mirror; he wondered whether she was thinking that, too. They had two more dances, and then Richard Harenger suggested that they should go. He paid the bill and they walked out. He noticed that she threaded her way through the crowd without a trace of self-consciousness. They got into a taxi and in ten minutes were at home.

"I'll go up the back way, sir," said Pritchard.

"There's no need to do that. Come up in the lift with me."

He took her up, giving the night porter an icy glance, so that he should not think it strange that he came back at that somewhat late hour with his parlourmaid, and with his latchkey let her into the flat.

"Well, good night, sir," she said. "Thank you very much. It's been a real treat for me."

"Thank *you*, Pritchard. I should have had a very dull evening by myself. I hope you've enjoyed your outing."

"That I have, sir, more than I can say."

It had been a success. Richard Harenger was satisfied with himself. It was a kindly thing for him to have done. It was a very agreeable sensation to give anyone so much real pleasure. His benevolence warmed him and for a moment he felt a great love in his heart for the whole human race.

"Good night, Pritchard," he said, and because he felt happy and good he put his arm round her waist and kissed her on the lips.

Her lips were very soft. They lingered on his, and she returned his kiss. It was the warm, hearty embrace of a healthy woman in the prime of life. He found it very pleasant, and he held her to him a little more closely. She put her arms round his neck.

As a general rule he did not wake till Pritchard came in with his letters, but next morning he woke at half past seven. He had a curious sensation that he did not recognize. He was accustomed to sleep with two pillows under his head, and he suddenly grew aware of the fact that he had only one. Then he remembered and with a start looked round. The other pillow was beside his own. Thank God, no sleeping head rested there, but it was plain that one had. His heart sank. He broke out into a cold sweat.

"My God, what a fool I've been!" he cried out loud.

How could he have done anything so stupid? What on earth had come over him? He was the last man to play about with servant girls. What a disgraceful thing to do! At his age and in his position. He had not heard Pritchard slip away. He must have been asleep. It wasn't even as if he'd liked her very much. She wasn't his type. And as he had said the other night, she rather bored him. Even now he only knew her as Pritchard. He had no notion what her first name was. What madness! And what was to happen now? The position was impossible. It was obvious he couldn't keep her, and yet to send her away for what was his fault as much as hers seemed shockingly unfair. How idiotic to lose the best parlourmaid a man ever had just for an hour's folly!

"It's that damned kindness of heart of mine," he groaned.

He would never find anyone else to look after his clothes so admirably or clean the silver so well. She knew all his friends' telephone numbers, and she understood wine. But of course she must go. She must see for herself that after what had happened things could never be the same. He would make her a handsome present and give her an excellent reference. At any minute she would be coming in now. Would she be arch, would she be familiar? Or would she put on airs? Perhaps even she wouldn't trouble to come in with his letters. It would be awful if he had to ring the bell and Mrs. Jeddy came in and said: "Pritchard's not up yet, sir, she's having a lie in after last night."

"What a fool I've been! What a contemptible cad!"

There was a knock at the door. He was sick with anxiety.

"Come in."

Richard Harenger was a very unhappy man.

Pritchard came in as the clock struck. She wore the print dress she was in the habit of wearing during the early part of the day.

"Good morning, sir," she said.

"Good morning."

She drew the curtains and handed him his letters and the papers. Her face was impassive. She looked exactly as she always looked. Her movements had the same competent deliberation that they always had. She neither avoided Richard's glance nor sought it.

"Will you wear your grey, sir? It came back from the tailor's yesterday."

"Yes."

He pretended to read his letters, but he watched her from under his eyelashes. Her back was turned to him. She took his vest and drawers and folded them over a chair. She took the studs out of the shirt he had worn the day before and studded a clean one. She put out some clean socks for him and placed them on the seat of a chair with the suspenders to match by the side. Then she put out his grey suit and attached the braces to the back buttons of the trousers. She opened his wardrobe and after a moment's reflection chose a tie to go with the suit. She collected on her arm the suit of the day before and picked up the shoes.

"Will you have breakfast now, sir, or will you have your bath first?"

"I'll have breakfast now," he said.

"Very good, sir."

With her slow quiet movements, unruffled, she left the room. Her face bore that rather serious, deferential, vacuous look it always bore. What had happened might have been a dream. Nothing in Pritchard's

demeanour suggested that she had the smallest recollection of the
night before. He gave a sigh of relief. It was going to be all right. She
need not go, she need not go. Pritchard was the perfect parlourmaid.
He knew that never by word nor gesture would she ever refer to the
fact that for a moment their relations had been other than those of
master and servant. Richard Harenger was a very happy man.

The Facts of Life

BY

W. SOMERSET MAUGHAM

IT WAS Henry Garnet's habit on leaving the city of an afternoon to
drop in at his club and play bridge before going home to dinner. He
was a pleasant man to play with. He knew the game well, and you
could be sure that he would make the best of his cards. He was a good
loser; and when he won was more inclined to ascribe his success to
his luck than to his skill. He was indulgent, and if his partner made
a mistake, could be trusted to find an excuse for him. It was surprising
then on this occasion to hear him telling his partner with unnecessary
sharpness that he had never seen a hand worse played; and it was
more surprising still to see him not only make a grave error himself,
an error of which you would never have thought him capable, but
when his partner, not unwilling to get a little of his own back, pointed
it out, insist against all reason and with considerable heat that he was
perfectly right. But they were all old friends, the men he was playing
with, and none of them took his ill humour very seriously. Henry
Garnet was a broker, a partner in a firm of repute, and it occurred to
one of them that something had gone wrong with some stock he was
interested in.

"How's the market today?" he asked.

"Booming. Even the suckers are making money."

It was evident that stocks and shares had nothing to do with Henry
Garnet's vexation; but something was the matter; that was evident,
too. He was a hearty fellow who enjoyed excellent health; he had
plenty of money; he was fond of his wife and devoted to his children.
As a rule he had high spirits, and he laughed easily at the nonsense
they were apt to talk while they played; but today he sat glum and

silent. His brows were crossly puckered, and there was a sulky look about his mouth. Presently, to ease the tension, one of the others mentioned a subject upon which they all knew Henry Garnet was glad to speak.

"How's your boy, Henry? I see he's done pretty well in the tournament."

Henry Garnet's frown grew darker.

"He's done no better than I expected him to."

"When does he come back from Monte?"

"He got back last night."

"Did he enjoy himself?"

"I suppose so; all I know is that he made a damned fool of himself."

"Oh. How?"

"I'd rather not talk about it if you don't mind."

The three men looked at him with curiosity. Henry Garnet scowled at the green baize.

"Sorry, old boy. Your call."

The game proceeded in a strained silence. Garnet got his bid, and when he played his cards so badly that he went three down not a word was said. Another rubber was begun, and in the second game Garnet denied a suit.

"Having none?" his partner asked him.

Garnet's irritability was such that he did not even reply, and when at the end of the hand it appeared that he had revoked, and that his revoke cost the rubber, it was not to be expected that his partner should let his carelessness go without remark.

"What the devil's the matter with you, Henry?" he said. "You're playing like a fool."

Garnet was disconcerted. He did not so much mind losing a big rubber himself, but he was sore that his inattention should have made his partner lose too. He pulled himself together.

"I'd better not play any more. I thought a few rubbers would calm me, but the fact is I can't give my mind to the game. To tell you the truth I'm in a hell of a temper."

They all burst out laughing.

"You don't have to tell us that, old boy. It's obvious."

Garnet gave them a rueful smile.

"Well, I bet you'd be in a temper if what's happened to me had happened to you. As a matter of fact I'm in a damned awkward situation, and if any of you fellows can give me any advice how to deal with it I'd be grateful."

"Let's have a drink and you tell us all about it. With a K.C., a Home Office official and an eminent surgeon—if we can't tell you how to deal with a situation, nobody can."

The K.C. got up and rang the bell for a waiter.

"It's about that damned boy of mine," said Henry Garnet.

Drinks were ordered and brought. And this is the story that Henry Garnet told them.

The boy of whom he spoke was his only son. His name was Nicholas, and of course he was called Nicky. He was eighteen. The Garnets had two daughters besides, one of sixteen and the other of twelve, but however unreasonable it seemed, for a father is generally supposed to like his daughters best, and though he did all he could not to show his preference, there was no doubt that the greater share of Henry Garnet's affection was given to his son. He was kind, in a chafing, casual way, to his daughters, and gave them handsome presents on their birthdays and at Christmas; but he doted on Nicky. Nothing was too good for him. He thought the world of him. He could hardly take his eyes off him. You could not blame him, for Nicky was a son that any parent might have been proud of. He was six foot two, lithe but muscular, with broad shoulders and a slim waist, and he held himself gallantly erect; he had a charming head, well placed on the shoulders, with pale brown hair that waved slightly, blue eyes with long dark lashes under well-marked eyebrows, a full red mouth and a tanned, clean skin. When he smiled he showed very regular and very white teeth. He was not shy, but there was a modesty in his demeanour that was attractive. In social intercourse he was easy, polite and quietly gay. He was the offspring of nice, healthy, decent parents, he had been well brought up in a good home, he had been sent to a good school, and the general result was as engaging a specimen of young manhood as you were likely to find in a long time. You felt that he was as honest, open and virtuous as he looked. He had never given his parents a moment's uneasiness. As a child he was seldom ill and never naughty. As a boy he did everything that was expected of him. His school reports were excellent. He was wonderfully popular, and he ended his career, with a creditable number of prizes, as head of the school and captain of the football team. But this was not all. At the age of fourteen Nicky had developed an unexpected gift for lawn tennis. This was a game that his father not only was fond of, but played very well, and when he discerned in the boy the promise of a tennis player he fostered it. During the holidays he had him taught by the best professionals, and by the time he was sixteen he had won a number of tournaments for boys of his age. He could beat his father so badly that only parental affection reconciled the older player to the poor show he put up. At eighteen Nicky went to Cambridge and Henry Garnet conceived the ambition that before he was through with the university he should play for it. Nicky had all the qualifications for becoming a great tennis player. He was tall, he had a long reach, he was quick on his feet and his timing was perfect. He realized instinctively where the ball was coming and, seemingly without hurry, was there to take it. He had a powerful serve, with a nasty break that made it difficult to return, and his forehand drive, low, long and accurate, was deadly. He was not so good on the backhand and his volleying was wild, but all through the summer before he went to Cambridge Henry Garnet made him work on these points under the best teacher in England. At the back of his mind, though he did not even mention it to Nicky, he cherished a further ambition, to see his son play at Wimbledon, and who could tell, perhaps be chosen to represent his country in the Davis Cup. A great lump came into Henry Garnet's throat as he saw in fancy his son leap over the net to shake hands with the American champion whom he had just defeated, and walk off the court to the deafening plaudits of the multitude.

As an assiduous frequenter of Wimbledon, Henry Garnet had a good many friends in the tennis world, and one evening he found himself at a city dinner sitting next to one of them, a Colonel Brabazon, and in due course began talking to him of Nicky and what chance there might be of his being chosen to play for his university during the following season.

"Why don't you let him go down to Monte Carlo and play in the spring tournament there?" said the Colonel suddenly.

"Oh, I don't think he's good enough for that. He's not nineteen yet, he only went up to Cambridge last October; he wouldn't stand a chance against all those cracks."

"Of course, Austin and Von Cramm and so on would knock spots off him, but he might snatch a game or two; and if he got up against some of the smaller fry there's no reason why he shouldn't win two or three matches. He's never been up against any of the first-rate players, and it would be wonderful practice for him. He'd learn a lot more than he'll ever learn in the seaside tournaments you enter him for."

"I wouldn't dream of it. I'm not going to let him leave Cambridge in the middle of a term. I've always impressed upon him that tennis is only a game and it mustn't interfere with work."

Colonel Brabazon asked Garnet when the term ended.

"That's all right. He'd only have to cut about three days. Surely that could be arranged. You see, two of the men we were depending on have let us down, and we're in a hole. We want to send as good a team as we can. The Germans are sending their best players, and so are the Americans."

"Nothing doing, old boy. In the first place Nicky's not good enough, and secondly, I don't fancy the idea of sending a kid like that to Monte Carlo without anyone to look after him. If I could get away myself I might think of it, but that's out of the question."

"I shall be there. I'm going as the nonplaying captain of the English team. I'll keep an eye on him."

"You'll be busy, and besides, it's not a responsibility I'd like to ask you to take. He's never been abroad in his life, and to tell you the truth, I shouldn't have a moment's peace all the time he was there."

They left it at that, and presently Henry Garnet went home. He was so flattered by Colonel Brabazon's suggestion that he could not help telling his wife.

"Fancy his thinking Nicky's as good as that. He told me he'd seen him play and his style was fine. He only wants more practice to get into the first flight. We shall see the kid playing in the semifinals at Wimbledon yet, old girl."

To his surprise Mrs. Garnet was not so much opposed to the notion as he would have expected.

"After all the boy's eighteen. Nicky's never got into mischief yet, and there's no reason to suppose he will now."

"There's his work to be considered; don't forget that. I think it would be a very bad precedent to let him cut the end of term."

"But what can three days matter? It seems a shame to rob him of a chance like that. I'm sure he'd jump at it if you asked him."

"Well, I'm not going to. I haven't sent him to Cambridge just to play tennis. I know he's steady, but it's silly to put temptation in his way. He's much too young to go to Monte Carlo by himself."

"You say he won't have a chance against these crack players, but you can't tell."

Henry Garnet sighed a little. On the way home in the car it had struck him that Austin's health was uncertain and that Von Cramm had his off days. Supposing, just for the sake of argument, that Nicky had a bit of luck like that—then there would be no doubt that he would be chosen to play for Cambridge. But of course that was all nonsense.

"Nothing doing, my dear. I've made up my mind, and I'm not going to change it."

Mrs. Garnet held her peace. But next day she wrote to Nicky, telling him what had happened, and suggested to him what she would do in his place if, wanting to go, he wished to get his father's consent. A day or two later Henry Garnet received a letter from his son. He was bubbling over with excitement. He had seen his tutor, who was a tennis player himself, and the Provost of his college, who happened to know Colonel Brabazon, and no objection would be made to his leaving before the end of term; they both thought it an opportunity that shouldn't be missed. He didn't see what harm he could come to, and if only, just this once, his father would stretch a point, well, next term, he promised faithfully, he'd work like blazes. It was a very pretty letter. Mrs. Garnet watched her husband read it at the breakfast table; she was undisturbed by the frown on his face. He threw it over to her.

"I don't know why you thought it necessary to tell Nicky something

I told you in confidence. It's too bad of you. Now you've thoroughly unsettled him."

"I'm so sorry. I thought it would please him to know that Colonel Brabazon had such a high opinion of him. I don't see why one should only tell people the disagreeable things that are said about them. Of course I made it quite clear that there could be no question of his going."

"You've put me in an odious position. If there's anything I hate it's for the boy to look upon me as a spoilsport and a tyrant."

"Oh, he'll never do that. He may think you rather silly and unreasonable, but I'm sure he'll understand that it's only for his own good that you're being so unkind."

"Christ," said Henry Garnet.

His wife had a great inclination to laugh. She knew the battle was won. Dear, oh dear, how easy it was to get men to do what you wanted. For appearance' sake Henry Garnet held out for forty-eight hours, but then he yielded, and a fortnight later Nicky came to London. He was to start for Monte Carlo next morning, and after dinner, when Mrs. Garnet and her elder daughter had left them, Henry took the opportunity to give his son some good advice.

"I don't feel quite comfortable about letting you go off to a place like Monte Carlo at your age practically by yourself," he finished, "but there it is, and I can only hope you'll be sensible. I don't want to play the heavy father, but there are three things especially that I want to warn you against: one is gambling, don't gamble; the second is money, don't lend anyone money; and the third is women, don't have anything to do with women. If you don't do any of those three things you can't come to much harm, so remember them well."

"All right, Father," Nicky smiled.

"That's my last word to you. I know the world pretty well, and believe me, my advice is sound."

"I won't forget it. I promise you."

"That's a good chap. Now let's go up and join the ladies."

Nicky beat neither Austin nor Von Cramm in the Monte Carlo tournament, but he did not disgrace himself. He snatched an unexpected victory over a Spanish player and gave one of the Austrians a closer match than anyone had thought possible. In the mixed doubles he got into the semifinals. His charm conquered everyone, and he vastly enjoyed himself. It was generally allowed that he showed promise, and Colonel Brabazon told him that when he was a little older and had had more practice with first-class players he would be a credit to his father. The tournament came to an end, and the day following he was to fly back to London. Anxious to play his best, he had lived very carefully, smoking little and drinking nothing, and going to bed early; but on his last evening he thought he would like to see something of the life in Monte Carlo of which he had heard so much. An official dinner was given to the tennis players, and after dinner with the rest of them he went into the Sporting Club. It was the first time he had been there. Monte Carlo was very full, and the rooms were crowded. Nicky had never before seen roulette played except in the pictures; in a maze he stopped at the first table he came to; chips of different sizes were scattered over the green cloth in what looked like a hopeless muddle; the croupier gave the wheel a sharp turn and with a flick threw in the little white ball. After what seemed an endless time the ball stopped and another croupier with a broad, indifferent gesture raked in the chips of those who had lost.

Presently Nicky wandered over to where they were playing *trente et quarante,* but he couldn't understand what it was all about, and he thought it dull. He saw a crowd in another room and sauntered in. A big game of baccara was in progress, and he was immediately conscious of the tension. The players were protected from the thronging bystanders by a brass rail; they sat round the table, nine on each side, with the dealer in the middle and the croupier facing him. Big money was changing hands. The dealer was a member of the Greek Syndicate. Nicky looked at his impassive face. His eyes were watchful, but his expression never changed whether he won or lost. It was a terrifying, strangely impressive sight. It gave Nicky, who had been thriftily brought up, a peculiar thrill to see someone risk a thousand pounds on the turn of a card and when he lost make a little joke and laugh. It was all terribly exciting. An acquaintance came up to him.

"Been doing any good?" he asked.

"I haven't been playing."

"Wise of you. Rotten game. Come and have a drink."

"All right."

While they were having it Nicky told his friend that this was the first time he had ever been in the rooms.

"Oh, but you must have one little flutter before you go. It's idiotic to leave Monte without having tried your luck. After all it won't hurt you to lose a hundred francs or so."

"I don't suppose it will, but my father wasn't any too keen on my coming at all, and one of the three things he particularly advised me not to do was to gamble."

But when Nicky left his companion he strolled back to one of the tables where they were playing roulette. He stood for a while looking at the losers' money being raked in by the croupier and the money that was won paid out to the winners. It was impossible to deny that it was thrilling. His friend was right, it did seem silly to leave Monte without putting something on the table just once. It would be an experience, and at his age you had to have all the experience you could get. He reflected that he hadn't promised his father not to gamble, he'd promised him not to forget his advice. It wasn't quite the same, was it? He took a hundred-franc note out of his pocket and rather shyly put it on number eighteen. He chose it because that was his age. With a wildly beating heart he watched the wheel turn; the little white ball whizzed about like a small demon of mischief; the wheel went round more slowly, the little white ball hesitated, it seemed about to stop, it went on again; Nicky could hardly believe his eyes when it fell into number eighteen. A lot of chips were passed over to him, and his hands trembled as he took them. It seemed to amount to a lot of money. He was so confused that he never thought of putting anything on the following round; in fact he had no intention of playing any more, once was enough; and he was surprised when eighteen again came up. There was only one chip on it.

"By George, you've won again," said a man who was standing near to him.

"Me? I hadn't got anything on."

"Yes, you had. Your original stake. They always leave it on unless you ask for it back. Didn't you know?"

Another packet of chips was handed over to him. Nicky's head reeled. He counted his gains: seven thousand francs. A queer sense of power seized him; he felt wonderfully clever. This was the easiest way of making money that he had ever heard of. His frank, charming face was wreathed in smiles. His bright eyes met those of a woman standing by his side. She smiled.

"You're in luck," she said.

She spoke English, but with a foreign accent.

"I can hardly believe it. It's the first time I've ever played."

"That explains it. Lend me a thousand francs, will you? I've lost everything I've got. I'll give it you back in half an hour."

"All right."

She took a large red chip from his pile and with a word of thanks disappeared. The man who had spoken to him before grunted.

"You'll never see that again."

Nicky was dashed. His father had particularly advised him not to lend anyone money. What a silly thing to do! And to somebody he'd never seen in his life. But the fact was, he felt at that moment such a love for the human race that it had never occurred to him to refuse. And that big red chip, it was almost impossible to realize that it had any value. Oh, well, it didn't matter, he still had six thousand francs, he'd just try his luck once or twice more, and if he didn't win he'd go home. He put a chip on sixteen, which was his elder sister's age, but it didn't come up; then on twelve, which was his younger sister's, and that didn't come up either; he tried various numbers at random, but without success. It was funny, he seemed to have lost his knack. He thought he would try just once more and then stop; he won. He made up all his losses and had something over. At the end of an hour, after various ups and downs, having experienced such thrills as he had never known in his life, he found himself with so many chips that they would hardly go in his pockets. He decided to go. He went to the changers' office, and he gasped when twenty thousand-franc notes were spread out before him. He had never had so much money in his life. He put it in his pocket and was turning away when the woman to whom he had lent the thousand francs came up to him.

"I've been looking for you everywhere," she said. "I was afraid you'd gone. I was in a fever, I didn't know what you'd think of me. Here's your thousand francs and thank you so much for the loan."

Nicky, blushing scarlet, stared at her with amazement. How he had misjudged her! His father had said, don't gamble; well, he had, and he'd made twenty thousand francs; and his father had said, don't lend anyone money; well, he had, he'd lent quite a lot to a total stranger, and she'd returned it. The fact was that he wasn't nearly such a fool as his father thought: he'd had an instinct that he could lend her the money with safety, and you see, his instinct was right. But he was so obviously taken aback that the little lady was forced to laugh.

"What is the matter with you?" she asked.

"To tell you the truth I never expected to see the money back."

"What did you take me for? Did you think I was a—cocotte?"

Nicky reddened to the roots of his wavy hair.

"No, of course not."

"Do I look like one?"

"Not a bit."

She was dressed very quietly, in black, with a string of gold beads round her neck; her simple frock showed off a neat, slight figure; she had a pretty little face and a trim head. She was made up, but not excessively, and Nicky supposed that she was not more than three or four years older than himself. She gave him a friendly smile.

"My husband is in the administration in Morocco, and I've come to Monte Carlo for a few weeks because he thought I wanted a change."

"I was just going," said Nicky because he couldn't think of anything else to say.

"Already!"

"Well, I've got to get up early tomorrow. I'm going back to London by air."

"Of course. The tournament ended today, didn't it? I saw you play, you know, two or three times."

"Did you? I don't know why you should have noticed me."

"You've got a beautiful style. And you looked very sweet in your shorts."

Nicky was not an immodest youth, but it did cross his mind that

perhaps she had borrowed that thousand francs in order to scrape acquaintance with him.

"Do you ever go to the Knickerbocker?" she asked.

"No. I never have."

"Oh, but you mustn't leave Monte without having been there. Why
don't you come and dance a little? To tell you the truth, I'm starving
with hunger, and I should adore some bacon and eggs."

Nicky remembered his father's advice not to have anything to do
with women, but this was different; you had only to look at the pretty
little thing to know at once that she was perfectly respectable. Her husband was in what corresponded, he supposed, to the civil service. His
father and mother had friends who were civil servants, and they and
their wives sometimes came to dinner. It was true that the wives were
neither so young nor so pretty as this one, but she was just as ladylike
as they were. And after winning twenty thousand francs he thought it
wouldn't be a bad idea to have a little fun.

"I'd love to go with you," he said. "But you won't mind if I don't
stay very long. I've left instructions at my hotel that I'm to be called
at seven."

"We'll leave as soon as ever you like."

Nicky found it very pleasant at the Knickerbocker. He ate his bacon
and eggs with appetite. They shared a bottle of champagne. They
danced, and the little lady told him he danced beautifully. He knew he
danced pretty well, and of course she was easy to dance with. As light
as a feather. She laid her cheek against his and when their eyes met
there was in hers a smile that made his heart go pit-a-pat. A coloured
woman sang in a throaty, sensual voice. The floor was crowded.

"Have you ever been told that you're very good-looking?" she asked.

"I don't think so," he laughed. "Gosh," he thought, "I believe she's
fallen for me."

Nicky was not such a fool as to be unaware that women often liked
him, and when she made that remark he pressed her to him a little
more closely. She closed her eyes, and a faint sigh escaped her lips.

"I suppose it wouldn't be quite nice if I kissed you before all these
people," he said.

"What do you think they would take me for?"

It began to grow late, and Nicky said that really he thought he ought to be going.

"I shall go too," she said. "Will you drop me at my hotel on your way?"

Nicky paid the bill. He was rather surprised at its amount, but with all that money he had in his pocket he could afford not to care, and they got into a taxi. She snuggled up to him, and he kissed her. She seemed to like it.

"By Jove," he thought, "I wonder if there's anything doing."

It was true that she was a married woman, but her husband was in Morocco, and it certainly did look as if she'd fallen for him. Good and proper. It was true also that his father had warned him to have nothing to do with women, but, he reflected again, he hadn't actually promised he wouldn't, he'd only promised not to forget his advice. Well, he hadn't; he was bearing it in mind that very minute. But circumstances alter cases. She was a sweet little thing; it seemed silly to miss the chance of an adventure when it was handed to you like that on a tray. When they reached the hotel he paid off the taxi.

"I'll walk home," he said. "The air will do me good after the stuffy atmosphere of that place."

"Come up a moment," she said. "I'd like to show you the photo of my little boy."

"Oh, have you got a little boy?" he exclaimed, a trifle dashed.

"Yes, a sweet little boy."

He walked upstairs after her. He didn't in the least want to see the photograph of her little boy, but he thought it only civil to pretend he did. He was afraid he'd made a fool of himself; it occurred to him that she was taking him up to look at the photograph in order to show him in a nice way that he'd made a mistake. He'd told her he was eighteen.

"I suppose she thinks I'm just a kid."

He began to wish he hadn't spent all that money on champagne at the night club.

But she didn't show him the photograph of her little boy after all. They had no sooner got into her room than she turned to him, flung her arms round his neck, and kissed him full on the lips. He had never in all his life been kissed so passionately.

"Darling," she said.

For a brief moment his father's advice once more crossed Nicky s mind, and then he forgot it.

Nicky was a light sleeper, and the least sound was apt to wake him. Two or three hours later he awoke and for a moment could not imagine where he was. The room was not quite dark, for the door of the bathroom was ajar, and the light in it had been left on. Suddenly he was conscious that someone was moving about the room. Then he remembered. He saw that it was his little friend, and he was on the point of speaking when something in the way she was behaving stopped him. She was walking very cautiously, as though she were afraid of waking him; she stopped once or twice and looked over at the bed. He wondered what she was after. He soon saw. She went over to the chair on which he had placed his clothes and once more looked in his direction. She waited for what seemed to him an interminable time. The silence was so intense that Nicky thought he could hear his own heart beating. Then, very slowly, very quietly, she took up his coat, slipped her hand into the inside pocket and drew out all those beautiful thousand-franc notes that Nicky had been so proud to win. She put the coat back and placed some other clothes on it so that it should look as though it had not been disturbed, then, with the bundle of notes in her hand, for an appreciable time stood once more stock-still. Nicky had repressed an instinctive impulse to jump up and grab her; it was partly surprise that had kept him quiet, partly the notion that he was in a strange hotel, in a foreign country, and if he made a row he didn't know what might happen. She looked at him. His eyes were partly closed, and he was sure that she thought he was asleep. In the silence she could hardly fail to hear his regular breathing. When she had reassured herself that her movements had not disturbed him, she stepped, with infinite caution, across the room. On a small table in the window a cineraria was growing in a pot. Nicky watched her now with his eyes wide open. The plant was evidently placed quite loosely in the pot, for, taking it by the stalks, she lifted it out; she put the bank notes in the bottom of the pot and replaced the plant. It was an excellent hiding place. No one could have guessed that anything was concealed under that richly flowering plant. She pressed the earth down with her fingers and then, very slowly, taking care not to make the smallest noise, crept across the room and slipped back into bed.

"Chéri," she said, in a caressing voice.

Nicky breathed steadily, like a man immersed in deep sleep. The little lady turned over on her side and disposed herself to slumber. But though Nicky lay so still, his thoughts worked busily. He was extremely indignant at the scene he had just witnessed, and to himself he spoke his thoughts with vigour.

"She's nothing but a damned tart. She and her dear little boy and her husband in Morocco. My eye! She's a rotten thief, that's what she is. Took me for a mug. If she thinks she's going to get away with anything like that, she's mistaken."

He had already made up his mind what he was going to do with the money he had so cleverly won. He had long wanted a car of his own and had thought it rather mean of his father not to have given him one. After all, a feller doesn't always want to drive about in the family bus. Well, he'd just teach the old man a lesson and buy one himself. For twenty thousand francs, two hundred pounds roughly, he could get a very decent second-hand car. He meant to get the money back, but just then he didn't quite know how. He didn't like the idea of kicking up a row, he was a stranger, in a hotel he knew nothing of; it might very well be that the beastly woman had friends there; he didn't mind facing anyone in a fair fight, but he'd look pretty foolish if someone pulled a gun on him. He reflected besides, very sensibly, that he had no proof the money was his. If it came to a showdown and she swore it was hers, he might very easily find himself hauled off to a police station. He really didn't know what to do. Presently by her regular breathing he knew that the little lady was asleep. She must have fallen asleep with an easy mind, for she had done her job without a hitch. It infuriated Nicky that she should rest so peacefully while he lay awake, worried to death. Suddenly an idea occurred to him. It was such a good one that it was only by the exercise of all his self-control that he prevented himself from jumping out of bed and carrying it out at once. Two could play at her game. She'd stolen his money; well, he'd steal it back again, and they'd be all square. He made up his mind to wait quite quietly until he was sure that deceitful woman was sound asleep. He waited for what seemed to him a very long time. She did not stir. Her breathing was as regular as a child's.

"Darling," he said at last.

No answer. No movement. She was dead to the world. Very slowly, pausing after every movement, very silently, he slipped out of bed. He stood still for a while, looking at her to see whether he had disturbed her. Her breathing was as regular as before. During the time he was waiting he had taken note carefully of the furniture in the room so that in crossing it he should not knock against a chair or a table and make a noise. He took a couple of steps and waited; he took a couple of steps more; he was very light on his feet and made no sound as he walked; he took fully five minutes to get to the window, and here he waited again. He started, for the bed slightly creaked, but it was only because the sleeper turned in her sleep. He forced himself to wait till he had counted one hundred. She was sleeping like a log. With infinite care he seized the cineraria by the stalks and gently pulled it out of the pot; he put his other hand in, his heart beat nineteen to the dozen as his fingers touched the notes, his hand closed on them and he slowly drew them out. He replaced the plant and in his turn carefully pressed down the earth. While he was doing all this he had kept one eye on the form lying in the bed. It remained still. After another pause he crept softly to the chair on which his clothes were lying. He first put the bundle of notes in his coat pocket and then proceeded to dress. It took him a good quarter of an hour, because he could afford to make no sound. He had been wearing a soft shirt with his dinner jacket, and he congratulated himself on this because it was easier to put on silently than a stiff one. He had some difficulty in tying his tie without a looking glass, but he very wisely reflected that it didn't really matter if it wasn't tied very well. His spirits were rising. The whole thing now began to seem rather a lark. At length he was completely dressed except for his shoes, which he took in his hand; he thought he would put them on when he got into the passage. Now he had to cross the room to get to the door. He reached it so quietly that he could not have disturbed the lightest sleeper. But the door had to be unlocked. He turned the key very slowly; it creaked.

"Who's that?"

The little woman suddenly sat up in bed. Nicky's heart jumped to his mouth. He made a great effort to keep his head.

"It's only me. It's six o'clock and I've got to go. I was trying not to wake you."

"Oh, I forgot."

She sank back onto the pillow.

"Now that you're awake I'll put on my shoes."

He sat down on the edge of the bed and did this.

"Don't make a noise when you go out. The hotel people don't like it. Oh, I'm so sleepy."

"You go right off to sleep again."

"Kiss me before you go." He bent down and kissed her. "You're a sweet boy and a wonderful lover. *Bon voyage.*"

Nicky did not feel quite safe till he got out of the hotel. The dawn had broken. The sky was unclouded, and in the harbour the yachts and the fishing boats lay motionless on the still water. On the quay fishermen were getting ready to start on their day's work. The streets were deserted. Nicky took a long breath of the sweet morning air. He felt alert and well. He also felt as pleased as Punch. With a swinging stride, his shoulders well thrown back, he walked up the hill and along the gardens in front of the Casino—the flowers in that clear light had a dewy brilliance that was delicious—till he came to his hotel. Here the day had already begun. In the hall porters with mufflers round their necks and berets on their heads were busy sweeping. Nicky went up to his room and had a hot bath. He lay in it and thought with satisfaction that he was not such a mug as some people might think. After his bath he did his exercises, dressed, packed and went down to breakfast. He had a grand appetite. No continental breakfast for him! He had grapefruit, porridge, bacon and eggs, rolls fresh from the oven, so crisp and delicious they melted in your mouth, marmalade and three cups of coffee. Though feeling perfectly well before, he felt better after that. He lit the pipe he had recently learnt to smoke, paid his bill and stepped into the car that was waiting to take him to the aerodrome on the other side of Cannes. The road as far as Nice ran over the hills, and below him was the blue sea and the coast line. He couldn't help thinking it damned pretty. They passed through Nice, so gay and friendly in the early morning, and presently they came to a long stretch of straight road that ran by the sea. Nicky had paid his bill, not with the money he had won the night before, but with the money his father had given him; he had changed a thousand francs to pay for supper at the Knickerbocker, but that deceitful little woman had returned him the thousand francs he had lent her, so that he still had twenty thousand-franc notes in his pocket. He thought he would like to have a look at them. He had so nearly lost them that they had a double value for him. He took them out of his hip pocket into which for safety's sake he had stuffed them when he put on the suit he was travelling in, and counted them one by one. Something very strange had happened to them. Instead of there being twenty notes, as there should have been, there were twenty-six. He couldn't understand it at all. He counted them twice more. There was no doubt about it; somehow or other he had twenty-six thousand francs instead of the twenty he should have had. He couldn't make it out. He asked himself if it was possible that he had won more at the Sporting Club than he had realized. But no, that was out of the question; he distinctly remembered the man at the desk laying the notes out in four rows of five, and he had counted them himself. Suddenly the explanation occurred to him; when he had put his hand into the flower pot, after taking out the cineraria, he had grabbed everything he felt there. The flower pot was the little hussy's money box, and he had taken out not only his own money, but her savings as well. Nicky leant back in the car and burst into a roar of laughter. It was the funniest thing he had ever heard in his life. And when he thought of her going to the flower pot sometime later in the morning when she awoke, expecting to find the money she had so cleverly got away with, and finding, not only that it wasn't there, but that her own had gone too, he laughed more than ever. And so far as he was concerned there was nothing to do about it, he knew neither her name nor the name of the hotel to which she had taken him. He couldn't return her money even if he wanted to.

"It serves her damned well right," he said.

This then was the story that Henry Garnet told his friends over the bridge table, for the night before, after dinner when his wife and daughter had left them to their port, Nicky had narrated it in full.

"And you know what infuriated me is that he's so damned pleased with himself. Talk of a cat swallowing a canary. And d'you know what he said to me when he'd finished? He looked at me with those innocent eyes of his and said: 'You know, Father, I can't help thinking there was something wrong about the advice you gave me. You said, don't gamble; well, I did, and I made a packet; you said, don't lend money; well, I did, and I got it back; and you said, don't have anything to do with women; well, I did, and I made six thousand francs on the deal.'"

It didn't make it any better for Henry Garnet that his three companions burst out laughing.

"It's all very well for you fellows to laugh, but you know, I'm in a damned awkward position. The boy looked up to me, he respected me, he took whatever I said as gospel truth, and now, I saw it in his eyes, he just looks upon me as a drivelling old fool. It's no good my saying one swallow doesn't make a summer; he doesn't see that it was just a fluke, he thinks the whole thing was due to his own cleverness. It may ruin him."

"You do look a bit of a damned fool, old man," said one of the others. "There's no denying that, is there?"

"I know I do, and I don't like it. It's so dashed unfair. Fate has no right to play one tricks like that. After all, you must admit that my advice was good."

"Very good."

"And the wretched boy ought to have burnt his fingers. Well, he hasn't. You're all men of the world, you tell me how I'm to deal with the situation now."

But they none of them could.

"Well, Henry, if I were you I wouldn't worry," said the lawyer. "My belief is that your boy's born lucky, and in the long run that's better than to be born clever or rich."

GEORGE SANTAYANA

The following essay was delivered at Oxford on the twenty-fourth of October, 1923, as the Herbert Spencer Lecture for that year. I quote from a recent letter from Mr. Santayana: "It was a curious occasion, that lecture of mine in Oxford. I was entrusted to the care of a scientific Don, doubtless of the committee for the Spencer Lectureship; and when I called at his house by appointment an hour before the time for the lecture, his wife said he was so sorry but had been called away to receive 4000 butterflies that had just arrived for him from South America. He turned up later, however, and took me to the Natural History Museum, to a lecture-room with a deep pit, and large maps on the walls, and instead of introducing me he only said, 'Oh, you might as well begin.' The audience was small, a few ladies, and a good many Indians and Japanese: However, I recognized old Professor Stewart of Christ Church and F. R. S. Schiller. This audience, however, was most sympathetic, didn't mind the length of the lecture, and applauded heartily at the end. But there was nothing Oxonian about the occasion: might have been at Singapoor."

Nor did very many people on this side of the water pay any attention to "The Unknowable." I remember that some months later a few copies of it in pamphlet form reached a small group of Serious Thinkers attending Columbia College. At that time a number of us were accepting the consolations of philosophy from the lips of such mentors as Frederick Woodbridge (the only philosopher I have ever met who looked completely like one), John Dewey (the only philosopher I have ever met who looked completely unlike one), and Irwin Edman, who, I believe, tipped us off to the essay, acting in his capacity of permanent advance agent for Santayana.

You won't believe this, but when we read "The Unknowable" we became highly excited. Some of us, I recall, committed to memory its final paragraph, in which the nature of substance, the mystery of

love, and the fascination of jewels are combined to yield one of the
most perfectly cadenced pieces of prose in our language.

I find myself, almost twenty years afterward, smiling, as perhaps
you are smiling, at the ludicrous picture of a dozen schoolboys going
into a lather over this profound metaphysical meditation. No doubt
our excitement was thoroughly unhealthy. We should have been agitated over the prospects of the football team. (I suppose some of us
who could double in brass were.) Yet I imagine that what the football team did that season is today of only remote interest, whereas
"The Unknowable" is still of considerable value.

Though I do not say that we understood everything Santayana was
saying, we had enough sense to realize that "The Unknowable" was
a masterpiece of its sort. It is still a masterpiece and I am still not
sure that I understand everything in it. Yet it is at no point obscure,
if at many points difficult. Those of my patient readers who have no
turn for speculation may skip it, and the heavens will not fall. Santayana will lack a reader or two, you will lack Santayana, and neither
you nor Santayana will be any the worse off.

I have included "The Unknowable" because I am fascinated by
the beautiful labyrinth of its argument and because I see no reason
why a collection such as this must necessarily confine itself to so-
called "easy" reading. Santayana (I quote again from his letter) says:
"I think it is one of the most reasonable things I have written, reasonable yet not cold, and I am encouraged to find that it has not been
altogether forgotten."

"The Unknowable," let me say at once, deals with the profoundest,
the most arcane problem that man in his most passionately meditative moments has put to himself. What is the nature of Reality?
What underlies the seeable, graspable flow of events we call experience? Is there a Substance, immutable and eternal, of which the
things that we "know" are the expressions, the projections, the inti-
mations? It is a question that engaged the subtlest intellects of the
Greeks and ancient Hindus. It continues persistently to engage us
during those fleeting instants when we act as rational beings. That
dour old systematist, Herbert Spencer, had his notion of Substance,
and it is Santayana's purpose in this essay to explain and vindicate it,

and to set it in a clearer and more impressive light than Spencer did.

During the last thirty years the reputation of Santayana has under-gone some curious vicissitudes. He was at one time frowned upon by professional philosophers (so often merely a dignified term for philo-sophical professors) because he wrote too well to be trustworthy. He was infra dig, I suppose, because he has always tried to transform the perspective of the metaphysician into the vision of the artist. To his mind a professional philosopher is a notion as absurd as a professional father or a professional child, or, indeed, a professional human being. For him a philosopher is what the Greeks said he was—a lover of wisdom. But this was enough to cut him off from the world of the academy.

Then, for a time, he was in the hands of a band of exquisites who swooned over his rhythms and treated him as if he were a seduction rather than a thinker. For years he was neglected, his influence on the course of American thought being not readily observable. Then came another sharp turn in the attitude of his audience: The Last Puritan, the work of a man of seventy-two, was published, and the remote, aristocratic Santayana became a best seller.

But all this while, it seems to me, his essential value remained un-changed. He is a profound interpreter of the strange constructs that man throws up in his imagination: the great symbolisms of art, reli-gion, science, philosophy. Santayana's irony has been overemphasized. He is a classic ironist but his irony is tinged with reverence. He is, I have no doubt, a poor systematist. But if he is no systematist, it is because he feels that a system is just another of those grandiose meta-phors invented by man that he may image in his own mind the nature of what Spencer called The Unknowable.

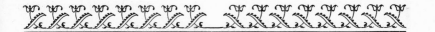

The Unknowable

BY

GEORGE SANTAYANA

Your kind invitation to deliver the Herbert Spencer Lecture of this year, apart from the honour and pleasure it brings me, enables me to perform a small act of piety. On the whole, with qualifications which will appear presently, I belong to Herbert Spencer's camp; and I am glad of so favourable an opportunity to offer a grain of propitiatory incense to his shade, which I feel to be wandering in our midst somewhat reproachfully. Fashion has completely deserted him, and the course of evolution in which he trusted has not taken his hints. Even where some philosophy of evolution is still in vogue, it is not his philosophy, but perhaps that of Hegel or Bergson, who conceive evolution as imposed on nature by some magic or dialectical force, contrary to an alleged helplessness in matter. Such devices were far removed from the innocence of Herbert Spencer, who dutifully gathered reports from every quarter and let them settle as they would in the broad levels of his system, as in geological strata; whence that Homeric sweep with which he pictures progress and decay, not in aversion from the severities of natural existence, but as the mechanical sediment of the tides of matter and motion, perpetually surging. Of course this epic movement, as Spencer describes it, is but a human perspective; he instinctively imposes his grandiloquent rhythms on things as he does his ponderous Latin vocabulary, or as Empedocles or Lucretius imposed their hexameters; but that is the case with every human system; it is and can be nothing but human discourse. Science and philosophy cast a net of words into the sea of being, happy in the end if they draw anything out besides the net itself, with some holes in it. The meshes of Spencer's net were not subtle; a thousand amiable human things

213

slipped through them like water, and compared with the studied en-
tanglements of more critical systems, his seem scandalously coarse and
wide: yet they caught the big fish. When I rub my eyes and look at
things candidly, it seems evident to me that this world is the sort of
world described by Herbert Spencer, not the sort of world described
by Hegel or Bergson. At heart these finer philosophers, like Plato, are
not seeking to describe the world of our daily plodding and commerce,
but to supply a visionary interpretation of it, a refuge from it in some
contrasted spiritual assurance, where the sharp facts vanish into a clarified drama or a pleasant trance. Far be it from me to deride the imagination, poetic or dialectical; but after all it is a great advantage for
a system of philosophy to be substantially true.

In political speculation, too, the times have turned their back on
Herbert Spencer. Everything he saw waxing is now visibly waning:
liberalism, individualism, faith in science, complacency at recent progress, assurance of further progress to come. Doubtless it is fortunate
for those who are not philosophers to share unreservedly the spirit of
their age. It must be exhilarating to stand on the hill-tops and point
the way to future generations, when you are confident that future generations must anyhow take that road. Such prophets have their reward.
They have seemed leaders in their day, they remain its representatives,
and hereafter they may prove a landmark to the historian or a find for
the antiquary. Time also has its revenges, and after an honest man has
been laughed at for a century or two as a simpleton or a scholastic, his
turn may come round again, and he may find keen advocates and
young defenders. But frankly, if in some respects Herbert Spencer's
views have so soon grown obsolete, I think he deserved his fate. A
philosopher should not be subject to the mood of the age in which he
happens to be born. When a man swims to eminence and to joyous
conviction on the crest of that wave, he must expect to be left high
and dry at the ebb-tide. A believer in evolution is indeed justified in
assuming that the latest view and the latest practice are the best so far;
but in consistency he must admit that the next view and subsequent
practice will be better still; so that his real faith is pinned by anticipation on an ultimate view and an ultimate practice, in which evolution
will reach its goal. Evolution, in the proper sense of this word, is not

a mere flux expected to be endless; evolution must have a goal, it must unfold a germ in a determinate direction towards an implicit ideal; otherwise there would be no progress involved, no means of distinguishing changes for the better from changes for the worse. I think it was a merit in Spencer to admit that evolution would culminate in a state from which any deviation would be decay; and he not only admitted such a goal in the abstract, but conceived it clearly. The goal was vital equilibrium, the adjustment and adaptation of living beings to their environment, or of their environment to them. The end of progress was harmony, that celestial harmony spoken of by a very different philosopher, which ran through all the gamut of the worlds, the diapason ending full, not exactly in man, but in any and every creature that might achieve a perfect harmony in nature. This confirms what I was saying just now about a system of philosophy—this philosophy of evolution, for instance—being but a human perspective. For the reindeer or the polar bear, evolution culminated in the glacial period; it culminated in the cities of Greece for one sort of man; it will culminate in other perfections, if there is plasticity enough in living creatures to adapt them to their conditions, before these conditions have passed away. Evolution, for any observer, will mean that strain in the total movement of nature which has ministered to the formation of his spirit, and to its full expression.

It is not, however, as a philosopher of evolution or as a political prophet that I wish to consider Herbert Spencer. I should like to confine myself, if it were possible, to one point in his system, not especially characteristic of his age nor of ours, a point in which he seems to me to have been a true philosopher such as any age might produce; for if nature has made a man observant, intelligent, and speculative, the times cannot prevent him from being so. I refer to his belief in a substance which by its secret operation, in infinite modes, kindles experience, so that all phenomena as they appear and all minds observing these appearances are secondary facts and not, as is often alleged, the fundamental or only realities. On the contrary, any experience is incidental to animal life and animal passions, which in turn are incidental to the general flux of substance in the world. Appearances and feelings and consciousness itself are in their nature desultory and unsubstantial, yet not groundless nor altogether mad, because substance creates and sustains them by its steady rhythms, so that they are truly expressive and, when intelligence arises, may become terms and symbols in true knowledge.

This is of course no new doctrine, but as old as the hills. It is an opinion which any man, if not otherwise prejudiced or indoctrinated, might well come to by himself. It was embraced by Spencer as a matter of course, and held perhaps all the more resolutely because he was not too respectful of academic tradition. Had he been expert in metaphysics and educated at a university, he might have missed the obvious.

Unfortunately, in wishing to pick out from Spencer's system this one ancient and familiar belief, and to defend it, I am arrested at once by an untoward circumstance. Herbert Spencer called this substance beneath all appearances the Unknowable. This negative appellation is evidently drawn from a critical and subjective philosophy, such as Spencer's was not. It belongs to the vocabulary of disappointment; it is a romantic word. It transports us far from the region of eager inquiry, experiment, statistics, miscellaneous information, and scientific enlightenment in which Spencer's other theories had bloomed. Why this anomaly? Why any metaphysical preface at all to a work of straightforward natural philosophy?

I think the reason was that Spencer, not being by nature a logician, bowed in logic to casual authorities, and relied too much, in this subject too, on the fashion of the hour. He supposed, as some do today, that the latest logic was the last. Dean Mansel, Sir William Hamilton, and Kant would never be superseded. He hardly considered the atmosphere, the implications, or the contradictions of the doctrines he quoted from those worthies; he appealed to them on one point, in order to discredit all their other arguments. Metaphysics should be proved, out of the mouths of the metaphysicians themselves, to be incompetent to revise his scientific speculations, or to refute his conclusions. He hardly cared, therefore, if the language of his metaphysical preface was that of his natural enemies, and perverse essentially: that fact seemed almost an advantage since it locked the gates against those enemies with their own bolts.

Yet words are weapons, and it is dangerous in speculation, as in politics, to borrow them from the arsenal of the enemy. In consenting to call substance unknowable, Spencer exposed himself to the derisive question how, if substance was unknowable, he ever came to know of its existence. Indeed, if the epithet were taken strictly, it would positively contradict and abolish belief in that tremendous reality on which he bestowed it, partly perhaps in reverence, and partly in haste to be done with reverence and to come to business. But Spencer did not take the epithet strictly, since he spoke of *modes* of the unknowable and regarded phenomena everywhere as its manifestations; and if we take the word knowledge in its natural sense (of which I shall speak presently) it is hard to see how anything could be better revealed than by being manifested everywhere. The fact is that relative and oblique designations, such as the unknowable or the unconscious, cannot be taken strictly: they cannot be intended to describe anything in its proper nature, but only in its accidental relation to something else— to a would-be knower who is unable to know it, or to an ulterior sensibility which as yet has not arisen. Nothing can be intrinsically unknowable; for if any one was tempted to imagine a substance such that it should antecedently defy description, inasmuch as that substance had no assignable character, he would be attributing existence to a nonentity. It would evidently make no difference in the universe whether a thing without any character were added to it or were taken away. If substance is to exist, it must have a character distinguishing it from nothing, and also from everything else. In saying this I do not mean to ignore those renowned philosophers who have maintained that the entire essence of substance is pure Being: I can easily conceive that in some other world pure Being should be all in all. Pure Being is itself a particular essence, the simplest essence of all, clearly distinguishable, both in definition and in experience, from every other essence, and loudly contrary to nothing, with which Hegel would identify it, not (I think) honestly; and if pure Being by chance were the essence of substance, substance would be so far from unknowable that it would be thoroughly well known, and we should always carry with us, as Spinoza observes, an adequate idea of it. That the substance of this world has a far more elaborate nature I believe can be easily proved; but I cannot enter here into that argument. It is easy to conceive, however, that the intrinsic nature of substance may be very recondite and very rich, so that the human mind has no occasion and no capacity to describe it adequately—and this perhaps comes nearer to Spencer's intention in calling it unknowable. In this sense not only God but the remoter parts of space and time, and probably the depths of matter, would be unknowable to man. Even then, however, the intrinsic nature of substance could offer no resistance to being discovered, if any one had the means and the wit to do so; and if substance remains largely unknown to mankind, the reason will not be any recalcitrancy on its part, but rather a casual coincidence in ourselves of curiosity with blindness, so that we earnestly desire to search the depths of substance, but cannot.

In this measure the emotion suggested by the term unknowable is a legitimate emotion. It expresses an integral part of the tragedy involved in being finite and mortal—perhaps in being a mind or spirit at all. Poets and philosophers sometimes talk as if life were an entertainment, a feast of ordered sensations; but the poets, if not the philosophers, know too well in their hearts that life is no such thing: it is a predicament. We are caught in it; it is something compulsory, urgent, dangerous, and tempting. We are surrounded by enormous, mysterious, only half-friendly forces. This is our experience in the dilemmas of conduct, in religion, in science, and in the arts; so that the usual sequel to agnosticism, when impatient people deny that the unknown exists, far from being a rational simplification, is a piece of arrant folly: one of those false exits in the comedy of thought which, though dramatic, are ignominious, because the mind must revert from them to the beginning of the scene, and play it over again on some other principle. All the reasons that originally suggested the belief in substance remain unimpaired, and suggest the same belief again and again. We are not less dependent than our forefathers on food, on circumstances, on our own bodies; the incubus of the not-ourselves is not lifted from us; or if in some respects we have acquired a greater dominion over nature, this only adds positive knowledge of substance to the dumb sense we had before of its environing presence. How far this understanding of substance shall go depends on the endowment of the proposed knower, and on the distance, scale, and connexions of the things he is attempting to describe. How far knowledge is possible, therefore, can never be determined without first knowing the circumstances; and the very notion of knowledge—by which I do not mean mere feeling or consciousness, but the cognizance which one existence can take of another—is a notion that never could be framed without confident experience of sundry objects known and of persons able to know them.

In saying this I am not merely expressing my own view of the matter; I am thinking of the agnosticism prevalent in Spencer's generation. It was no general scepticism; it did not, even in Kant, challenge the possibility of knowledge on account of the audacious claim which all transitive or informing knowledge puts forth in professing to report and describe something absent. On the contrary, such transitive and informing knowledge was still assumed to exist; the essential miracle of it was not denied, because it was not noticed. Everybody was assumed to know his own past, not merely to imagine it; everybody was assumed to know, not merely to imagine, the conscious existence of others, and the laws and phenomena of nature *ad infinitum*. But all these known facts, however remote and unobservable, were phenomena that had appeared, or might have appeared, to some human mind. What was condemned never to be known was only the environment of this experience, which experience had always supposed it possessed and observed, and which had been called matter, God, or the natural world. Yet the existence of these objects was not denied: had there really been no God, no matter, and no natural world, I do not see how incapacity to discover them could have been called agnosticism. The agnostic was haunted by ghosts of substance, filling his whole experience with a sense of discomfort, ignorance, and defeat. Those substances were real but elusive; and though he never saw them, the agnostic remembered only too well the tales once told concerning them, and secretly desired to have assurance of their truth; only he thought such assurance was eternally denied him by his psychological constitution. As speech has been called a means of concealing thought, so knowledge was a screen cutting off reality. Evidently this agnosticism, besides assuming true knowledge of much absent experience, presupposed accurate knowledge of the human mind and its categories, conceived to be unalterable; and it also presupposed a definition of that veiled reality definite enough to assure us that no definition of it would ever be given.

So much sure knowledge at home had a tendency to console the agnostic for his ignorance abroad. If metaphysics had closed its doors upon him, science was inviting him to a feast. Science was then believed to be so clear and unquestionable, and practically so beneficent, that human life would presently be filled to the brim with busy knowledge, busy wealth, and busy happiness. Mankind being thus happily occupied, like the busy bee, would have no reason to regret its ignorance of what did not concern it. Yet this contentment in agnosticism, so wise in its humility and so natural in an age of material progress, is fatal sooner or later to agnosticism itself. If you are not a wistful and distressed agnostic, you will forget ere long that you are an agnostic at all. Why should you believe in those ghosts of substance, if you never see them? There were once, or there seemed to be, substantial and formidable realities which everybody was sure of—God, matter, the natural world; but after literary psychology had proved that you could know nothing but your own ideas, and you found that, in spite of your incredulity, these ideas continued to flow as pleasantly as ever, what reason could you have to imagine the existence of anything else? Thus the agnostic who has lost his sense of bereavement will readily revert to dogmatism. He will relapse into the innocent habit of mind which regards what we see as existing substantially, and what we do not see as nothing.

You will not expect me, in these few minutes, to discuss the logic of idealism, but it is interesting to note how two important phases of this logic reappear in Spencer. One phase is the Socratic doctrine that knowledge is recognition. To know a thing, according to this view, is to be able to say what it is; in other words, to name and to classify it. The logical conclusion from this was drawn by Plato. He saw that the only true objects of knowledge were the types of being which we recognized things to possess. These types he called Ideas; earthly and transitory things could be understood only in so far as one or another of these Ideas was illustrated in them, or at least suggested by them in their confusion and imperfection. There is a curious approximation to this view in the Spencerian cosmology, where various principles of evolution are traced through all departments of nature, and represented as a sort of framework of eternal necessity on which the frail web of phenomena is stretched, and must be stretched in all future time. Law is the modern equivalent for the Ideas of Plato: there is no reason, save the plastic habit of the Hellenic imagination, why forms of motion or of relation should not have been counted amongst Platonic Ideas as honourably as the forms of animals or the categories of language. The radical divergence of modern rationalism from that of antiquity comes at another point. The modern is an agnostic in his idealism; he is subjective; he cannot believe that the laws that hold the world together are its true substance. They seem to him evidently figments of the mind, and he is driven to put substance in some nearer plane, a plane which on Socratic principles would be unknowable, since only laws or types of being can be defined in thought.

The other phase of idealistic logic which enters into Spencer's agnosticism is sensualism, or the doctrine that the only object of knowledge is the datum of sense. It is usual to identify this datum of sense, which is properly a visionary essence, with the sensation which reveals it, a sensation which is an event in somebody's personal experience and an historical fact. Sensations will then seem to be the substantial facts; for although they will remain unknowable in the sense of being indefinable, they will be felt and found, each at its own time; and this is the empirical criterion of reality and knowledge. But it is not clear how one sensation can know another, nor is it clear in what medium, if sensations are the only reality, they can arise or can be related; and a bottomless abyss of scepticism opens before anyone who takes the doctrine seriously that nothing can exist except sensations, each knowing itself only. Spencer was spared these perplexities by his robust faith in substance. Deeply influenced as he was by his idealistic friends, he could not forget that sensations had roots. They expressed bodily states, and effects of the environment. But as only laws or Platonic types could be defined, and only sensations could be felt, and as feeling and defining were the sole ways of knowing admitted by the two schools of idealistic logic, Spencer was confirmed in his conviction that only appearances were knowable. To be known in either of those ways is incongruous with the nature of substance. This fact does not militate against its existence; it militates against the illusion that anything existent can be known in either of those ways.

What jurisdiction can any feeling have, or any logic, over what shall arise or not arise in the universe? Even when we assert that the self-contradictory cannot exist, I suppose what we mean, if we are reasonable, is that some notion of ours, which contradicts itself, cannot be the true or complete description of the object we mean to describe by it. But often the objects to which we attempt to apply such notions are the things most indubitably existing in the world, such for instance as motion, and as this very fact of knowledge which we are now trying to understand. Motion and knowledge are facts perfectly notorious and familiar, although several great philosophers deny them to be possible, because the definitions they have given of them are self-contradictory. It is nothing against the existence of such things that they should be inexpressible in the terms of a particular logic, or unknowable to a stone. The lack of possible communication between two creatures is not necessarily a reproach to either. Even when they are sensitive, and are intelligent enough to take their sensations for signs of an external agent, the connexion may be too slight, or the scale too different, for mutual knowledge to be possible or important. But when it is important it is usually possible. We need but to sharpen our wits, and shake our minds loose from prejudice, trying new categories, until we come nearer to the heart of those substantial dynamic objects which confront us in action. This approach need not be by a miraculous divination of their essence, although when the object recognized is a mind like our own, such literal divination is not impossible. Usually, however, the approach is by refinements of adaptation, as in the moods and tenses of verbs, or the application of mathematics to nature; there is no similarity established of a pictorial sort between the symbol in the fancy and the fact in the world, but only a methodical correspondence in some one direction. If, however, we find that our senses and our logic are obdurate and incapable of further adaptations, we may reflect that all knowledge of fact, by its very privilege of transcending the data, is condemned to be external and symbolical, and that the most plastic and penetrating intellect, being still an animal function, will never discover the whole of things, either in their extent or in their structure. Things will not be unknown, since notice will have been taken of them and their appearance, in some respect, will have been recorded; we shall understand that there is one strain, at least, in their constitution and movement fitted to provoke our perception and to render our description applicable and correct. Even that intrinsic character of things, which remains undiscovered or inexpressible in our particular language, is a perfectly knowable character, and would be disclosed at any moment, in any particular, if a new observer turned up with the requisite organs, and a more sympathetic imagination.

Calling substance unknowable, then, is like calling a drum inaudible, for the shrewd reason that what you hear is the sound and not the drum. It is a play on words, and little better than a pun. In the sense in which what is heard is the sound, hearing is intuition: in the sense in which what is heard is the drum, hearing is an instance of animal faith, of that sort of perception which includes understanding and readiness to assume much that is not perceived, and to act on that assumption. Certainly if nature had confined our cognitive powers to intuition of absolute data, and we were incorrigibly æsthetic idiots, substance would be unknowable to us; but in that case we should not be agnostics about substance, since we should have not the least inkling that such a thing might exist, nor the least notion of its nature. But mankind has always had ideas of matter, of God or the gods, and of a natural world, full of hidden processes and powers; these objects, just because they existed, were necessarily removed from intuition; but everybody knew the quarter in which they lay and the circle of experiences in which each of them was manifested. Everybody knew what he meant by believing in them, and what sort of things they would be if it was really on them, and not on something quite different, that his action was directed. For instance, at this moment, not being able to discard the rude logic of my animal ancestors, I think I find indications before me of the four walls of this room and of you sitting within them, both you and the walls being possessed of a substantial existence, that is, having existed prior to my arrival in Oxford and existing apart, even now, from my summary intuitions of you, vague symbols to me of your being and of your presence. Nor does the

equal substantiality which I attribute to you and to the walls at all imply an identity of nature between the two. On the contrary, I should
be utterly lacking in sanity, as well as in civility, if I now turned my
back upon you and addressed the wall; yet on the hypothesis that my
perceptions do not convey knowledge of substance, but are intuitions
of pure ideas, it would be equally vain to address myself to you or to
the wall, since in either case I should be haranguing my own sensations. The fact that substantial, and substantially different, realities
must be posited beyond myself and my data, one sort amenable to persuasion and the other deaf, is something I assume because the enterprise of life in me at this moment demands that I should do so. I am
pledged by my instant adventure and by the general art of living
(which has a groundless ascendancy over all animals) to take for
granted that you are sitting there, admirable in your patience and inscrutable in your thoughts; and that just as in speaking to you I posit
your substantial existence, so you in your turn are kindly positing
mine, over and above the volatile sounds which you actually hear: and
I am sure you are intelligently recognizing me and my thoughts very
much for what we really are.

Thus the Spencerian Unknowable is unknowable only to idealists,
who identify knowledge with intuition, and, if they are consistent,
deny the capacity of thought to indicate anything external, whether an
event, a substance, or another actual thought. But these objects withdrawn from intuition are the objects of daily knowledge and of science: and Spencer believed he knew them very well. The scruples that
made him substitute the word unknowable for the word force or the
word force for the word matter, were the scruples of an idealist, such
as he did not intend to be. They sprang from the habit of reducing
things to their adventitious relation to ourselves, the habit of egotism;
as if the difficulty we may have in approaching them could constitute
their intrinsic being.

There was, however, a motive of quite another sort leading Spencer
to disguise the substance of things under the name of the Unknowable.
He wished to reconcile science with religion. It is easy to deride this
pretension in one who had so little sympathy with religious institutions
and with religious experience. Religion in the mass of mankind has

never been a mere sense of mystery. It has been a positive belief, and an experimental effort, directed on the means of salvation. A prophet, conscious of some promise or warning conveyed to him miraculously, cannot substitute for this specific faith an official assurance that science will never quite succeed in dissipating the mystery of things: it is not what he will never know that interests him, but what he thinks he has discovered. Genuine religion professes to have positive knowledge and to bring positive benefits: it is an art; and to ask it to be satisfied with knowing that no knowledge can penetrate to the heart of things is sheer mockery: the opposite is what religion instinctively asserts. Like science, religion is solid only in so far as by faith and art—the two wings of true knowledge—it can really survey human destiny and reveal the divine decrees on which human destiny depends. And yet I think that Herbert Spencer, in throwing somewhat contemptuously that sop to religion, was in fact silently reconciling religion with science behind his back and without suspecting it. The substance envisaged in science and that envisaged in religion have always been the same. The paths of discovery are different, but, if they convey true knowledge, they must ultimately converge upon the same facts, on the same ground of necessity in things. In the recognition of a universal substance far removed from the imagination and the will of men, yet creating this will and imagination at the appropriate places, and giving them their natural scope, there lies a quite positive religion, and by no means a new one. Substance, if we admit it at all, is by definition the source of our life and the dispenser to us of good and evil. Respect for it, then, is the beginning of wisdom, and harmony with it is the sign of salvation. I do not mean to suggest that *all* religion is addressed to such a real and formidable object. There are strains in religion of quite another quality. There is, for instance, a rapturous strain, the impulse to praise, to sing, to mythologize, to escape from all the limitations and cares of mortality into an ecstatic happiness. But I ask myself this question: What would ecstasy be but madness if it were not the voice of a substantial harmony with the substance of things and with its movement? Though substance may be forgotten, and only light and music may seem to remain, it is the massive harmonies in substance that justify those mystic feelings, if anything justifies them at all. If the spheres did not revolve according to law, the morning stars would not sing together; and the God of Aristotle would not think his eternal thoughts. Even enthusiasm, therefore, when not vapid, expresses respect for substance and happy union with its motion. Those prosaic terms of Spencer's—adaptation and equilibrium—really express admirably the basis of the most ecstatic emotions, when they are healthy and deserving of a place in human economy. It would be a sad compliment to pay to religion to identify it with fatuous and ephemeral heats, divorced from all perception of substance and of its true fertility. Religion of the sober, practical, manly sort, Roman piety, is emphatically reverence for the nature of things, for the ways of substance. How far such manly piety may have been misled by superstition, or by hasty and sentimental science, so as to distort the laws of the world and found a *false* religion, is a question of fact for soberer science to examine. If a traditional deity proves to be a living power, if it is the whole or a part of the substance actually confronting us, then serious piety will revere that deity and meditate on its ways. If on the contrary the only substance that controls our destiny or can reward our obedience is a natural substance, manifested in all nature and plastic to common arts, then a serious piety will study the ways and sing the praises of this natural substance. Piety is on the side of belief in substance: the existence of substance is the basis of piety. To set up in the place of substance any spontaneous ideas or pert exigences of our own is contrary to religion: a mind that professes to create matter, to create truth, and to create itself is a satanic mind. At least Lucifer and the ancient sceptics were disinterested, and disdained a world in which they did not believe; but modern rebels, religious or political, are without asceticism; like Doctor Faustus they are crammed with pretentious learning, they trust in magic and in their own will, covet all experience, and hanker for the promised land; but they will never see it except in a mirage if, in contempt of substance, they merely command it to appear.

There is a maxim which counsels a man lost in a wood to walk on steadily in any one direction, no matter which, lest by turning and turning in a circle he should never come out into the open. Spencer might have followed this maxim to advantage, and by sticking to his own cosmic principles he might have arrived at a theory of substance and of knowledge which would have been adequate to the facts, and potentially just also to the experience and logic of idealism (which are pathetically human), without departing at any point from the method of external observation or the doctrine of natural evolution. Knowledge, whatever else it may be, is certainly an incident in life. If all things were dead, no one of them could know another, much less itself. Now of the nature of life Spencer had a very just, if external, conception: life is a form of adaptation, a moving equilibrium, an adjustment of inner to outer relations. If a dog winces when struck, he is alive and has felt the blow; if a fly, when you try to catch it, escapes by flight, it has perceived the hand descending upon it. I am far from wishing to maintain a behaviourist psychology, or to say that in such observable cases of knowledge there is nothing that is not observable; on the contrary, I believe that every natural event has several ontological dimensions: it moves in the realm of matter, it is definable in the realm of truth, perhaps it flashes and burns for a moment in the realm of spirit, forming an actual feeling or thought. But the material facts, which biology might survey, are sufficient to determine the distribution of life and knowledge, as well as the distribution of all the other dimensions and values which the facts may involve. The state of our organs determines our sensations; our actions, or our perceptible impulses to act, determine our passions; our words enact and define our thoughts. Knowledge in its natural basis, bearing with it all its spiritual accompaniments, is thus a perfectly ascertainable fact of natural history. It is a relation of living bodies to their environment, such that the acts and words flowing from the body fit their external occasions, changing in a way relevant to these occasions but prompted by the native impulses of those bodies. Apart from such external adjustments there would be no telling whether the inner visions of any mind were knowledge or not. Intrinsically they are dream-images in any case; and they would never be anything more if directly or indirectly, by the action which accompanies them, they found no point of application in the material world.

The question what is knowable and what unknowable to any animal is accordingly easily answered by a biologist enjoying the requisite fa-

cilities for observation: if an animal possesses organs capable of dis-
criminating response to a determinate thing, that animal can know
this thing: if on the contrary the presence of this thing in influencing
the animal materially does not stimulate any reaction focused upon
that thing—any turning, or visible contemplation, or defensive movement, or pursuit—then the thing in question is unknowable to that
particular animal, and can never become an object of his thought, action, or desire. In the first case, when a fit reaction occurs, any sensuous image or any logical system which might then fill the mind would
express that reaction; and this expression would not be meaningless to
the active animal in whom it arose; he would instinctively understand
it to be the voice of the substance confronting him, his opposite partner
in the dance. Having announced its presence, and provoked in its host
some reaction of sense or fancy, that neighbour substance will have revealed itself in the only way in which anything existent and collateral
can be revealed at all—by producing some slight disturbance, which in
an active animal calls attention to its source; so that the intruder ac-
quires a reputation for good or ill, and a character in the social world.

Human experience is filled full with such appropriate comments on
neighbouring modes of substance, and with appropriate names and
sketches clapped upon events. Amongst these signs and tokens there
are some especially venerable symbols, those same ideas already mentioned of matter, of God, of the natural world, of various persons and
passions. These venerable symbols are characters attributed to substance
and its modes by the human imagination, after long experience and
much puzzled reflection: the degree of truth and precision which they
may possess will naturally vary, partly with the articulation they receive—the more articulate, the truer or the falser they will become—
and partly with the range of substantive being to which they are applied. Intrinsically they are all poetic ideas, fictions of the fancy; a
fact which does not prevent them from being true symbolically and
even literally, if they are so happily framed as to attribute to substance
no character which substance does not actually possess.

When people discuss the existence of matter or the existence of God,
the problem does not seem to me to be well stated. It is as if we began
to discuss the existence of our friends. In the material locus in which

we place the persons of our acquaintance there is undoubtedly something, and not something of any sort, but a mode of substance with precisely the active powers exerted upon us from that quarter. This reality is no less real than ourselves, being in dynamic interplay with the substance of our own being. To deny the reality of one's friends, though possible to a determined sceptic, is idle and in the end dishonest; because we can be sure of nothing and can believe nothing, if we do not allow ourselves to believe and to be sure that we are in contact with a substance not ourselves when we fight, love, or talk. This substance may be recognized and named without being at all comprehended; merely the different instincts awakened in its presence may suffice to distinguish it clearly, as when a child says John, mother, dog. It does not follow that these names, and the sentiment each mutely awakens, are similar to the substance they indicate, or form any part of that substance. Even the barking of the dog, not to speak of the dog himself, is not very like the bow-wow of the childish vocabulary. I see no necessity that our ideas of matter or of God should be truer than that; yet they have substantial and unequivocal objects. If, for instance, in denying that persons exist, a philosopher like Buddha had meant that the idea we commonly form of persons does not rightly describe the substance at work in those places, he might have been more than justified; a supposed spiritual substance called the soul is not easily to be found there; but he could hardly have maintained his negation if he had meant that there is no substance of any sort for which the idea of persons is a conventional mask. In fact Buddha himself implicitly believed in Karma, a principle of inheritance and continuity which was the parent of all illusions and the substance of our imaginary selves. No doubt this conception of Karma, like the notion of a person, needs to be clarified; but it is a splendid instrument of moral synthesis, and describes the operations of substance in one important respect, though doubtless without understanding the mechanism which actually subtends human character and moral inheritance.

Knowledge, then, is not knowledge of appearance, but appearances are knowledge of substance when they are taken for signs of it. The stuff and texture of knowledge, its verbal and pictorial terms, are flexible and subject to progressive correction. Thus the notion of matter, of God, of a human person, may continually vary, and may end by shedding completely the specious character it had at first: as, for instance, this Buddhistic notion of what a person really is, namely, a moral heritage, is a complete denial of several grosser definitions of a human spirit; but these reformed ideas and new names are meant to be applicable to the same object formerly conceived otherwise; for this reason they may be truer and better. In like manner the idea of matter or of God may be reformed; it may even be reformed so radically that a fresh word may be thought necessary to designate the new conception, and the old substance will receive a new name; but controversy is misguided if it turns on hypostatizing either idea, and asking which of them exists. The answer is, neither: what exists is the substance at work, and this substance is never an idea hypostatized. It is prior to all ideas and descriptions of it, the object that in their rivalry they are all endeavouring to report truly. In its local modes, or in its broad relations to some human interest, it bears without a murmur whatsoever names any one's tongue, in its pathetic spontaneity, may impose upon it; here it is called mother, there John, there bow-wow; in one broad aspect it is called matter, in another it is called God. When such names, in physics or in theology, are expanded into articulate systems, the question may arise whether they continue to be appropriate to the part or aspect of substance on which they were first bestowed: and this is a doubt for further study to solve, patiently directed upon the same object. A man may then honestly ask himself whether he believes in matter; meaning that he does not regard the conventional notion of matter as certainly applicable to the substance meant; or if he likes to startle the pious he may say he does not believe in God, because he may not regard the conventional notion of God, or perhaps any notion bred in the region of dramatic emotion, as honestly applicable to the substance actually operative in that sphere—say, in the sphere of momentous events and ultimate destiny. Evidently further study of momentous events, and further reflection on destiny, might decide this question for him, as further study of physics might decide the other; but whether we think fit to call substance there matter, and substance here God, or invent other names, substance will remain what it is; our appellations and ideas will have no power to create it where it is not, or to dislodge it or modify it where it is. Illusions have their own specious reality and physiognomy, curious as folklore is curious; but it is substance as it exists that is momentous, since it determines events, including our illusions and the disappointments they entail. I should be sorry to think for one moment that any philosopher, much less any religious man, could cling to his beliefs merely because they were his, or he liked them, or had defended them before. Of course every earnest mind recoils from self-deception and from the thought that its dearest feelings might go up in smoke; of course it is singly devoted to discovering the facts, whatever they may be, and to assuming towards them a brave and becoming attitude.

My conclusion accordingly is this: Belief in substance, besides being inevitable in daily life (which I think is the right place for philosophy), is vindicated by the adequacy and harmony of the view it gives us of existence; and the notion that substance is unknowable is reduced to a misunderstanding—intelligible but unfortunate—due to a confusion of knowledge with intuition. If by knowledge we understood an intuition containing no element of faith, but simply inspecting the obvious, then indeed all substance would be unknowable; but this necessary ignorance would then extend to every subsisting fact assumed in science and in daily life: not only would matter and God disappear from the scene, but the whole past and future would be denied, together with all that flux of experience which social intercourse, psychology, and history presuppose. Nothing would then be knowable save the feeling or image present at the moment to the mind; and even this would not be known for a fact or event in the world, but all that would be known in it, or through it, would be its own specious nature, the idea presented or the sensation felt. To limit knowledge to intuition of such obvious essences is to deny knowledge: it is to revoke the whole transitive intention or significance of ideas. The knowledge that mankind claims and rejoices in is of quite another sort; it consists in information about removed facts, intuitively undiscoverable. To a mortal creature, hounded by fate, and not merely engaged in seraphic contemplation, absent things are the things important to know; it is they that have created us, and can now feed or entice us; it is they that our moral nature hangs upon and looks to with respect.

I have sometimes wondered at the value ladies set upon jewels: as centres of light, jewels seem rather trivial and monotonous. And yet there is an unmistakable spell about these pebbles; they can be taken up and turned over; they can be kept; they are faithful possessions; the sparkle of them, shifting from moment to moment, is constant from age to age. They are substances. The same aspects of light and colour, if they were homeless in space, or could be spied only once and irrecoverably, like fireworks, would have a less comfortable charm. In jewels there is the security, the mystery, the inexhaustible fixity proper to substance. After all, perhaps I can understand the fascination they exercise over the ladies; it is the same that the eternal feminine exercises over us. Our contact with them is unmistakable, our contemplation of them gladly renewed, and pleasantly prolonged; yet in one sense they are unknowable; we cannot fathom the secret of their constancy, of their hardness, of that perpetual but uncertain brilliancy by which they dazzle us and hide themselves. These qualities of the jewel and of the eternal feminine are also the qualities of substance and of the world. The existence of this world—unless we lapse for a moment into an untenable scepticism—is certain, or at least it is unquestioningly to be assumed. Experience may explore it adventurously, and science may describe it with precision; but after you have wandered up and down in it for many years, and have gathered all you could of its ways by report, this same world, because it exists substantially and is not invented, remains a foreign thing and a marvel to the spirit: unknowable as a drop of water is unknowable, or unknowable like a person loved.

H. W. FOWLER

COMMENTARY

People who try to use the language with respect will do well to keep on hand the fattish, blue-bound volume known as H. W. Fowler's Dictionary of Modern English Usage. It should be a brain-side book for every writer, amateur as well as professional, since each of its 742 type-filled pages is a teacher of true humility. I refer to Fowler often, but not necessarily to solve a problem in usage, grammar, or pronunciation. I refer to it for spiritual sustenance. It shows me how bad a writer I am and encourages me to do better.

I am one of that dwindling band that believes the English language, flexible as it is, obeys certain laws and regulations. I do not believe writers are superior to these laws unless, like James Joyce, they have earned the right to that superiority. If a writer is vulgar in mind, sloppy in thought, and crude in manner, his language will betray him; his syntax will find him out. By examining his language with the kind of microscope Fowler supplies, he can spy upon his own defects of character and temperament.

I read, for example, the essays on Genteelisms and Hackneyed Phrases and I realize with a sense of shame that I have been guilty of many of them, not alone in speech but in formal prose. This does not argue that I am a character of black iniquity, but it does point to a tendency of mine to borrow the stale wit and ingenuity of others or to dress up linsey-woolsey thoughts in ostentatious finery. These are small faults of taste and tiny derelictions of morality. They are worth correcting.

Somerset Maugham sums up Fowler thus:

"I have read many books on English prose, but have found it hard to profit by them; for the most part they are vague, unduly theoretical, and often scolding. But you cannot say this of Fowler's Dictionary of Modern English Usage. It is a valuable work. I do not think anyone writes so well that he cannot learn much from it.

It is lively reading. Fowler liked simplicity, straightforwardness and common sense. He had no patience with pretentiousness. He had a sound feeling that idiom was the backbone of a language and he was all for the racy phrase. He was no slavish admirer of logic and was willing enough to give usage right of way through the exact demesnes of grammar."

I must add that Fowler is not only useful but diverting. He is himself, if something of a precisian, a sound writer, witty and ironical when he wishes to be (note, for example, the high comedy in his discourse on the Split Infinitive, here included), and able to make lucid the most subtle and difficult distinctions of usage and shades of linguistic feeling. He is also, on occasion, a vest-pocket essayist of no mean ability, as the little table on Wit, Humor, Irony, etc., indicates.

Naturally the few selections I have made give no complete idea of the worth of his dictionary, but they do afford a clue to the sort of pleasure you can get from the book if you happen to be the sort of person who gets pleasure from this sort of book.

Excerpts from "A Dictionary of Modern English Usage"

BY

H. W. FOWLER

GENTEELISM. By *genteelism* is here to be understood the substituting, for the ordinary natural word that first suggests itself to the mind, of a synonym that is thought to be less soiled by the lips of the common herd, less familiar, less plebeian, less vulgar, less improper, less apt to come unhandsomely betwixt the wind & our nobility. The truly genteel do not offer *beer*, but *ale;* invite one to *step*, not *come*, this way; take in not *lodgers*, but *paying guests;* send their boys not to *school*, but to *college;* never *help*, but *assist*, each other to potatoes; keep *stomachs* & *domestics* insteads of *bellies* & *servants;* & have quite forgotten that they could ever have been guilty of *toothpowder* & *napkins* & *underclothing*, of *before* & *except* & *about*, where nothing now will do for them but *dentifrice, serviette, lingerie, ere, save, anent.*

The reader need hardly be warned that the inclusion of any particular word in the small selection of genteelisms offered below does not imply that that word should never be used. All or most of these, & of the hundreds that might be classed with them, have their proper uses, in which they are not genteel, but natural. *Ale* is at home in historical novels, *ere* & *save* in poetry, *mirrors* in marble halls, *the military* in riots, *dentifrices* in druggists' lists, & so forth; but out of such contexts, & in the conditions explained above, the taint of gentility is on them. To illustrate a little more in detail, "He went out without shutting the door" is plain English; with *closing* substituted for *shutting* it becomes genteel; nevertheless, to *close* the door is justified if more is implied than the mere not leaving it open:—"Before beginning his

235

story, he crossed the room & closed the door," i.e. placed it so as to
obviate overhearing; "Six people sleeping in a small room with closed
windows," i.e. excluding air. Or again, "The schoolroom roof fell in,
& two of the boys (*or girls, or* children) were badly injured"; *scholars*
for boys &c. would be a genteelism, & a much more flagrant one than
closing in the previous example; yet *scholar* is not an obsolete or archaic word; it is no longer the natural English for a schoolboy or
schoolgirl, that is all.

The reader may now be left to the specimen list of genteelisms,
which he will easily increase for himself. The point is that, when the
word in the second column is the word of one's thought, one should
not consent to displace it by the word in the first column unless an improvement in the meaning would result.

Genteelisms	Normal words	Genteelisms	Normal words
ale	beer	lady-dog	bitch
anent	about	lady help	servant
assist	help	lingerie	underclothing
carafe	water-bottle	military, the	soldiers
cease	stop	mirror	looking-glass
chiropodist	corn-cutter	odour	smell
close	shut	paying guest	boarder
coal-vase	coal-scuttle	perspire, -ration	sweat
college	school	peruse	read
couch	sofa	place	put
dentifrice	toothpowder	preserve	jam
distingué	striking	proceed	go
domestic	servant	recreation	amusement
edifice	building	save	except
endeavour	try	scholar	boy &c.
ere	before	serviette	napkin
exclusive	select	step	come, go
expectorate	spit	stomach	belly
hither	here	sufficient	enough
inquire	ask	woolly	sweater
kinema	cinema	tipsy	drunk

HACKNEYED PHRASES. When *Punch* set down a heading that might be, & very likely has been, the title of a whole book, "Advice to those about to marry," & boiled down the whole contents into a single word, & that a surprise, the thinker of the happy thought deserved congratulations for a week; he hardly deserved immortality, but he has—anonymously, indeed—got it; a large percentage of the great British people cannot think of the dissuasive "don't" without remembering, &, alas! reminding others, of him. There are thousands to whose minds the cat cannot effect an entrance unaccompanied by "harmless necessary"; nay, in the absence of the cat, "harmless" still brings "necessary" in its train; & all would be well if the thing stopped at the mind, but it issues by way of the tongue, which is bad, or of the pen, which is worse. King David must surely writhe as often as he hears it told in Sheol what is the latest insignificance that may not be told in Gath. How many a time has Galileo longed to recant the recanting of his recantation, as "e pur si muove" was once more applied or misapplied! And the witty gentleman who equipped coincidence with her long arm has doubtless suffered even in this life at seeing that arm so mercilessly overworked.

The hackneyed phrases are counted by the hundred, & those registered below are a mere selection. Each of them comes to each of us at some moment in life with, for him, the freshness of novelty upon it; on that occasion it is a delight, & the wish to pass on that delight is amiable; but we forget that of any hundred persons for whom we attempt this good office, though there may be one to whom our phrase is new & bright, it is a stale offence to the ninety & nine.

The purpose with which these phrases are introduced is for the most part that of giving a fillip to a passage that might be humdrum without them; they do serve this purpose with some readers—the less discerning—though with the other kind they more effectually disserve it; but their true use when they come into the writer's mind is as danger-signals; he should take warning that when they suggest themselves it is because what he is writing is bad stuff, or it would not need such help; let him see to the substance of his cake, instead of decorating with sugarplums. In considering the following selection, the reader will bear in mind that he & all of us have our likes & our dislikes in this kind; he may find pet phrases of his own in the list, or miss his pet abominations; he should not on that account decline to accept a caution against the danger of the hackneyed phrase. Suffer a sea change./Sleep the sleep of the just./The cups that cheer but not inebriate./Conspicuous by his absence./The feast of reason./The flow of soul./A chartered libertine./A consummation devoutly to be wished./ All that was mortal of ——./Which would be laughable if it were not tragic./But that is another story./Had few equals & no superior./But it was not to be./Come into one's life./Has the defects of his qualities./Leave severely alone./Take in each other's washing./In her great sorrow./Metal more attractive./More sinned against than sinning./ There is balm in Gilead./Fit audience though few./My prophetic soul!/The scenes he loved so well./A work of supererogation./The irony of fate./The pity of it!/The psychological moment./Curses not loud but deep./More in sorrow than in anger./Heir of all the ages./ There's the rub./The curate's egg./To be or not to be./Hinc illae lacrimae./Filthy lucre./The outer man./The inner man./Of the —— persuasion./Too funny for words./Get no forrader./My better half./ Eagle eye./Young hopeful./Seriously incline./ Snapper-up of unconsidered trifles./The logic of facts, events./The tender mercies of./Olive branches./Pity 'tis, 'tis true./Have one's quiver full./In durance vile./ At the parting of the ways./Not wisely, but too well.

HUMOUR, WIT, SATIRE, SARCASM, INVECTIVE, IRONY, CYNICISM, THE SARDONIC. So much has been written upon the nature of some of these words, & upon the distinctions between pairs or trios among them (wit & humour, sarcasm & irony & satire), that it would be both presumptuous & unnecessary to attempt a further disquisition. But a sort of tabular statement may be of service against some popular misconceptions. No definition of the words is offered, but for each its motive or aim, its province, its method or means, & its proper audience, are specified. The constant confusion between sarcasm, satire, & irony, as well as that now less common between wit & humour, seems to justify this mechanical device of parallel classification; but it will be of use only to those who wish for help in determining which is the word that they really want.

	MOTIVE or AIM	PROVINCE	METHOD or MEANS	AUDIENCE
humour	Discovery	Human nature	Observation	The sympathetic
wit	Throwing light	Words & ideas	Surprise	The intelligent
satire	Amendment	Morals & manners	Accentuation	The self-satisfied
sarcasm	Inflicting pain	Faults & foibles	Inversion	Victim & bystand-er
invective	Discredit	Misconduct	Direct statement	The public
irony	Exclusiveness	Statement of facts	Mystification	An inner circle
cynicism	Self-justification	Morals	Exposure of na-kedness	The respectable
The sardonic	Self-relief	Adversity	Pessimism	Self

IRRELEVANT ALLUSION. We all know the people—for they are the majority, & probably include our particular selves—who cannot carry on the ordinary business of everyday talk without the use of phrases containing a part that is appropriate & another that is pointless or worse; the two parts have associated themselves together in their minds as making up what somebody has said, & what others as well as they will find familiar, & they have the sort of pleasure in producing the combination that a child has in airing a newly acquired word. There is indeed a certain charm in the grown-up man's boyish ebullience, not to be restrained by thoughts of relevance from letting the exuberant phrase jet forth. And for that charm we put up with it when one draws our attention to the methodical by telling us there is *method in the madness,* though method & not madness is all there is to see, when another's every winter is *the winter of* his *discontent,* when a third cannot complain of the *light* without calling it *religious* as well as *dim,* when for a fourth nothing can be *rotten* except *in the state of Denmark,* or when a fifth, asked whether he does not owe you 1/6 for that cabfare, *owns the soft impeachment.* Other phrases of the kind will be found in the article HACKNEYED PHRASES. A slightly fuller examination of a single example may be useful. The phrase *to leave severely alone* has two reasonable uses—one in the original sense of to leave alone as a method of severe treatment, i.e. to send to Coventry or show contempt for; & the other in contexts where *severely* is to be interpreted by contraries—to leave alone by way not of punishing the object, but of avoiding consequences for the subject. The straightfor-

ward meaning, & the ironical, are both good; anything between them,
in which the real meaning is merely to leave alone, & *severely* is no
more than an echo, is pointless & vapid & in print intolerable. Examples follow: (1, straightforward) *You must show him, by leaving him
severely alone, by putting him into a moral Coventry, your detestation
of the crime;* (2, ironical) *Fish of prey do not appear to relish the sharp
spines of the stickleback, & usually seem to leave them severely alone;*
(3, pointless) *Austria forbids children to smoke in public places; & in
German schools & military colleges there are laws upon the subject;
France, Spain, Greece, & Portugal, leave the matter severely alone.* It
is obvious at once how horrible the faded jocularity of N° 3 is in print;
&, though things like it come crowding upon one another in most conversation, they are not very easy to find in newspapers & books of any
merit; a small gleaning of them follows:—*The moral,* as Alice would
say, *appeared to be that, despite its difference in degree, an obvious
essential in the right kind of education had been equally lacking to
both these girls* (as Alice, or indeed as you or I, might say)./*Resignation became* a virtue of necessity *for Sweden* (If you do what you must
with a good grace, you make a virtue of necessity; without *make, a
virtue of necessity* is meaningless). /*I strongly advise the single work-
ing-man who would become a successful backyard poultry-keeper to
ignore* the advice of Punch, *& to secure a useful helpmate./ The beloved* lustige Wien [merry Vienna] *of his youth had* suffered a sea
change. *The green glacis . . . was blocked by ranges of grand new
buildings* (Ariel must chuckle at the odd places in which his *sea
change* turns up)./*Many of the celebrities who in that most frivolous
of watering-places* do congregate./*When about to quote Sir Oliver
Lodge's tribute to the late leader, Mr Law* drew, not a dial, *but what
was obviously a penny memorandum book from his pocket* (You want
to mention that Mr Bonar Law took a notebook out of his pocket; but
pockets are humdrum things; how give a literary touch? call it a *poke?*
no, we can better that; who was it drew what from his poke? why,
Touchstone a dial, to be sure! & there you are).

SPLIT INFINITIVE. The English-speaking world may be divided
into (1) those who neither know nor care what a split infinitive is;

(2) those who do not know, but care very much; (3) those who know & condemn; (4) those who know & approve; & (5) those who know & distinguish.

1. Those who neither know nor care are the vast majority, & are a happy folk, to be envied by most of the minority classes; "to really understand" comes readier to their lips & pens than "really to understand," they see no reason why they should not say it (small blame to them, seeing that reasons are not their critics' strong point), & they do say it, to the discomfort of some among us, but not to their own.

2. To the second class, those who do not know but do care, who would as soon be caught putting their knives in their mouths as splitting an infinitive but have hazy notions of what constitutes that deplorable breach of etiquette, this article is chiefly addressed. These people betray by their practice that their aversion to the split infinitive springs not from instinctive good taste, but from tame acceptance of the misinterpreted opinion of others; for they will subject their sentences to the queerest distortions, all to escape imaginary split infinitives. "To really understand" is a s.i.; "to really be understood" is a s.i.; "to be really understood" is not one; the havoc that is played with much well-intentioned writing by failure to grasp that distinction is incredible. Those upon whom the fear of infinitive-splitting sits heavy should remember that to give conclusive evidence, by distortions, of misconceiving the nature of the s.i. is far more damaging to their literary pretensions than an actual lapse could be; for it exhibits them as deaf to the normal rhythm of English sentences. No sensitive ear can fail to be shocked, if the following examples are read aloud, by the strangeness of the indicated adverbs. Why on earth, the reader wonders, is that word out of its place? He will find, on looking through again, that each has been turned out of a similar position, viz between the word *be* & a passive participle. Reflection will assure him that the cause of dislocation is always the same—all these writers have sacrificed the run of their sentences to the delusion that "to be really understood" is a split infinitive. It is not; & the straitest non-splitter of us all can with a clear conscience restore each of the adverbs to its rightful place:—He was proposed at the last moment as a candidate likely *gen-*

erally to be accepted./When the record of this campaign comes *dispassionately* to be written, & in just perspective, it will be found that . . ./The leaders have given instructions that the lives & property of foreigners shall *scrupulously* be respected./New principles will have *boldly* to be adopted if the Scottish case is to be met./This is a very serious matter, which clearly ought *further* to be inquired into./There are many points raised in the report which need *carefully* to be explored./Only two ways of escaping from the conflict without loss, by this time become too serious *squarely* to be faced, have ever offered themselves./The Headmaster of a public school possesses very great powers, which ought *most carefully & considerately* to be exercised./ The time to get this revaluation put through is when the amount paid by the State to the localities is *very largely* to be increased./But the party whose Leader in the House of Commons acts in this way cannot fail *deeply* to be discredited by the way in which he flings out & about these false charges.

3. The above writers are bogy-haunted creatures who for fear of splitting an infinitive abstain from doing something quite different, i.e. dividing *be* from its complement by an adverb. Those who presumably do know what split infinitives are, & condemn them, are not so easily identified, since they include all who neither commit the sin nor flounder about in saving themselves from it, all who combine with acceptance of conventional rules a reasonable dexterity. But when the dexterity is lacking, disaster follows. It does not add to a writer's readableness if readers are pulled up now & again to wonder—Why this distortion? Ah, to be sure, a non-split die-hard! That is the mental dialogue occasioned by each of the adverbs in the examples below. It is of no avail merely to fling oneself desperately out of temptation; one must *so* do it that no traces of the struggle remain; that is, sentences must be thoroughly remodelled instead of having a word lifted from its original place & dumped elsewhere:—What alternative can be found which the Pope has not condemned, & which will make it possible *to organize legally* public worship?/If it is to do justice between the various parties & not *unduly to burden* the State, it will . . ./It will, when better understood, tend *firmly to establish* relations between Capital & Labour./Both Ger-

many & England have done ill in not combining *to forbid flatly* hostilities./Nobody expects that the executive of the Amalgamated Society is going *to assume publicly* sackcloth & ashes./Every effort must be made *to increase adequately* professional knowledge & attainments./ We have had *to shorten somewhat* Lord Denbigh's letter./ The kind of sincerity which enables an author *to move powerfully* the heart would . . ./Safeguards should be provided *to prevent effectually* cosmopolitan financiers from manipulating these reserves.

4. Just as those who know & condemn the s.i. include many who are not recognizable, only the clumsier performers giving positive proof of resistance to temptation, so too those who know & approve are not distinguishable with certainty; when a man splits an infinitive, he may be doing it unconsciously as a member of our class 1, or he may be deliberately rejecting the trammels of convention & announcing that he means to do as he will with his own infinitives. But, as the following examples are from newspapers of high repute, & high newspaper tradition is strong against splitting, it is perhaps fair to assume that each specimen is a manifesto of independence:—It will be found possible *to considerably improve* the present wages of the miners without jeopardizing the interests of capital./Always providing that the Imperialists do not feel strong enough *to decisively assert* their power in the revolted provinces./But even so, he seems *to still be allowed* to speak at Unionist demonstrations./It is the intention of the Minister of Transport *to substantially increase* all present rates by means of a general percentage./The men in many of the largest districts are declared *to strongly favour* a strike if the minimum wage is not conceded.

It should be noticed that in these the separating adverb could have been placed outside the infinitive with little or in most cases no damage to the sentence-rhythm (*considerably* after *miners*, *decisively* after *power*, *still* with clear gain after *be*, *substantially* after *rates*, & *strongly* at some loss after *strike*), so that protest seems a safe diagnosis.

5. The attitude of those who know & distinguish is something like this: We admit that separation of *to* from its infinitive (viz *be, do, have, sit, doubt, kill,* or other verb inflexionally similar) is not in itself desirable, & we shall not gratuitously say either "to mortally wound"

or "to mortally be wounded"; but we are not foolish enough to confuse the latter with "to be mortally wounded", which is blameless English, nor "to just have heard" with "to have just heard", which is also
blameless. We maintain, however, that a real s.i., though not desirable
in itself, is preferable to either of two things, to real ambiguity, & to
patent artificiality. For the first, we will rather write "Our object is to
further cement trade relations" than, by correcting into "Our object is
further to cement . . .", leave it doubtful whether an additional object
or additional cementing is the point. And for the second, we take it
that such reminders of a tyrannous convention as "in not combining
to forbid flatly hostilities" are far more abnormal than the abnormality
they evade. We will split infinitives sooner than be ambiguous or artificial; more than that, we will freely admit that sufficient recasting will
get rid of any s.i. without involving either of those faults, & yet reserve to ourselves the right of deciding in each case whether recasting
is worth while. Let us take an example: "In these circumstances, the
Commission, judging from the evidence taken in London, has been
feeling its way to modifications intended to better equip successful
candidates for careers in India & at the same time to meet reasonable
Indian demands". To better equip? We refuse "better to equip" as a
shouted reminder of the tyranny; we refuse "to equip better" as ambiguous (*better* an adjective?); we regard "to equip successful candidates better" as lacking compactness, as possibly tolerable from an anti-
splitter, but not good enough for us. What then of recasting? "Intended
to make successful candidates fitter for" is the best we can do if the
exact sense is to be kept; it takes some thought to arrive at the correction; was the game worth the candle?

After this inconclusive discussion, in which, however, the author's
opinion has perhaps been allowed to appear with indecent plainness,
readers may like to settle for themselves whether, in the following sentence, "either to secure" followed by "to resign", or "to either secure"
followed by "resign", should have been preferred—an issue in which
the meaning & the convention are pitted against each other:—The
speech has drawn an interesting letter from Sir Antony MacDonnell,
who states that his agreement with Mr Wyndham was never cancelled,

& that Mr Long was too weak *either to secure* the dismissal of Sir Antony or himself to resign office.

It is perhaps hardly fair that this article should have quoted no split infinitives except such as, being reasonably supposed (as in 4) to be deliberate, are likely to be favourable specimens. Let it therefore conclude with one borrowed from a reviewer, to whose description of it no exception need be taken: "A book . . . of which the purpose is thus —with a deafening split infinitive—stated by its author:—'Its main idea is *to* historically, even while events are maturing, & divinely—from the Divine point of view—*impeach* the European system of Church & State.' "

WORN-OUT HUMOUR. "We are not amused"; so Queen Victoria baldly stated a fact that was disconcerting to someone; yet the thing was very likely amusing in its nature; it did not amuse the person whose amusement mattered, that was all. The writer's Queen Victoria is his public, & he would do well to keep a bust of the old Queen on his desk with the legend "We are not amused" hanging from it. His public will not be amused if he serves it up the small facetiae that it remembers long ago to have taken delight in. We recognize this about anecdotes, avoid putting on our friends the depressing duty of simulating surprise, & sort our stock into chestnuts & still possibles. Anecdotes are our pounds, & we take care of them; but of the phrases that are our pence we are more neglectful. Of the specimens of worn-out humour exhibited below nearly all have had point & liveliness in their time; but with every year that they remain current the proportion of readers who "are not amused" to those who find them fresh & new inexorably rises.

Such grammatical oddities as *muchly;* such puns as *Bedfordshire* & *the Land of Nod;* such allusions as the Chapter on Snakes in Iceland; such parodies as *To —— or not to ——;* such quotations as *On —— intent,* or *single blessedness,* or *suffer a sea change;* such oxymorons as *The gentle art of* doing something ungentle; such polysyllabic uncouthness as calling a person an *individual* or an old maid an *unappropriated blessing;* such needless euphemisms as *unmentionables* or a table's *limbs;* such meioses as *the herringpond,* or *Epithets the reverse of complimentary,* or "some" as a superlative; such playful archaisms as *hight* or *yclept;* such legalisms as *(the) said* ——, & *the same,* & *this deponent;* such shiftings of application as *innocent* or *guiltless of* hs, or *of the military persuasion,* or to *spell ruin* or *discuss a roast fowl* or *be too previous;* such metonymies as *the leather* & *the ribbons* for *ball* & *reins;* such metaphors as *timberyard* & *sky-pilot* & *priceless;* such zeugmas as *in top-boots & a temper;* such happy thoughts as *taking in each other's washing*—with all these we, i.e. the average adult, not only are not amused; we feel a bitterness, possibly because they remind us of the lost youth in which we could be tickled with a straw, against the scribbler who has reckoned on our having tastes so primitive.

C. K. OGDEN

COMMENTARY

Except by divine accident, book reviews are not works of literature. Called into being by trivial causes, they are generally written in haste and forgotten at the same tempo. In England, during the early nineteenth century, book reviews were massive and learned; sometimes three months might be taken in their composition. (They were often, one should add, extremely dull.) Today book reviews are at best informative, sprightly, and intelligent. At worst they are merely informative.

Perhaps they are not literature, not only because book reviewers are not first-rate writers but because a book review is the wrong length. It is difficult to say anything moving and memorable about a book in a thousand words. One needs either ten words or ten thousand. That is why the reviews I remember with most pleasure have been very long or very short. The little girl who wrote "This book tells me more about penguins than I am interested in knowing" was the author of a classic sentence and a classic book review. Those old single line crushers, "The only unity the book has was given it by the binder" and "There is too much space between the covers of this book"—these are good, direct-action reviews. If the truth were told, they would be appropriate to at least fifty per cent of the volumes that are accorded more extended treatment.

When I think of the best reviews I have read in the last twenty years, two come quickly to mind. One was a whopper of a job by Laurence Stallings in the Sun of perhaps twelve years ago. It performed several major operations on the autobiography of Emma Goldman, as a result of which the patient expired. It was cruel, but it was superb.

The other I am reprinting here. It appeared in the October 23, 1926, issue of The Saturday Review of Literature, rudely displacing practically all the other reviews scheduled for that week. The irate reader may well ask why at this late date I am digging up this mam-

moth commentary full of strange names and allusions and apoplectic
with erudition. I have one or two reasons ready, none of which, it
is quite possible, will seem cogent to anyone else.

In the first place, Mr. C. K. Ogden, its author, was handed what
is about the toughest assignment any reviewer can face: The Encyclopaedia Britannica. The mere possession of erudition (and it will
be seen that Mr. Ogden has what might almost be called a corner on
general information) will not suffice. You must make your erudition
comprehensible and you must make your erudition entertaining. I
submit that Mr. Ogden meets these three tests superbly. I draw particular attention to the fact that this lengthy comment on matters
which after all do not concern us vitally is not only interesting but
frequently funny. Through it blows like a favoring wind that amus-
ingly cheeky English urbanity which we now know to be the drawing-room face of stoical English courage.

Mr. Ogden's piece was thrown off hurriedly as a bit of journalism.
Yet it is full of good sense, good writing, and good humor. It is stuffed
with jokes and puns, some of them donnish, it is true, others fresh
and merry, one at least a most outrageous double-entendre. (No, find
it yourself.) A man so flexible and humane of temperament that he
can play games with the Britannica and at the same time accord it
the reverence that noble institution deserves is a phenomenon worthy
of your attention.

The minds of polymaths, though fascinating to the psychologist,
tend to repel us ordinary folk. It is difficult to pump up enthusiasm
over the personalities of such Know-Everythings as Macaulay, von
Ranke, or Lord Acton. C. K. Ogden, if less imposing than any of
these, has their same catholicity of intellectual interest. But his mind
remains playful, even skittish, and his learning sits lightly upon his
sentences. He will even teach you a new parlor game—the one he
calls Offs and Ons. It is fun to watch a brain like this at work.

It may also be of interest to some to note how shrewdly Ogden
called the intellectual turn fifteen years ago. His amiable strictures
on the Britannica's sins of omission in 1926 are indicative of the state
of vanguard knowledge at that time. For example, he scolds the
supplementary edition of the Britannica, which he is reviewing, for

omitting or treating insufficiently such names as Charles Peirce, Toscanini, Stokowski, Gershwin, Le Corbusier, Zaharoff, General Hoffmann, Laski, William Morton Wheeler, Tawney, T. S. Eliot, Rebecca West. Today it is a bit easier to estimate the importance of these figures. But in 1926 it required rare erudition, judgment, and boldness to be as certain of their worth as was C. K. Ogden.

Ogden is a Cambridge scholar. His special province is psychology and semantics. He is the author, with I. A. Richards, of The Meaning of Meaning (not recommended as light literature) and of a number of other books. His most important recent contribution is his invention of Basic English, a scientific vocabulary of about eight hundred common English words with which most ordinary discourse can be effectively conducted. Basic English has nothing in common with such "international languages" as Esperanto, Ido, or Volapük. It is an auxiliary, a tool constructed to serve as a supplement to existing languages. It is already being widely taught in Russia and parts of China and, properly used, may turn out a valuable aid in the gradual formation of that world-mindedness which must ensue if the present war is won by the democracies.

After the publication of the piece that follows, one of the Encyclopaedia Britannica people came to Henry Seidel Canby, then editor of The Saturday Review, in a state of considerable choler. He felt that the Ogden review might be considered prejudicial and talked of bringing suit. Dr. Canby inquired mildly what the grounds of complaint were. The other replied that Dr. Canby was responsible for having chosen an incompetent to write the review. "In that case," replied Dr. Canby very gently, "I suggest that you look up the Britannica article on Aesthetics and bring suit against yourself." The article in question was, of course, by C. K. Ogden.

The New Britannica

BY

C. K. OGDEN

BETWEEN the ages of ten and twenty-five the growing organism is prepared for the Battle with Death. So too with the Body of Knowledge. Between 1910 and 1925, it "just growed"—and after Topsy, the Autopsy. Its debonair grandsire the eighteenth, its heavy father the nineteenth, of a long line of centuries, were dissected and embalmed in those twelve monumental cenotaphs—the successive editions of the Encyclopædia Britannica as we have known it hitherto. But with the Resurrection at the dawn of the new century, a new Body was formed. Overshadowed in infancy, it grew slowly; but since 1910 its progress has been phenomenal, and now we can profitably take stock of the adolescent period, for the three new volumes of the Encyclopædia are before us.*

Once upon a time the writing of encyclopædias was a glorious adventure, and if your work ever reached a conclusion, *i.e.,* if you eventually got out of prison and could prevent the printers from mutilating your proofs at the last minute, you might even initiate a revolution. Diderot, as we know, was the Debs of Encyclopædism, and it is to Voltaire, who pronounced his achievement a compound of marble and wood, that we owe the description of the Royal supper-party in 1774 after the first twenty-one volumes had been suppressed. He tells us how the conversation turned on the nature of gunpowder; how Madame Pompadour complained that since the confiscation she had no idea

---

* The present survey deals only with the three new volumes. But these are intended to be regarded as supplementing the 11th Edition, 1910 (so as to supersede the War Volumes, 1921, known as the 12th Edition), and forming with it a complete 13th Edition.

what even her rouge or her stockings were made of; how the king thereupon sent for the volumes, and three servants eventually staggered in with a load which answered all the questions mooted; and how the next ten volumes were then sanctioned.

That was the moment chosen by "a society of gentlemen" in Scotland to launch the Encyclopædia Britannica. But with a very different motive, as is shown by the dedication of the two supplementary volumes in 1800, anent Diderot's "dissemination of the seeds of anarchy and atheism."—If they "shall in any degree counteract the tendency of that pestiferous work, even these two volumes will not be wholly unworthy of your Majesty's attention." Needless to say, no one has ever, before or since, accused the Britannica of radical or unsettling tendencies; nor are they likely to do so, as long as the judicious impartiality of Mr. Garvin is in evidence.

These three volumes, however, considerably larger in themselves than the entire first edition of 1771, are remarkable for the extent to which the barriers which have hitherto preserved the public from the inroads of modernity have been broken down. Thus, the Rev. J. M. Creed does not hesitate to expound Leuba's view that there is no essential difference between the so-called religious experience of the mystic and the illusions of narcotic intoxication: "Other psychologists have argued that religion is to be explained in terms of hallucinatory images formed by the mind, to which objective reality is wrongly ascribed." Diderot himself could scarcely ask for more.

This attempt to put at our disposal a means of understanding the material and intellectual forces which have made the past fifteen years amongst the most momentous in history must be pronounced a triumph of publishing and organization by everyone who realizes the labor and goodwill that have gone to its making. In particular, a notable advance can be recorded in all that pertains to the American scene, and here the name of Mr. Hooper has to be joined with those of the Editor and Mr. Holland in awarding to all their due meed of praise. The gradual widening of the Britannica horizon is also evident in the effort to meet the needs of the average family as well as of the librarian and the specialist.

Never, we feel, has such a comprehensive record of human endeavor been offered in so small a compass. Amongst the contributions which no one can afford to miss are the masterly architectural survey by the designer of Bush House, supplemented by the study of City planning (which might with advantage have referred to Le Corbusier's visions of the Paris of tomorrow); Leon Gaster's description of the possibilities of artificial light; Professor Raymond Pearl's discussion of the probabilities of artificial rejuvenation (though both he and Serge Voronoff are agreed that we cannot yet altogether escape Death—or even, be it added, add to our expectation of life); Stefansson's survey of Arctic resources; Henry Ford on Mass Production; Professor Rankine on Sound; Professor R. W. Gregory on Color and Race; and the formidable sextet on the various aspects of Evolution.

The section on Archæology is another notable triumph of composite work, though strangely enough so eminent and active an archæologist as Mr. Harold Peake is not indexed; the unique account of the new developments of air photography in the detection of ancient sites, by O. G. S. Crawford, is embellished by a convincing illustration.

Many would have favored the adoption of the same method for the War itself, and will deplore the practice of splitting up the various military episodes whereby the world was made a Safe for Democracy —to which we have apparently lost the key. The recurrence every few pages of a purely strategic narrative, under the name of some arbitrarily selected battle or campaign, in addition to elaborate studies of the various fronts and full military histories of the different belligerent powers, gives the impression that the Britannica has never been properly demobilized.

The articles on Economics and Social Science are naturally scattered, and number about two hundred, supplemented by over a hundred biographies. The right man for the subject, as in 1910, has been sought, regardless of prejudices, and the result is a sense of freshness and authority which rivals even that of the slightly more technical Engineering contributions. These, by the way, the literary reader should not shirk, for the marvels of modern engineering are often reflected in a brilliant linguistic technique for grappling with the most intricate mechanical constructions. The Currency and Finance section, in twenty-four divisions, will be as valuable to everyone concerned with

business and administration as the less complicated articles on commercial topics proper.

The practical note of Professor Ashley's central summary is echoed
in the thoughtful essays of T. E. Gregory, Sir Josiah Stamp, Gustav
Cassel, Moritz Julius Bonn, and even in the Cassandra-tones of Joseph
Caillaux. The international scope of the work, too, is here seen to
special advantage.

A special word of praise is necessary for many of the biographies.
Mr. Ervine, in particular, is in his element on the subject of Shaw,
and includes a brief excursus on the Shavian religion, showing how
American influences were twice paramount. Mr. D. G. Hogarth tells
the romantic story of Colonel Lawrence; and in the parallel column
the secret is out that the author of "The White Peacock" has written
a successful manual of modern history. In a word the new volumes
have, where suitable, sufficiently subordinated the formal character
which we associate with Encyclopædias to become readable and entertaining in the best sense.

Here is Trotsky assuring us that Lenin was courteous and attentive,
especially to the weak and oppressed, and to children, and Freud explaining why medical hostility could not check the progress of psychoanalysis. Dr. E. J. Dillon refuses to believe "that Izvolsky was responsible for the World War," and G. B. S. tweaks the beard of Capitalism
so violently that the editor has to launch a special bulletin to make
it quite clear that Wall Street is still hale and hirsute. The author of
"Thunder on the Left" gives us a brisk column on O. Henry, who
"often arouses the trained reader's amazement," while the sound
scholars who believe that our language is going to the dogs will hear
them barking in every line of Mr. Mencken's excellent essay on
Americanisms. Joyce's "Ulysses," it appears, is "little known to the
general public," Bela Kun "was a man of medium size, rather plump,"
and Noel Coward "has made himself an international figure." Mary
Pickford's violet eyes smile at us from her niche alongside Doug.,
and even Charlie's feet twinkle through a respectful black-type blurb.

In the exact sciences, of course, the high standard of the main Encyclopædia is fully maintained. Sir Ernest Rutherford and Sir J. J.
Thomson, the knights unerrant of physics, are ably assisted by Pro-

fessors Bohr, Eddington, McLennan, Millikan, and Soddy. To get
Mr. F. W. Aston to write, "Within a tumbler of water lies sufficient
energy to propel the *Mauretania* across the Atlantic and back at full
speed," and Einstein to assert that "we fare no better in our speculations than a fish which should strive to become clear as to what is
water," is an achievement after which any editor might claim a long
week-end.

Medicine, too, is well represented, and a fair balance is struck between the Clinicians and the Bacteriologists. Sir Humphrey Rolleston,
Professor L. F. Barker, Dr. Alexis Carrel, Hideyo Noguchi (Nogouchi
at II-474, as in both lists of contributors), Adolf Lorenz, Sir Almroth
Wright, and Dr. Kinnier Wilson, all contribute of their best. The last
named, by the way, has lately produced a manual for general practitioners embodying all the most recent work on speech defects, and
Piéron's summary of continental experience over the last decade, in
his popular exposition "Thought and the Brain," runs to over a
hundred pages; but in spite of the fact that one of the chief medical
results of the War was the stimulus it gave to Aphasia, even the
single allusion to Dr. Henry Head in these volumes (III-257) does
not get the subject indexed. Another missing entry is Chronaxy, with
its intriguing neurological implications; Bourguignon's contribution,
for example.

But let the reader beware of getting a false impression from any
captious remarks he may read by young men in a hurry to air their
own omniscience. Such an enterprise as this cannot be judged by one
or two lapses, however serious, nor yet by fifty. A few days ago the
Chinese delegate at Geneva, on the pretext of presenting to the League
of Nations a Chinese Encyclopædia, used his moments on the platform to insinuate a number of tuitional statements about gunboats
and cruisers on distant waters. Just as we cannot condemn the whole of
China even for such a lapse as this, so we may hesitate to decry the
Britannica because, as we shall contend, the analogy is not altogether
inapplicable. Its methods and its material may frequently be at fault,
but let us generously acknowledge the great stride an institution 158
years old has taken towards a renewal of those spacious days of
Encyclopædia-making, when Pierre Bayle would write down all that

he knew in alphabetical order, because he enjoyed doing it, with taste and gusto. Fresh breezes are blowing through these 3,000 pages, and a new and welcome spirit informs the majority of its 1,200 contributors. With this preamble, let us muster such reverence as befits an *advocatus diaboli* confronted by their labors.

II

A just criticism, we readily admit, makes much of good points and only mentions flaws for the purpose of future improvement. Our sole reason for adding a second part to this survey is the supreme importance and outstanding merits of the new Britannica. It would be an easy and a pleasant task to continue to lay stress on those merits, but for the discerning reader every further inch devoted to this edition is actually a further compliment. The following notes, then, are designed primarily for persons who are already in possession of the volumes and who expect from the *Saturday Review* some indication of the extent to which their record of modern achievement can claim to be "complete."

Since any such probe in these degenerate days is liable to be misinterpreted, let it be explained at the outset that the Britannica survives the test with flying colors—relatively to any other Encyclopædia in the world. But Homer's occasional surreptitious nod does not license the stertorous exhibitionism of his rivals. It is hardly necessary to state that the mention of an omission is not a demand for a biography. Every reader of the Britannica knows that only a very small proportion of those included are treated separately. Omissions are judged by the comparative standards set in these volumes themselves and by the public claims to completeness which have been made for them. In other words, 90 per cent of the names he has looked for in vain are regarded by the reviewer as more important than 30 per cent of the corresponding inclusions. It should be possible for an inquirer at once to discover from these three thousand pages whether and whereby they are able, notable, or noble, *i.e.,* whether their success is due to brains, behavior, or blood.

The Britannica does not regard itself as impressionistic or eclectic, and it is not so regarded. The reader who failed at once to find Low or Weyl might complain that American Administration and the Universe respectively had been inadequately treated; so the Britannica has exalted each in its own way. Britons must just accept the fact (though they may balk at the misplaced and misprinted entry "Weil's hypothesis"), but when they hear the *cognoscenti* acclaiming Sacharoff and Robeson they will find that here their needs have been less carefully considered, though in both fields ample space has been devoted to numerous lesser personalities.

The criticism, then, is one of judgment and correlation rather than of policy or intention. The Britannica, in fact, has doubled its value by opening its pages to modernity, but it is not surprising that in such an intellectual hurricane the editorial trireme rocks a trifle. Every little while the oars do not beat in unison, and a crab is caught. Imagine, for instance, a man "temperamentally desperate, loving extremes, . . . almost querulously criticizing the world's workings." There is in fact such a miserable specimen of humanity. His name, according to the Britannica biography, is Bertrand Arthur William Russell. He "has been peculiarly successful in eliciting from contemporary physics those theorems that are most consonant with his own temper." Bearing that in mind, locate now the most crucial article in the whole three volumes, the one that requires for its composition the acutest, the astutest, the most balanced, and the best informed mind in Christendom. There is such an article. It is on Knowledge itself—what we can know and how we know it. And whom does the editor select to write that article? The whole royal stable and all Cal's men will not induce me to give him away.

Something has gone wrong somewhere. As Mr. Russell himself writes: "I have read accounts of my own death in the newspapers, but I abstained from inferring that I was a ghost." Nay more: Mr. Russell visited Russia shortly after the war with the Labor delegation, and published a book expressing his disapproval of what he saw. He was subsequently appointed Professor of Philosophy in the University of Peking, being the first European thinker of first-class attainments to win the confidence of the East. The significance of such a contact for the future thought of the world has yet to be appreciated. The Britannica allows these events to be recorded as follows: "He travelled through China and Bolshevik Russia."

In the biography of F. H. Bradley we are informed that he "once and for all established the supremacy of idealism over realism, in dialectical controversy." On page 332 of Volume III, where modern thought says its last word, this is very properly contradicted—"It is a mistake to suppose that relativity adopts an idealistic picture of the world." But when we finally reach the Golden Gates behind which "there is found to be a residue not dependent upon the point of view of the observer" we are met by the magic word Tensors. The editors have presumably not noticed that after thus whetting our curiosity about this mysterious cosmic mantram, "the importance of which can hardly be exaggerated," the Britannica, though not elsewhere afraid of technicalities, leaves us in the lurch: for Professor Eddington, who likewise contracts a tensor just at this point (III-908a), also contracts his exegetic antennæ.

The Britannica has always featured the Population problem and Malthus himself adorned the supplement to the fifth edition. But it is too little known that Malthus was a clergyman and a Fellow of Jesus College, Cambridge. Consequently it is a new departure to be informed that Dr. Marie Stopes' "exhaustive treatise has been largely used by doctors and medical students." The Rev. Sir James Marchant is further inspired by his subject, Birth Control, to quote:

> By filching all the substance of the fit
> We make the rotten multiply as it.

Perhaps in the fourteenth edition he will rise to the worthier lines:

> There was an old woman who lived in a stew:
> She had so many children; she *didn't* know what to do.

The recent triumphs of Parasitology and the discovery of a virus or a tic in connection with so many of the ills to which flesh is heir seem to have led to a new and somewhat sinister form of medical optimism which might be christened *Virustics*. At any rate both Professor S. L.

Cummins (II-474), and still more confidently Dr. C. M. Wenyon (III-50b), as well as Dr. Tidy (I-978), envisage the complete virustication of Influenza.

Meanwhile we would have welcomed an article on the exorcism of the common cold, or of alopecia, to show just how far we really have progressed beyond our grandmothers. For though there is nearly a page of information and advice (how to move the bowels, etc.) should you be stricken by Phlebotomous fever in Malta, there is nothing to warn Americans against facing possible death by inoculation for typhoid prior to a European pleasure trip—and returning to find that the family has caught it in New York. Nor is anything said about Mongolian imbecility, for which this year's Bradshaw lecturer propounded so challenging an ætiology in 1924; about the effects of Noise and its abatement; or about Abrams' box.

Such reticence, when we reach topics which interest intelligent people not over-endowed with special knowledge, is distressing. Apart from an unindexed allusion, under Pragmatism, there is no mention of that outstanding American genius, Charles Santiago Sanders Peirce; nor of such pioneers of modern thought as Smith Ely Jelliffe, William A. White, Stewart Paton, G. M. Gould, Charles R. Stockard, R. W. Wood, and J. J. Putnam (Major Putnam's name by the way is also notably inconspicuous). Edward Carpenter fails to register, though throughout the period covered his influence on thought both in England and America has been considerable. More astonishing still is the fact that we search in vain for G. Lowes Dickinson and Rebecca West. And Stop, Look, Listen!—for Professor W. Z. Ripley (at whose whisper Wall Street winces) is not reckoned among the First Hundred Thousand of his compatriots. No wonder the Britannica suggests (I-420) that had Carpentier come to New York, he would have been a mere pork and beaner.

Though incorrigibly repetitive, the treatment of Armageddon is admittedly authoritative. We search, however, without success for any mention of General Hoffmann, the opponent of Ludendorff, whose book "The War of Lost Opportunities" is surely one of the most notable documents of the last ten years. His rôle in shaping recent history was presumably as great as that of, say Johann Friedrich (q.v.); which also applies to the Hon. James M. Beck, Frederic Coudert, Sir Geoffrey Butler, and Arthur Ponsonby. Nor do we find any allusion to the exploits of Nogales Bey. Rasputin is in, but not Burt Reese. It is curious, too, that J. B. S. Haldane's "Callinicus" is not mentioned even in the bibliography of the lengthy article on Chemical Warfare. That he himself is not in the index is, however, merely a mistake; for he is there confused with his father, the Vitalist—after the best traditions of the American press, which throughout the divorce proceedings against Cambridge University insisted on using photographs of the Oxford Professor in spectacles.

Marshal Foch asserts (II-950) that the British Tommy marched into battle "to the cry of 'Lusitania.'" We are more inclined to believe him when he declares that while soldiers wait in the trenches, "hours succeed hours, nights follow days, and weeks go by." It may be noted that though there is an arresting supernumerary article on War, like Pelion piled on Ossa, by Sir Ian Hamilton, there is no sign of a companion plea for Peace. A dirge on World Recovery and three despondent epithalamia on International Rapprochement do not adequately counterbalance the 70,000-word epic entitled World War; and by the same token the name Norman Angell is not in the index. Several of the 193 special military contributions look, or shall we say point, forward to the Next War. Two and a half pages, for example, are devoted to devices for attacking submerged hostile submarines, when your vessel is moving at a high speed, by means of paravanes equipped with automatic dynamometer switch trippers. In other words a highly technical article, dealing chiefly with offensive tactics in active warfare and quite likely to be out of date next year, gets more than twice the space devoted to the whole subject of Anæsthetics!

In their advertisements the Britannica Company referred to seventeen of their contributors as having won the Nobel Prize. We turn to the entry Nobel Prize to discover what standard it has maintained since 1910, but there is no such entry. To verify a hazy recollection that the Prime Minister of Great Britain recommended Mr. E. D. Morel, just before his death, for the said prize, we look the traitor up; no mention. The Congo, then: again the slippery scamp escapes us. The Union of Democratic Control, which he founded and whose committee afterwards virtually formed the British Cabinet; no mention. Quakers—with whom he plotted; no mention. Pacifism—in which he saw the hope of the future; no mention. Wearily we try the League of Nations—yes, Mr. Garvin allows us to hear of that.

Graham Wallas draws a blank. So does Dr. Eileen Power, most erudite and gracious of modern historians. Where then is the "New History" of which the biographer of James Harvey Robinson gives us a tantalizing glimpse? The "A. K. Travelling Fellowships," designed to broaden the minds of historians; no mention. Albert Kahn himself, who gave all that money? Nor Otto Kahn, who gave more still to still more deserving causes? Shame! Then Otto Beit, perhaps, whose generosity has made his name a household word amongst scientists? Or Arthur Serena, who founded so many costly chairs to make Italian thought and culture better known to the English-speaking world; not a word of either. And in spite of those chairs, neither Sante de Sanctis, nor Federigo Enriqués, nor Eugenio Rignano, nor Professor Luciani is known to the Britannica index, where even Gentile is misspelt. Such is gratitude—but perhaps Sir Basil Zaharoff, since he has both endowed learning and influenced the destinies of nations, is more fortunate; not even he.

As regards history, then, and the making of history the Britannica cannot be unequivocally congratulated. The lid is still down on J. L. Hammond, Montague Summers, G. G. Coulton, H. J. Laski, Norman Baynes, Alfred Zimmern, M. Dorothy George, Sir Samuel Dill, E. Lipson, Professors Gras, Arias, Brodnitz and Kosminsky, and R. H. Tawney. Not one of these prime determinants of twentieth century revaluations gets a mention. And you may read right through the index without finding the name of Mr. G. P. Gooch.

Reverting for a moment to Sir Basil's interest in Athens, Oxford and Monte Carlo (Harvard men can agree to symbolically omit the comma, since the Britannica omits Professor Kittredge), we are reminded of the classic game of chance known as Offs and Ons. You write down all the world-famous names you know that end in off, and for each that is not in the Encyclopædia index you score another point. The same with the Ons. My score to date, including Rachmaninoff and Carrie Nation, is twenty.

The English reader, like the dilettante, turns eagerly to the survey of American literature, where he had had so little opportunity of forming a just estimate; and he discovers a mine of valuable information. We note that America accepts E. E. Cummings, but England has not yet adopted T. S. Eliot—even as a critic. German literature is admirably covered by Soergel; but when we come to Britain we must confess that if the Britannica makes any claim to completeness, the omissions we have already recorded, where so many hundreds are admitted, would already give us pause. Moreover, here are ten names not one of which can be found in the index: Arthur Symons, Laurence Housman, R. Y. Tyrrell, Eden Phillpotts, Israel Zangwill, Rose Macaulay, Wyndham Lewis, Harold Munro, Alfred Noyes, Aldous Huxley. A careful search, however, does discover allusions to the last five in the main text, as well as of the unindexed Sir Owen Seaman (I-1010; though *Punch* "continued to reflect the prejudices rather than the judgments of the educated middle class." I-539). But let the American reader who so readily gets confused by Mr. and Mrs. Leonard Woolf, Humbert Wolfe, Wolfe the painter, Wolf the Maccabæan, and now "Turbott Wolfe," see what assistance he can get; for even with the aid of the text itself I have only tracked down a single Woolf, in Virginia (I-2008a).

Where more than a page is devoted to praise of Alice Meynell, someone might put in a word for England's most delectable emotionalist, Arthur Machen, though he did bring the Angels to Mons; or a line for that master of word-craft, Mr. Powys Mathers, though he did translate those "Nights" (Mardrus himself should appear); or a paragraph for the sophisticated satire of Norman Douglas, though he does live in Capri. And might not Edward M. C. Mackenzie (for so Mr. Compton Mackenzie appears in the index, where the reference at I-1008 should be added) be allowed some credit for his Phonograph record? Darrell Figgis, too; and the whole Sitwell family would seem to belong to the period covered, or vice versa.

But perhaps literature is, as they say, a matter of prejudices, and anyhow space had to be found for the news that "men, women, and children of all colors" answered the queen-mother's appeal for a Kitchener memorial.

Yet it cannot be a matter of space, for look at the biographies of Carlo Caneva, Luigi Capello, James Schoolcraft Sherman, or Count Casimir Badeni (who died in 1909 and gets as many inches as John Dewey), and the article on Choral singing which shows how "square-toed Choralism has been shaken to the roots" so that now "first rate work can be produced anywhere"—not only in Yorkshire. Now, too, "the dominions bid fair to follow the good example of the mother country," but "America has not yet produced a composer of outstanding choral works."

And need those homes of culture, the townships of Lancashire, advertize their parochial misfortunes at quite such length? In Preston, we are glad to learn, "much attention has been given to the health of the city and to the provision of hospitals, infant welfare centres, etc." We had already wondered whether the drainage problem was still engaging the attention of the Mayor. From Salford come tidings that "a wide new road was opened at Pendleton in 1925, and further road improvements were under consideration in 1926," while in Bolton "a Presbyterian Church and the Claremont Baptist Institute were erected in 1910." At Blackburn, "St. Jude's Church was built and its parish formed from that of St. Thomas in 1914." Blackpool has prepared "an ambitious scheme of development, including a 'social centre,' a restaurant, and a lake." What is Wigan going to do about it? A cafeteria perhaps?

The articles on the social side of Industry are for the most part hardly less uninspired than the disconnected oddments on international organization (Arbitration and the various Pacts). "Health," we read (III-463) "is needed for efficient work"; and Miss May Smith occupies two whole pages in elaborating the thesis that we cannot work for twenty-four hours a day. ("The physiological necessity for sleep prevented the complete working out of this principle.") We also learn that "a good industrial leader should possess vitality, sympathy, justice, and humor, as well as knowledge of the work." The late P. E. B. Jourdain, the paralytic mathematician, possessed all these qualities in a supreme degree. So, one would suppose, does Mr. Ring Lardner. The Girl Scouts, "known as Brownies," who are to be found under the Boy Scouts at page 423 of Vol. I, may, however, be without humor.

Everything, too, is provided for domestic bliss, from dish-washers to fire-extinguishers. The attempt to cope with Divorce strikes a layman as less adequate, and aspirants pressed for time would probably be better advised to go direct to Dudley Field Malone—another international name for the Editors to note on their cuffs.

Without a System, modern business would undoubtedly be back at 1910. By the best people, "motor-driven machines are used for endorsing large numbers of cheques. . . . Cheques are fed by hand one at a time." And again (III-1005d), "a stenographer employed in taking notes and transcribing letters, will do much more effective work than one who also keeps and files records": but will she abstain from putting commas between subjects and their verbs, Mr. Leffingwell? *Vivent les fourmis!* Our little friends the ants have reached an even higher degree of efficiency in the polycalic formicary.

Education is equally badly served. Lord Haldane and Professor Judd give us little idea of the ferment of new life which their stuffy summaries conceal. It is something that "Metaphysics" has vanished; but "Philosophy" remains, undisturbed by the fact that its foundations, too, have lately been removed; and Theology, unaware that Mr. Clive Bell's "significant form" has silently withdrawn before the shafts of linguistic analysis, is reduced to hoping that the even more naïve verbal projections of Otto may establish the existential validity of the numinous. In Logic we are asked to believe that the work of Driesch and Royce was the most important contribution between 1910 and 1921—though the articles on Knowledge, Mathematics, Philology, and Pragmatism fortunately combine to stultify this estimate.

Scepticism is gingerly tackled, but something must be done when the scientists are so disparaging about our eyes and ears. Thus "it is impossible to rely upon audition, handicapped as it is by the vagaries of the ear" (III-590). Sound, however, is not something which we hear. Nor is color what we see; that is only *visible* color. The really exciting colors, explains Professor Thorpe, are the *invisible* ones! Visible color, such as it is, receives inadequate treatment, however. The systems of Ross and Munsell, the experiments of Ladd-Franklin, and the work of Dr. Mary Collins are all passed over. Even in its biography of Ostwald the Britannica omits to record that the last ten years of his life have been devoted to Color, and to the publication of a number of fundamental studies bearing on a system of standardization which will only be superseded when the Tudor-Hart double inverted cones are finally available. The bibliographies are said to "provide lists of books carefully selected by the specialist who contributes the article." As one narcissist to another, I particularly commend the care with which Dr. Edridge-Green has selected his bibliography.

While it is indeed gratifying to have Dr. John B. Watson's crystallization of Behaviorism it is disappointing to find no mention of so profound and influential a thinker as Professor W. M. Wheeler, America's leading entomologist and perhaps her leading sociologist as well. Mr. Cornelius Newton Bliss and Mr. James Carrol Beckwith are dignified by full biographies, but Professors W. B. Cannon and C. Judson Herrick, who have contributed so brilliantly to our understanding of the body and mind of man, receive no word of appreciation. Sir Richard Burbidge secures a handsome tribute, but Major Darwin's life-service to Eugenics evokes no echo. Charles Frohman is immortalized at length, but Mr. Orage's decade of intellectual pioneering on the *New Age* is greeted with silence, and even his journal draws a blank; the same applies to Henry Goddard Leach, while Herbert Croly is indexed as Croley. Dean Keppel is side-stepped no less than J. O'Hara Cosgrave, Walkley, Hartley Withers, Bruce Richmond, and Norman Hapgood. Frank Harris suffers with them. Baron Corvo rings no bells, nor Panait Istrati, nor the Poet Laureate's "discovery" of Gerard Hopkins. Even capricoprophily avails Aleister Crowley naught, though his claims as poet are at least equal to those of Edna St. Vincent Millay; and it is a pity that Rudolph Valentino lived and died in vain.

Why, if Douglas Fairbanks, not Jackie Coogan, Billy Sunday, Sandow, Frank Crane, Pola Negri, Madame Nazimova, Emil Jannings, Raquel Meller and Mistinguette? I say nothing of the aristocracy of Variety—Lady Peel, Earl Carroll, and Lord George Sanger—though the Sanger circus, *pace* the index, does secure a mention at I-638d; but where are Mascagni and Toscanini, and where Jeritza? Surely those who stir the emotions of millions should have absolute precedence over the Philatelists and their acquisitive idiosyncrasies. More than a hundred words are consecrated to Aerophilosemy (q. v.) but Eugène

Goossens, who re-introduced Stravinsky to England, conducted the Russian Ballet, became the father of twins, thrice visited Rochester, and is now due in Hollywood, receives no recognition, though he should be in as a composer, quite apart from the allure of his *vie de bâton*. His predecessor in Hollywood, Sir Henry Wood, is equally unfortunate. So is Ysaÿe. Some would regard Mme Suggia as more than a John, but she might have been listed as that (II-610). John McCormack need only open his mouth for thirty minutes once a year to keep himself and family in food and clothing, but of those minutes the tens of thousands who hang on his lips cherish a lasting memory; yet he returns from his triumphs in China to find that the Britannica can dispense with him altogether. Ruth Draper is the outstanding personality of the American solipsist stage, but neither she nor her locally eminent medical brother (in spite of his concern for the Constitution, admitted at I-981) is allowed to snip half an inch off those treatises on square-toed Choralism and detonating Paravanes.

The Drama gets plenty of space; but unless we can assume that misprints occur in key articles, Mr. St. John Ervine might find a better predicate than "meritable" to apply to his own "Jane Clegg" (I-869c). Literary Criticism has not yet heard of I. A. Richards, nor Dancing of Margaret Morris or the Quadro Flamenco, though the Charleston "was already dying out in 1926." We find no allusion to Gurdjeff, and Geoffrey Toye's colleagues, Leopold Stokowski and Ernest Bloch, should at least be given half a line if so full a biography is to reward Sousa's services to music since 1910. Gershwin must get busy with some Out in the Cold Blues, nor has the editorial chariot swung low enough for Roland Hayes. Somewhere between Aesthetics and Atmospherics we had half expected to hear of Antheil, and somewhere between Albee and Ziegfeld we might have glimpsed Will Rogers or Florence Mills, but all three have escaped this gross reticulation. Amongst the scores of black and white bruisers whose form is analyzed at I-420, we miss the only one who has punched continuously since 1919 without striking his match, *viz* Tunney; while Fish is correspondingly absent from a further long list of successful black and white artists at I-539.

Since Science and Learning refuse to play at all with their eminent sons Professors Herbert A. Giles and E. W. Parker the sinologists, J. W. Postgate and Fritz Mauthner the protagonists of semantics, Flick and Feuter the historiographers, Jacques de Morgan and Déchelette the pre-historians, and since both von Buschan and von Uexküll are also absent from the index, the biography accorded to Professor Fitz-maurice-Kelly is all the more significant as a tribute to the progress of Hispanic philology. Fabre is in, but Donisthorpe, Bugnion, Emery and Escherich, no less than Mr. Ernest Thompson Seton, have natural-ized in vain; and Father Wasmann is apparently too myrmecophilous even to be entered as a symposiast in the Animal Intelligence contro-versy.

Having approached our Britannica from the standpoint of knowl-edge, let us now for a moment consider her in the family way. America is proud of her Cabots, but is given instead a single Lodge. Britain is proud of her golf champions and would like to see them indexed, but since even "Mr. R. T. Jones, commonly called 'Bobby,'" is not indexed in spite of all the nice things Darwin's grandson says about him on the same page, what can plain John Ball expect? And where is the rest of this potent English stock? Most of us remember how the heavens were first opened for them by the late Sir Robert Ball, the author of the astronomical articles in the 1910 Britannica. Neither he, nor W. W. Rouse Ball, the genial historian of Mathematics, nor C. T. Ball the Assyriologist, nor Sidney Ball who moulded the social thought of so many generations of Oxonians, nor J. Ball, the geog-rapher of Africa, is so much as alluded to; nor yet the Nottingham aces. No Balls at all, but discreet pages, covering both Whales and Earnings, by Bowley and Borley, a carillon of Bells, a long range of Hills, six Fishers, six Morgans, six Joneses (without Bobby), six Murrays, six Robertsons, seven Scotts, eight Millers, eight Walkers, nine Andersons, and fourteen Smiths.

After the family the nation, so let us once more vary the *venue* by a geographical approach and consider specifically the intellectual achievements of France. There is assuredly no prejudice as yet against our glorious ally and presumably every effort has been made to reflect and interpret her thought. Yet here is a list of names which everyone who knows anything of the movement of ideas must agree are hardly less significant than those of the Rev. Lyman Abbott, Mr. Owen Wister, Mr. Edward Arber, or John Strange Winter. Starting with the *doyen* of French letters, Ferdinand Brunot, we proceed as follows: Julien Benda, Henri Berr, René Berthelot, Georges Blondel, Léon Brunschwicg, René Cruchet, Georges Dumas, Espinas, Giard, Grand-jean, Goblot, Laignel-Lavastine, Lalande, Le Dantec, Milhaud, Mari-tain, Paulhan, Piaget, de Pressensé, Pradines, Rabaud, Rivière, Rougier, Segond, Séailles, concluding with Georges Sorel, whose "Reflexions on Violence" surely exercised more influence on this generation than all the works of Ferdinand Tönnies and Sir Frederick Wedmore combined.

Not one of these leaders of French thought can be found in the Britannica index! And where are Richepin, Henri de Régnier, Colette Willy, Dufy, and the builder of the Eiffel Tower? As for other domi-nating figures in the record of the last fifteen years, it would be hard to find more startling omissions than Auguste Forel, Léon Duguit, and Vilfredo Pareto, though an equally formidable trio consists of Rops, Lipps, and Stumpf (I would have added Wundt for euphony, were it not that he does happen to have caught the editor's fancy). But before we leave the subject of eminent Frenchmen we may note that Jules Romains (wrongly spelt without an s on five separate occasions) is not the real name of the author of "Dr. Knock," that he did not "make a reputation for himself" by that play, but was justly famous even ten years earlier, and that his much discussed work, "Eyeless Sight," was written under his own name of Louis Farigoule and should not be overlooked.

But would not the rectification of these omissions require more space than the Britannica had at its command? If so, much of the above would, of course, be irrelevant. Our point is, however, that judgment and adjustment alone are involved; or at most the extra space which would be available if such curiosities as "Time Sales" and "Hythe, Conference of" were reconsidered, the articles on Barracks and Canteens curtailed, and the experts on Ping Pong, Luck, and possibly Ballistics appropriately curbed! The index could then include such names as the following, who by all the canons of Encyclopædism belong to these eventful years, even if they figured to some extent in the older volumes. Sir Francis Younghusband, Iwan Bloch, Sir William Barrett, Professor James Sully, Professor William Smart, Vaihinger, H. B. Irving, A. H. Fried, Benjamin Kidd, Sir Victor Horsley, and Lady Welby. And what is psychiatry without Emil Kraepelin, phonetics without the researches of E. W. Scripture, the press without Mr. Swope, or sport without Babe Ruth, whose English counterpart, by the way, is wrongly listed as G. B. Hobbs?

Occasionally, as we have seen, the index may fail to do justice to the Britannica even where the giants are concerned. A glaring example is the case of Wolfgang Köhler who appears, wrongly spelt, at I-383, but *summa cum laude* at II-495. H. S. Jennings is in at I-382, Glotz at I-178, Professor Rothenstein can be found at II-6, and Mr. Rutherston at III-411, while Gilbert and Stanley Spencer both occur at III-8; thus scoring over Duveen and Berenson alike. Neither Meinong nor Husserl has really been omitted—except where we should expect them; the former, however, appears as Alexander instead of Alexius (II-190d). There is no excuse for such misleading omissions, when Kalkstickstoff (sic), *Stickstoffkalk* and two other chance synonyms for crude cyanamide are all gravely entered. Indeed the indexing as a whole seems to have been done on somewhat arbitrary principles, which, where arrangement and contents are equally arbitrary, is particularly to be deprecated.

In our opinion it would have been more important to be able to find quickly in these new volumes such names as Avenarius, F. C. Conybeare, W. A. Craigie, Edward J. Dent, Michael Farbman, Jane Harrison, and Baron Meyendorff (so far, we have only found the first two) than that "brilliant filly" Fifinella (Steinberg, *obiit* 1908), the gallant Shcherbackev (q. v.), or even the heroic Shtcherbachev (q. v.) who constitutes a good example of literary double-exposure.

In a work of this sort a complete and impeccable index is essential. But some articles, such as that of Mr. Cochran, seem hardly to have been judged worthy of attention, and another example is to be found in the Johns Hopkins column, where Doctor Wilmer may ultimately be located. Moorish names seem early to have been given up in despair, after an amusing attempt to index one misprint by another (Anoal, III-614c). We should be surprised to find that more than five per cent of the persons referred to in the bibliographies and bibliographical sections are indexed. Thus Mr. Garvin himself in his article on Capitalism (L-528b) singles out for recommendation a book which no American publisher can be persuaded to accept, Mr. M. H. Dobb's "Capitalist Enterprise and Social Progress" ("an acute critical analysis of the place of the entrepreneur"). Yet this able young Cambridge economist does not get into the index, whereas, for example, Carter G. Woodson, mentioned only in the bibliographical notes on Negro literature (I-111a), is duly inserted. Joseph Priestley is wrongly spelt in the index; Ellen Terry on the other hand, like the Ford Peace Ship, is not there at all, though the one is referred to in the full text at I-756 and the other at II-270 ("In 1915 he was convinced by certain peace advocates of foreign extraction," etc.; which the reader may compare with Mr. Lochner's version in "America's Don Quixote"). The Harvard notational relativist, H. M. Sheffer (II-830b), is not listed, nor is the dramatist H. M. Harwood (II-870, III-873), nor the chief references to Professor Elliot Smith (I-385, II-567), nor Charles M. Doughty's appearances as a geographer (I-1091, II-171).

Particularly unsystematic is the listing of periodicals. *Simplicissimus* appears in italics and quotes, *Jugend* not at all, though in the text they occur together. *Harper's Bazaar* and *Harper's Magazine* are in roman type, *The Century* in italics, while the *Forum* is nowhere to be found. Though Capablanca's prowess at chess is squarely dealt with, Bogoljuboff, who won the 1926 Tournament and is thrice referred to (I-602), must be content with that, like Euwe, Samisch, and others whose exploits with Rooks and Knights Mr. Van Vleit has so faithfully chronicled. Professor F. C. Burkitt, who seems to have been totally overlooked, will be sorry to see his son's name misspelt in the Editorial Preface.

Among five million words at least a dozen will always be errors or omissions. That proposition is proved once more in the case of the Britannica as follows: Duhamel should be *Georges* not George, Professor Lashley is *K. S.*, not L. S., and the foremost educationist of this century is *Georg*, not H., Kerschensteiner. Sydney Webb (I-390) should be *Sidney* and should receive fair treatment in the index (III-525, III-572) even if he was a failure in the Cabinet. Wicod (II-830) is a disconcerting misprint for the late Jean *Nicod* who should be indexed, and who also occurs at II-644d. Incidentally, if Wittgenstein is as important as Mr. Ramsey makes him in the article on Mathematics, he certainly deserves a biography. Kandinsky has been overlooked at I-190 and II-793, where he is wrongly spelt on both occasions. *Kurt* Koffka, please, not C. Koffka, Mr. Printer, for this is unfortunately the only reference to the brilliant apostle of *Gestalt* in the whole three volumes, and he is due back in America this week. A sentence has gone astray at I-1010d, complete should be *incomplete* at III-915c, and Pragmatistism *Pragmatism* at III-206c. I also note that Mr. Bernard Shaw is made to attribute war "on a scale which threatens not only civilization but human existence" to the "nobility" of capital. This rivals the famous printer's error, Hotario Bottomley, who does not get in even as Horatio, though he is now at large again.

In many cases there is no indication that the works of a foreign author are available in good English translations—a particularly striking example being Romain Rolland. This is presumably due to the fact that recourse has been had to foreign writers for many of these biographies. Tischner is recommended in the German and not the English edition by the writer of the article on Psychical Research, who, we think, is ill-advised in attaching so much importance to the "medium" Willy Schneider.

Students of the occult will notice that Houdini curtly dismisses all mediums, including "Margery" and the makers of "ectoplasm," in his brief article on Conjuring; and in general there is an abundance of piquant material scattered about for the curious reader. Thus the Britannica understands that a Tibetan lad is starting a small hydro-electric scheme in Lhasa (III-777c). Elsewhere it records that the Ringlings "set out from New York in four or five trains," this spring (I-637). It is interesting to know that America can claim the first five and twenty years of the life of Jacob Epstein (not to be confused with his patron, Mr. Jacob Epstein of Baltimore, the possessor of the Raphaels and the Rembrandts); we are given a superb picture of Lower Manhattan, some life-like Mendelian rats, and a faithful study of Musicians recording; and the colored illustrations add greatly to the impression of magnificence which pervades this stupendous undertaking.

For when all is said, these 5,000,000 words are a more worthy record of our time than anything that has hitherto been published. Mr. Garvin may not go down to history as the man who transformed Swords into Ploughshares, but at least he can be hailed as the man who took the initial sibilance out of Swords. Let us add wings to his words by promptly beckoning them to our shelves.

Only moderate notice was taken when Frank Moore Colby died in 1925. During his life he was no great seeker of society, and society has not sought him since his death. I do not suppose many people have read his essays: "Imaginary Obligations" (1904), "Constrained Attitudes" (1910), and "The Margin of Hesitation" (1921). Yet he was one of the best informal essayists produced in this country, the negligent master of a style witty, humorous, and urbane. With all this, American writers have hardly been conscious of his influence.

Perhaps to be "influential" in the modern journalistic sense, one must have in one's make-up at least a thin streak of vulgarity. Colby had none. During a period when complacence and mediocrity for the most part ruled the literary roost, he paid the penalty that comes of being almost puritanically conscientious.

Colby was not a professional writer. After a brief period of teaching at Columbia and New York University, he succeeded Harry Thurston Peck (there's another neglected figure for you) as editor of the New International Encyclopedia and the New International Yearbook. His trade, then, for the larger part of his mature life was that of an encyclopedist, which is, as he tells us, an executive rather than a literary job. From our point of view it was a silly waste of a fine brain, but Colby must have had his own reasons for doing what he did, and it is not for us to question them.

Perhaps this splitting of his life had its good points. It helped to produce in him a humorous attitude toward books and writers, the long, ironic view that the professional critic, busily, busily, busily reading all day long, tends to lose. This attitude has its limitations, too. Colby wrote at times like a gentleman scholar, as if he had been comfortably retired since infancy. But his detachment never weakened into mere elegance. He was too self-distrustful for that. Philip Littell, who knew him, wrote, "His was the face of a person having authority, to whom authority was distrustful, and who thought the idea that he himself possessed it altogether absurd."

Today the literature of discursive reflection seems on its last legs. We no longer ask of a writer whether he has an interesting mind; we ask what his mind stands for. Our public thinking is done for a purpose. We have not the time—or the time does not encourage us —to let our mind drift, its oars shipped, its rudder loose. Colby had the kind of discursive intellect that has ceased to be fashionable. He was as interested in how much play he could get out of it as in how much work it could produce. Perhaps that is the definition of a humorist, and Colby was one.

Like many humorists—Aristophanes was the first, and a good example—he was conservative. He was fond of ringing changes on his aphorism "A 'new thinker,' when studied closely, is merely a man who does not know what other people have thought." He was, I should judge, a fairly good classicist, in the eighteenth-century English manner, and because he was familiar with the standards set up by writers of the past, he was not for a moment taken in by the puerilities of current literary fashion. He is an excellent monitor for book reviewers, which is one reason I reread him often and with profit. He knows my tribe perfectly: "A critic is commonly a person who reads with an unusual show of feeling some very usual book, then tries to turn the writer's head completely or else to take it off." And of the great works of the past he has said with penetrating shrewdness, "The classics are not and never have been chiefly valuable as the means of success. They are obviously valued as the means of escaping its consequences." This is pretty much what Mortimer Adler teaches, though more systematically, in How to Read a Book.

If circumstances allow me to do another of these grab bags I should like to include some of Frank Moore Colby's writings on writing. You will find many of the best of them in a two-volume collection called The Colby Essays, selected and edited after his death by his friend Clarence Day. From these volumes I have chosen two pieces, neither of them critical. The first is "Trials of an Encyclopedist," diverting in itself and also useful as a mild counterblast to C. K. Ogden's review of the Britannica. After all, the encyclopedists have a case to make, too, and Colby makes it for them, though not perhaps precisely in the way they would prefer. I hope other readers will share my pleasure in Colby's account of his invented clergyman and the story of his adventure with the biologists.

The second selection, "Confessions of a Gallomaniac," is one of the most delicious pieces Colby ever wrote. Philip Littell praises it aptly when he says that the essay "as a whole is to Mark Twain on the German language what comedy is to farce." Its humor, so pure and true, links it with the humor of James Thurber.

Here, finally, is a small handful of Colbyisms that may give you the twist of his mind:

"Horace Walpole with his even flow of animal spites."

"Never burn an uninteresting letter is the first rule of British aristocracy."

"One learns little more about a man from the feats of his literary memory than from the feats of his alimentary canal."

"By rights, satire is a lonely and introspective occupation, for nobody can describe a fool to the life without much patient self-inspection."

"Self-esteem is the most voluble of the emotions."

"When a young American writer seems mad it is usually because an old one drives him almost crazy."

(Of H. G. Wells) "He is annoyed by the senseless refusal of almost everybody to shape his life in such a manner as will redound to the advantage of the beings who will people the earth a hundred thousand years hence."

Trials of an Encyclopedist

BY

FRANK MOORE COLBY

For the past twenty years, with occasional interruptions, I have been associated with encyclopedias either as a department editor or as an editor of the work as a whole.* I began by writing for an encyclopedia that has since gone into the junk-shop things beginning with the letter A. It may have been the Jewish month Abib. More likely it was one of those two familiar animals Aardvark and Aardwolf that are always at the mouth of every encyclopedia Hades. I don't remember my maiden effort—nor does anybody else. I didn't dream that twenty years later I should be worrying lest I hadn't said the latest thing about Zululand in an annual volume covering the year 1909. It began with a flirtation and ended in marriage. I am still what Dr. Johnson called the lexicographer—"a harmless drudge."

From the advertisements one would never guess that encyclopedias are made by human beings. Nor does a casual encounter with encyclopedia editors, of whom fortunately there are very few, always carry a strong conviction on that point. I am myself aware of being badly damaged by my calling. I feel drier after twenty years of it than I believe I should have felt after an equal time at some more gregarious occupation, and I fancy other people sometimes find me even drier

---

* This essay is one of the many that Colby published anonymously. It appeared in 1911, when he was forty-six, over the semi-transparent pseudonym of C. M. Francis. Colby was editor of the New International Encyclopedia, and of the International Year Book, and he used to say that after each new edition appeared his mind was so stuffed with facts that he had to pluck them out of his memory one by one, like slivers. Or he would vary the simile and complain that while the work was in progress his brain had felt like a coal-chute—tons of general information rattling through it in one long deafening roar. (Clarence Day, Jr., in his edition of *The Colby Essays*, 1926.)

275

than I feel. Twenty years among the barebones of all subjects, and seeing the full rotundity of none, must surely leave its mark upon one.

If it were a profession, it would be different. No one ever really means to be an encyclopedia editor. It merely happens to him. We do not hear children say they wish to be encyclopedia editors when they grow up. If we did we should probably punish them. No one ought ever to desire to be an encyclopedia editor. But though a peculiar calling, segregating and to a certain degree dehumanizing, it is not nearly so bad as might be inferred from advertisements and editorial announcements. Behind those smooth absurdities there often lurk actual men, withered perhaps, but fellow-beings nevertheless.

And so far as there is any honesty in them they will not confound their miscellaneous and unassimilated information with true knowledge. There is a good deal of nonsense talked about "varied learning," "enormous range of information," and so forth. If there really is a man who with any justice is entitled a "walking encyclopedia," I should be glad if some one would have a shot at him. It would scarcely be a case of homicide. Universality at the present stage of knowledge is a synonym for scatterbrains. Even in Diderot's time it was a doubtful compliment. No encyclopedia editor ever let so large a part of the work pass through his own head as Diderot, and certainly no encyclopedia editor ever had such a fiery head. The result was that his was not an encyclopedia in the present sense but a huge polemical pamphlet. Its attacks on the existing order were covert and indirect, because it was under governmental control; but by subterfuge, veiled irony, secret thrusts, Diderot never lost a chance to insinuate the spirit that was to overturn the Church and State. As to his universality Diderot confessed:

I know indeed a great enough number of things, but there is hardly any one who does not know his own subject better than I. This mediocrity in all fields is the result of an unbridled curiosity and of means so straitened that I could never give myself up wholly to a single branch of learning. I have been forced all my life to follow occupations for which I am not fitted and to leave aside those to which my taste calls me.

Sainte-Beuve, to be sure, says of him that he showed so much genius in his many-sidedness that "one is tempted to believe that he best fulfilled his destiny in thus scattering himself."

Nowadays Diderot's universality would be embarrassment. The modern editor is primarily an executive. His worth is in no wise measured by the span of his information—a narrow span at best. To know is impossible, but it is not impossible to know the men who should. Diderot's methods would ruin any modern encyclopedic enterprise. If I were a publisher I should distrust the omnivorous reader, still more a mind acquisitive of universal scraps. He would be more likely to consume the stock than organize it. He would be addicted to "drinking behind the bar."

Giants of learning are not at the present time needed for the work. For as Owen Meredith sang in lines too atrocious to be forgotten:

> A dwarf on a dead giant's shoulders sees more
> Than the live giant's eyesight availed to explore.

And I venture to say that a quite commonplace person, provided only that he had an open mind and plenty of time and money, could easily devise an encyclopedia today that should surpass all its predecessors.

Diderot gave the keynote to the present encyclopedia title list and its scope. There is no such break between the French encyclopedia and its successors in these respects as divided it from those which went before. Every encyclopedia maker turns as a matter of course to the title list of his predecessors. That is the way to begin and there is no trick about it. People have often asked me how the editor knows what titles to select. They do not stop to think that the majority of subjects in any one encyclopedia are in all the other encyclopedias. The editor is forever poring over the title lists of his predecessors. He may combine them in a single list or card catalog. He may sift into it the title lists of special reference books, as dictionaries of architecture, music and mechanic arts, reader's handbooks, or titles from the indexes of special treatises, and his department editors or contributors will swell the list from still more special sources. But the bulk of the titles remains the same from decade to decade.

The exercise of a rational judgment in selection is not the thing that surprises one who has seen encyclopedias in the making. The really amazing thing is their imitativeness and formalism. In every long-lived encyclopedia, titles are carried for a generation for no other reason than that they have been found in some preceding work. There is hardly a page of any encyclopedia, even the best, that does not include matters of less significance than something which has been left out.

In the department of biography, for instance, names of men and women are preserved merely as the result of the whim of some hack writer long since dead. If the late Leslie Stephen, in his much respected "Dictionary of National Biography," had in a sportive mood written three pages apiece on six purely imaginary British worthies— invented their names, dates, the books they wrote, the offices they held, their birthplaces and burial places—you would no doubt find them all in condensed form in the new edition of the "Britannica." At the next revision of "La Grande" they would probably appear in a concise French version, and the indefatigable "Brockhaus" and "Meyers" would surely catch them up. Posterity would be certain to encounter some of them.

I myself as a hack writer once invented a clergyman. That his title to fame might pass unchallenged, I said he was the author of the well-known hymn, "Leap, Leap, My Soul." No one cared to admit that that hymn was unfamiliar. I watched his life, carefully prepared in the encyclopedic style appropriate to clergymen, pass through the successive editorial stages. The article underwent the scrutiny of department editor, managing editor, editor-in-chief, and all the little sub-editors, and emerged unscathed; then it went into first proof, second proof, revise, and pages, and I pulled it out barely in time to save it from the plates. Otherwise he might have lived for fifty years in the hearts of his countrymen.

Hence to ask an encyclopedia editor how he knows what to put into his volume is greatly to embarrass the poor creature. He does not know what to put in. He has his precautions, his more or less elaborate system of subdivision and of checks. He can say that a certain title was taken from such and such a source, that it was assigned to the editor or contributor-in-chief of a certain department, that it was written by him or one of his collaborators, that it passed through the hands of a certain office editor whose duty it was to read all the articles of this and certain related departments, that the managing editor saw it, the editor-in-chief saw it, the editorial proofreader read it, and changed a noun from singular to plural, and the second proofreader read it, and caught two p's that were standing upside down. But he knows that many titles find their way into his work and into every other as the result of a foolish guess, and that all conceivable safeguards can only reduce the damage done by routine thinking, credulity, somnolence, conventionality, and imitativeness.

Luckily for him, encyclopedias are seldom criticized for this useless lumber. The great body of criticism is concentrated on omissions. Encyclopedia-making is a form of journalism—ponderous and intermittent, but journalism nevertheless. In order to tell people what they wish to know it casts its dragnet far and wide. Like the newspapers and magazines it tells a great deal that nobody wishes to know.

I know nothing of the peculiar problems that beset editors of dictionaries, encyclopedias of names, or special works of reference. I am speaking only of general encyclopedias, of which five have been my portion, all straining to be "universal" and one perishing miserably in the attempt, for lack of capital. In the course of this experience, one great difficulty has been the lack of intelligent adverse criticism. To be sure I have been aided by some censorious but able reviewers, who were willing to take pains in order to inflict them, and I recall one long, envenomed article which enabled me to revise an entire department to its great advantage. But in the press generally I have been insanely praised and so discouraged from doing better. Praise to an encyclopedia reviewer is the line of least resistance. To find fault he would have to read the text.

Still the best criticism is to be found in the reviews. That which comes to the editor's desk by mail is not reassuring as to the alertness of the public mind. The greater part of it is local or trivial. A church steeple is ten feet too low. A Western railway is not long enough. Somebody's relative is omitted. Correspondents in the West seem particularly engrossed in the sheer size of everything, and the omission of any large object situated in or near a Western town angers the inhabitants exceedingly.

I have been sometimes attacked on dogmatic or historical grounds. I have been accused of a deep-seated personal hatred of Ireland and of a determined purpose always to snub Australia. To state both sides of a disputed question fairly is not so safe as it seems. It angers the extremists on each side. It angers one party even to have the views of the other mentioned. State one side and the missiles all come only from the other. State both sides and you are exposed to a raking cross-fire from each. Nor is peace maintained always by preserving a mild demeanor. If you are calm you are sometimes doubly provocative. Many people lose their tempers merely from seeing you keep yours. "You are incapable," wrote one accuser, "of an honest statement of plain facts," and then substituted a new and hitherto private history of the heavens and the earth. I have learned to regard with suspicion anyone who inquires vehemently, "What are the facts?" That outward devotion to fact seems to increase with the power of misstatement, and it is a safe rule for an editor on reading a prefatory eulogy of truth in general to brace himself for some giant falsehoods in particular. . . . There is nothing stubborn about a fact. It is a time-server and a lickspittle and whenever it meets a fool it is ready to lay down its life for him.

It will do so sometimes for a genius. "It is my stern desire," said Ruskin, in one of his delightful letters to Mr. Norton, "to get at the pure facts, and nothing less or more, which gives me whatever power I have." Accordingly our Civil War was to him "a squabble between black and red ants," and Cervantes and Dickens were merely "mischievous," and Sainte-Beuve was a hopelessly "shallow" creature, and so on through a thousand charming vagaries (sternly pursued as "facts"), till he became quite mad, still convinced that he was merely judicious.

On the whole, however, the editor has little to fear from the *odium theologicum*. We are so used to free thought that restraint is hardly imaginable. It is not easy to picture Diderot with nine censors placed over him, "one of whom must be an orthodox theologian." Once the whole work was snatched away from him and turned over to the Jesuits, and it was only because they could not make head or tail of it that he got it back again. It goes without saying that in our day the state does not bother with such matters. The only tyrannical laws now are those of demand and supply. But it does seem rather remarkable that the people themselves are so good natured. Sects that presumably would desire proselytes or at least wish to defend themselves are in the main quite unconcerned with the statement of principles that undermine their foundations. The Catholic Church is, as it always has been, the most alert; but in this country at least it does not do much to stifle heresy at its source.

I remember years ago writing a school history intended for the use of both Catholics and Protestants. The publishers impressed on me the importance of presenting both sides fairly. Accordingly, as I was reared in the Protestant tradition, and knew very well that I could not help inclining to that point of view, I determined to seek counsel of the Jesuits. I submitted the proof to a Jesuit father, the head of a well-known American seminary, and, in a conversation with him afterward, warned him against the inevitable Protestant bias of my work. But what did he, breathing the latitudinarian air of this country, care for a Protestant bias? His suggested changes pertained, as I recall, to a few phrases about Tetzel and the Sale of Indulgences. Yet at a hundred points the book showed a spirit utterly at variance with Catholicism.

It has been much the same in editing encyclopedias. I have courted the criticism of both sides. Neither has seemed to care very much. I have taken the utmost pains to submit articles on delicate doctrinal points to both Protestants and Catholics, only to find on each side a weary and flaccid acquiescence. I have found the Jesuits more wide-awake than others. Yet they, as a matter of fact, questioned only the most obvious points—as in the case of that historical textbook. And this, though we all know that a Protestant or Roman Catholic color runs all through modern secular history in matters remote from definite doctrines. There is, of course, a Catholic and a Protestant view of the modern world. As Bishop Stubbs has said, history cannot be written later than the fourteenth century. All that follows is subject of present-day religious controversy.

We laugh at the Middle Ages for applying the test of orthodoxy to every branch of learning—an heretical or orthodox astronomy, a blas-

phemous view of the solar system, an irreligious physical law. I hazard
the question whether we have not gone to the opposite extreme. We
play at ostrich with one another. We hide one portion of our intellect
from the rest. We profess a principle of faith that makes our scientific
teaching ridiculous, and we accept as a matter of course scientific theories that would blow our churches into the air. We call it practical—
this intellectual hide-and-seek. As a matter of fact we prefer not to
know what our minds are up to.

Schoolmasters, as a recent English writer points out, treat a boy's
mind "as if it were a badger's pit. You put in the badger and you put
in the dog, and you wait to see which comes out first. They throw in
the Catechism and they throw in the Chemical Theory, and then they
wait to see whether he will turn out a Christian or an Atheist."

What interests me is not that we are constantly doing these things,
but that we are so sublimely, so complacently unconscious that we are
doing it—and that we think the Middle Ages so absurd. I contend that
the joke on human nature is permanent. Persecution was at least a
sign of personal interest. Tolerance is composed of nine parts of apathy
to one of brotherly love. We don't care to think where principles lead
to. Once I found on the margin of a seventeenth-century treatise on
mathematics, in the crabbed writing of some monkish reader, this
exclamation in Latin: "Luther and Melanchthon and those who think
with them be damned." Apropos of mathematics, mind you. Nowadays Christianity and its refutation live together in perfect amity in
the same mind. People make up little nosegays of doctrines for themselves out of the New Testament and Haeckel. I am not deploring the
decline of bigotry. I am merely pointing to the well-known fact, which
is brought out strongly in my experience as an encyclopedia editor,
that it has been replaced by the Religion of Sloppy-Mindedness.

Of course the direst problem of all is presented by modern special-
ism. The aim of the French Encyclopedia, as set forth in its prospectus,
was to serve as a reference library for every intelligent man on all subjects save his own. That has remained the aim of general encyclopedias
ever since. It is obvious that if every subject were written in such a
way as to appeal to the man who had specialized in it, few others
could make much out of it. But here is the difficulty: Though the

topics of a given science cannot be written for specialists, they must either be contributed by specialists or rest on their authority. The groundwork of any good encyclopedia must rest on special scholarship. I say any *good* encyclopedia. A bad one may make quite as much money, perhaps more. A financially successful encyclopedia may be made without any bothersome recourse to specialists. Buy up the plates of some dead predecessor, get four or five hack writers, and the thing is done, provided only you can swing a good force of those amazing hypnotists and prestidigitators—the subscription agents. Time and again they have told me they could sell anything, however bad; and from the books that they have sold, I know it is true. One of them went to a publisher and gave him this simple plan for a book. He said all that he asked was that it should have plenty of pictures of the Virgin Mary in it. He wanted merely to turn over the pages rapidly and sell it at the back door. Of course the subscription business as carried on in certain quarters is notorious—one of the scandals into which muck-rakers have not yet gone, hence still very fraudulent and comfortable.

Any good encyclopedia will carry specialization to the furthest point that is possible without sacrificing the interests of the layman. He is supposed to be a rather robust and intelligent layman willing to take some pains. The encyclopedia is not intended to coax the layman. It is not a baby pathfinder or a guide to little feet. Without some very formidable technicalities many subjects could not be treated at all. It is not the aim of an encyclopedia to do away with technicality or complexity, but only with that portion of it which inheres not in the subject itself but in the muddled mind of the man who writes about it. There is no less pedantry today than there ever was. I have never read a college textbook on any subject, science or other, that was free from it. It is human nature. I have never known a man who could so well digest his information that he did not occasionally show signs of flatulence. That is what pedantry means. That is why this is so hard a problem.

If one could find men of the Huxley type for every science it would be easy. Huxley liked to think himself a specialist. He called himself the "Reverend Father of Worms and Bishop of Annelida." But he elsewhere gave himself a better title—that of "something between a gladiator-general of science and a maid of all work." Huxley's mind would often wander gladly far from his specialty. Nowadays the man of worms is homesick when away from them. He is moreover disdainful of all elements that are accessible to laymen. He calls it popularizing to mention them. Popularizing has a bad name with specialists and they include in it almost every means for the diffusion of knowledge.

There is much to justify their contempt. Making things "readable" is often synonymous with making them silly. As a country we are much given to a sort of democratic insipidity. Witness the speeches of our public men, college presidents, culture courses, presidential messages, popular magazines. When we talk down, we talk too far down. Consider President Roosevelt* on the home and woman, and how there are good people and bad people, and how man should be manly and woman womanly. The most adroit politician we have had in a generation in the executive chair has talked more like a Sunday-school leaflet than any ruler or statesman ever did before.

Hence the embarrassment of the middleman of information, the encyclopedia editor, vibrating between specialist and layman, an object of suspicion to both. I am snubbed by the learned and yet not welcomed by the totally illiterate.

It may be merely an accident, but somehow I have always fared the worst among zoölogists and botanists. Naturally, an editor of an encyclopedia cannot have a sub-editor for every animal, but that is what the zoölogist apparently expected of me. Matters are far worse than in the days of Dr. Holmes's naturalist who flew into a rage because some one called him a Coleopterist. He was no smatterer, he said, trying to spread himself over the Coleoptera; he was a Scarabæist. Nowadays a zoölogist seeks out his animal in early life and henceforth stays with it. Often the intimacy between them is so great that it seems indelicate to intrude. I have known a bivalve and a man to develop interests in common so exclusively molluscous or bivalvular that no human being dared break in.

---

* Theodore, it need hardly be mentioned.—C. F.

When I tried to organize a department of biology, I soon found that it was impossible to thresh the matter out by correspondence. No one cared to be superficial enough to take charge of any branch of that subject, to say nothing of the whole. No man would leave his insect for that foolish, scattering popular subject, entomology. So one day I went to Washington, where biologists, I understood, were very thick and tame; and I had myself put up at a certain learned club, which seemed to be a sort of runway for biologists, where the layman might watch them as they came to drink. I have counted eight or ten distinct and mutually unintelligible varieties in the same room at once.

But when I came to meet them it was no easier. It was impossible to get the mosquito man away from his mosquito, the fossil horse man would not dismount, and the fish people, though kind, were firmly fishy. Day after day I was passed from one kind of biologist to another. . . . At length one man stooped so far as to help me with a plan, but it involved a subdivision of zoölogy into thirty departments with no one responsible for the whole. Less specialization than that would, he said, be vain and shallow. This would have left me alone to drive that herd of thirty rearing and plunging zoölogists.

I left Washington and again had recourse to correspondence. I wrote many letters, full of an Oriental flattery—abject grovelling letters in a style that I had learned as a layman addressing specialists. Finally I got a man to take charge of the department. It was understood that he might gather about him all the zoölogists he could find, but that he must be responsible for the whole department. He carried the work half through, then forgot it and sailed for Europe, chasing some insect, I suppose. In his absence I fell into the hands of a group of zoölogists whose eccentricities were scandalous. Part of the work had to be done over twice; part of it three times.

This illustrates the difficulty of making the knowledge of specialists available—not alluring, or exciting—but merely available to intelligent persons, even to persons of their own size, but of unlike experience. It is hard to convince many of them that the work is worth doing. It is a natural feeling but it is indulged to a point where it becomes a vice.

Bishop Stubbs once said that anything that he wrote that was readable was trivial and that anything worth while was unreadable. A great deal of the unreadable qualities in his writings, however, did not arise from having gone too deep into history. They arose from not having gone deep enough into the expressive capacities of the English language. Specialists must not be allowed to become completely inarticulate. Otherwise we shall have the state of things described by the old philosopher when he said: Those who tell do not know, and those who know don't tell.

Confessions of a Gallomaniac

BY

FRANK MOORE COLBY

DOWN TO THE OUTBREAK of the war I had no more desire to converse with a Frenchman in his own language than with a modern Greek. I thought I understood French well enough for my own purposes, because I had read it off and on for twenty years, but when the war aroused sympathies and sharpened curiosities that I had not felt before, I realized the width of the chasm that cut me off from what I wished to feel. Nor could it be bridged by any of the academic, natural, or commercial methods that I knew of. They were either too slow or they led in directions that I did not wish to go. I tried a phonograph, and after many bouts with it I acquired part of a sermon by Bossuet and real fluency in discussing a quinsy sore throat with a Paris physician, in case I ever went there and had one. I then took fourteen conversation lessons from a Mme. Carnet, and being rather well on in years at the start, I should, if I had kept on diligently, have been able at the age of eighty-five to inquire faultlessly my way to the post-office. I could already ask for butter and sing a song written by Henry IV— when my teacher went to France to take care of her half-brother's children. I will say this for Mme. Carnet. I came to understand perfectly the French for all her personal and family affairs. No human being has ever confided in me so abundantly as she did. No human being has ever so sternly repressed any answering confidences of my own. Her method of instruction, if it was one, was that of jealous, relentless, unbridled soliloquy.

Thrown on the world with no power of sustaining a conversation on any other subject than the members of the Carnet family, I nevertheless resolved to take no more lessons but to hunt down French people

287

and make them talk. What I really needed was a governess to take
me to and from my office and into the park at noon, but at my age
that was out of the question. Then began a career of hypocritical
benevolence. I scraped acquaintance with every Frenchman whom I
heard talking English very badly, and I became immensely interested
in his welfare. I formed the habit of introducing visiting Frenchmen
to French-speaking Americans, and sitting, with open mouth, in the
flow of their conversation. Then I fell in with M. Bernou, the commissioner who was over here buying guns, and whose English and my
French were so much alike that we agreed to interchange them. We
met daily for two weeks and walked for an hour in the park, each
tearing at the other's language. Our conversations, as I look back on
them, must have run about like this:

> "It calls to walk," said he, smiling brilliantly.
> "It is good morning," said I, "better than I had extended."
> "I was at you yestairday ze morning, but I deed not find."
> "I was obliged to leap early," said I, "and I was busy standing up
> straight all around the forenoon."
> "The book I prayed you send, he came, and I thank, but positively
> are you not deranged?"
> "Don't talk," said I. "Never talk again. It was really nothing any-
> where. I had been very happy, I reassure."
> "Pardon, I glide, I glode. There was the hide of a banane. Did I
> crash you?"
> "I noticed no insults," I replied. "You merely gnawed my arm."
> Gestures and smiles of perfect understanding.

I do not know whether Bernou, who like myself was middle-aged,
felt as I did on these occasions, but by the suppression of every
thought that I could not express in my childish vocabulary, I came to
feel exactly like a child. They said I ought to think in French and I
tried to do so, but thinking in French, when there is so little French
to think with, divests the mind of its acquisitions of forty years. Experience slips away for there are not words enough to lay hold of it.
Knowledge of good and evil does not exist; the sins have no names;

and the mind under its linguistic limitations is like a rather defective toy Noah's ark. From the point of view of Bernou's and my vocabulary, Central Park was as the Garden of Eden after six months—new and unnamed things everywhere. A dog, a tree, a statue taxed all our powers of description, and on a complex matter like a policeman our minds could not meet at all. We could only totter together a few steps in any mental direction. Yet there was a real pleasure in this earnest interchange of insipidities and they were highly valued on each side. For my part I shall always like Bernou, and feel toward him as my childhood's friend. I wonder if he noticed that I was an old, battered man, bothered with a tiresome profession. I certainly never suspected that he was. His language utterly failed to give me that impression.

After I lost Bernou I fastened upon an unfrocked priest who had come over here and gone into the shoe trade—a small, foxy man, who regarded me, I think, in the light of an aggressor. He wanted to become completely American and forget France, and as I was trying to reverse the process, I rather got in his way. He could talk of mediæval liturgies and his present occupation, but nothing in between, and as he spoke English very well, his practical mind revolted at the use of a medium of communication in which one of us almost strangled when there was another available in which we both were at ease. I could not pump much French out of him. He would burst into English rather resentfully. Then I took to the streets at lunch-time and tried news-dealers, book-shops, restaurants, invented imaginary errands, bought things that I did not want, and exchanged them for objects even less desirable. That kept a little conversation going day by day, but on the whole it was a dry season. It is a strange thing. There are more than thirty thousand of them in the city of New York, and I had always heard that the French are a clannish folk and hate to learn another language, but most of my overtures in French brought only English upon me. The more pains I took the more desirable it seemed to them that I should be spared the trouble of continuing. I was always diving into French and they were always pulling me out again. They thought they were humane.

French people hate broken French worse than most of us hate broken English. But when dragged out into the light of English I tried to

talk just as foolishly in order that they might think it was not really
my French that was the matter with me. Sometimes that worked quite
well. Finding me just as idiotic in my own language they went back
to theirs. It certainly worked well with my friend M. Bartet, a paralytic
tobacconist in the West Thirties near the river, to whom my relation
was for several months that of a grandchild, though I believe we were
of the same age. He tried to form my character by bringing me up on
such praiseworthy episodes of his early life as he thought I was able
to grasp.

Now at the end of a long year of these persistent puerilities I am
able to report two definite results: In the first place a sense of my
incapacity and ignorance infinitely vaster than when I began, and in
the second a profound distrust, possibly vindictive in its origin, of all
Americans in the city of New York who profess an acquaintance with
French culture, including teachers, critics, theater audiences, lecture
audiences, and patronesses of visiting Frenchmen.

It was perhaps true, as people said at the time, that a certain French
theatrical experiment in New York could not continue for the simple
reason that it was too good a thing for the theater-going public to support. It may be that the precise equivalent of the enterprise, even if not
hampered by a foreign language, could not have permanently endured.
Yet from what I saw of its audiences, critics, enthusiasts, and from
what I know of the American Gallophile generally, including myself,
I believe the linguistic obstacle to have been more serious than they
would have us suppose—serious enough to account for the situation
without dragging in our æsthetic incapacity. It was certainly an obstacle
that less than one-half of any audience ever succeeded in surmounting.

I do not mean that the rest of the audience got nothing out of it,
for so expressive were the players by other means than words, that
they often sketched the play out in pantomime. The physical activities
of the troupe did not arise, as some of the critics declared, from the
vivacity of the Gallic temperament; nor were they assumed, as others
believed, because in the seventeenth century French actors had been
acrobats. These somewhat exaggerated gestures were occasioned by the
perception that the majority of the spectators were beginners in French.

They were supplied by these ever-tactful people as a running translation for a large body of self-improving Americans.

I do not blame other Americans for dabbling in French, since I myself am the worst of dabblers, but I see no reason why any of us should
pretend that it is anything more than dabbling. The usual way of
reading French does not lead even to an acquaintance with French
literature. Everybody knows that words in a living language in order
to be understood have to be lived with. They are not felt as a part of
living literature when you see them pressed out and labeled in a glos-
sary, but only when you hear them fly about. A word is not a definite
thing susceptible of dictionary explanation. It is a cluster of associations, reminiscent of the sort of men that used it, suggestive of social
class, occupation, mood, dignity or the lack of it, primness, violences,
pedantries, or platitudes. It hardly seems necessary to say that words
in a living literature ought to ring in the ear with the sounds that
really belong to them, or that poetry without an echo cannot be felt.

It may be that there is no way out of it. Perhaps it is inevitable that
the colleges which had so long taught the dead languages as if they
were buried should now teach the living ones as if they were dead.
But there is no need of pretending that this formal acquaintance with
books results in an appreciation of literature. No sense of the intimate
quality of a writer can be founded on a verbal vacuum. His plots, his
place in literature, his central motives, and the opinion of his critics
could all be just as adequately conveyed, if his books were studied in
the language of the deaf and dumb. Of course, one may be drawn to
an author by that process but it would hardly be the artistic attraction
of literature; it is as if one felt drawn to a woman by an interest exclusively in her bones.

Elementary as these remarks may seem I offer them to Gallophiles
without apology. On the contrary I rather fear that I am writing over
their heads.

JAMES THURBER

I do not propose to explain Mr. James Thurber, or his doleful dogs, or his funny little men, or his terrifying little women. Explanations of humor are usually made by analytical fellows who substitute an awesome knowledge of why we should laugh for their own inability to do so. Philosophers of humor, like Sigmund Freud and Henri Bergson, often possess high intelligences which they employ with great dexterity on a problem which seems somehow to elude them. For humor is not perceived by the intelligence alone; often it is not perceived by the intelligence at all. The sudden interior burst of delight that comes of catching the humor of a remark or a situation seems ventral rather than cerebral. It is not an intellectual satisfaction, but one much more akin to the pleasure of consuming a good dinner.

The humor-analysts appear to think that a joke is related to a riddle. It is not; it is much more nearly related to a tickle. Those jokes which are like riddles, which have a complicated point, are precisely the jokes that have the shortest life and are least able to bear rehearing. Practically all radio humor is of this variety, and that is why it uses itself up so quickly. Radio gags of the Bob Hope order are often admirably clever, but on some people, including myself, they have the same effect as does a troupe of performing acrobats. Watching acrobats can be interesting, but it is also a little painful, because of empathy, the process by which you put yourself in the other fellow's place. It is also, when the act is over, in a way disappointing. You are left with an empty feeling, or no feeling at all. Gag humor has the same effect on me. I am lost in gap-mouthed wonder at Mr. Hope's rapid-fire quips. At the same time I am tense lest I lose the point of one of them, and I suffer lest Mr. Hope should fail to do the expected, to top his previous gag, or cap his stooge's remark. And when it is all over I find I am a trifle tired and vacant-minded.

True humor (and, mind, I am not explaining it) does something

292

to you, like great literature. It changes your feelings, usually in the
direction of greater well-being and general expansiveness. Instead of
tensing you, it relaxes you. It works not on the nerves and the brain
but on the heart and the imagination. It does not have a "point,"
which is a hard, direct thing. It suffuses an atmosphere, which is a
soft and subtle thing.

That is why good humor is enjoyable again and again. Once you
have "got the point" of something that has only "point" to offer,
you are through, but an atmosphere is no more exhaustible than a
fine landscape. The point of the fence-whitewashing chapter in
Tom Sawyer is that if you wish a person to perform a tiresome
job you should make it appear a hard-to-win privilege. The point
of it, however, has precious little to do with the humor, which you
can resavor even when you know the point in advance.

The humor of James Thurber (I am still not explaining it) is of
this subtle, atmospheric kind. It is the distillation of a rich temperament and so it is "rich" humor.

Perhaps it would be more correct to speak of two temperaments,
or, better, two sides of the same temperament. The Thurber of Let
Your Mind Alone and the Fables for Our Time shows one side.
The Thurber of My Life and Hard Times and The Male Animal * shows another. The first Thurber is the Sane Innocent; the
second is the Confused Innocent. Actually, Mr. Thurber is never
confused and never innocent. His confusion and his innocence,
though, are not just poses, but positions which he assumes in order
to allow his humor to play more readily.

The Sane Innocent is the Thurber who makes you laugh because
he sees through imposture (such as that of the self-improvement
school) from an angle that the rest of us would never think of. He is
to comedy what Dostoevsky's wise idiots are to tragedy. The pleasure
you get from this Thurber is the pleasure of sudden illumination.

The Confused Innocent is the Thurber who makes you laugh not
because he sees through things but, on the contrary, because he is
bewildered by them. (Actually, this bewilderment is merely a slyer

---

* Written in collaboration with J. C. Nugent.

form of understanding.) The pleasure you get from this Thurber is that wry and rueful satisfaction that comes of watching somebody make a fool of himself in a maze. Don Quixote and a drunk, Caspar Milquetoast and Mr. Pickwick, Mr. Disney's Dopey and Mr. Thurber's persecuted males—all are examples, on various levels, of the comedy of befuddlement.

You will note that I have still not explained the humor of James Thurber.

One of the staples of our writers is the Great American Eccentric Family. Examples: Mr. Caldwell's Tobacco Roaders, Thomas Wolfe's Gants, Kaufman and Hart's Sycamores, Mr. Saroyan's Saroyans— one could easily extend the list. There have been so many of these grotesques in the last decade that it almost seems as though they were called into being to redress a balance. During the period domi- nated by Sinclair Lewis and the realistic school the stupefying con- ventionality of American family life was the thing emphasized. The pendulum has swung back, and we are now hip-deep in grotesques.

My Life and Hard Times is about an eccentric family, too, but not a very eccentric one. The Thurbers are only slightly off-balance. Still, that small disequilibrium is enough to upset them and propel them into situations that are thoroughly and hilariously abnormal. "The little perils of routine living," in Thurber's phrase, form the base of his "autobiography." This is not to say that the Thurbers are ordinary people. It is to say that the Thurbers are mildly extraor- dinary people whose domestic lives from time to time burst into small volcanic eruptions of comic disaster.

This is especially true of a certain level of American life. It is pre- cisely such respectable middle-class inhabitants of Columbus, Ohio, whose public lives are models of modest deportment, that develop within the family circle a compensating environment of eccentricity. It takes a James Thurber, of course, to see how funny the other Thurbers are. They themselves probably have no inkling of the fig- ures they cut.

The humor of this book does not lie in the fact that crazy things happen. It lies in the fact that everybody in it is trying to be reasonable about the crazy things that happen. Mr. Thurber's mother, for example (a precious creation who must be waiting for her son to put her full-face into a book), is funny because she is so bent on rationalizing the odd cataclysms that shake her household. Her iron determination to be sensible amid this crowd of muddled maniacs is the root of her comicality. And the humor of Grandfather, of course, lies not in his fits of lunacy but in his spasms of sanity.

Everybody misunderstands everybody else—a tiny reflection of the whole universe of human discourse. The mishaps of misunderstanding generally yield farce. Here they yield true comedy, as in the incomparable Perth Amboy episode (which, just as a test, I have often tried to read through without breaking into laughter, failing each time); as in the story of the day the dam broke, which is a treatise by Le Bon translated by the comic spirit; as in the narratives of the night the bed fell on Father and the night the ghost got in.

Thurber is, true enough, a quiet writer who creates his effects with the most dexterous and light touches, but his understatement is a little different from the British variety, as one can see by comparing him with the much less funny P. G. Wodehouse. For one thing, he is subtler. For another, there is an odd, almost furtive touch of fancy that one does not find among the English. Here, for example, is a typical Thurber sentence: "In the early years of the nineteenth century, Columbus won out, as State capital, by only one vote over Lancaster, and ever since then has had the hallucination that it is being followed, a curious municipal state of mind which affects, in some way or other, all those who live there." No one but Thurber could have written this, and surely no Englishman, though the English are among Thurber's most devoted admirers.

My Life and Hard Times is so vivid and real as a family portrait that one sometimes forgets it is also a parody, a delicate parody on all the pompous, self-important autobiographies of the last fifteen years. Beyond all this, despite Thurber's disclaimer, it is a curiously intimate picture of a time and place—the comfortable, quiet, almost somnolent Middle West during the years just preceding the outbreak of the First World War. Finally, it is a fine piece of prose. It flows along so easily that only the attentive student marks how exactly Thurber manages his sentences so as to accommodate them to the effects he is after and the tempo he is setting.

There is one misconception about Thurber that I have always found it hard to understand. That is the notion that he is typical of a New Yorker school of humor. There is no New Yorker school of humor. I cannot conceive a more wildly disparate and ill-assorted group than, let us say, S. J. Perelman, Frank Sullivan, John O'Hara, Ruth McKenny, Arthur Kober, Wolcott Gibbs, and James Thurber. All of them abhor gags, except Perelman, who uses them for purposes of parody, but otherwise I can see nothing that unites them. Of the lot, Thurber is the most individual, the least a servant to formula. He has the most unexpected and, I should say, the wisest mind, and, though they all write well, Thurber is more than a good writer. He is an artist.

But enough of not explaining James Thurber. His life and hard times, given here in full, speak for themselves.

My Life and Hard Times

BY

JAMES THURBER

PREFACE TO A LIFE

BENVENUTO CELLINI said that a man should be at least forty years old before he undertakes so fine an enterprise as that of setting down the story of his life. He said also that an autobiographer should have accomplished something of excellence. Nowadays nobody who has a typewriter pays any attention to the old master's quaint rules. I myself have accomplished nothing of excellence except a remarkable and, to some of my friends, unaccountable expertness in hitting empty ginger ale bottles with small rocks at a distance of thirty paces. Moreover, I am not yet forty years old. But the grim date moves toward me apace; my legs are beginning to go, things blur before my eyes, and the faces of the rose-lipped maids I knew in my twenties are misty as dreams.

At forty my faculties may have closed up like flowers at evening, leaving me unable to write my memoirs with a fitting and discreet inaccuracy or, having written them, unable to carry them to the publisher's. A writer verging into the middle years lives in dread of losing his way to the publishing house and wandering down to the Bowery or the Battery, there to disappear like Ambrose Bierce. He has sometimes also the kindred dread of turning a sudden corner and meeting himself sauntering along in the opposite direction. I have known writers at this dangerous and tricky age to phone their homes from their offices, or their offices from their homes, ask for themselves in a low tone, and then, having fortunately discovered that they were "out," to collapse in hard-breathing relief. This is particularly true of writers of light pieces running from a thousand to two thousand words.

The notion that such persons are gay of heart and carefree is curiously untrue. They lead, as a matter of fact, an existence of jumpiness and apprehension. They sit on the edge of the chair of Literature. In the house of Life they have the feeling that they have never taken off their overcoats. Afraid of losing themselves in the larger flight of the two-volume novel, or even the one-volume novel, they stick to short accounts of their misadventures because they never get so deep into them but that they feel they can get out. This type of writing is not a joyous form of self-expression but the manifestation of a twitchiness at once cosmic and mundane. Authors of such pieces have, nobody knows why, a genius for getting into minor difficulties: they walk into the wrong apartments, they drink furniture polish for stomach bitters, they drive their cars into the prize tulip beds of haughty neighbors, they playfully slap gangsters, mistaking them for old school friends. To call such persons "humorists," a loose-fitting and ugly word, is to miss the nature of their dilemma and the dilemma of their nature. The little wheels of their invention are set in motion by the damp hand of melancholy.

Such a writer moves about restlessly wherever he goes, ready to get the hell out at the drop of a pie-pan or the lift of a skirt. His gestures are the ludicrous reflexes of the maladjusted; his repose is the momentary inertia of the nonplussed. He pulls the blinds against the morning and creeps into the smokey corners at night. He talks largely about small matters and smally about great affairs. His ears are shut to the ominous rumblings of the dynasties of the world moving toward a cloudier chaos than ever before, but he hears with an acute perception the startling sounds that rabbits make twisting in the bushes along a country road at night and a cold chill comes upon him when the comic supplement of a Sunday newspaper blows unexpectedly out of an areaway and envelops his knees. He can sleep while the commonwealth crumbles but a strange sound in the pantry at three in the morning will strike terror into his stomach. He is not afraid, or much aware, of the menaces of empire but he keeps looking behind him as he walks along darkening streets out of the fear that he is being softly followed by little men padding along in single file, about a foot and a half high, large-eyed, and whiskered.

It is difficult for such a person to conform to what Ford Madox Ford in his book of recollections has called the sole reason for writing one's memoirs: namely, to paint a picture of one's time. Your short-piece writer's time is not Walter Lippmann's time, or Stuart Chase's time, or Professor Einstein's time. It is his own personal time, circumscribed by the short boundaries of his pain and his embarrassment, in which what happens to his digestion, the rear axle of his car, and the confused flow of his relationships with six or eight persons and two or three buildings is of greater importance than what goes on in the nation or in the universe. He knows vaguely that the nation is not much good any more; he has read that the crust of the earth is shrinking alarmingly and that the universe is growing steadily colder, but he does not believe that any of the three is in half as bad shape as he is.

Enormous strides are made in star-measurement, theoretical economics, and the manufacture of bombing planes, but he usually doesn't find out about them until he picks up an old copy of "Time" on a picnic grounds or in the summer house of a friend. He is aware that billions of dollars are stolen every year by bankers and politicians, and that thousands of people are out of work, but these conditions do not worry him a tenth as much as the conviction that he has wasted three months on a stupid psychoanalyst or the suspicion that a piece he has been working on for two long days was done much better and probably more quickly by Robert Benchley in 1924.

The "time" of such a writer, then, is hardly worth reading about if the reader wishes to find out what was going on in the world while the writer in question was alive and at what might be laughingly called "his best." All that the reader is going to find out is what happened to the writer. The compensation, I suppose, must lie in the comforting feeling that one has had, after all, a pretty sensible and peaceful life, by comparison. It is unfortunate, however, that even a well-ordered life can not lead anybody safely around the inevitable doom that waits in the skies. As F. Hopkinson Smith long ago pointed out, the claw of the sea-puss gets us all in the end.

J. T.

Sandy Hook,
Connecticut,
September 25, 1933.

CHAPTER ONE

THE NIGHT THE BED FELL

I SUPPOSE that the high-water mark of my youth in Columbus, Ohio, was the night the bed fell on my father. It makes a better recitation (unless, as some friends of mine have said, one has heard it five or six times) than it does a piece of writing, for it is almost necessary to throw furniture around, shake doors, and bark like a dog, to lend the proper atmosphere and verisimilitude to what is admittedly a somewhat incredible tale. Still, it did take place.

It happened, then, that my father had decided to sleep in the attic one night, to be away where he could think. My mother opposed the notion strongly because, she said, the old wooden bed up there was unsafe: it was wobbly and the heavy headboard would crash down on father's head in case the bed fell, and kill him. There was no dissuading him, however, and at a quarter past ten he closed the attic door behind him and went up the narrow twisting stairs. We later heard ominous creakings as he crawled into bed. Grandfather, who usually slept in the attic bed when he was with us, had disappeared some days before. (On these occasions he was usually gone six or eight days and returned growling and out of temper, with the news that the federal Union was run by a passel of blockheads and that the Army of the Potomac didn't have any more chance than a fiddler's bitch.)

We had visiting us at this time a nervous first cousin of mine named Briggs Beall, who believed that he was likely to cease breathing when he was asleep. It was his feeling that if he were not awakened every hour during the night, he might die of suffocation. He had been accustomed to setting an alarm clock to ring at intervals until morning, but I persuaded him to abandon this. He slept in my room and I told him that I was such a light sleeper that if anybody quit breathing in the same room with me, I would wake instantly. He tested me the first night—which I had suspected he would—by holding his breath after my regular breathing had convinced him I was asleep. I was not asleep, however, and called to him. This seemed to allay his fears a little, but he took the precaution of putting a glass of spirits of camphor on a little table at the head of his bed. In case I didn't arouse him until he was almost gone, he said, he would sniff the camphor, a powerful reviver. Briggs was not the only member of his family who had his crotchets. Old Aunt Melissa Beall (who could whistle like a man, with two fingers in her mouth) suffered under the premonition that she was destined to die on South High Street, because she had been born on South High Street and married on South High Street. Then there was Aunt Sarah Shoaf, who never went to bed at night without the fear that a burglar was going to get in and blow chloroform under her door through a tube. To avert this calamity—for she was in greater dread of anesthetics than of losing her household goods—she always piled her money, silverware, and other valuables in a neat stack just outside her bedroom, with a note reading: "This is all I have. Please take it and do not use your chloroform, as this is all I have." Aunt Gracie Shoaf also had a burglar phobia, but she met it with more fortitude. She was confident that burglars had been getting into her house every night for forty years. The fact that she never missed anything was to her no proof to the contrary. She always claimed that she scared them off before they could take anything, by throwing shoes down the hallway. When she went to bed she piled, where she could get at them handily, all the shoes there were about her house. Five minutes after she had turned off the light, she would sit up in bed and say "Hark!" Her husband, who had learned to ignore the whole situation as long ago as 1903, would either be sound asleep or pretend to be sound asleep. In either case he would not respond to her tugging and pulling, so that presently she would arise, tiptoe to the door, open it slightly and heave a shoe down the hall in one direction, and its mate down the hall in the other direction. Some nights she threw them all, some nights only a couple of pair.

But I am straying from the remarkable incidents that took place during the night that the bed fell on father. By midnight we were all in bed. The layout of the rooms and the disposition of their occupants is important to an understanding of what later occurred. In the front room upstairs (just under father's attic bedroom) were my mother and my brother Herman, who sometimes sang in his sleep, usually "Marching Through Georgia" or "Onward, Christian Soldiers." Briggs Beall and myself were in a room adjoining this one. My brother Roy was in a room across the hall from ours. Our bull terrier, Rex, slept in the hall.

My bed was an army cot, one of those affairs which are made wide enough to sleep on comfortably only by putting up, flat with the middle section, the two sides which ordinarily hang down like the sideboards of a drop-leaf table. When these sides are up, it is perilous to roll too far toward the edge, for then the cot is likely to tip completely over, bringing the whole bed down on top of one, with a tremendous banging crash. This, in fact, is precisely what happened, about two o'clock in the morning. (It was my mother who, in recalling the scene later, first referred to it as "the night the bed fell on your father.")

Always a deep sleeper, slow to arouse (I had lied to Briggs), I was at first unconscious of what had happened when the iron cot rolled me onto the floor and toppled over on me. It left me still warmly bundled up and unhurt, for the bed rested above me like a canopy. Hence I did not wake up, only reached the edge of consciousness and went back. The racket, however, instantly awakened my mother, in the next room, who came to the immediate conclusion that her worst dread was realized: the big wooden bed upstairs had fallen on father. She therefore screamed, "Let's go to your poor father!" It was this shout, rather than the noise of my cot falling, that awakened Herman, in the same room with her. He thought that mother had become, for no apparent reason, hysterical. "You're all right, Mamma!" he shouted, trying to calm her. They exchanged shout for shout for perhaps ten seconds: "Let's go to your poor father!" and "You're all right!" That woke up Briggs. By this time I was conscious of what was going on, in a vague way, but did not yet realize that I was under my bed instead of on it. Briggs, awakening in the midst of loud shouts of fear and apprehension, came to the quick conclusion that he was suffocating and that we were all trying to "bring him out." With a low moan, he grasped the glass of camphor at the head of his bed and instead of sniffing it poured it over himself. The room reeked of camphor. "Ugf, ahfg," choked Briggs, like a drowning man, for he had almost succeeded in stopping his breath under the deluge of pungent spirits. He leaped out of bed and groped toward the open window, but he came up against one that was closed. With his hand, he beat out the glass, and I could hear it crash and tinkle on the alleyway below. It was at this juncture that I, in trying to get up, had the uncanny sensation of feeling my bed above me! Foggy with sleep, I now suspected, in my turn, that the whole uproar was being made in a frantic endeavor to extricate me from what must be an unheard-of and perilous situation. "Get me out of this!" I bawled. "Get me out!" I think I had the nightmarish belief that I was entombed in a mine. "Gugh," gasped Briggs, floundering in his camphor.

By this time my mother, still shouting, pursued by Herman, still shouting, was trying to open the door to the attic, in order to go up and get my father's body out of the wreckage. The door was stuck, however, and wouldn't yield. Her frantic pulls on it only added to the general banging and confusion. Roy and the dog were now up, the one shouting questions, the other barking.

Father, farthest away and soundest sleeper of all, had by this time been awakened by the battering on the attic door. He decided that the house was on fire. "I'm coming, I'm coming!" he wailed in a slow, sleepy voice—it took him many minutes to regain full consciousness. My mother, still believing he was caught under the bed, detected in his "I'm coming!" the mournful, resigned note of one who is preparing to meet his Maker. "He's dying!" she shouted.

"I'm all right!" Briggs yelled to reassure her. "I'm all right!" He still believed that it was his own closeness to death that was worrying mother. I found at last the light switch in my room, unlocked the door, and Briggs and I joined the others at the attic door. The dog, who never did like Briggs, jumped for him—assuming that he was the culprit in whatever was going on—and Roy had to throw Rex and hold him. We could hear father crawling out of bed upstairs. Roy pulled the attic door open, with a mighty jerk, and father came down the stairs, sleepy and irritable but safe and sound. My mother began to weep when she saw him. Rex began to howl. "What in the name of God is going on here?" asked father.

The situation was finally put together like a gigantic jigsaw puzzle. Father caught a cold from prowling around in his bare feet but there were no other bad results. "I'm glad," said mother, who always looked on the bright side of things, "that your grandfather wasn't here."

CHAPTER TWO

THE CAR WE HAD TO PUSH

MANY autobiographers, among them Lincoln Steffens and Gertrude Atherton, describe earthquakes their families have been in. I am unable to do this because my family was never in an earthquake, but we went through a number of things in Columbus that were a great deal like earthquakes. I remember in particular some of the repercussions of an old Reo we had that wouldn't go unless you pushed it for quite a way and suddenly let your clutch out. Once, we had been able to start the engine easily by cranking it, but we had had the car for so many years that finally it wouldn't go unless you pushed it and let your clutch out. Of course, it took more than one person to do this; it took sometimes as many as five or six, depending on the grade of the roadway and conditions underfoot. The car was unusual in that the clutch and brake were on the same pedal, making it quite easy to stall the engine after it got started, so that the car would have to be pushed again.

My father used to get sick at his stomach pushing the car, and very often was unable to go to work. He had never liked the machine, even when it was good, sharing my ignorance and suspicion of all automobiles of twenty years ago and longer. The boys I went to school with used to be able to identify every car as it passed by: Thomas Flyer, Firestone-Columbus, Stevens Duryea, Rambler, Winton, White Steamer, etc. I never could. The only car I was really interested in was one that the Get-Ready Man, as we called him, rode around town in: a big Red Devil with a door in the back. The Get-Ready Man was a lank unkempt elderly gentleman with wild eyes and a deep voice who used to go about shouting at people through a megaphone to prepare for the end of the world. "GET READY! GET READ-Y!" he would bellow. "THE WORLLLD IS COMING TO AN END!" His startling exhortations would come up, like summer thunder, at the most unexpected times and in the most surprising places. I remember once during Mantell's production of "King Lear" at the Colonial Theatre that the Get-Ready Man added his bawlings to the squealing of Edgar and the ranting of the King and the mouthing of the Fool, rising from somewhere in the balcony to join in. The theatre was in absolute darkness and there were rumblings of thunder and flashes of lightning offstage. Neither father nor I, who were there, ever completely got over the scene, which went something like this:

Edgar: Tom's a-cold.—O, do de, do de, do de!—Bless thee from whirlwinds, star-blasting, and taking . . . the foul fiend vexes!

> *(Thunder off.*

Lear: What! Have his daughters brought him to this pass?—
Get-Ready Man: Get ready! Get ready!
Edgar: Pillicock sat on Pillicock-hill:—

> Halloo, halloo, loo, loo!
> *(Lightning flashes.*

Get-Ready Man: The Worllld is com-ing to an End!
Fool: This cold night will turn us all to fools and madmen!
Edgar: Take heed o' the foul fiend: obey thy paren——
Get-Ready Man: Get *Rea*-dy!
Edgar: Tom's a-*cold*!
Get-Ready Man: The *Worr*-uld is coming to an end! . . .

They found him finally, and ejected him, still shouting. The Theatre, in our time, has known few such moments.

But to get back to the automobile. One of my happiest memories of it was when, in its eighth year, my brother Roy got together a great many articles from the kitchen, placed them in a square of canvas, and swung this under the car with a string attached to it so that, at a twitch, the canvas would give way and the steel and tin things would clatter to the street. This was a little scheme of Roy's to frighten father, who had always expected the car might explode. It worked perfectly. That was twenty-five years ago, but it is one of the few things in my life I would like to live over again if I could. I don't suppose that I can, now. Roy twitched the string in the middle of a lovely afternoon, on Bryden Road near Eighteenth Street. Father had closed his eyes and, with his hat off, was enjoying a cool breeze. The clatter on the asphalt was tremendously effective: knives, forks, can-openers, pie pans, pot lids, biscuit-cutters, ladles, egg-beaters fell, beautifully together, in a lingering, clamant crash. "Stop the *car!*" shouted father. "I can't," Roy said. "The engine fell out." "God Almighty!" said father, who knew what *that* meant, or knew what it sounded as if it might mean.

It ended unhappily, of course, because we finally had to drive back and pick up the stuff and even father knew the difference between the works of an automobile and the equipment of a pantry. My mother wouldn't have known, however, nor *her* mother. My mother, for instance, thought—or, rather, knew—that it was dangerous to drive an automobile without gasoline: it fried the valves, or something. "Now don't you dare drive all over town without gasoline!" she would say to us when we started off. Gasoline, oil, and water were much the same to her, a fact that made her life both confusing and perilous. Her greatest dread, however, was the Victrola—we had a very early one, back in the "Come Josephine in My Flying Machine" days. She had an idea that the Victrola might blow up. It alarmed her, rather than reassured her, to explain that the phonograph was run neither by gasoline nor by electricity. She could only suppose that it was propelled by some newfangled and untested apparatus which was likely to let go at any minute, making us all the victims and martyrs of the wild-eyed Edison's dangerous experiments. The telephone she was comparatively at peace with, except, of course, during storms, when for some reason or other she always took the receiver off the hook and let it hang. She came naturally by her confused and groundless fears, for her own mother lived the latter years of her life in the horrible suspicion that electricity was dripping invisibly all over the house. It leaked, she contended, out of empty sockets if the wall switch had been left on. She would go around screwing in bulbs, and if they lighted up she would hastily and fearfully turn off the wall switch and go back to her *Pearson's* or *Everybody's,* happy in the satisfaction that she had stopped not only a costly but a dangerous leakage. Nothing could ever clear this up for her.

Our poor old Reo came to a horrible end, finally. We had parked it too far from the curb on a street with a car line. It was late at night and the street was dark. The first streetcar that came along couldn't get by. It picked up the tired old automobile as a terrier might seize a rabbit and drubbed it unmercifully, losing its hold now and then but catching a new grip a second later. Tires booped and whooshed, the fenders queeled and graked, the steering-wheel rose up like a spectre and disappeared in the direction of Franklin Avenue with a melancholy whistling sound, bolts and gadgets flew like sparks from a Catherine wheel. It was a splendid spectacle but, of course, saddening to everybody (except the motorman of the streetcar, who was sore). I think some us broke down and wept. It must have been the weeping that caused grandfather to take on so terribly. Time was all mixed up in his mind; automobiles and the like he never remembered having seen. He apparently gathered, from the talk and excitement and weeping, that somebody had died. Nor did he let go of this delusion. He insisted, in fact, after almost a week in which we strove mightily to divert him, that it was a sin and a shame and a disgrace on the family to put the funeral off any longer. "Nobody is dead! The automobile is smashed!" shouted my father, trying for the thirtieth time to explain the situation to the old man. "Was he drunk?" demanded grandfather, sternly. "Was who drunk?" asked father. "Zenas," said grandfather. He had a name for the corpse now: it was his brother Zenas, who, as it happened, *was* dead, but not from driving an automobile while intoxicated. Zenas had died in 1866. A sensitive, rather poetical boy of twenty-one when the Civil War broke out, Zenas had gone to South America—"just," as he wrote back, "until it blows over." Returning after the war had blown over, he caught the same disease that was killing off the chestnut trees in those years, and passed away. It was the only case in history where a tree doctor had to be called in to spray a person, and our family had felt it very keenly; nobody else in the United States caught the blight. Some of us have looked upon Zenas' fate as a kind of poetic justice.

Now that grandfather knew, so to speak, who was dead, it became increasingly awkward to go on living in the same house with him as if nothing had happened. He would go into towering rages in which he threatened to write to the Board of Health unless the funeral were held at once. We realized that something had to be done. Eventually, we persuaded a friend of father's, named George Martin, to dress up in the manner and costume of the eighteen-sixties and pretend to be Uncle Zenas, in order to set grandfather's mind at rest. The impostor looked fine and impressive in sideburns and a high beaver hat, and not unlike the daguerreotypes of Zenas in our album. I shall never forget the night, just after dinner, when this Zenas walked into the living-room. Grandfather was stomping up and down, tall, hawk-nosed, round-oathed. The newcomer held out both his hands. "Clem!" he cried to grandfather. Grandfather turned slowly, looked at the intruder, and snorted. "Who air *you?*" he demanded in his deep, resonant voice. "I'm Zenas!" cried Martin. "Your brother Zenas, fit as a fiddle and sound as a dollar!" "Zenas, my foot!" said grandfather. "Zenas died of the chestnut blight in '66!"

Grandfather was given to these sudden, unexpected, and extremely lucid moments; they were generally more embarrassing than his other moments. He comprehended before he went to bed that night that the old automobile had been destroyed and that its destruction had caused all the turmoil in the house: "It flew all to pieces, Pa," my mother told him, in graphically describing the accident. "I knew 'twould," growled grandfather. "I allus told ye to git a Pope-Toledo."

CHAPTER THREE

THE DAY THE DAM·BROKE

MY MEMORIES of what my family and I went through during the 1913 flood in Ohio I would gladly forget. And yet neither the hardships we endured nor the turmoil and confusion we experienced can alter my feeling toward my native state and city. I am having a fine time now and wish Columbus were here, but if anyone ever wished a city was in hell it was during that frightful and perilous afternoon in 1913 when the dam broke, or, to be more exact, when everybody in town *thought* that the dam broke. We were both ennobled and demoralized by the experience. Grandfather especially rose to magnificent heights which can never lose their splendor for me, even though his reactions to the flood were based upon a profound misconception; namely, that Nathan Bedford Forrest's cavalry was the menace we were called upon to face. The only possible means of escape for us was to flee the house, a step which grandfather sternly forbade, brandishing his old army sabre in his hand. "Let the sons —— come!" he roared. Meanwhile hundreds of people were streaming by our house in wild panic, screaming "Go east! Go east!" We had to stun grandfather with the ironing board. Impeded as we were by the inert form of the old gentleman—he was taller than six feet and weighed almost a hundred and seventy pounds—we were passed, in the first half-mile, by practically everybody else in the city. Had grandfather not come to, at the corner of Parsons Avenue and Town Street, we would unquestionably have been overtaken and engulfed by the roaring waters—that is, if there had *been* any roaring waters. Later, when the panic had died down and people had gone rather sheepishly back to their homes and their offices, minimizing the distances they had run and offering various reasons for running, city engineers pointed out that even if the dam had broken, the water level would not have risen more than two additional inches in the West Side. The West Side was, at the time of the dam scare, under thirty feet of water—as, indeed, were all Ohio river towns during the great spring floods of twenty years ago. The East Side (where we lived and where all the running occurred) had never been in any danger at all. Only a rise of some ninety-five feet could have caused the flood waters to flow over High Street—the thoroughfare that divided the east side of town from the west—and engulf the East Side.

The fact that we were all as safe as kittens under a cookstove did not, however, assuage in the least the fine despair and the grotesque desperation which seized upon the residents of the East Side when the cry spread like a grass fire that the dam had given way. Some of the most dignified, staid, cynical, and clear-thinking men in town abandoned their wives, stenographers, homes, and offices and ran east. There are few alarms in the world more terrifying than "The dam has broken!" There are few persons capable of stopping to reason when that clarion cry strikes upon their ears, even persons who live in towns no nearer than five hundred miles to a dam.

The Columbus, Ohio, broken-dam rumor began, as I recall it, about noon of March 12, 1913. High Street, the main canyon of trade, was loud with the placid hum of business and the buzzing of placid businessmen arguing, computing, wheedling, offering, refusing, compromising. Darius Conningway, one of the foremost corporation lawyers in the Middle-West, was telling the Public Utilities Commission in the language of Julius Caesar that they might as well try to move the Northern star as to move him. Other men were making their little boasts and their little gestures. Suddenly somebody began to run. It may be that he had simply remembered, all of a moment, an engagement to meet his wife, for which he was now frightfully late. Whatever it was, he ran east on Broad Street (probably toward the Maramor Restaurant, a favorite place for a man to meet his wife). Somebody else began to run, perhaps a newsboy in high spirits. Another man, a portly gentleman of affairs, broke into a trot. Inside of ten minutes, everybody on High Street, from the Union Depot to the Courthouse was running. A loud mumble gradually crystallized

into the dread word "dam." "The dam has broke!" The fear was put
into words by a little old lady in an electric, or by a traffic cop, or by
a small boy: nobody knows who, nor does it now really matter. Two
thousand people were abruptly in full flight. "Go east!" was the cry
that arose—east away from the river, east to safety. "Go east! Go east!
Go east!"

Black streams of people flowed eastward down all the streets leading
in that direction; these streams, whose headwaters were in the dry-
goods stores, office buildings, harness shops, movie theatres, were fed
by trickles of housewives, children, cripples, servants, dogs, and cats,
slipping out of the houses past which the main stream flowed, shouting
and screaming. People ran out leaving fires burning and food cooking
and doors wide open. I remember, however, that my mother turned out
all the fires and that she took with her a dozen eggs and two loaves
of bread. It was her plan to make Memorial Hall, just two blocks away,
and take refuge somewhere in the top of it, in one of the dusty rooms
where war veterans met and where old battle flags and stage scenery
were stored. But the seething throngs, shouting "Go east!," drew her
along and the rest of us with her. When grandfather regained full
consciousness, at Parsons Avenue, he turned upon the retreating mob
like a vengeful prophet and exhorted the men to form ranks and stand
off the Rebel dogs, but at length he, too, got the idea that the dam
had broken and, roaring "Go east!" in his powerful voice, he caught
up in one arm a small child and in the other a slight clerkish man
of perhaps forty-two and we slowly began to gain on those ahead
of us.

A scattering of firemen, policemen, and army officers in dress uniforms—there had been a review at Fort Hayes, in the northern part
of town—added color to the surging billows of people. "Go east!" cried
a little child in a piping voice, as she ran past a porch on which
drowsed a lieutenant-colonel of infantry. Used to quick decisions,
trained to immediate obedience, the officer bounded off the porch and,
running at full tilt, soon passed the child, bawling "Go east!" The
two of them emptied rapidly the houses of the little street they were
on. "What is it? What is it?" demanded a fat, waddling man who
intercepted the colonel. The officer dropped behind and asked the

little child what it was. "The dam has broke!" gasped the girl. "The dam has broke!" roared the colonel. "Go east! Go east! Go east!" He was soon leading, with the exhausted child in his arms, a fleeing company of three hundred persons who had gathered around him from living-rooms, shops, garages, backyards, and basements.

Nobody has ever been able to compute with any exactness how many people took part in the great rout of 1913, for the panic, which extended from the Winslow Bottling Works in the south end to Clintonville, six miles north, ended as abruptly as it began and the bobtail and ragtag and velvet-gowned groups of refugees melted away and slunk home, leaving the streets peaceful and deserted. The shouting, weeping, tangled evacuation of the city lasted not more than two hours in all. Some few people got as far east as Reynoldsburg, twelve miles away; fifty or more reached the Country Club, eight miles away; most of the others gave up, exhausted, or climbed trees in Franklin Park, four miles out. Order was restored and fear dispelled finally by means of militiamen riding about in motor lorries bawling through megaphones: "The dam has *not* broken!" At first this tended only to add to the confusion and increase the panic, for many stampeders thought the soldiers were bellowing "The dam has now broken!," thus setting an official seal of authentication on the calamity.

All the time, the sun shone quietly and there was nowhere any sign of oncoming waters. A visitor in an airplane, looking down on the straggling, agitated masses of people below, would have been hard put to it to divine a reason for the phenomenon. It must have inspired, in such an observer, a peculiar kind of terror, like the sight of the *Marie Celeste,* abandoned at sea, its galley fires peacefully burning, its tranquil decks bright in the sunlight.

An aunt of mine, Aunt Edith Taylor, was in a movie theatre on High Street when, over and above the sound of the piano in the pit (a W. S. Hart picture was being shown), there rose the steadily increasing tromp of running feet. Persistent shouts rose above the tromping. An elderly man, sitting near my aunt, mumbled something, got out of his seat, and went up the aisle at a dogtrot. This started everybody. In an instant the audience was jamming the aisles. "Fire!" shouted a woman who always expected to be burned up in a theatre;

but now the shouts outside were louder and coherent. "The dam has broke!" cried somebody. "Go east!" screamed a small woman in front of my aunt. And east they went, pushing and shoving and clawing, knocking women and children down, emerging finally into the street, torn and sprawling. Inside the theatre, Bill Hart was calmly calling some desperado's bluff and the brave girl at the piano played "Row! Row! Row!" loudly and then "In My Harem." Outside, men were streaming across the Statehouse yard, others were climbing trees, a woman managed to get up onto the "These Are My Jewels" statue, whose bronze figures of Sherman, Stanton, Grant, and Sheridan watched with cold unconcern the going to pieces of the capital city.

"I ran south to State Street, east on State to Third, south on Third to Town, and out east on Town," my Aunt Edith has written me. "A tall spare woman with grim eyes and a determined chin ran past me down the middle of the street. I was still uncertain as to what was the matter, in spite of all the shouting. I drew up alongside the woman with some effort, for although she was in her late fifties, she had a beautiful easy running form and seemed to be in excellent condition. 'What is it?' I puffed. She gave me a quick glance and then looked ahead again, stepping up her pace a trifle. 'Don't ask me, ask God!' she said.

"When I reached Grant Avenue, I was so spent that Dr. H. R. Mallory—you remember Dr. Mallory, the man with the white beard who looks like Robert Browning?—well, Dr. Mallory, whom I had drawn away from at the corner of Fifth and Town, passed me. 'It's got us!' he shouted, and I felt sure that whatever it was *did* have us, for you know what conviction Dr. Mallory's statements always carried. I didn't know at the time what he meant, but I found out later. There was a boy behind him on rollerskates, and Dr. Mallory mistook the swishing of the skates for the sound of rushing water. He eventually reached the Columbus School for Girls, at the corner of Parsons Avenue and Town Street, where he collapsed, expecting the cold frothing waters of the Scioto to sweep him into oblivion. The boy on the skates swirled past him and Dr. Mallory realized for the first time what he had been running from. Looking back up the street, he could see no signs of water, but nevertheless, after resting a few minutes, he jogged on east again. He caught up with me at Ohio Avenue, where we rested together. I should say that about seven hundred people passed us. A funny thing was that all of them were on foot. Nobody seemed to have had the courage to stop and start his car; but as I remember it, all cars had to be cranked in those days, which is probably the reason."

The next day, the city went about its business as if nothing had happened, but there was no joking. It was two years or more before you dared treat the breaking of the dam lightly. And even now, twenty years after, there are a few persons, like Dr. Mallory, who will shut up like a clam if you mention the Afternoon of the Great Run.

CHAPTER FOUR

THE NIGHT THE GHOST GOT IN

THE ghost that got into our house on the night of November 17, 1915, raised such a hullabaloo of misunderstandings that I am sorry I didn't just let it keep on walking, and go to bed. Its advent caused my mother to throw a shoe through a window of the house next door and ended up with my grandfather shooting a patrolman. I am sorry, therefore, as I have said, that I ever paid any attention to the footsteps.

They began about a quarter past one o'clock in the morning, a rhythmic, quick-cadenced walking around the dining-room table. My mother was asleep in one room upstairs, my brother Herman in another; grandfather was in the attic, in the old walnut bed, which, as you will remember, once fell on my father. I had just stepped out of the bathtub and was busily rubbing myself with a towel when I heard the steps. They were the steps of a man walking rapidly around the dining-room table downstairs. The light from the bathroom shone down the back steps, which dropped directly into the dining-room; I could see the faint shine of plates on the plate-rail; I couldn't see the table. The steps kept going round and round the table; at regular intervals a board creaked, when it was trod upon. I supposed at first that it was my father or my brother Roy, who had gone to Indianapolis but were expected home at any time. I suspected next that it was a burglar. It did not enter my mind until later that it was a ghost.

After the walking had gone on for perhaps three minutes, I tiptoed to Herman's room. "Psst!" I hissed, in the dark, shaking him. "Awp," he said, in the low, hopeless tone of a despondent beagle—he always half suspected that something would "get him" in the night. I told him who I was. "There's something downstairs!" I said. He got up and followed me to the head of the back staircase. We listened together.

There was no sound. The steps had ceased. Herman looked at me in some alarm: I had only the bath towel around my waist. He wanted to go back to bed, but I gripped his arm. "There's something down there!" I said. Instantly the steps began again, circled the dining-room table like a man running, and started up the stairs toward us, heavily, two at a time. The light still shone palely down the stairs; we saw nothing coming; we only heard the steps. Herman rushed to his room and slammed the door. I slammed shut the door at the stairs top and held my knee against it. After a long minute, I slowly opened it again. There was nothing there. There was no sound. None of us ever heard the ghost again.

The slamming of the doors had aroused mother: she peered out of her room. "What on earth are you boys doing?" she demanded. Herman ventured out of his room. "Nothing," he said gruffly, but he was, in color, a light green. "What was all that running around downstairs?" said mother. So she had heard the steps, too! We just looked at her. "Burglars!" she shouted, intuitively. I tried to quiet her by starting lightly downstairs.

"Come on, Herman," I said.

"I'll stay with mother," he said. "She's all excited."

I stepped back onto the landing.

"Don't either of you go a step," said mother. "We'll call the police." Since the phone was downstairs, I didn't see how we were going to call the police—nor did I want the police—but mother made one of her quick, incomparable decisions. She flung up a window of her bedroom which faced the bedroom windows of the house of a neighbor, picked up a shoe, and whammed it through a pane of glass across the narrow space that separated the two houses. Glass tinkled into the bedroom occupied by a retired engraver named Bodwell and his wife. Bodwell had been for some years in rather a bad way and was subject to mild "attacks." Most everybody we knew or lived near had *some* kind of attacks.

It was now about two o'clock of a moonless night; clouds hung black and low. Bodwell was at the window in a minute, shouting, frothing a little, shaking his fist. "We'll sell the house and go back to Peoria," we could hear Mrs. Bodwell saying. It was some time before mother "got through" to Bodwell. "Burglars!" she shouted. "Burglars in the house!" Herman and I hadn't dared to tell her that it was not burglars but ghosts, for she was even more afraid of ghosts than of burglars. Bodwell at first thought that she meant there were burglars in his house, but finally he quieted down and called the police for us over an extension phone by his bed. After he had disappeared from the window, mother suddenly made as if to throw another shoe, not because there was further need of it but, as she later explained, because the thrill of heaving a shoe through a window glass had enormously taken her fancy. I prevented her.

The police were on hand in a commendably short time: a Ford sedan full of them, two on motorcycles, and a patrol wagon with about eight in it and a few reporters. They began banging at our front door. Flashlights shot streaks of gleam up and down the walls, across the yard, down the walk between our house and Bodwell's. "Open up!" cried a hoarse voice. "We're men from Headquarters!" I wanted to go down and let them in, since there they were, but mother wouldn't hear of it. "You haven't a stitch on," she pointed out. "You'd catch your death." I wound the towel around me again. Finally the cops put their shoulders to our big heavy front door with its thick beveled glass and broke it in: I could hear a rending of wood and a splash of glass on the floor of the hall. Their lights played all over the living-room and crisscrossed nervously in the dining-room, stabbed into hallways, shot up the front stairs and finally up the back. They caught me standing in my towel at the top. A heavy policeman bounded up the steps. "Who are you?" he demanded. "I live here," I said. "Well, whattsa matta, ya hot?" he asked. It was, as a matter of fact, cold; I went to my room and pulled on some trousers. On my way out, a cop stuck a gun into my ribs. "Whatta you doin' here?" he demanded. "I live here," I said.

The officer in charge reported to mother. "No sign of nobody, lady," he said. "Musta got away—whatt'd he look like?" "There were two or three of them," mother said, "whooping and carrying on and slamming doors." "Funny," said the cop. "All ya windows and doors was locked on the inside tight as a tick."

Downstairs, we could hear the tromping of the other police. Police were all over the place; doors were yanked open, drawers were yanked open, windows were shot up and pulled down, furniture fell with dull thumps. A half-dozen policemen emerged out of the darkness of the front hallway upstairs. They began to ransack the floor: pulled beds away from walls, tore clothes off hooks in the closets, pulled suitcases and boxes off shelves. One of them found an old zither that Roy had won in a pool tournament. "Looky here, Joe," he said, strumming it with a big paw. The cop named Joe took it and turned it over. "What is it?" he asked me. "It's an old zither our guinea pig used to sleep on," I said. It was true that a pet guinea pig we once had would never sleep anywhere except on the zither, but I should never have said so. Joe and the other cop looked at me a long time. They put the zither back on a shelf.

"No sign o' nuthin'," said the cop who had first spoken to mother. "This guy," he explained to the others, jerking a thumb at me, "was nekked. The lady seems historical." They all nodded, but said nothing; just looked at me. In the small silence we all heard a creaking in the attic. Grandfather was turning over in bed. "What's 'at?" snapped Joe. Five or six cops sprang for the attic door before I could intervene or explain. I realized that it would be bad if they burst in on grandfather unannounced, or even announced. He was going through a phase in which he believed that General Meade's men, under steady hammering by Stonewall Jackson, were beginning to retreat and even desert.

When I got to the attic, things were pretty confused. Grandfather had evidently jumped to the conclusion that the police were deserters from Meade's army, trying to hide away in his attic. He bounded out of bed wearing a long flannel nightgown over long woolen underwear, a nightcap, and a leather jacket around his chest. The cops must have realized at once that the indignant white-haired old man belonged in the house, but they had no chance to say so. "Back, ye cowardly dogs!" roared grandfather. "Back t' the lines, ye goddam lily-livered cattle!" With that, he fetched the officer who found the zither a flat-handed smack alongside his head that sent him sprawling. The others beat a retreat, but not fast enough; grandfather grabbed Zither's gun from its holster and let fly. The report seemed to crack the rafters; smoke filled the attic. A cop cursed and shot his hand to his shoulder. Some-how, we all finally got downstairs again and locked the door against the old gentleman. He fired once or twice more in the darkness and then went back to bed. "That was grandfather," I explained to Joe, out of breath. "He thinks you're deserters." "I'll say he does," said Joe.

The cops were reluctant to leave without getting their hands on somebody besides grandfather; the night had been distinctly a defeat for them. Furthermore, they obviously didn't like the "layout"; something looked—and I can see their viewpoint—phony. They began to poke into things again. A reporter, a thin-faced, wispy man, came up to me. I had put on one of mother's blouses, not being able to find anything else. The reporter looked at me with mingled suspicion and interest. "Just what the hell is the real lowdown here, Bud?" he asked. I decided to be frank with him. "We had ghosts," I said. He gazed at me a long time as if I were a slot machine into which he had, without results, dropped a nickel. Then he walked away. The cops followed him, the one grandfather shot holding his now-bandaged arm, cursing and blaspheming. "I'm gonna get my gun back from that old bird," said the zither-cop. "Yeh," said Joe. "You—and who else?" I told them I would bring it to the station house the next day.

"What was the matter with that one policeman?" mother asked, after they had gone. "Grandfather shot him," I said. "What for?" she demanded. I told her he was a deserter. "Of all things!" said mother. "He was such a nice-looking young man."

Grandfather was fresh as a daisy and full of jokes at breakfast next morning. We thought at first he had forgotten all about what had happened, but he hadn't. Over his third cup of coffee, he glared at Herman and me. "What was the idee of all them cops tarryhootin' round the house last night?" he demanded. He had us there.

CHAPTER FIVE

MORE ALARMS **AT NIGHT**

ONE of the incidents that I always think of first when I cast back over my youth is what happened the night that my father "threatened to get Buck." This, as you will see, is not precisely a fair or accurate description of what actually occurred, but it is the way in which I and the other members of my family invariably allude to the occasion. We were living at the time in an old house at 77 Lexington Avenue, in Columbus, Ohio. In the early years of the nineteenth century, Columbus won out, as state capital, by only one vote over Lancaster, and ever since then has had the hallucination that it is being followed, a curious municipal state of mind which affects, in some way or other, all those who live there. Columbus is a town in which almost anything is likely to happen and in which almost everything has.

My father was sleeping in the front room on the second floor next to that of my brother Roy, who was then about sixteen. Father was usually in bed by nine-thirty and up again by ten-thirty to protest bitterly against a Victrola record we three boys were in the habit of playing over and over, namely, "No News, or What Killed the Dog," a recitation by Nat Wills. The record had been played so many times that its grooves were deeply cut and the needle often kept revolving in the same groove, repeating over and over the same words. Thus: "ate some burnt hoss flesh, ate some burnt hoss flesh, ate some burnt hoss flesh." It was this reiteration that generally got father out of bed.

On the night in question, however, we had all gone to bed at about the same time, without much fuss. Roy, as a matter of fact, had been in bed all day with a kind of mild fever. It wasn't severe enough to cause delirium and my brother was the last person in the world to give way to delirium. Nevertheless, he had warned father when father went to bed that he *might* become delirious.

About three o'clock in the morning, Roy, who was wakeful, decided to pretend that delirium was on him, in order to have, as he later explained it, some "fun." He got out of bed and, going to my father's room, shook him and said, "Buck, your time has come!" My father's name was not Buck but Charles, nor had he ever been called Buck. He was a tall, mildly nervous, peaceable gentleman, given to quiet pleasures, and eager that everything should run smoothly. "Hmm?" he said, with drowsy bewilderment. "Get up, Buck," said my brother, coldly, but with a certain gleam in his eyes. My father leaped out of bed, on the side away from his son, rushed from the room, locked the door behind him, and shouted us all up.

We were naturally enough reluctant to believe that Roy, who was quiet and self-contained, had threatened his father with any such abracadabra as father said he had. My older brother, Herman, went back to bed without any comment. "You've had a bad dream," my mother said. This vexed my father. "I tell you he called me Buck and told me my time had come," he said. We went to the door of his room, unlocked it, and tiptoed through it to Roy's room. He lay in his bed, breathing easily, as if he were fast asleep. It was apparent at a glance that he did not have a high fever. My mother gave my father a look. "I tell you he did," whispered father.

Our presence in the room finally seemed to awaken Roy and he was (or rather, as we found out long afterward, pretended to be) astonished and bewildered. "What's the matter?" he asked. "Nothing," said my mother. "Just your father had a nightmare." "I did not have a nightmare," said father, slowly and firmly. He wore an old-fashioned, "side-slit" nightgown which looked rather odd on his tall, spare figure. The situation, before we let it drop and everybody went back to bed again, became, as such situations in our family usually did, rather more complicated than ironed out. Roy demanded to know what had happened, and my mother told him, in considerably garbled fashion, what father had told her. At this a light dawned in Roy's eyes. "Dad's got it backward," he said. He then explained that he had heard father get out of bed and had called to him. "I'll handle this,"

his father had answered. "Buck is downstairs." "Who is this Buck?" my mother demanded of father. "I don't know any Buck and I never said that," father contended, irritably. None of us (except Roy, of course) believed him. "You had a dream," said mother. "People have these dreams." "I did not have a dream," father said. He was pretty well nettled by this time, and he stood in front of a bureau mirror, brushing his hair with a pair of military brushes; it always seemed to calm father to brush his hair. My mother declared that it was "a sin and a shame" for a grown man to wake up a sick boy simply because he (the grown man: father) had got on his back and had a bad dream. My father, as a matter of fact, *had* been known to have nightmares, usually about Lillian Russell and President Cleveland, who chased him.

We argued the thing for perhaps another half-hour, after which mother made father sleep in her room. "You're all safe now, boys," she said, firmly, as she shut her door. I could hear father grumbling for a long time, with an occasional monosyllable of doubt from mother.

It was some six months after this that father went through a similar experience with me. He was at that time sleeping in the room next to mine. I had been trying all afternoon, in vain, to think of the name Perth Amboy. It seems now like a very simple name to recall and yet on the day in question I thought of every other town in the country, as well as such words and names and phrases as terra cotta, Walla-Walla, bill of lading, vice versa, hoity-toity, Pall Mall, Bodley Head, Schumann-Heink, etc., without even coming close to Perth Amboy. I suppose terra cotta was the closest I came although it was not very close.

Long after I had gone to bed, I was struggling with the problem. I began to indulge in the wildest fancies as I lay there in the dark, such as that there was no such town, and even that there was no such state as New Jersey. I fell to repeating the word "Jersey" over and over again, until it became idiotic and meaningless. If you have ever lain awake at night and repeated one word over and over, thousands and millions and hundreds of thousands of millions of times, you know the disturbing mental state you can get into. I got to thinking that there was nobody else in the world but me, and various other wild imaginings of that nature. Eventually, lying there thinking these outlandish thoughts, I grew slightly alarmed. I began to suspect that one might lose one's mind over some such trivial mental tic as a futile search for terra firma Piggly Wiggly Gorgonzola Prester John Arc de Triomphe Holy Moses Lares and Penates. I began to feel the imperative necessity of human contact. This silly and alarming tangle of thought and fancy had gone far enough. I might get into some kind of mental aberrancy unless I found out the name of that Jersey town and could go to sleep. Therefore, I got out of bed, walked into the room where father was sleeping, and shook him. "Um?" he mumbled. I shook him more fiercely and he finally woke up, with a glaze of dream and apprehension in his eyes. "What's matter?" he asked, thickly. I must, indeed, have been rather wild of eye, and my hair, which is unruly, becomes monstrously tousled and snarled at night. "Wha's it?" said my father, sitting up, in readiness to spring out of bed on the far side. The thought must have been going through his mind that all his sons were crazy, or on the verge of going crazy. I see that now, but I didn't then, for I had forgotten the Buck incident and did not realize how similar my appearance must have been to Roy's the night he called father Buck and told him his time had come. "Listen," I said. "Name some towns in New Jersey quick!" It must have been around three in the morning. Father got up, keeping the bed between him and me, and started to pull his trousers on. "Don't bother about dressing," I said. "Just name some towns in New Jersey." While he hastily pulled on his clothes—I remember he left his socks off and put his shoes on his bare feet—father began to name, in a shaky voice, various New Jersey cities. I can still see him reaching for his coat without taking his eyes off me. "Newark," he said, "Jersey City, Atlantic City, Elizabeth, Paterson, Passaic, Trenton, Jersey City, Trenton, Paterson—" "It has two names," I snapped. "Elizabeth and Paterson," he said. "No, no!" I told him, irritably. "This is one town with one name, but there are two words in it, like helter-skelter." "Helter-skelter," said my father, moving slowly toward the bedroom door and smiling in a faint, strained way which I understand now—but didn't then—was meant to humor me. When he was within a few paces of the door, he fairly leaped for it and ran out into the hall, his coat-tails and shoelaces flying. The exit stunned me. I had no notion that he thought I had gone out of my senses; I could only believe that he had gone out of *his* or that, only partially awake, he was engaged in some form of running in his sleep. I ran after him and I caught him at the door of mother's room and grabbed him, in order to reason with him. I shook him a little, thinking to wake him completely. "Mary! Roy! Herman!" he shouted. I, too, began to shout for my brothers and my mother. My mother opened her door instantly, and there we were at 3:30 in the morning grappling and shouting, father partly dressed, but without socks or shirt, and I in pajamas.

"*Now,* what?" demanded my mother, grimly, pulling us apart. She was capable, fortunately, of handling any two of us and she never in her life was alarmed by the words or actions of any one of us.

"Look out for Jamie!" said father. (He always called me Jamie when excited.) My mother looked at me.

"What's the matter with your father?" she demanded. I said I didn't know; I said he had got up suddenly and dressed and ran out of the room.

"Where did you think you were going?" mother asked him, coolly. He looked at me. We looked at each other, breathing hard, but somewhat calmer.

"He was babbling about New Jersey at this infernal hour of the night," said father. "He came to my room and asked me to name towns in New Jersey." Mother looked at me.

"I just asked him," I said. "I was trying to think of one and couldn't sleep."

"You see?" said father, triumphantly. Mother didn't look at him.

"Get to bed, both of you," she said. "I don't want to hear any more out of you tonight. Dressing and tearing up and down the hall at this hour in the morning!" She went back into the room and shut her door. Father and I went back to bed. "Are you all right?" he called to me. "Are you?" I asked. "Well, good night," he said. "Good night," I said.

Mother would not let the rest of us discuss the affair next morning at breakfast. Herman asked what the hell had been the matter. "We'll go on to something more elevating," said mother.

CHAPTER SIX

A SEQUENCE OF SERVANTS

WHEN I look back on the long line of servants my mother hired during the years I lived at home, I remember clearly ten or twelve of them (we had about a hundred and sixty-two, all told, but few of them were memorable). There was, among the immortals, Dora Gedd, a quiet, mousy girl of thirty-two who one night shot at a man in her room, throwing our household into an uproar that was equalled perhaps only by the goings-on the night the ghost got in. Nobody knew how her lover, a morose garage man, got into the house, but everybody for two blocks knew how he got out. Dora had dressed up in a lavender evening gown for the occasion and she wore a mass of jewelry, some of which was my mother's. She kept shouting something from Shakespeare after the shooting—I forget just what—and pursued the gentleman downstairs from her attic room. When he got to the second floor he rushed into my father's room. It was this entrance, and not the shot or the shouting, that aroused father, a deep sleeper always. "Get me out of here!" shouted the victim. This situation rapidly developed, from then on, into one of those bewildering involvements for which my family had, I am afraid, a kind of unhappy genius. When the cops arrived Dora was shooting out the Welsbach gas mantles in the living room, and her gentleman friend had fled. By dawn everything was quiet once more.

There were others. Gertie Straub: big, genial, and ruddy, a collector of pints of rye (we learned after she was gone), who came in after two o'clock one night from a dancing party at Buckeye Lake and awakened us by bumping into and knocking over furniture. "Who's down there?" called mother from upstairs. "It's me, dearie," said

Gertie, "Gertie Straub." "What are you *doing?*" demanded mother. "Dusting," said Gertie.

Juanemma Kramer was one of my favorites. Her mother loved the name Juanita so dearly that she had worked the first part of it into the names of all her daughters—they were (in addition to a Juanita) Juanemma, Juanhelen, and Juangrace. Juanemma was a thin, nervous maid who lived in constant dread of being hypnotized. Nor were her fears unfounded, for she was so extremely susceptible to hypnotic suggestion that one evening at B. F. Keith's theatre when a man on the stage was hypnotized, Juanemma, in the audience, was hypnotized too and floundered out into the aisle making the same cheeping sound that the subject on the stage, who had been told he was a chicken, was making. The act was abandoned and some xylophone players were brought on to restore order. One night, when our house was deep in quiet slumber, Juanemma became hypnotized in her sleep. She dreamed that a man "put her under" and then disappeared without "bringing her out." This was explained when, at last, a police surgeon whom we called in—he was the only doctor we could persuade to come out at three in the morning—slapped her into consciousness. It got so finally that any buzzing or whirring sound or any flashing object would put Juanemma under, and we had to let her go. I was reminded of her recently when, at a performance of the movie "Rasputin and the Empress," there came the scene in which Lionel Barrymore as the unholy priest hypnotizes the Czarevitch by spinning before his eyes a glittering watch. If Juanemma sat in any theatre and witnessed that scene she must, I am sure, have gone under instantly. Happily, she seems to have missed the picture, for otherwise Mr. Barrymore might have had to dress up again as Rasputin (which God forbid) and journey across the country to get her out of it—excellent publicity but a great bother.

Before I go on to Vashti, whose last name I forget, I will look in passing at another of our white maids (Vashti was colored). Belle Giddin distinguished herself by one gesture which fortunately did not result in the bedlam occasioned by Juanemma's hypnotic states or Dora Gedd's shooting spree. Belle burned her finger grievously, and purposely, one afternoon in the steam of a boiling kettle so that she could find out whether the pain-killer she had bought one night at a tent-show for fifty cents was any good. It was only fair.

Vashti turned out, in the end, to be partly legendary. She was a comely and sombre negress who was always able to find things my mother lost. "I don't know what's become of my garnet brooch," my mother said one day. "Yassum," said Vashti. In half an hour she had found it. "Where in the world was it?" asked mother. "In de yahd," said Vashti. "De dog mussa drug it out."

Vashti was in love with a young colored chauffeur named Charley, but she was also desired by her stepfather, whom none of us had ever seen but who was, she said, a handsome but messin' round gentleman from Georgia who had come north and married Vashti's mother just so he could be near Vashti. Charley, her fiancé, was for killing the stepfather but we counselled flight to another city. Vashti, however, would burst into tears and hymns and vow she'd never leave us; she got a certain pleasure out of bearing her cross. Thus we all lived in jeopardy, for the possibility that Vashti, Charley, and her stepfather might fight it out some night in our kitchen did not, at times, seem remote. Once I went into the kitchen at midnight to make some coffee. Charley was standing at a window looking out into the backyard; Vashti was rolling her eyes. "Heah he come! Heah he come!" she moaned. The stepfather didn't show up, however.

Charley finally saved up twenty-seven dollars toward taking Vashti away but one day he impulsively bought a .22 revolver with a mother-of-pearl handle and demanded that Vashti tell him where her mother and stepfather lived. "Doan go up dere, doan go *up* dere!" said Vashti. "Mah mothah is just as rarin' as he is!" Charley, however, insisted. It came out then that Vashti didn't have any stepfather; there was no such person. Charley threw her over for a yellow gal named Nancy: he never forgave Vashti for the vanishing from his life of a menace that had come to mean more to him than Vashti herself. Afterwards, if you asked Vashti about her stepfather or about Charley she would say, proudly, and with a woman-of-the-world air, "Neither one ob 'em is messin' round *me* any mo'."

Mrs. Doody, a huge, middle-aged woman with a religious taint, came into and went out of our house like a comet. The second night she was there she went berserk while doing the dishes and, under the impression that father was the Antichrist, pursued him several times up the backstairs and down the front. He had been sitting quietly over his coffee in the living room when she burst in from the kitchen waving a bread knife. My brother Herman finally felled her with a piece of Libby's cut-glass that had been a wedding present of mother's. Mother, I remember, was in the attic at the time, trying to find some old things, and, appearing on the scene in the midst of it all, got the quick and mistaken impression that father was chasing Mrs. Doody.

Mrs. Robertson, a fat and mumbly old colored woman, who might have been sixty and who might have been a hundred, gave us more than one turn during the many years that she did our washing. She had been a slave down South and she remembered having seen the troops marching—"a mess o' blue, den a mess o' gray." "What," my mother asked her once, "were they fighting about?" "Dat," said Mrs. Robertson, "Ah don't know." She had a feeling, at all times, that something was going to happen. I can see her now, staggering up from the basement with a basketful of clothes and coming abruptly to a halt in the middle of the kitchen. "Hahk!" she would say, in a deep, guttural voice. We would all hark; there was never anything to be heard. Neither, when she shouted "Look yondah!" and pointed a trembling hand at a window, was there ever anything to be seen. Father protested time and again that he couldn't stand Mrs. Robertson around, but mother always refused to let her go. It seems that she was a jewel. Once she walked unbidden, a dishpan full of wrung-out clothes under her arm, into father's study, where he was engrossed in some figures. Father looked up. She regarded him for a moment in silence. Then—"Look out!" she said, and withdrew. Another time, a murky winter afternoon, she came flubbering up the cellar stairs and bounced, out of breath, into the kitchen. Father was in the kitchen sipping some black coffee; he was in a jittery state of nerves from the effects of having had a tooth out, and had been in bed most of the day. "Dey is a death watch downstaihs!" rumbled the old colored lady. It developed that she had heard a strange "chipping" noise back of the furnace. "That was a cricket," said father. "Um-*hm*," said Mrs.

Robertson. "Dat was uh death watch!" With that she put on her hat and went home, poising just long enough at the back door to observe darkly to father, *"Dey ain't no way!"* It upset him for days.

Mrs. Robertson had only one great hour that I can think of—Jack Johnson's victory over Mistah Jeffries on the Fourth of July, 1910. She took a prominent part in the colored parade through the South End that night, playing a Spanish fandango on a banjo. The procession was led by the pastor of her church who, Mrs. Robertson later told us, had 'splained that the victory of Jack over Mistah Jeffries proved "de 'speriority ob de race." "What," asked my mother, "did he mean by that?" "Dat," said Mrs. Robertson, "Ah don't know."

Our other servants I don't remember so clearly, except the one who set the house on fire (her name eludes me), and Edda Millmoss. Edda was always slightly morose, but she had gone along for months, all the time she was with us, quietly and efficiently attending to her work, until the night we had Carson Blair and F. R. Gardiner to dinner —both men of importance to my father's ambitions. Then suddenly, while serving the entrée, Edda dropped everything and, pointing a quivering finger at father, accused him in a long rigmarole of having done her out of her rights to the land on which Trinity Church in New York stands. Mr. Gardiner had one of his "attacks" and the whole evening turned out miserably.

CHAPTER SEVEN

THE DOG THAT BIT PEOPLE

PROBABLY no one man should have as many dogs in his life as I have had, but there was more pleasure than distress in them for me except in the case of an Airedale named Muggs. He gave me more trouble than all the other fifty-four or five put together, although my moment of keenest embarrassment was the time a Scotch terrier named Jeannie, who had just had six puppies in the clothes closet of a fourth floor apartment in New York, had the unexpected seventh and last at the corner of Eleventh Street and Fifth Avenue during a walk she had insisted on taking. Then, too, there was the prize-winning French poodle, a great big black poodle—none of your little, untroublesome white miniatures—who got sick riding in the rumble seat of a car with me on her way to the Greenwich Dog Show. She had a red rubber bib tucked around her throat and, since a rain storm came up when we were half way through the Bronx, I had to hold over her a small green umbrella, really more of a parasol. The rain beat down fearfully and suddenly the driver of the car drove into a big garage, filled with mechanics. It happened so quickly that I forgot to put the umbrella down and I will always remember, with sickening distress, the look of incredulity mixed with hatred that came over the face of the particular hardened garage man that came over to see what we wanted, when he took a look at me and the poodle. All garage men, and people of that intolerant stripe, hate poodles with their curious hair cut, especially the pom-poms that you have got to leave on their hips if you expect the dogs to win a prize.

But the Airedale, as I have said, was the worst of all my dogs. He really wasn't my dog, as a matter of fact: I came home from a vacation one summer to find that my brother Roy had bought him while

331

I was away. A big, burly, choleric dog, he always acted as if he thought I wasn't one of the family. There was a slight advantage in being one of the family, for he didn't bite the family as often as he bit strangers. Still, in the years that we had him he bit everybody but mother, and he made a pass at her once but missed. That was during the month when we suddenly had mice, and Muggs refused to do anything about them. Nobody ever had mice exactly like the mice we had that month. They acted like pet mice, almost like mice somebody had trained. They were so friendly that one night when mother entertained at dinner the Friraliras, a club she and my father had belonged to for twenty years, she put down a lot of little dishes with food in them on the pantry floor so that the mice would be satisfied with that and wouldn't come into the dining room. Muggs stayed out in the pantry with the mice, lying on the floor, growling to himself—not at the mice, but about all the people in the next room that he would have liked to get at. Mother slipped out into the pantry once to see how everything was going. Everything was going fine. It made her so mad to see Muggs lying there, oblivious of the mice—they came running up to her—that she slapped him and he slashed at her, but didn't make it. He was sorry immediately, mother said. He was always sorry, she said, after he bit someone, but we could not understand how she figured this out. He didn't act sorry.

Mother used to send a box of candy every Christmas to the people the Airedale bit. The list finally contained forty or more names. Nobody could understand why we didn't get rid of the dog. I didn't understand it very well myself, but we didn't get rid of him. I think that one or two people tried to poison Muggs—he acted poisoned once in a while—and old Major Moberly fired at him once with his service revolver near the Seneca Hotel in East Broad Street—but Muggs lived to be almost eleven years old and even when he could hardly get around he bit a Congressman who had called to see my father on business. My mother had never liked the Congressman—she said the signs of his horoscope showed he couldn't be trusted (he was Saturn with the moon in Virgo)—but she sent him a box of candy that Christmas. He sent it right back, probably because he suspected it was trick candy. Mother persuaded herself it was all for the best that the dog had bitten him, even though father lost an important business association because of it. "I wouldn't be associated with such a man," mother said. "Muggs could read him like a book."

We used to take turns feeding Muggs to be on his good side, but that didn't always work. He was never in a very good humor, even after a meal. Nobody knew exactly what was the matter with him, but whatever it was it made him irascible, especially in the mornings. Roy never felt very well in the morning, either, especially before breakfast, and once when he came downstairs and found that Muggs had moodily chewed up the morning paper he hit him in the face with a grapefruit and then jumped up on the dining room table, scattering dishes and silverware and spilling the coffee. Muggs' first free leap carried him all the way across the table and into a brass fire screen in front of the gas grate but he was back on his feet in a moment and in the end he got Roy and gave him a pretty vicious bite in the leg. Then he was all over it; he never bit anyone more than once at a time. Mother always mentioned that as an argument in his favor; she said he had a quick temper but that he didn't hold a grudge. She was forever defending him. I think she liked him because he wasn't well. "He's not strong," she would say, pityingly, but that was inaccurate; he may not have been well but he was terribly strong.

One time my mother went to the Chittenden Hotel to call on a woman mental healer who was lecturing in Columbus on the subject of "Harmonious Vibrations." She wanted to find out if it was possible to get harmonious vibrations into a dog. "He's a large tan-colored Airedale," mother explained. The woman said that she had never treated a dog but she advised my mother to hold the thought that he did not bite and would not bite. Mother was holding the thought the very next morning when Muggs got the iceman but she blamed that slip-up on the iceman. "If you didn't think he would bite you, he wouldn't," mother told him. He stomped out of the house in a terrible jangle of vibrations.

One morning when Muggs bit me slightly, more or less in passing, I reached down and grabbed his short stumpy tail and hoisted him into the air. It was a foolhardy thing to do and the last time I saw my mother, about six months ago, she said she didn't know what possessed me. I don't either, except that I was pretty mad. As long as I held the dog off the floor by his tail he couldn't get at me, but he twisted and jerked so, snarling all the time, that I realized I couldn't hold him that way very long. I carried him to the kitchen and flung him onto the floor and shut the door on him just as he crashed against it. But I forgot about the backstairs. Muggs went up the backstairs and down the frontstairs and had me cornered in the living room. I managed to get up onto the mantelpiece above the fireplace, but it gave way and came down with a tremendous crash throwing a large marble clock, several vases, and myself heavily to the floor. Muggs was so alarmed by the racket that when I picked myself up he had disappeared. We couldn't find him anywhere, although we whistled and shouted, until old Mrs. Detweiler called after dinner that night. Muggs had bitten her once, in the leg, and she came into the living room only after we assured her that Muggs had run away. She had just seated herself when, with a great growling and scratching of claws, Muggs emerged from under a davenport where he had been quietly hiding all the time, and bit her again. Mother examined the bite and put arnica on it and told Mrs. Detweiler that it was only a bruise. "He just bumped you," she said. But Mrs. Detweiler left the house in a nasty state of mind.

Lots of people reported our Airedale to the police but my father held a municipal office at the time and was on friendly terms with the police. Even so, the cops had been out a couple of times—once when Muggs bit Mrs. Rufus Sturtevant and again when he bit Lieutenant-Governor Malloy—but mother told them that it hadn't been Muggs' fault but the fault of the people who were bitten. "When he starts for them, they scream," she explained, "and that excites him." The cops suggested that it might be a good idea to tie the dog up, but mother said that it mortified him to be tied up and that he wouldn't eat when he was tied up.

Muggs at his meals was an unusual sight. Because of the fact that if you reached toward the floor he would bite you, we usually put his food plate on top of an old kitchen table with a bench alongside the table. Muggs would stand on the bench and eat. I remember that my mother's Uncle Horatio, who boasted that he was the third man up

Missionary Ridge, was splutteringly indignant when he found out that we fed the dog on a table because we were afraid to put his plate on the floor. He said he wasn't afraid of any dog that ever lived and that he would put the dog's plate on the floor if we would give it to him. Roy said that if Uncle Horatio had fed Muggs on the ground just before the battle he would have been the first man up Missionary Ridge. Uncle Horatio was furious. "Bring him in! Bring him in now!" he shouted. "I'll feed the —— on the floor!" Roy was all for giving him a chance, but my father wouldn't hear of it. He said that Muggs had already been fed. "I'll feed him again!" bawled Uncle Horatio. We had quite a time quieting him.

In his last year Muggs used to spend practically all of his time outdoors. He didn't like to stay in the house for some reason or other—perhaps it held too many unpleasant memories for him. Anyway, it was hard to get him to come in and as a result the garbage man, the iceman, and the laundryman wouldn't come near the house. We had to haul the garbage down to the corner, take the laundry out and bring it back, and meet the iceman a block from home. After this had gone on for some time we hit on an ingenious arrangement for getting the dog in the house so that we could lock him up while the gas meter was read, and so on. Muggs was afraid of only one thing, an electrical storm. Thunder and lightning frightened him out of his senses (I think he thought a storm had broken the day the mantelpiece fell). He would rush into the house and hide under a bed or in a clothes closet. So we fixed up a thunder machine out of a long narrow piece of sheet iron with a wooden handle on one end. Mother would shake this vigorously when she wanted to get Muggs into the house. It made an excellent imitation of thunder, but I suppose it was the most roundabout system for running a household that was ever devised. It took a lot out of mother.

A few months before Muggs died, he got to "seeing things." He would rise slowly from the floor, growling low, and stalk stiff-legged and menacing toward nothing at all. Sometimes the Thing would be just a little to the right or left of a visitor. Once a Fuller Brush salesman got hysterics. Muggs came wandering into the room like Hamlet following his father's ghost. His eyes were fixed on a spot just to the left of the Fuller Brush man, who stood it until Muggs was about three slow, creeping paces from him. Then he shouted. Muggs wavered on past him into the hallway grumbling to himself but the Fuller man went on shouting. I think mother had to throw a pan of cold water on him before he stopped. That was the way she used to stop us boys when we got into fights.

Muggs died quite suddenly one night. Mother wanted to bury him in the family lot under a marble stone with some such inscription as "Flights of angels sing thee to thy rest" but we persuaded her it was against the law. In the end we just put up a smooth board above his grave along a lonely road. On the board I wrote with an indelible pencil "Cave Canem." Mother was quite pleased with the simple classic dignity of the old Latin epitaph.

CHAPTER EIGHT

UNIVERSITY DAYS

I PASSED all the other courses that I took at my University, but I could never pass botany. This was because all botany students had to spend several hours a week in a laboratory looking through a microscope at plant cells, and I could never see through a microscope. I never once saw a cell through a microscope. This used to enrage my instructor. He would wander around the laboratory pleased with the progress all the students were making in drawing the involved and, so I am told, interesting structure of flower cells, until he came to me. I would just be standing there. "I can't see anything," I would say. He would begin patiently enough, explaining how anybody can see through a microscope, but he would always end up in fury, claiming that I could *too* see through a microscope but just pretended that I couldn't. "It takes away from the beauty of flowers anyway," I used to tell him. "We are not concerned with beauty in this course," he would say. "We are concerned solely with what I may call the *mechanics* of flars." "Well," I'd say, "I can't see anything." "Try it just once again," he'd say, and I would put my eye to the microscope and see nothing at all, except now and again a nebulous milky substance—a phenomenon of maladjustment. You were supposed to see a vivid, restless clockwork of sharply defined plant cells. "I see what looks like a lot of milk," I would tell him. This, he claimed, was the result of my not having adjusted the microscope properly, so he would readjust it for me, or rather, for himself. And I would look again and see milk.

I finally took a deferred pass, as they called it, and waited a year and tried again. (You had to pass one of the biological sciences or you couldn't graduate.) The professor had come back from vacation brown as a berry, bright-eyed, and eager to explain cell-structure again to his classes. "Well," he said to me, cheerily, when we met in the first laboratory hour of the semester, "we're going to see cells this time, aren't we?" "Yes, sir," I said. Students to right of me and to left of me and in front of me were seeing cells; what's more, they were quietly drawing pictures of them in their notebooks. Of course, I didn't see anything.

"We'll try it," the professor said to me, grimly, "with every adjustment of the microscope known to man. As God is my witness, I'll arrange this glass so that you see cells through it or I'll give up teaching. In twenty-two years of botany, I—" He cut off abruptly for he was beginning to quiver all over, like Lionel Barrymore, and he genuinely wished to hold onto his temper; his scenes with me had taken a great deal out of him.

So we tried it with every adjustment of the microscope known to man. With only one of them did I see anything but blackness or the familiar lacteal opacity, and that time I saw, to my pleasure and amazement, a variegated constellation of flecks, specks, and dots. These I hastily drew. The instructor, noting my activity, came back from an adjoining desk, a smile on his lips and his eyebrows high in hope. He looked at my cell drawing. "What's that?" he demanded, with a hint of a squeal in his voice. "That's what I saw," I said. "You didn't, you didn't, you *did*n't!" he screamed, losing control of his temper instantly, and he bent over and squinted into the microscope. His head snapped up. "That's your eye!" he shouted. "You've fixed the lens so that it reflects! You've drawn your eye!"

Another course that I didn't like, but somehow managed to pass, was economics. I went to that class straight from the botany class, which didn't help me any in understanding either subject. I used to get them mixed up. But not as mixed up as another student in my economics class who came there direct from a physics laboratory. He was a tackle on the football team, named Bolenciecwcz. At that time Ohio State University had one of the best football teams in the country, and Bolenciecwcz was one of its outstanding stars. In order to be eligible to play it was necessary for him to keep up in his studies, a very difficult matter, for while he was not dumber than an ox he was not any smarter. Most of his professors were lenient and helped him along. None gave him more hints, in answering questions, or asked him simpler ones than the economics professor, a thin, timid man named Bassum. One day when we were on the subject of transportation and distribution, it came Bolenciecwcz's turn to answer a question. "Name one means of transportation," the professor said to him. No light came into the big tackle's eyes. "Just any means of transportation," said the professor. Bolenciecwcz sat staring at him. "That is," pursued the professor, "any medium, agency, or method of going from one place to another." Bolenciecwcz had the look of a man who is being led into a trap. "You may choose among steam, horse-drawn, or electrically propelled vehicles," said the instructor. "I might suggest the one which we commonly take in making long journeys across land." There was a profound silence in which everybody stirred uneasily, including Bolenciecwcz and Mr. Bassum. Mr. Bassum abruptly broke this silence in an amazing manner. "Choo-choo-choo," he said, in a low voice, and turned instantly scarlet. He glanced appealingly around the room. All of us, of course, shared Mr. Bassum's desire that Bolenciecwcz should stay abreast of the class in economics, for the Illinois game, one of the hardest and most important of the season, was only a week off. "Toot, toot, too-toooooot!" some student with a deep voice moaned, and we all looked encouragingly at Bolenciecwcz. Somebody else gave a fine imitation of a locomotive letting off steam. Mr. Bassum himself rounded off the little show. "Ding, dong, ding, dong," he said, hopefully. Bolenciecwcz was staring at the floor now, trying to think, his great brow furrowed, his huge hands rubbing together, his face red.

"How did you come to college this year, Mr. Bolenciecwcz?" asked the professor. "*Chuf*fa chuffa, *chuf*fa chuffa."

"M'father sent me," said the football player.

"What on?" asked Bassum.

"I git an 'lowance," said the tackle, in a low, husky voice, obviously embarrassed.

"No, no," said Bassum. "Name a means of transportation. What did you *ride* here on?"

"Train," said Bolenciecwcz.

"Quite right," said the professor. "Now, Mr. Nugent, will you tell us——"

If I went through anguish in botany and economics—for different reasons—gymnasium work was even worse. I don't even like to think about it. They wouldn't let you play games or join in the exercises with your glasses on and I couldn't see with mine off. I bumped into professors, horizontal bars, agricultural students, and swinging iron rings. Not being able to see, I could take it but I couldn't dish it out. Also, in order to pass gymnasium (and you had to pass it to graduate) you had to learn to swim if you didn't know how. I didn't like the swimming pool, I didn't like swimming, and I didn't like the swimming instructor, and after all these years I still don't. I never swam but I passed my gym work anyway, by having another student give my gymnasium number (978) and swim across the pool in my place. He was a quiet, amiable blond youth, number 473, and he would have seen through a microscope for me if we could have got away with it, but we couldn't get away with it. Another thing I didn't like about gymnasium work was that they made you strip the day you registered. It is impossible for me to be happy when I am stripped and being asked a lot of questions. Still, I did better than a lanky agricultural student who was cross-examined just before I was. They asked each student what college he was in—that is, whether Arts, Engineering, Commerce, or Agriculture. "What college are you in?" the instructor snapped at the youth in front of me. "Ohio State University," he said promptly.

It wasn't that agricultural student but it was another a whole lot like him who decided to take up journalism, possibly on the ground that when farming went to hell he could fall back on newspaper work. He didn't realize, of course, that that would be very much like falling back full-length on a kit of carpenter's tools. Haskins didn't seem cut out for journalism, being too embarrassed to talk to anybody and unable to use a typewriter, but the editor of the college paper assigned him to the cow barns, the sheep house, the horse pavilion, and the animal husbandry department generally. This was a genuinely big "beat," for it took up five times as much ground and got ten times as great a legislative appropriation as the College of Liberal Arts. The agricultural student knew animals, but nevertheless his stories were dull and colorlessly written. He took all afternoon on each of them, on account of having to hunt for each letter on the typewriter. Once in a while he had to ask somebody to help him hunt. "C" and "L," in particular, were hard letters for him to find. His editor finally got pretty much annoyed at the farmer-journalist because his pieces were so uninteresting. "See here, Haskins," he snapped at him one day. "Why is it we never have anything hot from you on the horse pavilion? Here we have two hundred head of horses on this campus—more than any other university in the Western Conference except Purdue—and yet you never get any real lowdown on them. Now shoot over to the horse barns and dig up something lively." Haskins shambled out and came back in about an hour; he said he had something. "Well, start it off snappily," said the editor. "Something people will read." Haskins set to work and in a couple of hours brought a sheet of typewritten paper to the desk; it was a two-hundred-word story about some disease that had broken out among the horses. Its opening sentence was simple but arresting. It read: "Who has noticed the sores on the tops of the horses in the animal husbandry building?"

Ohio State was a land grant university and therefore two years of military drill was compulsory. We drilled with old Springfield rifles and studied the tactics of the Civil War even though the World War was going on at the time. At 11 o'clock each morning thousands of freshmen and sophomores used to deploy over the campus, moodily creeping up on the old chemistry building. It was good training for the kind of warfare that was waged at Shiloh but it had no connection with what was going on in Europe. Some people used to think there was German money behind it, but they didn't dare say so or they would have been thrown in jail as German spies. It was a period of muddy thought and marked, I believe, the decline of higher education in the Middle West.

As a soldier I was never any good at all. Most of the cadets were glumly indifferent soldiers, but I was no good at all. Once General Littlefield, who was commandant of the cadet corps, popped up in front of me during regimental drill and snapped, "You are the main trouble with this university!" I think he meant that my type was the main trouble with the university, out ne may have meant me individually. I was mediocre at drill, certainly—that is, until my senior year. By that time I had drilled longer than anybody else in the Western Conference, having failed at military at the end of each preceding year so that I had to do it all over again. I was the only senior still in uniform. The uniform which, when new, had made me look like an interurban railway conductor, now that it had become faded and too tight made me look like Bert Williams in his bell-boy act. This had a definitely bad effect on my morale. Even so, I had become by sheer practise little short of wonderful at squad manoeuvres.

One day General Littlefield picked our company out of the whole regiment and tried to get it mixed up by putting it through one movement after another as fast as we could execute them: squads right, squads left, squads on right into line, squads right about, squads left front into line, etc. In about three minutes one hundred and nine men were marching in one direction and I was marching away from them at an angle of forty degrees, all alone. "Company, halt!" shouted General Littlefield. "That man is the only man who has it right!" I was made a corporal for my achievement.

The next day General Littlefield summoned me to his office. He was swatting flies when I went in. I was silent and he was silent too, for a long time. I don't think he remembered me or why he had sent for me, but he didn't want to admit it. He swatted some more flies, keeping his eyes on them narrowly before he let go with the swatter. "Button your coat!" he snapped. Looking back on it now I can see that he meant me although he was looking at a fly, but I just stood there. Another fly came to rest on a paper in front of the general and began rubbing its hind legs together. The general lifted the swatter cautiously. I moved restlessly and the fly flew away. "You startled him!" barked General Littlefield, looking at me severely. I said I was sorry. "That won't help the situation!" snapped the General, with cold military logic. I didn't see what I could do except offer to chase some more flies toward his desk, but I didn't say anything. He stared out the window at the faraway figures of co-eds crossing the campus toward the library. Finally, he told me I could go. So I went. He either didn't know which cadet I was or else he forgot what he wanted to see me about. It may have been that he wished to apologize for having called me the main trouble with the university; or maybe he had decided to compliment me on my brilliant drilling of the day before and then at the last minute decided not to. I don't know. I don't think about it much any more.

CHAPTER NINE

DRAFT BOARD NIGHTS

I LEFT the University in June, 1918, but I couldn't get into the army on account of my sight, just as grandfather couldn't get in on account of his age. He applied several times and each time he took off his coat and threatened to whip the men who said he was too old. The disappointment of not getting to Germany (he saw no sense in everybody going to France) and the strain of running around town seeing influential officials finally got him down in bed. He had wanted to lead a division and his chagrin at not even being able to enlist as a private was too much for him. His brother Jake, some fifteen years younger than he was, sat up at night with him after he took to bed, because we were afraid he might leave the house without even putting on his clothes. Grandfather was against the idea of Jake watching over him— he thought it was a lot of tomfoolery—but Jake hadn't been able to sleep at night for twenty-eight years, so he was the perfect person for such a vigil.

On the third night, grandfather was wakeful. He would open his eyes, look at Jake, and close them again, frowning. He never answered any question Jake asked him. About four o'clock that morning, he caught his brother sound asleep in the big leather chair beside the bed. When once Jake did fall asleep he slept deeply, so that grandfather was able to get up, dress himself, undress Jake, and put him in bed without waking him. When my Aunt Florence came into the room at seven o'clock, grandfather was sitting in the chair reading the *Memoirs of U. S. Grant* and Jake was sleeping in the bed. "He watched while I slept," said grandfather, "so now I'm watchin' while he sleeps." It seemed fair enough.

One reason we didn't want grandfather to roam around at night was that he had said something once or twice about going over to Lancaster, his old home town, and putting his problem up to "Cump"—that is, General William Tecumseh Sherman, also an old Lancaster boy. We knew that his inability to find Sherman would be bad for him and we were afraid that he might try to get there in the little electric runabout that had been bought for my grandmother. She had become, surprisingly enough, quite skilful at getting around town in it. Grandfather was astonished and a little indignant when he saw her get into the contraption and drive off smoothly and easily. It was her first vehicular triumph over him in almost fifty years of married life and he determined to learn to drive the thing himself. A famous old horseman, he approached it as he might have approached a wild colt. His brow would darken and he would begin to curse. He always leaped into it quickly, as if it might pull out from under him if he didn't get into the seat fast enough. The first few times he tried to run the electric, he went swiftly around in a small circle, drove over the curb, across the sidewalk, and up onto the lawn. We all tried to persuade him to give up, but his spirit was aroused. "Git that goddam buggy back in the road!" he would say, imperiously. So we would manoeuver it back into the street and he would try again. Pulling too savagely on the guiding-bar—to teach the electric a lesson—was what took him around in a circle, and it was difficult to make him understand that it was best to relax and not get mad. He had the notion that if you didn't hold her, she would throw you. And a man who (or so he often told us) had driven a four-horse McCormick reaper when he was five years old did not intend to be thrown by an electric runabout.

Since there was no way of getting him to give up learning to operate the electric, we would take him out to Franklin Park, where the roadways were wide and unfrequented, and spend an hour or so trying to explain the differences between driving a horse and carriage and driving an electric. He would keep muttering all the time; he never got it out of his head that when he took the driver's seat the machine flattened its ears on him, so to speak. After a few weeks, nevertheless, he got so he could run the electric for a hundred yards or so along a fairly straight line. But whenever he took a curve, he invariably pulled or pushed the bar too quickly and too hard and headed for a tree or a flower bed. Someone was always with him and we would never let him take the car out of the park.

One morning when grandmother was all ready to go to market, she called the garage and told them to send the electric around. They said that grandfather had already been there and taken it out. There was a tremendous to-do. We telephoned Uncle Will and he got out his Lozier and we started off to hunt for grandfather. It was not yet seven o'clock and there was fortunately little traffic. We headed for Franklin Park, figuring that he might have gone out there to try to break the car's spirit. One or two early pedestrians had seen a tall old gentleman with a white beard driving a little electric and cussing as he drove. We followed a tortuous trail and found them finally on Nelson Road, about four miles from the town of Shepard. Grandfather was standing in the road shouting, and the back wheels of the electric were deeply entangled in a barbed-wire fence. Two workmen and a farmhand were trying to get the thing loose. Grandfather was in a state of high wrath about the electric. "The —— — - —— backed up on me!" he told us.

But to get back to the war. The Columbus draft board never called grandfather for service, which was a lucky thing for them because they would have had to take him. There were stories that several old men of eighty or ninety had been summoned in the confusion, but somehow or other grandfather was missed. He waited every day for the call, but it never came. My own experience was quite different. I was called almost every week, even though I had been exempted from service the first time I went before the medical examiners. Either they were never convinced that it was me or else there was some clerical error in the records which was never cleared up. Anyway, there was usually a letter for me on Monday ordering me to report for examination on the second floor of Memorial Hall the following Wednesday at 9 P.M. The second time I went up, I tried to explain to one of the doctors that I had already been exempted. "You're just a blur to me," I said, taking off my glasses. "You're absolutely nothing to me," he snapped, sharply.

I had to take off all my clothes each time and jog around the hall with a lot of porters and bank presidents' sons and clerks and poets. Our hearts and lungs would be examined, and then our feet; and finally our eyes. That always came last. When the eye specialist got around to me, he would always say, "Why, you couldn't get into the service with sight like that!" "I know," I would say. Then a week or two later I would be summoned again and go through the same rigmarole. The ninth or tenth time I was called, I happened to pick up one of several stethoscopes that were lying on a table and suddenly, instead of finding myself in the line of draft men, I found myself in the line of examiners. "Hello, doctor," said one of them nodding. "Hello," I said. That, of course, was before I took my clothes off; I might have managed it naked, but I doubt it. I was assigned, or rather drifted, to the chest-and-lung section, where I began to examine every other man, thus cutting old Dr. Ridgeway's work in two. "I'm glad to have you here, doctor," he said.

I passed most of the men that came to me, but now and then I would exempt one just to be on the safe side. I began by making each of them hold his breath and then say "mi, mi, mi, mi," until I noticed Ridgeway looking at me curiously. He, I discovered, simply made them say "ah," and sometimes he didn't make them say anything. Once I got hold of a man who, it came out later, had swallowed a watch—to make the doctors believe there was something wrong with him inside (it was a common subterfuge: men swallowed nails, hairpins, ink, etc., in an effort to be let out). Since I didn't know what you were supposed to hear through a stethoscope, the ticking of the watch at first didn't surprise me, but I decided to call Dr. Ridgeway into consultation, because nobody else had ticked. "This man seems to tick," I said to him. He looked at me in surprise but didn't say anything. Then he thumped the man, laid his ear to his chest, and finally tried the stethoscope. "Sound as a dollar," he said. "Listen lower down," I told him. The man indicated his stomach. Ridgeway gave him a haughty, indignant look. "That is for the abdominal men to worry about," he said, and moved off. A few minutes later, Dr. Blythe Ballomy got around to the man and listened, but he didn't blink an eye; his grim expression never changed. "You have swallowed a watch, my man," he said, crisply. The draftee reddened in embarrassment and uncertainty. "On *purpose?*" he asked. "That I can't say," the doctor told him, and went on.

I served with the draft board for about four months. Until the summonses ceased, I couldn't leave town and as long as I stayed and appeared promptly for examination, even though I did the examining, I felt that technically I could not be convicted of evasion. During the daytime, I worked as publicity agent for an amusement park, the manager of which was a tall, unexpected young man named Byron Landis. Some years before, he had dynamited the men's lounge in the statehouse annex for a prank; he enjoyed pouring buckets of water on sleeping persons, and once he had barely escaped arrest for jumping off the top of the old Columbus Transfer Company building with a homemade parachute.

He asked me one morning if I would like to take a ride in the new Scarlet Tornado, a steep and wavy roller-coaster. I didn't want to but I was afraid he would think I was afraid, so I went along. It was about ten o'clock and there was nobody at the park except workmen and attendants and concessionaires in their shirtsleeves. We climbed into one of the long gondolas of the roller-coaster and while I was looking around for the man who was going to run it, we began to move off. Landis, I discovered, was running it himself. But it was too late to get out; we had begun to climb, clickety-clockety, up the first steep incline, down the other side of which we careened at eighty miles an hour. "I didn't know you could run this thing!" I bawled at my companion, as we catapulted up a sixty-degree arch and looped headlong into space. "I didn't either!" he bawled back. The racket and the rush of air were terrific as we roared into the pitch-black Cave of Darkness and came out and down Monohan's Leap, so called because a workman named Monohan had been forced to jump from it when caught between two approaching experimental cars while it was being completed. That trip, although it ended safely, made a lasting impression on me. It is not too much to say that it has flavored my life. It is the reason I shout in my sleep, refuse to ride on the elevated, keep jerking the emergency brake in cars other people are driving, have the sensation of flying like a bird when I first lie down, and in certain months can't keep anything on my stomach.

During my last few trips to the draft board, I went again as a draft prospect, having grown tired of being an examiner. None of the doctors who had been my colleagues for so long recognized me, not even Dr. Ridgeway. When he examined my chest for the last time, I asked him if there hadn't been another doctor helping him. He said there had been. "Did he look anything like me?" I asked. Dr. Ridgeway looked at me. "I don't think so," he said, "he was taller." (I had my shoes off while he was examining me.) "A good pulmonary man," added Ridgeway. "Relative of yours?" I said yes. He sent me on to Dr. Quimby, the specialist who had examined my eyes twelve or fifteen times before. He gave me some simple reading tests. "You could never get into the army with eyes like that," he said. "I know," I told him.

Late one morning, shortly after my last examination, I was awakened by the sound of bells ringing and whistles blowing. It grew louder and more insistent and wilder. It was the Armistice.

A NOTE AT THE END

The hard times of my middle years I pass over, leaving the ringing bells of 1918, with all their false promise, to mark the end of a special sequence. The sharp edges of old reticences are softened in the auto- biographer by the passing of time—a man does not pull the pillow over his head when he wakes in the morning because he suddenly re- members some awful thing that happened to him fifteen or twenty years ago, but the confusions and the panics of last year and the year before are too close for contentment. Until a man can quit talking loudly to himself in order to shout down the memories of blunderings and gropings, he is in no shape for the painstaking examination of distress and the careful ordering of event so necessary to a calm and balanced exposition of what, exactly, was the matter. The time I fell out of the gun room in Mr. James Stanley's house in Green Lake, New York, is, for instance, much too near for me to go into with any peace of mind, although it happened in 1925, the ill-fated year of "Horses, Horses, Horses" and "Valencia." There is now, I under- stand, a porch to walk out onto when you open the door I opened that night, but there wasn't then.

The mistaken exits and entrances of my thirties have moved me sev- eral times to some thought of spending the rest of my days wandering aimlessly around the South Seas, like a character out of Conrad, silent and inscrutable. But the necessity for frequent visits to my oculist and dentist has prevented this. You can't be running back from Singapore every few months to get your lenses changed and still retain the proper mood for wandering. Furthermore, my horn-rimmed glasses and my Ohio accent betray me, even when I sit on the terrasses of little tropical cafes, wearing a pith helmet, staring straight ahead, and twitching a muscle in my jaw. I found this out when I tried wandering around the West Indies one summer. Instead of being followed by

the whispers of men and the glances of women, I was followed by
bead salesmen and native women with postcards. Nor did any dark
girl, looking at all like Tondeleyo in "White Cargo," come forward
and offer to go to pieces with me. They tried to sell me baskets.

Under these circumstances it is impossible to be inscrutable and a
wanderer who isn't inscrutable might just as well be back at Broad
and High Streets in Columbus sitting in the Baltimore Dairy Lunch.
Nobody from Columbus has ever made a first rate wanderer in the
Conradean tradition. Some of them have been fairly good at disappearing for a few days to turn up in a hotel in Louisville with a bad
headache and no recollection of how they got there, but they always
scurry back to their wives with some cock-and-bull story of having lost
their memory or having gone away to attend the annual convention
of the Fraternal Order of Eagles.

There was, of course, even for Conrad's Lord Jim, no running away.
The cloud of his special discomfiture followed him like a pup, no
matter what ships he took or what wilderness he entered. In the path-
ways between office and home and home and the houses of settled people there are always, ready to snap at you, the little perils of routine
living, but there is no escape in the unplanned tangent, the sudden
turn. In Martinique, when the whistle blew for the tourists to get back
on the ship, I had a quick, wild, and lovely moment when I decided I
wouldn't get back on the ship. I did, though. And I found that somebody had stolen the pants to my dinner jacket.

R. B. CUNNINGHAME GRAHAM

Robert Bontine Cunninghame Graham, who died in 1936 at the age of eighty-four, could have been almost anything he pleased, had he wanted to. The essence of his life and character lies in the fact that he did not want to. He might have been a successful politician—with Keir Hardie he founded the Scottish Labor Party in 1890, and later served in Parliament. He might have been a notable explorer—in 1898, disguised as a Turkish doctor, he penetrated the mysterious fastnesses of Morocco. His ancestry, some say, made him the legitimate King of Scotland, but he never even cared to become the authentic grand laird appropriate to his station. He might have developed into a leading socialist revolutionary—he spent two months in prison on a charge of attacking the police during the Bloody Sunday riots in Trafalgar Square in November of 1887. And, finally, he might have become a great writer, had he devoted himself to the job.

But Cunninghame Graham, called by Conrad "the perfection of scorn," was the hidalgo type, holding a certain offhand amateurism the mark of true nobility of soul. In his life he did many things besides those I have listed. He was a rancher in the Argentine, a horse-trader for the British government, a fencing master in Mexico, a gentleman farmer in Scotland, and (what here concerns us) a voluminous writer of essays, sketches, short stories, travel books, and biographies, most of them on South American and Spanish themes.

His first book came out when he was forty-three, and thereafter he wrote only to please himself. His subjects were not popular and he was never widely read. This doubtless pleased him, as readers of the essay which follows will perceive. With what arrogant finality he writes, "Success, which touches nothing that it does not vulgarize, should be its own reward. In fact, rewards of any kind are but vulgarities." This attitude he preserved all his life. In London, during the great days of The Saturday Review, he would occasionally turn in a piece so brilliant that writers like George Bernard Shaw were glad that Cunninghame Graham's contributions were so infrequent, for had he put his mind to it he might have outshone all his colleagues.

But Cunninghame Graham preferred loneliness, a kind of noble melancholy, and the acquaintance of his own soul to pre-eminence in any of the fields he entered. He wanted to be Cunninghame Graham, not a writer, or a politician, or a farmer. He expressed himself primarily in action. Words, though he handled them so superbly, were a by-product. He belongs with Englishmen like Doughty, Richard Burton, T. E. Lawrence—solitary creatures, flawed artists, geniuses of adventure. His spiritual affiliations were largely with the Spanish conquistadores whose lives he studied so carefully. He was indeed more Spanish than Scottish. His grandmother was Spanish and he spoke Castilian before he learned English. But he acted Castilian all his life.

The piece I have chosen for this collection shows him at his most characteristic. It is a successful attack on success, the perfect expression of quixotism and the immortal charm of dead causes. As a piece of writing it seems to me marvelously effective, muscular with magnificent phrases ("the stolid Georges . . . sunk in their pudding and prosperity," "the prosperous Elizabeth, after a life of honours unwillingly surrendering her cosmetics up to death in a state bed"). Its picture of the deserted Cuban beach and the skeleton of the Spanish general has the grandeur of all truly chosen symbols. The prose has the ring of steel.

Success

BY

R. B. CUNNINGHAME GRAHAM

SUCCESS, WHICH TOUCHES NOTHING that it does not vulgarize, should be its own reward. In fact, rewards of any kind are but vulgarities.

We applaud successful folk, and straight forget them, as we do ballet-dancers, actors, and orators. They strut their little hour, and then are relegated to peerages, to baronetcies, to books of landed gentry, and the like.

Quick triumphs make short public memories. Triumph itself only endures the time the triumphal car sways through the street. Your nine days' wonder is a sort of five-legged calf, or a two-headed nightingale, and of the nature of a calculating boy—a seven months' prodigy, born out of time to his own undoing and a mere wonderment for gaping dullards who dislocate their jaws in ecstasy of admiration and then start out to seek new idols to adore. We feel that after all the successful man is fortune's wanton, and that good luck and he have but been equal to two common men. Poverty, many can endure with dignity. Success, how few can carry off, even with decency and without baring their innermost infirmities before the public gaze.

Caricatures in bronze and marble, and titles made ridiculous by their exotic style we shower upon all those who have succeeded, in war, in literature, or art; we give them money, and for a season no African Lucullus in Park Lane can dine without them. Then having given, feel that we have paid for service rendered, and generally withhold respect.

For those who fail, for those who have sunk still battling beneath the muddy waves of life, we keep our love, and that curiosity about

354

their lives which makes their memories green when the cheap gold is
dusted over, which once we gave success.

How few successful men are interesting! Hannibal, Alcibiades, with
Raleigh, Mithridates, and Napoleon, who would compare them for a
moment with their mere conquerors?

The unlucky Stuarts, from the first poet king slain at the ball play,
to the poor mildewed Cardinal of York, with all their faults, they leave
the stolid Georges millions of miles behind, sunk in their pudding and
prosperity. The prosperous Elizabeth, after a life of honours unwillingly surrendering her cosmetics up to death in a state bed, and Mary
laying her head upon the block at Fotheringay after the nine and forty
years of failure of her life (failure except of love), how many million
miles, unfathomable seas, and sierras upon sierras separate them?

And so of nations, causes and events. Nations there are as interesting in decadence, as others in their ten-percentish apogee are dull
and commonplace. Causes, lost almost from the beginning of the
world, but hardly yet despaired of, as the long struggle betwixt rich
and poor, which dullards think eternal, but which will one day be resolved, either by the absorption of the rich into the legions of the poor,
or vice versa, still remain interesting, and will do so whilst the unequal
combat yet endures.

Causes gone out of vogue, which have become almost as ludicrous
as is a hat from Paris of ten years ago; causes which hang in monumental mockery quite out of fashion, as that of Poland, still are more
interesting than is the struggle between the English and the Germans,
which shall sell gin and gunpowder to negroes on the Coast.

Even events long passed, and which right-thinking men have years
ago dismissed to gather dust in the waste spaces of their minds, may
interest or repel according as they may make for failure or success.

Failure alone can interest speculative minds. Success is for the millions of the working world, who see the engine in eight hours arrive
in Edinburgh from London, and marvel at the last improvement in
its wheels. The real interest in the matters being the forgotten efforts
of some alchemist who, with the majesty of law ever awake to burn
him as a witch, with the hoarse laughter of the practical and business

men still ringing in his ears, made his rude model of a steam engine, and perhaps lost his eyesight when it burst.

On a deserted beach in Cuba, not far from El Caney, some travellers not long ago came on a skeleton. Seated in a rough chair, it sat and gazed upon the sea. The gulls had roosted on the collar bones, and round the feet sea-wreck and dulse had formed a sort of wreath. A tattered Spanish uniform still fluttered from the bones, and a cigar-box set beside the chair held papers showing that the man had been an officer of rank. One of these gave the password of the day when he had lost his life, and as the travellers gazed upon the bones, a land crab peeped out of a hole just underneath the chair.

All up and down the coast were strewn the remnants of the pomp and circumstance of glorious war. Rifles with rusty barrels, the stocks set thick with barnacles, steel scabbards with bent swords wasted to scrap iron, fragments of uniforms and belts, ends of brass chains and bones of horses reft from their wind-swept prairies to undergo the agonies of transport in a ship, packed close as sardines in a box, and then left to die wounded with the vultures picking out their eyes. All, all, was there, fairly spread out as in a kindergarten, to point the lesson to the fools who write of war, if they had wit to see. Gun carriages half silted up with sand, and rusted broken Maxims, gave an air of ruin, as is the case wherever Titan man has been at play, broken his toys, and then set out to kill his brother fools.

Withal nothing of dignity about the scene; a stage unskilfully set out with properties all go up on the cheap; even the ribs and trucks of the decaying ships of what once had been Admiral Cervera's fleet stood roasting in the sun, their port-holes just awash, as they once roasted in the flames which burned them and their crews. Nothing but desolation in the scene, and yet a desolation of a paltry kind, not caused by time, by famine, pestilence, or anything which could impart an air of tragedy, only the desolation made by those who had respectively sent their poor helots out to fight, staying themselves smug and secure at home, well within reach of the quotations of the Stock Exchange.

So in his mouldering chair the general sat, his password antiquated and become as much the property of the first passer-by as an advertisement of "liver pills." His uniform, no doubt his pride, all rags; his sword (bought at some outfitter's) long stolen away and sold for drink by him who filched it; but yet the sun-dried bones, which once had been a man, were of themselves more interesting than were his living conquerors with their cheap air of insincere success.

The world goes out to greet the conqueror with flowers and with shouts, but first he has to conquer, and so draw down upon himself the acclamations of the crowd, who do not know that hundreds such as the man they stultify with noise have gloriously failed, and that the odium of success is hard enough to bear, without the added ignominy of popular applause. Who with a spark of humour in his soul can bear success without some irritation in his mind? But for good luck he might have been one of the shouters who run sweating by his car; doubts must assail him, if success has not already made him pachyder-matous to praise, that sublimate which wears away the angles of our self-respect, and leaves us smooth to catch the mud our fellows fling at us, in their fond adoration of accomplished facts. Success is but the recognition (chiefly by yourself) that you are better than your fellows are. A paltry feeling, nearly allied to the base scheme of punishments and of rewards which has made most faiths arid, and rendered actions noble in themselves mere huckstering affairs of fire insurance.

If a man put his life in peril for the Victoria Cross, or pass laborious days in laboratories tormenting dogs, only to be a baronet at last, a plague of courage and laborious days. Arts, sciences, and literature, with all the other trifles in which hard-working idle men make occu-pations for themselves, when they lead to material success, spoil their professor, and degrade themselves to piecework at so many pounds an hour.

Nothing can stand against success and yet keep fresh. Nations as well as individuals feel its vulgarizing power. Throughout all Europe, Spain alone still rears its head, the unspoiled race, content in philo-sophic guise to fail in all she does, and thus preserve the individual independence of her sons. Successful nations have to be content with their success, their citizens cannot be interesting. So many hundred feet of sanitary tubes a minute or an hour, so many wage-saving appli-cations of machinery, so many men grow rich; fancy a poet rich through rhyming, or a philosopher choked in banknotes, whilst writing his last scheme of wise philosophy. Yet those who fail, no matter how ingloriously, have their revenge on the successful few, by having kept themselves free from vulgarity, or by having died unknown.

A miner choked with firedamp in a pit, dead in the vain attempt to save some beer-mused comrade left behind entombed, cannot be vulgar, even if when alive he was a thief. Your crass successful man who has his statue set up in our streets (apparently to scare away the crows), and when he dies his column and a half in penny cyclopædias, turns interest to ashes by his apotheosis in the vulgar eye.

But the forgotten general sitting in his chair, his fleshless feet just lapping in the waves, his whitening bones fast mouldering into dust, nothing can vulgarize him; no fool will crown him with a tin-foiled laurel wreath, no poetaster sing his praise in maudlin ode or halting threnody, for he has passed into the realm of those who by misfortune claim the sympathy of writers who are dumb.

Let him sit on and rest, looking out on the sea, where his last vision saw the loss of his doomed country's fleet.

An archetype of those who fail, let him still sit watching the gulls fly screaming through the air, and mark the fish spring and fall back again with a loud crash, in the still waters of the tropic beach.

VIRGINIA WOOLF

COMMENTARY

On April 2, 1941, Virginia Woolf, fifty-nine years of age, left a note for her household and disappeared forever. Her suicide passed almost unremarked at a time when more momentous events were taking place every minute of the day. These events themselves may have helped her to her last exit, for her temperament, all delicate balance and vibration, was ill-adapted to the rough crash and strain of war. E. M. Forster said of her that she worked in a storm of atoms and seconds. But this is the Bomb Age. The atoms of personality, the seconds our individual hearts tick out, are crushed and dispersed under the impact of history being made too fast.

Perhaps Virginia Woolf, author of a sheaf of essays and a scattered half-dozen novels, had completed her work. With her vanishing the Bloomsbury school she helped to make transiently famous may be said to have closed its gates. The best writers of her generation—Lawrence, Joyce, Strachey—are dead; a marriage has been arranged between Aldous Huxley and Hollywood; E. M. Forster, the finest of living English novelists, is silent. Virginia Woolf's era is finished—a stupid, shallow way of saying that at the moment critics and readers are not paying much attention to it. Perhaps it is no more and no less finished than the preceding Edwardian era, which the essay here reprinted attacks with such charm and wit, if with only partial cogency.

Literary essays are usually a kind of dead language, kept in circulation by the determined efforts of a minority group. They do not seem to be written for people, but are communications, often of high permanent value, from one specialist to another. When a writer breaks through this formal mold and speaks of literature not as if it were a "subject," like paleography, but a passion, like love or hunger, the result is an essay like Virginia Woolf's "Mr. Bennett and Mrs. Brown." Its references may date, but its ideas, presented without

359

benefit of literary jargon, do not. It still seems to me a sound explanation of why novelists are interested in people, what interests them, and how they make you interested. All novels begin, as Virginia Woolf says, with an old lady in the corner opposite—the old lady she calls Mrs. Brown.

The Bennetts, the Wellses, and the Galsworthys, she thinks, forget all about Mrs. Brown. It may be that she is too hard on them. It is true that their reputations have declined, that they overstuff their books, that they edify and prophesy as much as they create character. Yet The Old Wives' Tale, I think, will be read for many years, despite its upholstery, and the Wells who wrote The History of Mr. Polly has created character as freshly as, if more simply than, did any Bloomsburian.

This does not controvert Virginia Woolf's thesis, of course, which stands even though she was a trifle unfair to her predecessors and perhaps a little rash in her confidence in her own generation. That great age of English literature on the verge of which she thought we were trembling in 1924 has not yet shown its head. Right now it looks as though it were indefinitely postponed.

Her work, like that of D. H. Lawrence and Lytton Strachey, has fallen into eclipse. I think it is too delicate and febrile to last; her sensibility was so great as often to obscure the sense, except for initiates. She used a private language, which is merely a barrier to be overcome if, as in the case of James Joyce, the private language expresses a large and generous sense of life. I do not feel this to be the case in her own novels, but my own obtuseness may be at fault. At any rate, her novels are not read as much as once they were, but her literary comments, of which "Mr. Bennett and Mrs. Brown" is one of the finest, remain as fresh and pertinent as ever.

Mr. Bennett and Mrs. Brown

BY

VIRGINIA WOOLF

It seems to me possible, perhaps desirable, that I may be the only person in this room* who has committed the folly of writing, trying to write, or failing to write, a novel. And when I asked myself, as your invitation to speak to you about modern fiction made me ask myself, what demon whispered in my ear and urged me to my doom, a little figure rose before me—the figure of a man, or of a woman, who said, "My name is Brown. Catch me if you can."

Most novelists have the same experience. Some Brown, Smith, or Jones comes before them and says in the most seductive and charming way in the world, "Come and catch me if you can." And so, led on by this will-o'-the-wisp, they flounder through volume after volume, spending the best years of their lives in the pursuit, and receiving for the most part very little cash in exchange. Few catch the phantom; most have to be content with a scrap of her dress or a wisp of her hair.

My belief that men and women write novels because they are lured on to create some character which has thus imposed itself upon them has the sanction of Mr. Arnold Bennett. In an article from which I will quote he says: "The foundation of good fiction is character-creating and nothing else. . . . Style counts; plot counts; originality of outlook counts. But none of these counts anything like so much as the convincingness of the characters. If the characters are real the novel will have a chance; if they are not, oblivion will be its portion. . . ." And he goes on to draw the conclusion that we have no young novelists of

---

*This essay was originally read before the Heretics club at Cambridge, May 18, 1924.—C. F.

first-rate importance at the present moment, because they are unable to create characters that are real, true, and convincing.

These are the questions that I want with greater boldness than discretion to discuss to-night. I want to make out what we mean when we talk about "character" in fiction; to say something about the question of reality which Mr. Bennett raises; and to suggest some reasons why the younger novelists fail to create characters, if, as Mr. Bennett asserts, it is true that fail they do. This will lead me, I am well aware, to make some very sweeping and some very vague assertions. For the question is an extremely difficult one. Think how little we know about character—think how little we know about art. But, to make a clearance before I begin, I will suggest that we range Edwardians and Georgians into two camps; Mr. Wells, Mr. Bennett, and Mr. Galsworthy I will call the Edwardians; Mr. Forster, Mr. Lawrence, Mr. Strachey, Mr. Joyce, and Mr. Eliot I will call the Georgians. And if I speak in the first person, with intolerable egotism, I will ask you to excuse me. I do not want to attribute to the world at large the opinions of one solitary, ill-informed, and misguided individual.

My first assertion is one that I think you will grant—that every one in this room is a judge of character. Indeed it would be impossible to live for a year without disaster unless one practised character-reading and had some skill in the art. Our marriages, our friendships depend on it; our business largely depends on it; every day questions arise which can only be solved by its help. And now I will hazard a second assertion, which is more disputable perhaps, to the effect that on or about December, 1910, human character changed.

I am not saying that one went out, as one might into a garden, and there saw that a rose had flowered, or that a hen had laid an egg. The change was not sudden and definite like that. But a change there was, nevertheless; and, since one must be arbitrary, let us date it about the year 1910. The first signs of it are recorded in the books of Samuel Butler, in *The Way of All Flesh* in particular; the plays of Bernard Shaw continue to record it. In life one can see the change, if I may use a homely illustration, in the character of one's cook. The Victorian cook lived like a leviathan in the lower depths, formidable, silent, obscure, inscrutable; the Georgian cook is a creature of sunshine and fresh air; in and out of the drawing-room, now to borrow *The Daily Herald,* now to ask advice about a hat. Do you ask for more solemn instances of the power of the human race to change? Read the *Agamemnon,* and see whether, in process of time, your sympathies are not almost entirely with Clytemnestra. Or consider the married life of the Carlyles, and bewail the waste, the futility, for him and for her, of the horrible domestic tradition which made it seemly for a woman of genius to spend her time chasing beetles, scouring saucepans, instead of writing books. All human relations have shifted—those between masters and servants, husbands and wives, parents and children. And when human relations change there is at the same time a change in religion, conduct, politics, and literature. Let us agree to place one of these changes about the year 1910.

I have said that people have to acquire a good deal of skill in character-reading if they are to live a single year of life without disaster. But it is the art of the young. In middle age and in old age the art is practised mostly for its uses, and friendships and other adventures and experiments in the art of reading character are seldom made. But novelists differ from the rest of the world because they do not cease to be interested in character when they have learnt enough about it for practical purposes. They go a step further; they feel that there is something permanently interesting in character in itself. When all the practical business of life has been discharged, there is something about people which continues to seem to them of overwhelming importance, in spite of the fact that it has no bearing whatever upon their happiness, comfort, or income. The study of character becomes to them an absorbing pursuit; to impart character an obsession. And this I find it very difficult to explain: what novelists mean when they talk about character, what the impulse is that urges them so powerfully every now and then to embody their view in writing.

So, if you will allow me, instead of analyzing and abstracting, I will tell you a simple story which, however pointless, has the merit of being true, of a journey from Richmond to Waterloo, in the hope that I may show you what I mean by character in itself; that you may realize the different aspects it can wear; and the hideous perils that beset you directly you try to describe it in words.

One night some weeks ago, then, I was late for the train and jumped into the first carriage I came to. As I sat down I had the strange and uncomfortable feeling that I was interrupting a conversation between two people who were already sitting there. Not that they were young or happy. Far from it. They were both elderly, the woman over sixty, the man well over forty. They were sitting opposite each other, and the man, who had been leaning over and talking emphatically to judge by his attitude and the flush on his face, sat back and became silent. I had disturbed him, and he was annoyed. The elderly lady, however, whom I will call Mrs. Brown, seemed rather relieved. She was one of those clean, threadbare old ladies whose extreme tidiness—everything buttoned, fastened, tied together, mended and brushed up—suggests more extreme poverty than rags and dirt. There was something pinched about her—a look of suffering, of apprehension, and, in addition, she was extremely small. Her feet, in their clean little boots, scarcely touched the floor. I felt that she had nobody to support her; that she had to make up her mind for herself; that, having been deserted, or left a widow, years ago, she had led an anxious, harried life, bringing up an only son, perhaps, who, as likely as not, was by this time beginning to go to the bad. All this shot through my mind as I sat down, being uncomfortable, like most people, at travelling with fellow passengers unless I have somehow or other accounted for them. Then I looked at the man. He was no relation of Mrs. Brown's I felt sure; he was of a bigger, burlier, less refined type. He was a man of business, I imagined, very likely a respectable corn-chandler from the North, dressed in good blue serge with a pocket-knife and a silk handkerchief, and a stout leather bag. Obviously, however, he had an unpleasant business to settle with Mrs. Brown; a secret, perhaps sinister business, which they did not intend to discuss in my presence.

"Yes, the Crofts have had very bad luck with their servants," Mr. Smith (as I will call him) said in a considering way, going back to some earlier topic, with a view to keeping up appearances.

"Ah, poor people," said Mrs. Brown, a trifle condescendingly. "My grandmother had a maid who came when she was fifteen and stayed till she was eighty" (this was said with a kind of hurt and aggressive pride to impress us both perhaps).

"One doesn't often come across that sort of thing nowadays," said Mr. Smith in conciliatory tones.

Then they were silent.

"It's odd they don't start a golf club there—I should have thought one of the young fellows would," said Mr. Smith, for the silence obviously made him uneasy.

Mrs. Brown hardly took the trouble to answer.

"What changes they're making in this part of the world," said Mr. Smith looking out of the window, and looking furtively at me as he did so.

It was plain, from Mrs. Brown's silence, from the uneasy affability with which Mr. Smith spoke, that he had some power over her which he was exerting disagreeably. It might have been her son's downfall, or some painful episode in her past life, or her daughter's. Perhaps she was going to London to sign some document to make over some property. Obviously against her will she was in Mr. Smith's hands. I was beginning to feel a great deal of pity for her, when she said, suddenly and inconsequently,

"Can you tell me if an oak-tree dies when the leaves have been eaten for two years in succession by caterpillars?"

She spoke quite brightly, and rather precisely, in a cultivated, inquisitive voice.

Mr. Smith was startled, but relieved to have a safe topic of conversation given him. He told her a great deal very quickly about plagues of insects. He told her that he had a brother who kept a fruit farm in Kent. He told her what fruit farmers do every year in Kent, and so on, and so on. While he talked a very odd thing happened. Mrs. Brown took out her little white handkerchief and began to dab her eyes. She was crying. But she went on listening quite composedly to what he was saying, and he went on talking, a little louder, a little angrily, as if he had seen her cry often before; as if it were a painful habit. At last it got on his nerves. He stopped abruptly, looked out of the window, then leant towards her as he had been doing when I got in, and said in a bullying, menacing way, as if he would not stand any more nonsense,

"So about that matter we were discussing. It'll be all right? George will be there on Tuesday?" ·

"We sha'n't be late," said Mrs. Brown, gathering herself together with superb dignity.

Mr. Smith said nothing. He got up, buttoned his coat, reached his bag down, and jumped out of the train before it had stopped at Clapham Junction. He had got what he wanted, but he was ashamed of himself; he was glad to get out of the old lady's sight.

Mrs. Brown and I were left alone together. She sat in her corner opposite, very clean, very small, rather queer, and suffering intensely. The impression she made was overwhelming. It came pouring out like a draught, like a smell of burning. What was it composed of—that overwhelming and peculiar impression? Myriads of irrelevant and incongruous ideas crowd into one's head on such occasions; one sees the person, one sees Mrs. Brown, in the centre of all sorts of different scenes. I thought of her in a seaside house, among queer ornaments: sea-urchins, models of ships in glass cases. Her husband's medals were on the mantelpiece. She popped in and out of the room, perching on the edges of chairs, picking meals out of saucers, indulging in long, silent stares. The caterpillars and the oak-trees seemed to imply all that. And then, into this fantastic and secluded life, broke Mr. Smith. I saw him blowing in, so to speak, on a windy day. He banged, he slammed. His dripping umbrella made a pool in the hall. They sat closeted together.

And then Mrs. Brown faced the dreadful revelation. She took her heroic decision. Early, before dawn, she packed her bag and carried it herself to the station. She would not let Smith touch it. She was wounded in her pride, unmoored from her anchorage; she came of gentlefolks who kept servants—but details could wait. The important thing was to realize her character, to steep oneself in her atmosphere. I had no time to explain why I felt it somewhat tragic, heroic, yet with a dash of the flighty, and fantastic, before the train stopped, and I watched her disappear, carrying her bag, into the vast blazing station. She looked very small, very tenacious; at once very frail and very heroic. And I have never seen her again, and I shall never know what became of her.

The story ends without any point to it. But I have not told you this anecdote to illustrate either my own ingenuity or the pleasure of travelling from Richmond to Waterloo. What I want you to see in it is this. Here is a character imposing itself upon another person. Here is Mrs. Brown making someone begin almost automatically to write a novel about her. I believe that all novels begin with an old lady in the corner opposite. I believe that all novels, that is to say, deal with character, and that it is to express character—not to preach doctrines, sing songs, or celebrate the glories of the British Empire, that the form of the novel, so clumsy, verbose, and undramatic, so rich, elastic, and alive, has been evolved. To express character, I have said; but you will at once reflect that the very widest interpretation can be put upon those words. For example, old Mrs. Brown's character will strike you very differently according to the age and country in which you happen to be born. It would be easy enough to write three different versions of that incident in the train, an English, a French, and a Russian. The English writer would make the old lady into a "character"; he would bring out her oddities and mannerisms; her buttons and wrinkles; her ribbons and warts. Her personality would dominate the book. A French writer would rub out all that; he would sacrifice the individual Mrs. Brown to give a more general view of human nature; to make a more abstract, proportioned, and harmonious whole. The Russian would pierce through the flesh; would reveal the soul—the soul alone, wandering out into the Waterloo Road, asking of life some tremendous question which would sound on and on in our ears after the book was finished. And then besides age and country there is the writer's temperament to be considered. You see one thing in character, and I another. You say it means this, and I that. And when it comes to writing each makes a further selection on principles of his own. Thus Mrs. Brown can be treated in an infinite variety of ways, according to the age, country, and temperament of the writer.

But now I must recall what Mr. Arnold Bennett says. He says that it is only if the characters are real that the novel has any chance of surviving. Otherwise, die it must. But, I ask myself, what is reality? And who are the judges of reality? A character may be real to Mr. Bennett and quite unreal to me. For instance, in this article he says that Dr. Watson in *Sherlock Holmes* is real to him: to me Dr. Watson is a sack stuffed with straw, a dummy, a figure of fun. And so it is with character after character—in book after book. There is nothing that people differ about more than the reality of characters, especially in contemporary books. But if you take a larger view I think that Mr. Bennett is perfectly right. If, that is, you think of the novels which seem to you great novels—*War and Peace, Vanity Fair, Tristram Shandy, Madame Bovary, Pride and Prejudice, The Mayor of Casterbridge, Villette*—if you think of these books, you do at once think of some character who has seemed to you so real (I do not by that mean so lifelike) that it has the power to make you think not merely of it itself, but of all sorts of things through its eyes—of religion, of love, of war, of peace, of family life, of balls in county towns, of sunsets, moonrises, the immortality of the soul. There is hardly any subject of human experience that is left out of *War and Peace* it seems to me. And in all these novels all these great novelists have brought us to see whatever they wish us to see through some character. Otherwise, they would not be novelists; but poets, historians, or pamphleteers.

But now let us examine what Mr. Bennett went on to say—he said that there was no great novelist among the Georgian writers because they cannot create characters who are real, true, and convincing. And there I cannot agree. There are reasons, excuses, possibilities which I think put a different colour upon the case. It seems so to me at least, but I am well aware that this is a matter about which I am likely to be prejudiced, sanguine, and near-sighted. I will put my view before you in the hope that you will make it impartial, judicial, and broad-minded. Why, then, is it so hard for novelists at present to create characters which seem real, not only to Mr. Bennett, but to the world at large? Why, when October comes round, do the publishers always fail to supply us with a masterpiece?

Surely one reason is that the men and women who began writing novels in 1910 or thereabouts had this great difficulty to face—that there was no English novelist living from whom they could learn their business. Mr. Conrad is a Pole; which sets him apart, and makes him, however admirable, not very helpful. Mr. Hardy has written no novel since 1895. The most prominent and successful novelists in the year

1910 were, I suppose, Mr. Wells, Mr. Bennett, and Mr. Galsworthy. Now it seems to me that to go to these men and ask them to teach you how to write a novel—how to create characters that are real—is precisely like going to a bootmaker and asking him to teach you how to make a watch. Do not let me give you the impression that I do not admire and enjoy their books. They seem to me of great value, and indeed of great necessity. There are seasons when it is more important to have boots than to have watches. To drop metaphor, I think that after the creative activity of the Victorian age it was quite necessary, not only for literature but for life, that someone should write the books that Mr. Wells, Mr. Bennett, and Mr. Galsworthy have written. Yet what odd books they are! Sometimes I wonder if we are right to call them books at all. For they leave one with so strange a feeling of incompleteness and dissatisfaction. In order to complete them it seems necessary to do something—to join a society, or, more desperately, to write a cheque. That done, the restlessness is laid, the book finished; it can be put upon the shelf, and need never be read again. But with the work of other novelists it is different. *Tristram Shandy* or *Pride and Prejudice* is complete in itself; it is self-contained; it leaves one with no desire to do anything, except indeed to read the book again, and to understand it better. The difference perhaps is that both Sterne and Jane Austen were interested in things in themselves; in character in itself; in the book in itself. Therefore everything was inside the book, nothing outside. But the Edwardians were never interested in character in itself; or in the book in itself. They were interested in something outside. Their books, then, were incomplete as books, and required that the reader should finish them, actively and practically, for himself.

Perhaps we can make this clearer if we take the liberty of imagining a little party in the railway carriage—Mr. Wells, Mr. Galsworthy, Mr. Bennett are travelling to Waterloo with Mrs. Brown. Mrs. Brown, I have said, was poorly dressed and very small. She had an anxious, harassed look. I doubt whether she was what you call an educated woman. Seizing upon all these symptoms of the unsatisfactory condition of our primary schools with a rapidity to which I can do no justice, Mr. Wells would instantly project upon the windowpane a vision

of a better, breezier, jollier, happier, more adventurous and gallant
world, where these musty railway carriages and fusty old women do
not exist; where miraculous barges bring tropical fruit to Camberwell
by eight o'clock in the morning; where there are public nurseries, foun-
tains, and libraries, dining-rooms, drawing-rooms, and marriages;
where every citizen is generous and candid, manly and magnificent,
and rather like Mr. Wells himself. But nobody is in the least like Mrs.
Brown. There are no Mrs. Browns in Utopia. Indeed I do not think
that Mr. Wells, in his passion to make her what she ought to be,
would waste a thought upon her as she is. And what would Mr. Galsworthy see? Can we doubt that the walls of Doulton's factory would
take his fancy? There are women in that factory who make twenty-
five dozen earthenware pots every day. There are mothers in the Mile
End Road who depend upon the farthings which those women earn.
But there are employers in Surrey who are even now smoking rich
cigars while the nightingale sings. Burning with indignation, stuffed
with information, arraigning civilization, Mr. Galsworthy would only
see in Mrs. Brown a pot broken on the wheel and thrown into the
corner. Mr. Bennett, alone of the Edwardians, would keep his eyes in
the carriage. He, indeed, would observe every detail with immense
care. He would notice the advertisements; the pictures of Swanage and
Portsmouth; the way in which the cushion bulged between the buttons; how Mrs. Brown wore a brooch which had cost three-and-ten-
three at Whitworth's bazaar; and had mended both gloves—indeed
the thumb of the left-hand glove had been replaced. And he would
observe, at length, how this was the non-stop train from Windsor
which calls at Richmond for the convenience of middle-class residents,
who can afford to go to the theatre but have not reached the social
rank which can afford motor-cars, though it is true, there are occasions
(he would tell us what), when they hire them from a company (he
would tell us which). And so he would gradually sidle sedately towards Mrs. Brown, and would remark how she had been left a little
copyhold, not freehold, property at Datchet, which, however, was
mortgaged to Mr. Bungay the solicitor—but why should I presume to
invent Mr. Bennett? Does not Mr. Bennett write novels himself? I
will open the first book that chance puts in my way—*Hilda Lessways*.

Let us see how he makes us feel that Hilda is real, true, and convincing, as a novelist should. She shut the door in a soft, controlled way, which showed the constraint of her relations with her mother. She was fond of reading *Maud;* she was endowed with the power to feel intensely. So far, so good; in his leisurely, sure-footed way Mr. Bennett is trying in these first pages, where every touch is important, to show us the kind of girl she was.

But then he begins to describe, not Hilda Lessways, but the view from her bedroom window, the excuse being that Mr. Skellorn, the man who collects rents, is coming along that way. Mr. Bennett proceeds:

"The bailiwick of Turnhill lay behind her; and all the murky district of the Five Towns, of which Turnhill is the northern outpost, lay to the south. At the foot of Chatterley Wood the canal wound in large curves on its way towards the undefiled plains of Cheshire and the sea. On the canal-side, exactly opposite to Hilda's window, was a flour-mill, that sometimes made nearly as much smoke as the kilns and the chimneys closing the prospect on either hand. From the flour-mill a bricked path, which separated a considerable row of new cottages from their appurtenant gardens, led straight into Lessways Street, in front of Mrs. Lessways' house. By this path Mr. Skellorn should have arrived, for he inhabited the farthest of the cottages."

One line of insight would have done more than all those lines of description; but let them pass as the necessary drudgery of the novelist. And now—where is Hilda? Alas. Hilda is still looking out of the window. Passionate and dissatisfied as she was, she was a girl with an eye for houses. She often compared this old Mr. Skellorn with the villas she saw from her bedroom window. Therefore the villas must be described. Mr. Bennett proceeds:

"The row was called Freehold Villas: a consciously proud name in a district where much of the land was copyhold and could only change owners subject to the payment of 'fines,' and to the feudal consent of a 'court' presided over by the agent of a lord of the manor. Most of the dwellings were owned by their occupiers, who, each an absolute monarch of the soil, niggled in his sooty garden of an evening amid the flutter of drying shirts and towels. Freehold Villas symbolized the final triumph of Victorian economics, the apotheosis of the prudent and industrious artisan. It corresponded with a Building Society Secretary's dream of paradise. And indeed it was a very real achievement. Nevertheless, Hilda's irrational contempt would not admit this."

Heaven be praised, we cry! At last we are coming to Hilda herself. But not so fast. Hilda may have been this, that, and the other; but Hilda not only looked at houses, and thought of houses; Hilda lived in a house. And what sort of a house did Hilda live in? Mr. Bennett proceeds:

"It was one of the two middle houses of a detached terrace of four houses built by her grandfather Lessways, the tea-pot manufacturer; it was the chief of the four, obviously the habitation of the proprietor of the terrace. One of the corner houses comprised a grocer's shop, and this house had been robbed of its just proportion of garden so that the seigneurial garden-plot might be triflingly larger than the other. The terrace was not a terrace of cottages, but of houses rated at from twenty-six to thirty-six pounds a year; beyond the means of artisans and petty insurance agents and rent-collectors. And further, it was well built, generously built; and its architecture, though debased, showed some faint traces of Georgian amenity. It was admittedly the best row of houses in that newly settled quarter of the town. In coming to it out of Freehold Villas Mr. Skellorn obviously came to something superior, wider, more liberal. Suddenly Hilda heard her mother's voice. . . ."

But we cannot hear her mother's voice, or Hilda's voice; we can only hear Mr. Bennett's voice telling us facts about rents and freeholds and copyholds and fines. What can Mr. Bennett be about? I have formed my own opinion of what Mr. Bennett is about—he is trying to make us imagine for him; he is trying to hypnotize us into the belief that, because he has made a house, there must be a person living there. With all his powers of observation, which are marvellous, with all his sympathy and humanity, which are great, Mr. Bennett has never once looked at Mrs. Brown in her corner. There she sits in the corner of the carriage—that carriage which is travelling, not from Richmond to Waterloo, but from one age of English literature to the next, for Mrs. Brown is eternal, Mrs. Brown is human nature, Mrs. Brown changes only on the surface, it is the novelists who get in and out—

there she sits and not one of the Edwardian writers had so much as looked at her. They have looked very powerfully, searchingly, and sympathetically out of the window; at factories, at Utopias, even at the decoration and upholstery of the carriage; but never at her, never at life, never at human nature. And so they have developed a technique of novel-writing which suits their purpose; they have made tools and established conventions which do their business. But those tools are not our tools, and that business is not our business. For us those conventions are ruin, those tools are death.

You may well complain of the vagueness of my language. What is a convention, a tool, you may ask, and what do you mean by saying that Mr. Bennett's and Mr. Wells's and Mr. Galsworthy's conventions are the wrong conventions for the Georgians? The question is difficult: I will attempt a short cut. A convention in writing is not much different from a convention in manners. Both in life and in literature it is necessary to have some means of bridging the gulf between the hostess and her unknown guest on the one hand, the writer and his unknown reader on the other. The hostess bethinks her of the weather, for generations of hostesses have established the fact that this is a subject of universal interest in which we all believe. She begins by saying that we are having a wretched May, and, having thus got into touch with her unknown guest, proceeds to matters of greater interest. So it is in literature. The writer must get into touch with his reader by putting before him something which he recognizes, which therefore stimulates his imagination, and makes him willing to coöperate in the far more difficult business of intimacy. And it is of the highest importance that this common meeting-place should be reached easily, almost instinctively, in the dark, with one's eyes shut. Here is Mr. Bennett making use of this common ground in the passage which I have quoted. The problem before him was to make us believe in the reality of Hilda Lessways. So he began, being an Edwardian, by describing accurately and minutely the sort of house Hilda lived in, and the sort of house she saw from the window. House property was the common ground from which the Edwardians found it easy to proceed to intimacy. Indirect as it seems to us, the convention worked admirably, and thousands of Hilda Lessways were launched upon the world by this means. For that age and generation, the convention was a good one.

But now, if you will allow me to pull my own anecdote to pieces, you will see how keenly I felt the lack of a convention, and how serious a matter it is when the tools of one generation are useless for the next. The incident had made a great impression on me. But how was I to transmit it to you? All I could do was to report as accurately as I could what was said, to describe in detail what was worn, to say, despairingly, that all sorts of scenes rushed into my mind, to proceed to tumble them out pell-mell, and to describe this vivid, this overmastering impression by likening it to a draught or a smell of burning. To tell you the truth, I was also strongly tempted to manufacture a three-volume novel about the old lady's son, and his adventures crossing the Atlantic, and her daughter, and how she kept a milliner's shop in Westminster, the past life of Smith himself, and his house at Sheffield, though such stories seem to me the most dreary, irrelevant, and humbugging affairs in the world.

But if I had done that I should have escaped the appalling effort of saying what I meant. And to have got at what I meant I should have had to go back and back and back; to experiment with one thing and another; to try this sentence and that, referring each word to my vision, matching it as exactly as possible, and knowing that somehow I had to find a common ground between us, a convention which would not seem to you too odd, unreal, and far-fetched to believe in. I admit that I shirked that arduous undertaking. I let my Mrs. Brown slip through my fingers. I have told you nothing whatever about her. But that is partly the great Edwardians' fault. I asked them—they are my elders and betters—How shall I begin to describe this woman's character? And they said, "Begin by saying that her father kept a shop in Harrogate. Ascertain the rent. Ascertain the wages of shop assistants in the year 1878. Discover what her mother died of. Describe cancer. Describe calico. Describe—" But I cried, "Stop! Stop!" And I regret to say that I threw that ugly, that clumsy, that incongruous tool out of the window, for I knew that if I began describing the cancer and the calico, my Mrs. Brown, that vision to which I cling though I know no way of imparting it to you, would have been dulled and tarnished and vanished for ever.

That is what I meant by saying that the Edwardian tools are the wrong ones for us to use. They have laid an enormous stress upon the fabric of things. They have given us a house in the hope that we may be able to deduce the human beings who live there. To give them their due, they have made that house much better worth living in. But if you hold that novels are in the first place about people, and only in the second about the houses they live in, that is the wrong way to set about it. Therefore, you see, the Georgian writer had to begin by throwing away the method that was in use at the moment. He was left alone there facing Mrs. Brown without any method of conveying her to the reader. But that is inaccurate. A writer is never alone. There is always the public with him—if not on the same seat, at least in the compartment next door. Now the public is a strange travelling companion. In England it is a very suggestive and docile creature, which, once you get it to attend, will believe implicitly what it is told for a certain number of years. If you say to the public with sufficient conviction, "All women have tails, and all men humps," it will actually learn to see women with tails and men with humps, and will think it very revolutionary and probably improper if you say "Nonsense. Monkeys have tails and camels humps. But men and women have brains, and they have hearts; they think and they feel,"—that will seem to it a bad joke, and an improper one into the bargain.

But to return. Here is the British public sitting by the writer's side and saying in its vast and unanimous way, "Old women have houses. They have fathers. They have incomes. They have servants. They have hot water bottles. That is how we know that they are old women. Mr. Wells and Mr. Bennett and Mr. Galsworthy have always taught us that this is the way to recognize them. But now with your Mrs. Brown —how are we to believe in her? We do not even know whether her villa was called Albert or Balmoral; what she paid for her gloves; or whether her mother died of cancer or of consumption. How can she be alive? No; she is a mere figment of your imagination."

And old women of course ought to be made of freehold villas and copyhold estates, not of imagination.

The Georgian novelist, therefore, was in an awkward predicament. There was Mrs. Brown protesting that she was different, quite different, from what people made out, and luring the novelist to her rescue by the most fascinating if fleeting glimpse of her charms; there were the Edwardians handing out tools appropriate to house building and house breaking; and there was the British public asseverating that they must see the hot water bottle first. Meanwhile the train was rushing to that station where we must all get out.

Such, I think, was the predicament in which the young Georgians found themselves about the year 1910. Many of them—I am thinking of Mr. Forster and Mr. Lawrence in particular—spoilt their early work because, instead of throwing away those tools, they tried to use them. They tried to compromise. They tried to combine their own direct sense of the oddity and significance of some character with Mr. Galsworthy's knowledge of the Factory Acts, and Mr. Bennett's knowledge of the Five Towns. They tried it, but they had too keen, too overpowering a sense of Mrs. Brown and her peculiarities to go on trying it much longer. Something had to be done. At whatever cost of life, limb, and damage to valuable property Mrs. Brown must be rescued, expressed, and set in her high relations to the world before the train stopped and she disappeared for ever. And so the smashing and the crashing began. Thus it is that we hear all round us, in poems and novels and biographies, even in newspaper articles and essays, the sound of breaking and falling, crashing and destruction. It is the prevailing sound of the Georgian age—rather a melancholy one if you think what melodious days there have been in the past, if you think of Shakespeare and Milton and Keats or even of Jane Austen and Thackeray and Dickens; if you think of the language, and the heights to which it can soar when free, and see the same eagle captive, bald, and croaking.

In view of these facts—with these sounds in my ears and these fancies in my brain—I am not going to deny that Mr. Bennett has some reason when he complains that our Georgian writers are unable to make us believe that our characters are real. I am forced to agree that they do not pour out three immortal masterpieces with Victorian regularity every autumn. But instead of being gloomy, I am sanguine. For this state of things is, I think, inevitable whenever from hoar old age or callow youth the convention ceases to be a means of communication between writer and reader, and becomes instead an obstacle and an impediment. At the present moment we are suffering, not from decay, but from having no code of manners which writers and readers accept as a prelude to the more exciting intercourse of friendship. The literary convention of the time is so artificial—you have to talk about the weather and nothing but the weather throughout the entire visit—that, naturally, the feeble are tempted to outrage, and the strong are led to destroy the very foundations and rules of literary society. Signs of this are everywhere apparent. Grammar is violated; syntax disintegrated; as a boy staying with an aunt for the week-end rolls in the geranium bed out of sheer desperation as the solemnities of the Sabbath wear on. The more adult writers do not, of course, indulge in such wanton exhibitions of spleen. Their sincerity is desperate, and their courage tremendous; it is only that they do not know which to use, a fork or their fingers. Thus, if you read Mr. Joyce and Mr. Eliot you will be struck by the indecency of the one, and the obscurity of the other. Mr. Joyce's indecency in *Ulysses* seems to me the conscious and calculated indecency of a desperate man who feels that in order to breathe he must break the windows. At moments, when the window is broken, he is magnificent. But what a waste of energy! And, after all, how dull indecency is, when it is not the overflowing of a super-abundant energy or savagery, but the determined and public-spirited act of a man who needs fresh air! Again, with the obscurity of Mr. Eliot. I think that Mr. Eliot has written some of the loveliest single lines in modern poetry. But how intolerant he is of the old usages and politenesses of society—respect for the weak, consideration for the dull! As I sun myself upon the intense and ravishing beauty of one of his lines, and reflect that I must make a dizzy and dangerous leap to the next, and so on from line to line, like an acrobat flying precariously from bar to bar, I cry out, I confess, for the old decorums, and envy the indolence of my ancestors who, instead of spinning madly through mid-air, dreamt quietly in the shade with a book. Again, in Mr. Strachey's books, *Eminent Victorians* and *Queen Victoria,* the effort and strain of writing against the grain and current of the times is visible too. It is much less visible, of course, for not only is he dealing with facts, which are stubborn things, but he has fabricated, chiefly from eighteenth-century material, a very discreet code of manners of his own, which allows him to sit at table with the highest in the land and to say a great many things under cover of that exquisite apparel which, had they gone naked, would have been chased by the men-servants from the room. Still, if you compare *Eminent Victorians* with some of Lord Macaulay's essays, though you will feel that Lord Macaulay is always wrong, and Mr. Strachey always right, you will also feel a body, a sweep, a richness in Lord Macaulay's essays which show that his age was behind him; all his strength went straight into his work; none was used for purposes of concealment or of conversion. But Mr. Strachey has had to open our eyes before he made us see; he has had to search out and sew together a very artful manner of speech; and the effort, beautifully though it is concealed, has robbed his work of some of the force that should have gone into it, and limited his scope.

For these reasons, then, we must reconcile ourselves to a season of failures and fragments. We must reflect that where so much strength is spent on finding a way of telling the truth the truth itself is bound to reach us in rather an exhausted and chaotic condition. Ulysses, Queen Victoria, Mr. Prufrock—to give Mrs. Brown some of the names she has made famous lately—is a little pale and dishevelled by the time her rescuers reach her. And it is the sound of their axes that we hear —a vigorous and stimulating sound in my ears—unless of course you wish to sleep, when, in the bounty of his concern, Providence has provided a host of writers anxious and able to satisfy your needs.

Thus I have tried, at tedious length, I fear, to answer some of the questions which I began by asking. I have given an account of some of the difficulties which in my view beset the Georgian writer in all his forms. I have sought to excuse him. May I end by venturing to remind you of the duties and responsibilities that are yours as partners in this business of writing books, as companions in the railway carriage, as fellow-travellers with Mrs. Brown? For she is just as visible to you who remain silent as to us who tell stories about her. In the course of your daily life this past week you have had far stranger and more interesting experiences than the one I have tried to describe. You have overheard scraps of talk that filled you with amazement. You have gone to bed at night bewildered by the complexity of your feelings.

In one day thousands of ideas have coursed through your brains; thousands of emotions have met, collided, and disappeared in astonishing disorder. Nevertheless, you allow the writers to palm off upon you a version of all this, an image of Mrs. Brown, which has no likeness to that surprising apparition whatsoever. In your modesty you seem to consider that writers are of different blood and bone from yourselves; that they know more of Mrs. Brown than you do. Never was there a more fatal mistake. It is this division between reader and writer, this humility on your part, these professional airs and graces on ours, that corrupt and emasculate the books which should be the healthy offspring of a close and equal alliance between us. Hence spring those sleek, smooth novels, those portentous and ridiculous biographies, that milk-and-watery criticism, those poems melodiously celebrating the innocence of roses and sheep which pass so plausibly for literature at the present time.

Your part is to insist that writers shall come down off their plinths and pedestals, and describe beautifully if possible, truthfully at any rate, our Mrs. Brown. You should insist that she is an old lady of unlimited capacity and infinite variety; capable of appearing in any place; wearing any dress; saying anything and doing heaven knows what. But the things she says and the things she does and her eyes and her nose and her speech and her silence have an overwhelming fascination, for she is, of course, the spirit we live by, life itself.

But do not expect just at present a complete and satisfactory presentment of her. Tolerate the spasmodic, the obscure, the fragmentary, the failure. Your help is invoked in a good cause. For I will make one final and surpassingly rash prediction—we are trembling on the verge of one of the great ages of English literature. But it can only be reached if we are determined never, never to desert Mrs. Brown.

HON. JOHN M. WOOLSEY

COMMENTARY

James Joyce dedicated his first play, now lost, to his own soul. The gesture, marrying arrogance to humility, is the trademark of his career, recently ended. At twenty he left his countrymen—"the most belated race in Europe," he overbitterly called them—and came home, as it were, to the Continent. At twenty, armed with the only weapons he permitted himself to use—"silence, exile, and cunning" —he began his pilgrimage.

I should think that James Joyce suffered more and longer than any other important artist of our time. Through it all, undeflectable, he kept intact his obligations to his own genius. He was a romantic artist of a type now going out of fashion, one who admitted no values more imperative than those of his own creative drive. His life was one of poverty, discouragement, constant literary setbacks, misunderstanding, physical pain, and near-blindness. All this he bore, and out of it came Ulysses, several great short stories, Finnegans Wake (which I confess baffles me), and a personal influence that helped to revolutionize the literatures of half a dozen countries.

For twelve years the customs authorities of our country refused to permit the entry of Ulysses, thus protecting you and me from the moral contamination that comes of contact with a masterpiece. Finally, on December 6, 1933, the ban was lifted by a decision of the United States District Court, the Honorable John M. Woolsey presiding. So at last we could all buy and read a long, difficult book which, from the point of view of the guardians of our morality, differed dangerously from other books in that it contained a half-dozen monosyllables of all work which English-speaking men, women, and most children at the two extremes of society have been using with unthinking casualness ever since the days of Henry VIII. So at last we could read this book, a whole literature in itself, the best and longest anecdote ever told about a Jew and an Irishman.

The decision in which the government of this country sustained a glorious defeat at the hands of Judge Woolsey is classic. Its final statement—"Ulysses may, therefore, be admitted into the United States"—is a declaration of historic importance, even though it only deals with a book most people will never read. The Peter Zenger case at the time seemed unimportant, but in retrospect we now realize it to be part of the charter of our liberties, for it established the principle of a free press.

It is not usual for novelists to take judges seriously in their novels. It is even rarer for judges to take novelists seriously in their decisions. Judge Woolsey based his opinion not on narrow legalistic grounds but on literary ones. The principle underlying his decision—though he does not so enunciate it, for it is an esthetic and not a juridical principle—is that a great work of art cannot be pornography. The important part of his comment is that in which he demonstrates Ulysses to be a work of art. The description of Joyce's aims and method—you will find it in Section IV of the decision—is high-grade literary analysis which puts us professional boys to shame, so clear, just, and perceptive is it. I also call your attention to the fact that the judge is not without his moments of sly humor. In fact, the entire decision deserves to be called a piece of literature, and that is why I have included it here.

The whole question of literary censorship will sooner or later be settled in one of two ways. A completely repressive government, such as that of Germany, will consider literature only in terms of its usefulness to the power of the state. That means a censorship so rigid as to achieve in the end the slow death of literature itself. A completely democratic government, which our grandchildren may live to see, will impose no restrictions at all. The legal definition of the word "obscene"—printed matter which tends "to stir the sex impulses"—is obviously ludicrous. The sex impulses of men and women are stirred daily by casual stimuli and suggestions that are far beyond the control of any regulating authority. It will take a long time, but the human race will sooner or later reach the conclusion that it is no more vicious or unnatural to possess stirrable sex impulses than it is to possess a normal appetite for food and drink. When that day comes there will be no more Ulysses cases. The path to that future day is pointed out to us in our own time by such men as Judge Woolsey.

A Decision of the United States District Court Rendered December 6, 1933, by Hon. John M. Woolsey Lifting the Ban on "Ulysses"

UNITED STATES DISTRICT COURT

SOUTHERN DISTRICT OF NEW YORK

United States of America,
Libelant

v.

One Book Called "Ulysses"
Random House, Inc.,
Claimant

OPINION

A. 110-59

On cross motions for a decree in a libel of confiscation, supplemented by a stipulation—hereinafter described—brought by the United States against the book "Ulysses" by James Joyce, under Section 305 of the Tariff Act of 1930, Title 19 United States Code, Section 1305, on the ground that the book is obscene within the meaning of that Section, and, hence, is not importable into the United States, but is subject to seizure, forfeiture and confiscation and destruction.

United States Attorney—by Samuel C. Coleman, Esq., and Nicholas Atlas, Esq., of counsel—for the United States, in support of motion for a decree of forfeiture, and in opposition to motion for a decree dismissing the libel.

Messrs. Greenbaum, Wolff & Ernst—by Morris L. Ernst, Esq., and Alexander Lindey, Esq., of counsel—attorneys for claimant Random House, Inc., in support of motion for a decree dismissing the libel, and in opposition to motion for a decree of forfeiture.

WOOLSEY, J:

The motion for a decree dismissing the libel herein is granted, and, consequently, of course, the Government's motion for a decree of forfeiture and destruction is denied.

Accordingly a decree dismissing the libel without costs may be entered herein.

I. The practice followed in this case is in accordance with the suggestion made by me in the case of *United States v. One Book Entitled "Contraception"*, 51 F. (2d) 525, and is as follows:

After issue was joined by the filing of the claimant's answer to the libel for forfeiture against "Ulysses", a stipulation was made between the United States Attorney's office and the attorneys for the claimant providing:

1. That the book "Ulysses" should be deemed to have been annexed to and to have become part of the libel just as if it had been incorporated in its entirety therein.

2. That the parties waived their right to a trial by jury.

3. That each party agreed to move for decree in its favor.

4. That on such cross motions the Court might decide all the questions of law and fact involved and render a general finding thereon.

5. That on the decision of such motions the decree of the Court might be entered as if it were a decree after trial.

It seems to me that a procedure of this kind is highly appropriate in libels for the confiscation of books such as this. It is an especially advantageous procedure in the instant case because on account of the length of "Ulysses" and the difficulty of reading it, a jury trial would have been an extremely unsatisfactory, if not an almost impossible, method of dealing with it.

II. I have read "Ulysses" once in its entirety and I have read those passages of which the Government particularly complains several times. In fact, for many weeks, my spare time has been devoted to the consideration of the decision which my duty would require me to make in this matter.

"Ulysses" is not an easy book to read or to understand. But there has been much written about it, and in order properly to approach the consideration of it it is advisable to read a number of other books which have now become its satellites. The study of "Ulysses" is, therefore, a heavy task.

III. The reputation of "Ulysses" in the literary world, however, warranted my taking such time as was necessary to enable me to satisfy myself as to the intent with which the book was written, for, of course, in any case where a book is claimed to be obscene it must first be determined, whether the intent with which it was written was what is called, according to the usual phrase, pornographic,—that is, written for the purpose of exploiting obscenity.

If the conclusion is that the book is pornographic that is the end of the inquiry and forfeiture must follow.

But in "Ulysses", in spite of its unusual frankness, I do not detect anywhere the leer of the sensualist. I hold, therefore, that it is not pornographic.

IV. In writing "Ulysses", Joyce sought to make a serious experiment in a new, if not wholly novel, literary genre. He takes persons of the lower middle class living in Dublin in 1904 and seeks not only to describe what they did on a certain day early in June of that year as they went about the City bent on their usual occupations, but also to tell what many of them thought about the while.

Joyce has attempted—it seems to me, with astonishing success—to show how the screen of consciousness with its ever-shifting kaleidoscopic impressions carries, as it were on a plastic palimpsest, not only what is in the focus of each man's observation of the actual things about him, but also in a penumbral zone residua of past impressions, some recent and some drawn up by association from the domain of the subconscious. He shows how each of these impressions affects the life and behavior of the character which he is describing.

What he seeks to get is not unlike the result of a double or, if that is possible, a multiple exposure on a cinema film which would give a clear foreground with a background visible but somewhat blurred and out of focus in varying degrees.

To convey by words an effect which obviously lends itself more appropriately to a graphic technique, accounts, it seems to me, for much of the obscurity which meets a reader of "Ulysses". And it also explains another aspect of the book, which I have further to consider, namely, Joyce's sincerity and his honest effort to show exactly how the minds of his characters operate.

If Joyce did not attempt to be honest in developing the technique which he has adopted in "Ulysses" the result would be psychologically misleading and thus unfaithful to his chosen technique. Such an attitude would be artistically inexcusable.

It is because Joyce has been loyal to his technique and has not funked its necessary implications, but has honestly attempted to tell fully what his characters think about, that he has been the subject of so many attacks and that his purpose has been so often misunderstood and misrepresented. For his attempt sincerely and honestly to realize his objective has required him incidentally to use certain words which are generally considered dirty words and has led at times to what many think is a too poignant preoccupation with sex in the thoughts of his characters.

The words which are criticized as dirty are old Saxon words known to almost all men and, I venture, to many women, and are such words as would be naturally and habitually used, I believe, by the types of folk whose life, physical and mental, Joyce is seeking to describe. In respect of the recurrent emergence of the theme of sex in the minds of his characters, it must always be remembered that his locale was Celtic and his season Spring.

Whether or not one enjoys such a technique as Joyce uses is a matter of taste on which disagreement or argument is futile, but to subject that technique to the standards of some other technique seems to me to be little short of absurd.

Accordingly, I hold that "Ulysses" is a sincere and honest book and I think that the criticisms of it are entirely disposed of by its rationale.

V. Furthermore, "Ulysses" is an amazing *tour de force* when one considers the success which has been in the main achieved with such a difficult objective as Joyce set for himself. As I have stated, "Ulysses" is not an easy book to read. It is brilliant and dull, intelligible and obscure by turns. In many places it seems to me to be disgusting, but although it contains, as I have mentioned above, many words usually considered dirty, I have not found anything that I consider to be dirt for dirt's sake. Each word of the book contributes like a bit of mosaic to the detail of the picture which Joyce is seeking to construct for his readers.

If one does not wish to associate with such folk as Joyce describes, that is one's own choice. In order to avoid indirect contact with them one may not wish to read "Ulysses"; that is quite understandable. But when such a real artist in words, as Joyce undoubtedly is, seeks to draw a true picture of the lower middle class in a European city, ought it to be impossible for the American public legally to see that picture?

To answer this question it is not sufficient merely to find, as I have found above, that Joyce did not write "Ulysses" with what is commonly called pornographic intent, I must endeavor to apply a more objective standard to his book in order to determine its effect in the result, irrespective of the intent with which it was written.

VI. The statute under which the libel is filed only denounces, in so far as we are here concerned, the importation into the United States from any foreign country of "any obscene book". Section 305 of the Tariff Act of 1930, Title 19 United States Code, Section 1305. It does not marshal against books the spectrum of condemnatory adjectives found, commonly, in laws dealing with matters of this kind. I am, therefore, only required to determine whether "Ulysses" is obscene within the legal definition of that word.

The meaning of the word "obscene" as legally defined by the Courts is: tending to stir the sex impulses or to lead to sexually impure and lustful thoughts. *Dunlop* v. *United States,* 165 U. S. 486, 501; *United States* v. *One Book Entitled "Married Love",* 48 F. (2d) 821, 824; *United States* v. *One Book Entitled "Contraception",* 51 F. (2d) 525, 528; and compare *Dysart* v. *United States,* 272 U. S. 655, 657; *Swearingen* v. *United States,* 161 U. S. 446, 450; *United States* v. *Dennett,* 39 F. (2d) 564, 568 (C. C. A. 2); *People* v. *Wendling,* 258 N. Y. 451, 453.

Whether a particular book would tend to excite such impulses and thoughts must be tested by the Court's opinion as to its effect on a person with average sex instincts—what the French would call *l'homme moyen sensuel*—who plays, in this branch of legal inquiry, the same role of hypothetical reagent as does the "reasonable man" in the law of torts and "the man learned in the art" on questions of invention in patent law.

The risk involved in the use of such a reagent arises from the inherent tendency of the trier of facts, however fair he may intend to be, to make his reagent too much subservient to his own idiosyncrasies. Here, I have attempted to avoid this, if possible, and to make my reagent herein more objective than he might otherwise be, by adopting the following course:

After I had made my decision in regard to the aspect of "Ulysses", now under consideration, I checked my impressions with two friends of mine who in my opinion answered to the above stated requirement for my reagent.

These literary assessors—as I might properly describe them—were called on separately, and neither knew that I was consulting the other. They are men whose opinion on literature and on life I value most highly. They had both read "Ulysses", and, of course, were wholly unconnected with this cause.

Without letting either of my assessors know what my decision was, I gave to each of them the legal definition of obscene and asked each whether in his opinion "Ulysses" was obscene within that definition.

I was interested to find that they both agreed with my opinion: that reading "Ulysses" in its entirety, as a book must be read on such a test as this, did not tend to excite sexual impulses or lustful thoughts but that its net effect on them was only that of a somewhat tragic and very powerful commentary on the inner lives of men and women.

It is only with the normal person that the law is concerned. Such a test as I have described, therefore, is the only proper test of obscenity in the case of a book like "Ulysses" which is a sincere and serious attempt to devise a new literary method for the observation and description of mankind.

I am quite aware that owing to some of its scenes "Ulysses" is a rather strong draught to ask some sensitive, though normal, persons to take. But my considered opinion, after long reflection, is that whilst in many places the effect of "Ulysses" on the reader undoubtedly is somewhat emetic, nowhere does it tend to be an aphrodisiac.

"Ulysses" may, therefore, be admitted into the United States.

WOOLSEY

UNITED STATES DISTRICT JUDGE

December 6, 1933

E. M. FORSTER

Of all the members of that fading Bloomsbury group of which Virginia Woolf was a prized ornament, it is E. M. Forster, to my mind, who has received the least attention and deserves the most. Some of the neglect allotted him is doubtless due to his own hypertrophied talent for privacy. Some of it results from his infertility. Mere productivity—witness the case of the pullulating Mr. Saroyan, the Mrs. Dionne of literature—often aids a writer to secure a reputation. The interval between Howards End (1910) and A Passage to India (1924) was so long that one forgot all about Forster, and there has been no novel from him since 1924. Finally, his work is so unaggressive that its voice is lost amid the general clamor.

Sooner or later such Forster books as A Room with a View and Howards End will be rediscovered and it will be found that they are no more dated than Pride and Prejudice. It will then also be found that, though the Forster universe is extremely limited—his people, if their unearned incomes disappeared, would simply disappear themselves—it is as truly and wittily pictured as the universe of any English novelist of our time. His style is as lucid, unobtrusive, and satisfying as a glass of water—and if more young American novelists studied him and fewer studied Thomas Wolfe, the quality of our literature would at once be improved.

E. M. Forster's mind is not easy to describe. It is indirect, it glances off things, it seems never to grasp firmly the object of its attention. Yet when it has finished its work, the object is there, caught cleanly, all ready for your inspection. His humor, too, is oblique, and needs careful watching lest it escape one. I could not hope to make his talent clear except by reprinting one of his novels complete, which is impossible. His short stories are not to my taste, for in them he surrenders to one of his few vices, a taste for the sentimentally fanciful.

But here are two pieces of light satire, very E. M. Forster. One of

them, "The Consolations of History," is conceived in his characteristically subtle, satiric vein, and exposes some of the pitiful roots
that lie beneath our appreciation of the past. The other, "My Own
Centenary," is an amiable but nonetheless pointed bit of mockery
in which English self-satisfaction is once more taken for a ride. The
novelty lies not in the content of the satire but in the vehicle Forster
has chosen, for offhand I do not remember that any other writer ever
wrote his own centenary address. The irony of the piece is underlined, I think, by its partial truth. For it is a fact that "his contemporaries did not recognize the greatness of Forster."

My Own Centenary

(FROM "THE TIMES" OF A.D. 2027)

BY

E. M. FORSTER

It is a hundred years ago today since Forster died; we celebrate his centenary indeed within a few months of the bicentenary of Beethoven, within a few weeks of that of Blake. What special tribute shall we bring him? The question is not easy to answer, and were he himself still alive he would no doubt reply, "My work is my truest memorial." It is the reply that a great artist can always be trusted to make. Conscious of his lofty mission, endowed with the divine gift of self-expression, he may rest content, he is at peace, doubly at peace. But we, we who are not great artists, only the recipients of their bounty—what shall we say about Forster? What can we say that has not already been said about Beethoven, about Blake? Whatever shall we say?

The Dean of Dulborough, preaching last Sunday in his own beautiful cathedral, struck perhaps the truest note. Taking as his text that profound verse in Ecclesiasticus, "Let us now praise famous men," he took it word by word, paused when he came to the word "famous," and, slowly raising his voice, said: "He whose hundredth anniversary we celebrate on Thursday next is famous, and why?" No answer was needed, none came. The lofty Gothic nave, the great western windows, the silent congregation—they gave answer sufficient, and passing on to the final word of his text, "men," the Dean expatiated upon what is perhaps the most mysterious characteristic of genius, its tendency to appear among members of the human race. Why this is, why, since it is, it is not accompanied by some definite outward sign through which it might be recognized easily, are questions not lightly to be raised. There can be no doubt that his contemporaries did not recognize the greatness of

Forster. Immersed in their own little affairs, they either ignored him, or forgot him, or confused him, or, strangest of all, discussed him as if he was their equal. We may smile at their blindness, but for him it can have been no laughing matter, he must have had much to bear, and indeed he could scarcely have endured to put forth masterpiece after masterpiece had he not felt assured of the verdict of posterity.

Sir Vincent Edwards, when broadcasting last night, voiced that verdict not uncertainly, and was fortunately able to employ more wealth of illustration than had been appropriate in Dulborough Minster for the Dean. The point he very properly stressed was our writer's loftiness of aim. "It would be impossible," he said, "to quote a single sentence that was not written from the very loftiest motive," and he drew from this a sharp and salutary lesson for the so-called writers of today. As permanent head of the Ministry of Edification, Sir Vincent has, we believe, frequently come into contact with the younger generation, and has checked with the kindliness of which he is a past-master their self-styled individualism—an individualism which is the precise antithesis of true genius. They confuse violence with strength, cynicism with open-mindedness, frivolity with joyousness—mistakes never made by Forster who was never gay until he had earned a right to be so, and only criticized the religious and social institutions of his time because they were notoriously corrupt. We know what the twentieth century was. We know the sort of men who were in power under George V. We know what the State was, what were the churches. We can as easily conceive of Beethoven as a Privy Councillor or of Blake as, forsooth, an Archbishop as of this burning and sensitive soul acquiescing in the deadening conditions of his age. What he worked for—what all great men work for—was for a New Jerusalem, a vitalized State, a purified Church; and the offertory at Dulborough last Sunday, like the success of Sir Edward's appeal for voluntary workers under the Ministry, show that he did not labour in vain.

The official ceremony is for this morning. This afternoon Lady Turton will unveil Mr. Boston Jack's charming statue in Kensington Gardens, and so illustrate another aspect of our national hero: his love of little children. It had originally been Mr. Boston Jack's intention to represent him as pursuing an ideal. Since, however, the Gardens are largely frequented by the young and their immediate supervisors, it was felt that something more whimsical would be in place, and a butterfly was substituted. The change is certainly for the better. It is true that we cannot have too many ideals. On the other hand, we must not have too much of them too soon, nor, attached as it will be to a long copper wire, can the butterfly be confused with any existing species and regarded as an incentive to immature collectors. Lady Turton will couple her remarks with an appeal for the Imperial Daisy Chain, of which she is the energetic Vice-President, and simultaneously there will be a flag collection throughout the provinces.

Dulborough, the Ministry of Edification, the official ceremony, Kensington Gardens! What more could be said? Not a little. Yet enough has been said to remind the public of its heritage, and to emphasize and define the central essence of these immortal works. And what is that essence? Need we say? Not their greatness—they are obviously great. Not their profundity—they are admittedly profound. It is something more precious than either: their nobility. Noble works, nobly conceived, nobly executed, nobler than the Ninth Symphony or the Songs of Innocence. Here is no small praise, yet it can be given, we are in the presence of the very loftiest, we need not spare or mince our words, nay, we will add one more word, a word that has been implicit in all that have gone before: like Beethoven, like Blake, Forster was essentially English, and in commemorating him we can yet again celebrate what is best and most permanent in ourselves.

The Consolations of History

E. M. FORSTER

IT IS PLEASANT to be transferred from an office where one is afraid of a sergeant-major into an office where one can intimidate generals, and perhaps this is why History is so attractive to the more timid amongst us. We can recover self-confidence by snubbing the dead. The captains and the kings depart at our slightest censure, while as for the "hosts of minor officials" who cumber court and camp, we heed them not, although in actual life they entirely block our social horizon. We cannot visit either the great or the rich when they are our contemporaries, but by a fortunate arrangement the palaces of Ujjain and the warehouses of Ormus are open for ever, and we can even behave outrageously in them without being expelled. The King of Ujjain, we announce, is extravagant, the merchants of Ormus unspeakably licentious . . . and sure enough Ormus is a desert now and Ujjain a jungle. Difficult to realize that the past was once the present, and that, transferred to it, one would be just the same little worm as today, unimportant, parasitic, nervous, occupied with trifles, unable to go anywhere or alter anything, friendly only with the obscure, and only at ease with the dead; while up on the heights the figures and forces who make History would contend in their habitual fashion, with incomprehensible noises or in ominous quiet. "There is money in my house . . . there is no money . . . no house." That is all that our sort can ever know about doom. The extravagant king, the licentious merchants—they escape, knowing the ropes.

If only the sense of actuality can be lulled—and it sleeps for ever in most historians—there is no passion that cannot be gratified in the past. The past is devoid of all dangers, social and moral, and one can meet

394

with perfect ease not only kings, but people who are even rarer on one's visiting list. We are alluding to courtesans. It is seemly and decent to meditate upon dead courtesans. Some, like Aspasia, are in themselves a liberal education, and turning from these as almost too awful one can still converse unblamed with their sisters. There is no objection, for instance, against recalling the arrangements of the sixteenth-century Hindu kingdom of Vijayanagar. The courtesans of Vijayanagar were beautiful and rich—one of them left over £32,000. They were highly esteemed, which also seems right; some were housemaids, others cooks, and five hundred were attached on a peace basis to the army, "all great musicians, dancers and acrobats, and very quick and nimble at their performances." In war the number was increased; indeed, the king sent the entire of the personable population into the field, judging that its presence would enhearten the troops. So many ladies hampered his strategy, it is true, but the opposing army was equally hampered, and when its soldiers ran away, its ladies sat still, and accrued to the victors. With existence as it threatens today—a draggled mass of elderly people and barbed wire—it is agreeable to glance back at those enchanted carnages, and to croon over conditions that we now subscribe to exterminate. Tight little faces from Oxford, fish-shaped faces from Cambridge—we cannot help having our dreams. Was life then warm and tremendous? Did the Vijayanagar Government really succeed in adjusting the balance between society and sex? —a task that has baffled even Mrs. Humphry Ward. We cannot tell; we can only be certain that it acted with circumspection and pomposity, and that most of its subjects did not know what it was up to. The myriads of nonentities who thronged its courts and camps, and were allotted inferior courtesans or none at all—alas! it is with these alone that readers of my pages can claim kinship.

Yet sweet though it is to dally with the past, one returns to the finer pleasures of morality in the end. The schoolmaster in each of us awakes, examines the facts of History, and marks them on the result of the examination. Not all the marks need be bad. Some incidents, like the Risorgimento, get excellent as a matter of course, while others, such as the character of Queen Elizabeth, get excellent in the long run. Nor must events be marked at their face value. Why was it right of Drake to play bowls when he heard the Armada was approaching, but wrong of Charles II to catch moths when he heard that the Dutch Fleet had entered the Medway? The answer is "Because Drake won." Why was it right of Alexander the Great to throw away water when his army was perishing, but wrong of Marie Antoinette to say "Let them eat cake"? The answer is "Because Marie Antoinette was executed." Why was George Washington right because he would not tell a lie, and Jael right because she told nothing else? Answers on similar lines. We must take a larger view of the past than of the present, because when examining the present we can never be sure what is going to pay. As a general rule, anything that ends abruptly must be given bad marks; for instance, the fourth century B.C. at Athens, the year 1492 in Italy, and the summer of 1914 everywhere. A civilization that passes quickly must be decadent, therefore let us censure those epochs that thought themselves so bright, let us show that their joys were hectic and their pleasures vile, and clouded by the premonition of doom. On the other hand, a civilization that does not pass, like the Chinese, must be stagnant, and is to be censured on that account. Nor can one approve anarchy. What then survives? Oh, a greater purpose, the slow evolution of Good through the centuries—an evolution less slow than it seems, because a thousand years are as yesterday, and consequently Christianity was only, so to speak, established on Wednesday last. And if this argument should seem flimsy (it is the Bishop of London's, not our own—he put it into his Christmas sermon) one can at all events return to an indubitable triumph of evolution—oneself, sitting untouched and untouchable in the professorial chair, and giving marks to men.

Sweet then is dalliance, censure sweeter. Yet sweetest of all is pity, because it subtly combines the pleasures of the other two. To pity the dead because they are dead is to experience an exquisite pleasure, identical with the agreeable heat that comes to the eyes in a churchyard. The heat has nothing to do with sorrow, it has no connection with anything that one has personally known and held dear. It is half a sensuous delight, half gratified vanity, and Shakespeare knew what he was about when he ascribed such a sensation to the fantastical Armado. They had been laughing at Hector, and Armado, with every appearance of generosity, exclaims: "The sweet war-man is dead and rotten; sweet chucks, beat not the bones of the buried; when he breathed he was a man." It was his happiest moment; he had never felt more certain either that he was alive himself, or that he was Hector. And it is a happiness that we can all experience until the sense of actuality breaks in. Pity wraps the student of the past in an ambrosial cloud, and washes his limbs with eternal youth. "Dear dead women with such hair too," but not "I feel chilly and grown old." That comes with the awakening.

SARAH ORNE JEWETT

Willa Cather, in her fine preface to the Mayflower Edition of the Best Stories of Sarah Orne Jewett, writes: "If I were asked to name three American books which have the possibility of a long, long life, I would say at once, The Scarlet Letter, Huckleberry Finn, and The Country of the Pointed Firs. I can think of no others that confront time and change so serenely. The latter book seems to me fairly to shine with the reflection of its long, joyous future." I do not suppose many would agree that Sarah Orne Jewett belongs in the company of Mark Twain and Hawthorne, but there is something in her tender genre work, a Vermeer quality, that may perhaps keep her memory quietly alive after many more vigorous talents have been forgotten.

Sarah Orne Jewett died years ago, in 1909. Her stories of old New England, a New England long since vanished, are also of long ago. She cultivated well and truly a tiny patch of ground. I read her first twenty years back; I have now reread her, and nothing seems lost.

The inclusion of one of her stories may be put down to a whim. I thought it might be interesting to confront my readers with a tale so old-fashioned, so sentimental, so simple as this, for most of the reading in this book is not old-fashioned or sentimental or simple. Perhaps the minds of writers like Hemingway, Steinbeck, and Katherine Anne Porter, so patently of our own time, will appear in sharper relief when set against the mind of a writer like Sarah Orne Jewett.

But quite candidly I doubt that many readers will care for this story. I suppose some will laugh at it, if good-naturedly. This is a fine time of day, one can hear them saying, to ask us to read a tale about a cow, a little girl, an old lady, a young man who hunts birds, a pine tree, and a white heron. Understanding their skepticism, I cannot share it. True, the materials of "The White Heron" are ordinary enough. Yet I hope that for some these ordinary materials will add up to something, to a kind of New England fairy tale, moral, like all fairy tales, and carrying with it, over the gulf of more than fifty years, the scent of beauty.

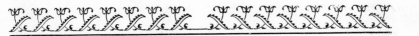

A White Heron

BY

SARAH ORNE JEWETT

THE WOODS were already filled with shadows one June evening, just before eight o'clock, though a bright sunset still glimmered faintly among the trunks of the trees. A little girl was driving home her cow, a plodding, dilatory, provoking creature in her behavior, but a valued companion for all that. They were going away from the western light, and striking deep into the dark woods, but their feet were familiar with the path, and it was no matter whether their eyes could see it or not.

There was hardly a night the summer through when the old cow could be found waiting at the pasture bars; on the contrary, it was her greatest pleasure to hide herself away among the high huckleberry bushes, and though she wore a loud bell she had made the discovery that if one stood perfectly still it would not ring. So Sylvia had to hunt for her until she found her, and call Co'! Co'! with never an answering Moo, until her childish patience was quite spent. If the creature had not given good milk and plenty of it, the case would have seemed very different to her owners. Besides, Sylvia had all the time there was, and very little use to make of it. Sometimes in pleasant weather it was a consolation to look upon the cow's pranks as an intelligent attempt to play hide and seek, and as the child had no playmates she lent herself to this amusement with a good deal of zest. Though this chase had been so long that the wary animal herself had given an unusual signal of her whereabouts, Sylvia had only laughed when she came upon Mistress Moolly at the swamp-side, and urged her affectionately homeward with a twig of birch leaves. The old cow was not inclined to wander farther, she even turned in the right direction for once as they left the pasture, and stepped along the road at a good pace. She was quite ready to be milked now, and seldom stopped to browse. Sylvia wondered what her grandmother would say because they were so late. It was a great while since she had left home at half past five o'clock, but everybody knew the difficulty of making this errand a short one. Mrs. Tilley had chased the hornéd torment too many summer evenings herself to blame any one else for lingering, and was only thankful as she waited that she had Sylvia, nowadays, to give such valuable assistance. The good woman suspected that Sylvia loitered occasionally on her own account; there never was such a child for straying about out-of-doors since the world was made! Everybody said that it was a good change for a little maid who had tried to grow for eight years in a crowded manufacturing town, but, as for Sylvia herself, it seemed as if she never had been alive at all before she came to live at the farm. She thought often with wistful compassion of a wretched dry geranium that belonged to a town neighbor.

" 'Afraid of folks,' " old Mrs. Tilley said to herself, with a smile, after she had made the unlikely choice of Sylvia from her daughter's houseful of children, and was returning to the farm. " 'Afraid of folks,' they said! I guess she won't be troubled no great with 'em up to the old place!" When they reached the door of the lonely house and stopped to unlock it, and the cat came to purr loudly, and rub against them, a deserted pussy, indeed, but fat with young robins, Sylvia whispered that this was a beautiful place to live in, and she never should wish to go home.

The companions followed the shady wood-road, the cow taking slow steps, and the child very fast ones. The cow stopped long at the brook to drink, as if the pasture were not half a swamp, and Sylvia stood still and waited, letting her bare feet cool themselves in the shoal water, while the great twilight moths struck softly against her. She waded on through the brook as the cow moved away, and listened to the thrushes with a heart that beat fast with pleasure. There was a stirring in the great boughs overhead. They were full of little birds and beasts that seemed to be wide-awake, and going about their world, or else saying good-night to each other in sleepy twitters. Sylvia herself felt sleepy as she walked along. However, it was not much farther to the house, and the air was soft and sweet. She was not often in the woods so late as this, and it made her feel as if she were a part of the gray shadows and the moving leaves. She was just thinking how long it seemed since she first came to the farm a year ago, and wondering if everything went on in the noisy town just the same as when she was there; the thought of the great red-faced boy who used to chase and frighten her made her hurry along the path to escape from the shadow of the trees.

Suddenly this little woods-girl is horror-stricken to hear a clear whistle not very far away. Not a bird's whistle, which would have a sort of friendliness, but a boy's whistle, determined, and somewhat aggressive. Sylvia left the cow to whatever sad fate might await her, and stepped discreetly aside into the bushes, but she was just too late. The enemy had discovered her, and called out in a very cheerful and persuasive tone, "Halloa, little girl, how far is it to the road?" and trembling Sylvia answered almost inaudibly, "A good ways."

She did not dare to look boldly at the tall young man, who carried a gun over his shoulder, but she came out of her bush and again followed the cow, while he walked alongside.

"I have been hunting for some birds," the stranger said kindly, "and I have lost my way, and need a friend very much. Don't be afraid," he added gallantly. "Speak up and tell me what your name is, and whether you think I can spend the night at your house, and go out gunning early in the morning."

Sylvia was more alarmed than before. Would not her grandmother consider her much to blame? But who could have foreseen such an accident as this? It did not appear to be her fault, and she hung her head as if the stem of it were broken, but managed to answer "Sylvy," with much effort when her companion again asked her name.

Mrs. Tilley was standing in the doorway when the trio came into view. The cow gave a loud moo by way of explanation.

"Yes, you'd better speak up for yourself, you old trial! Where'd she tucked herself away this time, Sylvy?" Sylvia kept an awed silence; she knew by instinct that her grandmother did not comprehend the gravity of the situation. She must be mistaking the stranger for one of the farmer-lads of the region.

The young man stood his gun beside the door, and dropped a heavy game-bag beside it; then he bade Mrs. Tilley good-evening, and repeated his wayfarer's story, and asked if he could have a night's lodging.

"Put me anywhere you like," he said. "I must be off early in the morning, before day; but I am very hungry, indeed. You can give me some milk at any rate, that's plain."

"Dear sakes, yes," responded the hostess, whose long slumbering hospitality seemed to be easily awakened. "You might fare better if you went out on the main road a mile or so, but you're welcome to what we've got. I'll milk right off, and you make yourself at home. You can sleep on husks or feathers," she proffered graciously. "I raised them all myself. There's good pasturing for geese just below here towards the ma'sh. Now step round and set a plate for the gentleman, Sylvy!" And Sylvia promptly stepped. She was glad to have something to do, and she was hungry herself.

It was a surprise to find so clean and comfortable a little dwelling in this New England wilderness. The young man had known the horrors of its most primitive housekeeping, and the dreary squalor of that level of society which does not rebel at the companionship of hens. This was the best thrift of an old-fashioned farmstead, though on such a small scale that it seemed like a hermitage. He listened eagerly to the old woman's quaint talk, he watched Sylvia's pale face and shining gray eyes with ever growing enthusiasm, and insisted that this was the best supper he had eaten for a month; then, afterward, the new-made friends sat down in the doorway together while the moon came up.

Soon it would be berry-time, and Sylvia was a great help at picking. The cow was a good milker, though a plaguy thing to keep track of, the hostess gossiped frankly, adding presently that she had buried four children, so that Sylvia's mother, and a son (who might be dead) in California were all the children she had left. "Dan, my boy, was a great hand to go gunning," she explained sadly. "I never wanted for pa'tridges or gray squer'ls while he was to home. He's been a great wand'rer, I expect, and he's no hand to write letters. There, I don't blame him. I'd ha' seen the world myself if it had been so I could.

"Sylvia takes after him," the grandmother continued affectionately, after a minute's pause. "There ain't a foot o' ground she don't know her way over, and the wild creatur's counts her one o' themselves. Squer'ls she'll tame to come an' feed right out o' her hands, and all sorts o' birds. Last winter she got the jay-birds to bangeing here, and I believe she'd 'a' scanted herself of her own meals to have plenty to throw out amongst 'em, if I hadn't kep' watch. Anything but crows, I tell her, I'm willin' to help support,—though Dan he went an' tamed one o' them that did seem to have reason same as folks. It was round here a good spell after he went away. Dan an' his father they didn't hitch,—but he never held up his head ag'in after Dan had dared him an' gone off."

The guest did not notice this hint of family sorrows in his eager interest in something else.

"So Sylvy knows all about birds, does she?" he exclaimed, as he looked round at the little girl who sat, very demure but increasingly sleepy, in the moonlight. "I am making a collection of birds myself. I have been at it ever since I was a boy." (Mrs. Tilley smiled.) "There are two or three very rare ones I have been hunting for these five years. I mean to get them on my own ground if they can be found."

"Do you cage 'em up?" asked Mrs. Tilley doubtfully, in response to this enthusiastic announcement.

"Oh, no, they're stuffed and preserved, dozens and dozens of them," said the ornithologist, "and I have shot or snared every one myself. I caught a glimpse of a white heron three miles from here on Saturday, and I have followed it in this direction. They have never been found in this district at all. The little white heron, it is," and he turned again to look at Sylvia with the hope of discovering that the rare bird was one of her acquaintances.

But Sylvia was watching a hop-toad in the narrow footpath.

"You would know the heron if you saw it," the stranger continued eagerly. "A queer tall white bird with soft feathers and long thin legs. And it would have a nest perhaps in the top of a high tree, made of sticks, something like a hawk's nest."

Sylvia's heart gave a wild beat; she knew that strange white bird, and had once stolen softly near where it stood in some bright green swamp grass, away over at the other side of the woods. There was an open place where the sunshine always seemed strangely yellow and hot, where tall, nodding rushes grew, and her grandmother had warned her that she might sink in the soft black mud underneath and never be heard of more. Not far beyond were the salt marshes and beyond those was the sea, the sea which Sylvia wondered and dreamed about, but never had looked upon, though its great voice could often be heard above the noise of the woods on stormy nights.

"I can't think of anything I should like so much as to find that heron's nest," the handsome stranger was saying. "I would give ten dollars to anybody who could show it to me," he added desperately, "and I mean to spend my whole vacation hunting for it if need be. Perhaps it was only migrating, or had been chased out of its own region by some bird of prey."

Mrs. Tilley gave amazed attention to all this, but Sylvia still watched the toad, not divining, as she might have done at some calmer time, that the creature wished to get to its hole under the doorstep, and was much hindered by the unusual spectators at that hour of the evening. No amount of thought, that night, could decide how many wished-for treasures the ten dollars, so lightly spoken of, would buy.

The next day the young sportsman hovered about the woods, and Sylvia kept him company, having lost her first fear of the friendly lad, who proved to be most kind and sympathetic. He told her many things about the birds and what they knew and where they lived and what they did with themselves. And he gave her a jack-knife, which she thought as great a treasure as if she were a desert-islander. All day long he did not once make her troubled or afraid except when he brought down some unsuspecting singing creature from its bough. Sylvia would have liked him vastly better without his gun; she could not understand why he killed the very birds he seemed to like so much. But as the day waned, Sylvia still watched the young man with loving admiration. She had never seen anybody so charming and delightful; the woman's heart, asleep in the child, was vaguely thrilled by a dream of love. Some premonition of that great power stirred and swayed these young foresters who traversed the solemn woodlands with soft-footed silent care. They stopped to listen to a bird's song; they pressed

forward again eagerly, parting the branches,—speaking to each other
rarely and in whispers; the young man going first and Sylvia following, fascinated, a few steps behind, with her gray eyes dark with
excitement.

She grieved because the longed-for white heron was elusive, but she
did not lead the guest, she only followed, and there was no such thing
as speaking first. The sound of her own unquestioned voice would
have terrified her,—it was hard enough to answer yes or no when
there was need of that. At last evening began to fall, and they drove
the cow home together, and Sylvia smiled with pleasure when they
came to the place where she heard the whistle and was afraid only the
night before.

II

Half a mile from home, at the farther edge of the woods, where the
land was highest, a great pine-tree stood, the last of its generation.
Whether it was left for a boundary mark, or for what reason, no one
could say; the woodchoppers who had felled its mates were dead and
gone long ago, and a whole forest of sturdy trees, pines and oaks and
maples, had grown again. But the stately head of this old pine towered
above them all and made a landmark for sea and shore miles and
miles away. Sylvia knew it well. She had always believed that whoever climbed to the top of it could see the ocean; and the little girl had
often laid her hand on the great rough trunk and looked up wistfully
at those dark boughs that the wind always stirred, no matter how hot and
still the air might be below. Now she thought of the tree with a new excitement, for why, if one climbed it at break of day, could not one see
all the world, and easily discover whence the white heron flew, and
mark the place, and find the hidden nest?

What a spirit of adventure, what wild ambition! What fancied triumph and delight and glory for the later morning when she could
make known the secret! It was almost too real and too great for the
childish heart to bear.

All night the door of the little house stood open, and the whippoorwills came and sang upon the very step. The young sportsman and his

old hostess were sound asleep, but Sylvia's great design kept her broad awake and watching. She forgot to think of sleep. The short summer night seemed as long as the winter darkness, and at last when the whippoorwills ceased, and she was afraid the morning would after all come too soon, she stole out of the house and followed the pasture path through the woods, hastening toward the open ground beyond, listening with a sense of comfort and companionship to the drowsy twitter of a half-awakened bird, whose perch she had jarred in passing. Alas, if the great wave of human interest which flooded for the first time this dull little life should sweep away the satisfactions of an existence heart to heart with nature and the dumb life of the forest!

There was the huge tree asleep yet in the paling moonlight, and small and hopeful Sylvia began with utmost bravery to mount to the top of it, with tingling, eager blood coursing the channels of her whole frame, with her bare feet and fingers, that pinched and held like bird's claws to the monstrous ladder reaching up, up, almost to the sky itself. First she must mount the white oak tree that grew alongside, where she was almost lost among the dark branches and the green leaves heavy and wet with dew; a bird fluttered off its nest, and a red squirrel ran to and fro and scolded pettishly at the harmless housebreaker. Sylvia felt her way easily. She had often climbed there, and knew that higher still one of the oak's upper branches chafed against the pine trunk, just where its lower boughs were set close together. There, when she made the dangerous pass from one tree to the other, the great enterprise would really begin.

She crept out along the swaying oak limb at last, and took the daring step across into the old pine-tree. The way was harder than she thought; she must reach far and hold fast, the sharp dry twigs caught and held her and scratched her like angry talons, the pitch made her thin little fingers clumsy and stiff as she went round and round the tree's great stem, higher and higher upward. The sparrows and robins in the woods below were beginning to wake and twitter to the dawn, yet it seemed much lighter there aloft in the pine-tree, and the child knew that she must hurry if her project were to be of any use.

The tree seemed to lengthen itself out as she went up, and to reach farther and farther upward. It was like a great main-mast to the voyaging earth; it must truly have been amazed that morning through all its ponderous frame as it felt this determined spark of human spirit creeping and climbing from higher branch to branch. Who knows how steadily the least twigs held themselves to advantage this light, weak creature on her way! The old pine must have loved his new dependent. More than all the hawks, and bats, and moths, and even the sweet-voiced thrushes, was the brave, beating heart of the solitary gray-eyed child. And the tree stood still and held away the winds that June morning while the dawn grew bright in the east.

Sylvia's face was like a pale star, if one had seen it from the ground, when the last thorny bough was past, and she stood trembling and tired but wholly triumphant, high in the tree-top. Yes, there was the sea with the dawning sun making a golden dazzle over it, and toward that glorious east flew two hawks with slow-moving pinions. How low they looked in the air from that height when before one had only seen them far up, and dark against the blue sky. Their gray feathers were as soft as moths; they seemed only a little way from the tree, and Sylvia felt as if she too could go flying away among the clouds. Westward, the woodlands and farms reached miles and miles into the distance; here and there were church steeples, and white villages; truly it was a vast and awesome world.

The birds sang louder and louder. At last the sun came up bewilderingly bright. Sylvia could see the white sails of ships out at sea, and the clouds that were purple and rose-colored and yellow at first began to fade away. Where was the white heron's nest in the sea of green branches, and was this wonderful sight and pageant of the world the only reward for having climbed to such a giddy height? Now look down again, Sylvia, where the green marsh is set among the shining birches and dark hemlocks; there where you saw the white heron once you will see him again; look, look! a white spot of him like a single floating feather comes up from the dead hemlock and grows larger, and rises, and comes close at last, and goes by the land-mark pine with steady sweep of wing and outstretched slender neck and crested head. And wait! wait! do not move a foot or a finger, little girl, do not send an arrow of light and consciousness from your two eager eyes, for the heron has perched on a pine bough not far

beyond yours, and cries back to his mate on the nest, and plumes hi
feathers for the new day!

The child gives a long sigh a minute later when a company o
shouting cat-birds comes also to the tree, and vexed by their flutterin
and lawlessness the solemn heron goes away. She knows his secre
now, the wild, light, slender bird that floats and wavers, and goes bac
like an arrow presently to his home in the green world beneath. Thes
Sylvia, well satisfied, makes her perilous way down again, not darinş
to look far below the branch she stands on, ready to cry sometimes
because her fingers ache and her lamed feet slip. Wondering over ano
over again what the stranger would say to her, and what he would
think when she told him how to find his way straight to the heron's
nest.

"Sylvy, Sylvy!" called the busy old grandmother again and again,
but nobody answered, and the small husk bed was empty, and Sylvia
had disappeared.

The guest waked from a dream, and remembering his day's pleasure
hurried to dress himself that it might sooner begin. He was sure
from the way the shy little girl looked once or twice yesterday that
she had at least seen the white heron, and now she must really be
persuaded to tell. Here she comes now, paler than ever, and her worn
old frock is torn and tattered, and smeared with pine pitch. The
grandmother and the sportsman stand in the door together and question her, and the splendid moment has come to speak of the dead
hemlock-tree by the green marsh.

But Sylvia does not speak after all, though the old grandmother
fretfully rebukes her, and the young man's kind appealing eyes are
looking straight into her own. He can make them rich with money;
he has promised it, and they are poor now. He is so well worth making
happy, and he waits to hear the story she can tell.

No, she must keep silence! What is it that suddenly forbids her and
makes her dumb? Has she been nine years growing, and now, when
the great world for the first time puts out a hand to her, must she
thrust it aside for a bird's sake? The murmur of the pine's green
branches is in her ears, she remembers how the white heron came

flying through the golden air and how they watched the sea and the morning together, and Sylvia cannot speak; she cannot tell the heron's secret and give its life away.

Dear loyalty, that suffered a sharp pang as the guest went away disappointed later in the day, that could have served and followed him and loved him as a dog loves! Many a night Sylvia heard the echo of his whistle haunting the pasture path as she came home with the loitering cow. She forgot even her sorrow at the sharp report of his gun and the piteous sight of thrushes and sparrows dropping silent to the ground, their songs hushed and their pretty feathers stained and wet with blood. Were the birds better friends than their hunter might have been,—who can tell? Whatever treasures were lost to her, woodlands and summer-time, remember! Bring your gifts and graces and tell your secrets to this lonely country child!

RING LARDNER

COMMENTARY

Ring Lardner spent most of his adult life among ballplayers, prize fighters, Great White Highwaymen, songwriters, wealthy Long Islanders, and upper-class bridge- and golf-players. He saw these people at their worst, during the Boom Decade, during which our national behavior hit a record low. Though he never left them, he didn't like them, and his short stories are the record of that dislike. The odd thing is that when he wanted to be just funny, he could shut off his irritation and write pieces that still make you laugh. But oftener you find yourself laughing on the wrong side of your face.

William Bolitho divided Lardner's population into fools and swine. That's a little offhand, but there's much truth in it. Lardner went a long way on sheer dislike alone. I don't think he even cared much for himself, but he was wrong there, because his work, though he may never have realized it, projects a picture of an extraordinarily honest, intelligent, charming person, if also an unhappy one.

It's hard to remember half a dozen sympathetic Lardner characters. Somewhere he refers to "this special police dog," which "was like most of them and hated everybody." Lardner himself was a sort of police dog, but his hatred was not mere crabbedness. It was an expression of his insight into American life on certain levels as it revealed itself during a sordid era.

Lardner's aim is deadly because he is cold. There is almost no emotion. His satire is negative; that is why it never caused a revolution in American manners, as Main Street did. No one is uneasy under the whiplash of Lardner's scorn, for he is not really worked up about anything. Paradoxically that is one of the reasons that enabled this complete misanthrope to appear in the most popular and genial of our weekly magazines. He never rails at the crowd because he has passed beyond raillery.

He has a uniform method of attack. He takes some national trait which is ordinarily treated with good-natured humor and reduces it to its basic viciousness. Pullman-washroom sociability is revealed as a vulgar garrulity which conceals a brutal egotism ("Sun Cured"). Simple boy-and-girl calf love is shown to have its roots in colossal selfishness ("Some Like Them Cold"). The practical joker, that standby of amiable American humor, turns out to be cruel and heartless ("Haircut," "The Maysville Minstrel"). The wife who is proud of her husband's achievements betrays herself as a witless bore ("Who Dealt?"). The lavish hospitality which members of the American upper strata are supposed to extend to each other is analyzed and found to conceal nosiness, lack of imagination, possessiveness, and, if you go deep enough, actual antagonism ("Liberty Hall").

Lardner is best-natured in his baseball stories, for he really loved the game. But his love never prevented him from seeing through it. He had a press-bench eye. He saw baseball, as he saw all American sport, as a focal point drawing together bonehead and sharper. For entertainment purposes he chooses to devote most of his attention to the bonehead ("You Know Me Al"), but when he elects to attack a professionalized sport without any gloves on, we get "Champion." The direct, vicious hatred that animates "Champion" is far removed from the reined-in fascination underlying a fight yarn like Hemingway's "Fifty Grand." The two stories are equally effective, but one feels that Lardner is far closer to the facts of American sport than is Hemingway. He does not inject himself into the story. He has his eye coldly fixed on the object, whereas Hemingway, despite the famous lean, pared style, is lyrical.

Lardner is a great master of mimicry, catching to the life our flat, democratic speech. The effect of "Lardner's Ringlish" is often humorous but more often satiric. If the mind of a boob is fuzzy and banal, the best way to get it over is to make the boob open his mouth and talk.

To see how instrumental is his style, note how he handles our traditional humor of exaggeration. When Mark Twain exaggerates, it is to secure an effect of comic absurdity, but when Lardner says, "He give her a look that you could pour on a waffle," the mad metaphor has the power to fill us with a distaste for all sentimental affection.

Even a simple, forthright line like "French trains run like they was on pogo sticks" conceals an undercurrent of exacerbation.

One of Lardner's worlds is filled with soreheads and kickers; it is a land in a never-ending state of civil war. Any two Lardner characters, when they get together, are apt to quarrel about something. He is the epic recorder of bicker.

This appears most clearly in his treatment of marriage. If his men are mainly niggling pewts garrulously trying to impress the world with their nonexistent virtues, his women are mainly egotists of the most predatory type, barren of glamor, charm, humor, and sexual attractiveness. His vision is narrow and distorted, but it is powerful. In his stories middle-class marriage is filled with hypocrisy, selfishness, and constant antagonism between husband and wife. For proof I suggest a rereading of "The Love Nest," which I have selected as a typical Lardner story. Passion, sentiment, generosity, sympathy, and humor are barred, leaving only the four components of comic-strip marital comedy: contentiousness, henpecking, gold-digging, and that peculiar, hopeless irony of the American male which for Lardner is his chief defense against the onslaughts of the female.

In the face of Lardner's perfectly clear simon-pure, deliberate misanthropy it is a little difficult to understand how readers could ever have welcomed him as a standard, "popular" humorist. The world he shows us is a world of mental sadists, fourflushers, intolerable gossipers, meal-ticket females, interfering morons, brainless flirts, liars, brutes, spiteful snobs, vulgar climbers, dishonest jockeys, selfish children, dipsomaniacal chorus girls, senile chatterers, idiotically complacent husbands, mean arrivistes, drunks, snoopers, poseurs, and bridge-players. Yet, despite his bitterness, he is a top-notch humorist on some occasions, as he is a great satirist on almost all.

The Love Nest

BY

RING LARDNER

"I'LL TELL YOU what I'm going to do with you, Mr. Bartlett," said the great man. "I'm going to take you right out to my home and have you meet the wife and family; stay to dinner and all night. We've got plenty of room and extra pajamas, if you don't mind them silk. I mean that'll give you a chance to see us just as we are. I mean you can get more that way than if you sat here a whole week, asking me questions."

"But I don't want to put you to a lot of trouble," said Bartlett.

"Trouble!" The great man laughed. "There's no trouble about it. I've got a house that's like a hotel. I mean a big house with lots of servants. But anyway I'm always glad to do anything I can for a writing man, especially a man that works for Ralph Doane. I'm very fond of Ralph. I mean I like him personally besides being a great editor. I mean I've known him for years and when there's anything I can do for him, I'm glad to do it. I mean it'll be a pleasure to have you. So if you want to notify your family——"

"I haven't any family," said Bartlett.

"Well, I'm sorry for you! And I bet when you see mine, you'll wish you had one of your own. But I'm glad you can come and we'll start now so as to get there before the kiddies are put away for the night. I mean I want you to be sure and see the kiddies. I've got three."

"I've seen their pictures," said Bartlett. "You must be very proud of them. They're all girls, aren't they?"

"Yes, sir; three girls. I wouldn't have a boy. I mean I always wanted girls. I mean girls have got a lot more zip to them. I mean they're a lot zippier. But let's go! The Rolls is downstairs and if we start now

413

we'll get there before dark. I mean I want you to see the place while it's still daylight."

The great man—Lou Gregg, president of Modern Pictures, Inc.—escorted his visitor from the magnificent office by a private door and down a private stairway to the avenue, where the glittering car with its glittering chauffeur waited.

"My wife was in town today," said Gregg as they glided northward, "and I hoped we could ride out together, but she called up about two and asked would I mind if she went on home in the Pierce. She was through with her shopping and she hates to be away from the house and the kiddies any longer than she can help. Celia's a great home girl. You'd never know she was the same girl now as the girl I married seven years ago. I mean she's different. I mean she's not the same. I mean her marriage and being a mother has developed her. Did you ever see her? I mean in pictures?"

"I think I did once," replied Bartlett. "Didn't she play the young sister in 'The Cad'?"

"Yes, with Harold Hodgson and Marie Blythe."

"I thought I'd seen her. I remember her as very pretty and vivacious."

"She certainly was! And she is yet! I mean she's even prettier, but of course she ain't a kid, though she looks it. I mean she was only seventeen in that picture and that was ten years ago. I mean she's twenty-seven years old now. But I never met a girl with as much zip as she had in those days. It's remarkable how marriage changes them. I mean nobody would ever thought Celia Sayles would turn out to be a sit-by-the-fire. I mean she still likes a good time, but her home and kiddies come first. I mean her home and kiddies come first."

"I see what you mean," said Bartlett.

An hour's drive brought them to Ardsley-on-Hudson and the great man's home.

"A wonderful place!" Bartlett exclaimed with a heroic semblance of enthusiasm as the car turned in at an *arc de triomphe* of a gateway and approached a white house that might have been mistaken for the Yale Bowl.

"It ought to be!" said Gregg. "I mean I've spent enough on it. I mean these things cost money."

He indicated with a gesture the huge house and Urbanesque landscaping.

"But no amount of money is too much to spend on home. I mean it's a good investment if it tends to make your family proud and satisfied with their home. I mean every nickel I've spent here is like so much insurance; it insures me of a happy wife and family. And what more can a man ask!"

Bartlett didn't know, but the topic was forgotten in the business of leaving the resplendent Rolls and entering the even more resplendent reception hall.

"Forbes will take your things," said Gregg. "And, Forbes, you may tell Dennis that Mr. Bartlett will spend the night." He faced the wide stairway and raised his voice. "Sweetheart!" he called.

From above came the reply in contralto: "Hello, sweetheart!"

"Come down, sweetheart. I've brought you a visitor."

"All right, sweetheart, in just a minute."

Gregg led Bartlett into a living-room that was five laps to the mile and suggestive of an Atlantic City auction sale.

"Sit there," said the host, pointing to a balloon-stuffed easy chair, "and I'll see if we can get a drink. I've got some real old Bourbon that I'd like you to try. You know I come from Chicago and I always liked Bourbon better than Scotch. I mean I always preferred it to Scotch. Forbes," he addressed the servant, "we want a drink. You'll find a full bottle of that Bourbon in the cupboard."

"It's only half full, sir," said Forbes.

"Half full! That's funny! I mean I opened it last night and just took one drink. I mean it ought to be full."

"It's only half full," repeated Forbes, and went to fetch it.

"I'll have to investigate," Gregg told his guest. "I mean this ain't the first time lately that some of my good stuff has disappeared. When you keep so many servants, it's hard to get all honest ones. But here's Celia!"

Bartlett rose to greet the striking brunette who at this moment made

an entrance so Delsarte as to be almost painful. With never a glance
at him, she minced across the room to her husband and took a half
interest in a convincing kiss.

"Well, sweetheart," she said when it was at last over.

"This is Mr. Bartlett, sweetheart," said her husband. "Mr. Bartlett,
meet Mrs. Gregg."

Bartlett shook his hostess's proffered two fingers.

"I'm so pleased!" said Celia in a voice reminiscent of Miss Claire's
imitation of Miss Barrymore.

"Mr. Bartlett," Gregg went on, "is with Mankind, Ralph Doane's
magazine. He is going to write me up; I mean us."

"No, you mean you," said Celia. "I'm sure the public is not interested
in great men's wives."

"I am sure you are mistaken, Mrs. Gregg," said Bartlett politely.
"In this case at least. You are worth writing up aside from being a
great man's wife."

"I'm afraid you're a flatterer, Mr. Bartlett," she returned. "I have
been out of the limelight so long that I doubt if anybody remembers
me. I'm no longer an artist; merely a happy wife and mother."

"And I claim, sweetheart," said Gregg, "that it takes an artist to
be that."

"Oh, no, sweetheart!" said Celia. "Not when they have you for
a husband!"

The exchange of hosannahs was interrupted by the arrival of Forbes
with the tray.

"Will you take yours straight or in a high-ball?" Gregg inquired
of his guest. "Personally I like good whisky straight. I mean mixing
it with water spoils the flavor. I mean whisky like this, it seems like
a crime to mix it with water."

"I'll have mine straight," said Bartlett, who would have preferred
a high-ball.

While the drinks were being prepared, he observed his hostess more
closely and thought how much more charming she would be if she had
used finesse in improving on nature. Her cheeks, her mouth, her eyes,
and lashes had been, he guessed, far above the average in beauty
before she had begun experimenting with them. And her experiments

had been clumsy. She was handsome in spite of her efforts to be handsomer.

"Listen, sweetheart," said her husband. "One of the servants has been helping himself to this Bourbon. I mean it was a full bottle last night and I only had one little drink out of it. And now it's less than half full. Who do you suppose has been at it?"

"How do I know, sweetheart? Maybe the groceryman or the iceman or somebody."

"But you and I and Forbes are the only ones that have a key. I mean it was locked up."

"Maybe you forgot to lock it."

"I never do. Well, anyway, Bartlett, here's a go!"

"Doesn't Mrs. Gregg indulge?" asked Bartlett.

"Only a cocktail before dinner," said Celia. "Lou objects to me drinking whisky, and I don't like it much anyway."

"I don't object to you drinking whisky, sweetheart. I just object to you drinking to excess. I mean I think it coarsens a woman to drink. I mean it makes them coarse."

"Well, there's no argument, sweetheart. As I say, I don't care whether I have it or not."

"It certainly is great Bourbon!" said Bartlett, smacking his lips and putting his glass back on the tray.

"You bet it is!" Gregg agreed. "I mean you can't buy that kind of stuff any more. I mean it's real stuff. You help yourself when you want another. Mr. Bartlett is going to stay all night, sweetheart. I told him he could get a whole lot more of a line on us that way than just interviewing me in the office. I mean I'm tongue-tied when it comes to talking about my work and my success. I mean it's better to see me out here as I am, in my home, with my family. I mean my home life speaks for itself without me saying a word."

"But, sweetheart," said his wife, "what about Mr. Latham?"

"Gosh! I forgot all about him! I must phone and see if I can call it off. That's terrible! You see," he explained to Bartlett, "I made a date to go up to Tarrytown tonight, to K. L. Latham's, the sugar people. We're going to talk over the new club. We're going to have a golf club that will make the rest of them look like a toy. I mean a real golf club! They want me to kind of run it. And I was to go up there tonight and talk it over. I'll phone and see if I can postpone it."

"Oh, don't postpone it on my account!" urged Bartlett. "I can come out again some other time, or I can see you in town."

"I don't see how you *can* postpone it, sweetheart," said Celia. "Didn't he say old Mr. King was coming over from White Plains? They'll be mad at you if you don't go."

"I'm afraid they would resent it, sweetheart. Well, I'll tell you. You can entertain Mr. Bartlett and I'll go up there right after dinner and come back as soon as I can. And Bartlett and I can talk when I get back. I mean we can talk when I get back. How is that?"

"That suits me," said Bartlett.

"I'll be as entertaining as I can," said Celia, "but I'm afraid that isn't very entertaining. However, if I'm too much of a bore, there's plenty to read."

"No danger of my being bored," said Bartlett.

"Well, that's all fixed then," said the relieved host. "I hope you'll excuse me running away. But I don't see how I can get out of it. I mean with old King coming over from White Plains. I mean he's an old man. But listen, sweetheart—where are the kiddies? Mr. Bartlett wants to see them."

"Yes, indeed!" agreed the visitor.

"Of course you'd say so!" Celia said. "But we *are* proud of them! I suppose all parents are the same. They all think their own children are the only children in the world. Isn't that so, Mr. Bartlett? Or haven't you any children?"

"I'm sorry to say I'm not married."

"Oh, you poor thing! We pity him, don't we, sweetheart? But why aren't you, Mr. Bartlett? Don't tell me you're a woman hater!"

"Not now, anyway," said the gallant Bartlett.

"Do you get that, sweetheart? He's paying you a pretty compliment."

"I heard it, sweetheart. And now I'm sure he's a flatterer. But I must hurry and get the children before Hortense puts them to bed."

"Well," said Gregg when his wife had left the room, "would you say she's changed?"

"A little, and for the better. She's more than fulfilled her early promise."

"I think so," said Gregg. "I mean I think she was a beautiful girl and now she's an even more beautiful woman. I mean wifehood and maternity have given her a kind of a—well, you know—I mean a kind of a pose. I mean a pose. How about another drink?"

They were emptying their glasses when Celia returned with two of her little girls.

"The baby's in bed and I was afraid to ask Hortense to get her up again. But you'll see her in the morning. This is Norma and this is Grace. Girls, this is Mr. Bartlett."

The girls received this news calmly.

"Well, girls," said Bartlett.

"What do you think of them, Bartlett?" demanded their father. "I mean what do you think of them?"

"They're great!" replied the guest with creditable warmth.

"I mean aren't they pretty?"

"I should say they are!"

"There, girls! Why don't you thank Mr. Bartlett?"

"Thanks," murmured Norma.

"How old are you, Norma?" asked Bartlett.

"Six," said Norma.

"Well," said Bartlett. "And how old is Grace?"

"Four," replied Norma.

"Well," said Bartlett. "And how old is baby sister?"

"One and a half," answered Norma.

"Well," said Bartlett.

As this seemed to be final, "Come, girls," said their mother. "Kiss daddy good night and I'll take you back to Hortense."

"I'll take them," said Gregg. "I'm going up-stairs anyway. And you can show Bartlett around. I mean before it gets any darker."

"Good night, girls," said Bartlett, and the children murmured a good night.

"I'll come and see you before you're asleep," Celia told them. And after Gregg had led them out, "Do you really think they're pretty?" she asked Bartlett.

"I certainly do. Especially Norma. She's the image of you," said Bartlett.

"She looks a little like I used to," Celia admitted. "But I hope she doesn't look like me now. I'm too old looking."

"You look remarkably young!" said Bartlett. "No one would believe you were the mother of three children."

"Oh, Mr. Bartlett! But I mustn't forget I'm to 'show you around.' Lou is so proud of our home!"

"And with reason," said Bartlett.

"It *is* wonderful! I call it our love nest. Quite a big nest, don't you think? Mother says it's too big to be cosy; she says she can't think of it as a home. But I always say a place is whatever one makes of it. A woman can be happy in a tent if they love each other. And miserable in a royal palace without love. Don't you think so, Mr. Bartlett?"

"Yes, indeed."

"Is this really such wonderful Bourbon? I think I'll just take a sip of it and see what it's like. It can't hurt me if it's so good. Do you think so, Mr. Bartlett?"

"I don't believe so."

"Well, then, I'm going to taste it and if it hurts me it's your fault." Celia poured a whisky glass two-thirds full and drained it at a gulp.

"It *is* good, isn't it?" she said. "Of course I'm not much of a judge as I don't care for whisky and Lou won't let me drink it. But he's raved so about this Bourbon that I did want to see what it was like. You won't tell on me, will you, Mr. Bartlett?"

"Not I!"

"I wonder how it would be in a high-ball. Let's you and I have just one. But I'm forgetting I'm supposed to show you the place. We won't have time to drink a high-ball and see the place too before Lou comes down. Are you so crazy to see the place?"

"Not very."

"Well, then, what do you say if we have a high-ball? And it'll be a secret between you and I."

They drank in silence and Celia pressed a button by the door.

"You may take the bottle and tray," she told Forbes. "And now," she said to Bartlett, "we'll go out on the porch and see as much as we can see. You'll have to guess the rest."

Gregg, having changed his shirt and collar, joined them.

"Well," he said to Bartlett, "have you seen everything?"

"I guess I have, Mr. Gregg," lied the guest readily. "It's a wonderful place!"

"We like it. I mean it suits us. I mean it's my idear of a real home. And Celia calls it her love nest."

"So she told me," said Bartlett.

"She'll always be sentimental," said her husband.

He put his hand on her shoulder, but she drew away.

"I must run up and dress," she said.

"Dress!" exclaimed Bartlett, who had been dazzled by her flowered green chiffon.

"Oh, I'm not going to really dress," she said. "But I couldn't wear this thing for dinner!"

"Perhaps you'd like to clean up a little, Bartlett," said Gregg. "I mean Forbes will show you your room if you want to go up."

"It might be best," said Bartlett.

Celia, in a black lace dinner gown, was rather quiet during the elaborate meal. Three or four times when Gregg addressed her, she seemed to be thinking of something else and had to ask, "What did you say, sweetheart?" Her face was red and Bartlett imagined that she had "sneaked" a drink or two besides the two helpings of Bourbon and the cocktail that had preceded dinner.

"Well, I'll leave you," said Gregg when they were in the living-room once more. "I mean the sooner I get started, the sooner I'll be back. Sweetheart, try and keep your guest awake and don't let him die of thirst. *Au revoir,* Bartlett. I'm sorry, but it can't be helped. There's a fresh bottle of the Bourbon, so go to it. I mean help yourself. It's too bad you have to drink alone."

"It *is* too bad, Mr. Bartlett," said Celia when Gregg had gone.

"What's too bad?" asked Bartlett.

"That you have to drink alone. I feel like I wasn't being a good hostess to let you do it. In fact, I refuse to let you do it. I'll join you in just a little wee sip."

"But it's so soon after dinner!"

"It's never too soon! I'm going to have a drink myself and if you don't join me, you're a quitter."

She mixed two life-sized high-balls and handed one to her guest.

"Now we'll turn on the radio and see if we can't stir things up. There! No, no! Who cares about the old baseball! Now! This is better! Let's dance."

"I'm sorry, Mrs. Gregg, but I don't dance."

"Well, you're an old cheese! To make me dance alone! 'All alone, yes, I'm all alone.'"

There was no affectation in her voice now and Bartlett was amazed at her unlabored grace as she glided around the big room.

"But it's no fun alone," she complained. "Let's shut the damn thing off and talk."

"I love to watch you dance," said Bartlett.

"Yes, but I'm no Pavlowa," said Celia as she silenced the radio. "And besides, it's time for a drink."

"I've still got more than half of mine."

"Well, you had that wine at dinner, so I'll have to catch up with you."

She poured herself another high-ball and went at the task of "catching up."

"The trouble with you, Mr.—now isn't that a scream! I can't think of your name."

"Bartlett."

"The trouble with you, Barker—do you know what's the trouble with you? You're too sober. See? You're too damn sober! That's the whole trouble, see? If you weren't so sober, we'd be better off. See? What I can't understand is how you can be so sober and me so high."

"You're not used to it."

"Not used to it! That's the cat's pajamas! Say, I'm like this half the time, see? If I wasn't, I'd die!"

"What does your husband say?"

"He don't say because he don't know. See, Barker? There's nights when he's out and there's a few nights when I'm out myself. And there's other nights when we're both in and I pretend I'm sleepy and

I go up-stairs. See? But I don't go to bed. See? I have a little party all by myself. See? If I didn't, I'd die!"

"What do you mean, you'd die?"

"You're dumb, Barker! You may be sober, but you're dumb! Did you fall for all that apple sauce about the happy home and the contented wife? Listen, Barker—I'd give anything in the world to be out of this mess. I'd give anything to never see him again."

"Don't you love him any more? Doesn't he love you? Or what?"

"Love! I never did love him! I didn't know what love was! And all his love is for himself!"

"How did you happen to get married?"

"I was a kid; that's the answer. A kid and ambitious. See? He was a director then and he got stuck on me and I thought he'd make me a star. See, Barker? I married him to get myself a chance. And now look at me!"

"I'd say you were fairly well off."

"Well off, am I? I'd change places with the scum of the earth just to be free! See, Barker? And I could have been a star without any help if I'd only realized it. I had the looks and I had the talent. I've got it yet. I could be a Swanson and get myself a marquis; maybe a prince! And look what I did get! A self-satisfied, self-centered ——! I thought he'd *make* me! See, Barker? Well, he's made me all right; he's made me a chronic mother and it's a wonder I've got any looks left.

"I fought at first. I told him marriage didn't mean giving up my art, my life work. But it was no use. He wanted a beautiful wife and beautiful children for his beautiful home. Just to show us off. See? I'm part of his chattels. See, Barker? I'm just like his big diamond or his cars or his horses. And he wouldn't stand for his wife 'lowering' herself to act in pictures. Just as if pictures hadn't made him!

"You go back to your magazine tomorrow and write about our love nest. See, Barker? And be sure and don't get mixed and call it a baby ranch. Babies! You thought little Norma was pretty. Well, she is. And what is it going to get her? A rich —— of a husband that treats her like a ——! That's what it'll get her if I don't interfere. I hope I don't last long enough to see her grow up, but if I do, I'm going to advise her to run away from home and live her own life. And *be* somebody! Not a *thing* like I am! See, Barker?"

"Did you ever think of a divorce?"

"Did I ever think of one! Listen—but there's no chance. I've got nothing on him, and no matter what he had on me, he'd never let the world know it. He'd keep me here and torture me like he does now, only worse. But I haven't done anything wrong, see? The men I might care for, they're all scared of him and his money and power. See, Barker? And the others are just as bad as him. Like fat old Morris, the hotel man, that everybody thinks he's a model husband. The reason he don't step out more is because he's too stingy. But I could have him if I wanted him. Every time he gets near enough to me, he squeezes my hand. I guess he thinks it's a nickel, the tight old ——! But come on, Barker. Let's have a drink. I'm running down."

"I think it's about time you were running up—up-stairs," said Bartlett. "If I were you, I'd try to be in bed and asleep when Gregg gets home."

"You're all right, Barker. And after this drink I'm going to do just as you say. Only I thought of it before you did, see? I think of it lots of nights. And tonight you can help me out by telling him I had a bad headache."

Left alone, Bartlett thought a while, then read, and finally dozed off. He was dozing when Gregg returned.

"Well, well, Bartlett," said the great man, "did Celia desert you?"

"It was perfectly all right, Mr. Gregg. She had a headache and I told her to go to bed."

"She's had a lot of headaches lately; reads too much, I guess. Well, I'm sorry I had this date. It was about a new golf club and I had to be there. I mean I'm going to be president of it. I see you consoled yourself with some of the Bourbon. I mean the bottle doesn't look as full as it did."

"I hope you'll forgive me for helping myself so generously," said Bartlett. "I don't get stuff like that every day!"

"Well, what do you say if we turn in? We can talk on the way to town tomorrow. Though I guess you won't have much to ask me. I guess you know all about us. I mean you know all about us now."

"Yes, indeed, Mr. Gregg. I've got plenty of material if I can just handle it."

Celia had not put in an appearance when Gregg and his guest were ready to leave the house next day.

"She always sleeps late," said Gregg. "I mean she never wakes up very early. But she's later than usual this morning. Sweetheart!" he called up the stairs.

"Yes, sweetheart," came the reply.

"Mr. Bartlett's leaving now. I mean he's going."

"Oh, good-by, Mr. Bartlett. Please forgive me for not being down to see you off."

"You're forgiven, Mrs. Gregg. And thanks for your hospitality."

"Good-by, sweetheart!"

"Good-by, sweetheart!"

ERNEST HEMINGWAY

"The Snows of Kilimanjaro" is one of Hemingway's most recent short stories. I think it is also his best, far superior to "The Killers," "The Undefeated," and "Fifty Grand," which are the usual pets of anthologists. It goes deeper than any of them and its technique is not so patent. All the old Hemingway bitterness is still there, but also greater understanding. The story stands the test of several readings.

So much has been written about Hemingway that I do not suppose the reader is unduly anxious to read any more. If he does not wish to, he need not; he will find "The Snows of Kilimanjaro" waiting for him a few pages further on. For those dogged few who read everything in a book, whether they like it or not, I address a word of explanation to account for the inclusion of what immediately follows. In January, 1933, The Nation published a longish essay by me called "Ernest Hemingway: An American Byron." It was not, as you will see, a very good essay, and it was (you will see this even more quickly) a youthful essay, but it said some true things, I still believe, about the Hemingway of that period. I reproduce it here in condensed form. I also reproduce a review of For Whom the Bell Tolls that appeared in The New Yorker of October 26, 1940. It is by comparing these two estimates, written almost eight years apart, that you get, I think, a reasonably clear picture of Hemingway's growth.

Here is the early piece. Remember, this was long, long ago, in 1933.

"There is always a lost generation; and there is always a book in which it finds itself. The brilliance of his writing accounts only in part for Hemingway's success. Had he written half as well, but in the same manner and about the same subjects, he would have become just as celebrated. He has triumphed more as hero than as artist. Hemingway is a man born in his due time, embodying the mute longings and confused ideals of a large segment of his own and the succeeding generation. He is the unhappy warrior that many men would like to be. About him has sprung up a real contemporary hero-myth; young men by the thousand are concerned with the importance of being Ernest.

"Why is Hemingway news? It is because this young Lochinvar out of the Middle West is a hero. It is because he apparently creates a new tradition for those who have rejected the old ones. He provides a modern and more violent romanticism of the nineteenth century. He takes a spiritual malaise and translates it into something vivid, vital, even splendid, giving to bitterness an exuberance that joy itself cannot match.

"The generation for which Hemingway so ably speaks is not only the generation that lost itself in the Argonne or among the hassocks of Gertrude Stein's drawing room. A part, probably a major part, of the succeeding generation is equally lost today, in the crisis. Hemingway's present readers, I would hazard a guess, are largely under thirty. Though to this group the war can mean little more than something in a book, they feel as vitally maimed as the hero of The Sun Also Rises. They are the defeated and the betrayed, so disillusioned as to have no desire to attack their betrayers. They are too deeply wounded for the easy salve of sophistication. The values with which they have been inoculated they discover to be false. The culture which they have been instructed to flaunt as the badge of their superiority proves hollow. Since most of the grand words have collapsed, they throw them all overboard. They become rebels who smile at reform and offer a bitter shrug to revolution.

"Where are these young people to place the animal faith deeply grounded beneath all their tragic rejections? In historical crises, when the flesh of the dominant system has withered away and laid bare the bones of chaos, the superior individual either makes common cause with his fellows in some attempt at a finer order or, as in the novels of Hemingway, retreats upon his instincts. He abandons, as Hemingway puts it, all efforts "to save the world." He cultivates those primal emotions which cannot betray him, as his hands and feet cannot betray him. Among these emotions may be the fear of death and the delight in it, the stoic joy of battle and the pleasurable acceptance of the flesh and the muscles. In the last analysis he worships his reflexes, tending to exalt any activity which introspection cannot corrode. He reverts, however subtly, to the primitive and even the brutal, because on these levels he finds no echo of the culture which has cheated him. He attempts to cling to the hands of the clock, to become a nonpolitical animal, an individualist contemning all creeds, individualism included.

"He is at home in all countries. He puts his faith in simple things rather than in complicated words. He seeks the companionship and tries to share the experiences of booze-fighters, killers, athletes, and sportsmen, men who lead careers of physical sensation, cut off from the main current of the life of their time. He may even cultivate a special interest in the reactions of animals, creatures unspoiled by the general infection of the world. Above all, he looks for a hero, one who does all this with efficiency and elegance and presents a convincing rationale of his behavior.

"Hemingway is the hero thrown up by the American ferment. Hemingway is the modern primitive, who makes as fresh a start with the emotions as his forefathers did with the soil. He is the frontiersman of the loins, heart, and biceps, the stoic Red Indian minus traditions, scornful of the past, bare of sentimentality, catching the muscular life in a plain and muscular prose. He is the hero who distrusts heroism. He is the prophet of those who are without faith.

"If we compare Hemingway with a great poet who died a little over a century ago, we get an interesting insight into the manner in which similar epochs evoke similar personalities. In the imagination of young Europeans, Byron in his time occupied a place strikingly like Hemingway's position today.

"Both Byron and Hemingway awake to find themselves famous at twenty-five. Both cut themselves off at an early age from their native lands. Byron adopts Greece and Italy; Hemingway celebrates Spain. In Greece Byron finds the fatal theater in which to stage his worship of liberty. In Spain Hemingway discovers the shrine for his cult of violence, and, later, an object in which to repose his political faith. Both are attracted by the glory of military life, and meet with disillu-

sion. Both are prepossessing examples of maleness and both exploit
an athleticism which wins for them—as much to Byron's satisfaction
as to Hemingway's disgust—a matinee-idol popularity. Both are attracted to wild and romantic places—Byron to the Swiss mountains
and the Greek coast, Hemingway to Montana, the Ozarks, Spain.

"But there is a deeper similarity which history itself points out for
us. Byron is a product of the post-Napoleonic period. His defiant
romanticism focuses the turmoil, the disillusion, and the bitterness
which flooded Europe after her first great imperialist civil war. Hemingway is no less clearly a product of the second breakdown, and the
hard, tense quality of his romanticism marks the difference in spiritual tone between 1825 and 1925. But the two are distinctly postwar
men, typical of a period of violently shifting values. Driven by the
surrounding chaos in upon their own sensations, they inevitably
charge their work with this very chaos from which they seek to
escape. Byron, writhing under the spell of the Judeo-Christian myth,
prefers to think himself 'damned.' The Manfred pose is impossible
to the more sophisticated Hemingway. But at the heart of both lies
a tragic sense of defeat, vitalized by a burning rebellion.

"This rebellion they express in an open defiance of conventional
morality—Byron with the grandiose gesture of the aristocrat, Hemingway with the casualness of the hard-boiled reporter. In controversy
both employ an acidulous style, and each, using the language of his
day, goes as far as postal regulations will permit. They are both concerned with the odder aspects of sex. Byron's florid incest obsession,
through partly rooted in, his biography, is as much a reflection of
what was then literary fashion as Hemingway's bitter-comic preoccupation with homosexuality, nymphomania, and impotence. Both
laugh off their lostness with a certain wild morbidity. Byron drinks
from skulls. Hemingway enjoys a nice cold riot in bloody hospital
scenes and testicle feasts.

"Byron is torn between a very real love for the grand words of his
epoch—liberty, freedom, the chainless mind—and Don Juan's cynicism, which negates them all. In Hemingway a not dissimilar opposition exists. In A Farewell to Arms he writes: 'Abstract words such
as glory, honor, courage, or hallow were obscene beside the concrete

names of villages, the numbers of roads, the names of rivers, the numbers of regiments, and the dates.' One can see part of his nature seeking a new set of phrases, finding them perhaps in the Spanish pundonor, in the romantic accent he gives to the death concept, and in the very vocabulary of disillusion itself.

"In the value hierarchy of Hemingway and Byron passion, action, and violence reign supreme. Both exalt sport, though with Byron this is owing partly to his clubfoot and partly to his Tory, country-gentleman tradition. Neither has much capacity for logical reflection, and Goethe's oft-quoted remark about Byron's thinking powers may be applied with some justice to Hemingway. This lack of interest in rational analysis, however, is responsible for a great deal of the drive and power in the work of the two writers. Both admire the noble, the chivalric individual. ('Nothing ever happens to the brave.') This admiration is founded on the notion of the superior virtues of a trained caste. Byron finds this ideal in his cloudy Oriental princes, Hemingway in his matadors. There is a real cousinship between Manolo, the undefeated bullfighter, and Byron's corsairs. Finally, like Byron, Hemingway expresses the aspirations of that portion of his generation which genuinely feels itself lost and is eager to admire a way of life which combines lostness with courage and color. Both Byron and Hemingway have an unforced faculty for creating an aura of violence, waywardness, and independence which dazzles the imagination of those among their readers who suffer, in Charles du Bos' admirable phrase, from 'the need of fatality.'"

And here is what I, a representative reader and reviewer, felt about Hemingway seven years later:

"It's not inaccurate to say that Hemingway's For Whom the Bell Tolls is A Farewell to Arms with the background, instead, the Spanish Civil War. The hero, Robert Jordan, a young American Loyalist sympathizer, recalls Frederic Henry. Like Henry, he is antiheroically heroic, antiromantically romantic, very male, passionate, an artist of action, Mercutio modernized. Though the heroine, Maria, reminds one rather less of Catherine Barkley, the two women have much in common. Also, in both books the mounting interplay of death and sex is a major theme, the body's intense aliveness as it senses its own destruction.

"But there, I think, the resemblance ends. For this book is not merely an advance on A Farewell to Arms. It touches a deeper level than any sounded in the author's other books. It expresses and releases the adult Hemingway, whose voice was first heard in the groping To Have and Have Not. It is by a better man.

"The story opens and closes with Robert Jordan lying flat on the pine-needle floor of a Spanish forest. When we first meet him he is very much alive and planning the details of his job, which is to join forces with a band of Spanish guerrillas and with their aid blow up an important bridge at the precise instant that will most help the Loyalist advance on Segovia. When we last see him he has fulfilled his mission and is facing certain death. Between the opening and closing pass three days and three nights. Between the opening and closing pass a lifetime for Robert and Maria and something very much like a lifetime for the reader. 'I suppose,' thinks Robert, 'it is possible to live as full a life in seventy hours as in seventy years.' The full life lived by Robert and Maria spills over into your own mind as you read, so that the three days and three nights are added to your life, and you are larger and more of a person on page 471 than you were on page 1. That is one test of a first-rate work of fiction.

"For Whom the Bell Tolls is about serious people engaged in serious actions. The word 'serious' (a favorite among Spaniards) occurs again and again. The thoughts of Robert, even at his most sardonic, are serious thoughts. 'There are necessary orders that are no fault of yours and there is a bridge and that bridge can be the point on which the future of the human race can turn. As it can turn on everything that happens in this war.' It is a stern and grave reflection, sterner, graver than anything in A Farewell to Arms. The title itself is part of a grave reflection from the Devotions of John Donne. That we may see on what a new and different level of emotion Hemingway now works, I quote the sentence from which the title is taken: 'No man is an Iland, intire of it selfe; every man is a peece of the Continent, a part of the maine; if a Clod bee washed away by the Sea, Europe is the lesse, as well as if a Promontorie were, as well as if a Mannor of thy friends or of

thine owne were; any mans death diminishes me, because I am
involved in Mankinde; And therefore never send to know for whom
the bell tolls; It tolls for thee.'

"This utterance (I suppose it is one of the greatest sentences in
English) is about death and says yes to life. That men confer
value on life by feeling deeply each other's mortality is the underlying theme of the novel. Here is something other than Hemingway's old romantic absorption in death, though growing out of it.
Remember that For Whom the Bell Tolls is an anti-Fascist
novel. 'Any mans death diminishes me, because I am involved in
Mankinde.' All of what the dictator most profoundly and re-
ligiously disbelieves is in that sentence. Hemingway is no fool. He
portrays many of the Loyalists as cowards, brutes, and politicians
—as they undoubtedly were. He portrays some of the Fascists as
men of twisted nobility—as they undoubtedly were. But he knows
that the war, at its deepest level (the first battle of the war now
on your front pages), is a war between those who deny life and
those who affirm it. And if it is not yet such a war, it must become
so, or it will, no matter who wins, have been fought in vain. I take
that to be the central feeling of For Whom the Bell Tolls, and
that is why the book is more than a thrilling novel about love and
death and battle and a finer work than A Farewell to Arms.

"It is interesting to watch in this book a certain process of ethe-
realization. Just as the Wagnerian death fascination of Death in
the Afternoon changes here into something purer, so the small-
boy Spartanism and the parade of masculinity which weakened the
earlier books are transformed into something less gross, something
—Hemingway would despise the word—spiritual. And yet this is
by far the most sensual of all his books, the most truly passionate.

"This process of purification extends even to minor matters. In
Hemingway's other books, for example, drinking is described as
a pleasure, as a springboard for wit, as a help to love, as fun, as
madness. There is much drinking in For Whom the Bell Tolls,
and none of it is solemn, but it becomes at times a serious thing.
Liquor, drunk by these Spanish guerrillas before a battle, is a noble
and necessary pleasure. Drinking has dignity.

"Dignity also is what each of the characters possesses, from
Fernando, who wears it like another skin, down to Augustín,
whose every third word is an obscenity. Each has his own dignity,

which means worth, and that dignity is gradually lifted to the surface by the harsh touch of death, as the grain of a fine wood reveals itself with polishing. Anselmo, the Shakespearean old man who fears his own cowardice ('I remember that I had a great tendency to run at Segovia') and comes through at the end to a good and sound death; Rafael, the gypsy, unreliable, gluttonous, wild; El Sordo, the deaf guerrilla leader; Andrés, the Bulldog of Villaconejos; Pablo, the sad-faced revolutionary with the spayed spirit, the treacherous heart, and the subtle, ingrown mind; Pilar, the greatest character in the book, with her ugliness, her rages, her terrible memories, her vast love for the Republic, her understanding and envy of the young Robert and Maria; Maria herself, knitting her spirit together after her rape by the Falangists, finding the purpose of her young life in the three days and nights with her American lover—each of these (all of them flawed, some of them brutal, one of them treacherous) has a value, a personal weight that Hemingway makes us feel almost tangibly, so that their lives and deaths are not incidents in a story but matters of moment to us who are 'involved in Mankinde.'

"For Whom the Bell Tolls rises above A Farewell to Arms in another way. The love story in A Farewell to Arms is the book. Chapters like that describing the retreat from Caporetto or that beautiful scene of the conversation with the old man at the billiard table are mere set pieces and might conceivably have been used in some other novel. But the love of Robert and Maria is a structural part of For Whom the Bell Tolls. It is not 'love interest,' nor is it the whole story, either; it is an integral portion of three days and three nights of life lived by two young people facing death. Furthermore, though this love does not rise above passion, it endows passion with an end and a meaning. In the great scene just before Robert goes out to blow up the bridge, knowing that he will almost surely die, when he makes love to Maria, describing, his heart breaking, the fine life he knows they will never lead, he arrives at an identification of which Hemingway's other heroes were incapable: 'I love thee as I love all that we have fought for. I love thee as I love liberty and dignity and the rights of all men to work and not be hungry.'

"Fine as the Italians were in A Farewell to Arms, these Spaniards are finer. 'There is no people,' thinks Robert, 'like them when they are good and when they go bad there is no people that is worse.' And here they are, good and bad. They are in some ways like Russians, the pre-Soviet Russians, very philosophic and confessional and poetical. But they are not soft; indeed, the Spanish fury to kill, to kill as a pure act of faith, is one of the dominating emotions of the book. And their language is superb, translated literally out of its elegant and formal original, a trick which sounds as if it might be atrocious and turns out one hundred per cent effective. As a matter of fact, I would imagine For Whom the Bell Tolls to be as excellent a Spanish novel as it is an American one.

"I have no idea whether it is a 'great' book. But I know there are great things in it and that the man who wrote it is a bigger man than he was five years ago. There are some technical flaws. For example, the chapters describing the disorganization and political chicanery of the Loyalist command impede the story. But the faults are far outweighed by a dozen episodes that invade the memory and settle there: El Sordo's last fight on the hilltop; any of the love scenes; the struggle at the bridge; Pilar's dreadful story of Pablo's killing of the Fascists; Maria's recital of the noble death of her mother and father; Pilar's memories of her life among the bullfighters; the astounding conversation—this is a set piece, but it's forgivable—about 'the smell of death'; and the final scene, in which Robert, his left leg smashed, alone and on the threshold of delirium, trains his machine gun on the advancing Fascists and prepares himself, knowing at last why he is doing so, to die.

"So I do not much care whether or not this is a 'great' book. I feel that it is what Hemingway wanted it to be: a true book. It is written with only one prejudice—a prejudice in favor of the common human being. But that is a prejudice not easy to arrive at and which only major writers can movingly express.

"Robert's mission is to blow up a bridge, and he does so. Oddly, it is by the blowing up of just such bridges that we may be able to cross over into the future."

The Snows of Kilimanjaro

BY

ERNEST HEMINGWAY

Kilimanjaro is a snow-covered mountain 19,710 feet high, and is said to be the highest mountain in Africa. Its western summit is called the Masai "Ngàje Ngài," the House of God. Close to the western summit there is the dried and frozen carcass of a leopard. No one has explained what the leopard was seeking at that altitude.

"THE MARVELOUS thing is that it's painless," he said. "That's how you know when it starts."

"Is it really?"

"Absolutely. I'm awfully sorry about the odor though. That must bother you."

"Don't! Please don't."

"Look at them," he said. "Now is it sight or is it scent that brings them like that?"

The cot the man lay on was in the wide shade of a mimosa tree and as he looked out past the shade onto the glare of the plain there were three of the big birds squatted obscenely, while in the sky a dozen more sailed, making quick-moving shadows as they passed.

"They've been there since the day the truck broke down," he said. "Today's the first time any have lit on the ground. I watched the way they sailed very carefully at first in case I ever wanted to use them in a story. That's funny now."

"I wish you wouldn't," she said.

"I'm only talking," he said. "It's much easier if I talk. But I don't want to bother you."

"You know it doesn't bother me," she said. "It's that I've gotten so

435

very nervous not being able to do anything. I think we might make it as easy as we can until the plane comes."

"Or until the plane doesn't come."

"Please tell me what I can do. There must be something I can do."

"You can take the leg off and that might stop it, though I doubt it. Or you can shoot me. You're a good shot now. I taught you to shoot, didn't I?"

"Please don't talk that way. Couldn't I read to you?"

"Read what?"

"Anything in the book bag that we haven't read."

"I can't listen to it," he said. "Talking is the easiest. We quarrel and that makes the time pass."

"I don't quarrel. I never want to quarrel. Let's not quarrel any more. No matter how nervous we get. Maybe they will be back with another truck today. Maybe the plane will come."

"I don't want to move," the man said. "There is no sense in moving now except to make it easier for you."

"That's cowardly."

"Can't you let a man die as comfortably as he can without calling him names? What's the use of slanging me?"

"You're not going to die."

"Don't be silly. I'm dying now. Ask those bastards." He looked over to where the huge, filthy birds sat, their naked heads sunk in the hunched feathers. A fourth planed down, to run quick-legged and then waddle slowly toward the others.

"They are around every camp. You never notice them. You can't die if you don't give up."

"Where did you read that? You're such a bloody fool."

"You might think about some one else."

"For Christ's sake," he said, "that's been my trade."

He lay then and was quiet for a while and looked across the heat shimmer of the plain to the edge of the bush. There were a few Tommies that showed minute and white against the yellow and, far off, he saw a herd of zebra, white against the green of the bush. This was a pleasant camp under big trees against a hill, with good water, and close by, a nearly dry water hole where sand grouse flighted in the mornings.

"Wouldn't you like me to read?" she asked. She was sitting on a canvas chair beside his cot. "There's a breeze coming up."

"No thanks."

"Maybe the truck will come."

"I don't give a damn about the truck."

"I do."

"You give a damn about so many things that I don't."

"Not so many, Harry."

"What about a drink?"

"It's supposed to be bad for you. It said in Black's to avoid all alcohol. You shouldn't drink."

"Molo!" he shouted.

"Yes Bwana."

"Bring whiskey-soda."

"Yes Bwana."

"You shouldn't," she said. "That's what I mean by giving up. It says it's bad for you. I know it's bad for you."

"No," he said. "It's good for me."

So now it was all over, he thought. So now he would never have a chance to finish it. So this was the way it ended in a bickering over a drink. Since the gangrene started in his right leg he had no pain and with the pain the horror had gone and all he felt now was a great tiredness and anger that this was the end of it. For this, that now was coming, he had very little curiosity. For years it had obsessed him; but now it meant nothing in itself. It was strange how easy being tired enough made it.

Now he would never write the things that he had saved to write until he knew enough to write them well. Well, he would not have to fail at trying to write them either. Maybe you could never write them, and that was why you put them off and delayed the starting. Well he would never know, now.

"I wish we'd never come," the woman said. She was looking at him holding the glass and biting her lip. "You never would have gotten anything like this in Paris. You always said you loved Paris. We could have stayed in Paris or gone anywhere. I'd have gone anywhere. I said I'd go anywhere you wanted. If you wanted to shoot we could have gone shooting in Hungary and been comfortable."

"Your bloody money," he said.

"That's not fair," she said. "It was always yours as much as mine. I left everything and I went wherever you wanted to go and I've done what you wanted to do. But I wish we'd never come here."

"You said you loved it."

"I did when you were all right. But now I hate it. I don't see why that had to happen to your leg. What have we done to have that happen to us?"

"I suppose what I did was to forget to put iodine on it when I first scratched it. Then I didn't pay any attention to it because I never infect. Then, later, when it got bad, it was probably using that weak carbolic solution when the other antiseptics ran out that paralyzed the minute blood vessels and started the gangrene." He looked at her, "What else?"

"I don't mean that."

"If we would have hired a good mechanic instead of a half baked kikuyu driver, he would have checked the oil and never burned out that bearing in the truck."

"I don't mean that."

"If you hadn't left your own people, your goddamned Old Westbury, Saratoga, Palm Beach people to take me on——"

"Why, I loved you. That's not fair. I love you now. I'll always love you. Don't you love me?"

"No," said the man. "I don't think so. I never have."

"Harry, what are you saying? You're out of your head."

"No. I haven't any head to go out of."

"Don't drink that," she said. "Darling, please don't drink that. We have to do everything we can."

"You do it," he said. "I'm tired."

Now in his mind he saw a railway station at Karagatch and he was standing with his pack and that was the headlight of the Simplon-

Orient cutting the dark now and he was leaving Thrace then after the retreat. That was one of the things he had saved to write, with, in the morning at breakfast, looking out the window and seeing snow on the mountains in Bulgaria and Nansen's Secretary asking the old man if it were snow and the old man looking at it and saying, No, that's not snow. It's too early for snow. And the Secretary repeating to the other girls, No, you see. It's not snow and them all saying, It's not snow we were mistaken. But it was the snow all right and he sent them on into it when he evolved exchange of populations. And it was snow they tramped along in until they died that winter.

It was snow too that fell all Christmas week that year up in the Gauertal, that year they lived in the woodcutter's house with the big square porcelain stove that filled half the room, and they slept on mattresses filled with beech leaves, the time the deserter came with his feet bloody in the snow. He said the police were right behind him and they gave him woolen socks and held the gendarmes talking until the tracks had drifted over.

In Schrunz, on Christmas day, the snow was so bright it hurt your eyes when you looked out from the weinstube and saw every one coming home from church. That was where they walked up the sleigh-smoothed urine-yellowed road along the river with the steep pine hills, skis heavy on the shoulder, and where they ran that great run down the glacier above the Madlener-haus, the snow as smooth to see as cake frosting and as light as powder and he remembered the noiseless rush the speed made as you dropped down like a bird.

They were snow-bound a week in the Madlener-haus that time in the blizzard playing cards in the smoke by the lantern light and the stakes were higher all the time as Herr Lent lost more. Finally he lost it all. Everything, the skischule money and all the season's profit and then his capital. He could see him with his long nose, picking up the cards and then opening, "Sans Voir." There was always gambling then. When there was no snow you gambled and when there was too much you gambled. He thought of all the time in his life he had spent gambling.

But he had never written a line of that, nor of that cold, bright Christmas day with the mountains showing across the plain that

Barker had flown across the lines to bomb the Austrian officers' leave train, machine-gunning them as they scattered and ran. He remembered Barker afterwards coming into the mess and starting to tell about it. And how quiet it got and then somebody saying, "You bloody murderous bastard."

Those were the same Austrians they killed then that he skied with later. No not the same. Hans, that he skied with all that year, had been in the Kaiser-Jägers and when they went hunting hares together up the little valley above the saw-mill they had talked of the fighting on Pasubio and of the attack on Pertica and Asalone and he had never written a word of that. Nor of Monte Corno, nor the Siete Commum, nor of Arsiedo.

How many winters had he lived in the Voralberg and the Arlberg? It was four and then he remembered the man who had the fox to sell when they had walked into Bludenz, that time to buy presents, and the cherry-pit taste of good kirsch, the fast-slipping rush of running powder-snow on crust, singing "Hi! Ho! said Rolly!" as you ran down the last stretch to the steep drop, taking it straight, then running the orchard in three turns and out across the ditch and onto the icy road behind the inn. Knocking your bindings loose, kicking the skis free and leaning them up against the wooden wall of the inn, the lamplight coming from the window, where inside, in the smoky, new-wine smelling warmth, they were playing the accordion.

"Where did we stay in Paris?" he asked the woman who was sitting by him in a canvas chair, now, in Africa.

"At the Crillon. You know that."

"Why do I know that?"

"That's where we always stayed."

"No. Not always."

"There and at the Pavillion Henri-Quatre in St. Germain. You said you loved it there."

"Love is a dunghill," said Harry. "And I'm the cock that gets on it to crow."

"If you have to go away," she said, "is it absolutely necessary to kill off everything you leave behind? I mean do you have to take away everything? Do you have to kill your horse, and your wife and burn your saddle and your armour?"

"Yes," he said. "Your damned money was my armour. My Swift and my Armour."

"Don't."

"All right. I'll stop that. I don't want to hurt you."

"It's a little bit late now."

"All right then. I'll go on hurting you. It's more amusing. The only thing I ever really liked to do with you I can't do now."

"No, that's not true. You liked to do many things and everything you wanted to do I did."

"Oh, for Christ sake stop bragging, will you?"

He looked at her and saw her crying.

"Listen," he said. "Do you think that it is fun to do this? I don't know why I'm doing it. It's trying to kill to keep yourself alive, I imagine. I was all right when we started talking. I didn't mean to start this, and now I'm crazy as a coot and being as cruel to you as I can be. Don't pay any attention, darling, to what I say. I love you, really. You know I love you. I've never loved any one else the way I love you."

He slipped into the familiar lie he made his bread and butter by.

"You're sweet to me."

"You bitch," he said. "You rich bitch. That's poetry. I'm full of poetry now. Rot and poetry. Rotten poetry."

"Stop it. Harry, why do you have to turn into a devil now?"

"I don't like to leave anything," the man said. "I don't like to leave things behind."

It was evening now and he had been asleep. The sun was gone behind the hill and there was a shadow all across the plain and the small animals were feeding close to camp; quick dropping heads and switching tails, he watched them keeping well out away from the bush now. The birds no longer waited on the ground. They were all perched heavily in a tree. There were many more of them. His personal boy was sitting by the bed.

"Memsahib's gone to shoot," the boy said. "Does Bwana want?"

"Nothing."

She had gone to kill a piece of meat and, knowing how he liked to watch the game, she had gone well away so she would not disturb this little pocket of the plain that he could see. She was always thoughtful, he thought. On anything she knew about, or had read, or that she had ever heard.

It was not her fault that when he went to her he was already over. How could a woman know that you meant nothing that you said; that you spoke only from habit and to be comfortable? After he no longer meant what he said, his lies were more successful with women than when he had told them the truth.

It was not so much that he lied as that there was no truth to tell. He had had his life and it was over and then he went on living it again with different people and more money, with the best of the same places, and some new ones.

You kept from thinking and it was all marvellous. You were equipped with good insides so that you did not go to pieces that way, the way most of them had, and you made an attitude that you cared nothing for the work you used to do, now that you could no longer do it. But, in yourself, you said that you would write about these people; about the very rich; that you were really not of them but a spy in their country; that you would leave it and write of it and for once it would be written by some one who knew what he was writing of. But he would never do it, because each day of not writing, of comfort, of being that which he despised, dulled his ability and softened his will to work so that, finally, he did no work at all. The people he knew now were all much more comfortable when he did not work. Africa was where he had been happiest in the good time of his life, so he had come out here to start again. They had made this safari with the minimum of comfort. There was no hardship; but there was no luxury and he had thought that he could get back into training that way. That in some way he could work the fat off his soul the way a fighter went into the mountains to work and train in order to burn it out of his body.

She had liked it. She said she loved it. She loved anything that was exciting, that involved a change of scene, where there were new people and where things were pleasant. And he had felt the illusion of returning strength of will to work. Now if this was how it ended, and he knew it was, he must not turn like some snake biting itself because its back was broken. It wasn't this woman's fault. If it had not been she it would have been another. If he lived by a lie he should try to die by it. He heard a shot beyond the hill.

She shot very well this good, this rich bitch, this kindly caretaker and destroyer of his talent. Nonsense. He had destroyed his talent himself. Why should he blame this woman because she kept him well? He had destroyed his talent by not using it, by betrayals of himself and what he believed in, by drinking so much that he blunted the edge of his perceptions, by laziness, by sloth, and by snobbery, by pride and by prejudice, by hook and by crook. What was this? A catalogue of old books? What was his talent anyway? It was a talent all right but instead of using it, he had traded on it. It was never what he had done, but always what he could do. And he had chosen to make his living with something else instead of a pen or a pencil. It was strange, too, wasn't it, that when he fell in love with another woman, that woman should always have more money than the last one? But when he no longer was in love, when he was only lying, as to this woman, now, who had the most money of all, who had all the money there was, who had had a husband and children, who had taken lovers and been dissatisfied with them, and who loved him dearly as a writer, as a man, as a companion and as a proud possession; it was strange that when he did not love her at all and was lying, that he should be able to give her more for her money than when he had really loved.

We must all be cut out for what we do, he thought. However you make your living is where your talent lies. He had sold vitality, in one form or another, all his life and when your affections are not too involved you give much better value for the money. He had found that out but he would never write that, now, either. No, he would not write that, although it was well worth writing.

Now she came in sight, walking across the open toward the camp. She was wearing jodhpurs and carrying her rifle. The two boys had a Tommie slung and they were coming along behind her. She was still a good-looking woman, he thought, and she had a pleasant body. She had a great talent and appreciation for the bed, she was not pretty, but he liked her face, she read enormously, liked to ride and shoot and, certainly, she drank too much. Her husband had died when she was still a comparatively young woman and for a while she had devoted herself to her two just-grown children, who did not need her and were embarrassed at having her about, to her stable of horses, to books, and to bottles. She liked to read in the evening before dinner and she drank Scotch and soda while she read. By dinner she was fairly drunk and after a bottle of wine at dinner she was usually drunk enough to sleep.

That was before the lovers. After she had the lovers she did not drink so much because she did not have to be drunk to sleep. But the lovers bored her. She had been married to a man who had never bored her and these people bored her very much.

Then one of her two children was killed in a plane crash and after that was over she did not want the lovers, and drink being no anæsthetic she had to make another life. Suddenly, she had been acutely frightened of being alone. But she wanted some one that she respected with her.

It had begun very simply. She liked what he wrote and she had always envied the life he led. She thought he did exactly what he wanted to. The steps by which she had acquired him and the way in which she had finally fallen in love with him were all part of a regular progression in which she had built herself a new life and he had traded away what remained of his old life.

He had traded it for security, for comfort too, there was no denying that, and for what else? He did not know. She would have bought him anything he wanted. He knew that. She was a damned nice woman too. He would as soon be in bed with her as any one; rather with her, because she was richer, because she was very pleasant and appreciative and because she never made scenes. And now this life that she had built again was coming to a term because he had not used iodine two weeks ago when a thorn had scratched his knee as they moved forward trying to photograph a herd of waterbuck standing, their heads up, peering while their nostrils searched the air, their ears spread wide to hear the first noise that would send them rushing into the bush. They had bolted, too, before he got the picture.

Here she came now.

He turned his head on the cot to look toward her. "Hello," he said.

"I shot a Tommy ram," she told him. "He'll make you good broth and I'll have them mash some potatoes with the Klim. How do you feel?"

"Much better."

"Isn't that lovely? You know I thought perhaps you would. You were sleeping when I left."

"I had a good sleep. Did you walk far?"

"No. Just around behind the hill. I made quite a good shot on the Tommy."

"You shoot marvellously, you know."

"I love it. I've loved Africa. Really. If *you're* all right it's the most fun that I've ever had. You don't know the fun it's been to shoot with you. I've loved the country."

"I love it too."

"Darling, you don't know how marvellous it is to see you feeling better. I couldn't stand it when you felt that way. You won't talk to me like that again, will you? Promise me?"

"No," he said. "I don't remember what I said."

"You don't have to destroy me. Do you? I'm only a middle-aged woman who loves you and wants to do what you want to do. I've been destroyed two or three times already. You wouldn't want to destroy me again, would you?"

"I'd like to destroy you a few times in bed," he said.

"Yes. That's the good destruction. That's the way we're made to be destroyed. The plane will be here tomorrow."

"How do you know?"

"I'm sure. It's bound to come. The boys have the wood all ready and the grass to make the smudge. I went down and looked at it again today. There's plenty of room to land and we have the smudges ready at both ends."

"What makes you think it will come tomorrow?"

"I'm sure it will. It's overdue now. Then, in town, they will fix up

your leg and then we will have some good destruction. Not that
dreadful talking kind."

"Should we have a drink? The sun is down."

"Do you think you should?"

"I'm having one."

"We'll have one together. *Molo, letti dui whiskey-soda!*" she called.

"You'd better put on your mosquito boots," he told her.

"I'll wait till I bathe . . ."

While it grew dark they drank and just before it was dark and there
was no longer enough light to shoot, a hyena crossed the open on his
way around the hill.

"That bastard crosses there every night," the man said. "Every
night for two weeks."

"He's the one makes the noise at night. I don't mind it. They're
a filthy animal though."

Drinking together, with no pain now except the discomfort of
lying in one position, the boys lighting a fire, its shadow jumping on
the tents, he could feel the return of acquiescence in this life of pleasant
surrender. She *was* very good to him. He had been cruel and unjust
in the afternoon. She was a fine woman, marvellous really. And just
then it occurred to him that he was going to die.

It came with a rush; not as a rush of water nor of wind; but of a
sudden evil-smelling emptiness and the odd thing was that the hyena
slipped lightly along the edge of it.

"What is it, Harry?" she asked him.

"Nothing," he said. "You had better move over to the other side.
To windward."

"Did Molo change the dressing?"

"Yes. I'm just using the boric now."

"How do you feel?"

"A little wobbly."

"I'm going in to bathe," she said. "I'll be right out. I'll eat with
you and then we'll put the cot in."

So, he said to himself, we did well to stop the quarrelling. He had
never quarrelled much with this woman, while with the women that
he loved he had quarrelled so much they had finally, always, with

the corrosion of the quarrelling, killed what they had together. He had loved too much, demanded too much, and he wore it all out.

•

He thought about alone in Constantinople that time, having quarrelled in Paris before he had gone out. He had whored the whole time and then, when that was over, and he had failed to kill his loneliness, but only made it worse, he had written her, the first one, the one who left him, a letter telling her how he had never been able to kill it. . . . How when he thought he saw her outside the Regence one time it made him go all faint and sick inside, and that he would follow a woman who looked like her in some way, along the Boulevard, afraid to see it was not she, afraid to lose the feeling it gave him. How every one he had slept with had only made him miss her more. How what she had done could never matter since he knew he could not cure himself of loving her. He wrote this letter at the Club, cold sober, and mailed it to New York asking her to write him at the office in Paris. That seemed safe. And that night missing her so much it made him feel hollow sick inside, he wandered up past Taxim's, picked a girl up and took her out to supper. He had gone to a place to dance with her afterward, she danced badly, and left her for a hot Armenian slut, that swung her belly against him so it almost scalded. He took her away from a British gunner subaltern after a row. The gunner asked him outside and they fought in the street on the cobbles in the dark. He'd hit him twice, hard, on the side of the jaw and when he didn't go down he knew he was in for a fight. The gunner hit him in the body, then beside his eye. He swung with his left again and landed and the gunner fell on him and grabbed his coat and tore the sleeve off and he clubbed him twice behind the ear and then smashed him with his right as he pushed him away. When the gunner went down his head hit first and he ran with the girl because they heard the M. P.'s coming. They got into a taxi and drove out to Rimmily Hissa along the Bosphorus, and around, and back in the cool night and went to bed and she felt as over-ripe as she looked but smooth, rose-petal, syrupy, smooth-bellied, big-breasted and needed no pillow under her buttocks, and he left her before she was awake looking blousy enough in the first daylight and turned up at the Pera Palace with a black eye, carrying his coat because one sleeve was missing.

That same night he left for Anatolia and he remembered, later on that trip, riding all day through fields of the poppies that they raised for opium and how strange it made you feel, finally, and all the distances seemed wrong, to where they had made the attack with the newly arrived Constantine officers, that did not know a god-damned thing, and the artillery had fired into the troops and the British observer had cried like a child.

That was the day he'd first seen dead men wearing white ballet skirts and upturned shoes with pompons on them. The Turks had come steadily and lumpily and he had seen the skirted men running and the officers shooting into them and running then themselves and he and the British observer had run too until his lungs ached and his mouth was full of the taste of pennies and they stopped behind some rocks and there were the Turks coming as lumpily as ever. Later he had seen the things that he could never think of and later still he had seen much worse. So when he got back to Paris that time he could not talk about it or stand to have it mentioned. And there in the café as he passed was that American poet with a pile of saucers in front of him and a stupid look on his potato face talking about the Dada movement with a Roumanian who said his name was Tristan Tzara, who always wore a monocle and had a headache, and, back at the apartment with his wife that now he loved again, the quarrel all over, the madness all over, glad to be home, the office sent his mail up to the flat. So then the letter in answer to the one he'd written came in on a platter one morning and when he saw the handwriting he went cold all over and tried to slip the letter underneath another. But his wife said, "Who is that letter from, dear?" and that was the end of the beginning of that.

He remembered the good times with them all, and the quarrels. They always picked the finest places to have the quarrels. And why had they always quarrelled when he was feeling best? He had never written any of that because, at first, he never wanted to hurt any one and then it seemed as though there was enough to write without it. But he had always thought that he would write it finally. There was so much to write. He had seen the world change; not just the events;

although he had seen many of them and had watched the people, but
he had seen the subtler change and he could remember how the people
were at different times. He had been in it and he had watched it and
it was his duty to write of it; but now he never would.

"How do you feel?" she said. She had come out from the tent now
after her bath.

"All right."

"Could you eat now?" He saw Molo behind her with the folding
table and the other boy with the dishes.

"I want to write," he said.

"You ought to take some broth to keep your strength up."

"I'm going to die tonight," he said. "I don't need my strength up."

"Don't be melodramatic, Harry, please," she said.

"Why don't you use your nose? I'm rotted half way up my thigh
now. What the hell should I fool with broth for? Molo bring whiskey-
soda."

"Please take the broth," she said gently.

"All right."

The broth was too hot. He had to hold it in the cup until it cooled
enough to take it and then he just got it down without gagging.

"You're a fine woman," he said. "Don't pay any attention to me."

She looked at him with her well-known, well-loved face from
Spur and *Town and Country,* only a little the worse for drink, only
a little the worse for bed, but *Town and Country* never showed those
good breasts and those useful thighs and those lightly small-of-back-
caressing hands, and as he looked and saw her well known pleasant
smile, he felt death come again. This time there was no rush. It was
a puff, as of a wind that makes a candle flicker and the flame go tall.

"They can bring my net out later and hang it from the tree and
build the fire up. I'm not going in the tent tonight. It's not worth
moving. It's a clear night. There won't be any rain."

So this was how you died, in whispers that you did not hear. Well,
there would be no more quarrelling. He could promise that. The one
experience that he had never had he was not going to spoil now. He
probably would. You spoiled everything. But perhaps he wouldn't.

"You can't take dictation, can you?"

"I never learned," she told him.

"That's all right."

There wasn't time, of course, although it seemed as though it telescoped so that you might put it all into one paragraph if you could get it right.

There was a log house, chinked white with mortar, on a hill above the lake. There was a bell on a pole by the door to call the people in to meals. Behind the house were fields and behind the fields was the timber. A line of lombardy poplars ran from the house to the dock. Other poplars ran along the point. A road went up to the hills along the edge of the timber and along that road he picked blackberries. Then that log house was burned down and all the guns that had been on deer foot racks above the open fire place were burned and afterwards their barrels, with the lead melted in the magazines, and the stocks burned away, lay out on the heap of ashes that were used to make lye for the big iron soap kettles, and you asked Grandfather if you could have them to play with, and he said, no. You see they were his guns still and he never bought any others. Nor did he hunt any more. The house was rebuilt in the same place out of lumber now and painted white and from its porch you saw the poplars and the lake beyond; but there were never any more guns. The barrels of the guns that had hung on the deer feet on the wall of the log house lay out there on the heap of ashes and no one ever touched them.

In the Black Forest, after the war, we rented a trout stream and there were two ways to walk to it. One was down the valley from Triberg and around the valley road in the shade of the trees that bordered the white road, and then up a side road that went up through the hills past many small farms, with the big Schwarzwald houses, until that road crossed the stream. That was where our fishing began.

The other way was to climb steeply up to the edge of the woods and then go across the top of the hills through the pine woods, and then out to the edge of a meadow and down across this meadow to the bridge. There were birches along the stream and it was not big, but narrow, clear and fast, with pools where it had cut under the roots of the birches. At the Hotel in Triberg the proprietor had a fine season. It was very pleasant and we were all great friends. The next year came the inflation and the money he had made the year before was not enough to buy supplies to open the hotel and he hanged himself.

You could dictate that, but you could not dictate the Place Contrescarpe where the flower sellers dyed their flowers in the street and the dye ran over the paving where the autobus started and the old men and the women, always drunk on wine and bad marc; and the children with their noses running in the cold; the smell of dirty sweat and poverty and drunkenness at the Café des Amateurs and the whores at the Bal Musette they lived above. The Concièrge who entertained the trooper of the Garde Républicaine in her loge, his horse-hair-plumed helmet on a chair. The locataire across the hall whose husband was a bicycle racer and her joy that morning at the Crémerie when she had opened L'Auto and seen where he placed third in Paris-Tours, his first big race. She had blushed and laughed and then gone upstairs crying with the yellow sporting paper in her hand. The husband of the woman who ran the Bal Musette drove a taxi and when he, Harry, had to take an early plane the husband knocked upon the door to wake him and they each drank a glass of white wine at the zinc of the bar before they started. He knew his neighbors in that quarter then because they all were poor.

Around that Place there were two kinds: the drunkards and the sportifs. The drunkards killed their poverty that way; the sportifs took it out in exercise. They were the descendants of the Communards and it was no struggle for them to know their politics. They knew who had shot their fathers, their relatives, their brothers, and their friends when the Versailles troops came in and took the town after the Commune and executed any one they could catch with calloused hands, or who wore a cap, or carried any other sign he was a working man. And in that poverty, and in that quarter across the street from a Boucherie Chevaline and a wine co-operative he had written the start of all he was to do. There never was another part of Paris that he loved like that, the sprawling trees, the old white plastered houses painted brown below, the long green of the autobus in that round square, the purple flower dye upon the paving, the sudden drop down the hill of the rue Cardinal Lemoine to the River, and the other way the narrow crowded world of the rue Mouffetard. The street that ran up toward the Panthéon and the other that he always took with the bicycle, the only asphalted street in all that quarter, smooth under the tires, with the high narrow houses and the cheap tall hotel where Paul Verlaine had died. There were only two rooms in the apartments where they lived and he had a room on the top floor of that hotel that cost him sixty francs a month where he did his writing, and from it he could see the roofs and chimney pots and all the hills of Paris.

From the apartment you could only see the wood and coal man's place. He sold wine too, bad wine. The golden horse's head outside the Boucherie Chevaline where the carcasses hung yellow gold and red in the open window, and the green painted co-operative where they bought their wine; good wine and cheap. The rest was plaster walls and the windows of the neighbors. The neighbors who, at night, when some one lay drunk in the street, moaning and groaning in that typical French ivresse that you were propaganded to believe did not exist, would open their windows and then the murmur of talk.

"Where is the policeman? When you don't want him the bugger is always there. He's sleeping with some concièrge. Get the Agent." Till some one threw a bucket of water from a window and the moaning stopped. "What's that? Water. Ah, that's intelligent." And the windows shutting. Marie, his femme de ménage, protesting against the eight-hour day saying, "If a husband works until six he gets only a little drunk on the way home and does not waste too much. If he works only until five he is drunk every night and one has no money. It is the wife of the working man who suffers from this shortening of hours."

"Wouldn't you like some more broth?" the woman asked him now.

"No, thank you very much. It is awfully good."

"Try just a little."

"I would like a whiskey-soda."

"It's not good for you."

"No. It's bad for me. Cole Porter wrote the words and the music. This knowledge that you're going mad for me."

"You know I like you to drink."

"Oh yes. Only it's bad for me."

When she goes, he thought, I'll have all I want. Not all I want but all there is. Ayee he was tired. Too tired. He was going to sleep a little while. He lay still and death was not there. It must have gone around another street. It went in pairs, on bicycles, and moved absolutely silently on the pavements.

No, he had never written about Paris. Not the Paris that he cared about. But what about the rest that he had never written?

What about the ranch and the silvered gray of the sage brush, the quick, clear water in the irrigation ditches, and the heavy green of the alfalfa. The trail went up into the hills and the cattle in the summer were shy as deer. The bawling and the steady noise and slow moving mass raising a dust as you brought them down in the fall. And behind the mountains, the clear sharpness of the peak in the evening light and, riding down along the trail in the moonlight, bright across the valley. Now he remembered coming down through the timber in the dark holding the horse's tail when you could not see and all the stories that he meant to write.

About the half-wit chore boy who was left at the ranch that time and told not to let any one get any hay, and that old bastard from the Forks who had beaten the boy when he had worked for him stopping to get some feed. The boy refusing and the old man saying he would beat him again. The boy got the rifle from the kitchen and shot him when he tried to come into the barn and when they came back to the ranch he'd been dead a week, frozen in the corral, and the dogs had eaten part of him. But what was left you packed on a sled wrapped in a blanket and roped on and you got the boy to help you haul it, and the two of you took it out over the road on skis, and sixty miles down to town to turn the boy over. He having no idea that he would be arrested. Thinking he had done his duty and that you were his friend and he would be rewarded. He'd helped to haul

*the old man in so everybody could know how bad the old man had
been and how he'd tried to steal some feed that didn't belong to him,
and when the sheriff put the handcuffs on the boy he couldn't believe
it. Then he'd started to cry. That was one story he had saved to
write. He knew at least twenty good stories from out there and he
had never written one. Why?*

"You tell them why," he said.

"Why what, dear?"

"Why nothing."

She didn't drink so much, now, since she had him. But if he lived
he would never write about her, he knew that now, Nor about any
of them. The rich were dull and they drank too much, or they played
too much backgammon. They were dull and they were repetitious. He
remembered poor Julian and his romantic awe of them and how he
had started a story once that began, "The very rich are different from
you and me." And how some one had said to Julian, Yes, they have
more money. But that was not humorous to Julian. He thought they
were a special glamorous race and when he found they weren't it
wrecked him just as much as any other thing that wrecked him.

He had been contemptuous of those who wrecked. You did not have
to like it because you understood it. He could beat anything, he
thought, because no thing could hurt him if he did not care.

All right. Now he would not care for death. One thing he had
always dreaded was the pain. He could stand pain as well as any
man, until it went on too long, and wore him out, but here he had
something that had hurt frightfully and just when he had felt it breaking him, the pain had stopped.

*He remembered long ago when Williamson, the bombing officer,
had been hit by a stick bomb some one in a German patrol had
thrown as he was coming in through the wire that night and, screaming, had begged every one to kill him. He was a fat man, very brave,
and a good officer, although addicted to fantastic shows. But that
night he was caught in the wire, with a flare lighting him up and his
bowels spilled out into the wire, so when they brought him in, alive,*

they had to cut him loose. Shoot me, Harry. For Christ sake shoot me.
They had had an argument one time about our Lord never sending
you anything you could not bear and some one's theory had been that
meant that at a certain time the pain passed you out automatically.
But he had always remembered Williamson, that night. Nothing
passed out Williamson until he gave him all his morphine tablets that
he had always saved to use himself and then they did not work right
away.

Still this now, that he had, was very easy; and if it was no worse
as it went on there was nothing to worry about. Except that he would
rather be in better company.

He thought a little about the company that he would like to have.

No, he thought, when everything you do, you do too long, and do
too late, you can't expect to find the people still there. The people
all are gone. The party's over and you are with your hostess now.

I'm getting as bored with dying as with everything else, he thought.

"It's a bore," he said out loud.

"What is, my dear?"

"Anything you do too bloody long."

He looked at her face between him and the fire. She was leaning
back in the chair and the firelight shone on her pleasantly lined face
and he could see that she was sleepy. He heard the hyena make a
noise just outside the range of the fire.

"I've been writing," he said. "But I got tired."

"Do you think you will be able to sleep?"

"Pretty sure. Why don't you turn in?"

"I like to sit here with you."

"Do you feel anything strange?" he asked her.

"No. Just a little sleepy."

"I do," he said.

He had just felt death come by again.

"You know the only thing I've never lost is curiosity," he said to her.

"You've never lost anything. You're the most complete man I've
ever known."

"Christ," he said. "How little a woman knows. What is that? Your intuition?"

Because, just then, death had come and rested its head on the foot of the cot and he could smell its breath.

"Never believe any of that about a scythe and a skull," he told her. "It can be two bicycle policemen as easily, or be a bird. Or it can have a wide snout like a hyena."

It had moved up on him now, but it had no shape any more. It simply occupied space.

"Tell it to go away."

It did not go away but moved a little closer.

"You've got a hell of a breath," he told it. "You stinking bastard."

It moved up closer to him still and now he could not speak to it, and when it saw he could not speak it came a little closer, and now he tried to send it away without speaking, but it moved in on him so its weight was all upon his chest, and while it crouched there and he could not move, or speak, he heard the woman say, "Bwana is asleep now. Take the cot up very gently and carry it into the tent."

He could not speak to tell her to make it go away and it crouched now, heavier, so he could not breathe. And then, while they lifted the cot, suddenly it was all right and the weight went from his chest.

It was morning and had been morning for some time and he heard the plane. It showed very tiny and then made a wide circle and the boys ran out and lit the fires, using kerosene, and piled on grass so there were two big smudges at each end of the level place and the morning breeze blew them toward the camp and the plane circled twice more, low this time, and then glided down and levelled off and landed smoothly and, coming walking toward him, was old Compton in slacks, a tweed jacket and a brown felt hat.

"What's the matter, old cock?" Compton said.

"Bad leg," he told him. "Will you have some breakfast?"

"Thanks. I'll just have some tea. It's the Puss Moth you know. I won't be able to take the Memsahib. There's only room for one. Your lorry is on the way."

Helen had taken Compton aside and was speaking to him. Compton came back more cheery than ever.

"We'll get you right in," he said. "I'll be back for the Mem. Now I'm afraid I'll have to stop at Arusha to refuel. We'd better get going."

"What about the tea?"

"I don't really care about it you know."

The boys had picked up the cot and carried it around the green tents and down along the rock and out onto the plain and along past the smudges that were burning brightly now, the grass all consumed, and the wind fanning the fire, to the little plane. It was difficult getting him in, but once in he lay back in the leather seat, and the leg was stuck straight out to one side of the seat, where Compton sat. Compton started the motor and got in. He waved to Helen and to the boys and, as the clatter moved into the old familiar roar, they swung around with Compie watching for wart-hog holes and roared, bumping, along the stretch between the fires and with the last bump rose and he saw them all standing below, waving, and the camp beside the hill, flattening now, and the plain spreading, clumps of trees, and the bush flattening, while the game trails ran now smoothly to the dry waterholes, and there was a new water that he had never known of. The zebra, small rounded backs now, and the wildebeeste, big-headed dots seeming to climb as they moved in long fingers across the plain, now scattering as the shadow came toward them, they were tiny now, and the movement had no gallop, and the plain was as far as you could see, gray-yellow now and ahead old Compie's tweed back and the brown felt hat. Then they were over the first hills and the wildebeeste were trailing up them, and then they were over mountains with sudden depths of green-rising forest and the solid bamboo slopes, and then the heavy forest again, sculptured into peaks and hollows until they crossed, and hills sloped down and then another plain, hot now, and purple brown, bumpy with heat and Compie looking back to see how he was riding. Then there were other mountains dark ahead.

And then instead of going on to Arusha they turned left, he evidently figured that they had the gas, and looking down he saw a pink sifting cloud, moving over the ground, and in the air, like the first snow in a blizzard, that comes from nowhere, and he knew the locusts were coming up from the South. Then they began to climb and they were going to the East it seemed, and then it darkened and they were in a storm, the rain so thick it seemed like flying through a waterfall, and then they were out and Compie turned his head and grinned and pointed and there, ahead, all he could see, as wide as all the world, great, high, and unbelievably white in the sun, was the square top of Kilimanjaro. And then he knew that there was where he was going.

Just then the hyena stopped whimpering in the night and started to make a strange, human, almost crying sound. The woman heard it and stirred uneasily. She did not wake. In her dream she was at the house on Long Island and it was the night before her daughter's début. Somehow her father was there and he had been very rude. Then the noise the hyena made was so loud she woke and for a moment she did not know where she was and she was very afraid. Then she took the flashlight and shone it on the other cot that they had carried in after Harry had gone to sleep. She could see his bulk under the mosquito bar but somehow he had gotten his leg out and it hung down alongside the cot. The dressings had all come down and she could not look at it.

"Molo," she called, "Molo! Molo!"

Then she said, "Harry, Harry!" Then her voice rising, "Harry! Please, Oh Harry!"

There was no answer and she could not hear him breathing.

Outside the tent the hyena made the same strange noise that had awakened her. But she did not hear him for the beating of her heart.

JOHN STEINBECK

I can't understand why some reviewers persist in classing John Stein-
beck as a hard-boiled writer. I guess it must be because he uses direct
English and because so many of his characters are socially submerged
—as if itinerant workers and tramps were necessarily more hard-
boiled than other people. Actually, if resistance to emotion is the
true mark of the hard-boiled writer, Steinbeck is soft-boiled, and no
bad thing either. Far from being tough, he is exceptionally sensitive,
not merely to the cruder, or what one might call large-muscle, emo-
tions but to those subtleties of feeling that are the stock in trade of
writers like Chekhov, D. H. Lawrence, and Katherine Mansfield.

I know of no better proof of this than "The Red Pony," a heart-
breakingly true picture of boyhood. The Grapes of Wrath excepted,
it is the finest writing Steinbeck has so far done. To my mind it is far
superior to the overpublicized Of Mice and Men, which is one of
those stories that hit you in the solar plexus the first time you read
it and makes mighty little impression the second time. Of Mice
and Men betrays Steinbeck's one major fault—a weakness for theatri-
cal contrivance. You will find the weakness again in that tawdry end-
ing of The Grapes of Wrath, when the young girl, who has only a
day or two before given birth to a dead child, offers the milk of her
breasts to a starving man.

But in "The Red Pony" there is no hint of contrivance. All is
warm, intimate, unworked over. The story tells itself; the emotion
comes through as if there were no art medium between you and the
mind of little Jody. It says a great deal, this tale, about life and death
—about forgotten elementals, such as the old paisano's dignified
assumption that he has a right to die in the place where he was
born, about the relationship that may exist between a human being
and a loved animal, about fathers and sons, about small boys and
what's in their heads and their capacity for joy and for suffering. It

says all this very quietly and indirectly, and it says it in a way that stays with you.

The two brief excerpts from The Grapes of Wrath—"Dust" and "The Turtle"—will be familiar to all readers of the book. They are the contemporary equivalent, lean, intense, of the old-fashioned "purple patch."

The Red Pony

BY

JOHN STEINBECK

I. THE GIFT

At DAYBREAK Billy Buck emerged from the bunkhouse and stood for a moment on the porch looking up at the sky. He was a broad, bandy-legged little man with a walrus mustache, with square hands, puffed and muscled on the palms. His eyes were a contemplative, watery grey and the hair which protruded from under his Stetson hat was spiky and weathered. Billy was still stuffing his shirt into his blue jeans as he stood on the porch. He unbuckled his belt and tightened it again. The belt showed, by the worn shiny places opposite each hole, the gradual increase of Billy's middle over a period of years. When he had seen to the weather, Billy cleared each nostril by holding its mate closed with his forefinger and blowing fiercely. Then he walked down to the barn, rubbing his hands together. He curried and brushed two saddle horses in the stalls, talking quietly to them all the time; and he had hardly finished when the iron triangle started ringing at the ranch house. Billy stuck the brush and currycomb together and laid them on the rail, and went up to breakfast. His action had been so deliberate and yet so wasteless of time that he came to the house while Mrs. Tiflin was still ringing the triangle. She nodded her grey head to him and withdrew into the kitchen. Billy Buck sat down on the steps, because he was a cow-hand, and it wouldn't be fitting that he should go first into the dining-room. He heard Mr. Tiflin in the house, stamping his feet into his boots.

The high jangling note of the triangle put the boy Jody in motion. He was only a little boy, ten years old, with hair like dusty yellow grass and with shy polite grey eyes, and with a mouth that worked when he thought. The triangle picked him up out of sleep. It didn't occur to him to disobey the harsh note. He never had: no one he knew ever had. He brushed the tangled hair out of his eyes and skinned his nightgown off. In a moment he was dressed—blue chambray shirt and overalls. It was late in the summer, so of course there were no shoes to bother with. In the kitchen he waited until his mother got from in front of the sink and went back to the stove. Then he washed himself and brushed back his wet hair with his fingers. His mother turned sharply on him as he left the sink. Jody looked shyly away.

"I've got to cut your hair before long," his mother said. "Breakfast's on the table. Go on in, so Billy can come."

Jody sat at the long table which was covered with white oilcloth washed through to the fabric in some places. The fried eggs lay in rows on their platter. Jody took three eggs on his plate and followed with three thick slices of crisp bacon. He carefully scraped a spot of blood from one of the egg yolks.

Billy Buck clumped in. "That won't hurt you," Billy explained. "That's only a sign the rooster leaves."

Jody's tall stern father came in then and Jody knew from the noise on the floor that he was wearing boots, but he looked under the table anyway, to make sure. His father turned off the oil lamp over the table, for plenty of morning light now came through the windows.

Jody did not ask where his father and Billy Buck were riding that day, but he wished he might go along. His father was a disciplinarian. Jody obeyed him in everything without questions of any kind. Now, Carl Tiflin sat down and reached for the egg platter.

"Got the cows ready to go, Billy?" he asked.

"In the lower corral," Billy said. "I could just as well take them in alone."

"Sure you could. But a man needs company. Besides your throat gets pretty dry." Carl Tiflin was jovial this morning.

Jody's mother put her head in the door. "What time do you think to be back, Carl?"

"I can't tell. I've got to see some men in Salinas. Might be gone till dark."

The eggs and coffee and big biscuits disappeared rapidly. Jody followed the two men out of the house. He watched them mount their horses and drive six old milk cows out of the corral and start over the hill toward Salinas. They were going to sell the old cows to the butcher.

When they had disappeared over the crown of the ridge Jody walked up the hill in back of the house. The dogs trotted around the house corner hunching their shoulders and grinning horribly with pleasure. Jody patted their heads—Doubletree Mutt with the big thick tail and yellow eyes, and Smasher, the shepherd, who had killed a coyote and lost an ear in doing it. Smasher's one good ear stood up higher than a collie's ear should. Billy Buck said that always happened. After the frenzied greeting the dogs lowered their noses to the ground in a business-like way and went ahead, looking back now and then to make sure that the boy was coming. They walked up through the chicken yard and saw the quail eating with the chickens. Smasher chased the chickens a little to keep in practice in case there should ever be sheep to herd. Jody continued on through the large vegetable patch where the green corn was higher than his head. The cow-pumpkins were green and small yet. He went on to the sagebrush line where the cold spring ran out of its pipe and fell into a round wooden tub. He leaned over and drank close to the green mossy wood where the water tasted best. Then he turned and looked back on the ranch, on the low, white-washed house girded with red geraniums, and on the long bunkhouse by the cypress tree where Billy Buck lived alone. Jody could see the great black kettle under the cypress tree. That was where the pigs were scalded. The sun was coming over the ridge now, glaring on the white-wash of the houses and barns, making the wet grass blaze softly. Behind him, in the tall sagebrush, the birds were scampering on the ground, making a great noise among the dry leaves; the squirrels piped shrilly on the side-hills. Jody looked along at the farm buildings. He felt an uncertainty in the air, a feeling of change and of loss and of the gain of new and unfamiliar things. Over the hillside two big black buzzards sailed low to the ground and their shadows slipped smoothly and quickly ahead of them. Some animal had died in the vicinity. Jody knew it. It might be a cow or it might be the remains of a rabbit. The buzzards overlooked nothing. Jody hated them as all decent things hate them, but they could not be hurt because they made away with carrion.

After a while the boy sauntered down hill again. The dogs had long ago given him up and gone into the brush to do things in their own way. Back through the vegetable garden he went, and he paused for a moment to smash a green muskmelon with his heel, but he was not happy about it. It was a bad thing to do, he knew perfectly well. He kicked dirt over the ruined melon to conceal it.

Back at the house his mother bent over his rough hands, inspecting his fingers and nails. It did little good to start him clean to school for too many things could happen on the way. She sighed over the black cracks in his fingers, and then gave him his books and his lunch and started him on the mile walk to school. She noticed that his mouth was working a good deal this morning.

Jody started his journey. He filled his pockets with little pieces of white quartz that lay in the road, and every so often he took a shot at a bird or at some rabbit that had stayed sunning itself in the road too long. At the crossroads over the bridge he met two friends and the three of them walked to school together, making ridiculous strides and being rather silly. School had just opened two weeks before. There was still a spirit of revolt among the pupils.

It was four o'clock in the afternoon when Jody topped the hill and looked down on the ranch again. He looked for the saddle horses, but the corral was empty. His father was not back yet. He went slowly, then, toward the afternoon chores. At the ranch house, he found his mother sitting on the porch, mending socks.

"There's two doughnuts in the kitchen for you," she said. Jody slid to the kitchen, and returned with half of one of the doughnuts already eaten and his mouth full. His mother asked him what he had learned in school that day, but she didn't listen to his doughnut-muffled answer. She interrupted, "Jody, tonight see you fill the wood-box clear full. Last night you crossed the sticks and it wasn't only about half full. Lay the sticks flat tonight. And Jody, some of the hens are hiding eggs, or else the dogs are eating them. Look about in the grass and see if you can find any nests."

Jody, still eating, went out and did his chores. He saw the quail
come down to eat with the chickens when he threw out the grain. For
some reason his father was proud to have them come. He never allowed any shooting near the house for fear the quail might go away.

When the wood-box was full, Jody took his twenty-two rifle up to
the cold spring at the brush line. He drank again and then aimed the
gun at all manner of things, at rocks, at birds on the wing, at the big
black pig kettle under the cypress tree, but he didn't shoot for he had
no cartridges and wouldn't have until he was twelve. If his father had
seen him aim the rifle in the direction of the house he would have put
the cartridges off another year. Jody remembered this and did not
point the rifle down the hill again. Two years was enough to wait for
cartridges. Nearly all of his father's presents were given with reservations which hampered their value somewhat. It was good discipline.

The supper waited until dark for his father to return. When at last
he came in with Billy Buck, Jody could smell the delicious brandy on
their breaths. Inwardly he rejoiced, for his father sometimes talked to
him when he smelled of brandy, sometimes even told things he had
done in the wild days when he was a boy.

After supper, Jody sat by the fireplace and his shy polite eyes sought
the room corners, and he waited for his father to tell what it was he
contained, for Jody knew he had news of some sort. But he was disappointed. His father pointed a stern finger at him.

"You'd better go to bed, Jody. I'm going to need you in the morning."

That wasn't so bad. Jody liked to do the things he had to do as long
as they weren't routine things. He looked at the floor and his mouth
worked out a question before he spoke it. "What are we going to do
in the morning, kill a pig?" he asked softly.

"Never you mind. You better get to bed."

When the door was closed behind him, Jody heard his father and
Billy Buck chuckling and he knew it was a joke of some kind. And
later, when he lay in bed, trying to make words out of the murmurs in the other room, he heard his father protest, "But, Ruth, I
didn't give much for him."

Jody heard the hoot-owls hunting mice down by the barn, and he

heard a fruit tree limb tap-tapping against the house. A cow was lowing when he went to sleep.

When the triangle sounded in the morning, Jody dressed more
quickly even than usual. In the kitchen, while he washed his face and
combed back his hair, his mother addressed him irritably. "Don't you
go out until you get a good breakfast in you."

He went into the dining-room and sat at the long white table. He
took a steaming hotcake from the platter, arranged two fried eggs on
it, covered them with another hotcake and squashed the whole thing
with his fork.

His father and Billy Buck came in. Jody knew from the sound on
the floor that both of them were wearing flat-heeled shoes, but he
peered under the table to make sure. His father turned off the oil lamp,
for the day had arrived, and he looked stern and disciplinary, but Billy
Buck didn't look at Jody at all. He avoided the shy questioning eyes
of the boy and soaked a whole piece of toast in his coffee.

Carl Tiflin said crossly, "You come with us after breakfast!"

Jody had trouble with his food then, for he felt a kind of doom in
the air. After Billy had tilted his saucer and drained the coffee which
had slopped into it, and had wiped his hands on his jeans, the two men
stood up from the table and went out into the morning light together,
and Jody respectfully followed a little behind them. He tried to keep
his mind from running ahead, tried to keep it absolutely motionless.

His mother called, "Carl! Don't you let it keep him from school."

They marched past the cypress, where a singletree hung from a limb
to butcher the pigs on, and past the black iron kettle, so it was not a
pig killing. The sun shone over the hill and threw long, dark shadows
of the trees and buildings. They crossed a stubble-field to shortcut to
the barn. Jody's father unhooked the door and they went in. They had
been walking toward the sun on the way down. The barn was black as
night in contrast and warm from the hay and from the beasts. Jody's
father moved over toward the one box stall. "Come here!" he ordered.
Jody could begin to see things now. He looked into the box stall and
then stepped back quickly.

A red pony colt was looking at him out of the stall. Its tense ears were forward and a light of disobedience was in its eyes. Its coat was rough and thick as an airedale's fur and its mane was long and tangled. Jody's throat collapsed in on itself and cut his breath short.

"He needs a good currying," his father said, "and if I ever hear of you not feeding him or leaving his stall dirty, I'll sell him off in a minute."

Jody couldn't bear to look at the pony's eyes any more. He gazed down at his hands for a moment, and he asked very shyly, "Mine?" No one answered him. He put his hand out toward the pony. Its grey nose came close, sniffing loudly, and then the lips drew back and the strong teeth closed on Jody's fingers. The pony shook its head up and down and seemed to laugh with amusement. Jody regarded his bruised fingers. "Well," he said with pride—"Well, I guess he can bite all right." The two men laughed, somewhat in relief. Carl Tiflin went out of the barn and walked up a side-hill to be by himself, for he was embarrassed, but Billy Buck stayed. It was easier to talk to Billy Buck. Jody asked again—"Mine?"

Billy became professional in tone. "Sure! That is, if you look out for him and break him right. I'll show you how. He's just a colt. You can't ride him for some time."

Jody put out his bruised hand again, and this time the red pony let his nose be rubbed. "I ought to have a carrot," Jody said. "Where'd we get him, Billy?"

"Bought him at a sheriff's auction," Billy explained. "A show went broke in Salinas and had debts. The sheriff was selling off their stuff."

The pony stretched out his nose and shook the forelock from his wild eyes. Jody stroked the nose a little. He said softly, "There isn't a —saddle?"

Billy Buck laughed. "I'd forgot. Come along."

In the harness room he lifted down a little saddle of red morocco leather. "It's just a show saddle," Billy Buck said disparagingly. "It isn't practical for the brush, but it was cheap at the sale."

Jody couldn't trust himself to look at the saddle either, and he couldn't speak at all. He brushed the shining red leather with his fingertips, and after a long time he said, "It'll look pretty on him though." He thought of the grandest and prettiest things he knew. "If he hasn't a name already, I think I'll call him Gabilan Mountains," he said.

Billy Buck knew how he felt. "It's a pretty long name. Why don't you just call him Gabilan? That means hawk. That would be a fine name for him." Billy felt glad. "If you will collect tail hair, I might be able to make a hair rope for you sometime. You could use it for a hackamore."

Jody wanted to go back to the box stall. "Could I lead him to school, do you think—to show the kids?"

But Billy shook his head. "He's not even halter-broke yet. We had a time getting him here. Had to almost drag him. You better be starting for school though."

"I'll bring the kids to see him here this afternoon," Jody said.

Six boys came over the hill half an hour early that afternoon, running hard, their heads down, their forearms working, their breath whistling. They swept by the house and cut across the stubble-field to the barn. And then they stood self-consciously before the pony, and then they looked at Jody with eyes in which there was a new admiration and a new respect. Before today Jody had been a boy, dressed in overalls and a blue shirt—quieter than most, even suspected of being a little cowardly. And now he was different. Out of a thousand centuries they drew the ancient admiration of the footman for the horseman. They knew instinctively that a man on a horse is spiritually as well as physically bigger than a man on foot. They knew that Jody had been miraculously lifted out of equality with them, and had been placed over them. Gabilan put his head out of the stall and sniffed them.

"Why'n't you ride him?" the boys cried. "Why'n't you braid his tail with ribbons like in the fair?" "When you going to ride him?"

Jody's courage was up. He too felt the superiority of the horseman. "He's not old enough. Nobody can ride him for a long time. I'm going to train him on the long halter. Billy Buck is going to show me how."

"Well, can't we even lead him around a little?"

"He isn't even halter-broke," Jody said. He wanted to be completely alone when he took the pony out the first time. "Come and see the saddle."

They were speechless at the red morocco saddle, completely shocked out of comment. "It isn't much use in the brush," Jody explained. "It'll look pretty on him though. Maybe I'll ride bareback when I go into the brush."

"How you going to rope a cow without a saddle horn?"

"Maybe I'll get another saddle for every day. My father might want me to help him with the stock." He let them feel the red saddle, and showed them the brass chain throat-latch on the bridle and the big brass buttons at each temple where the headstall and brow band crossed. The whole thing was too wonderful. They had to go away after a little while, and each boy, in his mind, searched among his possessions for a bribe worthy of offering in return for a ride on the red pony when the time should come.

Jody was glad when they had gone. He took brush and currycomb from the wall, took down the barrier of the box stall and stepped cautiously in. The pony's eyes glittered, and he edged around into kicking position. But Jody touched him on the shoulder and rubbed his high arched neck as he had always seen Billy Buck do, and he crooned, "So-o-o Boy," in a deep voice. The pony gradually relaxed his tenseness. Jody curried and brushed until a pile of dead hair lay in the stall and until the pony's coat had taken on a deep red shine. Each time he finished he thought it might have been done better. He braided the mane into a dozen little pigtails, and he braided the forelock, and then he undid them and brushed the hair out straight again.

Jody did not hear his mother enter the barn. She was angry when she came, but when she looked in at the pony and at Jody working over him, she felt a curious pride rise up in her. "Have you forgot the wood-box?" she asked gently. "It's not far off from dark and there's not a stick of wood in the house, and the chickens aren't fed."

Jody quickly put up his tools. "I forgot, ma'am."

"Well, after this do your chores first. Then you won't forget. I expect you'll forget lots of things now if I don't keep an eye on you."

"Can I have carrots from the garden for him, ma'am?"

She had to think about that. "Oh—I guess so, if you only take the big tough ones."

"Carrots keep the coat good," he said, and again she felt the curious rush of pride.

Jody never waited for the triangle to get him out of bed after the coming of the pony. It became his habit to creep out of bed even before his mother was awake, to slip into his clothes and to go quietly down to the barn to see Gabilan. In the grey quiet mornings when the land and the brush and the houses and the trees were silver-grey and black like a photograph negative, he stole toward the barn, past the sleeping stones and the sleeping cypress tree. The turkeys, roosting in the tree out of coyotes' reach, clicked drowsily. The fields glowed with a grey frost-like light and in the dew the tracks of rabbits and of field mice stood out sharply. The good dogs came stiffly out of their little houses, hackles up and deep growls in their throats. Then they caught Jody's scent, and their stiff tails rose up and waved a greeting—Double-tree Mutt with the big thick tail, and Smasher, the incipient shepherd —then went lazily back to their warm beds.

It was a strange time and a mysterious journey, to Jody—an extension of a dream. When he first had the pony he liked to torture himself during the trip by thinking Gabilan would not be in his stall, and worse, would never have been there. And he had other delicious little self-induced pains. He thought how the rats had gnawed ragged holes in the red saddle, and how the mice had nibbled Gabilan's tail until it was stringy and thin. He usually ran the last little way to the barn. He unlatched the rusty hasp of the barn door and stepped in, and no matter how quietly he opened the door, Gabilan was always looking at him over the barrier of the box stall and Gabilan whinnied softly and stamped his front foot, and his eyes had big sparks of red fire in them like oakwood embers.

Sometimes, if the work horses were to be used that day, Jody found Billy Buck in the barn harnessing and currying. Billy stood with him and looked long at Gabilan and he told Jody a great many things about horses. He explained that they were terribly afraid for their feet, so that one must make a practice of lifting the legs, and patting the hooves and ankles to remove their terror. He told Jody how horses love conversation. He must talk to the pony all the time, and tell him the reasons for everything. Billy wasn't sure a horse could understand everything that was said to him, but it was impossible to say how much was understood. A horse never kicked up a fuss if some one he liked explained things to him. Billy could give examples, too. He had known, for instance, a horse nearly dead beat with fatigue to perk up when told it was only a little farther to his destination. And he had known a horse paralyzed with fright to come out of it when his rider told him what it was that was frightening him. While he talked in the mornings, Billy Buck cut twenty or thirty straws into neat three-inch lengths and stuck them into his hatband. Then during the whole day, if he wanted to pick his teeth or merely to chew on something, he had only to reach up for one of them.

Jody listened carefully, for he knew and the whole country knew that Billy Buck was a fine hand with horses. Billy's own horse was a stringy cayuse with a hammer head, but he nearly always won the first prizes at the stock trials. Billy could rope a steer, take a double half-hitch about the horn with his riata, and dismount, and his horse would play the steer as an angler plays a fish, keeping a tight rope until the steer was down or beaten.

Every morning, after Jody had curried and brushed the pony, he let down the barrier of the stall, and Gabilan thrust past him and raced down the barn and into the corral. Around and around he galloped, and sometimes he jumped forward and landed on stiff legs. He stood quivering, stiff ears forward, eyes rolling so that the whites showed, pretending to be frightened. At last he walked snorting to the water-trough and buried his nose in the water up to the nostrils. Jody was proud then, for he knew that was the way to judge a horse. Poor horses only touched their lips to the water, but a fine spirited beast put his whole nose and mouth under, and only left room to breathe.

Then Jody stood and watched the pony, and he saw things he had never noticed about any other horse, the sleek, sliding flank muscles and the cords of the buttocks, which flexed like a closing fist, and the shine the sun put on the red coat. Having seen horses all his life, Jody had never looked at them very closely before. But now he noticed the moving ears which gave expression and even inflection of expression to the face. The pony talked with his ears. You could tell exactly how he felt about everything by the way his ears pointed. Sometimes they were stiff and upright and sometimes lax and sagging. They went back when he was angry or fearful, and forward when he was anxious and curious and pleased; and their exact position indicated which emotion he had.

Billy Buck kept his word. In the early fall the training began. First there was the halter-breaking, and that was the hardest because it was the first thing. Jody held a carrot and coaxed and promised and pulled on the rope. The pony set his feet like a burro when he felt the strain. But before long he learned. Jody walked all over the ranch leading him. Gradually he took to dropping the rope until the pony followed him unled wherever he went.

And then came the training on the long halter. That was slower work. Jody stood in the middle of a circle, holding the long halter. He clucked with his tongue and the pony started to walk in a big circle, held in by the long rope. He clucked again to make the pony trot, and again to make him gallop. Around and around Gabilan went thundering and enjoying it immensely. Then he called, "Whoa," and the pony stopped. It was not long until Gabilan was perfect at it. But in many ways he was a bad pony. He bit Jody in the pants and stomped on Jody's feet. Now and then his ears went back and he aimed a tremendous kick at the boy. Every time he did one of these bad things, Gabilan settled back and seemed to laugh to himself.

Billy Buck worked at the hair rope in the evenings before the fireplace. Jody collected tail hair in a bag, and he sat and watched Billy slowly constructing the rope, twisting a few hairs to make a string and rolling two strings together for a cord, and then braiding a number of cords to make the rope. Billy rolled the finished rope on the floor under his foot to make it round and hard.

The long halter work rapidly approached perfection. Jody's father, watching the pony stop and start and trot and gallop, was a little bothered by it.

"He's getting to be almost a trick pony," he complained. "I don't like trick horses. It takes all the—dignity out of a horse to make him do tricks. Why, a trick horse is kind of like an actor—no dignity, no character of his own." And his father said, "I guess you better be getting him used to the saddle pretty soon."

Jody rushed for the harness-room. For some time he had been riding the saddle on a sawhorse. He changed the stirrup length over and over, and could never get it just right. Sometimes, mounted on the sawhorse in the harness-room, with collars and hames and tugs hung all about him, Jody rode out beyond the room. He carried his rifle across the pommel. He saw the fields go flying by, and he heard the beat of the galloping hoofs.

It was a ticklish job, saddling the pony the first time. Gabilan hunched and reared and threw the saddle off before the cinch could be tightened. It had to be replaced again and again until at last the pony let it stay. And the cinching was difficult, too. Day by day Jody tightened the girth a little more until at last the pony didn't mind the saddle at all.

Then there was the bridle. Billy explained how to use a stick of licorice for a bit until Gabilan was used to having something in his mouth. Billy explained, "Of course we could force-break him to everything, but he wouldn't be as good a horse if we did. He'd always be a little bit afraid, and he wouldn't mind because he wanted to."

The first time the pony wore the bridle he whipped his head about and worked his tongue against the bit until the blood oozed from the corners of his mouth. He tried to rub the headstall off on the manger. His ears pivoted about and his eyes turned red with fear and with general rambunctiousness. Jody rejoiced, for he knew that only a mean-souled horse does not resent training.

And Jody trembled when he thought of the time when he would first sit in the saddle. The pony would probably throw him off. There was no disgrace in that. The disgrace would come if he did not get right up and mount again. Sometimes he dreamed that he lay in the dirt and cried and couldn't make himself mount again. The shame of the dream lasted until the middle of the day.

Gabilan was growing fast. Already he had lost the long-leggedness of the colt; his mane was getting longer and blacker. Under the constant currying and brushing his coat lay as smooth and gleaming as orange-red lacquer. Jody oiled the hoofs and kept them carefully trimmed so they would not crack.

The hair rope was nearly finished. Jody's father gave him an old pair of spurs and bent in the side bars and cut down the strap and took up the chainlets until they fitted. And then one day Carl Tiflin said:

"The pony's growing faster than I thought. I guess you can ride him by Thanksgiving. Think you can stick on?"

"I don't know," Jody said shyly. Thanksgiving was only three weeks off. He hoped it wouldn't rain, for rain would spot the red saddle.

Gabilan knew and liked Jody by now. He nickered when Jody came across the stubble-field, and in the pasture he came running when his master whistled for him. There was always a carrot for him every time.

Billy Buck gave him riding instructions over and over. "Now when you get up there, just grab tight with your knees and keep your hands away from the saddle, and if you get throwed, don't let that stop you. No matter how good a man is, there's always some horse can pitch him. You just climb up again before he gets to feeling smart about it. Pretty soon, he won't throw you no more, and pretty soon he *can't* throw you no more. That's the way to do it."

"I hope it don't rain before," Jody said.

"Why not? Don't want to get throwed in the mud?"

That was partly it, and also he was afraid that in the flurry of bucking Gabilan might slip and fall on him and break his leg or his hip. He had seen that happen to men before, had seen how they writhed on the ground like squashed bugs, and he was afraid of it.

He practiced on the sawhorse how he would hold the reins in his left hand and a hat in his right hand. If he kept his hands thus busy, he couldn't grab the horn if he felt himself going off. He didn't like to think of what would happen if he did grab the horn. Perhaps his father and Billy Buck would never speak to him again, they would be so ashamed. The news would get about and his mother would be ashamed too. And in the school yard—it was too awful to contemplate.

He began putting his weight in a stirrup when Gabilan was saddled, but he didn't throw his leg over the pony's back. That was forbidden until Thanksgiving.

Every afternoon he put the red saddle on the pony and cinched it tight. The pony was learning already to fill his stomach out unnaturally large while the cinching was going on, and then to let it down when the straps were fixed. Sometimes Jody led him up to the brush line and let him drink from the round green tub, and sometimes he led him up through the stubble-field to the hilltop from which it was possible to see the white town of Salinas and the geometric fields of the great valley, and the oak trees clipped by the sheep. Now and then they broke through the brush and came to little cleared circles so hedged in that the world was gone and only the sky and the circle of brush were left from the old life. Gabilan liked these trips and showed it by keeping his head very high and by quivering his nostrils with interest. When the two came back from an expedition they smelled of the sweet sage they had forced through.

Time dragged on toward Thanksgiving, but winter came fast. The clouds swept down and hung all day over the land and brushed the hilltops, and the winds blew shrilly at night. All day the dry oak leaves drifted down from the trees until they covered the ground, and yet the trees were unchanged.

Jody had wished it might not rain before Thanksgiving, but it did. The brown earth turned dark and the trees glistened. The cut ends of the stubble turned black with mildew; the haystacks greyed from exposure to the damp, and on the roofs the moss, which had been all summer as grey as lizards, turned a brilliant yellow-green. During the week of rain, Jody kept the pony in the box stall out of the dampness, except for a little time after school when he took him out for exercise and to drink at the water-trough in the upper corral. Not once did Gabilan get wet.

The wet weather continued until little new grass appeared. Jody walked to school dressed in a slicker and short rubber boots. At length one morning the sun came out brightly. Jody, at his work in the box stall, said to Billy Buck, "Maybe I'll leave Gabilan in the corral when I go to school today."

"Be good for him to be out in the sun," Billy assured him. "No animal likes to be cooped up too long. Your father and me are going back on the hill to clean the leaves out of the spring." Billy nodded and picked his teeth with one of his little straws.

"If the rain comes, though—" Jody suggested.

"Not likely to rain today. She's rained herself out." Billy pulled up his sleeves and snapped his arm bands. "If it comes on to rain—why a little rain don't hurt a horse."

"Well, if it does come on to rain, you put him in, will you, Billy? I'm scared he might get cold so I couldn't ride him when the time comes."

"Oh sure! I'll watch out for him if we get back in time. But it won t rain today."

And so Jody, when he went to school, left Gabilan standing out in the corral.

Billy Buck wasn't wrong about many things. He couldn't be. But he was wrong about the weather that day, for a little after noon the clouds pushed over the hills and the rain began to pour down. Jody heard it start on the schoolhouse roof. He considered holding up one finger for permission to go to the outhouse and, once outside, running for home to put the pony in. Punishment would be prompt both at school and at home. He gave it up and took ease from Billy's assurance that rain couldn't hurt a horse. When school was finally out, he hurried home through the dark rain. The banks at the sides of the road spouted little jets of muddy water. The rain slanted and swirled under a cold and gusty wind. Jody dog-trotted home, slopping through the gravelly mud of the road.

From the top of the ridge he could see Gabilan standing miserably in the corral. The red coat was almost black, and streaked with water. He stood head down with his rump to the rain and wind. Jody arrived running and threw open the barn door and led the wet pony in by his forelock. Then he found a gunny sack and rubbed the soaked hair and rubbed the legs and ankles. Gabilan stood patiently, but he trembled in gusts like the wind.

When he had dried the pony as well as he could, Jody went up to the horse and brought hot water down to the barn and soaked the grain in it. Gabilan was not very hungry. He nibbled at the hot mash, but he was not very much interested in it, and still shivered now and then. A little steam rose from his damp back.

It was almost dark when Billy Buck and Carl Tiflin came home. "When the rain started we put up at Ben Herche's place, and the rain never let up all afternoon," Carl Tiflin explained. Jody looked reproachfully at Billy Buck and Billy felt guilty.

"You said it wouldn't rain," Jody accused him.

Billy looked away. "It's hard to tell, this time of year," he said, but his excuse was lame. He had no right to be fallible, and he knew it.

"The pony got wet, got soaked through."

"Did you dry him off?"

"I rubbed him with a sack and I gave him hot grain."

Billy nodded in agreement.

"Do you think he'll take cold, Billy?"

"A little rain never hurt anything," Billy assured him.

Jody's father joined the conversation then and lectured the boy a little. "A horse," he said, "isn't any lap-dog kind of thing." Carl Tiflin hated weakness and sickness, and he held a violent contempt for helplessness.

Jody's mother put a platter of steaks on the table and boiled potatoes and boiled squash, which clouded the room with their steam. They sat down to eat. Carl Tiflin still grumbled about weakness put into animals and men by too much coddling.

Billy Buck felt bad about his mistake. "Did you blanket him?" he asked.

"No. I couldn't find any blanket. I laid some sacks over his back."

"We'll go down and cover him up after we eat, then." Billy felt better about it then. When Jody's father had gone in to the fire and his mother was washing dishes, Billy found and lighted a lantern. He and Jody walked through the mud to the barn. The barn was dark and warm and sweet. The horses still munched their evening hay. "You hold the lantern!" Billy ordered. And he felt the pony's legs and tested the heat of the flanks. He put his cheek against the pony's grey muzzle and then he rolled up the eyelids to look at the eyeballs and he lifted the lips to see the gums, and he put his fingers inside the ears. "He don't seem so chipper," Billy said. "I'll give him a rubdown."

Then Billy found a sack and rubbed the pony's legs violently and he rubbed the chest and the withers. Gabilan was strangely spiritless. He submitted patiently to the rubbing. At last Billy brought an old cotton comforter from the saddle-room, and threw it over the pony's back and tied it at neck and chest with string.

"Now he'll be all right in the morning," Billy said.

Jody's mother looked up when he got back to the house. "You're late up from bed," she said. She held his chin in her hard hand and brushed the tangled hair out of his eyes and she said, "Don't worry about the pony. He'll be all right. Billy's as good as any horse doctor in the country."

Jody hadn't known she could see his worry. He pulled gently away from her and knelt down in front of the fireplace until it burned his stomach. He scorched himself through and then went in to bed, but it was a hard thing to go to sleep. He awakened after what seemed a long time. The room was dark but there was a greyness in the window like that which precedes the dawn. He got up and found his overalls and searched for the legs, and then the clock in the other room struck two. He laid his clothes down and got back into bed. It was broad daylight when he awakened again. For the first time he had slept through the ringing of the triangle. He leaped up, flung on his clothes and went out of the door still buttoning his shirt. His mother looked after him for a moment and then went quietly back to her work. Her eyes were brooding and kind. Now and then her mouth smiled a little but without changing her eyes at all.

Jody ran on toward the barn. Halfway there he heard the sound he dreaded, the hollow rasping cough of a horse. He broke into a sprint then. In the barn he found Billy Buck with the pony. Billy was rubbing its legs with his strong thick hands. He looked up and smiled gaily. "He just took a little cold," Billy said. "We'll have him out of it in a couple of days."

Jody looked at the pony's face. The eyes were half closed and the lids thick and dry. In the eye corners a crust of hard mucus stuck. Gabilan's ears hung loosely sideways and his head was low. Jody put out his hand, but the pony did not move close to it. He coughed again and his whole body constricted with the effort. A little stream of thin fluid ran from his nostrils.

Jody looked back at Billy Buck. "He's awful sick, Billy."

"Just a little cold, like I said," Billy insisted. "You go get some breakfast and then go back to school. I'll take care of him."

"But you might have to do something else. You might leave him."

"No, I won't. I won't leave him at all. Tomorrow's Saturday. Then you can stay with him all day." Billy had failed again, and he felt badly about it. He had to cure the pony now.

Jody walked up to the house and took his place listlessly at the table. The eggs and bacon were cold and greasy, but he didn't notice it. He ate his usual amount. He didn't even ask to stay home from school. His mother pushed his hair back when she took his plate. "Billy'll take care of the pony," she assured him.

He moped through the whole day at school. He couldn't answer any questions nor read any words. He couldn't even tell anyone the pony was sick, for that might make him sicker. And when school was finally out he started home in dread. He walked slowly and let the other boys leave him. He wished he might continue walking and never arrive at the ranch.

Billy was in the barn, as he had promised, and the pony was worse. His eyes were almost closed now, and his breath whistled shrilly past an obstruction in his nose. A film covered that part of the eyes that was visible at all. It was doubtful whether the pony could see any more. Now and then he snorted, to clear his nose, and by the action seemed to plug it tighter. Jody looked dispiritedly at the pony's coat. The hair lay rough and unkempt and seemed to have lost all of its old luster. Billy stood quietly beside the stall. Jody hated to ask, but he had to know.

"Billy, is he—is he going to get well?"

Billy put his fingers between the bars under the pony's jaw and felt about. "Feel here," he said and he guided Jody's fingers to a large lump under the jaw. "When that gets bigger, I'll open it up and then he'll get better."

Jody looked quickly away, for he had heard about that lump. "What is it the matter with him?"

Billy didn't want to answer, but he had to. He couldn't be wrong three times. "Strangles," he said shortly, "but don't you worry about that. I'll pull him out of it. I've seen them get well when they were worse than Gabilan is. I'm going to steam him now. You can help."

"Yes," Jody said miserably. He followed Billy into the grain room and watched him make the steaming bag ready. It was a long canvas nose bag with straps to go over a horse's ears. Billy filled it one-third full of bran and then he added a couple of handfuls of dried hops. On top of the dry substance he poured a little carbolic acid and a little turpentine. "I'll be mixing it all up while you run to the house for a kettle of boiling water," Billy said.

When Jody came back with the steaming kettle, Billy buckled the straps over Gabilan's head and fitted the bag tightly around his nose. Then through a little hole in the side of the bag he poured the boiling water on the mixture. The pony started away as a cloud of strong steam rose up, but then the soothing fumes crept through his nose and into his lungs, and the sharp steam began to clear out the nasal passages. He breathed loudly. His legs trembled in an ague, and his eyes closed against the biting cloud. Billy poured in more water and kept the steam rising for fifteen minutes. At last he set down the kettle and took the bag from Gabilan's nose. The pony looked better. He breathed freely, and his eyes were open wider than they had been.

"See how good it makes him feel," Billy said. "Now we'll wrap him up in the blanket again. Maybe he'll be nearly well by morning."

"I'll stay with him tonight," Jody suggested.

"No. Don't you do it. I'll bring my blankets down here and put them in the hay. You can stay tomorrow and steam him if he needs it."

The evening was falling when they went to the house for their supper. Jody didn't even realize that some one else had fed the chickens and filled the wood-box. He walked up past the house to the dark brush line and took a drink of water from the tub. The spring water was so cold that it stung his mouth and drove a shiver through him. The sky above the hills was still light. He saw a hawk flying so high that it caught the sun on its breast and shone like a spark. Two blackbirds were driving him down the sky, glittering as they attacked their enemy. In the west, the clouds were moving in to rain again.

Jody's father didn't speak at all while the family ate supper, but after Billy Buck had taken his blankets and gone to sleep in the barn, Carl

Tiflin built a high fire in the fireplace and told stories. He told about the wild man who ran naked through the country and had a tail and ears like a horse, and he told about the rabbit-cats of Moro Cojo that hopped into the trees for birds. He revived the famous Maxwell brothers who found a vein of gold and hid the traces of it so carefully that they could never find it again.

Jody sat with his chin in his hands; his mouth worked nervously, and his father gradually became aware that he wasn't listening very carefully. "Isn't that funny?" he asked.

Jody laughed politely and said, "Yes, sir." His father was angry and hurt, then. He didn't tell any more stories. After a while, Jody took a lantern and went down to the barn. Billy Buck was asleep in the hay, and, except that his breath rasped a little in his lungs, the pony seemed to be much better. Jody stayed a little while, running his fingers over the red rough coat, and then he took up the lantern and went back to the house. When he was in bed, his mother came into the room.

"Have you enough covers on? It's getting winter."

"Yes, ma'am."

"Well, get some rest tonight." She hesitated to go out, stood uncertainly. "The pony will be all right," she said.

Jody was tired. He went to sleep quickly and didn't awaken until dawn. The triangle sounded, and Billy Buck came up from the barn before Jody could get out of the house.

"How is he?" Jody demanded.

Billy always wolfed his breakfast. "Pretty good. I'm going to open that lump this morning. Then he'll be better maybe."

After breakfast, Billy got out his best knife, one with a needle point. He whetted the shining blade a long time on a little carborundum stone. He tried the point and the blade again and again on his calloused thumb-ball, and at last he tried it on his upper lip.

On the way to the barn, Jody noticed how the young grass was up and how the stubble was melting day by day into the new green crop of volunteer. It was a cold sunny morning.

As soon as he saw the pony, Jody knew he was worse. His eyes were

closed and sealed shut with dried mucus. His head hung so low that
his nose almost touched the straw of his bed. There was a little groan
in each breath, a deep-seated, patient groan.

Billy lifted the weak head and made a quick slash with the knife.
Jody saw the yellow pus run out. He held up the head while Billy
swabbed out the wound with weak carbolic acid salve.

"Now he'll feel better," Billy assured him. "That yellow poison is
what makes him sick."

Jody looked unbelieving at Billy Buck. "He's awful sick."

Billy thought a long time what to say. He nearly tossed off a careless
assurance, but he saved himself in time. "Yes, he's pretty sick," he said
at last. "I've seen worse ones get well. If he doesn't get pneumonia,
we'll pull him through. You stay with him. If he gets worse, you can
come and get me."

For a long time after Billy went away, Judy stood beside the pony,
stroking him behind the ears. The pony didn't flip his head the way
he had done when he was well. The groaning in his breathing was
becoming more hollow.

Doubletree Mutt looked into the barn, his big tail waving provoca-
tively, and Jody was so incensed at his health that he found a hard
black clod on the floor and deliberately threw it. Doubletree Mutt went
yelping away to nurse a bruised paw.

In the middle of the morning, Billy Buck came back and made another steam bag. Jody watched to see whether the pony improved this
time as he had before. His breathing eased a little, but he did not raise
his head.

The Saturday dragged on. Late in the afternoon Jody went to the
house and brought his bedding down and made up a place to sleep in
the hay. He didn't ask permission. He knew from the way his mother
looked at him that she would let him do almost anything. That night
he left a lantern burning on a wire over the box stall. Billy had told
him to rub the pony's legs every little while.

At nine o'clock the wind sprang up and howled around the barn.
And in spite of his worry, Jody grew sleepy. He got into his blankets
and went to sleep, but the breathy groans of the pony sounded in his
dreams. And in his sleep he heard a crashing noise which went on and

on until it awakened him. The wind was rushing through the barn. He sprang up and looked down the lane of stalls. The barn door had blown open, and the pony was gone.

He caught the lantern and ran outside into the gale, and he saw Gabilan weakly shambling away into the darkness, head down, legs working slowly and mechanically. When Jody ran up and caught him by the forelock, he allowed himself to be led back and put into his stall. His groans were louder, and a fierce whistling came from his nose. Jody didn't sleep any more then. The hissing of the pony's breath grew louder and sharper.

He was glad when Billy Buck came in at dawn. Billy looked for a time at the pony as though he had never seen him before. He felt the ears and flanks. "Jody," he said, "I've got to do something you won't want to see. You run up to the house for a while."

Jody grabbed him fiercely by the forearm. "You're not going to shoot him?"

Billy patted his hand. "No. I'm going to open a little hole in his windpipe so he can breathe. His nose is filled up. When he gets well, we'll put a little brass button in the hole for him to breathe through."

Jody couldn't have gone away if he had wanted to. It was awful to see the red hide cut, but infinitely more terrible to know it was being cut and not to see it. "I'll stay right here," he said bitterly. "You sure you got to?"

"Yes. I'm sure. If you stay, you can hold his head. If it doesn't make you sick, that is."

The fine knife came out again and was whetted again just as carefully as it had been the first time. Judy held the pony's head up and the throat taut, while Billy felt up and down for the right place. Jody sobbed once as the bright knife point disappeared into the throat. The pony plunged weakly away and then stood still, trembling violently. The blood ran thickly out and up the knife and across Billy's hand and into his shirtsleeve. The sure square hand sawed out a round hole in the flesh, and the breath came bursting out of the hole, throwing a fine spray of blood. With the rush of oxygen, the pony took a sudden strength. He lashed out with his hind feet and tried to rear, but Jody held his head down while Billy mopped the new wound with carbolic salve. It was a good job. The blood stopped flowing and the air puffed out the hole and sucked it in regularly with a little bubbling noise.

The rain brought in by the night wind began to fall on the barn roof. Then the triangle rang for breakfast. "You go up and eat while I wait," Billy said. "We've got to keep this hole from plugging up."

Jody walked slowly out of the barn. He was too dispirited to tell Billy how the barn door had blown open and let the pony out. He emerged into the wet grey morning and sloshed up to the house, taking a perverse pleasure in splashing through all the puddles. His mother fed him and put dry clothes on. She didn't question him. She seemed to know he couldn't answer questions. But when he was ready to go back to the barn she brought him a pan of steaming meal. "Give him this," she said.

But Jody did not take the pan. He said, "He won't eat anything," and ran out of the house. At the barn, Billy showed him how to fix a ball of cotton on a stick, with which to swab out the breathing hole when it became clogged with mucus.

Jody's father walked into the barn and stood with them in front of the stall. At length he turned to the boy. "Hadn't you better come with me? I'm going to drive over the hill." Jody shook his head. "You better come on, out of this," his father insisted.

Billy turned on him angrily. "Let him alone. It's his pony, isn't it?"

Carl Tiflin walked away without saying another word. His feelings were badly hurt.

All morning Jody kept the wound open and the air passing in and out freely. At noon the pony lay wearily down on his side and stretched his nose out.

Billy came back. "If you're going to stay with him tonight, you better take a little nap," he said. Jody went absently out of the barn. The sky had cleared to a hard thin blue. Everywhere the birds were busy with worms that had come to the damp surface of the ground.

Jody walked to the brush line and sat on the edge of the mossy tub. He looked down at the house and at the old bunkhouse and at the dark cypress tree. The place was familiar, but curiously changed. It wasn't itself any more, but a frame for things that were happening. A cold wind blew out of the east now, signifying that the rain was over for a little while. At his feet Jody could see the little arms of new weeds spreading out over the ground. In the mud about the spring were thousands of quail tracks.

Doubletree Mutt came sideways and embarrassed up through the vegetable patch, and Jody, remembering how he had thrown the clod, put his arm about the dog's neck and kissed him on his wide black nose. Doubletree Mutt sat still, as though he knew some solemn thing was happening. His big tail slapped the ground gravely. Jody pulled a swollen tick out of Mutt's neck and popped it dead between his thumb-nails. It was a nasty thing. He washed his hands in the cold spring water.

Except for the steady swish of the wind, the farm was very quiet. Jody knew his mother wouldn't mind if he didn't go in to eat his lunch. After a little while he went slowly back to the barn. Mutt crept into his own little house and whined softly to himself for a long time.

Billy Buck stood up from the box and surrendered the cotton swab. The pony still lay on his side and the wound in his throat bellowsed in and out. When Jody saw how dry and dead the hair looked, he knew at last that there was no hope for the pony. He had seen the dead hair before on dogs and on cows, and it was a sure sign. He sat heavily on the box and let down the barrier of the box stall. For a long time he kept his eyes on the moving wound, and at last he dozed, and the afternoon passed quickly. Just before dark his mother brought a deep dish of stew and left it for him and went away. Jody ate a little of it, and, when it was dark, he set the lantern on the floor by the pony's head so he could watch the wound and keep it open. And he dozed again until the night chill awakened him. The wind was blowing fiercely, bringing the north cold with it. Jody brought a blanket from his bed in the hay and wrapped himself in it. Gabilan's breathing was quiet at last; the hole in his throat moved gently. The owls flew through the hayloft, shrieking and looking for mice. Jody put his hands down on his head and slept. In his sleep he was aware that the wind had increased. He heard it slamming about the barn.

It was daylight when he awakened. The barn door had swung open. The pony was gone. He sprang up and ran out into the morning light.

The pony's tracks were plain enough, dragging through the frostlike dew on the young grass, tired tracks with little lines between them where the hoofs had dragged. They headed for the brush line halfway up the ridge. Jody broke into a run and followed them. The sun shone on the sharp white quartz that stuck through the ground here and there. As he followed the plain trail, a shadow cut across in front of him. He looked up and saw a high circle of black buzzards, and the slowly revolving circle dropped lower and lower. The solemn birds soon disappeared over the ridge. Jody ran faster then, forced on by panic and rage. The trail entered the brush at last and followed a winding route among the tall sage bushes.

At the top of the ridge Jody was winded. He paused, puffing noisily. The blood pounded in his ears. Then he saw what he was looking for. Below, in one of the little clearings in the brush, lay the red pony. In the distance, Jody could see the legs moving slowly and convulsively. And in a circle around him stood the buzzards, waiting for the moment of death they know so well.

Jody leaped forward and plunged down the hill. The wet ground muffled his steps and the brush hid him. When he arrived, it was all over. The first buzzard sat on the pony's head and its beak had just risen dripping with dark eye fluid. Jody plunged into the circle like a cat. The black brotherhood arose in a cloud, but the big one on the pony's head was too late. As it hopped along to take off, Jody caught its wing tip and pulled it down. It was nearly as big as he was. The free wing crashed into his face with the force of a club, but he hung on. The claws fastened on his leg and the wing elbows battered his head on either side. Jody groped blindly with his free hand. His fingers found the neck of the struggling bird. The red eyes looked into his face, calm and fearless and fierce; the naked head turned from side to side. Then the beak opened and vomited a stream of putrefied fluid. Jody brought up his knee and fell on the great bird. He held the neck to the ground with one hand while his other found a piece of sharp white quartz. The first blow broke the beak sideways and black blood spurted from the twisted, leathery mouth corners. He struck again and missed. The red fearless eyes still looked at him, impersonal and unafraid and detached. He struck again and again, until the buzzard lay dead, until its head was a red pulp. He was still beating the dead bird when Billy Buck pulled him off and held him tightly to calm his shaking.

Carl Tiflin wiped the blood from the boy's face with a red bandana. Jody was limp and quiet now. His father moved the buzzard with his toe. "Jody," he explained, "the buzzard didn't kill the pony. Don't you know that?"

"I know it," Jody said wearily.

It was Billy Buck who was angry. He had lifted Jody in his arms, and had turned to carry him home. But he turned back on Carl Tiflin. " 'Course he knows it," Billy said furiously, "Jesus Christ! man, can't you see how he'd feel about it?"

II. THE GREAT MOUNTAINS

In the humming heat of a midsummer afternoon the little boy Jody listlessly looked about the ranch for something to do. He had been to the barn, had thrown rocks at the swallows' nests under the eaves until every one of the little mud houses broke open and dropped its lining of straw and dirty feathers. Then at the ranch house he baited a rat trap with stale cheese and set it where Doubletree Mutt, that good big dog, would get his nose snapped. Jody was not moved by an impulse of cruelty; he was bored with the long hot afternoon. Doubletree Mutt put his stupid nose in the trap and got it smacked, and shrieked with agony and limped away with blood on his nostrils. No matter where he was hurt, Mutt limped. It was just a way he had. Once when he was young, Mutt got caught in a coyote trap, and always after that he limped, even when he was scolded.

When Mutt yelped, Jody's mother called from inside the house, "Jody! Stop torturing that dog and find something to do."

Jody felt mean then, so he threw a rock at Mutt. Then he took his slingshot from the porch and walked up toward the brush line to try to kill a bird. It was a good slingshot, with store-bought rubbers, but while Jody had often shot at birds, he had never hit one. He walked up through the vegetable patch, kicking his bare toes into the dust. And on the way he found the perfect slingshot stone, round and slightly

flattened and heavy enough to carry through the air. He fitted it into
the leather pouch of his weapon and proceeded to the brush line. His
eyes narrowed, his mouth worked strenuously; for the first time that
afternoon he was intent. In the shade of the sagebrush the little birds
were working, scratching in the leaves, flying restlessly a few feet and
scratching again. Jody pulled back the rubbers of the sling and advanced cautiously. One little thrush paused and looked at him and
crouched, ready to fly. Jody sidled nearer, moving one foot slowly after
the other. When he was twenty feet away, he carefully raised the sling
and aimed. The stone whizzed; the thrush started up and flew right
into it. And down the little bird went with a broken head. Jody ran
to it and picked it up.

"Well, I got you," he said.

The bird looked much smaller dead than it had alive. Jody felt a
little mean pain in his stomach, so he took out his pocket-knife and
cut off the bird's head. Then he disemboweled it, and took off its wings;
and finally he threw all the pieces into the brush. He didn't care about
the bird, or its life, but he knew what older people would say if they
had seen him kill it; he was ashamed because of their potential opinion. He decided to forget the whole thing as quickly as he could, and
never to mention it.

The hills were dry at this season, and the wild grass was golden, but
where the spring-pipe filled the round tub and the tub spilled over,
there lay a stretch of fine green grass, deep and sweet and moist. Jody
drank from the mossy tub and washed the bird's blood from his hands
in cold water. Then he lay on his back in the grass and looked up at
the dumpling summer clouds. By closing one eye and destroying perspective he brought them down within reach so that he could put up
his fingers and stroke them. He helped the gentle wind push them
down the sky; it seemed to him that they went faster for his help. One
fat white cloud he helped clear to the mountain rims and pressed it
firmly over, out of sight. Jody wondered what it was seeing, then. He
sat up the better to look at the great mountains where they went piling
back, growing darker and more savage until they finished with one
jagged ridge, high up against the west. Curious secret mountains; he
thought of the little he knew about them.

"What's on the other side?" he asked his father once.

"More mountains, I guess. Why?"

"And on the other side of them?"

"More mountains. Why?"

"More mountains on and on?"

"Well, no. At last you come to the ocean."

"But what's in the mountains?"

"Just cliffs and brush and rocks and dryness."

"Were you ever there?"

"No."

"Has anybody ever been there?"

"A few people, I guess. It's dangerous, with cliffs and things. Why, I've read there's more unexplored country in the mountains of Monterey County than any place in the United States." His father seemed proud that this should be so.

"And at last the ocean?"

"At last the ocean."

"But," the boy insisted, "but in between? No one knows?"

"Oh, a few people do, I guess. But there's nothing there to get. And not much water. Just rocks and cliffs and greasewood. Why?"

"It would be good to go."

"What for? There's nothing there."

Jody knew something was there, something very wonderful because it wasn't known, something secret and mysterious. He could feel within himself that this was so. He said to his mother, "Do you know what's in the big mountains?"

She looked at him and then back at the ferocious range, and she said, "Only the bear, I guess."

"What bear?"

"Why the one that went over the mountain to see what he could see."

Jody questioned Billy Buck, the ranch hand, about the possibility of ancient cities lost in the mountains, but Billy agreed with Jody's father.

"It ain't likely," Billy said. "There'd be nothing to eat unless a kind of people that can eat rocks live there."

That was all the information Jody ever got, and it made the mountains dear to him, and terrible. He thought often of the miles of ridge after ridge until at last there was the sea. When the peaks were pink in the morning they invited him among them: and when the sun had gone over the edge in the evening and the mountains were a purple-like despair, then Jody was afraid of them; then they were so impersonal and aloof that their very imperturbability was a threat.

Now he turned his head toward the mountains of the east, the Gabilans, and they were jolly mountains, with hill ranches in their creases, and with pine trees growing on the crests. People lived there, and battles had been fought against the Mexicans on the slopes. He looked back for an instant at the Great Ones and shivered a little at the contrast. The foothill cup of the home ranch below him was sunny and safe. The house gleamed with white light and the barn was brown and warm. The red cows on the farther hill ate their way slowly toward the north. Even the dark cypress tree by the bunkhouse was usual and safe. The chickens scratched about in the dust of the farm-yard with quick waltzing steps.

Then a moving figure caught Jody's eye. A man walked slowly over the brow of the hill, on the road from Salinas, and he was headed toward the house. Jody stood up and moved down toward the house too, for if someone was coming, he wanted to be there to see. By the time the boy had got to the house the walking man was only halfway down the road, a lean man, very straight in the shoulders. Jody could tell he was old only because his heels struck the ground with hard jerks. As he approached nearer, Jody saw that he was dressed in blue jeans and in a coat of the same material. He wore clodhopper shoes and an old flat-brimmed Stetson hat. Over his shoulder he carried a gunny sack, lumpy and full. In a few moments he had trudged close enough so that his face could be seen. And his face was as dark as dried beef. A mustache, blue-white against the dark skin, hovered over his mouth, and his hair was white, too, where it showed at his neck. The skin of his face had shrunk back against the skull until it defined bone, not flesh, and made the nose and chin seem sharp and fragile. The eyes were large and deep and dark, with eyelids stretched tightly over them. Irises and pupils were one, and very black, but the eyeballs were brown. There were no wrinkles in the face at all. This old man wore a blue denim coat buttoned to the throat with brass buttons, as all men do who wear no shirts. Out of the sleeves came strong bony wrists and hands gnarled and knotted and hard as peach branches. The nails were flat and blunt and shiny.

The old man drew close to the gate and swung down his sack when he confronted Jody. His lips fluttered a little and a soft impersonal voice came from between them.

"Do you live here?"

Jody was embarrassed. He turned and looked at the house, and he turned back and looked toward the barn where his father and Billy Buck were. "Yes," he said, when no help came from either direction.

"I have come back," the old man said. "I am Gitano, and I have come back."

Jody could not take all this responsibility. He turned abruptly, and ran into the house for help, and the screen door banged after him. His mother was in the kitchen poking out the clogged holes of a colander with a hairpin, and biting her lower lip with concentration.

"It's an old man," Jody cried excitedly. "It's an old *paisano* man, and he says he's come back."

His mother put down the colander and stuck the hairpin behind the sink board. "What's the matter now?" she asked patiently.

"It's an old man outside. Come on out."

"Well, what does he want?" She untied the strings of her apron and smoothed her hair with her fingers.

"I don't know. He came walking."

His mother smoothed down her dress and went out, and Jody followed her. Gitano had not moved.

"Yes?" Mrs. Tiflin asked.

Gitano took off his old black hat and held it with both hands in front of him. He repeated, "I am Gitano, and I have come back."

"Come back? Back where?"

Gitano's whole straight body leaned forward a little. His right hand described the circle of the hills, the sloping fields and the mountains, and ended at his hat again. "Back to the rancho. I was born here, and my father, too."

"Here?" she demanded. "This isn't an old place."

"No, there," he said, pointing to the western ridge. "On the other side there, in a house that is gone."

At last she understood. "The old 'dobe that's washed almost away, you mean?"

"Yes, *señora*. When the rancho broke up they put no more lime on the 'dobe, and the rains washed it down."

Jody's mother was silent for a little, and curious homesick thoughts ran through her mind, but quickly she cleared them out. "And what do you want here now, Gitano?"

"I will stay here," he said quietly, "until I die."

"But we don't need an extra man here."

"I can not work hard any more, *señora*. I can milk a cow, feed chickens, cut a little wood; no more. I will stay here." He indicated the sack on the ground beside him. "Here are my things."

She turned to Jody. "Run down to the barn and call your father."

Jody dashed away, and he returned with Carl Tiflin and Billy Buck behind him. The old man was standing as he had been, but he was resting now. His whole body had sagged into a timeless repose.

"What is it?" Carl Tiflin asked. "What's Jody so excited about?"

Mrs. Tiflin motioned to the old man. "He wants to stay here. He wants to do a little work and stay here."

"Well, we can't have him. We don't need any more men. He's too old. Billy does everything we need."

They had been talking over him as though he did not exist, and now, suddenly, they both hesitated and looked at Gitano and were embarrassed.

He cleared his throat. "I am too old to work. I come back where I was born."

"You weren't born here," Carl said sharply.

"No. In the 'dobe house over the hill. It was all one rancho before you came."

"In the mud house that's all melted down?"

"Yes. I and my father. I will stay here now on the rancho."

"I tell you you won't stay," Carl said angrily. "I don't need an old man. This isn't a big ranch. I can't afford food and doctor bills for an old man. You must have relatives and friends. Go to them. It is like begging to come to strangers."

"I was born here," Gitano said patiently and inflexibly.

Carl Tiflin didn't like to be cruel, but he felt he must. "You can eat here tonight," he said. "You can sleep in the little room of the old bunkhouse. We'll give you your breakfast in the morning, and then you'll have to go along. Go to your friends. Don't come to die with strangers."

Gitano put on his black hat and stooped for the sack. "Here are my things," he said.

Carl turned away. "Come on, Billy, we'll finish down at the barn. Jody, show him the little room in the bunkhouse."

He and Billy turned back toward the barn. Mrs. Tiflin went into the house, saying over her shoulder, "I'll send some blankets down."

Gitano looked questioningly at Jody. "I'll show you where it is," Jody said.

There was a cot with a shuck mattress, an apple box holding a tin lantern, and a backless rocking-chair in the little room of the bunk-house. Gitano laid his sack carefully on the floor and sat down on the bed. Jody stood shyly in the room, hesitating to go. At last he said,

"Did you come out of the big mountains?"

Gitano shook his head slowly. "No, I worked down the Salinas Valley."

The afternoon thought would not let Jody go. "Did you ever go into the big mountains back there?"

The old dark eyes grew fixed, and their light turned inward on the years that were living in Gitano's head. "Once—when I was a little boy. I went with my father."

"Way back, clear into the mountains?"

"Yes."

"What was there?" Jody cried. "Did you see any people or any houses?"

"No."

"Well, what was there?"

Gitano's eyes remained inward. A little wrinkled strain came between his brows.

"What did you see in there?" Jody repeated.

"I don't know," Gitano said. "I don't remember."

"Was it terrible and dry?"

"I don't remember."

In his excitement, Jody had lost his shyness. "Don't you remember anything about it?"

Gitano's mouth opened for a word, and remained open while his brain sought the word. "I think it was quiet—I think it was nice."

Gitano's eyes seemed to have found something back in the years, for they grew soft and a little smile seemed to come and go in them.

"Didn't you ever go back in the mountains again?" Jody insisted.

"No."

"Didn't you ever want to?"

But now Gitano's face became impatient. "No," he said in a tone that told Jody he didn't want to talk about it any more. The boy was held by a curious fascination. He didn't want to go away from Gitano. His shyness returned.

"Would you like to come down to the barn and see the stock?" he asked.

Gitano stood up and put on his hat and prepared to follow.

It was almost evening now. They stood near the watering trough while the horses sauntered in from the hillsides for an evening drink. Gitano rested his big twisted hands on the top rail of the fence. Five horses came down and drank, and then stood about, nibbling at the dirt or rubbing their sides against the polished wood of the fence. Long after they had finished drinking an old horse appeared over the brow of the hill and came painfully down. It had long yellow teeth; its hooves were flat and sharp as spades, and its ribs and hip-bones jutted out under its skin. It hobbled up to the trough and drank water with a loud sucking noise.

"That's old Easter," Jody explained. "That's the first horse my father ever had. He's thirty years old." He looked up into Gitano's old eyes for some response.

"No good any more," Gitano said.

Jody's father and Billy Buck came out of the barn and walked over. "Too old to work," Gitano repeated. "Just eats and pretty soon dies."

Carl Tiflin caught the last words. He hated his brutality toward old Gitano, and so he became brutal again.

"It's a shame not to shoot Easter," he said. "It'd save him a lot of pains and rheumatism." He looked secretly at Gitano, to see whether he noticed the parallel, but the big bony hands did not move, nor did the dark eyes turn from the horse. "Old things ought to be put out of their misery," Jody's father went on. "One shot, a big noise, one big pain in the head maybe, and that's all. That's better than stiffness and sore teeth."

Billy Buck broke in. "They got a right to rest after they worked all of their life. Maybe they like to just walk around."

Carl had been looking steadily at the skinny horse. "You can't imagine now what Easter used to look like," he said softly. "High neck, deep chest, fine barrel. He could jump a five-bar gate in stride. I won a flat race on him when I was fifteen years old. I could of got two hundred dollars for him any time. You wouldn't think how pretty he was." He checked himself, for he hated softness. "But he ought to be shot now," he said.

"He's got a right to rest," Billy Buck insisted.

Jody's father had a humorous thought. He turned to Gitano. "If ham and eggs grew on a side-hill I'd turn you out to pasture too," he said. "But I can't afford to pasture you in my kitchen."

He laughed to Billy Buck about it as they went on toward the house. "Be a good thing for all of us if ham and eggs grew on the side-hills."

Jody knew how his father was probing for a place to hurt in Gitano. He had been probed often. His father knew every place in the boy where a word would fester.

"He's only talking," Jody said. "He didn't mean it about shooting Easter. He likes Easter. That was the first horse he ever owned."

The sun sank behind the high mountains as they stood there, and the ranch was hushed. Gitano seemed to be more at home in the evening. He made a curious sharp sound with his lips and stretched one of his hands over the fence. Old Easter moved stiffly to him, and Gitano rubbed the lean neck under the mane.

"You like him?" Jody asked softly.

"Yes—but he's no damn good."

The triangle sounded at the ranch house. "That's supper," Jody cried. "Come on up to supper."

As they walked up toward the house Jody noticed again that Gitano's body was as straight as that of a young man. Only by a jerkiness in his movements and by the scuffling of his heels could it be seen that he was old.

The turkeys were flying heavily into the lower branches of the cypress tree by the bunkhouse. A fat sleek ranch cat walked across the road carrying a rat so large that its tail dragged on the ground. The quail on the side-hills were still sounding the clear water call.

Jody and Gitano came to the back steps and Mrs. Tiflin looked out through the screen door at them.

"Come running, Jody. Come in to supper, Gitano."

Carl and Billy Buck had started to eat at the long oilcloth-covered table. Jody slipped into his chair without moving it, but Gitano stood holding his hat until Carl looked up and said, "Sit down, sit down. You might as well get your belly full before you go on." Carl was afraid he might relent and let the old man stay, and so he continued to remind himself that this couldn't be.

Gitano laid his hat on the floor and diffidently sat down. He wouldn't reach for food. Carl had to pass it to him. "Here, fill yourself up." Gitano ate very slowly, cutting tiny pieces of meat and arranging little pats of mashed potato on his plate.

The situation would not stop worrying Carl Tiflin. "Haven't you got any relatives in this part of the country?" he asked.

Gitano answered with some pride, "My brother-in-law is in Monterey. I have cousins there, too."

"Well, you can go and live there, then."

"I was born here," Gitano said in gentle rebuke.

Jody's mother came in from the kitchen, carrying a large bowl of tapioca pudding.

Carl chuckled to her, "Did I tell you what I said to him? I said if ham and eggs grew on the side-hills I'd put him out to pasture, like old Easter."

Gitano stared unmoved at his plate.

"It's too bad he can't stay," said Mrs. Tiflin.

"Now don't you start anything," Carl said crossly.

When they had finished eating, Carl and Billy Buck and Jody went into the living-room to sit for a while, but Gitano, without a word of farewell or thanks, walked through the kitchen and out the back door. Jody sat and secretly watched his father. He knew how mean his father felt.

"This country's full of these old *paisanos,*" Carl said to Billy Buck.

"They're damn good men," Billy defended them. "They can work older than white men. I saw one of them a hundred and five years old, and he could still ride a horse. You don't see any white men as old as Gitano walking twenty or thirty miles."

"Oh, they're tough, all right," Carl agreed. "Say, are you standing up for him too? Listen, Billy," he explained, "I'm having a hard enough time keeping this ranch out of the Bank of Italy without taking on anybody else to feed. You know that, Billy."

"Sure, I know," said Billy. "If you was rich, it'd be different."

"That's right, and it isn't like he didn't have relatives to go to. A brother-in-law and cousins right in Monterey. Why should I worry about him?"

Jody sat quietly listening, and he seemed to hear Gitano's gentle voice and its unanswerable, "But I was born here." Gitano was mysterious like the mountains. There were ranges back as far as you could see, but behind the last range piled up against the sky there was a great unknown country. And Gitano was an old man, until you got to the dull dark eyes. And in behind them was some unknown thing. He didn't ever say enough to let you guess what was inside, under the eyes. Jody felt himself irresistibly drawn toward the bunkhouse. He slipped from his chair while his father was talking and he went out the door without making a sound.

The night was very dark and far-off noises carried in clearly. The hamebells of a wood team sounded from way over the hill on the county road. Jody picked his way across the dark yard. He could see a light through the window of the little room of the bunkhouse. Because the night was secret he walked quietly up to the window and peered in. Gitano sat in the rocking-chair and his back was toward the window. His right arm moved slowly back and forth in front of him. Jody pushed the door open and walked in. Gitano jerked upright and, seizing a piece of deerskin, he tried to throw it over the thing in his lap, but the skin slipped away. Jody stood overwhelmed by the thing in Gitano's hand, a lean and lovely rapier with a golden basket hilt. The blade was like a thin ray of dark light. The hilt was pierced and intricately carved.

"What is it?" Jody demanded.

Gitano only looked at him with resentful eyes, and he picked up the fallen deerskin and firmly wrapped the beautiful blade in it.

Jody put out his hand. "Can't I see it?"

Gitano's eyes smoldered angrily and he shook his head.

"Where'd you get it? Where'd it come from?"

Now Gitano regarded him profoundly, as though he pondered. "I got it from my father."

"Well, where'd he get it?"

Gitano looked down at the long deerskin parcel in his hand. "I don' know."

"Didn't he ever tell you?"

"No."

"What do you do with it?"

Gitano looked slightly surprised. "Nothing. I just keep it."

"Can't I see it again?"

The old man slowly unwrapped the shining blade and let the lamp-light slip along it for a moment. Then he wrapped it up again. "You go now. I want to go to bed." He blew out the lamp almost before Jody had closed the door.

As he went back toward the house, Jody knew one thing more sharply than he had ever known anything. He must never tell anyone about the rapier. It would be a dreadful thing to tell anyone about it, for it would destroy some fragile structure of truth. It was a truth that might be shattered by division.

On the way across the dark yard Jody passed Billy Buck. "They're wondering where you are," Billy said.

Jody slipped into the living-room, and his father turned to him. "Where have you been?"

"I just went out to see if I caught any rats in my new trap."

"It's time you went to bed," his father said.

Jody was first at the breakfast table in the morning. Then his father came in, and last, Billy Buck. Mrs. Tiflin looked in from the kitchen. "Where's the old man, Billy?" she asked.

"I guess he's out walking," Billy said. "I looked in his room and he wasn't there."

"Maybe he started early to Monterey," said Carl. "It's a long walk."

"No," Billy explained. "His sack is in the little room."

After breakfast Jody walked down to the bunkhouse. Flies were flashing about in the sunshine. The ranch seemed especially quiet this morning. When he was sure no one was watching him, Jody went into the little room, and looked into Gitano's sack. An extra pair of long cotton underwear was there, an extra pair of jeans and three pairs of worn socks. Nothing else was in the sack. A sharp loneliness fell on Jody. He walked slowly back toward the house. His father stood on the porch talking to Mrs. Tiflin.

"I guess old Easter's dead at last," he said. "I didn't see him come down to water with the other horses."

In the middle of the morning Jess Taylor from the ridge ranch rode down.

"You didn't sell that old gray crowbait of yours, did you, Carl?"

"No, of course not. Why?"

"Well," Jess said. "I was out this morning early, and I saw a funny thing. I saw an old man on an old horse, no saddle, only a piece of rope for a bridle. He wasn't on the road at all. He was cutting right up straight through the brush. I think he had a gun. At least I saw something shine in his hand."

"That's old Gitano," Carl Tiflin said. "I'll see if any of my guns are missing." He stepped into the house for a second. "Nope, all here. Which way was he heading, Jess?"

"Well, that's the funny thing. He was heading straight back into the mountains."

Carl laughed. "They never get too old to steal," he said. "I guess he just stole old Easter."

"Want to go after him, Carl?"

"Hell no, just save me burying that horse. I wonder where he got the gun. I wonder what he wants back there."

Jody walked up through the vegetable patch, toward the brush line. He looked searchingly at the towering mountains—ridge after ridge after ridge until at last there was the ocean. For a moment he thought he could see a black speck crawling up the farther ridge. Jody thought of the rapier and of Gitano. And he thought of the great mountains. A longing caressed him, and it was so sharp that he wanted to cry to get it out of his breast. He lay down in the green grass near the round tub at the brush line. He covered his eyes with his crossed arms and lay there a long time, and he was full of a nameless sorrow.

III. THE PROMISE

In a mid-afternoon of spring, the little boy Jody walked martially along the brush-lined road toward his home ranch. Banging his knee against the golden lard bucket he used for school lunch, he contrived a good bass drum, while his tongue fluttered sharply against his teeth to fill in snare drums and occasional trumpets. Some time back the other members of the squad that walked so smartly from the school had turned into the various little canyons and taken the wagon roads to their own home ranches. Now Jody marched seemingly alone, with high-lifted knees and pounding feet; but behind him there was a phantom army with great flags and swords, silent but deadly.

The afternoon was green and gold with spring. Underneath the spread branches of the oaks the plants grew pale and tall, and on the hills the feed was smooth and thick. The sagebrushes shone with new silver leaves and the oaks wore hoods of golden green. Over the hills there hung such a green odor that the horses on the flats galloped madly, and then stopped, wondering; lambs, and even old sheep, jumped in the air unexpectedly and landed on stiff legs, and went on eating; young clumsy calves butted their heads together and drew back and butted again.

As the grey and silent army marched past, led by Jody, the animals stopped their feeding and their play and watched it go by.

Suddenly Jody stopped. The grey army halted, bewildered and nervous. Jody went down on his knees. The army stood in long uneasy ranks for a moment, and then, with a soft sigh of sorrow, rose up in a faint grey mist and disappeared. Jody had seen the thorny crown of a horny-toad moving under the dust of the road. His grimy hand went out and grasped the spiked halo and held firmly while the little beast struggled. Then Jody turned the horny-toad over, exposing its pale gold stomach. With a gentle forefinger he stroked the throat and chest until the horny-toad relaxed, until its eyes closed and it lay languorous and asleep.

Jody opened his lunch pail and deposited the first game inside. He moved on now, his knees bent slightly, his shoulders crouched; his bare feet were wise and silent. In his right hand there was a long grey rifle. The brush along the road stirred restively under a new and unexpected population of grey tigers and grey bears. The hunting was very good, for by the time Jody reached the fork of the road where the mail box stood on a post, he had captured two more horny-toads, four little grass lizards, a blue snake, sixteen yellow-winged grasshoppers and a brown damp newt from under a rock. This assortment scrabbled unhappily against the tin of the lunch bucket.

At the road fork the rifle evaporated and the tigers and bears melted from the hillsides. Even the moist and uncomfortable creatures in the lunch pail ceased to exist, for the little red metal flag was up on the mail box, signifying that some postal matter was inside. Jody set his pail on the ground and opened the letter box. There was a Montgomery Ward catalog and a copy of the *Salinas Weekly Journal*. He slammed the box, picked up his lunch pail and trotted over the ridge and down into the cup of the ranch. Past the barn he ran, and past the used-up haystack and the bunkhouse and the cypress tree. He banged through the front screen door of the ranch house calling, "Ma'am, ma'am, there's a catalog."

Mrs. Tiflin was in the kitchen spooning clabbered milk into a cotton bag. She put down her work and rinsed her hands under the tap. "Here in the kitchen, Jody. Here I am."

He ran in and clattered his lunch pail on the sink. "Here it is. Can I open the catalog, ma'am?"

Mrs. Tiflin took up the spoon again and went back to her cottage cheese. "Don't lose it, Jody. Your father will want to see it." She scraped the last of the milk into the bag. "Oh, Jody, your father wants to see you before you go to your chores." She waved a cruising fly from the cheese bag.

Jody closed the new catalog in alarm. "Ma'am?"

"Why don't you ever listen? I say your father wants to see you."

The boy laid the catalog gently on the sink board. "Do you—is it something I did?"

Mrs. Tiflin laughed. "Always a bad conscience. What did you do?"

"Nothing, ma'am," he said lamely. But he couldn't remember, and besides it was impossible to know what action might later be construed as a crime.

His mother hung the full bag on a nail where it could drip into the sink. "He just said he wanted to see you when you got home. He's somewhere down by the barn."

Jody turned and went out the back door. Hearing his mother open the lunch pail and then gasp with rage, a memory stabbed him and he trotted away toward the barn, conscientiously not hearing the angry voice that called him from the house.

Carl Tiflin and Billy Buck, the ranch hand, stood against the lower pasture fence. Each man rested one foot on the lowest bar and both elbows on the top bar. They were talking slowly and aimlessly. In the pasture half a dozen horses nibbled contentedly at the sweet grass. The mare, Nellie, stood backed up against the gate, rubbing her buttocks on the heavy post.

Jody sidled uneasily near. He dragged one foot to give an impression of great innocence and nonchalance. When he arrived beside the men he put one foot on the lowest fence rail, rested his elbows on the second bar and looked into the pasture too. The two men glanced sideways at him.

"I wanted to see you," Carl said in the stern tone he reserved for children and animals.

"Yes, sir," said Jody guiltily.

"Billy, here, says you took good care of the pony before it died." No punishment was in the air. Jody grew bolder. "Yes, sir, I did."

"Billy says you have a good patient hand with horses."

Jody felt a sudden warm friendliness for the ranch hand.

Billy put in, "He trained that pony as good as anybody I ever seen." Then Carl Tiflin came gradually to the point. "If you could have another horse would you work for it?"

Jody shivered. "Yes, sir."

"Well, look here, then. Billy says the best way for you to be a good hand with horses is to raise a colt."

"It's the *only* good way," Billy interrupted.

"Now, look here, Jody," continued Carl. "Jess Taylor, up to the ridge ranch, has a fair stallion, but it'll cost five dollars. I'll put up the money, but you'll have to work it out all summer. Will you do that?"

Jody felt that his insides were shriveling. "Yes, sir," he said softly.

"And no complaining? And no forgetting when you're told to do something?"

"Yes, sir."

"Well, all right, then. Tomorrow morning you take Nellie up to the ridge ranch and get her bred. You'll have to take care of her, too, till she throws the colt."

"Yes, sir."

"You better get to the chickens and the wood now."

Jody slid away. In passing behind Billy Buck he very nearly put out his hand to touch the blue-jeaned legs. His shoulders swayed a little with maturity and importance.

He went to his work with unprecedented seriousness. This night he did not dump the can of grain to the chickens so that they had to leap over each other and struggle to get it. No, he spread the wheat so far and so carefully that the hens couldn't find some of it at all. And in the house, after listening to his mother's despair over boys who fill their lunch pails with slimy, suffocated reptiles, and bugs,

he promised never to do it again. Indeed, Jody felt that all such foolish-
ness was lost in the past. He was far too grown up ever to put horny-
toads in his lunch pail any more. He carried in so much wood and
built such a high structure with it that his mother walked in fear of
an avalanche of oak. When he was done, when he had gathered eggs
that had remained hidden for weeks, Jody walked down again past
the cypress tree, and past the bunkhouse toward the pasture. A fat
warty toad that looked out at him from under the watering trough
had no emotional effect on him at all.

Carl Tiflin and Billy Buck were not in sight, but from a metallic
ringing on the other side of the barn Jody knew that Billy Buck was
just starting to milk a cow.

The other horses were eating toward the upper end of the pasture,
but Nellie continued to rub herself nervously against the post. Jody
walked slowly near, saying, "So, girl, so-o, Nellie." The mare's ears
went back naughtily and her lips drew away from her yellow teeth.
She turned her head around; her eyes were glazed and mad. Jody
climbed to the top of the fence and hung his feet over and looked
paternally down on the mare.

The evening hovered while he sat there. Bats and nighthawks
flicked about. Billy Buck, walking toward the house carrying a full
milk bucket, saw Jody and stopped. "It's a long time to wait," he said
gently. "You'll get awful tired waiting."

"No I won't, Billy. How long will it be?"

"Nearly a year."

"Well, I won't get tired."

The triangle at the house rang stridently. Jody climbed down from
the fence and walked to supper beside Billy Buck. He even put out
his hand and took hold of the milk bucket to help carry it.

The next morning after breakfast Carl Tiflin folded a five-dollar bill
in a piece of newspaper and pinned the package in the bib pocket of
Jody's overalls. Billy Buck haltered the mare Nellie and led her out
of the pasture.

"Be careful now," he warned. "Hold her up short here so she can't
bite you. She's crazy as a coot."

Jody took hold of the halter leather itself and started up the hill toward the ridge ranch with Nellie skittering and jerking behind him. In the pasturage along the road the wild oat heads were just clearing their scabbards. The warm morning sun shone on Jody's back so sweetly that he was forced to take a serious stiff-legged hop now and then in spite of his maturity. On the fences the shiny blackbirds with red epaulets clicked their dry call. The meadowlarks sang like water, and the wild doves, concealed among the bursting leaves of the oaks, made a sound of restrained grieving. In the fields the rabbits sat sunning themselves, with only their forked ears showing above the grass heads.

After an hour of steady uphill walking, Jody turned into a narrow road that led up a steeper hill to the ridge ranch. He could see the red roof of the barn sticking up above the oak trees, and he could hear a dog barking unemotionally near the house.

Suddenly Nellie jerked back and nearly freed herself. From the direction of the barn Jody heard a shrill whistling scream and a splintering of wood, and then a man's voice shouting. Nellie reared and whinnied. When Jody held to the halter rope she ran at him with bared teeth. He dropped his hold and scuttled out of the way, into the brush. The high scream came from the oaks again, and Nellie answered it. With hoofs battering the ground the stallion appeared and charged down the hill trailing a broken halter rope. His eyes glittered feverishly. His stiff, erected nostrils were as red as flame. His black, sleek hide shone in the sunlight. The stallion came on so fast that he couldn't stop when he reached the mare. Nellie's ears went back; she whirled and kicked at him as he went by. The stallion spun around and reared. He struck the mare with his front hoof, and while she staggered under the blow, his teeth raked her neck and drew an ooze of blood.

Instantly Nellie's mood changed. She became coquettishly feminine. She nibbled his arched neck with her lips. She edged around and rubbed her shoulder against his shoulder. Jody stood half-hidden in the brush and watched. He heard the step of a horse behind him, but before he could turn, a hand caught him by the overall straps and lifted him off the ground. Jess Taylor sat the boy behind him on the horse.

"You might have got killed," he said. "Sundog's a mean devil sometimes. He busted his rope and went right through a gate."

Jody sat quietly, but in a moment he cried, "He'll hurt her, he'll kill her. Get him away!"

Jess chuckled. "She'll be all right. Maybe you'd better climb off and go up to the house for a little. You could get maybe a piece of pie up there."

But Jody shook his head. "She's mine, and the colt's going to be mine. I'm going to raise it up."

Jess nodded. "Yes, that's a good thing. Carl has good sense sometimes."

In a little while the danger was over. Jess lifted Jody down and then caught the stallion by its broken halter rope. And he rode ahead, while Jody followed, leading Nellie.

It was only after he had unpinned and handed over the five dollars, and after he had eaten two pieces of pie, that Jody started for home again. And Nellie followed docilely after him. She was so quiet that Jody climbed on a stump and rode her most of the way home.

The five dollars his father had advanced reduced Jody to peonage for the whole late spring and summer. When the hay was cut he drove a rake. He led the horse that pulled on the Jackson-fork tackle, and when the baler came he drove the circling horse that put pressure on the bales. In addition, Carl Tiflin taught him to milk and put a cow under his care, so that a new chore was added night and morning.

The bay mare Nellie quickly grew complacent. As she walked about the yellowing hillsides or worked at easy tasks, her lips were curled in a perpetual fatuous smile. She moved slowly, with the calm importance of an empress. When she was put to a team, she pulled steadily and unemotionally. Jody went to see her every day. He studied her with critical eyes and saw no change whatever.

One afternoon Billy Buck leaned the many-tined manure fork against the barn wall. He loosened his belt and tucked in his shirt-tail and tightened the belt again. He picked one of the little straws from his hatband and put it in the corner of his mouth. Jody, who was helping Doubletree Mutt, the big serious dog, to dig out a gopher, straightened up as the ranch hand sauntered out of the barn.

"Let's go up and have a look at Nellie," Billy suggested.

Instantly Jody fell into step with him. Doubletree Mutt watched them over his shoulder; then he dug furiously, growled, sounded little sharp yelps to indicate that the gopher was practically caught. When he looked over his shoulder again, and saw that neither Jody nor Billy was interested, he climbed reluctantly out of the hole and followed them up the hill.

The wild oats were ripening. Every head bent sharply under its load of grain, and the grass was dry enough so that it made a swishing sound as Jody and Billy stepped through it. Halfway up the hill they could see Nellie and the iron-grey gelding, Pete, nibbling the heads from the wild oats. When they approached, Nellie looked at them and backed her ears and bobbed her head up and down rebelliously. Billy walked to her and put his hand under her mane and patted her neck, until her ears came forward again and she nibbled delicately at his shirt.

Jody asked, "Do you think she's really going to have a colt?"

Billy rolled the lids back from the mare's eyes with his thumb and forefinger. He felt the lower lip and fingered the black, leathery teats. "I wouldn't be surprised," he said.

"Well, she isn't changed at all. It's three months gone."

Billy rubbed the mare's flat forehead with his knuckle while she grunted with pleasure. "I told you you'd get tired waiting. It'll be five months more before you can even see a sign, and it'll be at least eight months more before she throws the colt, about next January."

Jody sighed deeply. "It's a long time, isn't it?"

"And then it'll be about two years more before you can ride."

Jody cried out in despair, "I'll be grown up."

"Yep, you'll be an old man," said Billy.

"What color do you think the colt'll be?"

"Why, you can't ever tell. The stud is black and the dam is bay. Colt might be black or bay or gray or dappled. You can't tell. Sometimes a black dam might have a white colt."

"Well, I hope it's black and a stallion."

"If it's a stallion, we'll have to geld it. Your father wouldn't let you have a stallion."

"Maybe he would," Jody said. "I could train him not to be mean."

Billy pursed his lips, and the little straw that had been in the corner of his mouth rolled down to the center. "You can't ever trust a stallion," he said critically. "They're mostly fighting and making trouble. Sometimes when they're feeling funny they won't work. They make the mares uneasy and kick hell out of the geldings. Your father wouldn't let you keep a stallion."

Nellie sauntered away, nibbling the drying grass. Jody skinned the grain from a grass stem and threw the handful into the air, so that each pointed, feathered seed sailed out like a dart. "Tell me how it'll be, Billy. Is it like when the cows have calves?"

"Just about. Mares are a little more sensitive. Sometimes you have to be there to help the mare. And sometimes if it's wrong, you have to—" he paused.

"Have to what, Billy?"

"Have to tear the colt to pieces to get it out, or the mare'll die."

"But it won't be that way this time, will it, Billy?"

"Oh, no. Nellie's thrown good colts."

"Can I be there, Billy? Will you be certain to call me? It's my colt."

"Sure, I'll call you. Of course I will."

"Tell me how it'll be."

"Why, you've seen the cows calving. It's almost the same. The mare starts groaning and stretching, and then, if it's a good right birth, the head and forefeet come out, and the front hoofs kick a hole just the way the calves do. And the colt starts to breathe. It's good to be there, 'cause if its feet aren't right maybe he can't break the sac, and then he might smother."

Jody whipped his leg with a bunch of grass. "We'll have to be there, then, won't we?"

"Oh, we'll be there, all right."

They turned and walked slowly down the hill toward the barn. Jody was tortured with a thing he had to say, although he didn't want to. "Billy," he began miserably, "Billy, you won't let anything happen to the colt, will you?"

And Billy knew he was thinking of the red pony, Gabilan, and of how it died of strangles. Billy knew he had been infallible before that.

and now he was capable of failure. This knowledge made Billy much less sure of himself than he had been. "I can't tell," he said roughly. "All sorts of things might happen, and they wouldn't be my fault. I can't do everything." He felt badly about his lost prestige, and so he said, meanly, "I'll do everything I know, but I won't promise anything. Nellie's a good mare. She's thrown good colts before. She ought to this time." And he walked away from Jody and went into the saddle-room beside the barn, for his feelings were hurt.

Jody traveled often to the brushline behind the house. A rusty iron pipe ran a thin stream of spring water into an old green tub. Where the water spilled over and sank into the ground there was a patch of perpetually green grass. Even when the hills were brown and baked in the summer that little patch was green. The water whined softly into the trough all the year round. This place had grown to be a center-point for Jody. When he had been punished the cool green grass and the singing water soothed him. When he had been mean the biting acid of meanness left him at the brushline. When he sat in the grass and listened to the purling stream, the barriers set up in his mind by the stern day went down to ruin.

On the other hand, the black cypress tree by the bunkhouse was as repulsive as the water-tub was dear; for to this tree all the pigs came, sooner or later, to be slaughtered. Pig killing was fascinating, with the screaming and the blood, but it made Jody's heart beat so fast that it hurt him. After the pigs were scalded in the big iron tripod kettle and their skins were scraped and white, Jody had to go to the water-tub to sit in the grass until his heart grew quiet. The water-tub and the black cypress were opposites and enemies.

When Billy left him and walked angrily away, Jody turned up toward the house. He thought of Nellie as he walked, and of the little colt. Then suddenly he saw that he was under the black cypress, under the very singletree where the pigs were hung. He brushed his dry-grass hair off his forehead and hurried on. It seemed to him an unlucky thing to be thinking of his colt in the very slaughter place, especially after what Billy had said. To counteract any evil result of that bad conjunction he walked quickly past the ranch house, through the chicken yard, through the vegetable patch, until he came at last to the brushline.

He sat down in the green grass. The trilling water sounded in his ears. He looked over the farm buildings and across at the round hills, rich and yellow with grain. He could see Nellie feeding on the slope. As usual the water place eliminated time and distance. Jody saw a black, long-legged colt, butting against Nellie's flanks, demanding milk. And then he saw himself breaking a large colt to halter. All in a few moments the colt grew to be a magnificent animal, deep of chest, with a neck as high and arched as a sea-horse's neck, with a tail that tongued and rippled like black flame. This horse was terrible to everyone but Jody. In the schoolyard the boys begged rides, and Jody smilingly agreed. But no sooner were they mounted than the black demon pitched them off. Why, that was his name, Black Demon! For a moment the trilling water and the grass and the sunshine came back, and then . . .

Sometimes in the night the ranch people, safe in their beds, heard a roar of hoofs go by. They said, "It's Jody, on Demon. He's helping out the sheriff again." And then . . .

The golden dust filled the air in the arena at the Salinas Rodeo. The announcer called the roping contests. When Jody rode the black horse to the starting chute the other contestants shrugged and gave up first place, for it was well known that Jody and Demon could rope and throw and tie a steer a great deal quicker than any roping team of two men could. Jody was not a boy any more, and Demon was not a horse. The two together were one glorious individual. And then . . .

The President wrote a letter and asked them to help catch a bandit in Washington. Jody settled himself comfortably in the grass. The little stream of water whined into the mossy tub.

The year passed slowly on. Time after time Jody gave up his colt for lost. No change had taken place in Nellie. Carl Tiflin still drove her to a light cart, and she pulled on a hay rake and worked the Jackson-fork tackle when the hay was being put into the barn.

The summer passed, and the warm bright autumn. And then the

frantic morning winds began to twist along the ground, and a chill came into the air, and the poison oak turned red. One morning in September, when he had finished his breakfast, Jody's mother called him into the kitchen. She was pouring boiling water into a bucket full of dry midlings and stirring the materials to a steaming paste.

"Yes, ma'am?" Jody asked.

"Watch how I do it. You'll have to do it after this every other morning."

"Well, what is it?"

"Why, it's warm mash for Nellie. It'll keep her in good shape."

Jody rubbed his forehead with a knuckle. "Is she all right?" he asked timidly.

Mrs. Tiflin put down the kettle and stirred the mash with a wooden paddle. "Of course she's all right, only you've got to take better care of her from now on. Here, take this breakfast out to her!"

Jody seized the bucket and ran, down past the bunkhouse, past the barn, with the heavy bucket banging against his knees. He found Nellie playing with the water in the trough, pushing waves and tossing her head so that the water slopped out on the ground.

Jody climbed the fence and set the bucket of steaming mash beside her. Then he stepped back to look at her. And she was changed. Her stomach was swollen. When she moved, her feet touched the ground gently. She buried her nose in the bucket and gobbled the hot breakfast. And when she had finished and had pushed the bucket around the ground with her nose a little, she stepped quietly over to Jody and rubbed her cheek against him.

Billy Buck came out of the saddle-room and walked over. "Starts fast when it starts, doesn't it?"

"Did it come all at once?"

"Oh, no, you just stopped looking for a while." He pulled her head around toward Jody. "She's goin' to be nice, too. See how nice her eyes are! Some mares get mean, but when they turn nice, they just love everything." Nellie slipped her head under Billy's arm and rubbed her neck up and down between his arm and his side. "You better treat her awful nice now," Billy said.

"How long will it be?" Jody demanded breathlessly.

The man counted in whispers on his fingers. "About three months," he said aloud. "You can't tell exactly. Sometimes it's eleven months to the day, but it might be two weeks early, or a month late, without hurting anything."

Jody looked hard at the ground. "Billy," he began nervously, "Billy, you'll call me when it's getting born, won't you? You'll let me be there, won't you?"

Billy bit the tip of Nellie's ear with his front teeth. "Carl says he wants you to start right at the start. That's the only way to learn. Nobody can tell you anything. Like my old man did with me about the saddle blanket. He was a government packer when I was your size, and I helped him some. One day I left a wrinkle in my saddle blanket and made a saddle-sore. My old man didn't give me hell at all. But the next morning he saddled me up with a forty-pound stock saddle. I had to lead my horse and carry that saddle over a whole damn mountain in the sun. It darn near killed me, but I never left no wrinkles in a blanket again. I couldn't. I never in my life since then put on a blanket but I felt that saddle on my back."

Jody reached up a hand and took hold of Nellie's mane. "You'll tell me what to do about everything, won't you? I guess you know everything about horses, don't you?"

Billy laughed. "Why I'm half horse myself, you see," he said. "My ma died when I was born, and being my old man was a government packer in the mountains, and no cows around most of the time, why he just gave me mostly mare's milk." He continued seriously, "And horses know that. Don't you know it, Nellie?"

The mare turned her head and looked full into his eyes for a moment, and this is a thing horses practically never do. Billy was proud and sure of himself now. He boasted a little. "I'll see you get a good colt. I'll start you right. And if you do like I say, you'll have the best horse in the county."

That made Jody feel warm and proud, too; so proud that when he went back to the house he bowed his legs and swayed his shoulders as horsemen do. And he whispered, "Whoa, you Black Demon, you! Steady down there and keep your feet on the ground."

The winter fell sharply. A few preliminary gusty showers, and then a strong steady rain. The hills lost their straw color and blackened under the water, and the winter streams scrambled noisily down the canyons. The mushrooms and puffballs popped up and the new grass started before Christmas.

But this year Christmas was not the central day to Jody. Some undetermined time in January had become the axis day around which the months swung. When the rains fell, he put Nellie in a box stall and fed her warm food every morning and curried her and brushed her.

The mare was swelling so greatly that Jody became alarmed. "She'll pop wide open," he said to Billy.

Billy laid his strong square hand against Nellie's swollen abdomen. "Feel here," he said quietly. "You can feel it move. I guess it would surprise you if there were twin colts."

"You don't think so?" Jody cried. "You don't think it will be twins, do you, Billy?"

"No, I don't, but it does happen, sometimes."

During the first two weeks of January it rained steadily. Jody spent most of his time, when he wasn't in school, in the box stall with Nellie. Twenty times a day he put his hand on her stomach to feel the colt move. Nellie became more and more gentle and friendly to him. She rubbed her nose on him. She whinnied softly when he walked into the barn.

Carl Tiflin came to the barn with Jody one day. He looked admiringly at the groomed bay coat, and he felt the firm flesh over ribs and shoulders. "You've done a good job," he said to Jody. And this was the greatest praise he knew how to give. Jody was tight with pride for hours afterward.

The fifteenth of January came, and the colt was not born. And the twentieth came; a lump of fear began to form in Jody's stomach. "Is it all right?" he demanded of Billy.

"Oh, sure."

And again, "Are you sure it's going to be all right?"

Billy stroked the mare's neck. She swayed her head uneasily. "I told you it wasn't always the same time, Jody. You just have to wait."

When the end of the month arrived with no birth, Jody grew frantic. Nellie was so big that her breath came heavily, and her ears were close together and straight up, as though her head ached. Jody's sleep grew restless, and his dreams confused.

On the night of the second of February he awakened crying. His mother called to him, "Jody, you're dreaming. Wake up and start over again."

But Jody was filled with terror and desolation. He lay quietly a few moments, waiting for his mother to go back to sleep, and then he slipped his clothes on, and crept out in his bare feet.

The night was black and thick. A little misting rain fell. The cypress tree and the bunkhouse loomed and then dropped back into the mist. The barn door screeched as he opened it, a thing it never did in the daytime. Jody went to the rack and found a lantern and a tin box of matches. He lighted the wick and walked down the long straw-covered aisle to Nellie's stall. She was standing up. Her whole body weaved from side to side. Jody called to her, "So, Nellie, so-o, Nellie," but she did not stop her swaying nor look around. When he stepped into the stall and touched her on the shoulder she shivered under his hand. Then Billy Buck's voice came from the hayloft right above the stall.

"Jody, what are you doing?"

Jody started back and turned miserable eyes up toward the nest where Billy was lying in the hay. "Is she all right, do you think?"

"Why sure, I think so."

"You won't let anything happen, Billy, you're sure you won't?"

Billy growled down at him, "I told you I'd call you, and I will. Now you get back to bed and stop worrying that mare. She's got enough to do without you worrying her."

Jody cringed, for he had never heard Billy speak in such a tone. "I only thought I'd come and see," he said. "I woke up."

Billy softened a little then. "Well, you get to bed. I don't want you bothering her. I told you I'd get you a good colt. Get along now."

Jody walked slowly out of the barn. He blew out the lantern and set it in the rack. The blackness of the night, and the chilled mist struck him and enfolded him. He wished he believed everything Billy said as he had before the pony died. It was a moment before his eyes, blinded by the feeble lantern-flame, could make any form of the darkness. The damp ground chilled his bare feet. At the cypress tree the roosting turkeys chattered a little in alarm, and the two good dogs responded to their duty and came charging out, barking to frighten away the coyotes they thought were prowling under the tree.

As he crept through the kitchen, Jody stumbled over a chair. Carl called from his bedroom, "Who's there? What's the matter there?"

And Mrs. Tiflin said sleepily, "What's the matter, Carl?"

The next second Carl came out of the bedroom carrying a candle, and found Jody before he could get into bed. "What are you doing out?"

Jody turned shyly away. "I was down to see the mare."

For a moment anger at being awakened fought with approval in Jody's father. "Listen," he said, finally, "there's not a man in this country that knows more about colts than Billy. You leave it to him."

Words burst out of Jody's mouth. "But the pony died——"

"Don't you go blaming that on him," Carl said sternly. "If Billy can't save a horse, it can't be saved."

Mrs. Tiflin called, "Make him clean his feet and go to bed, Carl. He'll be sleepy all day tomorrow."

It seemed to Jody that he had just closed his eyes to try to go to sleep when he was shaken violently by the shoulder. Billy Buck stood beside him, holding a lantern in his hand. "Get up," he said. "Hurry up." He turned and walked quickly out of the room.

Mrs. Tiflin called, "What's the matter? Is that you, Billy?"

"Yes, ma'am."

"Is Nellie ready?"

"Yes, ma'am."

"All right, I'll get up and heat some water in case you need it."

Jody jumped into his clothes so quickly that he was out the back door before Billy's swinging lantern was halfway to the barn. There was a rim of dawn on the mountain-tops, but no light had penetrated into the cup of the ranch yet. Jody ran frantically after the lantern and caught up to Billy just as he reached the barn. Billy hung the lantern to a nail on the stall-side and took off his blue denim coat. Jody saw that he wore only a sleeveless shirt under it.

Nellie was standing rigid and stiff. While they watched, she crouched. Her whole body was wrung with a spasm. The spasm passed. But in a few moments it started over again, and passed.

Billy muttered nervously, "There's something wrong." His bare hand disappeared. "Oh, Jesus," he said. "It's wrong."

The spasm came again, and this time Billy strained, and the muscles stood out on his arm and shoulder. He heaved strongly, his forehead beaded with perspiration. Nellie cried with pain. Billy was muttering, "It's wrong. I can't turn it. It's way wrong. It's turned all around wrong."

He glared wildly toward Jody. And then his fingers made a careful, careful diagnosis. His cheeks were growing tight and grey. He looked for a long questioning minute at Jody standing back of the stall. Then Billy stepped to the rack under the manure window and picked up a horseshoe hammer with his wet right hand.

"Go outside, Jody," he said.

The boy stood still and stared dully at him.

"Go outside, I tell you. It'll be too late."

Jody didn't move.

Then Billy walked quickly to Nellie's head. He cried, "Turn your face away, damn you, turn your face."

This time Jody obeyed. His head turned sideways. He heard Billy whispering hoarsely in the stall. And then he heard a hollow crunch of bone. Nellie chuckled shrilly. Jody looked back in time to see the hammer rise and fall again on the flat forehead. Then Nellie fell heavily to her side and quivered for a moment.

Billy jumped to the swollen stomach; his big pocket-knife was in his hand. He lifted the skin and drove the knife in. He sawed and ripped at the tough belly. The air filled with the sick odor of warm living entrails. The other horses reared back against their halter chains and squealed and kicked.

Billy dropped the knife. Both of his arms plunged into the terrible ragged hole and dragged out a big, white, dripping bundle. His teeth tore a hole in the covering. A little black head appeared through the tear, and little slick, wet ears. A gurgling breath was drawn, and then another. Billy shucked off the sac and found his knife and cut the string. For a moment he held the little black colt in his arms and looked at it. And then he walked slowly over and laid it in the straw at Jody's feet.

Billy's face and arms and chest were dripping red. His body shivered and his teeth chattered. His voice was gone; he spoke in a throaty whisper. "There's your colt. I promised. And there it is. I had to do it —had to." He stopped and looked over his shoulder into the box stall. "Go get hot water and a sponge," he whispered. "Wash him and dry him the way his mother would. You'll have to feed him by hand. But there's your colt, the way I promised."

Jody stared stupidly at the wet, panting foal. It stretched out its chin and tried to raise its head. Its blank eyes were navy blue.

"God damn you," Billy shouted, "will you go now for the water? *Will you go?*"

Then Jody turned and trotted out of the barn into the dawn. He ached from his throat to his stomach. His legs were stiff and heavy. He tried to be glad because of the colt, but the bloody face, and the haunted, tired eyes of Billy Buck hung in the air ahead of him.

Dust

FROM "THE GRAPES OF WRATH" BY

JOHN STEINBECK

To THE red country and part of the gray country of Oklahoma, the last rains came gently, and they did not cut the scarred earth. The plows crossed and recrossed the rivulet marks. The last rains lifted the corn quickly and scattered weed colonies and grass along the sides of the roads so that the gray country and the dark red country began to disappear under a green cover. In the last part of May the sky grew pale and the clouds that had hung in high puffs for so long in the spring were dissipated. The sun flared down on the growing corn day after day until a line of brown spread along the edge of each green bayonet. The clouds appeared, and went away, and in a while they did not try any more. The weeds grew darker green to protect themselves, and they did not spread any more. The surface of the earth crusted, a thin hard crust, and as the sky became pale, so the earth became pale, pink in the red country and white in the gray country.

In the water-cut gullies the earth dusted down in dry little streams. Gophers and ant lions started small avalanches. And as the sharp sun struck day after day, the leaves of the young corn became less stiff and erect; they bent in a curve at first, and then, as the central ribs of strength grew weak, each leaf tilted downward. Then it was June, and the sun shone more fiercely. The brown lines on the corn leaves widened and moved in on the central ribs. The weeds frayed and edged back toward their roots. The air was thin and the sky more pale; and every day the earth paled.

In the roads where the teams moved, where the wheels milled the ground and the hooves of the horses beat the ground, the dirt crust broke and the dust formed. Every moving thing lifted the dust into

the air: a walking man lifted a thin layer as high as his waist, and a
wagon lifted the dust as high as the fence tops, and an automobile
boiled a cloud behind it. The dust was long in settling back again.

When June was half gone, the big clouds moved up out of Texas
and the Gulf, high heavy clouds, rain-heads. The men in the fields
looked up at the clouds and sniffed at them and held wet fingers up to
sense the wind. And the horses were nervous while the clouds were up.
The rain-heads dropped a little spattering and hurried on to some other
country. Behind them the sky was pale again and the sun flared. In the
dust there were drop craters where the rain had fallen, and there were
clean splashes on the corn, and that was all.

A gentle wind followed the rain clouds, driving them on northward,
a wind that softly clashed the drying corn. A day went by and the
wind increased, steady, unbroken by gusts. The dust from the roads
fluffed up and spread out and fell on the weeds beside the fields, and
fell into the fields a little way. Now the wind grew strong and hard
and it worked at the rain crust in the corn fields. Little by little the
sky was darkened by the mixing dust, and the wind felt over the earth,
loosened the dust, and carried it away. The wind grew stronger. The
rain crust broke and the dust lifted up out of the fields and drove gray
plumes into the air like sluggish smoke. The corn threshed the wind
and made a dry, rushing sound. The finest dust did not settle back to
earth now, but disappeared into the darkening sky.

The wind grew stronger, whisked under stones, carried up straws
and old leaves, and even little clods, marking its course as it sailed
across the fields. The air and the sky darkened and through them the
sun shone redly, and there was a raw sting in the air. During a night
the wind raced faster over the land, dug cunningly among the rootlets
of the corn, and the corn fought the wind with its weakened leaves
until the roots were freed by the prying wind and then each stalk settled wearily sideways toward the earth and pointed the direction of the
wind.

The dawn came, but no day. In the gray sky a red sun appeared, a
dim red circle that gave a little light, like dusk; and as that day advanced, the dusk slipped back toward darkness, and the wind cried
and whimpered over the fallen corn.

Men and women huddled in their houses, and they tied handker-chiefs over their noses when they went out, and wore goggles to pro-tect their eyes.

When the night came again it was black night, for the stars could not pierce the dust to get down, and the window lights could not even spread beyond their own yards. Now the dust was evenly mixed with the air, an emulsion of dust and air. Houses were shut tight, and cloth wedged around doors and windows, but the dust came in so thinly that it could not be seen in the air, and it settled like pollen on the chairs and tables, on the dishes. The people brushed it from their shoulders. Little lines of dust lay at the door sills.

In the middle of that night the wind passed on and left the land quiet. The dust-filled air muffled sound more completely than fog does. The people, lying in their beds, heard the wind stop. They awak-ened when the rushing wind was gone. They lay quietly and listened deep into the stillness. Then the roosters crowed, and their voices were muffled, and the people stirred restlessly in their beds and wanted the morning. They knew it would take a long time for the dust to settle out of the air. In the morning the dust hung like fog, and the sun was as red as ripe new blood. All day the dust sifted down from the sky, and the next day it sifted down. An even blanket covered the earth. It settled on the corn, piled up on the tops of the fence posts, piled up on the wires; it settled on roofs, blanketed the weeds and trees.

The people came out of their houses and smelled the hot stinging air and covered their noses from it. And the children came out of the houses, but they did not run or shout as they would have done after a rain. Men stood by their fences and looked at the ruined corn, drying fast now, only a little green showing through the film of dust. The men were silent and they did not move often. And the women came out of the houses to stand beside their men—to feel whether this time the men would break. The women studied the men's faces secretly, for the corn could go, as long as something else remained. The children stood near by, drawing figures in the dust with bare toes, and the chil-dren sent exploring senses out to see whether men and women would break. The children peeked at the faces of the men and women, and then drew careful lines in the dust with their toes. Horses came to the watering troughs and nuzzled the water to clear the surface dust. After a while the faces of the watching men lost their bemused perplexity and became hard and angry and resistant. Then the women knew that they were safe and that there was no break. Then they asked, What'll we do? And the men replied, I don't know. But it was all right. The women knew it was all right, and the watching children knew it was all right. Women and children knew deep in themselves that no misfortune was too great to bear if their men were whole. The women went into the houses to their work, and the children began to play, but cautiously at first. As the day went forward the sun became less red. It flared down on the dust-blanketed land. The men sat in the doorways of their houses; their hands were busy with sticks and little rocks. The men sat still—thinking—figuring.

The Turtle

FROM "THE GRAPES OF WRATH" BY

JOHN STEINBECK

THE CONCRETE HIGHWAY was edged with a mat of tangled, broken, dry grass, and the grass heads were heavy with oat beards to catch on a dog's coat, and foxtails to tangle in a horse's fetlocks, and clover burrs to fasten in sheep's wool; sleeping life waiting to be spread and dispersed, every seed armed with an appliance of dispersal, twisting darts and parachutes for the wind, little spears and balls of tiny thorns, and all waiting for animals and for the wind, for a man's trouser cuff or the hem of a woman's skirt, all passive but armed with appliances of activity, still, but each possessed of the anlage of movement.

The sun lay on the grass and warmed it, and in the shade under the grass the insects moved, ants and ant lions to set traps for them, grasshoppers to jump into the air and flick their yellow wings for a second, sow bugs like little armadillos, plodding restlessly on many tender feet. And over the grass at the roadside a land turtle crawled, turning aside for nothing, dragging his high-domed shell over the grass. His hard legs and yellow-nailed feet threshed slowly through the grass, not really walking, but boosting and dragging his shell along. The barley beards slid off his shell, and the clover burrs fell on him and rolled to the ground. His horny beak was partly open, and his fierce, humorous eyes, under brows like fingernails, stared straight ahead. He came over the grass leaving a beaten trail behind him, and the hill, which was the highway embankment, reared up ahead of him. For a moment he stopped, his head held high. He blinked and looked up and down. At last he started to climb the embankment. Front clawed feet reached forward but did not touch. The hind feet kicked his shell along, and it scraped on the grass, and on the gravel.

As the embankment grew steeper and steeper, the more frantic were the efforts of the land turtle. Pushing hind legs strained and slipped, boosting the shell along, and the horny head protruded as far as the neck could stretch. Little by little the shell slid up the embankment until at last a parapet cut straight across its line of march, the shoulder of the road, a concrete wall four inches high. As though they worked independently the hind legs pushed the shell against the wall. The head upraised and peered over the wall to the broad smooth plain of cement. Now the hands, braced on top of the wall, strained and lifted, and the shell came slowly up and rested its front end on the wall. For a moment the turtle rested. A red ant ran into the shell, into the soft skin inside the shell, and suddenly head and legs snapped in, and the armored tail clamped in sideways. The red ant was crushed between body and legs. And one head of wild oats was clamped into the shell by a front leg. For a long moment the turtle lay still, and then the neck crept out and the old humorous frowning eyes looked about and the legs and tail came out. The back legs went to work, straining like elephant legs, and the shell tipped to an angle so that the front legs could not reach the level cement plain. But higher and higher the hind legs boosted it, until at last the center of balance was reached, the front tipped down, the front legs scratched at the pavement, and it was up. But the head of wild oats was held by its stem around the front legs.

Now the going was easy, and all the legs worked, and the shell boosted along, waggling from side to side. A sedan driven by a forty-year-old woman approached. She saw the turtle and swung to the right, off the highway, the wheels screamed and a cloud of dust boiled up. Two wheels lifted for a moment and then settled. The car skidded back onto the road, and went on, but more slowly. The turtle had jerked into its shell, but now it hurried on, for the highway was burning hot.

And now a light truck approached, and as it came near, the driver saw the turtle and swerved to hit it. His front wheel struck the edge of the shell, flipped the turtle like a tiddly-wink, spun it like a coin, and rolled it off the highway. The truck went back to its course along the right side. Lying on its back, the turtle was tight in its shell for a long time. But at last its legs waved in the air, reaching for something to pull it over. Its front foot caught a piece of quartz and little by little the shell pulled over and flopped upright. The wild oat head fell out and three of the spearhead seeds stuck in the ground. And as the turtle crawled on down the embankment, its shell dragged dirt over the seeds. The turtle entered a dust road and jerked itself along, drawing a wavy shallow trench in the dust with its shell. The old humorous eyes looked ahead, and the horny beak opened a little. His yellow toe nails slipped a fraction in the dust.

M. F. FISHER

It is as interesting as it is unprofitable to speculate on what writers will concern themselves with ten thousand years from now. Humanity (well, my guess is as good as yours) will be unified and so there will be no literature based on racial or national differences. Money and the class struggle will both have been liquidated; imagine what that will do to the novel. There will be no neuroses or mental conflicts, so a rearisen Sophocles or Dostoevsky will have nothing to write about. The individual will probably have been submerged in an efficient mass society—no more lyric poetry. The professors may even have fixed up love so that there will be more than enough to go round and nobody will be unhappy enough (or happy enough) to be inspired to write romances.

One theme will remain—maybe. That's eating. The way things look now, the palate and the alimentary canal are set for life, for the life of man. The curious pleasure that comes of chewing and swallowing miscellaneous masses of nutritive molecules will probably still exist ten thousand years hence, unless the human anatomy has been radically remodeled and streamlined in the interval.

That means the literature of gastronomy, one of the oldest forms of literature we know of, will still be popular. Not that good books about food are common, though you would imagine the subject, which interests everybody, would inspire a great deal of fine writing. The fact is that most food books (I am not here speaking of cookbooks or recipe collections, which belong to the literature of knowledge, not to the literature of power) are written by gourmets for gourmets. Even so delightful a volume as P. Morton Shand's A Book of Food has a touch of the esoteric. Or, if such books are not full of gastronomic chi-chi, they are full of a certain unpalatable fake-hearty Rabelaisianism.

That is why I sing the praises of Serve It Forth, by a young woman named M. F. K. Fisher. It is a book as charming as it is unpretentious—good talk about good food by one who does not believe that you need temperament to like your soup.

Mrs. Fisher wrote it in a mild huff after discovering "that no self-respecting restaurateur will pay more than a tolerant and patronizing half-attention to a woman's ideas for a good dinner." The huff was a lucky one. Serve It Forth avoids all the pitfalls mentioned in its first chapter. It does not "begin with witty philosophizing on the pleasures of the table" or end with a suggested menu "for an intimate dinner given to seven gentlemen who know his wife, by a wealthy old banker who feels horns pricking up gently from his bald skull." It does not show pictures of its author "standing beside a quaint old inn near Oxford or a quaint old inn near Cannes." It was not written by two young men who "are young and full of intellectual fun and frolic, and making a gastronomic tour on bicycles." From its pages there does not rise "a reek, a heady stench of truffles, Château Yquem, and quails financière."

In a dozen brief chapters, not too stuffy with facts, Mrs. Fisher manages to sketch the history of food, from the Emperor Shennung's great cookbook, the Hon-Zo (about 2800 B.C.), up to the celebrated period of Carême. To ensure easy digestion, she interlards these chapters with others, more personal than historical, and these latter make the book the rare and flavorous thing it is. There is a first-rate essay on the potato, and another one which raises, but does not settle, the whole puzzling question of the social status of vegetables—why, for example, should cabbage be infra dig, and why is broccoli tony? There is a charming chapter, called "Borderland," that deals with the "secret eatings" each of us has a passion for. (Somehow I always remember Mary MacLane, "the Butte Bashkirtseff," and her morbid craving for a cold boiled potato extracted from the icebox at two in the morning and eaten in the fingers, without salt or butter.) Mrs. Fisher's private vice runs to sections of tangerine, carefully de-strung, slowly melted to a hot, voluptuous plumpness on a radiator, and then placed for a few minutes on packed snow, to ensure the forming of an icy, paper-thin shell of sweetness.

I like, too, the story of how Papa Papazi prepared snails, not to mention the one about the snails that exploded, or the one about the last virgin woman truffle-hunter in France.

Of recipes, as is proper in such a book, there are but a handful, carefully chosen for their nonpracticality. They are not intended for use. They have but an incantatory value: they are food to stimulate the very imaginations of our palates. Such a recipe is that for the authentic Dijon pain d'épice, according to which the paste, worked up on a base of old black honey (prepared, no doubt, by some old black bees), is supposed to ripen in a cold temperature for several months or even years. To those seeking desperately a novel dish for a most special occasion, I recommend one startling recipe Mrs. Fisher dug up out of a six-hundred-year-old manuscript. It's very simple: "Take a capon and a little pig and smite them in the waist. Sew the hind part of one on the fore quarters of the other, and stuff, and roast, and serve them forth."

The two finest chapters in Serve It Forth happen, I think, to be literature. They are really tales. One is achingly sad, one is muscularly gay. The finer of them, "The Standing and the Waiting," slight as it is, is perfectly written and reveals a gift of phrase (who can forget Mrs. Fisher's Chinese "eating pâté in a trance of philosophical nausea"?) that should make Mrs. Fisher as good a writer as she is probably a cook.

The Standing and the Waiting

BY

M. F. K. FISHER

It was at the top of the stairs that I first felt something wrong. Until then all had been as I last knew it: the archway, the irregular honey-coloured courtyard, the rounded trees in tubs. The stairs, too, were the same, bending round and back over themselves in several shallow flights; and at the top was the familiar glass box with trout, a plate of mushrooms, and some steaks laid carelessly across the cold-pipes that made its bottom.

We looked for a moment into the box, Chexbres with the hurried, timid appraisal of a man who is in a strange place and conscious of being watched for his reactions to it by another person to whom it is familiar, I with the proud worry of a woman who fears she has too much boasted.

Would the dishes be as exciting, as satisfying? Would the wine still be the best wine? And I, would I be accepted, a loving admirer, or would I now be long forgotten?

Well, the glass box was the same. Chexbres flipped me a quick smile of reassurance. We went along the ugly tiled corridor, past the water-closets where I felt a sudden hilarious memory of my mother's consternation when she had first entered them and found them full of men all chatting, easing themselves, belching appreciatively.

I started to tell Chexbres of her face, puckered in an effort to look broad-minded. We turned the first abrupt corner of the hall, the corner where the kitchens started.

One of the doors opened. A rat-like boy darted out, ducking his head and grinning shyly as he passed us. I refused to look at Chexbres, for I knew that he had smelled, as I had, as alas! I had, that faint trail of bad air following after the scullion like the silver of a snail, bad air rising noxiously from the hidden dirty corners of the kitchens.

I finished the story of my mother's dauntless face, as we hurried on down the long dim corridor.

"There are two dining-rooms for the *pensionnaires*," I chattered foolishly, "and the *pensionnaires* are everybody—like the mayor and the rich brothel-keepers and carpenters and Chinese students.

"And here is Ribaudot's office."

I was trying to sound casual, but I felt very nervous. Oh, to have talked so much of the restaurant, to have boasted! And then that little ominous whiff! Or had Chexbres noticed it?

I tapped nonchalantly on the half-open glass door of the small, incredibly disordered room.

"Come in, then!" The voice was cross and muffled.

We pushed into the office. By the dim window two cooks in very tall hats sat with their bare arms leaning on a table covered with empty dishes. A cradled bottle lay in front of them. They smiled impersonally.

Ribaudot stood clumsily with one leg still half under the table, his hands leaning on his tall desk.

"Come in, come in," he said, more pleasantly. He wiped his mouth, and peered politely at us.

"How do you do—good afternoon, Monsieur Ribaudot. I am sure you don't remember me: Madame Fischer, who used so often to dine here? I used to come here with——"

"Oh, of course! Why, of course!" He smiled warmly, but I could see that he did not remember. I shrugged inside, and while I introduced Chexbres as a fervent student of gastronomy, and we all chattered and assured each other of remembrance and good will, I looked for change.

If the whiff, the faint bad trail, had caught Ribaudot, it was not yet evident. His office was filled with the conglomerate cooling odours of a good meal, and he himself with the first leisurely torpor of perfect digestion. Yes, of course he looked older, perhaps thinner, uncombed as ever, though, and still modestly sure of being a great *restaurateur*.

"And Charles, little Charles?" I asked, suddenly.

Several looks crossed in the air. Chexbres looked at me, warmly, smiling at my nostalgic probings and at what I had told him of the waiter Charles. I looked first at Chexbres, thanking him for recognizing the name, and assuring him that even if Charles were long dead, he had still been the ultimate, the impeccable peak of all waiters. Then I saw Ribaudot look swiftly at the two silent cooks and they at him, a look—a look—I felt very sad and puzzled.

Ribaudot interrupted me.

"The little Charles?" he asked, blandly. "Ah, you remember the little old Charles?" His voice was noncommittal. "But certainly he is here. We will call him."

Through my half-hearted protestations he walked majestically the three paces to the door, and disappeared. The air was still full of crossed meaningful looks. I wondered very much, and watched Chexbres' impassive interest in the framed diplomas on the walls. I tried to feel impassive, too.

Chexbres turned. Charles stood in the doorway, breathing quickly, a rumpled napkin over one arm. Oh, I had forgotten how small—but hadn't he been fatter? Yes, old, the little *old* Charles.

I went quickly toward him, watching his pouchy face lighten quickly from peevish bewilderment to pleasure.

"Howdedo, Charles. I don't know if you remember——"

"O my God! Oh, pardon, pardon, but it is the little American student, the little lady!"

Behind me, Chexbres laughed to hear me called little as I peered down on Charles, he up at me, timidly still, but recognizing me.

"And you, Madame? And how long is it? And you, are you well? Has it been two years? *Six?* Impossible! But it is good, pardon me for saying so, but it is good to see you!"

He stopped suddenly, looking confusedly at the two silent cooks, and then at Ribaudot. He seemed to shrink even smaller.

"Monsieur Ribaudot," I said, "would it be possible to command a dinner for this evening, and ask for the services of Charles?"

"But certainly, certainly!" He pulled a pad of paper toward him, and started to make squiggles on it.

"Until eight tonight, then, Charles. And the old table in the corner —was it Number Four?"

I turned to Ribaudot again. He seemed to know me at last, and to be trying to comfort me, to soften life for me. And all the time we discussed food so pleasantly I wondered at Charles' quick, poignant, wet look of—of gratitude?—as he hurried back to his work.

I felt sad, but said nothing to Chexbres. Instead, we talked of Burgundian architecture, not even mentioning the Burgundian meal we had so long planned.

At eight o'clock the small dining-room was full, except for our waiting table. As we sat down I saw in one easy glance that the people were no different after six years. There was the old woman with a dog and a dancing-boy on her way to Cannes, and the table of American school-teachers eating from a guide-book. And there were the two big young Englishmen in brown and grey, looking embarrassed before their larks on toast.

At the table under the mirror sat a college professor; the College Professor, twirling a glass of Corton, the pedagogic connoisseur, sipping alone in solemn appreciation, sure that his accent was as refined as his taste.

There were two tables of French people, gay and hungry. I remembered that their faces would grow red, later on.

A Chinese eating truffled *pâté* in a trance of philosophical nausea, two Lesbians drinking Vichy, three silent *pensionnaires,* a priest—the hard white lights burned down on all of us, the mirror reflected our monotonous gestures, the grey walls picked out our pale natures and the warmth of colour and odour and taste before us on the white tables.

"This is a good room," Chexbres murmured, lowering his eyelids and straightening a straight fork. "I like small rooms. Small rooms, for eating—or mountain-sides."

"Good evening! Ah, 'sieur-'dame, you are here!"

Charles stood by the table, breathing fast. His minute moustache was newly stiff with wax, and his hair was plastered in a thin replica of the debonair curlicues he used to wear. He beamed anxiously at us.

"Does—is everything as you wished?"

"Everything is perfect, Charles!" I wondered if my voice were too fervent. "Now we will start with a little glass of Dubonnet, please."

When he had gone, Chexbres said: "You are known, my dear! You should be much flattered—or I for being with you."

He smiled, the sweet-tongued self-mocker, at me and at the table, and I looked with less haste at the tall crystal tulips to hold wine, at the napkins folded like pheasants, at the inky menu big as a newspaper, and our own little typewritten one on top of it, at the flowers——

Flowers *chez* Ribaudot, Ribaudot who hated any foreign odours near his plates? Never before—no, we were the only diners with flowers on our table.

On the little serving-board beside us, Charles fussed clumsily with a new bottle of Dubonnet. Finally it was open. He poured it with a misjudged flourish. Purple spread on the cloth. I looked quickly, without meaning to, at Chexbres, but he was watching the quiet colour in his glass. Perhaps he had not seen, had not realized, the fumblings of my perfect waiter?

He raised his *apéritif*. His eyes were wide and candid.

"I drink to our pasts—to yours and mine. And to ours. The wine is strong. Time is strong, too." He bowed slightly. "I grow solemn—or sententious."

I laughed at him. "I'm not afraid of time."

"Don't boast."

"I'm not boasting. Really, I'm glad six years—oh, it's too complicated. But this tastes good. I'm hungry."

"And this will be a good meal, worth waiting even longer than six years for. Do you know," he asked naïvely, "that I've never before had a menu written just for me? It's very exciting."

I felt my self-confidence sweep back, as he meant it to.

"And flowers," he went on. "I've had flowers on my table, but never the only ones, in a room of such important people."

We looked vaguely, amicably, at the stiff little bouquet, mimosa and a purplish rosebud and a short twig of cypress.

Charles steamed beside us, with a tall pitcher of soup. While he served it, it spilled from the trembling cups into the saucers. I felt a flash of intense irritation: wet saucers, God! how they irritate me. I looked straight into his eyes.

They were not wet and grateful now. They were desperate eyes, bloodshot, frantic, desperate. I cringed away.

"Oh, Chexbres," I whispered, "don't mind the spilling! Don't! It's that he's nervous. His hand's shaking because of that, I know."

You are lying to save your own boastful face, too, I said inside. You know Charles is drunk. Yes, Charles, the perfect waiter, spilling soup and drunk, and it hurts your pride.

"Maybe his feet hurt him," I went on very fast. "I know you hate soup in saucers. But you know I've heard that waiters do stranger things than most criminals, simply because their feet hurt."

"Yes, I'm sure," Chexbres agreed, vaguely. "This is really delicious, my dear.

"You know," he said, in a suddenly direct voice, "I can't understand why most people are put off at first by the coloured tiles on the roofs of Burgundy. It seems to me they're a definite outcropping of the plebeian in architecture, like the frescoes of Swiss interiors during the same period."

For a moment I felt rebuffed. But almost at once I knew he was right. Six years—six hundred years . . . architecture was better.

We talked, and well, and all the dinner was most excellent, and the wine was like music on our tongues. Time was forgotten, and its signals, too. But I noticed, with a kind of fifth eye, that Charles' hand grew steady, and his own eye clear, until by the end of the meal I dared preen myself upon his delicate sure touch.

"Have you ever seen that better done?" I asked Chexbres.

"No. No, he is wonderful. He is an artist."

We watched as in a blissful dream the small fat hands moving like magic among bottles and small bowls and spoons and plates, stirring, pouring, turning the pan over the flame just so, just so, with the face bent keen and intent above.

"It's like a brain operation," Chexbres said, "—the hard light, the excitement, the great surgeon. Thank you for bringing me here. It's worth——"

It was done. We tasted. We nodded silently, and smiled at Charles, and he looked almost like the old Charles again, very self-sure. I felt happy.

After coffee, I laughed to think of us sitting there almost the last, and at what I was going to do.

"Chexbres, you think I've shown off, but that was only the beginning! Now I really do show off, and all for your benefit."

We smiled at each other, very effortless and calm.

"Charles," I called, warning Chexbres quickly, "You have never tasted the local *marc,* remember!

"Charles, what do you think has been the sad experience—but first, are we keeping you too late?"

I waved my hand at the now empty room, dim in every corner but ours, and at a scullery boy scrubbing the hall. I felt expansive, warm from the wine, at ease in Time.

"Oh, but what an idea!" Charles exploded. "Excuse me for chiding you, Madame, but what an idea! Madame, you must know that for you to have another good meal *chez* Ribaudot, and to go away remembering it and me, I would gladly stay here until morning—no, until tomorrow night, by God!"

Chexbres and I bowed courteously. Charles did, too.

"And the sad experience, Madame?"

"Oh, thank you for recalling me. I had almost forgotten. Charles, last night we had a stroke of luck that was unfortunate—I should say almost desolating. I, who wished to introduce our good friend Monsieur Chexbres to the famous *marc* of Burgundy, was served with a glass of some strange liquid—thank God I had the good sense to taste it before letting Monsieur come near it!—some strange liquid, pale, cut, rank, which could never——"

"Ah, but I know! I know where!" Charles beamed, flourishing his napkin with glee.

"Oh, but naturally I would not be so indiscreet as to mention the name of the miserable restaurant," I protested, rhetorically. I glanced at Chexbres exultantly: the scene was beautiful.

"No need, no need, Madame! A restaurant serving the good *marc* so insultingly, and to you, a connoisseur" (here I bowed graciously) "and to this poor gentleman a sure amateur having his first taste (here Chexbres lowered his eyes modestly)—"ah, such poisonous conduct, my God! could only be at" (and here Charles leaned very close to us in the empty room and hissed) "could only be at La Tour!"

He stood off, triumphant. I pressed a little line into the tablecloth with my thumb nail, smirking, murmuring, "Of course I say nothing, no names!" in complete agreement. I could feel Chexbres' appreciation all round me.

"But, *but* 'dame, we must rectify that infected that—pardon me— that stinking behaviour!"

I sighed faintly. It had worked!

"Yes, my idea, too. But no ordinary *marc,* Charles, no liqueur served on any one's order. This must be——"

"Yes, very special," he finished for me. "Trust me, Madame. It may take a few extra minutes. A little more *filtre,* perhaps, while I am gone?"

Chexbres and I sat wordless, looking mildly and somnolently at each other. We sipped at the bitter black coffee. A rickety old ventilator whirred in the ceiling, and the boy cleaning the hall bumped his bucket against the tiles. Lights went out, except over our table.

Charles tiptoed back, wheezing, but his face full of life. He held a filthy old green bottle, not picturesquely crusted, but filthy. Silently he poured a little dark brown liquid into a large glass. He swirled it round. Chexbres reached for it.

"Permit me, sir," Charles halted him, "permit me to suggest that Madame taste it."

I winked slightly at Chexbres, and took up the glass. I tried to look like a connoisseur, a little pompous probably. I sipped, and then I could only look beatifically delighted, for it was the cleanest, smoothest distillation that I had ever met.

"Ah!"

Charles sighed. I had told him. He poured the glass almost half full, at least twice as full as he should have, and with a jubilant look disappeared into the wet dark hall.

"Chexbres, now *I* shall be solemn. But I have never been served with such *marc!* Not even Ribaudot would serve that to his best friends, to any one less than the mayor or maybe the Holy Ghost. Where did Charles get it?"

Chexbres let it run under his tongue, and sat nodding ecstatically at me. I could almost see it seeping through his head, in and around in a hot tonic tide, and then down his throat.

"Dear sweet gentle Jesus!" he remarked, softly.

"Oh, I'm glad we came, Chexbres. After all, I mean."

We both drank at the one glass, and talked peacefully under the one white light. Finally the *marc* was gone. Charles appeared, carrying the filthy bottle.

"Oh, no more, no more! Really, we couldn't——"

He stopped very still, and looked at me.

"Madame, you must drink one glass. Please!" he said, in a quiet voice, almost muttering. "Please drink this glass from me. It is I, Charles, who offer it to you and to Monsieur Chexbres."

"But—it is so late, and—" The thought of swallowing one more mouthful closed my throat, almost.

"I have said I would stay until tomorrow for you. I would stay until the end of the world, truly." He looked at me calmly, standing between us and the dark doorway. Beyond him I could see nothing, and there was not a sound anywhere, except the three of us breathing rather cautiously.

"Thank you," Chexbres said, warmly. "Madame was afraid only of detaining you too long, Charles. Otherwise we could sit for ever, too, drinking this miraculous liqueur."

He held out the glass. With a hand steady as oak, Charles poured it to the brim, a good half-pint of strong *marc*.

"Thank you, Charles," I said. "I want never to leave, here where I have so often been happy. It may be six years again. Will you prepare the bill, please?"

We knew we must drink it all. It was like smouldering fire, wonderful still, but hard now to swallow. We sat without moving, conscious suddenly of exhaustion, and of being perhaps too full of food, with all the heady wine-life gone out of us.

Charles came back, with the little sheet of flimsy paper on a plate. I wondered about the tip: in a way I felt like not leaving one, because he seemed more than a waiter now. But when he brought back change, I left it all on the plate.

"Thank you, Madame," he said, and did not pick it up. He stood watching us sip resolutely at the *marc*. Finally I looked up at him.

"Madame, thank you, thank you for coming again."

I wanted not to be personal, so I said, "But why not? All people who love good food come to Ribaudot's again."

"Yes," he stuttered slightly, "but—pardon me—but I mean thank you for asking for me. You don't know——"

"Oh, Charles, it is we who are fortunate, to have your services." I felt very polished and diplomatic, but at the same time sincere, sincere as hell under the weariness and all the *marc*.

"No, no—I mean, you will never know what it meant, tonight, to have you ask for me, little old Charles. And now, good evening."

Chexbres asked, quickly, "But we will pass this way again, and soon we hope, and then of course——?"

"Ah, who knows?" Charles raised his eyebrows toward his thinning curlicue of hair, restrained a gesture to stroke his little whiff of moustache, smiled debonairly at us, and disappeared finally into the black corridor.

"I thought he said he would wait until tomorrow night," I murmured, flippantly. Then I felt rather ashamed, and apologized. "He'll probably be waiting at the end of the hall, the top of the stairs, to help us with our coats."

Chexbres said nothing, but slowly drank down the rest of the *marc*. The chairs squawked wildly as we stood up. The sound was almost good in that silent room.

In the corridor we saw a dim light, and as we went by Ribaudot's office, his silhouette was sharp against the frosted glass, bent over his high desk.

"I know where the coats are," I whispered, and we tiptoed down the hall.

"Is it Madame Fischer?" His voice came muffled through the door. He opened it, blinking at us, with his hair mussed.

"Oh, I'm sorry! I do hope we haven't kept you," I said, in confusion.

He looked very tenderly at us. "No. And have you dined well? I am glad. I have your coats in here."

We stood awkwardly in the doorway while he crossed the little room to the table where the two cooks had sat in the afternoon. Our coats were piled on it, to one side, and a stiff ugly bouquet of mimosa and two purplish rosebuds and a twig of cypress stood by them. I looked dully at it, wishing I were home in bed, very tired.

"It was good of you to remember Ribaudot," he said.

"It was very natural. Who does not?"

"Ah, things nowadays—the affairs—" but he bowed, acceptance calm on his face.

"And the poor old Charles. It was especially good for him. I see you and I shared the honour of flowers from him." He looked impersonally at the ugly bouquet. "Yes, I fired Charles today, just before your first visit. He is on his way to the South by now.

"Permit me to help you with your scarf. It was sad—a fine waiter once, a brave little man always—but what will you do? Everything changes. Everything passes.

"Good-night. Good-night, sir and Madame, and thank you. And good-bye."

"Au revoir, we hope," I called as we walked away from him towards the dark.

"Who knows?" He shrugged, and closed the glass door.

In the long hall corruption hung faint and weakly foul on the still air. The stairs were deep, with the empty glass box like a dark ice cube, and we breathed freely once out in the courtyard.

It was filled with moonlight. The trees in tubs were black, and through the archway the tower of the palace gleamed and glowed against the black sky.

Chexbres took my hand gently, and pointed to the roofs, coloured tiles, Burgundian, drained of their colour now, but plainly patterned. I began to cry.

César

BY

M. F. K. FISHER

For one reason or another it is thought advisable to change the names of real people when you write about them. I can do that sometimes, but not now. And of course there is no reason why I should. César is very real: he lives more surely than most men; and if he does read about himself in any book, which is doubtful, he will at the most be amused.

I cannot remember how we first met him. He was the butcher in a village of fishermen. We were foreigners, who stayed in the village several weeks. It is probably strange that we knew César so well, and he us.

The women of the village hated him and were afraid of him, but, "All I do is reach through my window at night," said César, "and there's a fine piece of woman waiting for me in the dark street. Any time, every night, I pluck them in."

The women hated him for two reasons. He had been very cruel to his termagant wife. She fled from him finally, and the two sons with her, after a fight between them and their father.

They were very strong men, all three, and when they were angry they swelled with muscle and spleen. César chased them out, all howling maledictions.

Later one of the sons crept back and stabbed at his father, but César broke the dagger between his fists and gave the pieces to his son's mistress, one night after he had plucked her through his window.

But it was sorrow for the poor wife, even if she was a foul-mouthed shrew, that made the village women hate César. That was the first reason. The second was that the men in the village loved César more than they did their women or their sons or even their boats.

They loved him for a thousand reasons and one reason. César was all that every man wants secretly to be: strong, brave; foul, cruel, reckless; desired by women and potent as a goat; tender and very sweet with children; feared by the priest, respected by the mayor; utterly selfish and as generous as a prince; gay. César was man, Man noble and monstrous again after so many centuries.

Once a week, two or three times a week, we'd walk down the one street, after noon dinner. All the boats beached on one side of us, all the doorsteps empty on the other, desertion would lie like dust in the air, with here and there a woman peering sourly from a dark room.

Madame Revenusso or Madame Médin, maybe, would call sullenly that César was looking for Monsieur Fischer.

Al's face would flash with joy, like a torch or a trumpet call. He'd hurry away. I'd go home alone, understanding some of the village women's jealous anger.

César's meat shop was behind the chapel, in a dirty alley. It was seldom peopled: women would buy no cuts from him, the devil, and even if they had wanted to he was always saving the best for himself. Probably he ran the shop because it was an easy way to have good meat ready to hand.

Back of the store, there was one large room. It was dark, spotless, full of clean cold air from stone walls and floor, and almost bare. Under the lone window was César's big bed, very conveniently arranged for his carnal nocturnes. A wide ledge jutted from two walls, wide enough to sit on or lie on. There were one or two chairs on the scrubbed tiles of the floor, nuisances to stumble over in the room's darkness.

In the centre was the heart, the yolk, the altar, the great stone fireplace flat and high as a table, with an iron top for pots and a grill. And the whole ceiling of the room was its chimney, rising to a point and a far hole above the fire, like an ancient ducal kitchen.

It was there, to that big dark room, that the men would come, usually in the afternoon. I never saw them there, nor the room, neither, but I know they came to it as quickly as they could, very joyfully. César would say "Come!" and they would hurry.

On the stove there was always something steaming in a great black pot—a stew of tiny opaque whitebait, or tripe jugged in sour white wine, or succulent scraps whose origin César leeringly would not tell.

Piled on a chair, or on the floor near the stove, were steaks as thick as your fist, or four or five lamb's legs, or a kid ready to broil. On the stone ledge were two kegs of wine, or three, or bottles never counted.

The fire was hot, the steam rose toward the roof.

César stood taller and broader than any other man before his stove, stirring, basting, smelling. His voice was mightier.

"Drink!" he cried out. "Drink, eat!" And he roared with joy.

In the other houses women snapped at their children or perked their heads towards the chapel alley. When they heard songs and wild laughter, or more alarming silence, they sighed and looked black. If there'd only been bad strumpets there behind the butcher shop, they would have comprehended, but just men—it was unnatural.

If their husbands came home before dark, they would not eat fish soup and bread with the children. If they came too late for that, they leaped fiercely and silently on the sleeping women, or stood for a long time looking through the shutters at the sea, their faces very gentle and intent.

The women hated César.

The mornings after, they cackled maliciously when his shop stayed closed until noon, and when he finally opened its wide door, they looked sideways at his tired thick face.

"M'sieur César appears ill today," they would greet him, oilily.

"Ill? My God, no, dear Madame Dirtypot! Two quarts of purgative water is all I need—or three. And I'd advise the same for your husband—but in proportion, in proportion, my good Mrs. Soilskirt. I'd say a half-glass. More would tear his vitals clean off, with more loss to you than to him, eh, Madame Foulface?"

César's eyes, almost shut, gleamed wickedly, and he hoisted up his big sagging belly with lewd relish.

Then his face cleared. A young woman came towards him, with a warm little naked child on one arm. César called her.

"Célèstine! How goes it with your new rascal?"

He paid no attention to her stiff mouth and forehead, but looked lovingly at the tiny brown baby she had.

"Oh, he is a beauty, but a beauty, so strong and straight! Célèstine, you've done a fine job here. That's right, girl—smile. César is your good friend, really. And this child! He is a grand fellow, I tell you. Here, come to me, you little beautiful limb of the devil!"

César stood in the strong white sunlight, his two bottles of physic forgotten. The naked baby in his arms grinned up at him candidly while he murmured to it. He turned it across his arm, and ran his huge hand over its firm little bottom.

"My God!" he exclaimed, suddenly, "what a delicious, truly what a delicious morsel that would be, broiled!"

With an outraged squawk Célèstine tore her baby from him and scuttled away. César yelled with laughter, belched mightily, and went toward his shop, his physic under his arms.

Whenever a strange creature came up in the nets, some sea beast's child or watery vegetable, the fishermen carried it to César.

He'd poke it, smell it, inevitably taste it. If he spat it out, they'd nod wisely. Poison! If he gulped it down alive, or cooked it up into a queer stew, they'd talk for days, admiringly. Brave man to eat a mass of purple jelly with a little green-toothed mouth in its middle!

But do you remember, and their eyes would glisten with amazed delight, do you remember the time the crocodile died at the big zoo in the city, and César was called to skin it, and brought himself back a fine thick steak from it? Ah, do you remember?

The time came for us to go. We asked César to come to our house to eat a last supper.

I felt awkward, because I was a woman—but there was no other place for me to eat. César felt awkward for the same reason.

He came with a coat on, and a pink shirt, and silently handed me a massive filet of beef. I left the room with it, and heard him talking to Al, but when I came back he stopped.

The meal was strained at the beginning, but we had plenty of good wine, and the meat was the best I have ever tasted.

César put down his knife and fork.

"She likes it, she likes good food!" he said, wonderingly, to Al. "She cannot be a real woman!"

After that things were very pleasant. He took off his coat, and we ate and drank and talked, all a good deal.

"I hear you are married," César remarked. "It is a filthy lie, naturally?"

"But of course we are married," Al protested. "We have been married for several years."

César peered incredulously at us, and then laughed.

"Ridiculous! And why? Children, you are not married, I say— because marriage is a rotten business, and you are not rotten." He spat neatly over his huge pink shoulder. "If you were married, Alfred, Alfred-the-Penguin, my Al, would not be a real man, happy. And he is. And you," he glared at me, "would not be sitting knowing good meat between your teeth. And you are.

"Therefore, my two peculiar little foreign children, you are not married! No, you are brother and sister, living in sinful glory!"

He laughed until the whole room shook, and tipped a full bottle of wine down his throat.

"I shall die soon," he said, "and when I die, every man in the village will laugh for many days. Do you know why? Because they'll have all my wine to drink, barrels and casks of it, to drink to my commands, and they'll all try to drink as I would, as I've taught them.

"Yes, they'll drink for me, to float my soul to Purgatory. And the biggest cask of wine will be my coffin. My friends know. They'll put me in it and bury me deep, and they and all the women, too, will weep."

He was silent for a minute, and then roared another laugh.

"And grapes will grow up from me," he cried, "and by God, what wine I'll make!"

Al and I looked and recognized there a ghost with us, another Man from whose dead heart had sprung a vine. Was he César, was César that dim great figure who heard of Pan's death and cried tears as big as ostrich eggs?

We parted merrily, with no farewells.

About a year later, a shabby post card came from the village on the Mediterranean coast. It was stiffly pencilled.

"My friends in Sinful Glory, plant a tree somewhere for César." Since then we have planted many, almost all for him.

I imagine that every writer who has a dozen unsalable short stories in the bottom drawer has played with the notion of stringing together a modern Decameron. The form has always seemed to me dull, and so has Boccaccio, the most overpraised writer of an overpraised literary epoch. When I say that Miss Christina Stead's Salzburg Tales are far better than the Decameron, I intend nothing but disrespect to Boccaccio, prince of bores.

Miss Stead impales literary butterflies on the needles of malicious paragraphs, weaves medieval legends that sound as if you had looked in upon them years ago through the dim pages of the Gesta Romanorum, relates funny stories about goldfish that predict the fluctuations of the stock market, and tricks venerable jokes out until they become tiny, twinkling masterpieces of gargoyle humor.

The Salzburg Tales consists of forty adult fairy stories, bearing aloft (to steal a phrase from the author) "the hundred flowers of her unpremeditated virtuosity." Gnomelike mockery alternates with a luxuriance of chills and fevers. A "partisan of the improbable," she dares to tell stories of morbid, impassioned lovers, bleeding hearts, imps and triskelions, Don Juan as a matador, sparrows in love, ghosts and gazelles and the caverns of the dead. And she gets away with it, partly because of the beauty of the style, which occasionally softens into lushness, and partly because a faint ring of mockery sounds behind the heaviest and most shadowy of her gothic portals.

Yet the best thing in the book is not the tales themselves (a few of them are tediously complex) but forty pages of introductory matter, in which she characterizes in a page or paragraph the personages, gathered together at a Salzburg Festival, into whose mouths the tales are put. For wit, fancy, variety, light-brushwork satire, and almost offensive polish, these miniature novels are inimitable. There is nothing medieval about them; they are shrewdly cosmopolitan, jewelwork by a contemporary La Bruyère. I include here this introductory section and suggest that you get the book and try the tales themselves, in some mood that rejects the probable, the plain, the quotidian.

It is easy to say that Miss Stead is no artist, but rather an artificer, yet her artificiality is so easy, she is so airily confident in her romanticism, claiming nothing for it, charging it with no message, that in the end the most commonsensical reader is likely, for a luxurious moment, to smile with pleasure at the paradox of her Philosopher when he says, "I only tell fairy tales, for I would rather be seen in their sober vestments than in the prismatic unlikelihood of reality."

The Salzburg Tales

BY

CHRISTINA STEAD

THE PROLOGUE

SALZBURG, old princely and archiepiscopal city, and its fortress Hohen-Salzburg, lie among the mountains of the Tyrol, in Salzburg Province, in Austria. The river Salzach, swift and yellow from the glaciers and streaming mountain valleys, flows between baroque pleasure-castles standing in glassy lakes, and peasant villages pricked in their vineyards, and winds about to reflect the citadel rising in its forests, single eminence in the plain. The river divides the city, leaving a wooded mound on either hand, rushes noisily under the bridges between Italian domes and boulevarded banks, and rolls out, placid, fast and deep, towards the Bavarian plain and the rain-burdened evening sky.

Yesterday morning, the city flashed like an outcrop of rock-crystals in its cliffs by the river: in the evening, rain-clouds sat on the Kapuzinerberg and the Mönchsberg and squirted their black waters on the town and beat down the mild leafage of the woods. This morning the clouds rolled away with troutside gleams under a fresh wind, and the river, risen a foot in the night, and roaring like the wind, is again calm and yellow. And now, on this last day of July, the townspeople look at the red walls of the naked Tyrol far off and at the giant peak of the Untersberg, like a hatchet in the air, and all their conversation is that they hope it will be fine for the first day of the August festival, the great event of Salzburg men.

Now the streets are full: bands of German students in blue linen coats with rucksacks and staves lope through the town at a round pace, counting the monuments and ignoring the tourists; foreign women in summer dresses peer in jewellers' windows full of Swiss

547

clocks and edelweiss pressed under glass, foreign gentlemen buy tufts
of reindeer hair to put in their hats, and trout-flies; the milk-wagons
are busy, the elegants sit in the cafés and drink coffee with cream,
and the men going home from work on their bicycles glance thirstily
in the low leaded panes of beer-cellars on the Linzergasse, and see
severe Berlin merchants and tall blond American college boys drinking
good Salzburg beer. A stage has been put up in the Cathedral Place for
the Miracle Play of "Jedermann," German bands are playing Mozart
and Wagner in all the cafés, the Residenz Platz is packed with visitors
waiting to hear the Glockenspiel at six o'clock ring out its antique
elfin tunes, tourists pop in and out of the house at number nine,
Getreide-gasse, where Mozart was born, musicians and actors are walking and talking under the thick trees on the river-bank, and even the
poor people in the new pink and blue stucco houses, built in a marsh
on the Josef-Mayburger Kai, look at the red sunset and count busily
for the hundredth time the little profit they will make on the Viennese lady who has rented a room from them for the duration of the
Festival.

Opposite the fortress, across the river, is the yellow-walled Capuchin
convent in its tall wood. One has to pay a few groschen each day at the
convent gate to enter the wood. Within the gate, transported there
from Vienna, stands the little wooden hut in which Mozart wrote "The
Magic Flute." Higher up the hill is a fine outlook towards Bavaria,
and on the crest of the hill in the grounds of an ancient house built
of beams and hung with vines, in which the monks formerly dwelt, is
a vantage-point commanding the city and its environs.

In this wood the visitors to the August Festival walk often, and often
sit long, in groups, listening to the innumerable bells of the town
ringing through the wood, and talking, in the fresh mornings. The
wood is tranquil in its brown hollows and full of sandalled Capuchin
monks drawing wagons of wood, and woodcutters who have to take
their carts and horses down the steep Calvary Way beyond the convent gate to reach the streets of the town. Sometimes by the covered
well in the tall-wooded hollow are heard foreign voices relating sono-
rously the marvellous and dark and bloody annals of the town, or some
long-spun story brought in their packs with them from overseas, while

the soft Austrian breeze entreats the leaves in the tops of the trees, squirrels scrabble in the roots and wild violets and sun-coloured fungi fill the hollows. So passionate a love awakes in the stranger's breast as he scarcely feels for his native land, for the incomparable beauty of these wild peaks, these rose walls two thousand feet in air and this mediæval fortress hanging footless on an adamantine rock against the unweathered cliffs of the Untersberg: and as he walks, meditative, along some lowland or upland path, listening to the distant voices, the bells and the diminutive rustlings, he passes an old inhabitant with large brown eyes, sitting immobile on a log, who says politely in his sweet dialect, "Good-day," as he would to a son of the city come from a foreign shore.

THE PERSONAGES

A FRESH wind blew in the woods, the pigeons massed in the Residenz Platz, tooting because the sky was bright, and the fountain dropped loudly on the weedgrown stones. The people went through an archway into the Domplatz where "Jedermann" of the poet Hofmansthal was to be played in the open air before the cathedral. Actors in mediæval costumes ran about in the nearby streets and disappeared quickly in a little door at the back of the cathedral, or were seen leaning momentarily over the high cornices of the roofs of the Domplatz. In the courtyard of the fortress, high up in the air, tourists looking like flies or sparrows hung over the wall and peered at the Domplatz, trying to make out whether the play had begun, and whether many people had paid for seats. In the middle of the front seat sat the Archbishop of Salzburg, tall, plump and dressed in red, with white linen and white hands: he greeted distinguished visitors like a prince welcoming talent to his court. Near him on the same seat sat the superior from the Capuchin Convent and the Mayor of Salzburg; but these three great persons, who divided the town into three parts between them, told no tales in the Capuchin Wood.

The FESTIVAL DIRECTOR came in from the Cathedral bareheaded, warm with his last instructions to the actors. He bowed to the Archbishop and remarked that the pontifical sun shone on their labours, in a voice unctuous but constrained, for he was small and stout, while the Archbishop was firm, large and grey as a gravestone: likewise the sun shone in the Director's face and made it red, and he was aware that the Archbishop did not give a benedicite for his style. Courteously he bent his head once more to the Archbishop's chest and said, he hoped his Grace would applaud the Miracle Play of Everyman which they were about to put on again, and that, while indoors one tricked the eye with fat columns and a giant cornice to suggest boundless space, here his stage was two bare boards, for he had to present simple verities, and otherwise his theatre was exalted above fame by the redoubtable acts of Salzburg's Princes of the Church. Meanwhile, the Director cast glances about him, conscious of whispers and of people standing on tiptoe to see him. He murmured discreetly to the Mayor the hiding-places of his actors concealed on the roofs and explained to a monk that the church-bells of the town would be silent now until the play was done. Then, he glanced over the audience, standing three-quarters on to the Archbishop still with a gracious air which yet lacked polish, for he was a ready, practical man of elephantine dreams, who tried to give the imagination a footrest on earth: and he was always casting off from his thick, square shoulders set on his thick long torso, presentiments of trouble, of criticism and of failure. His eye grouped the audience quickly this way and that like the parting of thick hair with a comb. Here were the art patrons, rich amateurs, people of fashion, the Viennese, Berliners, New Yorkers, here the musicians, conductors and actors, there the poor, the townspeople from the boarding-houses, Cook's tourists: beyond the rope were the *Naturfreunde,* and in the background some wretched of the town, and peasants come in from the mountains wearing great black hats and bell-bottomed trousers, and monks and college students, and fishermen, and conscripts from the barracks down the river, and idling shopboys and shopgirls escaped for half an hour. Smiling, bowing and turning in the sun like a buoy in the bay, the Director backed away from the Archbishop and sat down a few seats away, waiting for the play to begin.

After the Festival Director came the VIENNESE CONDUCTOR, with another Conductor from Munich. The Viennese Conductor was like a tasselled reed, with shoulders and hands spreading outwards, delicate hips and a soft, long, feline stride: he sometimes took shorter steps and sometimes longer as if to show that in him the passion of rhythm was constant but tidal. He looked this way and that as he bowed obsequiously over his companion's conversation, smiling to himself on the side, as if he had a tiding of joy in his sleeve, and gathering in the ladies' glances; it might have been harvest-time and he a reaping-hook. Bowing, with long bright looks of adulation, he acknowledged

the distinguished guests, and stooped with manner consciously rich
and theatrical to the Archbishop, for whom he did not give a fig. He
took the hand of an aged prima donna and looked as if he would
faint from excessive admiration; and then he walked on indifferently,
dropping all this behind him, like a dolphin in the waves, going on
from easy conquest to easy conquest, speaking of violins and sunshine,
of Max Reinhardt and overtones, of Mozart and Apollo, easily, wittily,
with everything said in reverse, in order to amuse. He was thirty years
of age and had conducted orchestras since the age of six. He delighted
especially in chamber concerts where the atmosphere was intimate and
the women were near enough to study his attitudes, how he swooned
with ecstasy one moment and closed his eyes wearily at another, how
his eyes sparkled when the soft theme rose on the strings, and again,
how he snapped his fingers quickly, impatient to hear the quick tread
of the bows getting through the thicket of notes in soldierly unison:
now he waved them off with both hands, entreating them not to assail
his silken nerves with such boisterousness, now he bowed to them, and
scooped them out of the basin of the orchestra, then he smiled like a
lover to one, and gave a snaky look to another; he gathered them in
his arms like a woman gathering chickens in her apron, he danced up
and down on his toes as if he were a reed alone bearing the tremendous
harmonies of the wild. At the end, turning from the performers, he
bowed like an Eastern prince to the audience, as much as to say, "This
is what I draw out of mere things of catgut, wood and silver," and
when the stormy applause arose, he at once, with the same bright look,
and an abnegatory gesture, deplored it and deferred to it—"Are we
not here for the cause of art alone—for the soul, not for the laurels";
and all the time he smiled to himself as if to say, "My little ones, you
ignorant pusses, my tympanum vibrates like a film of air, all this is
a thousand times more exquisite to me"; and then he turned to the
orchestra and made them rise with the gesture of a good host who
leaves no one in the shade, and thanked them himself, disregarding
their amused glances and bluff haste to be packed up and gone. He
was a wonderful actor of concertos.

These two conductors then passed up a side aisle and sat into their
places like two bars of music well-fallen.

After them came the ITALIAN SINGER, a gentleman of fifty years or more, with a ravaged wrinkled face, like a mask of tragedy carved in wood; he wore a blue silk shirt and a gold bracelet. When he spoke it might be in a whisper, or cavernously, or gruffly: the ear was at first repelled by the harsh voice and soon after was surprised and seduced by its rich, tormented and varying tones. He seemed to be weeping internally even when he broke into his slow, great smile of an Easter Island idol. He was a famous singer and had once been the rival of the greatest singer in the world. For years the balance went up and down between them, but into his clear, far-sounding notes came whisperings and rich lachrymose overtones; disease marched on him in full array. Yet even now, thrilling and deathly to hear were the infernal rustlings of his great stage-whisper. The sun silvered his smooth, black hair and his low, satanic forehead. He had an antique cast: one would have said some giant warrior who had kept watch on the walls of Carthage. His melancholy great eyes, deepset, scaled the castle-walls as if pursuing a bird of prey into the air. His large mouth drew down the curtain of gloom; but in an instant the scene was changed with his brilliant teeth flashing at a pretty neighbour. He bowed gravely to the apostolic damask.

Next came two women. The first was a FRENCHWOMAN, tall, slender and fair, from the south of France, and boasting in her veins an English blood that sprinkled the soil at Poitiers. Her hair was yellow and curled, and her high nose looked out between her fine cheekbones, like a thorn between two buds. Her eyes were blue and clear as water, her skin was golden with a brown shade beneath, and her lips were full, small and prettily painted. She was dressed in a costume of black and white silk in small stripes like hairs laid close together, with a belt of red leather and silver. She wore high-heeled black slippers and the finest silk stockings ever seen; they were of pewter grey. She wore a blue fox fur and a pair of white gloves, and when she took off her gloves, which were always clean, she had on a silver chased ring for a wedding ring and a platinum ring with a diamond as large as a shoe-button, for she thought she might one day have to fly in some sudden uprising of the farmers, or some political disorder in the south, or in war, or pestilence; her family was so old that they had seen every kind of trouble. When she spoke she spoke excellently, with a firm, caressing voice; to everything she said she gave an aphoristic turn; her conversation disarmed the jealous, dismayed the dull and sharpened with salt the wit of the witty. She was a very good Catholic and met the Archbishop with frank pleasure. She had already visited by eight o'clock in the morning every Catholic altar in the town. She had been to Lourdes, to Lisieux and Rome and to all the famous places of pilgrimage, travelling richly like a great lady, to fall on the stones of some obscure chapel and receive a wafer from some hasty priest. Yet she always had a tolerant smile for unbelievers and jested smartly with those who laughed at her piety. Whatever was brought against the fathers of the church, the scholarship, beliefs or promises of the church, against local credulity or pontifical honour, she turned against the accuser with the sharp thrust of a tongue for debate. In company she had no equal; she was benevolent and polished in repartee, in anecdote pithy and wise, and in her tales, circumstantial and rotund with a long line of development and a sentimental conclusion. There was nothing she loved so much as to be with her dressmaker or her friends. When she was with her friends, who were of all classes and temperaments, she forgave them all their errors and she exerted herself to amuse them. When she sat mistress at a table the wines were numerous, course followed course with succulent fleshes, subtle sauces and new garnishings, and compliment followed compliment with fresh blandishments; at the end she had always some little flask of liqueur brought from her own vines, dated and named and tended at home, which kept her guests sitting hour after hour from evening till daylight, without anyone noticing where the hours had flown.

With the Frenchwoman came a DOCTRESS, a Scottish woman from Inverness, jolly, fresh-complexioned and round, tall, with a small waist and wide bosom; with ginger hair and russet eyelids and eyes like cats'-eyes. Her hair was long and loosely wound on her round head. She wore a brown straw hat with flowers in it, a brown, yellow and cream dress amply draped without much fashion, small shoes of kid, with copper buckles, and long kid gloves. She was perhaps thirty-eight years old, and gay, lively and affectionate to the companion of the moment. She liked to be with men, she smoked cigarettes and drank

milk, laughed heartily at all that was said and told plenty of lively
stories herself: but if she did not think enough attention was paid
her she showed the spitfire under the skin; a grain of mustard-seed
under her tongue put a scornful tang into what she said: she would
have liked to be honey-voiced but she was too impatient: her voice
would break in the middle of a flattery and she would snap her fingers
and say no more. She had got her degree in Medical School after several failures. She had gone into the Government medical service, gave
lectures in schools to embarrassed adolescents and taught nose-blowing
to kindergartners. She went round the country with a pair of calipers
and a measuring stick, taking the height and cranial capacity of schoolchildren. She liked pretty little girls but detested little boys with their
ink, their coils of string, their stamps and smells. She expected to go
on in the Department until the age of retirement, for she did not
think of marrying, although she was a pretty woman and liked a
house of her own. Her most sentimental amusement was to walk in
the evening with some middle-aged man of distinction with black or
silver hair and white linen and clothes of a good cut, and listen to
his sonorous sentiments, dispute his personalities and agree at bottom
with all he said. The stars made her salty, but they made her wise.
She opened her eyes in the dark like a cat; it seemed that an immense
affectionate understanding could have sprung up in her cold bosom,
but that was only her comfortable fat. She was like the Frenchwoman
in this, that she had strong prejudices she liked to discuss publicly;
and she liked tales: but the Doctress preferred scandalous stories and
her ideas came out of a slipshod imagination, with an evident intention of pleasing only herself, whereas the Frenchwoman far exceeded
any other woman there in the telling of tales.

Next came in an ENGLISH GENTLEMAN, born and bred on an estate
in one of the southern counties, a laureate in Greek and Latin poetry,
who spoke of race horses and foxhounds in unconscious hexameters.
He wore a suit of Scottish tweed in a large check pattern, a brown
shirt in a small check pattern and a cream tie with a fine check; and
he had no idea of the value of money. His small pale-thatched head,
the size and appearance of a rock melon almost, he made as insignificant as possible by wearing an unsuitable (but correct) hat: his slender

six-foot-two he reduced by a studied crouch; his natural wit he veiled in an impenetrably bad accent taught at home, cultivated at Eton, brought to mysterious flower at Balliol and improved out of his own fantasy. His intelligence was only occasionally allowed to gleam through a moving cloud of flippancies and racing metaphors: his natural benevolence and soft heart he would have concealed if he had known how they were naked: he pretended, with all the ardour of his nature, to a vapid cynicism, but he could never learn the art. He carried a fine snakewood cane with a gold initial, and was ready to wink and pull his blond moustache at any lady who came his way.

After the English country gentleman came two women. One was forty years of age and spoke English with an Irish accent. She wore a silk coatee, a silk dress flowered in a small pattern, a hat with a blue velvet ribbon and forget-me-nots, and worn, brown kid gloves; and she carried a large brown leather bag. She had a paperwhite skin and greying hair, and she spoke with confidence rare phrases of guide-book German to help out her description of all she had seen in Europe. She had on her small wrist, from which a round bone stuck out, a gilt bracelet set with malachite, and on her foulard corsage, flat and draped, she wore a large Victorian brooch, with a moonstone heart set in gold filigree. Above, on her bare, wind-blown neck, pitted with a web of goose-flesh, like shagrin, hung a plain gold cross such as little girls get to wear to Sunday School. She ambled along in high-heeled kid shoes with six or seven straps, which she had bought in an expensive Dublin shop. She almost wept talking about the Falls of Schaffhausen and the castled crag of Drachenfels, for she had asked Thomas Cook to include these in her itinerary and it would cost her seventeen pounds extra. She wished to see the Pitti Palace, the tomb of Virgil and the David of Michel-Angelo, whom she called, clearing her throat, "mik-kel-anghelo."

The second woman, a SCHOOLTEACHER, was fifty years old, taller, thinner, with no rings on her fingers, but gloves of brown silk net. She sailed along on her long legs, like a bare pole on a smooth sea. She nodded her head, smiling with purplish lips at her companion's chatter, and smoothed down her brown skirt of crêpe-de-chine, with attention; she held her shoulders straight, plumped out her frilled blouse and looked in the mirrors of shops as they passed, at her straight hair, the colour of gold-bearing sand, done up in a neat coil, and tilted more fashionably her expensive brown satin toque. Wherever she moved she gave out buff or yellow shades. She put her hand to her side and felt it, for she had a pain there, and she smiled still more obligingly at her garrulous friend. She had been a highschool mistress for thirty years and now lived in a pretty town house with a flower garden, and on the walls the prints of the Medici Society, of Botticelli and the Dutch painters. She ate delicately of chicken, salad and jelly; she never spoke loudly, and an allusion, however discreet, to immodest subjects troubled and shocked her. Although she was a good scholar and an apt learner and believed in modernism, so that her pupils were always reading the most recent books put out, her intricate, delicate and tenuous mind somehow transformed all she had learned into a kind of mediæval manuscript with the modern instances as a cynical and even comic gloss. She said she believed in a Divinity not in God. Liberal, rationalist, philanthropist, she called herself, and she remained as foolishly credulous as a girl of fifteen: she had read all the white, blue, green, brown and yellow books published on crime, war, drugs, prostitution and atrocities, and she still believed in the sacredness of patriotic passion and the perspicacity of private interest. She thought these evils which she read about, but never saw, could be stamped out by strong-minded old ladies with fat pocketbooks. She always wept when clergymen and publicists spoke of the welfare of man. She presented with the same equanimity to the jovial misses of her school, the system of Bergson and the little flowers of St. Francis of Assisi. She now nodded to her friend, recommended a German liner for Ireland, said she had heard the Falls of Schaffhausen were much spoiled, and all the time under the fortress, now in shade on this side, and the mountain-pierced sky, the sun and the breeze seemed to repeat to her the simple poetical ideas of the play of "Jedermann," which she had just read. She spoke German fluently and listened attentively to the remarks of the bands of young people, so that she could use their words as an illustration of the ideas of modern youth abroad, when she gave her address to the Headmistress's Association in her own country.

There came in next the Poet. He was tall, spare and ill, with hollow cheeks and eyes. He liked to rake through muck for a jewel; he exalted things like himself, useless and attenuated in form. His expiring sensibility preferred obscure verbal tingle-tongle to intelligible verse, suggestiveness of syllable-sequence to the banality of grammar, phantoms flying out of a dark cloud to the bright, close-embroidered visions of reason, with their everyday woof and warp. To stimulate his dying talent and hope, he proclaimed the advent of mathematics into poetry, when symbols would serve for concepts and kill rhetoric. He published manifestoes proclaiming a gentlemen's revolution, the virgin birth and the divine right of an aristocratic, analphabetic, table-rapping soul; he protested against the cult of the working man, although he made use of those portions of his vocabulary which permitted him to shock and mystify. With a feverish ear for assonances and puns and a moribund imagination he tried to pierce the clouds that hung over his lethargic soul, or to transform them into shapes of fantasy. He borrowed phrases from all the sciences and religions, he got his colours from the plush, chalices, laces, windows and stone angels of churches and tried to revive his appetites with ever wilder perversities. He was a man deathly sick; he had struggled all his life against extreme poverty and he retreated from it farther and farther into the night, bringing up in his dreams images of bounding youth and female beauty as a last hunger for life; and in despair, ruined with drugs (which he had first bought to calm neuralgia) wasted his days and nights without knowing their number nor the seasons that passed over his head, in the luxurious apartment in which a wealthy patron kept him. When they asked him to tell a tale, he began in a lively way, but soon his voice dropped and he pointed to his companion, a pale, lively boy, also a poet, who had remained unnoticed till that moment.

Beside the seats stood a band of school and college girls, travelling through Europe in their long vacation. They imagined that, in general, the real was the contrary of the apparent, for they had all suffered gross deceptions when very young. They were atheists, anarchists and hard as nails, they said; they were profane, sacrilegious and low at one moment, and the next, obscure, lofty, and as technical with their artistic and psychological terms as a magician's apprentices wrinkling their brows in the smoke of his devil's kitchen. Being in their first soft and dazzling youth, with strength untried and impertinence unreproved, and savage with their ripe passions, they called love rough names and suspected their friends of psychological and even moral perversions from every sentence uttered in conversation. They bandied about the names and works of all the high priests of music, letters and art, placing them into a rigid hierarchy which no one questioned, but which varied from week to week; but they were ignorant of any principle of æsthetics or of the problems of composition. They were fanciers of the infinitely precious, the shockingly immodest and the undiscoverably insignificant; they reproved symbolists and incoherent poets for lost chances of obscurity, and themselves wrote verses full of childish images and rhythms, using a vocabulary of a thousand words which had been signed with their seal and signature. They read, on their trips along the country roads and in the students' hostels, passionate and polite verses, sang sea-chanties, discussed exotic religions and did physical exercises together, naked.

There was one of them, a girl of sixteen, whose Eastern face was the shape of the most beautiful and secret of triangles: her eyes and hair were equally bold, wild and black, and she seemed to bear under her ivory skin the blue which she had knitted into her grotesque garments. A cobalt blue and black sweater, badly-knitted, ravelled, with dropped stitches, and skin-tight, covered the smooth triangle of her thorax: her breasts stood out like small bosses on a breastplate, and her waist was not more than eighteen inches round although she wore no corset. Her skirt of cobalt blue serge, impatiently tightened at the waist with an old belt, wrapped round her like a chrysalis skin, gave her greater and more singular beauty, since beneath it, perfectly moulded, could be seen her pear-shaped hips. Her legs were not long, but thin, and her feet and hands, both bare, were burned dark-brown. A scowling, affronted and bitter expression contracted her childish face; she had a loud, threatening voice, in which was nevertheless a twanging, that might have come from an Æolian harp. Her companions had her manners, for the most part, but not her harsh beauty, and they did not arouse love, pity and horror as she did.

Yet one of them was curious to see. She was a girl of seventeen with a sunburnt, fair skin, a ready blush and pale blue eyes with large pupils

from which came an intense liquid glare unusual in blue-eyed persons.
Her hair was the flax-colour common in Norway and hung round her
face on her shoulders straight and plain, unwashed and unbrushed, in
strands; but she had bound round her head a band of coloured woollen
flowers she had bought at a village in the Tyrol; and this, with her
blue dress, her knapsack, plump coarse face with large bones and bare
brown feet, gave her the appearance of a country girl transported
there from the far north. She ordered her friends about, arranged
everything to suit her convenience and took a seat which she had not
paid for, but which was empty: then in the hearing of half a hundred
people, she began to read a letter she had received from Wisconsin,
from her mother, that morning, laughing at its stupidity, describing, in
parenthesis, her mother's slavery in a tenement kitchen and her father's
life, labouring for forty years in a factory; she laughed pleasantly and
pictured her mother as a sow routing in the mud, and her father as a
mule tied to a turn-table: "That is what they are, exactly," she cried,
"if we are to be Behaviourists!" But she was a brave and adventurous
girl and so vigorous that no miseries could move her.

There was near them, with her father, a SCHOOLGIRL of different
breeding. She had fair hair curling round her ears and her face seemed
to be made by a dollmaker: her small nose turned up and her large,
pale, well-shaped mouth weighted well her cream, untinted face. Her
eyebrows were long, crescent-shaped and dark, and the flesh swelled
under the eyebrow like an almond lying above the eye. Her eye was
large and grey. She had the attentive, startled looks of a rabbit-girl, a
soft and trustful smile; and in everything she did appeared so strong
a desire to sleep on a faithful heart that both men and women looked
after her with a tender smile. She spoke in a hesitating voice, almost
under her breath, and her throat creaked and whirred out of pure
timidity; and when she had once stated her opinion she at once deferred to another and deplored her haste in statement. Only in matters
of behaviour her opinion was strong, her judgments were harsh, her
rules inflexible: and her rule of behaviour was this, that no one should
hurt a fly, and that no one should tell a lie. Her shoulders were broad,
her arms white and her breast soft and prominent. Her waist was
narrow and her hips round like a clock: she had little flesh and that

was light and almost translucent, but it was elegantly massed and disposed. Among the valleys one can see a little landscape, verdant, hilly and lovely to the eye, which has no rocks, thick, bristling woods, sharp precipices or loud streams, and over which the clouds, hours and seasons, pass with a thousand superficial moods while beneath the place is always soft and mild. She was like that. Her legs were not long, but her feet were very small and she always wore expensive shoes, with thin leathers and small toes, and with high heels like threads. Her pale, small hands had large round nails like rock-crystal. She always wore a scarf over her shoulders, which were rounded a bit, as if in modesty; out of timidity she blinked when she was spoken to suddenly. But although she was not vain and not assured like the others, she was full of romantic ideas and was anxious to please, so that if they asked her to amuse them, she did not demur but did her best to speak.

Then there stood behind the rope a band of German youths and girls on a walking trip. The youths wore thick woollen stockings, white, green and blue, embroidered in cross-stitch, linen coats in white or blue and heavy corduroy shorts, the shorts very dirty. The girls wore short socks, discoloured with dust, skirts and sweaters; they wore no corsets, and some of them wore no belts; they had no hats; their faces were brown and dirty. In town, over their blouses they wore blue linen coats or a shawl: they leaned forward as they walked, tramping heavily, with sweating cheeks and wrinkled foreheads, like peasant women who must carry a great burden up a mountain-side. Sometimes they all sang together; they yodelled in the mountains. They stopped at cheap wayside houses to drink bad beer and eat some meat stew with heavy piquant sauce: or they went into a chapel to pray, the men taking off their mountain hats of felt and clanking over the flagged pavement with their hobnailed boots till they reached the altar; the women, kneeling down farther back, bending their fair, unkempt heads, their large bellies and bosoms unstayed, while the studded soles of their boots turned up in line along the bench. These students stood at the barrier in the cathedral place and waited, for this day and hour had been carefully reckoned with in their schedules. When an hour had passed they would be on their way with their road-maps flapping, in celluloid cases, on their hips. They could not afford lodging or entertainments; they were all poor, and though most were University students, some were unemployed, and some were clerks and factory hands. They had to be on their way long before sunset. They had many exhausting miles by cloudy thicket and mountain stream, on hobnailed boots or leather-soled bare feet uphill and down dale, to cities, rivers and mountain outlooks, to cathedrals, birthplaces of famous men and picturesque old streets, such as are starred in Baedeker, before they could return, contented, to their homes. Their cheeks were lean, some were hollow, their stomachs were bad and their breaths sour: their clothing was scanty and they had only a few marks between them, but their legs and arms were thick, muscular and brown; and when some-one said, for instance, "Cologne Cathedral is a masterpiece," each could say, "I have seen it: it is marvellous!" This was their reward.

They were to sleep that night in a cabin on a hillside, built by a society of round-walkers, and had only to get the key from the guardian in the village, to enter into their own demesne. The cabin was between two hills on a green hummock, among summer gardens: there was a smell of honeysuckle in the air, convolvuluses grew over the walls and birds and insects went in and out of the untenanted cottage by a window left unfastened. They would not know that; but, falling heavily on the benches and floor of the cabin, would sleep like beasts in the dark, snoring, and flinging their limbs about in their exhaustion; but seeing perhaps in their dreams when the first fatigue had passed, the fantastic spire of some great cathedral, lacy on a blue sky, the cryptic black marble door closing in the sarcophagus of a great man, or a wide outlook over a blue mountain lake, that was starred in Baedeker. O passionate and devout race! They had no time to pause: they told no tales. They passed on and went back to their dull, oppressed lives, their ambitions pacified with their conquests over boulders and nettles, until the next vacation.

But there was a GERMAN STUDENT who had travelled with them from Innsbruck only: not a fair, lantern-jawed, blue-eyed youth, such as they all were, but one with a chubby face and red cheeks and fine manners, who raised women's hands to his lips when he saluted them. He was a student in philosophy. He squirmed with delight at the sight of a little bit of tracery in a clerestory, and went into fits over the counter-

point of Brahms: he had the sententiousness of a cherub when he declared that El Greco was a *back number* and the tricks of a water
spaniel in the water when he sang from Richard Strauss's operas. He
loved singing and he had a mild will but absolute judgment. He worshipped famous people and ran after women, who were his despair.
His skin was white, his hair black and he wore fine clothes; he could
not bear the least sight of blood but he was happy one day to give his
handkerchief to tie up the leg of a dog run over by a cart: and whenever he heard a shot rumble in the hills and saw the birds fly scattered
out of the trees, he said, "O, my goodness, my goodness, isn't that
dreadful? It should never be allowed."

He brought in with him a LAWYER from Buda-Pesth, a swagger
beau who spent his nights in night-clubs and paid attention to every
woman he met, dark or fair, pretty or plain, sweet or forbidding, out
of incontinence. He read all the gossip sheets and liked to pretend that
he could find out the truth of every affair in the city, by fraud, bribery,
threats and natural cunning. He believed whatever his client believed,
affected to be cynical and saturnine, speaking in innuendoes; or jovial,
sly and hail-fellow-well-met, according to the case. He soothed and
flattered his client as if the client were a prince and he the prince's
vizier. He examined a contract so closely for a flaw or deceitful intent,
that he often missed the nature of the business and he was astonished
to observe that a business could be unsound when a contract was water-
tight. He loved to crack a walnut with a sledge-hammer. He gulped
down all the information thrown at him, went ahead in business and
conversation by leaps and bounds, was called for that a bounder, loved
to interrupt a business conversation with a quotation from his school-
book poets, read the memoirs of diplomats with fervour and credulity,
rejoiced at the crashing fall of magnates and kings, and was an ardent
patriot and a conservative voter. He was like a man who has got into a
pair of bewitched shoes by accident and must always be hopping and
pirouetting, curtseying and leaping in the air, malapropos. He was a
handsome young man of thirty-two with thick curly hair, brown eyes
and a red mouth: he wore a morning coat in the morning and an
eyeglass and evening dress every evening. He had learned, in two or
three hours, all about the people in the hotel, and he now flattered and

fawned on them shamelessly; he went about the place with dancing steps and his head in the air, delighted to be able to show his glittering talents to so cultivated a crowd. He was not a bad man, but very foolish: he was rich, because he had married a rich wife: he flattered her to her heart's content, and was a gay man about town.

Now he was laughing excessively at every word that fell out of the mouth of the PHILOSOPHER. The philosopher was heir to a noble house, but not rich: he lived from his lectures and his writings. He was odd in appearance, with a bloodless face and a receding chin and an underlip that dropped engagingly like a young foal's. His hands were the colour of bleached bone, and when he stood, he stood not straight, but shifting from one foot to the other like a schoolboy reciting a piece. Nothing astonished his admirers so much as the sight of him. He was received like a grandee in every country in the world and his books on history and moral philosophy, written clearly, picturesquely, with an economy of words, and full of quaint, moral notions often caught during illicit revels nightly in a sphere without morals, delighting pastors and schoolteachers, were translated into every language. He had rapid soft speech and caressing manners like an adolescent boy, but he was nearly fifty years old. Ladies were very partial to him, saying that he looked harmless, but knowing quite well that he was ardent, well-born, enterprising and in a sphere beyond prejudices. He had no difficulty; he never had to eat green fruit although he was poor: the best and ripest fruit fell into his lap from the highest and best-tended trees, London was his orchard, the world was his estate. He ate very well and was one of the first gentlemen of the realm, but his shoes were often down-at-heel and he did not give a rap for it. He liked popularity, but he was happy in his soul, and unpopularity was the same thing to him, he thought. He would go to gaol for his opinions, he said: and because he liked to flout opinions in fee entail and mock inherited gentility, he never visited the House of Lords, which he called the prosiest and least select of all private clubs. He was not married and had no children.

There was also a MATHEMATICIAN born in Finland, educated in France, America and Germany, who taught in Spain. He had lived all his life in schools and universities, and knew the rough and tumble of life only as a thorny proposition. His brown, thick skin was pitted with smallpox; his hair was so thick and tufty that it fell into his eyes and he could not wear a hat. His eyes were deep-blue and narrowed under brows like dried peony follicles, dark, twisted and cleft sidelong: he was of Tartar blood. He had a large library of books in four languages; many languages he read well but did not speak with ease. He had a slight impediment in his speech and in revenge he invented a story to this effect, that after the establishment of Grimm's Law, Grimm broke his heart at the incorrect deformation of primitive tongues by the vulgar, wooden-eared and thick-tongued, that he went mad and went to a mountain fastness where he established *Grimm's Anarchy* and taught to a simple people a language without rhyme or reason: in this way arose the Basque tongue. For every anomaly he invented an amusing reason. All day he sat before a quire of paper writing and figuring in a crabbed script, in his leisure hours he read to his young wife. He pitied women for their thwarted ambitions, and found many diamonds of plain truth in the sand of their conversation. He meditated everything a long time: he liked to sleep twelve hours a day and dream. He was wrathful at the errors of men, at fatuity, lunacy and dishonour, because he was forced to doubt the perfection of his own organism. He was in his relations with his friends violent, partial in love or hate, easily offended and given to bloody ideas of revenge like a schoolboy. He liked the cloistered academic path he would tread all his life: from windows of universities he looked out speculatively on every kind of activity. He was not indulgent but he was kind. He had cold feet because he liked to sit hours by himself spinning his web with his head in his own web. He dreamed at night of curious manipulations of logic and letters from which he got the supple solutions of theorems. He liked mathematical tricks and logical puzzles: at dinner, with his coffee he would puzzle his friends with *"the class of all classes."* Then he would laugh, show his white teeth and begin to sing themes from Bach in a sonorous humming tone, or he would go to the piano and play with a firm, delicate, improvising touch. He liked to play chess and learn the grammars of languages. He had a brother he loved so dearly he would have died for him. He calculated his brother's chances of survival with a slide-rule and his birthday, according to the Julian calendar. He could calculate very well, both what he owed and what was owed him. He liked to eat well, go in his friends' automobiles, wear silk shirts not overpriced, and entertain his friends generously, for by spending money he could be potent while supine. He was thin and flexible as a fishing-rod but his grace was disguised in suits of expensive tweed cloth, cut in pompous fashion. The cloth was chosen for the sober intricacy of its pattern, but the colours, violet, blue, russet and green, were always at variance with the rest of his turn-out and with the fashion; he lived in a world of black and white, and when he turned his attention to colours, he was without prejudices. His house was barely furnished as a hermit's cell, so that his wife could polish her mind and not brass fittings; but he bought electrical contrivances of every sort, out of curiosity, and liked to fossick in ironmongery shops and bring home patent egg-shellers and butter-coolers, or anything that was ingenious. He kept his work in pigeon-holes and sent by registered post to trusted colleagues his original ideas for their criticism, but he was careful not to mention his ideas in mixed company; he knew mathematicians are not honest and have sharp ears.

If he found fault in persons he thought perfect before, he suffered for days; he came back to the imperfection again and again to understand how he could have been deceived at first, or else, what strange rule of harmony permitted these flaws to reign in organisms that pleased him.

In the middle block, which is the most expensive, sat a Berlin business man with his wife, richly furred and gloved, although not in the best style either of Paris or Vienna. Her great round face was heavily topped by uncut blonde hair and a fashionable sunhat, while he sat uncovered and mopped with a silk initialled handkerchief his bald cranium shaped like a sea-elephant's.

His lady's tongue, flowered head, and stout bosom under a lace front, all niddle-noddled; he barked his responses in stiff Berlin German, and sniffed the perfume and eyed the white silk of a bare-armed Society girl who sat with a lapdog, indifferent on his left hand. A long white glove covered her warm arm in the most fashionable wrinkles: when she asked for a glass of milk at the ambulant milkstore or for a book of verse at the bookseller's, her voice lisped softer than milk and sweeter than verses. Always a sort of natural fresh odour came from her as one seems to come from green fields, even when they are a long way off and no wind is blowing.

This young lady turned her back to the Berliner (at which his wife sighed pleasantly), and answered the young Viennese woman beside her, who asked her in that liquid German certainly invented by the Rhine maidens, when the play would begin. This young Viennese woman was dressed in costly Swiss embroidery and embroidered gloves. Her bronzed hair was neatly curled; she wore a small crocheted hat: her little white and black shoes shone like snakes' heads, with their jet stones. She wore a wedding-ring and a necklace of crystals. She began to confide in the Berlin girl the social confidences and hurried conventional raptures of one who is a little fluttered and uneasy, and whose social station is not assured.

"What a crowd is here this year! They say the American President's financial advisers all are here: there are five millionaires. . . . The first performance of *Don Juan* this evening will unquestionably be brilliant! . . . I am here with my husband," said the Viennese lady: "he has some business in the south," and she licked her dark red lips and looked appealing at her confidante. The Berlin girl's practised eyes turned for a moment to her lapdog while she said to herself, "She is here with her lover, on an escapade"; then she prattled sociably on with an indefinite note of patronage: not indeed, for the escapade, but for the weak confidence.

The afternoon shadows drew a little nearer. The Viennese beauty, young, appealing and lonely, drew a bizarre embroidered scarf round her bust and sighed.

Stolidly, in the same row, but in the cheapest seat, with a sharp nose and weary and uncoloured face, with drab hair and a blue dress, a young woman clerk from Cologne shaded her eyes and read a French literary review. She raised her eyes patiently from time to time to the back of the stage, quizzed the elegants with the critical looks of an ambitious white-collar who has had to buy every luxury with soul-deadening parsimony; she was palely but precisely aware of a growing antipathy for a Jewish citizen of Vienna who sat beside her, in Tyrolean mountain costume, chortling at his fine seat, declaiming with a soft lisp and holding his wife's gloved hand.

There came late into his seat a thickset, cheerful DOCTOR from New York, who had just come from a conference in Constantinople on hay-fever. His teeth, his starched linen, his jewelled shirt-studs, his finger-nails and his shoe-tops all shone as he walked. When he talked, he often spread the square stubbed fingers of his small hand in a round gesture, and he had the shadowy smile of the Mona Lisa hovering un-consciously in the folds of his firm mouth. He was very rich; he loved art and music; he had at his home in New York a private gallery; he attracted to his home by cajolery and good suppers, twice a week, a trio of musicians with whom he practised quartets. He was so strong that he would keep them sitting there till their backs cracked, their wrists were sprained, their eyes dropped and they were obliged to kick over his music-stands by stealth to interrupt him. When he began to play his quartet, to pursue an indigent painter in whose work he fancied he saw a profitable streak, or to make a scatter-diagram of temperatures, his eyes shone and he became insensible to other things, like a figure of stone. He knew to the least detail the soft scenes pic-tured by Sisley and the dazzling suns of Van Gogh, but he would walk through fields and by streams and villages unconscious if the sun, moon or stars shone, or if his way was lighted by rainbows, northern lights, lightning or roman candles, for his walks only served to develop his theories on art and his dexterity in determining the coefficient of correlation between two sets of facts. He had taken up all his hobbies late, after a mild youth, and he went at them with the pleasure and abandon of a mastiff pup chasing chickens.

There was also there a Chinaman, the FOREIGN CORRESPONDENT of a French newspaper. He spoke five languages, and all without a foreign accent. He had studied in Universities in America, France and Ger-many. He was a passionate patriot, but he said little about his own country in Western European society, preferring to talk about his childhood when he had lived in sheltered calm. He had a high fore-head and round eyes with arched brows like the warriors in old paint-ings; he wore European dress. He spoke in clear tones like a clapper falling on thin ivory; his red mouth smiled sweetly though with

melancholy, and everything he said came out with compressed visionary epithets, as if his imagination flowered impetuously, quicker than
the tongue. He expected many more years of trouble for his country:
this cloud sat over all he said and thought. He sat shining and neat in
black clothes and shining shoes, with smooth hair and bright eyes, resembling a newt or other smart black water animal, or a legendary
dragon very small, carved on an urn of genii from the old tales.

Next came sliding and bustling across the centre of the place, from
beneath the archway, a small-footed man with a thin face. Whenever
the centenary of the birth or death of a great composer of music approached, he flew about the world with propaganda, forming commit-
tees, cajoling Departments of Education and of the Fine-Arts, flattering musicians, bribing publishing companies, engaging publicists,
writing, speaking, wheedling, persuading, his head swarming with
wily, original schemes for making the world take an interest in Haydn,
Brahms, Schubert, or whatever other musician was a hundred years
born or dead. It was he who first conceived the idea of finishing the
Unfinished Symphony, and he who wrote and distributed to schoolmasters, mayors and representatives of the people, the *Few Thoughts
on the Place of Music in the Home and in the Market-place,* in which
he worked the threads of patriotism and the family, public education
and private sensibility, Schubert and the wares of gramophone companies. He had a fine ear, long with a large orifice, and he sang in an
angelic falsetto which resembled at will a wood or string instrument,
or a desert voice rising through the sharp edges of the sand. He knew
many thousand themes from the master musicians and many peasant
songs and single strains picked up here and there on the earth: he had
as friends all the musicians and was able to make a child understand a
theme. He loved to sit in a large audience and be moved with its emotions, as if his heart was a silver disc recording an orchestral piece. He
was as sympathetic as a nervous beauty to his hearers and endeavoured
to enchant all by showing the glittering facets of his talents. His eyes
with animal intensity and sagacity, blue and oval, darted left and right:
he got into his seat with the movement of a bird settling into a thick
tree, disappearing in the crowd. His clothes had cost him a great deal
but seemed unsuitable to his movements and habit of mind: he should

have worn a smock, or Persian trousers. His shoe might have concealed
the long tip of a seraphic wing or the long toe of a satyr's foot. When
Death approached in the Miracle Play, he shuddered and cast his eyes
discreetly from side to side to see how the audience took it, and when
the heavenly bells and voices rang out, his eyes sent out points of light
and his dark-veined thin hand played delicately from the soft pale wrist
on which was a gold chain. He had a dark crafty profile, like an ancient Venetian, with a long, pointed nose and thin lips; he was as attentive as a lizard. He hummed ever and again to himself like syrinx
when the tide is rising in the reeds. He was full of tales as the poets
of Persia: he unwound endlessly his fabrics, as from a spool the silks
of Arabia. He was a publicist, a salesman, but of so peculiar a sort,
specialising in the centenaries of famous men, that they invented a
name and called him THE CENTENARIST.

There was near him, amused by him, sitting with the five millionaires, youngest of the six wealthy men that the other guests in derision
called the *Gold Trust,* a very thin young man, with a long Dutch nose;
a BANKER he was, from London. He had a sea-going yacht, three motor-
cars, a house in Grosvenor Square, a house in the country, three race
horses and twelve servants: he gave five hundred guineas for a horse-
race and a silver cup for polo, and he went each weekend to France to
get the sun. But in town his chief amusement was to go to the pictures
with his wife seven times a week. He abhorred the opera which he
thought was noisy and the theatre which he thought oldfashioned and
wordy. He lived in the depths of his house alone with his wife; and
they went about as inseparable as twins. He dined off an omelette and
a chop badly served by his lazy and spoiled French chef, and sipped a
glass of bad, red wine from a bin in the pantry furnished by his thief
of a butler. He knew his servants robbed him but could not bear to
sack them (he said), because they would thereby lose their jobs. He
did not like to go to friends' houses to dine for he could not understand
the sense of their flippancies and their high-church passions drove him
mad; and he never entertained, for he liked to live at home with his
wife alone.

If he met a pretty girl, he looked for a rich husband for her to marry:
if he was amused by a journalist he mentioned his name to some cabi-

net minister to get him influence: if he thought an author hard-working and mild, he would think about his case, telling him, perhaps, that he could work quicker if he took the stories out of the Arabian Nights and simply changed the names, and local colour, such as the degree of heat and the type of costume. He had stolen his brother's shillings when they were in the nursery together and had only been beaten by his brother's squirrel secretiveness. He never read a book; and he had passed through the costliest and most famous schools of his land and all their bosh (he said) had fallen off him like water off a duck's back. But in banking he knew all that he should know. His natural ingenuity was so complex and so wakeful that if a clerk made an error of twopence he made fourpence out of it; if the world was prosperous he promoted gambling-circles, rotary movements and publishing houses, lent money to liberal professors and ne'er-do-weel geniuses and made fortunes in speculation in fraudulent inventions exploited on the exchange; and if the world was black and most men were ruined, he laid in stocks of fat, flour, and cotton, speculated in armaments and cheap shirts and got back his money from the liberal professors now turned conservative. If a king lay at death's door, he bought a bolt of crape, if a peasant girl in adolescent delirium saw the Virgin at her furrow's end, he started an omnibus line. He understood only one thing, Profit; he thought all men thought as he did, and that their bank-balances were the measure of their brains. He would risk half his fortune on a throw, turn head-over-heels in the air in an aeroplane, tell anyone in the world to go to Hell, laugh at princes and throw tax-collectors out the door, but he suffered excessively from toothache because he feared the dentist's chair: and he was convinced that his luck depended on numbers, events, persons, odd things he encountered; his head accountant was forced to wear the same tie for six weeks because it preserved a liberal state of mind in the Government in a difficult time: his chauffeur was obliged to carry for nine months the same umbrella, rain, hail or shine, because the umbrella depressed the market in a stock he had sold short.

There was with him a SOLICITOR from London. He liked to walk in the City on a sunny morning swinging his cane and rubbing shoulders with the crowd in Throgmorton Street. He loved a little chat, with a

legal joke and a neat personality, and a little cup of tea. He lived at
Streatham and always wore light clothes, although his income was not
large, because he was blond, delicate and pale-faced. He acted the male
lead in private theatricals in a Y.M.C.A. Literary Club and played
tennis on Saturday afternoons. In the train in the morning, he read
the exchanges, recommended a purchase of Witwatersrand, asked why
the Government was riding the fence in the present crisis, and knew
the sporting news. His highest ambition was to come by a great deal
of money one day and go shares with some reliable client in a bill-
broking business. He wrote a genial solicitor's letters, leaving not a
single knot to catch his foot in, and even in conversation his remarks
were without prejudice. His clients' secrets were inviolate with him,
but if a wealthy client had a well-cut suit and told him a good joke
he would let the brush tail of a strong-scented affair peep through his
thicket of discretion. His integrity was spotless; and he always saw
that his clients were properly protected. His knowledge of the law was
exact so that he could circumvent it with grace, but it was necessary
to ask his services with a merry smiling countenance and a round,
periphrastic style. He kept a little diary at home, neat as a sandwich
bar, where he noted the events of a life spent among the great, fruity
with sagacious little aphorisms. He strolled out on Sunday afternoons
with his wife along the hedges and explained the masonic ritual of
his business.

There was a DANISH WOMAN, a bookbinder in Paris. She had bright
blue eyes and a large nose; her large head was covered with curls. She
talked all day and recounted hundreds of tales, mostly improbable, like
a female Munchhausen: she was usually gay, but sometimes a weird
melancholy fell on her, like the gloomy shades of the north. She loved
cats and bright-coloured leathers, dyes and gilt. Her workshop, though
in a cold and dirty apartment in a tumble-down building by the river,
was always humming with talk, hammer-taps, the creaking of presses
and the roaring of flames in the stove; and was as cheerful as the
common-room of the knights in heroic times, when they lived and
slept by the fires and their swords jingled. The walls were covered
with papers she painted and dyed, and with pictures of Copenhagen,
and caricatures by her pupils. She was lively as a trooper at night, and

drank wine, beer, punch, champagne, vodka and every strong drink they had at the table, until she rolled under it. She was as free as a brother with men; but she was modest, she blushed if a man looked at her boldly, was faithful to her husband, and would stare for hours at modern books, with their naked men, women and truths, red, gay, astonished and abashed.

With her was a young ARCHITECT, a gentle creature, modest and shy, whose restless fingers designed without end, even as they tapped on his knee, and who covered his walls, trunks, letters, easels and restaurant tables with the motifs of his irrepressible fantasy. He had built in Russia where the workers' cities are made of glass, aluminum, stone and tile, and in Amsterdam in the garden-cities, and in Paris where they build houses of glass and each stone is chiselled by hand, and in New York where they tear down twenty-five storey buildings in which the heating is expensive to put up thirty-five storey buildings in which the heating is more scientifically planned, and in Hollywood where the porches must frame beauties and the bathrooms are designed for Houdini; in seaports where the tiles must be wavy-bendy to correspond with the waves of the sea, on mountain-tops where the beetling walls must fit in with the craggy scenery, and in wheat-growing areas where the silos, towering in the fields, must look like a mightier cathedral. He had blossomed out, in his morning sun of success, and was the darling of poets and rich amateurs. His curly black hair fell over a white and red face, and his heart was simple, although he wrote cryptic verses. He danced like a feather; when by himself he capered, sent up darts, and sang, for he liked to be alone; but when he worked in a room with other draughtsmen, he was bemused, putting down his first strokes with diffidence as if afraid to spoil perfection, until the plan burst out in final clarity, like a rocket in his forehead.

An OLD LADY was there because her third husband had been a conductor in Vienna, and, dying, had left her with plenty of money and a taste for elevated society. She took scores to every performance, always turned over the page before the conductor and nodded over the last page. She wore a long gold chain and a lorgnette and an expensive hat made of satin, feathers, straw and tulle, all mixed and mummified together: no one could imagine what octogenarian designer and what antediluvian stock of unfashionable materials had been drawn upon to make her hat. Perhaps the old lady, this Frau Hofrat, designed her own hats, or had them made by her maid, taken over from the service of some ex-Empress. She was dignified at table, took mineral waters and powders, and was pleasantly condescending to the young. She cleared her throat often, and wore a high white lace collar and a chased gold band which supported her old dun throat.

There was an OLD MAN who liked company and joined in all the conversations to show he was a spark and an accomplished trifler. He dressed with coquetry. His thin, bent head nodded every few minutes like a tremulous head of oats, and the skin hung down on his neck. He wore soft gloves; his handkerchief and thin silver hair were perfumed with a thin, fine scent. His shoes were polished like glass and his clothes pressed every morning by a valet who travelled with him. When he was at home he exacted a special service of his five sons: each one had to call on him at his home, in a morning coat, wearing a flower and a bowler hat to pay his father his respects and kiss the hand of his mother. The old man had disinherited his youngest son, a Liberal Deputy, who refused to do this. Abroad, he treated everyone with caressing condescension but he was cold to waiters. His manners were so fine that one would have thought they had been invented specially to suit his frame: he wore them like a handmade shirt next his skin. He thought estates were bestowed by divine mandate and that those born to high estate should show that God had chosen well. Not even the wines, painters and race horses he fancied gave him the pleasure that he had from contemplating a fine family-tree; he imagined that he could tell noble birth even in a monster, if a monster were born in a great family. He allowed that it was inoffensive for a beautiful woman or an artist, low-born, to climb out of their natural sphere, because, on the one hand, women's empiry is always brief and rarely disturbs an inheritance, and on the other hand, artists are like the alchemists his fathers kept, who spun money out of thin air, sunshine, spoof.

He still let his bright brown eyes, clear as enamel, rove over the women's faces, feet and bosoms, and he heaved delicate sighs before them, as if a zephyr were blowing up a banked fire, or as if autumnal breaths were there, succeeding summer, but with winter yet a long way off. He put his hands under his coat-tails and told the men embroidered anecdotes of the old days.

There was a CRITIC OF MUSIC too, a columnist, who knew a musician's art by the way he whirled his stool, pulled at his collar, shrugged his shoulders, spread his hands, or looked in profile; by his manager or his bows; and in music he knew the difference between staccato and glissando, between Chopin and Rimsky-Korsakov, between fat playing and lean playing. He disliked versatile performers, he liked those who had a single doctrine of art and who wrote it down in words. But he had a fine ear: he could hear a whisper in the farthest corner of a concert hall, and if he heard it he would frown tremendously: and he could hear the opinions of other critics three seats away, even in a tumult. He could hear the fluid in the tube of a barometer rising and falling and the rise and fall of the tides of opinion. He could predict fashions in music a year away, and describe his state of mind at a concert in such sympathetic terms that the majority of people imagined he had heard the music. He was, truth to tell, a very poor musician, but a good journalist and a natural prestidigitateur: he could squeeze blood out of a stone, make a dinner out of a bar-room invention, and borrow money at a chess-table. He had once taken to agriculture and grown potato-plants with potatoes in the leaves and to cattle-raising and bred a calf with two heads. This experience had given him such confidence that he expected to conquer every subject with like ease, producing miracles. The calf should have been blamed for his musical criticisms.

A quiet man was there, a NATURALIST, who had come over the mountains on a walking-tour, with his lens and collecting-case. His ear was so fine that he could hear caterpillars eating leaves and crickets burrowing in the earth and buds starting out of nodes. He was a Russian, gay, full of songs which he sang by himself in the open. He had always walking with him a SCHOOLBOY to whose ires, fires and laments he listened with the attention and objections of a naturalist.

A PUBLIC STENOGRAPHER was passing through Salzburg on her way home to a rural village in England because, she said, she should see the sights before she got too old. She had a large office in Geneva and hired out for occasional work translators, accountants and typists, both

men and women. She wore black cotton gloves and buff cotton stockings and a navy-blue silk dress which she thought nice for all occasions.
She had greying hair arranged in scallops round her long face: her
skin was the colour of young corn in the cob and wrinkled round the
eyes. Her mouth was terra cotta and she had a faint rufous patch on
each cheek which never deepened, but which faded when she worked
on some late job, through the night. She had met all the personalities
of the League of Nations since 1920: she knew the gay gossip of the
town, how they all sat at little tables, alone, during important events
so that they should not gab; how a Balkan minister had walked in
the bright sunlight with his umbrella up because he had news of his
recall. She knew their little miseries, and if they wore spats, and how
they should be handled when they wanted to make a speech. She knew
the right word to suggest to fill a space, for the League of Nations has
a word for everything. She knew how to take a rebuff from bridling
vanity; but she looked everyone in the eye with her small brown eyes,
for she was old, tried and quite ignorant of the world. She had eaten
for fifteen years, at midday and in the evening, in the same large, public restaurant where they had a printed card with perhaps two hundred
dishes to choose from. In the face of all those diners, of the changing
waiters and of the generous menu, she had learned to hold her countenance and maintain a negligent pose as well as any pretty darling in
a young ladies' school, but she walked with rapid, dry strides, not
sinuously like those, because she had often to hurry to a man in the
throes of delivery; her arms were thin, muscular and rough skinned as
a shark's fin with too much exercise. At night, over a shaving of
cheese, dry and old, with a bitter, mouldy flavour caught in the restaurant's damp pantry (but which she thought was the natural flavour
of the cheese since it had been served so for fifteen years), and over a
small cup of black coffee, her single exotic habit caught in forty years
abroad, she would lean forward her long neck out of a halter of
Madeira embroidery and would amuse herself with anecdotes of the
comic, pathetic and marvellous, in her long dull life. She knew a for-
tune-teller who had predicted her life for ten years (those ten years,
she had sat at a typewriter); she speculated about love and its thick
mystery; she recalled breaths of the supernatural which had blown on

her cheek, and the great strokes of luck which had passed within a hand's-breadth of humble workers she had known. She knew clerks who had made immense sums, even a thousand dollars, by intercepting a private telephone call passing between heads of firms and accountants who had correctly calculated a firm's position from a disguised balance-sheet; she knew telegraph girls who had predicted European wars. She could not understand why these darlings of fate had not afterwards had a brilliant career and had their names in the papers, or had not at least become heads of their departments; she supposed it was due to a freakishness of their star, to pernicious anæmia in the seat of ambition.

She had once, she remembered out of forty years, drunk a very fine drink in a German family, curaçao, she believed, with cream and orange-juice, and in her opinion, no drink could be like that, not even champagne; but she had never tasted it again. Very coy she had been, on first going into Germany, when invited by a girl to take beer in public; but coming out, she had slapped down her money at a bar in the French railway-station and said, "A bock," and laughed, with her sister, to think what they would say at home in England, to that. Workmen had offered her another and she had accepted out of comradeship.

Then she had long winter tales. She had gone home to a new apartment late at night, in a storm of rain or snow, and found the window open and seen an apparition weeping on the mantelpiece—long afterwards she had learned that a girl had received a letter from her mother, dead immediately afterwards, in the room. She had tales of cats gone mad with hunger in cellars, running up the walls in frenzy and clinging to the ceiling, their red eyes glaring in the dark; and of seeing her dead grandmother's ghost, many a time, sitting in the corner darning ghostly socks in a flowered work-basket; of seeing an immaterial personage passing by the hearth leading a great greyhound, the night her mother died. She had once slept in a students' hostel in a foreign land and awakened to hear a coach driving up with the jingling of bits and the sounds of passengers getting down; and had been astonished at the survival of coaching in this land. Later in the night, someone had walked from a door in her room to her bedside, crying; she thought it the girl next door and had comforted it. But in the morning she had

found that there was no door there, but a gas-meter; and that no coach
had arrived. Returning that way months later she had heard that an
old passage had been discovered, covered in behind the gas-meter, and
in the passage a man had been murdered who had come by the coach
in the old days. She knew, too, country girls, the daughters of clergymen and honest as the day, who had seen past generations rise in the
wayside grass, and children who had seen bloody hands appear on
plastered walls in haunted houses. All these tales she told in a quiet
musing tone with no sign of nervousness: she told about the old bridge
that collapsed near her home and a fatal card-party in the village, the
discovery of an adultery by dreams; and a hundred curious things such
as the Society for Psychical Research used to discuss solemnly. She told
it so naturally, with such an air of belief, that the hearers at hot midday gave a shiver of surprise and superstition. Behind her lay the
ghostly tradition of English literature, the genius of the Brontës, the
popularity of Scott and the mad gifts of Protestantism, but she did not
know it. When she had told her tale, she would blow her nose in a
cheap lawn handkerchief with machine-made lace and say, "This was
given me by a man I did work for, an Under-Secretary," and add, "I
often think if I could tell these things to a writer he could write them
up." She would say, listening to a conversation, "What is happening
in the world? O, dear, who knows what will happen? The world is so
mixed up: you would think I should know more than you, working
in Geneva, but I know less than anybody else."

After her thin, black figure, there entered late a stalwart young man
with dark eyes and rubicund in a furred motoring-coat, who put his
automobile behind the Cathedral. His self-possession and the professional glance he cast on the audience, drew glances. He greeted many
people in the crowd, bowing from the waist to some, laughing heartily
at others, shaking hands again. He had a bounding, healthy look and
when he smiled, brilliant teeth made his dark face seem darker. He
was the Viennese singer who played the part of "Don Juan." With
him was a thin, sharp-nosed, thick-browed chap with thin hair, very
much wrinkled, jealous and salty as a long-tongued woman; a Trans-
lator he was, who translated all the modern books, flighty, scandalous
and political, that were written. He was extremely laborious, verifying

each word with a dozen notes at the foot of the page, and bitter, stinging with a thousand imagined affronts, and cruel, ready for a thousand expected attacks. He would run down even his dearest friends for the pleasure of saying something original on his own account, and he cried like a child, at home, if he was found out in a fault of grammar.

There was a POLICE COMMISSIONER, a lively, political journalist, a moke of all trades who worked ambitiously in any shafts offered him, thinking he would one day have a chance to sit on the driver's seat and show a long head despite his ass's ears. He had been a Minister in a Government, but he drove one day into some too, too slippery mass of garbage, and he had been obliged to take a long rest in the country in the clover, biding his time. In the country, he had improved his manners, taken an eye-glass, studied fine eating, invented a few dishes, written two romances and a book of aphorisms and learned to seem wise by ignoring questions. He had a wife with whom he lived at times in hotels, and then the pair would quarrel so loudly that everyone would rap on the walls and the manager, red in face, would endeavour to silence the domestic ululations, pacifying madam, expostulating with the gentleman, bidding him remember the next elections. And when his wife was ill and went to a sanatorium in Switzerland, the Commissioner published in modern literary journals, post-dada-ist laments on his tubercular love. When he had put his finger successfully into several lucrative scandals in Persia, Thibet and China, he retired for a season again, but now to Biarritz, where he met the best people, including princes of the blood, cinema stars, champion Aberdeen terriers and bathing-suits by Patou and distinguished himself at water-polo. His supporters then thought him groomed for another public appearance and he emerged as Police Commissioner and was given the Order of Merit by the king of his country. There, he revolutionised the police, introduced military discipline, gave military pay, studied machine-guns and tear-gas bombs and went on long voyages. During these, he visited America and studied their automatic prisons and the adroit way they broadcast robberies so that their police can give the burglar a fair avenue of escape; went to London, admired Dartmoor and crossed the crossing at the Bank; went to Paris to see how they provide one policeman for each citizen, and visited the Quai d'Orsay where they entertained him at dinner: went to Germany and learned how to turn recidivists into citizens by kindness, and how to discover non-existent documents. Then he returned home, made a secret report, was fêted in the streets, received bouquets, an Order, and proposals of marriage from ladies, invented a new dish, appeared in the films, improved the munition factories and once more went into retirement to be groomed for a coup d'état. This man of his time had come to Salzburg to polish himself off by rubbing shoulders with the cultivated, and to meet the Gold Trust. In the meantime, he spread sedulously his reputation for caustic repartee and looked through the proofs of a slight volume of neo-symbolist poems dedicated to his Lady of the Snows.

There was, among many, a MUSICIAN there, a tall, broad-shouldered man with florid thick neck and face, who suffered from his antipathy to innumerable conductors. He would sweat at the beginning of a concert, lose his handkerchief, fish for it in all his pockets, cough, sweat, drop his music, tug at his tie, roll his piano-stool too low, sigh and get red to the roots of his hair. Only when his fingers touched the keyboard did he get calm again, and then the delight he felt at being at rest pervaded all his music. This musician was a kindly man, modest and unpretentious. He did not like to shine, but to drink beer and sit with a friend or two: his clothes were not smart, he was always embarrassed when eating in society, and he could never think of a witty reply. Nevertheless, when he began to speak, at last, and he was at his ease, it was the same thing as with his music; his ideas rolled out freely without a hitch and an elevated, regretful and sometimes revolutionary sentiment was heard in his words.

There was, among the last who came in when the actors were assembled on the stage, an AMERICAN BROKER who had been, when young, an orator for the Democratic Party, and a musical prodigy, but he had left the orchestra because musicians have to enter the theatre through a side-door while the front-door is reserved for the do-nothings, the spectators; and he had left off speaking for the Democratic Party at the age of fifteen, when he was employed to go about the country to raise funds for the starving Armenians. He then invented the famous slogan:—

> For hungry Armenians, American bread;
> For sick Armenians, an American bed;
> An American winding sheet for the Armenian dead."

After this, he became private secretary to a man who invented a new type of female screw and thus made millions, and when the millionaire retired to his estates, our friend entered the office of a large broking and banking firm on Wall Street and devoted himself there to the various branches of high finance, that is, literature, the fine arts, the entertainment of senators, and duplicate book-keeping by high-powered electrical Lunar machines. On fine days he cut up ticker tape and threw it out of the window so that Tammany Hall would be able to justify the salaries it gave its street cleaners which were from 5,000 to 10,-000 dollars a year for casual labour; and on wet days he went about putting gilt edges on South American certificates. He was a tall, slender gentleman with chestnut hair; he was educated at Groton and at Harvard, and wore a real pearl stud and the sign of Phi Beta Kappa on his watch-chain. He had an air of extreme refinement, although he spoke German with a perfect accent, and it was rumoured that he would be admitted to the Tennis and Racket Club. But, in private life, as they said in the magazines which gave his biography, he loved only big game fishing and exotic literature. When he spoke, his bright, brown eyes rolled, his tongue wallowed through a heavy swell of epithets and he had a jolly, rollicking style among men. He was a man whose feet were on earth, and who liked the smell of earth.

And there was last of all, a TOWN COUNCILLOR of Salzburg, a very pleasant, honest and cultivated man, to whom everything must be ascribed: for he accompanied the men they called the Gold Trust, and the American Broker, and others into the Capuchin Wood the next morning. When they reached the outlook over the city and sat down, he began, by accident, to relate the history of a humble man who had lived in Salzburg and been a friend of his; and that was the first story told.

Each novelist has his own method of exploring a world. Nevertheless, the methods tend to fall into a few categories, which of course overlap, and some of these categories may be expressed by simple diagrams.

For example, the basic narrative pattern—it is also the first, for it is Homer's—may be indicated thus:

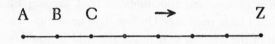

This is a picture of the adventure story, centered in an individual hero, who starts at A and has various experiences, B, C, D, and so on up to Z, which represents the conclusion of the story. Often B, C, D, and the rest are obstacles that he must overcome to reach Z. Z is frequently the heroine. The narrative line A-Z is strictly chronological: that is, B follows A in time, C follows B, etc. Nothing could be simpler, but the product may be anything from Superman to Tom Jones. When the incidents are largely physical we get the picaresque novel, of which Le Sage's Gil Blas is a pure example. But the obstacles or experiences may also be mainly mental, in which case we get the development-novel, of which the middle-period books of H. G. Wells—Marriage, Tono-Bungay, The Research Magnificent —are excellent specimens.

Now, here is another diagram:

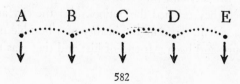

This is meant to show the pattern of the psychological novel. The interest is not in progressive adventure, whether physical or mental, but in the total exploration of the minds of the characters, here shown as A, B, C, etc. The arrows indicate the direction of that exploration, downward into the unconscious. The narrative often is a-chronological, with cutbacks, dream episodes, and so on, as in Proust. The novels of Virginia Woolf are fair examples of this method, which was in part stimulated by the discoveries of Freud. It is at present rather out of fashion.

Certain novels, such as Vicki Baum's Grand Hotel and Thornton Wilder's Bridge of San Luis Rey, use a trick form, really an adaptation of the detective story. We might picture it this way and call it the convergent novel:

In the detective story each of the arrows represents a clue (disguised as a character) and each of them—except for the red herrings—points toward the solution, indicated by the dot at the center. In Wilder's story, the dot is the fall of the bridge.

Here is a picture of still another kind of novel, very popular about a decade ago:

This is the social novel, in which the individual hero and heroine are submerged in the class or group. The simplest kind of social novel is shown in the diagram. A is one class, perhaps the working class; B may represent the capitalist class. A and B are lines of force that

are bound to collide—a strike, a walkout, a riot, a revolution. Zola's
Germinal is a classic example of this kind of book, and dozens of
others will occur to you offhand.

Tired of little pictures? Here's one more:

A

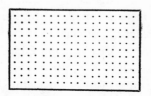

With a single exception (the mythical or symbolic novel, such as
Thomas Mann's Joseph and His Brothers, or James Joyce's Finnegans Wake, whose method is so complicated that only a tesseract
could serve as diagram), this represents the most involved form of
narrative I know. It is peculiarly the expression of the twentieth century, although it has a precursor in Emile Zola's Rougon-Macquart
series. Let us call it the collective novel. Here also, as in the social
novel, individuals are subordinated, but even more so. The collective novel does not aim so much to tell a story as to describe a society. It combines the viewpoint of anthropology and sociology with
the methods of fiction.

The diagram, in a rough way, attempts to illustrate this. The rectangle A represents the field of investigation. In the case of Dos
Passos' U.S.A., for example, that would be postwar America. Each
horizontal dotted line stands for a single element or institution or
movement that played an important role in forming the society the
author is reproducing. Each vertical line, we may say, represents a
key character whose career intersects the line of the movement or
institution.

Now, the collective novel attempts to give a complete picture of
a society. It cannot, of course, do so, but that is the ideal it approaches. The nearer complete the picture, the more horizontal and
vertical lines we would have to draw within rectangle A. Obviously

we can in theory draw an infinite number of such lines, just as the collective novelist can in theory describe a near-infinity of characters and institutions.

And this at last brings us to Jules Romains. Of all writers, living or dead, he has filled the rectangle most densely. He is the greatest of collective novelists and to my mind one of the greatest of living novelists. At this writing there have been published in English nine volumes of his series, Men of Good Will, ably translated by Warre B. Wells. Each of these is made up of two of the original French volumes. There will be at least six, and probably even more, of the latter before the series comes to an end, making a minimum of 6000 pages. This is the most gigantic unified effort in the whole of the world's literature, for Zola's Rougon-Macquart series has only a mechanical coherence and Balzac's Human Comedy really breaks down into separate volumes.

Romains endeavors in Men of Good Will to portray not characters but "life in the twentieth century, our own life as modern men." Obviously he must choose a terrain: it is France from 1908 to, one may presume, the present, or very close to it. He is writing, he says, "one single novel, and its plot has been drafted in advance."

For almost twenty years this novelist, poet, dramatist, and authority on extraretinal vision has proclaimed the doctrine of "unanimism." Long ago he waved farewell to the individual and to the family as literary units. Society itself and those bonds, tenuous or brutal, which hold society together form his theme. If there is a hero of his epic it may be said to be Paris, focus of European civilization as we knew it up to 1939.

I propose to offer a running summary of all the volumes so far available in English. The casual reader need not pay any attention to this summary, but it may be of some slight use to those who seriously intend to go through the entire series, an undertaking that involves a considerable amount of time.

In the first volume, composed of the two parts "The Sixth of October" and "Quinette's Crime," Romains introduces us to a large number of characters (sixty, to be exact), most of whom will continue to play their parts throughout the series. At once he reveals that omniscience which is his hallmark.

We meet in this first section the haut monde of society and finance, represented by the Saint-Papouls, the de Champcenais, and Sammécaud. We watch the actress Germaine Baader considering the attractions of her body and the security of her investments. The deputy Gurau, Germaine's lover, opens up for us the world of European politics. Two of the chief characters who thread the entire series—the students Jerphanion and Jallez—make their first appearance. The central intrigue is provided by the crime of the bookbinder, Quinette. Quinette, with his carefully kept beard, his electric health belt, his introspection, becomes the very image, the ghastly pattern, of the defeated intellectual of our day, forced to find in violent action some outlet for his own lack of balance.

Before the penetrating gaze of Jules Romains few aspects of life seem to remain sealed. He seizes upon the contour and temperature of a street crowd. For eight breathless pages (I have included them in this book), he makes us inhabit the mind of eleven-year-old Louis Bastide as he trundles his hoop through the streets of Paris on a beautiful October day of 1908. Romains draws a circle which circumscribes prostitutes and financiers, political idealists and politicians, murderers and actresses, policemen, students, manicurists, cabinetmakers—human life in all its diversity and density.

The second volume, Passion's Pilgrims, is, if possible, finer than the first, more acute, more subtle, richer in characters, and less dependent for its interest on the Quinette intrigue, which smells ever so slightly of melodrama. The scene remains Paris, the time the autumn of 1908. The wonder and complexity of Paris (one of the major motifs of the series) reach us through the alert and sensitive minds of Jerphanion and Jallez. Quinette, the intellectual criminal, treads his subtle, perverse path into the inner circles of revolutionary intrigue. This gives Romains a chance to expose the political cancers of Europe just before the First World War. What we know of the contemporary state of European capitalism is suddenly illuminated as we spy upon the private lives of the oil magnates, Sammécaud and de Champcenais. We watch the liberal politician Gurau, as, without knowing it, he sells out to the oil industry. The hypnotic dream of monopoly is illustrated, from another point of view, by the street urchin Wazemmes and the entrepreneur Haverkamp, who begin the task of establishing a corner in Paris real estate. And somehow, though the tone of this volume is not at all grim or foreboding, we feel in every chapter the first faint stirrings of an imminent European cataclysm.

The dominating theme, however, is neither war, politics, nor industry, for Passion's Pilgrims is primarily concerned with the varieties of erotic experience. Here Romains' virtuosity nears the incredible. He is equally successful whether he depicts the provincial Jerphanion writhing in the coils of youthful lust, or Jallez sentimentally retrieving in imagination his boyhood romance, or Madame de Champcenais hysterically frigid before the advances of Sammécaud, or the old maid Mlle Bernardine cruelly revealing to a young virgin the final secret of physical love, or the manicurist Renée casually explaining the basis of a healthy, sensual marriage.

Passion, politics, industry, revolution—even these do not begin to exhaust the themes Romains handles with such confident power. He seems to have lived for years on intimate terms, not so much with a variety of characters as with the whole population of a great city: society romancers, poules de luxe, professors of literature, secret-service agents, real-estate speculators, schoolgirls, manicurists, abbés, chauffeurs, coachmen, nymphomaniacal lady novelists, revolutionaries, milliner's assistants, poets, orators, and dogs.

As we begin the third volume, The Proud and the Meek, a gnawing discomfort begins to unsettle us. There is something a trifle terrifying about this Javert's eye that remembers where all the bodies, every last one, are hidden.

It is of interest, even instructive, for us to be neatly wedged beneath the adulterous bed of Marie de Champcenais and Roger Sammécaud; to be smuggled into a closet from which we overlook the cold, exultant play of Haverkamp's mind and the career of his body in a house of convenience; furtive and silent, to assist at the rites of Madame Camille, abortionist and seller of secret herbs; to

spy upon the soul of the mystic Abbé Jeanne; like the devil on two
sticks, to peep in upon the roofless homes of a Parisian workers'
quarter; or with godlike calm to watch four crooks float a bond
issue that will ruin a million simple Frenchmen.

But, we catch ourselves asking uneasily, where will all this end?
Here is this superb Romains, more confident now than ever, thread-
ing humanity's steeplechase maze as if crossing a drawing room,
passing with negligent ease from Sammécaud's pied-à-terre to a real-
estate promoter's conference room, grasping indifferently the sorrowful delight of a mother gazing upon her little son's undersize bed,
the premature conscientiousness of nine-year-old Louis Bastide, the
twilight mentality of the de Champcenais idiot boy, the upsurge of
revolutionary feeling in Jerphanion, the sexual calculus of a high-
grade lady of pleasure. When, each of us asks with a wild start, does
he reach me? When will he surprise me in parlor, bedroom, or bath?
When will he uncover, with his frightening impartiality, those
hoarded secrets and hidden shames my complacence imagined unique
and incommunicable?

As a matter of fact, part of the fascination of Men of Good Will,
especially marked in this third section, lies in the constant stimulus
given our sense of recognition. On almost every page there is something to make us mutter, "There, by the grace of Romains, go I."
Our feeling that this man knows everything is merely a translation
of the fact that he remembers things we have experienced or guessed
at and then forgotten. The mind of Jules Romains is among other
things a one hundred per cent efficient filing system in which is
docketed, under a thousand related heads, the life of modern man.
Possibly there is also even an entry for the fall of sparrows.

The second section of The Proud and the Meek makes us realize
that if Romains lacks Proust's subtlety and poetry, he is superior to
him in his social knowledge and sympathies. The Bastides represent
a world in which work is the obsessive value. It is extremely clever of
Romains here to make his chief character a child of nine, rather than
an adult; through Louis' dawning consciousness, we slowly discover,
instead of being told, the acid fact that society may be the enemy
of man.

Once or twice, as this Nile among novels continues on its way, Romains gives himself a sort of breathing spell in the form of a volume devoid of high points. It is necessary, for a true Romains admirer, to take these duller volumes along with the higher-pitched ones; they are just as essential to his grand design. The fourth volume, The World from Below, belongs to this class.

The first part of The World from Below is called "The Lonely," a title which is a gratuitously sappy nonequivalent for the precise "Recherche d'une Église" of the original. Some of "the proud" of Volume Three reappear. But the chief part of the book is devoted to Jerphanion and Jallez, who, it is an easy guess, represent two elements in the personality of Romains as a youth. Jerphanion, typifying the lost generation of the time, is on the lookout for a "church." His quest leads him to Socialism and more particularly to Freemasonry, which occupied the mind of the intellectuals to a degree we in America, who lump Masons with Elks, Odd Fellows, and Rotarians, can hardly understand. Jallez, on the other hand, represents nonpolitical, introspective youth. His entire life at this point is obsessed by a dangerous and frustrated love affair.

The second part, "Provincial Interlude," is a showpiece. It is almost as if Romains were saying, "To convince you that I am not bounded by the streets of Paris, I'm going to describe in detail the manners of the squirearchy, expose a complicated financial scandal involving the clergy of a provincial town, deliver up the private thoughts of a farmer, and follow the fortunes of a local election." He does all this with the greatest of ease, but the tricks are not as interesting as they might be, and the relation of these elaborate manipulations to the whole scheme is foggy.

In the fifth volume, The Earth Trembles, the tempo changes. The book appeared in 1936, when Europe was stirring uneasily under the threat of war and the imminence of revolution. The Earth Trembles opens in 1910 and runs through 1911, but the reader gets a weird notion that Romains was writing contemporary history.

One notes, too, the increased seriousness of the tone. The individual men and women now reveal their symbolic values in a giant historical process. Thus the politician Gurau is, to be sure, studied as a fallible human being, suffering from eczema, tortured by ambition, narcotized by daydreams, and enfeebled by sensuality, but he is studied also as an example of how a "friend of the people" is corrupted by power into assuming a position which today is called Fascist.

Similarly, each of the other characters is made to yield a meaning above and beyond his unique personality. Edmond Maillecottin, latheworker in a mass-production auto factory, is shown, true enough, in a complex web of personal relations, but his importance to us lies more in the fact that through him we get a clear picture of the mind of a class-conscious proletarian, a picture drawn not by a writer of tracts but by a novelist.

Light episodes are sparse and there are only a few of those trick set pieces that Romains will occasionally touch off merely to exhibit the unfailing powers of his technique. For instance, there is a description of how a woman feels during the birth of a baby. The problem has been a challenge to many male novelists. I know of none except Romains who has followed it up with a perfectly unhesitating record of how the baby feels during the process.

We might expect Romains to be at home in the luxurious milieu of the Champcenais, but in this volume he proves himself no less conversant with the life of the industrial suburbs to the north of Paris, where the trade-union movement is slowly recruiting its revolutionary strength. He makes an easy transition to provincial France, where the agile Abbé Mionnet is involved in a bit of scandal; thence to a secret organization, half pacifist, half anarchist, all a little unreal; thence to the heart of French politics, where we listen to Briand, Delcassé, Tardieu, Jaurès planning, equivocating, fearing, hoping; thence to the superworld of Zulpicher, a great industrialist, armaments manufacturer, and war fomenter, to whom all these other people are merely slight conveniences or petty obstacles. The decayed politics surrounding election to the French Academy, the sewer of venal Paris journalism, the life of the students (for Jerphanion and Jallez, with their walks and talks, their gradual growth into typical "men of good will," still help to hold the narrative together), the mad yet logical French parliamentary system, the atmosphere of a first-rate house of prostitution, the forced marches of the French Army in Morocco, the boudoir conversations of smart women, and always Paris, and again Paris—these are a few of the matters and milieus upon which Romains touches with a sure hand.

In this volume there is less drama, but more magnitude, less bravura work and more seriousness. We are approaching Sarajevo. Europe holds its breath. What was life like in those years of painful breath-holding? Romains tells us, and as he does so he appears, by that miracle only great novelists command, to be writing of ourselves.

Volume Six, The Depths and the Heights, has passages and chapters superior to anything that has gone before. I wish I could include some of them in this collection but, torn from their context, they would lose much of their force. More than ever we are struck by the phenomenal quality of Romains' genius. He seems to me to dwarf all living imaginative writers except Thomas Mann. The real titans—Mann, Tolstoy, Dickens, Balzac—have a certain mark of greatness upon them, easy to recognize. They combine a passion for the exact detail with a never-failing grasp of a large idea. They are jewelers and architects at once. In their pages the large and the little reinforce each other constantly. I believe Romains shows this mark of greatness.

In "To the Gutter" (the first half of The Depths and the Heights), a certain number of minor threads continue their slow unwinding. Jerphanion and Jallez, the nearest thing to main characters in a novel based on the denial of the idea of main characters, act as choruses and editorial voices, write each other long, intellectual letters, deepen in knowledge, advance ignorantly to their great life experience—the time is two years before the outbreak of the Great War. The Left politician, Gurau, as he becomes more powerful, becomes more entrenched in the very system he has sworn to alter. Gurau is the fictional representation of one of the most characteristic figures of our time: the liberal politician who keeps on compromising till he finds himself part of the reaction. Gurau is Clemenceau, he is Briand, he is MacDonald. If the records of these personages should disappear from history, we should still be able, at

some future date, to reconstruct their characters, even the outlines of
their careers, from Romains' cool and pitiless study of Gurau.

But it is the literary, not the political, mind that is the main concern of "To the Gutter." George Allory, a second-rate Bourget (which
is to say a third-rate novelist), fails, after much wirepulling, to be
elected to the Academy. (Academy politics, by the way, are subjected
to a dose of satire that will forever prevent Romains from becoming
one of the Forty—hardly a tragic circumstance.) The blow shatters
the last remnants of organization in Allory's already feeble moral
character. Impelled by the sinister Mme Raymonde, he sinks bit by
bit to the level of a vicieux, committing finally a tawdry sexual offense
that leads him to attempt suicide. Whatever talent, whatever sensi-
tivity he has, becomes debased and discolored in the service of his
own moral decadence. The study of Allory's degeneration is typically
French, almost mathematical in its rigor, subtle, quite shocking, and
quite unshocked. Huysmans would have admired it and would have
been incapable of its coolness and clarity.

In "To the Stars" (the second half of The Depths and the
Heights), the minor developments are overshadowed by the story of
Dr. Viaur. Allory is a study in decadence, Viaur a study of creative
energy in general and of scientific genius in particular. Interested in
antisepsis and the revitalizing of damaged tissue, Viaur is suddenly
switched from the path he has laid out for himself by his discovery
of a freak patient, one Vidalencque, who can stop his own heart vol-
untarily. Viaur becomes obsessed by the case and embarks on a long
series of experiments which are ultimately, one gathers, to change the
whole course of biological theory.

I, a layman knowing practically nothing of physiology and biology,
find Viaur convincing. Experts may not. But I'd place bets on Romains. After all, he has had a long scientific training and himself
conducted original investigations in extraretinal vision and related
problems. Romains gives you detail. He shirks nothing, is technical
when he must be so, never writes down. In short, this is a serious, not
a literary, study of genius. I know of nothing like it in fiction, and
in nonfiction it is rivaled only by Jules Henri Poincaré's classic account of the way the mathematical imagination works. As for other

fictional portrayals of genius—Jean Christophe, for one—it makes them look like pinchbeck. The complicated tracing of the way in which training, curiosity, imagination, intuition, information, and skepticism all merge in Viaur's mind to create almost symphonically a new scientific truth—I find this one of the peaks of modern fiction.

The seventh volume, Death of a World, carries the story, or stories, up to mobilization day in 1914. Obviously it marks something in the nature of a turning point in the series. From now on the multiple rays of Romains' characters are to be focused in the burning glass of war. Lives which seemed so individual, even wayward—Quinette, Haverkamp—prepare to empty their tiny tributaries into the vast stream of history. Characters who already possess historical meaning, whether invented, like Gurau, or real, like Jaurès and Cardinal Merry del Val, will have that meaning augmented and clarified by the universal experience of 1914–18. The pattern of Romains' seeming labyrinth begins to establish itself. You feel at last that the author has foreseen everything, and with relief you place yourself unreservedly in his hands.

Death of a World consists of two books—"Mission to Rome" and "The Black Flag." The Romains method remains constant: each of the books makes use first of a dominating theme or story that gives its narrative continuity, and second of a group of minor incidents which pick up characters previously more fully treated and carry them one step farther. "Mission to Rome" deals mainly with the subtle, worldly Abbé Mionnet and his expedition. The Roman adventures into which Mionnet is drawn offer Romains an opportunity to unlock for us another of his apparently inexhaustible series of universes—in this case, Roman ecclesiastical and near-ecclesiastical society. Some of the lighter scenes may recall Thornton Wilder's charming The Cabala, but Romains is deeper and broader. I should add that his picture of the higher clergy is not entirely flattering. In fact, not to put too fine a point upon it, some of it is scandalous.

The second part, "The Black Flag," is atmospheric rather than narrative—that on-the-eve-of-war atmosphere curiously compounded of boredom, lassitude, desperation, fear, and curiosity. Europe is waiting; the world is coming to an end.

Of Verdun, the eighth volume, I think one may maintain that, whether or not it is the greatest novel so far written about the First World War, it is clearly the most adult. By contrast the best of the other war novels appear in retrospect a shade callow. Hatred, pity, and indignation (I'm thinking of All Quiet on the Western Front) form an inadequate equipment for the novelist who would write greatly about a great conflict. A certain maturity of vision is needed, at times even a certain almost cold detachment. To see war steadily and see it whole—the author of War and Peace turned the trick, and perhaps Romains comes as close as any to doing it for our time. Verdun is not a record of one man's indignation. It is not emotional crusading. Epic, not lyrical, it is a war novel in the grand style.

For me it tops any other in three basic particulars. First, Romains has a firm intellectual grasp of the problems of war qua war. That is, he has gone to the trouble of mastering the general strategical ideas in accordance with which the conflict was waged. Second, his angle of vision is enormously wide, so that you get the impression of something like total perspective. Finally—lest all this sound too inhuman —he cuts to the core of the emotions of the fighting soldier, exposing it without prejudice, endeavoring to illuminate rather than to shock.

Romains' understanding of the meaning of Verdun is attested by the endorsement of Pétain, at that time a Frenchman, who took over the command of the sector at the outbreak of the German attack and organized the victory. But the reader does not need the approval of Pétain. He can feel for himself that Romains' mind must have dominated a chaos of reports, communiqués, official narratives, specialists' interpretations, long before pen was set to paper. The first three chapters of Verdun, for example, are brilliant military essays which explain in dramatic terms how the struggle developed, contrary to all expectations, into a stalemate involving millions, so that the whole concept of war underwent a complete change. "The war will be won by the side that can last fifteen minutes longer than the other" was the judgment of high military officials on both sides. Along with Romains' incisive feeling for the attritive nature of 1914–18 goes his understanding of the gigantic order of the war's operations, of the part which chance is bound to play in so incalculably large a field, of the proportion of useful actions to actions whose only purpose is to satisfy some petty official vanity, of the manner in which a new idea percolates through the military hierarchy, and, generally, of the complex way in which a thousand technical factors and a thousand psychological factors intertwine to produce the unbelievable phenomenon of whole nations engaged in mutual murder. The generals, or at any rate the intelligent ones, understand these things, but, of course, won't or can't tell; the Remarques do not know enough. Romains seems to add the dramatic sense of a Remarque to the strategical and tactical sense of a good military mind.

But Verdun is more than the clear analysis of a great battle. It is a motion picture of a great battle and the events leading up to it, a picture taken with a wide-angle lens. No single novel can give the war complete, but Verdun comes close to it. Romains' omniscience, which in some of the earlier volumes may have smacked of the exhibitionist, here comes into serious play with serious effect. Nothing seems to elude him: the look and smell of an old trench, a combination of cemetery, junk pile, and midden; how it feels to have a mine explode near you; the behind-the-lines life of a general; two deputies being thoroughly deceived on a visit of inspection to the front; the minds of the big boys—the cheerful cherub Joffre, the intelligent, suffering Galliéni, the anxious, hesitating Wilhelm II, the cool, executive Pétain; the minds of the men in the trenches; the carpe diem outlook of the airmen; the action of a 305 gun; tea-table strategy in a Paris salon; Haverkamp the profiteer, figuring out his millions over partridge and Burgundy; the strange, slow, almost unmilitary advance of the German infantry on the Verdun positions; the trench-ward march of the French soldiers from the rear and the reverse stream of refugees clogging the Voie Sacrée; the common soldiers' grouse against the civilians; Maillecottin the munitions worker, stricken with guilt as his earnings increase; Wazemmes the royalist, killed as he charges, singing, ironically enough, the "Marseillaise"; Maykosen the international journalist, trying to explain things to the Kaiser; the Abbé Jeanne finding excuses for God's part in the war; the whole sweep and range of the battle, photographed by a lens that has also the quality of an X ray.

But military grasp and encyclopedic knowledge would not be enough to give Verdun stature. To them, Romains adds a profound instinct for the springs of human action in an environment of death. Using Jerphanion, now a second lieutenant, as his mouthpiece, Romains endeavors to answer the root question: how can men stand war? For the tragedy lies not in the fact that men suffer in war but in the fact that they suffer war. "Whence do I draw sufficient courage to endure it?" writes Jerphanion to Jallez. For Jerphanion, the thinking man, "nothing can be worth this," and yet, he continues, "it is now proved beyond power of contradiction that millions of men can tolerate, for an indefinite period and without spontaneously rising in revolt, an existence more terrible and more degraded than any that the numberless revolutions of history were held to have terminated forever."

What deters the men from doing the sensible thing—disarming their officers and walking home—is a complex set of factors. In the first place, it is not so much the fear of court-martial that stops them as a generalized, intangible, but overshadowing fear of society, of what "they" (and particularly the women) will say. Also, war is in a horrible way its own best propagandist. The soldier becomes used to what he does. Indeed, it releases in him certain drives that civil life would have forever repressed. "What we're seeing now," says Jerphanion—and the words are much truer today—"is the re-emergence of the warrior spirit in the bosom of society." This warrior spirit is more than a rebirth of the urge to kill, it is a paralysis of the capacity to feel what killing means. "One of the most extraordinary things in the trenches"—I am again quoting Jerphanion—"is the apparent inability of the soldier to imagine any connection between the tiny movement necessary to release a projectile—whether it's a single bullet, a machine-gun belt, or a trench-mortar shell—a movement that's usually the result of sheer boredom or momentary nerves, and the effect caused at the other end of the trajectory in the shape of smashed heads or torn bodies."

But that man may engage in this "universal crime," he must be more than subject to social pressure, more than merely afraid of punishment, more than callous. He must have a private mythology, a personal faith or skepticism all his own, a little cave in his mind into which he can retreat when the horror becomes too much. Jerphanion has his, and each man under him and above him has his. Jerphanion explains to Jallez how each soldier constructs and then clings to his own special philosophy. It is this fixed idea that is his last stand. It is this fixed idea that explains how men could face the hell of the German artillery bombardment of Verdun and not go mad. This section, I think, is classic. It says more than most novels of the war say in their whole length about the profound impulses that enable men to abandon their humanity. I have included it in this book.

Verdun, though many of the old characters of the series reappear, is not a book about individuals. It is a book about a battle in which guns are as important as men, and men in the mass more important than personalities. Its scale is stepped up from that of the earlier volumes. Niceties of psychological penetration go by the board. A moment of history is grasped almost in its entirety. Though death and disaster are the materials of the narrative, it is in a way less exciting than some of the other, lighter volumes have been. Romains is not out to startle or surprise or shock or touch you but to make you understand, to make you understand a whole way of living and feeling grotesquely and horribly peculiar to our own century, which has apparently adopted murder as its norm of experience.

Aftermath, ninth in the series, is a letdown from the magnificences of his Verdun. Part of Aftermath is pretty dull, particularly its second volume, "The Sweets of Life." I say this with regret; indignor quandoque bonus dormitat Homerus.

However, Romains is not precisely nodding in the first half of Aftermath, which is a dadaist crime thriller of great sophistication, even though overelaborated. Here we again meet our old friend Quinette, the homicidal bookbinder we first encountered eight volumes back. Quinette is a murder-for-murder's-saker. He is an esthetic killer. So far he has avoided detection. On the principle that it takes an artist to catch an artist, Romains now introduces a weird character named Vorge, a dadaist poet whose fantastic imagination is given over to images of destruction, sadism, murder, and insanity. In the quiet, unobtrusive bookbinder, Vorge's intuition recognizes a kindred spirit.

Romains devotes a couple of hundred pages to the manner in which
Vorge establishes his domination over Quinette.

The Vorge-Quinette story, I think, is intended to carry a certain
weight of symbolism. The nihilist disintegration of conscience after
the First World War is reflected in Vorge and his circle. They represent the eccentric, the "art" form of the will to death which the Fascists have organized and exploited in political and military patterns.

The second half of the book is disappointing. It deals mainly with
a lyrical love affair between the introspective Jallez and a little maiden
of the people, Antonia. There's too much pedantic soul-searching on
Jallez' part to please our downright American tastes, I fear. In fact,
Jallez, who up to this point has been one of Romains' most appealing
creations, seems to be slowly turning into an intellectual prig. Perhaps it's only a phase. Romains is too wise a bird to let one of his
main characters get out of hand. In general you come to feel that the
author is having trouble in starting this postwar section of the series.
There are a great many threads to tie up, a whole new atmosphere to
project, perhaps even a new tempo to establish. The volume seems
uncertain, tentative, but once Romains gets up steam, I think, its
sequels will not disappoint us. I'm convinced that when Men of
Good Will at last reaches its appointed end we will see in it a coherence of parts and a unity of conception which are as yet only half
apparent.

Shortcomings Romains has, obviously. He exhibits wide sympathy
but little passion, irony but little humor. Occasionally the mania for
analysis gets the better of him and the body of the novel stiffens suddenly when it should move free and relaxed. He has been reproached
by some for the detachment of his social viewpoint. In so far as his
political sympathies may be descried, they are enlisted sincerely on
the side of the weak and the suffering. One cannot render a final
judgment on his social and political views, which, whatever they are,
undoubtedly underlie the whole of his vast collective epic. The very
title of his book, however, gives us the clue to his political position,
as does the simple fact that he now lives in our country. Romains,
with his great humanity, his deep political insight, and his profound
knowledge of the history of his time, is obviously opposed to those

who would be the first to destroy the very culture that has created him.

The three excerpts that follow can give one no more idea of the vastness and the momentum of the whole work than has my own flat summary. They are presented simply as brilliant pieces of writing that happen to be comprehensible in themselves. The first exposes the mind of a little boy of the working class. The second, which is an essay—there are many essays in Men of Good Will, just as there are in Tom Jones—describes the permanent France, the France that will still be there when "the wave of the future" has ebbed back into the ooze from which it came. The third, one of the great pieces of modern French prose, is as revealing in relation to today's events as it is in relation to Verdun. My hope is that these three brief chapters plus the résumé you have just waded through may induce some to engage in a great adventure—the reading of the entire vast, magnificent Men of Good Will.

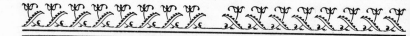

A Little Boy's Long Journey

FROM "MEN OF GOOD WILL" BY

JULES ROMAINS

CLANRICARD HAD not seen Louis Bastide passing with his hoop. Louis Bastide had come up the rue Clignancourt from the corner of the rue Ordener, running all the way. The slope was very steep. Horses had to take it at a walk; and they pulled their loads up in jerks, straining for all they were worth and striking sparks out of the stones. One day little Louis had been there when a fire-engine with magnificent horses arrived at a gallop and attacked the slope. A few yards up the hill, they had to slow down like everybody else.

So it was obviously very difficult to roll a hoop up such a slope. It needed plenty of enthusiasm and stout-heartedness at the beginning; and then a determination not to weaken, not to give way to your tiredness—to say nothing of great skill in handling your stick.

When he got out of school, Louis Bastide had gone straight home to his parents, who lived in the rue Duhesme, on the third floor, quite near the boulevard Ornano. He kissed his mother and showed her his copy-books and the report on his work and conduct. He did not ask for anything, but his eyes shone. His mother looked at his pale little cheeks and at the fine sun outside; and she tried not to let him see how pleased she was that he wanted to go out and play.

"All right," she said, "take your hoop. Mind the traffic. Be home by five o'clock."

The hoop was big and substantial—too big for Louis's size. But he had chosen it himself after mature consideration. Long before buying it he had seen it in the window of a bazaar, and he had said to himself that nobody could want a finer hoop—perhaps because of the strong, healthy look of the wood, whose colour was clear and whose joints were well fitted. You had only to look at it to realize how it would run and jump.

Its dimensions had given him something to think about. But Louis expected to go on growing for some years yet; and he could not imagine that a hoop of which he got very fond might some day cease to be dear to him and simply strike him as a child's trivial toy. His only reason for ever discarding it would be its getting too small for him. In choosing a rather big one, Louis was taking thought for the future.

He went down the stairs, with the hoop hanging from his shoulder. Once he was out in the street, he stood it in the middle of the sidewalk, very straight up, holding it lightly with the fingers of his left hand. Then he gave it a smart tap. The hoop rolled away. The end of the stick caught up with it at once, keeping it in the right direction; and after that Bastide and his hoop had run one after the other; rather like a child running after a dog that he has on a leash; and also rather like a rider who lets himself be carried along by his horse, but at the same time keeps on spurring and guiding him.

When you have played for a long time with a hoop, as Louis Bastide had done, and you have had the luck to find one of which you are very fond, you come to realize that things are quite different from going out in the ordinary way. Try and run by yourself; you will be tired in a few minutes. With a hoop, you can keep tiredness at bay indefinitely. You feel as though you were holding on to something, almost as though you were being carried along. If you happen to feel tired for a moment, it seems as though the hoop imparted strength to you in a friendly kind of way.

Besides, you don't have to run fast all the time. If you know how to do it, you can go almost at a walking pace. The trouble is to keep the hoop from falling to the right or left; or clinging to the legs of a passer-by, who struggles like a rat in a trap; or lying down flat on the ground after going through extraordinary contortions. You must know how to use your stick, how to give the hoop very gentle taps, just as though you were stroking it and helping it on its way. Above all, in between your taps, you must keep control over any tendency of the hoop to waver, with the help of your stick, which must just graze the edge of it on one side or the other all the time, keeping it on the move or changing its speed, with the end of the stick held ready to intervene quickly at any point where the hoop threatens to fall into a lurch.

Louis Bastide need not have kept all these details in his mind, for he had been playing with the hoop for a long time, and he had become skilled enough in handling it to trust to most of his actions being automatic. But there was a background of conscientiousness, of thoroughness in him which prevented him from doing anything in the least important without taking pains over it. Nor could he help taking pains even over his pleasures. Once he was interested in anything, he applied himself to it passionately, and the smallest details struck him with pulsating clearness, with a sharpness which made every one of them something unforgettable.

He was born to be a man with the utmost presence of mind. But his capacity for taking pains did not prevent him from taking fire. If his control of the hoop never ceased for a moment to be an operation of scientific exactitude, performed in a sphere of pitiless clarity, his running through the streets became an adventure luxuriant and mysterious, whose connecting thread resembled that of dreams, and whose inexplicable ups and downs led him little by little, and turn by turn, to moments of enthusiasm, or of intoxication, or of a melancholy in itself uplifting.

Once he had crossed the boulevard, he followed the rue Championnet. It was, at that time, a rather out-of-the-way street, still full of whiteness and brightness. There were scarcely any tall houses. There were low, long buildings, opening on inside courtyards, with nothing but a window or a peep-hole in a door looking out on the street now and then. It was a street with gateways, with fences. A street whose habitual silence was broken only by the occasional rumbling passing of a three-horse truck.

The sidewalk was bright, and wide enough; and also it was empty. The long wall which ran on your right accompanied you like a comrade. There were only three or four lamp-posts between you and the next crossing. All this street was full of easiness, of security, of mute benevolence. The sky above it was spacious. The smoke of a factory, in the distance, emerged almost pure white and displayed itself to the right of the tall chimney like a banner floating in the breeze.

Happy the child of Paris who had the run of this quiet street. He could see the sky and the smoke. The sky, still blue and sunny, told you, all the same, that night was coming. It bent down over the roofs of the sheds, and so it came quite close to you. But away there where the smoke was, it was glorious, deep, distant.

That beloved sky, towards which your eyes kept straying, which you kept on finding from time to time—this evening it was like your idea of the future. It did not promise anything, but it contained, somehow or other, all kinds of promises which the heart of a child of Paris could divine. It reminded him of certain hazy but still remembered happinesses that he had known when he was still quite small, still more of a child than he was now, that were already a part of his memory, even while he was running behind his hoop, that were already his own personal, incomparable, secret past.

How lovely that smoke was! A quite regular series of puffs that rolled up and then spread out. Something like those magnificent clouds of summer, but with a will of their own, an aim of their own, an aspiration of their own. They conveyed to you the idea of a spring; and then that chimney, which you could see sticking out of the city—it was as though the source of the clouds, coming to birth in the depths of Paris, had been borne up there into the sky.

Sometimes the hoop took it into its head to run away. The end of the stick pursued it without succeeding in catching up with it; and the hoop leant over a little, it veered about. It behaved just like an animal which loses its head as it runs. You must know how to catch up with it not too impatiently. Otherwise you ran the risk of running it up against a wall or of knocking it over.

When the time came to leave the sidewalk and cross the street, it was a delight to wait for the hoop's little leap and watch over it. It was exactly as though you were dealing with a sensitive, nervous beast. And afterwards, until it reached the opposite sidewalk, it never stopped leaping on the stones, in their cracks, with all kinds of capricious irregularities and changes of direction.

Louis Bastide pretended that he had a mission to accomplish. Somebody had commissioned him to follow a certain course, to carry something, or perhaps to herald something. But the itinerary was not easy.

He had to keep to it, respecting all its unexpectedness, all its oddness, both because this was a law and also because there were dangers and enemies to be avoided.

Here was the immense wall of the freight station, and the rue des Poissonniers, whose gas-lamps were so strange. They had a crown, like kings; a halo, like martyrs. Louis's mission demanded that he should turn to the left, across the street, and go towards the fortifications, following the long wall and passing underneath those strange gas-lamps.

The day was declining a little. The street was beginning to be filled with bluish shadows and with an almost cold air. The sky remained luminous, but it was farther away. There was no further question of the promises that it might hold for a boy who raised his eyes. Louis slowed down to a little running step, very regular, scarcely faster than the walk of a grown-up. The hoop visibly helped him. That kind of slender wheel, which could run so fast, slackened its pace so as not to tire Bastide. At this rate he could keep on going to the other end of Paris.

The bridge over the Ceinture railway, encircling the city. What had his mission to say? That he should not cross it, but turn to the left along the rue Béliard.

The rue Béliard reminded you of a road running out into the country. Far away, in the provinces, there must be many a road like this, where travellers and coaches passed along at the fall of day. Louis remembered an engraving in a school-book; and also a picture in a postal almanac; and, most of all, a drawing in an old catalogue of the Magasins du Bon Marché.

It was fine to have got as far away as this. The houses at the side of the road looked at you with astonishment. They all looked at your face and said to themselves: "How tired he must be!" But they were wrong if they imagined that Louis had come there for their benefit. His goal was far beyond, and he must get there before night, "before night overtook him," as the books said.

The most that Louis would do was to call a brief halt here. The courier would not even dismount from his horse. He would let his beast go slowly, quite slowly; and as he passed the trough, he would let him drink a little. If anybody questioned him, he would make no reply; or he would content himself with "evasive words."

Thus his gallant little horse, so faithful to its master, recovered its breath. It was better not to pay any attention to the cutting of the Ceinture railway, which lay to the right. Otherwise, the spell would be broken. Unless, indeed, you thought of mountains. In mountain country the railway, penetrating any number of tunnels, made its way to a village. Once a day at the most, the mountaineers watched for the arrival of the train.

In the inn, which was that shed surrounded by a bank, opposite the cut, people were drinking and playing cards as they waited. They might be hunters who had come down from the mountain. They had not come down to take the train; for nothing in the world would they leave their own country-side; but, still, they were waiting.

Louis imagined himself going into the inn for a moment. He left his hoop outside, leaning against the wall; but he kept his stick in his hand, just as you keep your whip. "A glass of wine, sir?" "Yes, but I won't sit down, because I haven't time. . . . Good health! . . . Is it freezing in the mountains?" "Yes, they say that right at the top the pass is covered with snow. But you'll get through, if you don't let the night overtake you."

The courier set out on his way again. Here began the road that ran up into the mountains, that led to the pass blocked by snow.

How fine it was, a street that went up straight in front of you and ended far away in the sky! This one was particularly fine, because it was never-ending and made you think of a great precipice beyond it. Louis's father called it "chaussée" Clignancourt, not just "street" like the others. Louis did not know why, but he was not surprised that this marvellous street should have a name all to itself.

His mission now was to get to the top of it before he was "overtaken by the night"; higher even than he could see; right up to the top of the hill of Montmartre. Then it would be his mission to make a kind of reconnaissance by following the end of the rue Lamarck, like a road cut in a rock, from which you could see the whole of Paris across the new gardens.

Long before he reached the slope, there was still a fair distance on level ground, and, since the hoop was bowling along without his touching it, as though the wind were pushing it, Louis imposed a quite moderate pace upon himself. On the other hand, he made a vow not to slacken up the slope until he reached the pass "blocked by snow." After that he would be free to proceed as he chose. He would have left the road. He would be on paths where it was permissible and even prudent to dismount.

But that was still a very long way off! Bastide needed all his courage, and also all his skill. He resisted the temptation to go fast. He approached the dangerous street-crossings carefully. His mother had warned him to mind the traffic. Louis had no desire to be killed; but his mother's despair if he were killed frightened him even more than the idea of death. The stretcher being carried upstairs; "My little Louis! My poor little boy!" The wreck of the hoop, which they might put with his body; the stick, which he might still clasp in his hand.

Still, it is difficult to evade a law which you have laid down for yourself. Cross the boulevard Ornano with his hoop hanging from his shoulder—that was something which Louis could not bring himself to do. He even had a feeling that he would be punished in some way or other if he did. The laws which you lay down for yourself, or, rather, the orders which come to you from some mysterious depths in yourself, will not suffer you to infringe them or play tricks with them. You risk much less in disobeying a visible master.

Louis had the right to stop, he and his hoop, the one supporting the other. But so long as the course was not finished, the hoop must not leave the ground, must not cease to be in contact with the ground; for if it did, he would cease to be "true" to himself.

The rue Marcadet in its turn was successfully negotiated. The long climb began. Louis, who knew very little about any other neighbourhood, thought that in the whole of Paris there could not be any slope which it was more honourable to conquer. He who was capable of scaling it, without the hoop that he guided falling down or running away, need not be dismayed anywhere.

But the passers-by lacked brains. If they understood the value of the test, they would not hesitate about getting out of the way, instead of making those annoyed faces, or looking at the boy with contemptuous pity.

So it was that Louis Bastide came to the half-way house of the rue Custine. He saw Clanricard and saluted him hastily, raising his hand to his béret. The master was looking the other way. Bastide, very fond of him as he was, could not possibly stop. The private law which he had formulated for himself at the bottom of the slope required that he should reach the "pass blocked by snow" without a halt. He would have liked to be able to explain to his master that he was not imposing such an effort on himself just for fun.

So he kept his stride and did not allow himself to take breath until he was at the top of the street.

After that it was almost a rest. Louis had the right to go up the rue Muller at walking pace. To help his hoop to keep its balance, he could even support it gently with his left hand, with the tips of his fingers grazing the edge of the wood. On mountain paths the most skilful horseman dismounts and, taking his horse, however good he may be, by the bridle, guides him and helps him not to stumble. All this was inside the rules.

When he reached the bottom of the rue Sainte-Marie, he asked himself whether he should go up the street itself or up the steps. He chose the steps. The other way was much longer and offered no opportunity of picking up new threads of adventure. So far as going up a flight of steps like this with a hoop was concerned, the rule to be followed was self-evident. While Louis himself used the steps, keeping as far over to the left as possible, the hoop made use of the granite curb. He helped it with stick and hand. It was a delicate manœuvre, the more so in that the principal role devolved upon the left hand. The hoop might escape you and hop backwards; in a series of hops it might run away altogether and go and get smashed under a carriage. But, to avert such a misfortune, it sufficed to be very careful—in other words, to be very fond of your hoop.

As he climbed up the steps, Louis met a keener air, less tainted with darkness. The cliff of houses on his right rose in successive surges, following the rhythm of the steps, and at its peak still received a slanting but dazzling light. The windows of the upper floors were still burning with reflections. Without stirring from their rooms women could watch the sunset.

And the boy wanted to raise himself up faster, as though up there, on the cornice of the hill, were all the joy, all the games, all the adventures of the future. The very noise of Paris passed into his body, though he was not aware of listening to it. Up with you, nimble hoop! Trains whistled in the suburbs in the plain. The child of the low streets recognized their cries without noticing them, as though he had been born among sea-birds. Roofs innumerable creaked in the wind; their creakings and cracklings sounded above the rustle of the leaves in the precipitous gardens. Like all these noises, the hoop, too, bounded and mounted. The child of Paris, as he stopped to take breath, drank in a sound of destinies that came to him from everywhere.

Portrait of France in July '14

FROM "MEN OF GOOD WILL" BY

JULES ROMAINS

THUS IT was that this nation of decent folk, of men rather badly dressed, not too well washed, and somewhat undersized, prepared to march once again into the pages of History.

The west end of Paris got ready with a bright air of gallantry. Beautiful women, crossing the Place de l'Étoile in their cars, gazed dreamily at the Arc de Triomphe. Retired colonels who had seen the war of '70 and served in the campaign of Madagascar screwed their monocles into their eyes and raised their walking-sticks in a gesture of swagger. Racecourse habitués, their grey top hats set at rather a more rakish angle than usual, made a point of discussing the favourite's chances as calmly as though their hearts were not already beating to the sound of the charge and the booming of the guns.

The farther one went towards the east, however, the more definitely did one become aware of a troubled undercurrent. One was vaguely conscious of ideas in the light of which complacency felt sick. Perhaps one was permitting them to raise their uneasy heads now for the last time, before letting one's feeling sink to the level of everyone else's, before calmly, like everyone else, crossing the threshold of a heroic age into that great echoing hall of heroisms, that side-show of freaks, both men and women, on whose behalf the newspapers were already playing the showman: "Just about to begin. . . . Fifteen wild savages in a state of nature. . . . Step up, ladies and gentlemen!"

History was no stranger to us. From the open-air restaurants of Montmartre men had already seen, in former days, the Prussian batteries spouting flame from beyond Saint-Denis or Stains. From the open-air restaurants of Belleville their fellows had watched the mili-

tiamen marching to be swallowed up in the battle of Champigny.
From a certain mound near Charonne, just above the ruined buildings, anxious eyes had followed the flashes on the far slopes of Châtil-
lon and been terrified at times by the sight of a shell crashing into
some house on the left bank. Men had helped the gunners drag their
pieces up the rue du Télégraphe and set them on the ramparts. Later
still had come a time when changed circumstances had meant changed
targets for the guns of Paris, when the foe had been no longer Prussian, but French troops marching from Versailles. But at such a distance of time the details were all confused. It sufficed for those others
to remember, those crowded, indistinguishable subjects of the Kaiser,
square-heads beneath spiked helmets, that they were men without fear
in their hearts, ready at a word to march.

City of taut nerves. City in which the memories of History had had
no time to fade, of History in its last new garb. City placed always at
the point of danger. When the wind blew from the east—on summer
days when the children played ball on the slopes of Romainville—it
could come in a short three hours from the enemy lines, nor find its
way impeded. The plain lay open to its onset; "Blow freely above my
spaces," said the plain. City that must sleep always with one eye open.
Strange must have been the thoughts of those who set her there, the
kings of long ago; and of those others, older still, half-wild men with
long moustaches and great spears and bodies swathed in skins. Farther off, in the deep heart of the land, they might have found high
mountains to serve them in the place of walls. Ah, if only the kings
had been cunning, had built their Paris among the slag-heaps and
the mines, the Prussians might have whistled for their victory. But
could anyone seriously regret the choice? Could anyone think of Paris,
of the Paris of the Parisians, set among the slag-heaps and the mines?
A fine thing that would have been! If things are as they are, it is because a destiny has guided them.

This exposed city, with her flank ever open to the attacks of History
—again and again she has tried to clothe her nakedness with walls,
but always they have been breached—this city is where she is because a
fate has set her there, and it would be ungracious to complain over-

much, since there is so much beauty in her choice of a site, marked out at a meeting-place of many ways. The rivers called for her, and the open plains. The folk, wandering at first, and later settled on their lands, craved her presence. The people of the mountains found it good that their capital should be builded in a valley low and fruitful. Thinking of her, men have been ever influenced more by considerations of convenience, of splendour, of adornment, than of possible danger. Famous throughout the world as a place of pleasure, she has ever known a destiny of peril. At her back, wide-stretching miles rise to slow uplands; before her the plains of the north-east lie bare, so that she resembles one of those churches that we see perched on a cliff-top's farthest edge, gazing out to sea—a Notre-Dame du Péril.

And, like her metropolis, all France is a meeting-place of ways, a country ill placed for security, but proud of her post of danger and of honour, a country set on the extreme point of a lean and bony continent which narrows away from the great cow's flanks of Asia until at last it fronts the Western Ocean. But though she stands at this far end of a mass of land, she is neither cabined nor confined; is neither the cul-de-sac of Europe, a backwater whither the flood of wandering folk have drifted when all other lands were full, nor an island to which men have, as it were, swum when naught but safety mattered, or when the spirit of adventurous daring drove them onwards in search of new worlds to conquer.

All the peoples who moved slowly through the centuries from east to west were bound, unless they settled elsewhere on their journey, to come at last to France. Not a race, not a wandering tribe, but some time or other found itself within her borders and stood on her high terraces above the Ocean, feeling the chill air on naked bodies, sniffing the winds that blew from far immensities, and all the damp sweetness of the gardened land. Many of them turned back again like wild beasts that, from the prison of fair meadows, long for the freedom of open spaces; but in the hearts of all of them the moist sweetness left its memory, so that, when the desire to wander seized upon them once again, it was always to these Western gardens, to these Ocean terraces, that they tried once more to come.

Vaguely France has always known of this lure she exercises, has taken thought, though casually, with herself, has felt, now and again, a passing fear of these invading strangers. Sometimes the knowledge has filled her with pride. She has found it but natural that her lands should be more constantly sought than any others of the world, nor thought it hard to pardon those who, from time to time, have disturbed her peace.

But on her perilous situation, which so often has cost her dear, she has never brooded with a dark, aggressive pride; has never said to herself: "I am the rampart of a continent; through me the world breathes in the airs of Ocean"; nor, when what was once for her "the world" became the "Old World," did she say: "The part of bastion to a continent thrust forth to meet the challenge of new lands is mine and must be mine to play alone, whatever the cost. Shamelessly have all the races of the Old World invaded my privacies, crept into my bosom, mixed the stream of their lives with mine; therefore now, tirelessly and of right, warm with their blood and avid with their greed, will I greet what is to come from worlds still young." By force and forethought she might have made of all her coastline between the Pas-de-Calais and Brittany, between Finisterre and the Pyrenees, a lurking trap, facing two ways, to catch and hold the wanderer, with, at its back, netted by roads and canals and railway lines, a land fed by skilled farmers, rich in factories laboriously installed, dotted with overcrowded harbour towns; a double-headed tentacle planted there at the far limit of Europe, into whose clutches the Atlantic must, willy-nilly, have surrendered her rich and aimless freights, her fleets of treasure ships at sea without a goal. But to accomplish such an end she would have had to pursue, through long generations, one of those great plans, at once blindly wrought yet cunningly devised, which set a seal on nature's work by forcing things to a determined shape, feeling a slow way to achievement, harnessing necessity to wily ends, leaving to chance no right but that of choosing between two or three alternative channels dug to make doubly sure that the rich waters shall flow in set courses and not escape elsewhere.

But to realize such an ambition she would have needed what she has never had, a grandiose self-seeking that never leaves a task but at completion. Obstinate she may have been, and mad at times, but of the unswerving schemer she has never shown a trace. When the delirium of glory has seized on her, it has always been with the desire to accomplish some deed islanded in History, without past or future, some enterprise envisaged against every rule of caution, and for ever at the beck and call of chance: a Europe called to arms, a young Corsican leading the nation to the world's far ends, just because, with his men from Brittany and Auvergne, he wished to build again, and on a greater scale, the realm of Charlemagne. Or it might be that suddenly she held it to be a point of honour to conquer at one blow more distant lands than Spain had ever done. But since, with the prize all but in her grasp, she grew sick of adventure, nothing of Canada has remained to her but an isle of fisher-folk, and of the West Indies but a strip of land barely large enough to flaunt her flag. Finding no satisfaction in schemes fashioned with an eye to the future, she has taken pleasure in what came her way, and, flushed with the excitement of the moment, has grown to see in passing triumphs a compensation for the longer view. She constructed the Suez Canal, and all but made its twin in Panama; but the ideal of linking her own two seas, north and south, by waterways she has obstinately regarded as a madman's dream to which never again would she set her hand. She has equipped with railways all the new countries, taking in exchange their gold, but she has never seriously considered joining Paris and the Western Ocean with what should have been the great trunk line of Europe. And with an easy negligence she still faces the wide new world, not with a string of overpeopled harbour towns fitted to draw to her the trade of all the world, but with desolate plains, and woods, and fields of vine.

Once, perhaps, in a century her pride has found a vent; but between whiles she has let it sleep, preferring the self-love that turns in upon itself. Prudent and capricious she has been by turns; more sensible than any of her neighbours, but victim, now and then, of fits of petulance. She has always been more willing to lose her money by believing in the illusions of others than by using it to back her own, which she has ever seen with too clear a vision. Economical by temperament, she has been led to waste her substance on ill-planned schemes. Intending peace, she has more than once been forced into a war by some movement that has caught her unawares.

True it is that, through the ages, samples of all the hardiest and most adventurous races of Europe have drifted into the hexagon of France, as later they were to filter across into the vast quadrilateral of America, but they never, unlike those men beyond the seas, found an empty land awaiting them. From the first they were confronted by the squat folk of the mountains already thick upon the ground, a stubborn people content to live on little, good fighters and tenacious of their rights in a land where they had settled long before anybody else. To these, the earliest inhabitants, words meant nothing. It mattered little to them that their country was the point at which all roads of the Old World met, the great assembly-ground of the West, the sea strand on which the men of countless lands could breathe free air, a terrace set above the Ocean. They cared only about holding what they had, and sending the intruders back whence they had come. And when, in their despite, the intruders stayed, it was, in their turn, to become even more sensitive than their predecessors to the call of the new homeland; to pretend that they had never known any other.

This mixture of blood has been common to all the provinces of France, but it was achieved without bitterness, and in no two places have its ingredients been exactly the same. Brittany, Normandy, Auvergne, Burgundy, Gascony and Provence, all are alike in so far as all contain the product of a mixed heritage. But in some places the squat men of the mountains still form the heart of the race, having absorbed each new wave of migration, while elsewhere it is some other intruding stock that has become predominant, though never twice the same, nor in the same proportions. The one constant rule has been that each of the new peoples came soon to forget its origins. There was room for every mixture of strain, and, in places, for pockets even of the unsullied aborigines. Here and there the old blood has kept itself pure in some hidden cranny, and ten thousand years of History are seen to have been as nothing. The accidents of the land have permitted this interplay of race; have, to some extent, conditioned it by the variety of its features, its natural divisions, its watersheds, its slopes, so that in places certain arrangements have been almost automatic, while in others natural obstacles have forced life to adapt itself to the requirements of the surrounding earth.

France is a land of valleys, majestic, almost royal of contour, but not drawn on a scale of vastness. No one of them is central to the whole country, nor drains it from end to end. It is a land, too, of many mountains, easy of access, yet forming many self-contained areas. The highest of them make its frontiers and repel invasion. The great plains are few, and lie far apart, so that the mixture of races obtaining in one rarely overflows into another, and intercommunication is exceptional. This fact has led to the coexistence of many agglomerations, no one of which has remained definite for long. It is a land of many provinces, yet few small cantons shut away from the world, since, with minor exceptions in the mountain tracts, communities have been separated by obstacles rather than by imprisoning walls, while what walls there have been have never been impenetrable. Since, therefore, the soil is fruitful, many peasant communities have taken root, varying in kind, yet all, in different ways, settled and obstinate. Jostled in the course of History they may have been, but they have clung desperately to their homes, refusing, whatever legend may say to the contrary, to be uprooted. Some individuals have migrated to the cities, but they have never taken their roots with them. Now and again the ancient stock may have shown a trace of withering, but it has never been torn from its native earth.

True to the lie of the land, these peasant communities have set their boundaries, marking canton from canton, village from village, but also field from field, each man staking his claim to what would suffice him for a livelihood. No work, however hard, on the rolling plough-lands has broken the spirit of these tillers of the soil, nor has the power of overlords, sweeping like a harrow over the vast acres, dispossessed these farmers of their fields. France is a land of peasant proprietors some of whom may have been called serfs when the word was in fashion, but none of whom have ever really been slaves.

Her people come from a race of peasants who, through the centuries, have loved their tiny holdings—each district having its own methods of demarcation and enclosure, jealously held to since the first settling of the tribes. Knowing they are in matters of boundaries, great disputers in questions of division, curious in all matters of usage and strict in its meticulous observance. Ready at all times they are to listen to the law's interpreters, or to peer through spectacles at its written authority. The "Code," for them, is an animal only less attractive than the cow. They like to see lines of ownership sharp drawn, and so, to avoid injustice and, better still, to avoid inequality, they incline to make all shares the same. Privilege, the lion's part, the superior claim of the eldest born—these things are anathema to them, and similarly all rights that are not clearly based, the justification for which has been lost in the misty distances of the past and cannot be hammered out in talk around a table. In this category they include the claim of any one man to issue orders to another, to demand tithes of his produce, or to live off his labour. They are a race of small-holders, of jurists, of equal shareholders in the family estate, of free men. A race which has created the communes of France, yet has always striven to have community of ownership in as few things as possible.

These are the men who love work, so it be in their own fields and for their own advantage; who delight in the vision of the task as it emerges to the call of their tools and grows to perfection, even preferring the small profit made in the sweat of their brows, but without fear or favour, to the wage which a man must take blindly, which may come conjoined with fraud and treachery in its concealing envelope. Handymen all of them, Jacks of all trades since the days of the cave-dwellers. Still, they have had to accept the age of factories, though it went against the grain for them to do so. No people were ever less intended by nature to form part of the long stream that, morning and night, crowds the suburban thoroughfares. Work, yes—since work is man's destiny; sixteen hours a day if need be when the harvest calls—but not the slavery of the shops. To war, likewise, they will submit, since war, so they are told, is sometimes necessary—but not to the barrack yard. At the heart of the proletarian here in France has ever dwelt the essential farmer; beneath the soldier's uniform has always beat the heart of a rebel drilled by authority and furiously resentful.

It was they who made the great Revolution, not to bring to birth some vague new world fated to end in disenchantment, but to reform injustices of ancient date, to have done, once and for all, with old wrongs, to make it possible for men to discuss everything under the sun freely around a table. They had no quarrel with their King, nor would ever have driven him from his throne and killed him had he but listened to the voice of reason and consented to be the guardian of the law and the protector of free men. Since then they have made other, smaller revolutions, partly, no doubt, because their nerves were on edge, partly, perhaps, on occasion, to satisfy a taste for violence left as a heritage from '89; but whatever the cause, it has never lain in the desire to set all things in ruin. Rather has it sprung from a longing to protest against the violation by others of a contract, to re-establish order on a firmer basis. At bottom the French peasant proprietor is neither a conservative nor a revolutionary. He may lose respect for institutions which have outlived their usefulness, but he sees no reason to believe that what men have never tried must necessarily be better than what they have always known. Anarchy he detests, and would rather, if it came to a choice, suffer from an excess of discipline, hoping that a chance may come later of restoring a truer balance. Law and order he does not worship, but in so far as they can justify themselves, he loves them.

When it seemed probable that the age of factories had come to stay, those whom the world now calls "proletarians" saw that they had been fooled; that the cities were poor substitutes for their native villages, that the Great Revolution had foreseen nothing of what was to come; that it had taken very few years for new masters and new abuses to arise in the place of those from which their fathers had shaken themselves free. And since they could not go back to their villages, where none knew them, they talked, like their brothers in other countries, of the possibility of making a new beginning, calling it the "Social Revolution." But no more than formerly did they wish to hurl themselves blindly into the arms of a new world. Their object was mainly that of redressing wrongs, of suppressing the policy of the lion's share and the claim of primogeniture, of re-establishing an equality of inheritance, of clothing once more in flesh and blood the essential landowner who had lain dormant beneath the skin of the proletarian.

France has long been the most lay-minded of countries, for she was the first to discover that civil society can function in its every part without the meddling of priests, and that prayers may be offered to

God, morning and evening, by the member of Parliament, the chief
of police, and the paterfamilias. She might well have been, too, the
least religious, capable as she is, like the Chinese, of dispensing with
everything that is not of this world, yet at the same time of finding
this world a pleasant place in which to live. But she has always liked
to take stock of things, nor has ever lacked a passion for creation and
for vast, sweeping movements of the intellect, with the result that she
has been able to approach God by way of the mind, to build for Him
the loveliest churches in the world, and to give Him an honourable
place in the great systems of her philosophy.

Furthermore, she has ever been the one country in which people of
vision, with an interest in maintaining ancient privileges, have seen
clearly and calmly the value of religion in the purely social scheme.
Having at first decided that it would be enough to keep it alive among
the masses as a quieting influence, without themselves having to submit to its unnecessary discipline, these people soon made the second
discovery that, in a land where even the smallest fry were gifted with
extreme subtlety of intelligence, the best way of maintaining piety
among the lower orders was to give an example of it themselves. They
resumed, therefore, the practices of their faith, and, as often happens in
such cases, found that belief followed automatically. But since the
smaller fry, with their genuine subtlety of intelligence, had, from the
beginning, seen through the whole manœuvre and realized the contempt for themselves which it implied, they refused to take the sequel
at its face value. Pricked to suspicion by the attitude of the clergy in
every political struggle, they grew accustomed, by degrees, to looking
on religion as one of those weapons employed by the possessing classes
to keep them in poverty and subjection. Consequently, in the great
cities and in many parts of the country men lost their faith as well as
the habit of religious observance, and, finding that none of those dis-
asters befell them which had been foretold, grew obstinate in their
attitude of agnosticism. So much was this so that France became almost the only country—Italy being a bad second—in which religion
was identified in men's minds with a definite political and social outlook; where, for instance, a Socialist leader who should happen to men-

tion the name of God at a meeting would have been suspected of having lost his reason.

But it is also the one country in which religion might be taken seriously, because it is the one country in which it is quite impossible for a mind with any claim to seriousness to retain or to discover a belief in God without first asking itself whether it is being tricked by considerations of social utility, and because the natural intelligence of the French people, averse as it is to all mental slovenliness and superficial cleverness, keeps them from remaining in a state of complacent satisfaction, suspended half-way between faith and incredulity. France, indeed, has produced a peculiarly national type of mysticism, which has always been more exacting than any other, since it has never ceased to be on its guard against the hysteria of the flesh and the visions of an exaggerated sensibility.

There is no human excellence of which this people—with the mixed blood of all Europe in its veins—has not shown itself to be capable, or, at least, of becoming so. But, except in certain outstanding instances, such, for example, as literature, fashion, and the arts of the kitchen, it has rarely tried to assert itself. Too often have Frenchmen been satisfied with the mediocre, or rather with a facile and careless achievement. Every now and then, in a sudden burst of activity, they have realized that some particular department of human endeavour was important and glorious, and that it was intolerable that they should be contented to occupy a back place among its practitioners. When that has happened, suddenly, with a promptness which their rivals have found disconcerting, they have forced their way to the front, amazed to find pre-eminence, after all, so simple a matter. For instance, after long remaining satisfied to be a country well in the wake of its neighbours, in which an occasional painter of fine, if rather academic, inspiration broke through the tradition of an easy pictorial grace, France all at once decided to show the world what a genuine national school might achieve, with the result that, to the amazement of all, she has produced most of the first-rate painters of Europe for over a century. Without any apparent difficulty, painting has become a peculiarly French art, notwithstanding the fact that the Frenchman is

still, of all Europeans, the least susceptible to colour. Similarly, during
the last thirty years, she has grown sick of occupying an inferior place
in the world of music. Without even having the time to teach her own
people to sing or her village bands to play in tune, she is now well
on the way to claim a monopoly in the contemporary field.

It is, therefore, as well for a man to be on his guard in describing and
summing up the French nation, or in foretelling its future. A good
rule, before committing himself to any statement, would be to realize
that, in her case, a number of contradictory formulas are simultaneously true. In matters relating to the past, contradictions have a way
of seeming natural or of escaping attention altogether. No one, for
instance, finds it difficult to accept the fact that this nation of peasants,
in whose veins runs the blood of a stocky mountain ancestry, should
have given birth to a proud aristocracy and been the one country in
the world where life for a privileged few reached its highest expression
of subtlety and elegance; nor yet that a race given, above all others,
to a close domesticity should have carried to perfection the arts of
social intercourse, of conversation, and of fine manners. No one is
surprised that these small-holders and careful tradesmen with a reputation for miserliness should, ever since the Middle Ages, have coun-
tenanced and financed so many works of mere magnificence that their
country can show thousands of grandiose cities and luxurious buildings,
a few dozen of which would have satisfied any of its neighbours. No
one is surprised when it learns that this nation of doubters and
mockers built the cathedrals and organized the Crusades; that these
confirmed stay-at-homes and fastidious sensualists have waged so
many wars merely to please a king or an emperor; that the inventors
of patriotism, the cry of *"Vive la Nation!"* and the mania of Monsieur
Chauvin could also declare themselves, almost in the same breath, to be
the champions of Universal Peace and the International Republic;
that a people so pleased with itself and so completely absorbed in its
own affairs could more than once have set itself to preach a gospel
through the length and breadth of Europe.

Preach a gospel? Yes, the worst of it has always been that, with their
fatal gift for turning the moment to account, they have ever been too

ready to begin the old game over again. It took them, in 1914, not longer than a week to convince themselves that if History was calling them to arms, it was as the result of no sinister concatenation of mishaps and misunderstandings, no mere interplay of the Forces of Economics and the Influences of the Powers that Be. It did not take them six days to persuade themselves that the bugles were blowing to the last great battle for Liberty, Justice, and Civilization. The voice of History, they decided, was summoning them to take a part in the supreme struggle, begun a hundred and twenty years earlier, but again and again interrupted and postponed, of Democracy against Absolutism, to join in the marshalling of the Peoples against the Kings and the Emperors. The object to be attained was not so much the defeat of the Germans and the Austrians as the striking of the fetters from their limbs. Even at the meetings and in the papers of the revolutionary Left, now that the cry of History had sounded, all references to imperialist guilt, to the joint conspiracy of the capitalist governments, to the indifference which good working-class men should show to the criminal call of patriotism, were soon seen to be out of fashion. All these over-recent cries of an academic ideology writhed like strips of tinfoil in a furnace and vanished, touching the flames with a faint and fugitive discoloration. No longer was it a question of the class war, of Socialism, of conflicting theories, but only of a Crusade, of the freeing of the Holy Sepulchre.

Eastwards, welded to the land of France, its spear-head, its terraced watch-tower on the Ocean fringe, lay the Continent. Europe, lean and bony, rich and turbulent, close-knit yet divided, one but never united, a place of Kings, of Emperors, and of Peoples. Neither the Kings, the Emperors, nor the Peoples knew really why they set such store on battle, nor for what end they fought. None of them had ever clearly viewed the miracle of this continent, nor stopped deeply to consider the more fragile miracle that had determined its position in the world. This Europe, their Europe, which had become the mother and the teacher of all the countries of the earth, the source of all thought, of all invention, the guardian of all the high secrets of mankind, was less precious to them now than was a flag, a national song, an accident of language, a frontier line, the name of a battle to be graven on a stone, a deposit of phosphates, the comparative statistics of ocean tonnage, or the pleasure of humiliating a neighbour.

And that is why, on the 1st of August, at half past four in the afternoon, Jean Jerphanion, a man sprung from the ancient stock of France, and one among the many million inhabitants of Europe, standing with his young wife beside his uncle Crouziols, heard the bell of Saint-Julien Chapteuil, a canton similar to a hundred others, sounding for the peasants of this age-old land the tocsin cry of "Mobilize!"

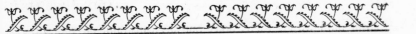

How Verdun Managed to Hold Out

FROM "MEN OF GOOD WILL" BY
JULES ROMAINS

ON LEAVING the boulevards, they wandered down to the quays beside the Seine and, as pilgrims might, moved slowly along the left bank towards Notre-Dame. Jerphanion thus found himself on his direct road home.

"Look here," he said to Jallez, "if you're free this evening, why not come and dine with us? Odette's made no preparations, but that doesn't matter. I'll buy something on the way. Odette'll be delighted to see you. She wanted to come with me to our appointment. It was I who asked her to let me meet you alone. I felt sure that we should talk frankly about all our concerns. As you know, she is very intelligent. There's nothing she can't understand, and in fact I never hide anything from her. But there are certain harshnesses of judgment, certain bitternesses, certain extremes of suffering, that I soft-pedal when I am with her, because they would rouse in her such a terror of despair that she would cry suddenly aloud: 'You mustn't go back!'"

Jallez was caught in a quick wave of emotion at the hint of tragedy which his friend's last words had disclosed.

"Of course I'll come," he said. "I have such happy memories of hours spent with you two when—there still seemed a hope of happiness for the world. We've spoken so much about the war that perhaps we can turn the conversation to other subjects before Odette, eh?"

"If you like . . . we'll see. . . . If you've anything in your mind that might offer a little comfort for the future, anything that might bring the prospect of peace a little nearer . . . it would be very welcome."

"I'll do my best, old man."

"But until we get there, don't put any constraint on yourself. Ask me anything you still want to know."

Jallez spoke with considerable hesitation:

"No . . . I feel that I'm raking things up unnecessarily . . . things that you'd much rather forget while you're here."

"Not at all. . . . Just the reverse, in fact. I like getting it off my chest. During all this hideous experience I've become more than ever convinced that Epictetus, Marcus Aurelius . . . Pascal . . . were right. There's only one really heroic remedy for an excess of misery: to think the misery through honestly to the end. I told myself that I would keep a journal, in imitation of the philosopher Emperor; but I lacked the strength of character. A conversation such as we've just had takes its place. Besides, I've never forgotten what you once said on the subject of 'bearing witness.' Do you remember? It was on the day of our first walk together, our very first, in the neighbourhood of the rue Claude-Bernard and the avenue des Gobelins. . . . The *Road to Emmaus*. . . . The light striking the top of a wall. . . . Doesn't it all come back? . . . What beauty we knew then! How lovely life could be! . . . And look at us now, creatures of shreds and patches! . . . Selfishly speaking, the greatest comfort I could have found in this war would have been to have you beside me in the trenches, as I have had good old Fabre . . . so that we might have 'borne witness' together . . . so that, at certain moments, I might have been able to say: 'Do you see this? . . . Did you see that? . . .' But fate ruled otherwise. . . . It is terribly important, though, for me to be able, in spite of everything, to make you a witness . . . to think all these things with you beside me. . . . One of the Disciples at Emmaus was absent from the room when the Figure appeared. His comrade, who witnessed all, could not rest until he had explained what he had seen, until he had made the moment 'live again' for him. That was what he was after—to make the moment live again for his friend. . . . So please go on; ask away."

His face took on the expression of a man setting himself to listen intently. At the same time, in an access of melting tenderness, his eyes took in the magnificent pageant of the river, closed at its far end by the mass of Notre-Dame.

"You've told me much that I find thrilling," said Jallez in measured tones; "but there is a good deal that still remains obscure. I don't yet understand the nature of that strength which can support millions of men in the life of an endless purgatory. You have mentioned the trivial aids, the little thoughts that buoy them up. . . . But are they really enough to account for what is happening? These men of yours are such as we all have known: men cradled, more or less, by civilization. It was not idealism that swept them along. . . . Enthusiasm? For a few days, perhaps, but not for years. How does it come about that these coddled, these matter-of-fact homunculi can endure so much, and over such long periods?"

"The first step was what counted. Once you've begun a thing, it exercises a terrible authority over you. That is one of the laws of existence about which I have fewest doubts. But if one's honest with oneself, one's got to admit that there is yet another authority which governs everything else. One's always realizing that one has somehow avoided mentioning it. Why? . . . Because it's axiomatic? . . . Because one's shy about putting it into words? . . . Even when one does take it into account one disguises it in borrowed plumage that gives it an air more flattering to self-pride: one calls it duty, patriotism, and so forth. . . . Its true name is something much cruder: nothing more or less than the pressure of society. Society today has willed that men should suffer and die on the battlefield. Well then, they just suffer and die. That's all there is to it. At other periods it has willed other things, and men have acted accordingly. The only disconcerting feature about what is happening now is this: that for a long time now men have been told that society no longer had this mystic power over them; that they had certain absolute rights as individuals; that no one could any longer demand of them anything that was not wholly reasonable from the point of view of their own personal existence. Now, from such a point of view, it does seem unreasonable that a man should be asked to give his life—in other words, his all—just to defend that part of the collective interest, often a very small part, which concerns him as an individual. Let him do it if he is moved to do it of his own free will, but no one can 'reasonably' demand it of him. Well, the only explanation to account for what we are seeing is that mankind has not yet learned to take this new theory at its face value. Certainly no one has been sufficiently assured to claim immunity as a right."

"Perhaps you're right. What seems so extraordinary to me is that this pressure should at all times be strong enough to overcome even physical fear."

"It might be truer to say that man's fear of society is still stronger than his fear of shells."

"I suppose that's it. . . . The soldier says to himself: 'If I refuse to go forward, if I run away, I shall be shot.' "

"That's not it exactly, either. . . . Some do have to think something like that; but for most of them such deliberate argument is unnecessary. Their fear of society is not a physical fear. It concerns the spirit rather than the body. Man is so made that usually fear for his body is less strong than fear that touches his spirit."

"Even to the extent of controlling his immediate reactions? . . . You start going over the top . . . shells are bursting all around . . . you find yourself in a machine-gun's field of fire. . . ."

"The point is that the mystical, the spiritual, fear of society can take forms which themselves produce immediate response. On one side of the balance is the fear of shells; on the other the fear of what your pals, what your officer, what your men, if you happen to be an officer, will think. In some ways it needs more courage to make the average man face being dubbed a coward than to get him to stand up to shell-fire."

They spoke of fear. Jerphanion maintained that at the front everyone was afraid, just as everyone is cold when it freezes, the only difference in the way fear manifested itself being due to variations in temperament. The constant presence of danger did, of course, harden men to a certain degree of insensitiveness, but not always. Often, indeed, it had just the opposite effect, screwed the nerves up to an abnormal pitch of exasperation, giving an added horror to anticipation.

"And then, you see, one never entirely gets rid of the fear one has had on previous occasions. The thought of the advance in which I was wounded last year still terrifies me. If I had to go over the top again, I should be far more frightened than I was the first time. Fear, too, has

its periods; it goes in waves. There are days when one trembles all
over, when one just can't control one's limbs, and other days when one
is almost indifferent. Why it's impossible to say. I've found out that
one of the best cures for fear is to say to oneself that it's completely
useless (the same holds true of courage). One goes on saying to oneself:
'Don't be a fool. Is your stomach in your boots? Are you all strung
up? Do your teeth want to chatter? Well, that won't make the slightest difference to the trajectory of the next shell or the path of the next
bullets. It's merely so much fatigue the more.' On such occasions one
tries to behave as though it were simply a question of going out in the
rain, harmless, ordinary rain. It falls in big, heavy drops, but one just
thinks of something else, like a cop huddled up in his cloak at a street-
crossing. . . . See the kind of thing I mean? . . . Or else one tries to
imagine that one is a pedestrian stranded in a swirl of cars in the
middle of the Place de la Concorde. Each of them, dashing at full
speed across the square, is more than capable of killing a man; and
since they are all converging from different directions, it seems that
before five minutes are out, one must crush the poor wayfarer. . . .
And yet, if you're a hardened Parisian, you don't tremble, your teeth
don't chatter. . . . You realize the guile of my system? One just pretends to believe that each shell will miss one as each car misses one,
and that one can be killed only by the particular projectile loosed with
that deliberate object by some mysterious power. . . . You remember
Napoleon's famous phrase about the bullet that hadn't yet been cast?
It's not much of a self-deception, but it works. Little things like that
are all one has left in such situations. . . . I'm not sure, if it comes to
that, that it is so little. It's just fatalism in a new dress. 'I've got a feeling that destiny has not willed that I should die today. If it has, then
there's nothing I can do about it, so why worry?' When one's lived
some time under the constant threat of danger, one begins to realize
that fatalism is a necessary drug, just as alcohol is a necessary stimulant
to a man on an arctic expedition. One of the secret virtues of fatalism
is that it implies, against one's better judgment, a belief in the supernatural. 'If destiny has so far taken charge of me as to fix the moment
of my death, it's not likely that it's going to leave me in the lurch
afterwards. It will take me through to another stage. The adventure

isn't finished yet.' Fundamentally all that man asks is that the adventure should not be ended. He doesn't want to know what happens next; he's perfectly willing to let the future remain a mystery. So long as the adventure is not finished, he can bear anything. The shells hurtling down on the trench, the advancing wave of which he forms a part, the storm of 77's and machine-gun bullets which will probably knock him over two yards farther on and leave him with his head smashed to pulp near that little tree—all these things become merely an episode. . . . You've no idea, my dear Jallez, of the depths of inherited belief that are stirred by such tornadoes of death."

"Yes, I have, and the thought moves me deeply." (Far ahead, but nearer now than it had been, rose Notre-Dame, with its gargoyles and its dreaming spires.)

"What I want to make you realize is the way that all these ideas swarm and jostle and come and go, quite arbitrarily, in a man's mind. That's why all formulas that try to generalize our reactions to life in the front line are false. There may be some men gifted with an abnormal strength of mind, whose attitude never varies . . . but they can't be many. . . . I can look back now, for instance, and see myself as I was on the second of those foodless days in the valley of Haudromont, about ten o'clock in the morning. A good many 77's were falling. Heavy shrapnel was bursting high up between our trenches and the crest to our rear, which meant that the bullets had a good chance of coming straight down into what shelter we had. As a matter of fact, I had one killed and four wounded that morning. But my own mood was one of almost complete resignation. I could hear the snapping of the branches, the burst of shells in the damp earth. It was as though I were standing aside from my own destiny. What might happen to me seemed no longer to have any significance. I didn't even have to take refuge behind my little tricks of mental comfort. My attitude was something that had been produced without any conscious exercise of my will. 'This is marvellous,' I said to myself; 'this is how a man ought to feel. Let's hope it continues.' And then, two hours later, when, if anything, the shelling was rather less intense, I found myself in a mood of hysterical and undisciplined excitement. But note this: that these ups and downs of the spirit can often have very awkward sequels. A man may be perfectly impotent in the face of shell-fire; still, the care or the speed with which he takes certain precautions may result in his being killed within the next three minutes, or finding himself still alive at the day's end. During those periods of superb indifference he may scorn to crouch or lie flat, may carelessly show his head above the parapet. When he becomes excited, on the other hand, he may get himself killed as the result of a clumsy excess of precautions, such as changing his position every few minutes, and the like. But the body is wiser than the mind. It draws the necessary inferences, adjusts the balance, looks after its own safety. The man of calm resignation and the hysterical worrier, taking the lead successively in each one of us, perform almost precisely the same automatic movements of self-preservation."

They were walking very slowly. Every few moments they stopped, the better to pick out for scrutiny some particular idea, just as wood-cutters pause to choose one log rather than another.

A little later, after an effort, which clearly showed in the expression of his face, to assemble his ideas, Jerphanion said:

"I've been pondering again that question of yours. . . . Yes, the great operative influence is, I'm quite sure, the sense of social pressure. A man's got to stay where he is. He's caught like a rat in a trap, in a tangle of intersecting threads—the fear of a firing squad, a sense of shame, of dishonour, the moral impossibility of doing otherwise, a sort of mystical terror—on all sides he is hemmed in. Naturally, he is free, if he pleases, to be transported by ecstasy, free to declare that he is where he is because he wants to do his duty, because he loves his country. He is free *into the bargain* to accept his presence there as an act of will. . . . And that will may be perfectly sincere. . . . If we were intent on splitting hairs, we could prove easily enough that even this free and sincere will to sacrifice was something that he would never have come by unaided, that it is the product of that silly nonsense called education, or, in other words, of society's most cunning trick to mould a man to its design. But never mind. That's not what I meant. . . . No. . . . My point is that man is like any other animal: when there's no alternative, he gives in. Even the wild beasts give in under such conditions. . . . Men can screw themselves up to resist or to rebel when the au-

thority that enjoins obedience shows signs of weakness. It may be all
very depressing, but it's true. In the old days my 'optimism' wouldn't
let me believe it. But the war has only too clearly shown me that I was
wrong. Where now is man's vaunted spirit of revolt, of 'revolution'?
Isn't it obvious that all such talk was never anything but a bad joke?
The 'governed' make revolutions not when the governors most abuse
their privileges, but when, having been guilty of abuses—not, perhaps,
very grave abuses—they lack the courage to abide by their actions. . . .
As my friend Griollet said, just think of the revolutionary fervour displayed by men like Pataud, Puget, Merrheim, and all the working-
class leaders when they risked nothing. . . . Are they quite so keen
now? Show me a single factory hand conscripted on war work, no
matter how militant he was in days gone by, who refuses to turn out
shells or agitates for a munition strike among his pals to stop the
slaughter of the proletariat. . . . If the governments of the world don't
deduce from what's happening certain philosophic and cynically Machi-
avellian truths for use in the post-war period, that'll only be because
they are incapable of digesting any lesson of experience. In short, man
is an animal who does what he is made to do very much more readily
than one is inclined to believe. But once he has realized that, whatever
happens, he has got to do what he is told, he likes nothing so much
as to believe that the initial order came from himself. . . ."

Jerphanion paused a moment, then continued:

"To be fair, one must recognize that, in a sense, it does. No matter
how strong or how cunning the collective will may be, it could not
compel, and continue to compel, the individual to actions that were at
complete variance with his nature. One must always reckon, for instance, with the love of destruction, which is deeply rooted in humanity. Man loves to demolish what he has himself created. Don't mothers
say: 'Children are so destructive'? Think of the rows we used to make
over the food at college. Most of us were only too delighted to discover
once or twice a term that the stew was uneatable, because it gave us
an excuse for throwing our plates on the ground and smashing them.
Men are always ready to revenge themselves on the increasing complexity of material civilization. The ordered life of society forces us to
give too much time to the making of too many things, and compels us

to an over-nice exercise of care in using them. Bang, bang, bang, go the guns—partly to give release to the nerves of men who have heard nothing since childhood but 'Don't touch that!' 'Don't upset that!' 'Don't break that!' . . . Then there's an emotion of a totally different kind to reckon with—humanity's liking for sacrifice. I'm convinced that it exists, that it is no mere fantasy of a morbid literary taste. It's the only thing that can explain the success, the fanatical success, that cruel religions have always had. No matter how ferocious the inventions of their leaders, whether lay or priestly, there has never been any lack of willing victims. No master has ever succeeded in getting men to accept such things against their wishes. The most dearly loved leaders have always been the most bloodthirsty. There has never ceased to be a deep complicity between martyr and executioner. Certain German theorists—you know more about these things than I do—have assumed a connexion between this taste for sacrifice and sexual perversion. That is being unnecessarily ingenious. I have studied my own reactions and those of others in the course of this war. My impression is that, unless they are under the strict control of reason, men are an easy prey to the attraction, the lure, of great emotional thrills. For anyone in the prime of life there is no thrill comparable to the horror of being tortured and killed. . . . The anticipation of some such thrill does, of course, explain most perversions and the delight of the sexual act in general. And, apropos of sex, you must always remember that among the influences that conspire to keep the soldier in the trenches, exposed to constant shell-fire, sex is by no means the least. . . ."

"Hm!" interrupted Jallez. "Isn't that a bit far-fetched? . . . You can't have much time to think about sex, surely?"

"In the crude, carnal sense, no—except when we are in quiet rest-billets. But the thought of women never leaves us. I'm not talking of the girls in pink undies cut out of the *Vie Parisienne* and pinned up in every hut and every dug-out . . . though they are not without their significance. I'm talking of the idea that women exist, 'way back, out of the war zone. . . ."

"Whom it's up to you to defend?"

"Well, yes, if you like to put it that way, but it's not quite that, not so sentimental as that. . . . What I mean is that we're always conscious of them standing, as it were, on the walls of some ancient fortified city, watching and criticizing. . . ."

"Isn't that all a bit literary? Aren't you rather modulating on a traditional theme?"

"No. When the common or garden poilu dreams of getting a soft job, one argument above all others makes him pause, especially if he happens to be young. . . . I've used it myself, more shame to me, in talking to country lads; and that is: 'What'll the girls at home say? They'll never look at you again.' Carry that same motive a little further, think of it as animating the man going over the top with his rifle at the trail. 'The women are watching,' he says to himself; 'watching to see whether I'm making as good a showing as the rest . . . watching to see whether I turn tail . . . whether I'm going to sneak into a shell-hole while the others go forward.' And if that constant obsession is not enough, there are always the war 'godmothers'—that admirable invention of the people at home for keeping the soldier in a constant state of slightly amorous excitation which, it is supposed, will be ultimately translated into patriotic ardour. Think of all those 'godmothers' going to bed with their protégés when they're on leave, and kissing them good-bye at the end of it, with a 'Be brave, darling,' which merely means: 'Do the sensible thing and get yourself killed. . . .' How thrilling it must be for all these women, many of them no longer young, to have such interludes of love with fresh, virile boys, always with the thought at the back of their minds that the lover is going from their arms straight to death. . . . The purely sensual delight of the female insect. Sweep away all women—women in the narrow sense of the word—from the back areas; leave no one there but mothers, old men, and children (to make use of the categories beloved of the official mind), and I don't mind betting that the war would soon be over."

"It's certainly worth thinking about," said Jallez. "What it all comes to is that war touches springs that lie deep at the heart of humanity."

"Of course it does. In a way that's all it does. But even that's not the only thing I'm after. The frightful thing about war is that, as a subject, it's inexhaustible. One's eye is always being caught by some new aspect of the business. My real point is this: that for the men in the trenches—for all of them, that is, who are above the purely animal

level, for whom, as you must see for yourself, it is most necessary to
find an explanation—the idea that they must stay where they are and
get on with their job because there is no real alternative is not enough
to keep them in spirits, to prevent their moral collapse. Each one of
them has got to find some effective suggestion that will touch him personally, some thought, some fixed idea, the secret of which is known
to him alone, the essence of which he can absorb drop by drop. Sometimes he has several among which he can take his choice. No sooner
does one begin to lose its potency than he can change over to others.
Take my own case, for instance. For quite a while I managed very
comfortably on the idea that I was the kind of man who could 'rise
superior to circumstances'—the circumstances in question being partly
composed of mental distress, partly of bodily discomfort. 'I'd like,' said
I, 'to see those circumstances to which I could not rise superior!' While
shrapnel pattered round me (it was at the time when a good deal of
shrapnel was being used), I would recite to myself like a sort of magic
formula, those terrific lines of Horace:

> *Si fractus illabatur orbis*
> *Impavidum ferient ruinæ. . . .*

It really is a magic formula. And then, one day, it no longer worked.
My mental distress became too great, my fear became too great, and
I just wanted to burst into tears and cry 'Mamma!' like a little boy.
. . . Then take the young second lieutenant fresh from Saint-Cyr, all
innocence and splendid bravery, who says to himself: 'If France is conquered, life will be impossible. I shall feel personally dishonoured. Far
rather would I have my name on a headstone with the words: "Died
on the field of honour," than live on disgraced.' Another example is
that of the reservist with a taste for serious reading and an equipment
of large-hearted ideals, the kind of man who says to himself: 'This is
the war that will end war. We are bringing peace to the whole world.
Thanks to our sacrifice, our children will be spared knowledge of such
horrors.' Standing next to him in the same trench will be some fellow
who thinks: 'This is the end of the world. We're all in for it. What
does it matter if I get killed a little sooner or a little later?' Another

there may be who believes in a coming reign of justice, who is still convinced that victory for the democracies will mean freedom for the oppressed everywhere in the world, the end of the domination of money and social iniquity, who would be willing even to die if only he could be sure that his death would mean greater happiness for men yet unborn. Then there's the sentimentalist, for whom nothing counts but personal relationships, whose world is made up of just a few dear friends, who argues: 'Most of my pals are dead. If they all go, what is there left to live for?' There's the man whose wife left him as soon as he was called up, and ran off with someone else; who gets no letters and no parcels; who feels himself too old to start life afresh, who would just as soon be dead, for whom the very fact of danger is a distraction, because it gives him the illusion that life is still sweet. There is the man who exists in a world of dreams and takes things as they come. 'Everything is predestined,' says he; 'I always knew it. No use fighting against fate. We must just go with the tide.' There is the man who has never had a chance, who has always felt himself to be the victim of injustice and insult, who has always envied the good fortune of others, who so relishes the taste of equality bred of a general misery that he pays but lip service to the desire for peace with all the bitterness that it will bring for him in its train. Close beside him is another in whom the war has waked a deep-seated strain of pessimism, who thinks sincerely: 'The universe is a foul absurdity. It was always pretty obvious, but the war has proved it beyond the shadow of a doubt. Why cling to a foul absurdity?' or: 'Humanity is the work of the Devil, a blot on the face of the earth, born for murder and self-slaughter. So much the worse for humanity (and for me, who am part of humanity and so of the whole putrescent mess).' There is the fanatical Catholic, who thinks: 'This is God's punishment wrought on a corrupt and faithless generation. If God has decided that I too must pay the penalty, even for the faults of others, who am I to question His will?' There is the gentle Catholic who carries tucked away in his pack a tiny edition of the *Imitation,* who, when night falls, says his prayers in his shell-hole, very quietly, so that no one shall notice him, and murmurs: 'Let me suffer, as You suffered, Jesu mine. Why should I be spared, since You suffered a thousand deaths hanging on Your cross? Give me strength that I may be not too unworthy of You.' Finally, there is the man"—and Jerphanion made a gesture towards Notre-Dame, which was now immediately opposite them, across the river, its pinnacles just touched by the fading day—"who says: 'All that matters to me in this world is the language of France, the cathedrals of our French country-side, the quays of the Seine, landscapes that can be found nowhere else in the world, a way of life that is unique. If all that is to be taken away, life has no longer any point. If, by dying, I can ensure that all these things will live on after me, then death is right and proper. . . .' Picture to yourself trench after trench filled with men thinking such thoughts, and you will find the answer to your question. . . . That is why Verdun still stands."

ROGER MARTIN DU GARD

If intelligence *is the word for Jules Romains, integrity is the word for Roger Martin du Gard. The two men between them exemplify the finest qualities of what was a short while ago the contemporary French novel, and those who follow its course cannot risk ignorance of either. There are many who rank Martin du Gard above Romains and would, indeed, place him among the three or four greatest living novelists. However one estimates Martin du Gard's stature, there will be few readers to disagree with his own comment, made when, in 1937, the Swedish Academy awarded him the Nobel Prize. He told the members of the Academy that he presumed they wished to reward "an independent writer who had escaped the fascination of partisan ideologies, an investigator as objective as is humanly possible, as well as a novelist striving to express the tragic quality of individual lives." This is continental candor, but it is true.*

There are certain evident resemblances between The World of the Thibaults *and* Men of Good Will. *Both are lengthy. Both are in part studies of prewar French society. Both are written with that calm but not chilly intellectual detachment to which apparently only French novelists still possess the key. In both the drama of medical science plays a large part.*

But the differences are acute. Romains is unrolling a social panorama whose aim is completeness. Martin du Gard paints a picture, broad and inclusive, of a middle-class French family. Romains seems devoid of moral prejudices and so far his work reveals no underlying moral system. Martin du Gard is obviously affected by the values of that same bourgeois Catholic conservatism whose roots he exposes with such analytical patience. Romains is (for me) the greater writer, further ranging and, in the best sense, more sophisticated. He also has at his command a dazzling variety of techniques, to which the more plodding Martin du Gard cannot lay claim.

The head of the Thibault family is Oscar Thibault, fanatically

Catholic, patriarchal, intensely conservative, a family tyrant minus the Clarence Day charm but possessed of an inner strength and narrow-minded integrity which even his pair of rebellious sons must respect. The elder son, Antoine, a doctor, is a man of action, a Goethean type to whom experience and activity are ends in themselves. The younger son, Jacques, is more complex and, one must add, less successfully characterized. He is unbalanced, capable of decisive shifts of temperament, born to be a novelist. The varying tensions between the three Thibaults, plus the love affairs of Jacques and Antoine, furnish the main threads of the first half of the story.

When Martin du Gard sticks to his Thibaults, to the class of which he is himself a product, he is on sure ground. When he tries his hand at a character such as Rachel, Antoine's Jewish mistress, he is less certain. The tone becomes forced and even melodramatic. The high points of the book are not the love passages—though Martin du Gard's understanding of adolescence is simply phenomenal—but those connected with sickness and death: Antoine performing a split-second dining-room-table operation on a little girl; Pastor Gregory, the Christian healer, saving little Jenny de Fontanin by an act of faith; and the unforgettable sickness, death, and funeral of old Oscar. This last series of scenes comprises two hundred pages; it is as ruthless as surgery, with not a detail omitted—a piece of mountingly tense realistic writing for which I know of no exact parallel in the modern novel.

The first half of The World of the Thibaults is called, in the two-volume translation, simply "The Thibaults." The second half is titled "Summer 1914."

As "Summer 1914" opens, we see Jacques in Geneva, deeply involved with a group of international revolutionaries, some of whom are conspiring to avert the imminent European war, some of whom are planning to use it as a steppingstone to a general social overturn. Jacques is not a true revolutionary but rather a flaming humanitarian for whom socialism is a religious gospel. His views are widely at variance with those of Antoine, who, though sadly troubled by the exploitation and misery he sees around him, has no solution except to trust "the leaders." Antoine seeks escape in his comfortable labo-

ratory and a feverish erotic life. Jacques deceives himself into a belief
that fiery café-table programs and conspiratorial activities in behalf
of the Second International are the keys to a happy world future.
The war comes. Both men fail. Jacques, in a frenzied gesture recalling the magnificent suicide flight of the anti-Fascist poet-aviator
Lauro de Bosis, flies over the lines in August, 1914, dropping peace
pamphlets, and is unwittingly killed by one of his own countrymen.
Antoine, gassed, dies a horrible, lingering death, every detail of which
he notes in his diary. This diary, or epilogue, forming the concluding
section of "Summer 1914," is the most powerful piece of writing in
the whole enormous book.

The movement of "Summer 1914" is slow. While Jacques and
Antoine and the women they love are the characters upon whom the
plot depends, the author is less interested in them than in painting
a truly gigantic picture of France and, by implication, Europe on the
eve of the war. This involves a great deal of political discussion, por-
traits of Jaurès and other leaders, and descriptions of the Brussels
Congress, which was supposed to head off the war. It also involves
a minute tracing of the complex diplomatic maneuvers of the late
summer of that year. Martin du Gard's interpretation is that of the
revisionist school. He believes in the theory of divided guilt. While not
absolving Germany, he certainly does not place the blame squarely
on her shoulders. If there is a single villain, it is Russia, but it would
be more accurate to say that he blames European capitalism in general, a capitalism too blind to control itself but too strong to be
curbed by the growing yet futile strength of labor. "Summer 1914"
might be subtitled "The Tragedy and Death of the Second International."

Much of this has been the subject of innumerable histories and
essays. I cannot feel that Martin du Gard completely succeeds in
animating it. He is exquisitely just and painstakingly detailed, but it
is when he is most just and most detailed that he somehow ceases to
be a novelist. In "The Thibaults" the emphasis was all on individuals and their relation to society; in "Summer 1914" society itself
almost usurps the canvas. For me, there is a certain loss of power and
originality.

But when Martin du Gard concentrates he approaches magnificence: in his study of the Fontanin family, in his agonizingly perceptive account of the love between Anne and Antoine, in his heartbreaking record of the slow decay of the mind and body of Antoine.

As a whole, The World of the Thibaults is unquestionably an impressive work. That world is now dead, its final hours having lasted from 1918 to 1939. Someone had to write its epitaph, and for that epitaph to be clear it was necessary to go back to the roots of the Thibault world in the nineteenth and early twentieth centuries. This was Martin du Gard's task, to which he has now devoted two decades of his life. The task, presenting almost insuperable difficulties, has been completed with honor.

Martin du Gard is not a great stylist; he writes rather conservatively, even traditionally. His value lies not in the originality of his prose but in the honesty and integrity of his social viewpoint. He is less clever than Romains, and—I must say it—less interesting and far less various. Still, his work has a certain solidity that some prefer to brilliance. You may not read him with absorption; you will read him with respect.

It is rather hard to select any section of the whole tremendous work that will give you any idea of Martin du Gard. He does not deal in set pieces as does Romains; he writes more evenly and, of course, his story is more conventionally integrated. I have chosen the operation chapter, exciting in itself and a superb study of the character of Antoine. It shows you, by the way, what a real artist can do with medical material. Dr. A. J. Cronin please note.

An Excerpt from
"The World of the Thibaults"

BY

ROGER MARTIN DU GARD

WHEN THE TAXI pulled up near the Tuileries in front of the house in the Rue d'Alger where the Chasles lived, Antoine had pieced together, from the concierge's flustered explanations, an outline of the accident. The victim was a little girl who used to meet "M. Jules" each evening on his way back. Had she tried to cross the Rue de Rivoli on this occasion, as M. Jules was late in coming home? A delivery tri-car had knocked her down and passed over her body. A crowd had gathered and a newspaper-vender who was present had recognized the child by her plaited hair, and furnished her address. She had been carried unconscious to the flat.

M. Chasle, crouching in a corner of the taxi, shed no tears, but each new detail drew from him a racking sob, half muffled by the hand he pressed against his mouth.

A crowd still lingered round the doorway. They made way for M. Chasle, who had to be helped up the stairs as far as the top landing by his two companions. A door stood open at the end of a corridor, down which M. Chasle made his way on stumbling feet. The concierge stood back to let Antoine pass, and touched him on the arm.

"My wife, who's got a head on her shoulders, ran off to fetch the young doctor who dines at the restaurant next door. I hope she found him there."

Antoine nodded approval and followed M. Chasle. They crossed a sort of anteroom, redolent of musty cupboards, then two low rooms with tiled floors; the light was dim and the atmosphere stifling despite the open windows giving on a courtyard. In the further room Antoine

640

had to edge round a circular table where a meal for four was laid on a strip of dingy oilcloth. M. Chasle opened a door and, entering a brightly lit room, stumbled forward with a piteous cry: ˙

"Dédette! Dédette!"

"Now, Jules!" a raucous voice protested.

The first thing Antoine noticed was the lamp which a woman in a pink dressing-gown was lifting with both hands; her ruddy hair, her throat and forehead were flooded with the lamplight. Then he observed the bed on which the light fell, and shadowy forms bending above it. Dregs of the sunset, filtering through the window, merged in the halo of the lamp, and the room was bathed in a half-light where all things took the semblance of a dream. Antoine helped M. Chasle to a chair and approached the bed. A young man wearing pince-nez, with his hat still on, was bending forward and slitting up with a pair of scissors the blood-stained garments of the little girl. Her face, ringed with matted hair, lay buried in the bolster. An old woman on her knees was helping the doctor.

"Is she alive?" Antoine asked.

The doctor turned, looked at him, and hesitated; then mopped his forehead.

"Yes." His tone lacked assurance.

"I was with M. Chasle when he was sent for," Antoine explained, "and I've brought my first-aid kit. I'm Dr. Thibault," he added in a whisper, "house-physician at the Children's Hospital."

The young doctor rose and was about to make way for Antoine.

"Carry on! Carry on!" Antoine drew back a step. "Pulse?"

"Almost imperceptible," the doctor replied, intent once more on his task.

Antoine raised his eyes towards the red-haired young woman, saw the anxiety in her face, and made a suggestion.

"Wouldn't it be best to telephone for an ambulance and have your child taken at once to my hospital?"

"No!" an imperious voice answered him.

Then Antoine descried an old woman standing at the head of the bed—was it the child's grandmother?—and scanning him intently with eyes limpid as water, a peasant's eyes. Her pointed nose and resolute features were half submerged in a vast sea of fat that heaved in billowy folds upon her neck.

"I know we look like paupers," she continued in a resigned tone, "but, believe me, even folk like us would rather die at home in our own beds. Dédette shan't go to the hospital."

"But why not, Madame?" Antoine protested.

She straightened up her back, thrust out her chin, and sadly but sternly rebuked him.

"We prefer not," was all she said.

Antoine tried to catch the eye of the younger woman, but she was busy brushing off the flies that obstinately settled on her glowing cheeks, and seemed of no opinion. He decided to appeal to M. Chasle. The old fellow had fallen on his knees in front of the chair to which Antoine had led him; his head was buried on his folded arms as though to shut out all sights from his eyes, and, from his ears, all sounds. The old lady, who was keenly watching Antoine's movements, guessed his intention and forestalled him.

"Isn't that so, Jules?"

M. Chasle started.

"Yes, Mother."

She looked at him approvingly and her voice grew mothering.

"Don't stay there, Jules. You'd be much better in your room."

A pallid forehead rose into view, eyes tremulous behind their spectacles; then, without a protest, the poor old fellow stood up and tiptoed from the room.

Antoine bit his lips. Meanwhile, pending an occasion further to insist, he took off his coat and rolled up his sleeves above the elbows. Then he knelt at the bedside. He seldom took thought without at the same time beginning to take action—such was his incapacity for long deliberation on any issue raised, and such his keenness to be up and doing. The avoidance of mistakes counted less with him than bold decision and prompt activity. Thought, as he used it, was merely the lever that set an act in motion—premature though it might be.

Aided by the doctor and the old woman's trembling hands, he had soon stripped off the child's clothing; pale, almost grey, her body lay beneath their eyes in its frail nakedness. The impact of the car must have been very violent, for she was covered with bruises, and a black streak crossed her thigh transversely from hip to knee.

"It's the right leg," Antoine's colleague observed. Her right foot was twisted, bent inwards, and the whole leg was spattered with blood and deformed, shorter than the other one.

"Fracture of the femur?" suggested the doctor.

Antoine did not answer. He was thinking. "That's not all," he said to himself; "the shock is too great for that. But what can it be?" He tapped her knee-cap, then ran his fingers slowly up her thigh; suddenly there spurted through an almost imperceptible lesion on the inner side of the thigh, some inches above the knee, a jet of blood.

"That's it," he said.

"The femoral artery!" the other exclaimed.

Antoine rose quickly to his feet. The need to make, unaided, a decision gave him a new access of energy and, as ever when others were present, his sense of power intensified. A surgeon? he speculated. No, we'd never get her alive to the hospital. Then who? I? Why not? And, anyhow, there's no alternative.

"Will you try a ligature?" asked the doctor, piqued by Antoine's silence.

But Antoine did not heed his question. It must be done, he was thinking, and without a moment's delay; it may be too late already, who knows? He threw a quick glance round him. A ligature. What can be used? Let's see. The red-headed girl hasn't a belt; no loops on the curtains. Something elastic. Ah, I have it! In a twinkling he had thrown off his waistcoat and unfastened his braces. Snapping them with a jerk, he knelt down again, made with them a tourniquet, and clamped it tightly round the child's groin.

"Good! Two minutes' breathing-time," he said as he rose. Sweat was pouring down his cheeks. He knew that every eye was fixed on him. "Only an immediate operation," he said decisively, "can save her life. Let's try!"

The others moved away at once from the bed—even the woman with the lamp, even the young doctor, whose face had paled.

Antoine clenched his teeth, his eyes narrowed and grew hard, he seemed to peer into himself. Must keep calm, he mused. A table? That round table I saw, coming in.

"Bring the lamp!" he cried to the young woman, then turned to the doctor. "You there—come with me!" He strode quickly into the next room. Good, he said to himself; here's our operating-theatre. With a quick gesture he cleared the table, stacked the plates in a pile. "That's for my lamp." Like a general in charge of a campaign, he allotted each thing its place. "Now for our little patient." He went back to the bedroom. The doctor and the young woman hung on his every gesture and followed close behind him. Addressing the doctor, he pointed to the child:

"I'll carry her. She's light as a feather. Hold up her leg, you."

As he slipped his arms under the child's back and carried her to the table, she moaned faintly. He took the lamp from the red-haired woman and, removing the shade, stood it on the pile of plates. As he surveyed the scene, a thought came suddenly and went: "I'm a wonderful fellow!" The lamp gleamed like a brazier, reddening the ambient shadow, where only the young woman's glowing cheeks and the doctor's pince-nez showed up as high-lights; its rays fell harshly on the little body, which twitched spasmodically. The swarming flies seemed worked up to frenzy by the oncoming storm. Heat and anxiety brought beads of sweat to Antoine's brow. Would she live through it? he wondered, but some dark force he did not analyse buoyed up his faith; never had he felt so sure of himself.

He seized his bag and, taking out a bottle of chloroform and some gauze, handed the former to the doctor.

"Open it somewhere. On the sideboard. Take off the sewing-machine. Get everything out."

As he turned, holding the bottle, he noticed two dim figures in the dark doorway, the two old women like statues posted there. One, M. Chasle's mother, had great, staring eyes, an owl's eyes; the other was pressing her breast with her clasped hands.

"Go away!" he commanded. They retreated some steps into the shadows of the bedroom, but he pointed to the other end of the flat. "No. Out of the room. That way." They obeyed, crossed the room, vanished without a word.

"Not you!" he cried angrily to the red-haired woman, who was about to follow them.

She turned on her heel and, for a moment, he took stock of her. She had a handsome, rather fleshy face, touched with a certain dignity, it seemed, by grief; an air of calm maturity that pleased him. Poor woman! he could not help thinking. . . . But I need her!

"You're the child's mother?" he asked.

"No." She shook her head.

"All the better."

As he spoke he had been soaking the gauze and now he swiftly stretched it over the child's nose. "Stand there, and keep this." He handed her the bottle. "When I give the signal, you'll pour some more of it on."

The air grew heavy with the reek of chloroform. The little girl groaned, drew a deep breath or two, grew still.

A last look round. The field was clear; the rest lay with the surgeon's skill. Now that the crucial moment had come, Antoine's anxieties vanished as if by magic. He went to the sideboard where the doctor, holding the bag, was laying on a napkin the last of its contents. "Let's see," he murmured, as though to gain a few seconds' respite. "There's the instrument-box; good. The scalpel, the artery-forceps. A packet of gauze, cotton-wool, that'll do. Alcohol. Caffeine. Tincture of iodine. And so forth. . . . All's ready. Let's begin." And yet again there came to him that sense of buoyancy, of boundless confidence, of vital energies tautened to breaking-point, and, crowning all, a proud awareness of being lifted high above his workaday self.

Raising his head, he looked his junior for a moment in the eyes. "Have you the nerve?" his eyes seemed to inquire. "It's going to be a tough job. Now for it!"

The young man did not flinch. And now he hung on Antoine's gestures with servile assiduity. Well he knew that in this operation lay their only hope, but never would he have dared to take the risk, alone. With Antoine, however, nothing seemed impossible.

He's not so bad, this young chap, thought Antoine. Lucky for me! Let's see. A basin? No matter—this will do as well. Grasping the bottle of iodine he sluiced his arms up to the elbow with the liquid.

"Your turn!" He passed the bottle to the doctor, who was feverishly polishing the lenses of his pince-nez.

A vivid lightning flash, closely followed by a deafening clap of thunder, lit up the window.

"A bit previous, the applause," Antoine said to himself. "I hadn't even taken up my lancet. The young woman didn't turn a hair. It'll cool things down; good for our nerves. Must be pretty nearly a hundred degrees in this room."

He had laid out a series of compresses round the injured limb, delimiting the operative field. Now he turned towards the young woman.

"A whiff of chloroform. That'll do. Right!"

She obeys orders, he mused, like a soldier under fire. Women! Then, fixing his eyes on the swollen little thigh, he swallowed his saliva and raised the scalpel.

"Here goes!"

With one neat stroke he cut the skin.

"Swab!" he commanded the doctor bending beside him. "What a thin child!" he said to himself. "Well, we'll be there all the sooner. Hallo, there's little Dédette starting snoring! Good! Better be quick about it. Now for the retractors."

"Now, you," he said aloud, and the other let fall the blood-stained swabs of cotton-wool and, grasping the retractors, held the wound open.

Antoine paused a moment. "Good!" he murmured. "My probe? Here it is. In Hunter's canal. The classical ligation; all's well. Zip! Another flash! Must have landed pretty near. On the Louvre. Perhaps on the 'gentlemen at Saint-Roch.'" He felt quite calm—no more anxiety for the child, none for death's imminence—and cheerfully repeated under his breath: "The ligature of the femoral artery in Hunter's canal."

Zip! There goes another! Hardly any rain, either. It's stifling. Artery injured at the site of the fracture; the end of the bone tore it open. Simple as anything. Still she hadn't much blood to spare. He glanced at the little girl's face. Hallo! Better hurry up. Simple as anything—but could be fatal, too. A forceps; right! Another; that will do. Zip! These flashes are getting a bore; cheap effect! I've only plaited silk;

must make the best of it. Breaking a tube, he pulled out the skein and made a ligature beside each forceps. Splendid! Almost finished now. The collateral circulation will be quite enough, especially at that age. I'm really wonderful! Can I have missed my vocation? I've all the makings of a surgeon, sure enough; a great surgeon. In the silent interval between two thunder-claps dying into the distance, the sharp metallic click of scissors snipping the loose ends of the silk was audible. Yes; quickness of eye, coolness, energy, dexterity. Suddenly he picked up his ears and his cheeks paled.

"The devil!" he muttered under his breath.

The child had ceased to breathe.

Brushing aside the woman, he tore away the gauze from the unconscious child's face and pressed his ear above her heart. Doctor and young woman waited in suspense, their eyes fixed on Antoine.

"No!" he murmured. "She's breathing still."

He took the child's wrist, but her pulse was so rapid that he did not attempt to count it. "Ouf!" He drew a deep breath, the lines of anxiety deepened on his forehead. The two others felt his gaze pass across their faces, but he did not see them.

He rapped out a brief command.

"You, doctor, remove the forceps, put on a dressing, and then undo the tourniquet. Quickly. You, Madame, get me some note-paper—no, you needn't; I've my note-book." He wiped his hands feverishly with a wad of cotton-wool. "What's the time? Not nine yet. The pharmacist's open. You'll have to hurry."

She stood before him, waiting; her tentative gesture—to wrap the dressing-gown more closely round her body—told him of her reluctance at going thus, half dressed, into the streets, and for the fraction of a second a picture of the opulent form under the garment held his imagination. He scribbled a prescription, signed it. "A two-pint ampoule. As quickly as you can."

"And if—?" she stammered.

"If the pharmacist's shut, ring, and keep on hammering on the door till they open. Be quick!"

She was gone. He followed her with his eyes to make sure she was running, then addressed the doctor.

"We'll try the saline. Not subcutaneously; that's hopeless now. Intravenously. Our last hope." He took two small phials from the sideboard.

"You've removed the tourniquet? Right. Give her an injection of camphor to begin with, then the caffeine—only half of it for her, poor kid! Only, for God's sake, be quick about it!"

He went back to the child and took her thin wrist between his fingers; now he could feel nothing more than a vague, restless fluttering. "It's got past counting," he said to himself. And suddenly a feeling of impotence, of sheer despair, swept over him.

"God damn it!" he broke out. "To think it went off perfectly—and it was all no use!"

The child's face became more livid with every second. She was dying. Antoine observed, beside the parted lips, two slender strands of curling hair, lighter than gossamer, that rose and fell; anyhow, she was breathing still.

He watched the doctor giving the injections. Neat with his fingers, he thought, considering his short sight. But we can't save her. Vexation rather than grief possessed him. He had the callousness common to doctors, for whom the sufferings of others count only as so much new experience, or profit, or professional advantage; men to whose fortunes death and pain are frequent ministers.

But then he thought he heard a banging door and ran towards the sound. It was the young woman coming back with quick, lithe steps, trying to conceal her breathlessness. He snatched the parcel from her hands.

"Bring some hot water." He did not even pause to thank her.

"Boiled?"

"No. To warm the solution. Be quick!"

He had hardly opened the parcel when she returned, bringing a steaming saucepan.

"Good! Excellent!" he murmured, but did not look towards her.

No time to lose. In a few seconds he had nipped off the tips of the ampoule and slipped on the rubber tubing. A Swiss barometer in carved wood hung on the wall. With one hand he unhooked it, while with the other he hung the ampoule on the nail. Then he took the saucepan of hot water, hesitated for the fraction of a second, and looped the rubber tubing round the bottom of it. That'll heat the saline as it flows through, he said to himself. Smart idea, that! He glanced towards the other doctor to see if he had noticed what he had done. At last he came back to the child, lifted her inert arm, and sponged it with iodine. Then, with a stroke of his scalpel, he laid bare the vein, slipped his probe beneath it and inserted the needle.

"It's flowing in all right," he cried. "Take her pulse. I'll stay where I am."

The ten minutes that followed seemed an eternity. No one moved or spoke.

Streaming with sweat, breathing rapidly, with knitted brows, Antoine waited, his gaze riveted on the needle. After a while he glanced up at the ampoule.

"How much gone?"

"Nearly a pint."

"The pulse?"

The doctor silently shook his head.

Five more minutes passed, five minutes more of sickening suspense. Antoine looked up again.

"How much left?"

"Just over half a pint."

"And the pulse?"

The doctor hesitated.

"I'm not sure. I almost think . . . it's beginning to come back a little."

"Can you count it?"

A pause.

"No."

If only the pulse came back! sighed Antoine. He would have given ten years of his own life to restore life to this little corpse. Wonder what age she is. Seven? And, if I save her, she'll fall a victim to consumption within the next ten years, living in this hovel. But shall I save her? It's touch and go; her life hangs on a thread. Still—damn it!—I've done all I could. The saline's flowing well. But it's too late. There's nothing more to be done, nothing else to try. We can only wait. . . . That red-haired girl did her bit. A good-looker. She's not the child's mother; who can she be then? Chasle never breathed a word about all these people. Not his daughter, I imagine. Can't make head or tail of it! And that old woman, putting on airs. . . . Anyhow, they made themselves scarce, good riddance! Curious how one suddenly gets them in hand. They all knew the sort of man they had to deal with. The strong hand of a masterful man. But it was up to me to bring it off. Shall I now? No, she lost too much blood on the way here. No signs of improvement so far, worse luck! Oh, damn it all!

His gaze fell on the child's pale lips and the two strands of golden hair, rising and falling still. The breathing struck him as a little better. Was he mistaken? Half a minute passed. Her chest seemed to flutter with a faint sigh which slowly died into the air, as though a fragment of her life were passing with it. For a moment Antoine stared at her in perplexity. No, she was breathing still. Nothing to be done but to wait, and keep on waiting.

A minute later she sighed again, more plainly now.

"How much left?"

"The ampoule's almost empty."

"And the pulse? Coming back?"

"Yes."

Antoine drew a deep breath.

"Can you count it?"

The doctor took out his watch, settled his pince-nez, and, after a minute's silence, announced:

"A hundred and forty. A hundred and fifty, perhaps."

"Better than nothing!" The exclamation was involuntary, for Antoine was straining every nerve to withstand the flood of huge relief that surged across his mind. Yet it was not imagination; the improvement was not to be gainsaid. Her breathing was steadier. It was all he could do to stay where he was; he had a childish longing to sing or whistle. *Better than nothing tra-la-la*—he tried to fit the words to the tune that had been haunting him all day. *In my heart tra-la-la. In my heart sleeps* . . . Sleeps—sleeps *what?* Got it. *The pale moonlight.*

> In my heart sleeps the pale moonlight
> Of a lovely summer night . . .

The cloud of doubt lifted, gave place to radiant joy.

"The child's saved," he murmured. "She's *got to be* saved!"

. . . a lovely summer night!

"The ampoule's empty," the doctor announced.

"Capital!"

Just then the child, whom his eyes had never left, gave a slight shudder. Antoine turned almost gaily to the young woman, who, leaning against the sideboard, had been watching the scene with steady eyes for the past quarter of an hour.

"Well, Madame!" he cried with affected gruffness. "Gone to sleep have we? And how about the hot-water bottle?" He almost smiled at her amazement. "But, my dear lady, nothing could be more obvious. A bottle, piping hot, to warm her little toes!"

A flash of joy lit up her eyes as she hastened from the room.

Then Antoine, with redoubled care and gentleness, bent down and drew out the needle, and with the tips of his fingers applied a compress to the tiny wound. He ran his fingers along the arm from which the hand still hung limp.

"Another injection of camphor, old man, just to make sure; and then we'll have played our last card. Shouldn't wonder," he added under his breath, "if we've pulled it off." Once more that sense of power that was half joy elated him.

The woman came back carrying a jar in her arms. She hesitated, then, as he said nothing, came and stood by the child's feet.

"Not like that!" said Antoine, with the same brusque cheerfulness. "You'll burn her. Give it here. Just imagine my having to show you how to wrap up a hot-water bottle!"

Smiling now, he snatched up a rolled napkin that caught his eye and, flinging the ring onto the sideboard, wrapped the jar in it and pressed it to the child's feet. The red-haired woman watched him, taken aback by the boyish smile that made his face seem so much younger.

"Then she's—saved?" she ventured to ask.

He dared not affirm it as yet.

"I'll tell you in an hour's time." His voice was gruff, but she took his meaning and cast on him a bold, admiring look.

For the third time Antoine asked himself what this handsome girl could be doing in the Chasle household. Then he pointed to the door.

"What about the others?"

A smile hovered on her lips.

"They're waiting."

"Hearten them up a bit. Tell them to go to bed. You too, Madame, you'd better take some rest."

"Oh, as far as I'm concerned . . ." she murmured, turning to go.

"Let's get the child back to bed," Antoine suggested to his colleague. "The same way as before. Hold up her leg. Take the bolster away; we'd better keep her head down. The next thing is to rig up some sort of a gadget. . . . That napkin, please, and the string from the parcel. Some sort of extension, you see. Slip the string between the rails; handy things these iron bedsteads. Now for a weight. Anything will do. How about this saucepan? No, the flat-iron there will be better. We've all we need here. Yes, hand it over. Tomorrow we'll improve on it. Meanwhile it will do if we stretch the leg a bit, don't you think so?"

The young doctor did not reply. He gazed at Antoine with spellbound awe—the look that Martha may have given the Saviour when Lazarus rose from the tomb. His lips worked and he stammered timidly:

"May I . . . shall I arrange your instruments?" The faltered words breathed such a zeal for service and for devotion that Antoine thrilled with the exultation of an acknowledged chief. They were alone. Antoine went up to the younger man and looked him in the eyes.

"You've been splendid, my dear fellow."

The young man gasped. Antoine, who felt even more embarrassed than his colleague, gave him no time to put in a word.

"Now you'd better be off home; it's late. There's no need for two of us here." He hesitated. "We may take it that she's saved, I think. That's my opinion. However, for safety's sake, I'll stay here for the night, if you'll permit me." The doctor made a vague gesture. "If you permit me, I repeat. For I don't forget that she's your patient. Obviously. I only gave a hand, as there was nothing else for it. That's so, eh? But from tomorrow on I leave her in your hands. They're competent hands and I have no anxiety." As he spoke he led the doctor towards the door. "Will you look in again towards noon? I'll come back when I'm done at the hospital and we will decide on the treatment to follow."

"Sir, it's . . . it's been a privilege for me to . . . to . . ."

Never before had Antoine been "sirred" by a colleague, never before been treated with such deference. It went to his head, like generous wine, and unthinkingly he held out both hands towards the young man. But in the nick of time he regained his self-control.

"You've got a wrong impression," he said in a subdued tone. "I'm only a learner, a novice—like you. Like so many others. Like everyone. Groping our way. We do our best—and that's all there is to it!"

A. E. COPPARD

COMMENTARY

William Blake called certain of his poems Songs of Innocence and others Songs of Experience. Tales may be similarly divided. Some storytellers—most of them, perhaps—draw their narratives from experience, their own or another's, and the mark of that experience is detectable in the stories. They are, we say, "real." The stories of Somerset Maugham belong to this class. Other storytellers, more rarely to be found, apparently invent their tales out of whole cloth; everything in them seems "thought up" and bears the stamp of invention, fancy, remoteness from verifiable experience. Such stories are often "romantic." A man may write well or poorly in either category, though the greatest tales are probably tales of experience.

To the second class, the class of "innocence," belong the strange stories of A. E. Coppard, an Englishman who produces little and whose more recent work lacks the decisive freshness and originality of his first few volumes. His tales bear out whatever truth there is in Bacon's oft-quoted assertion that "There is no excellent beauty that hath not some strangeness in the proportion." He is sometimes strange to the point of eeriness, as in his best-known short story, "Adam and Eve and Pinch Me." When he attempts anything like realism, he is apt to come a cropper. When he steers a middle course between the completely believable and the completely unreal, he is most successful.

The three Coppard tales here offered have for me that magical quality of which I have spoken elsewhere in this volume. The magic is quite minor, but it is magic nonetheless. The illuminated toy church in "Felix Tincler," the mother of "Arabesque" squeezing the milk of her breasts into the fire, the man undoing the hair of Dusky Ruth as she sits in her chair in the taproom—these pictures, ever since I encountered them years ago, have lain quietly in the back of my mind with that same odd persistence possessed by one's lovely or terrible memories of childhood. Not great stories, they are

654

touched with wonder. Ford Madox Ford once wrote: "Mr. Coppard is almost the first English writer to get into English prose the peculiar quality of English lyric poetry." That is very well said.

The effect of "Felix Tincler" results from the ingenious way in which the child's charming innocence, symbolized by the little church, and his impending doom, symbolized by the orphanage, are counterpointed, until the situation is resolved by the dreadful clangor of the bell.

Arabesque is a form of ornamentation based on interlacing lines and curves. Note how Coppard's story so named bears out its title. The Utamaro color print carries over to the man's recollection of himself as a child caressing his mother; the playing mouse interlaces with the memory of the mother in front of the fire; the mother with her bleeding stumps ties into the climax of the story; Cassia putting her hand against Filip's breast recalls his mother again; and so on. If there were not deep feeling in "Arabesque" this would all seem prearranged and mechanical, but there is deep feeling.

"Dusky Ruth" seems to me the best of the three tales, the best Coppard ever wrote, and one of the most curiously moving stories I know. Perhaps its secret lies in the fact that it tells of one of those imagined adventures that every man in his hidden heart (I cannot speak for women) would like to have had and to be able, many years afterward, to remember.

Felix Tincler

BY

A. E. COPPARD

THE child was to have a birthday to-morrow and was therefore not uneasy about being late home from school this afternoon. He had lost his pencil case, a hollow long round thing it was, like a rolling-pin, only it had green and yellow rings painted upon it. He kept his marbles in it and so he was often in a trouble about his pencils. He had not tried very much to find the pencil case because the boys "deludered" him—that's what his father always said. He had asked Heber Gleed if he had seen it—he had strange suspicions of that boy—but Heber Gleed had sworn so earnestly that the greengrocer opposite the school had picked it up, he had even "saw him do it," that Felix Tincler went into Mr. Gobbit's shop, and when the greengrocer lady appeared in answer to the ring of the door bell he enquired politely for his pencil case. She was tall and terrible with a squint and, what was wórse, a large velvety mole with hairs sprouting from it. She immediately and with inexplicable fury desired him to flee from her greengrocer shop, with a threat of alternative castigation in which a flat iron and a red-hot pick-axe were to figure with unusual and unpleasant prominence. Well, he had run out of Mr. Gobbit's shop and there was Heber Gleed standing in the road giggling derisively at him. Felix walked on alone looking in the gutters and areas for his pencil case until he encountered another friendly boy who took him to dig in a garden where they grew castor-oil plants. When he went home it was late; as he ran along under the high wall of the orphanage that occupied one end of his street its harsh peevish bell clanged out six notes. He scampered past the great gateway under the dismal arch that always filled him with uneasiness, he never passed it without feeling the sad trouble that

656

a prison might give. He stepped into his own pleasant home, a little mute, and a little dirty in appearance; but at six years of age in a home so comfortable and kind the eve of the day that is to turn you into seven is an occasion great enough to yield an amnesty for peccadilloes. His father was already in from work, he could hear him singing. He gave his mother the sprigs he had picked from the castor-oil plant and told her about the pencil case. The meal was laid upon the table, and while mother was gone into the kitchen to boil the water for tea he sat down and tried to smooth out the stiff creases in the white table cloth. His father was singing gaily in the scullery as he washed and shaved.

> *High cockalorum,*
> *Charlie ate the spinach . . .*

He ceased for a moment to give the razor a vigorous stropping and then continued:

> *High cockalorum,*
> *High cockalee . . .*

Felix knew that was not the conclusion of the song. He listened, but for some moments all that followed was the loud crepitation of a razor searching a stubborn beard and the sigh of the kettle. Then a new vigour seized the singer:

> *But mother brought the pandy down*
> *And bate the gree . . .*

Again that rasping of chin briefly intervened, but the conclusion of the cropping was soon denoted by the strong rallentando of the singer:

> *. . . dy image,*
> *High cock—alorum,*
> *High cock—a—lee.*

Mrs. Tincler brought in the teapot and her husband followed her with his chin tightly shaven but blue, crying with mock horror:

"Faylix, my son! that is seven years old to-morrow! look at him, Mary, the face of him and the hands of him! I didn't know there was a bog in this parish; is it creeping in a bog you have been?"

The boy did not blench at his father's spurious austerity, he knew he was the soul of kindness and fun.

"Go wash yourself at the sink," interposed his mother. Kevin Tincler, taking his son by the hand, continued with mocking admonishment: "All the fine copybooks of the world that you've filled up with that blather about cleanliness and holiness, the up strokes very thin and the down strokes very thick! What was it, Mary, he has let it all out of his mind?"

"Go and wash, Felix, and come quickly and have your tea," laughed Mary Tincler.

"Ah, but what was it—in that grand book of yours?"

The boy stood, in his short buff tunic, regarding his father with shy amusement. The small round clear-skinned face was lovely with its blushes of faint rose; his eyes were big and blue, and his head was covered with thick curling locks of rich brown hair.

"Cleanliness comes next to godliness," he replied.

"Does it so, indeed?" exclaimed his father. "Then you're putting your godliness in a pretty low category!"

"What a nonsense," said Mary Tincler as the boy left them.

The Irishman and his dark-eyed Saxon wife sat down at the table waiting for their son.

"There's a bit of a randy in the Town Gardens to-night, Mary, dancing on the green, fireworks! When the boy is put to bed we'll walk that way."

Mary expressed her pleasure, but then declared she could not leave the boy alone in his bed.

"He'll not hurt, Mary, he has no fear in him. Give him the birthday gift before we go. Whisht, he's coming!"

The child, now clean and handsome, came to his chair and looked up at his father sitting opposite to him.

"Holy Mother!" exclaimed the admiring parent, "it's the neck of a swan he has. Faylix Tincler, may you live to be the father of a bishop!"

After tea his father took him upon the downs for an hour. As they left their doorway a group of the tidy but wretched orphans was marching back into their seminary, little girls moving in double columns behind a stiff-faced woman. They were all dressed alike in garments of charity, exact as pilchards. Grey capes, worsted stockings, straw hats with blue bands round them, and hard boots. The boys were coming in from a different direction, but all of them, even the minutest, were clad in corduroy trousers and short jackets high throated like a gaoler's. This identity of garment was contrary to the will of God, for He had certainly made their pinched bodies diverse enough. Some were short, some tall, dark, fair, some ugly, others handsome. The sight of them made Felix unhappy, he shrank into himself, until he and his father had slipped through a gap in a hedge and were going up the hill that stretched smoothly and easily almost from their very door. The top of the down hereabouts was quiet and lovely, but a great flank of it two miles away was scattered over with tiny white figures playing very deliberately at cricket. Pleasant it was up there in the calm evening, and still bright, but the intervening valley was full of grey ungracious houses, allotments, railway arches, churches, graveyards, and schools. Worst of all was the dull forbidding aspect of the Orphanage down beyond the roof of their own house.

They played with a ball and had some wrestling matches until the declining day began to grow dim even on the hill and the fat jumbo clouds over the town were turning pink. If those elephants fell on him —what would they do? Why they'd mix him up like ice-cream! So said his father.

"Do things ever fall out of the sky?"

"Rain," said Mr. Tincler.

"Yes, I know."

"Stars—maybe."

"Where do they go?"

"Oh, they drop on the hills but ye can never find 'em."

"Don't Heaven ever?"

"What, drop down! No," said Mr. Tincler, "it don't. I have not heard of it doing that, but maybe it all just stoops down sometimes, Faylix, until it's no higher than the crown of your hat. Let us be going home now and ye'll see something this night."

"What is it?"

"Wait, Faylix, wait!"

As they crossed from the hill Mary, drawing down the blinds, signalled to them from the window.

"Come along, Felix," she cried, and the child ran into the darkened room. Upon the table was set a little church of purest whiteness. Kevin had bought it from an Italian hawker. It had a wonderful tall steeple and a cord that came through a hole and pulled a bell inside. And that was not all; the church was filled with light that was shining through a number of tiny arched windows, blue, purple, green, violet, the wonderful windows were everywhere. Felix was silent with wonder; how could you get a light in a church that hadn't a door! Then Mary lifted the hollow building from the table; it had no floor, and there was a nightlight glowing in one of her patty-pans filled with water. The church was taken up to bed with him in the small chamber next his parents' room and set upon a bureau. Kevin and Mary then went off to the "bit of devilment" in the town gardens.

Felix kept skipping from his bed, first to gaze at the church, and then to lean out of the window in his night-shift, looking for the lamplighter who would come to the street lamp outside. The house was the very last and the lamp was the very last one on the roads that led from the town and went poking out into the steady furze-covered downs. And as the lamp was the very last to be lit darkness was always half-fallen by the time the old man arrived at his journey's end. He carried a pole with a brass tube on its top. There were holes in the brass tube showing gleams of light. The pole rested upon his shoulders as he trudged along, humming huskily.

"Here he is," cried Felix, leaning from the window and waving a white arm. The dull road, empty of traffic, dim as his mother's pantry by day, curved slightly, and away at the other end of the curve a jet of light had sprung into the gloom like a bright flower bursting its sheath; a black figure moved along towards him under the Orphanage wall. Other lamps blossomed with light and the lamplighter, approaching the Tinclers' lamp, thrust the end of his pole into the lantern, his head meanwhile craning back like the head of a horse that has been pulled violently backwards. He deftly turned the tap; with a tiny dull explosion that sounded like a doormat being beaten against the wall in the next street the lamp was lit and the face of the old man sprang into vague brilliance, for it was not yet utterly dark. Vague as the light was, the neighbouring hills at once faded out of recognition and became black bulks of oblivion.

"Oi . . . Oi . . ." cried the child, clapping his hands. The old man's features relaxed, he grunted in relief, the pole slid down in his palm. As the end of it struck the pavement a sharp knock he drew an old pipe from his pocket and lit it quite easily, although one of his hands was deficient of a thumb and some fingers. He was about to travel back into the sparkling town when Felix called to him:

"Soloman! Soloman!"

"Goo an to yer bed, my little billycock, or you'll ketch a fever."

"No, but what's this?" Felix was pointing to the ground below him. The old man peered over the iron railings into the front garden that had just sufficient earth to cherish four deciduous bushes, two plants of marigold, and some indeterminate herbs. In the dimness of their shadows a glowworm beamed clearly.

"That?" exclaimed he; "Oh, s'dripped off the moon, yas, right off, moon's wasting away, you'll see later on if you'm watch out for it, s'dripped off the moon, right off." Chuckling, he blew out the light at the end of his pole, and went away, but turned at intervals to wave his hand towards the sky, crying "Later on, right off!" and cackling genially until he came to a tavern.

The child stared at the glowworm and then surveyed the sky, but the tardy moon was deep behind the hills. He left the open window and climbed into bed again. The house was empty, but he did not mind, father and mother had gone to buy him another birthday gift. He did not mind, the church glowed in its corner on the bureau, the street lamp shined all over the ceiling and a little bit upon the wall where the splendid picture of Wexford Harbour was hanging. It was not gloomy at all, although the Orphanage bell once sounded very piercingly. Sometimes people would stroll by, but not often, and he would hear them mumbling to each other. He would rather have a Chinese lantern first, and next to that a little bagpipe, and next to that a cockatoo with a yellow head, and then a Chinese lantern, and then. . . . He awoke; he thought he heard a heavy bang on the door as if somebody had thrown a big stone. But when he looked out of the window there was nobody to be seen. The little moon-drip was still lying in the dirt, the sky was softly black, the stars were vivid, only the lamp dazzled his eyes and he could not see any moon. But as he yawned he saw just over the downs a rich globe of light moving very gradually towards him, swaying and falling, falling in the still air. To the child's dazzled eyes the great globe, dropping towards him as if it would crush the house, was shaped like an elephant, a fat squat jumbo with a green trunk. Then to his relief it fell suddenly from the sky right on to the down where he and father had played. The light was extinguished and black night hid the fire-balloon.

He scrambled back into bed again, but how he wished it was morning so that he could go out and capture the old elephant—he knew he would find it! When at last he slept he sank into a world of white churches that waved their steeples like vast trunks, and danced with elephants that had bellies full of fire and hidden bells that clanged impetuously to a courageous pull of each tail. He did not wake again until morning was bright and birds were singing. It was early, but it was his birthday. There were no noises in the street yet, and he could not hear his father or mother moving about. He crawled silently from his bed and dressed himself. The coloured windows in the little white fane gleamed still but it looked a little dull now. He took the cake that mother always left at his bedside and crept down the stairs. There he put on his shoes and, munching the cake, tiptoed to the front door. It was not bolted, but it was difficult for him to slip back the latch quietly, and when at last it was done and he stood upon the step he was doubly startled to hear a loud rapping on the knocker of a house a few doors away. He sidled quickly but warily to the corner of the street, crushing the cake into his pocket, and then peeped back. It was more terrible than he had anticipated! A tall policeman stood outside that house, bawling to a woman with her hair in curl papers who was lifting the sash of an upper window. Felix turned and ran through the gap in the hedge and onwards up the hill. He did not wait; he thought he heard the policeman calling out "Tincler!" and he ran faster and faster, then slower and more slow as the down steepened, until he was able to sink down breathless behind a clump of the furze, out of sight and out of hearing. The policeman did not appear to be following him; he moved on up the hill and through the soft smooth alleys of the furze until he reached the top of the down, searching always for the white elephant which he knew must be hidden close there and nowhere else, although he had no clear idea in his mind of the appearance of his mysterious quarry. Vain search, the elephant was shy or cunning and eluded him. Hungry at last and tired he sat down and leaned against a large ant hill close beside the thick and perfumed furze. Here he ate his cake and then lolled, a little drowsy, looking at the few clouds in the sky and listening to birds. A flock of rooks was moving in straggling flight towards him, a wide flat changing skein, like a curtain of crape that was being pulled and stretched delicately by invisible fingers. One of the rooks flapped just over him; it had a small round hole right through the feathers of one wing—what was that for? Felix was just falling to sleep, it was so soft and comfortable there, when a tiny noise, very tiny but sharp and mysterious, went "Ping!" just by his ear, and something stung him lightly in the neck. He knelt up, a little startled, but he peered steadily under the furze. "Ping!" went something again and stung him in the ball of the eye. It made him blink. He drew back; after staring silently at the furze he said very softly, "Come out!" Nothing came; he beckoned with his forefinger and called aloud with friendliness, "Come on, come out!" At that moment his nose was almost touching a brown dry sheath of the furze bloom, and right before his eyes the dried flower burst with the faint noise of "Ping!" and he felt the shower of tiny black seeds shooting against his cheek. At once he comprehended the charming mystery of the furze's dispersal of its seeds, and he submitted himself to the fairylike bombardment with great glee, forgetting even the elephant until in one of the furze alleys he came in sight of a heap of paper that fluttered a little heavily. He went towards it; it was so large that he could not make out its shape or meaning. It was a great white

bag made of paper, all crumpled and damp, with an arrangement of
wire where the hole was, and some burned tow fixed in it. But at last
he was able to perceive the green trunk, and it also had pink eyes! He
had found it and he was triumphant! There were words in large black
letters painted upon it which he could not read, except one word which
was CURE. It was an advertisement fire-balloon relating to a specific
for catarrh. He rolled the elephant together carefully, and carrying
the mass of it clasped in his two arms he ran back along the hill
chuckling to himself, "I'm carrying the ole elephant." Advancing
down the hill to his home he was precariously swathed in a drapery
of balloon paper. The door stood open; he walked into the kitchen.
No one was in the kitchen, but there were sharp straight voices speaking in the room above. He thought he must have come into the wrong
house, but the strange noises frightened him into silence; he stood
quite still listening to them. He had dropped the balloon and it unfolded upon the floor, partly revealing the astounding advertisement of

PEASEGOOD'S PODOPHYLLIN

The voices above were unravelling horror upon horror. He knew
by some divining instinct that tragedy was happening to him, had indeed already enveloped and crushed him. A mortar had exploded at
the fireworks display, killing and wounding people that he knew.

"She had a great hole of a wound in the soft part of her thigh as
you could put a cokernut in . . ."

"God a'mighty . . ."

"Died in five minutes, poor thing."

"And the husband . . . they couldn't . . . ?"

"No, couldn't identify . . . they could not identify him . . . only by
some papers in his pocket."

"And he'd got a little bagpipe done up in a package . . . for their
little boy . . ."

"Never spoke a word. . . ."

"Never a word, poor creature."

"May Christ be good to 'em."

"Yes, yes," they all said softly.

The child walked quietly up the stairs to his mother's bedroom. Two policemen were there making notes in their pocket books, their helmets lying on the unused bed. There were also three or four friendly women neighbours. As he entered the room the gossip ceased abruptly. One of the women gasped "O Jesus!" and they seemed to huddle together, eyeing him as if he had stricken them with terror. With his fingers still upon the handle of the door he looked up at the taller policeman and said:

"What's the matter?"

The policeman did not reply immediately; he folded up his notebook, but the woman who had gasped came to him with a yearning cry and wrapped him in her protecting arms with a thousand kisses.

"Ye poor lamb, ye poor little orphan, whatever 'ull become of ye!"

At that moment the bell of the Orphanage burst into a peal of harsh impetuous clangour and the policemen picked up their helmets from the bed.

Arabesque: The Mouse

BY

A. E. COPPARD

IN THE main street amongst tall establishments of mart and worship
was a high narrow house pressed between a coffee factory and a bootmaker's. It had four flights of long dim echoing stairs, and at the top,
in a room that was full of the smell of dried apples and mice, a man
in the middle age of life had sat reading Russian novels until he
thought he was mad. Late was the hour, the night outside black and
freezing, the pavements below empty and undistinguishable when he
closed his book and sat motionless in front of the glowing but flameless
fire. He felt he was very tired, yet he could not rest. He stared at a
picture on the wall until he wanted to cry; it was a colour-print by
Utamaro of a suckling child caressing its mother's breasts as she sits
in front of a blackbound mirror. Very chaste and decorative it was, in
spite of its curious anatomy. The man gazed, empty of sight though
not of mind, until the sighing of the gas-jet maddened him. He got
up, put out the light, and sat down again in the darkness trying to compose his mind before the comfort of the fire. And he was just about to
begin a conversation with himself when a mouse crept from a hole in
the skirting near the fireplace and scurried into the fender. The man
had the crude dislike for such sly nocturnal things, but this mouse was
so small and bright, its antics so pretty, that he drew his feet carefully
from the fender and sat watching it almost with amusement. The
mouse moved along the shadows of the fender, out upon the hearth,
and sat before the glow, rubbing its head, ears, and tiny belly with its
paws as if it were bathing itself with the warmth, until, sharp and
sudden, the fire sank, an ember fell, and the mouse flashed into its hole.
The man reached forward to the mantelpiece and put his hand

upon a pocket lamp. Turning on the beam, he opened the door of a cupboard beside the fireplace. Upon one of the shelves there was a small trap baited with cheese, a trap made with a wire spring, one of those that smashed down to break the back of ingenuous and unwary mice.

"Mean—so mean," he mused, "to appeal to the hunger of any living thing just in order to destroy it."

He picked up the empty trap as if to throw it in the fire.

"I suppose I had better leave it though—the place swarms with them." He still hesitated. "I hope that little beastie won't go and do anything foolish." He put the trap back quite carefully, closed the door of the cupboard, sat down again and extinguished the lamp.

Was there anyone else in the world so squeamish and foolish about such things! Even his mother, mother so bright and beautiful, even she had laughed at his childish horrors. He recalled how once in his childhood, not long after his sister Yosine was born, a friendly neighbour had sent him home with a bundle of dead larks tied by the feet "for supper." The pitiful inanimity of the birds had brought a gush of tears; he had run weeping home and into the kitchen, and there he had found the strange thing doing. It was dusk; mother was kneeling before the fire. He dropped the larks.

"Mother!" he exclaimed softly.

She looked at his tearful face.

"What's the matter, Filip?" she asked, smiling too at his astonishment.

"Mother! What are you doing?"

Her bodice was open and she was squeezing her breasts; long thin streams of milk spurted into the fire with a plunging noise.

"Weaning your little sister," laughed mother. She took his inquisitive face and pressed it against the delicate warmth of her bosom, and he forgot the dead birds behind him.

"Let me do it, mother," he cried, and doing so he discovered the throb of the heart in his mother's breast. Wonderful it was for him to experience it, although she could not explain it to him.

"Why does it do that?"

"If it did not beat, little son, I should die and the Holy Father would take me from you."

"God?"

She nodded. He put his hand upon his own breast. "Oh, feel it, Mother!" he cried. Mother unbuttoned his little coat and felt the gentle *tick tick* with her warm palm.

"Beautiful!" she said.

"Is it a good one?"

She kissed his smiling lips. "It is good if it beats truly. Let it always beat truly, Filip; let it always beat truly."

There was the echo of a sigh in her voice, and he had divined some grief, for he was very wise. He kissed her bosom in his tiny ecstasy and whispered soothingly: "Little mother! little mother!" In such joys he forgot his horror of the dead larks; indeed he helped mother to pluck them and spit them for supper.

It was a black day that succeeded, and full of tragedy for the child. A great bay horse with a tawny mane had knocked down his mother in the lane, and a heavy cart had passed over her, crushing both her hands. She was borne away moaning with anguish to the surgeon who cut off the two hands. She died in the night. For years the child's dreams were filled with the horror of the stumps of arms, bleeding unendingly. Yet he had never seen them, for he was sleeping when she died.

While this old woe was come vividly before him he again became aware of the mouse. His nerves stretched upon him in repulsion, but he soon relaxed to a tolerant interest, for it was really a most engaging little mouse. It moved with curious staccato scurries, stopping to rub its head or flicker with its ears; they seemed almost transparent ears. It spied a red cinder and skipped innocently up to it . . . sniffing . . . sniffing . . . until it jumped back scorched. It would crouch as a cat does, blinking in the warmth, or scamper madly as if dancing, and then roll upon its side rubbing its head with those pliant paws. The melancholy man watched it until it came at last to rest and squatted meditatively upon its haunches, hunched up, looking curiously wise, a pennyworth of philosophy; then once more the coals sank with a rattle and again the mouse was gone.

The man sat on before the fire and his mind filled again with unaccountable sadness. He had grown into manhood with a burning generosity of spirit and rifts of rebellion in him that proved too exacting for his fellows and seemed mere wantonness to men of casual rectitudes. "Justice and Sin," he would cry, "Property and Virtue—incompatibilities! There can be no sin in a world of justice, no property in a world of virtue!" With an engaging extravagance and a certain clear-eyed honesty of mind he had put his two and two together and seemed then to rejoice, as in some topsy-turvy dream, in having rendered unto Cæsar, as you might say, the things that were due to Napoleon! But this kind of thing could not pass unexpiated in a world of men having an infinite regard for Property and a pride in their traditions of Virtue and Justice. They could indeed forgive him his sins, but they could not forgive him his compassions. So he had to go seek for more melodious-minded men and fair unambiguous women. But rebuffs can deal more deadly blows than daggers; he became timid—a timidity not of fear but of pride—and grew with the years into misanthropy, susceptible to trivial griefs and despairs, a vessel of emotion that emptied as easily as it filled, until he came at last to know that his griefs were half deliberate, his despairs half unreal, and to live but for beauty—which is tranquillity—to put her wooing hand upon him.

Now, while the mouse hunts in the cupboard, one fair recollection stirs in the man's mind—of Cassia and the harmony of their only meeting, Cassia who had such rich red hair, and eyes, yes, her eyes were full of starry inquiry like the eyes of mice. It was so long ago that he had forgotten how he came to be in it, that unaccustomed orbit of vain vivid things—a village festival, all oranges and houp-la. He could not remember how he came to be there, but at night, in the court hall, he had danced with Cassia—fair and unambiguous indeed!—who had come like the wind from among the roses and swept into his heart.

"It is easy to guess," he had said to her, "what you like most in the world."

She laughed. "To dance? Yes, and you . . . ?"

"To find a friend."

"I know, I know," she cried, caressing him with recognitions. "Ah,

at times I quite love my friends—until I begin to wonder how much
they hate me!"

He had loved at once that cool pale face, the abundance of her
strange hair as light as the autumn's clustered bronze, her lilac dress
and all the sweetness about her like a bush of lilies. How they had
laughed at the two old peasants whom they had overheard gabbling of
trifles like sickness and appetite!

"There's a lot of nature in a parsnip," said one, a fat person of the
kind that swells grossly when stung by a bee, "a lot of nature when
it's young, but when it's old it's like everything else."

"True it is."

"And I'm very fond of vegetables, yes, and I'm very fond of bread."

"Come out with me," whispered Cassia to Filip, and they walked
out in the blackness of midnight into what must have been a garden.

"Cool it is here," she said, "and quiet, but too dark even to see your
face—can you see mine?"

"The moon will not rise until after dawn," said he, "it will be white
in the sky when the starlings whistle in your chimney."

They walked silently and warily about until they felt the chill of the
air. A dull echo of the music came to them through the walls, then
stopped, and they heard the bark of a fox away in the woods.

"You are cold," he whispered, touching her bare neck with timid
fingers. "Quite, quite cold," drawing his hand tenderly over the curves
of her chin and face. "Let us go in," he said, moving with discretion
from the rapture he desired. "We will come out again," said Cassia.

But within the room the ball was just at an end, the musicians were
packing up their instruments and the dancers were flocking out and
homewards, or to the buffet which was on a platform at one end of
the room. The two old peasants were there, munching hugely.

"I tell you," said one of them, "there's nothing in the world for it
but the grease of an owl's liver. That's it, that's it! Take something
on your stomach now, just to offset the chill of the dawn!"

Filip and Cassia were beside them, but there were so many people
crowding the platform that Filip had to jump down. He stood then
looking up adoringly at Cassia, who had pulled a purple cloak around
her.

"For Filip, Filip, Filip," she said, pushing the last bite of her sandwich into his mouth, and pressing upon him her glass of Loupiac. Quickly he drank it with a great gesture, and, flinging the glass to the wall, took Cassia into his arms, shouting: "I'll carry you home, the whole way home, yes, I'll carry you!"

"Put me down!" she cried, beating his head and pulling his ear, as they passed among the departing dancers. "Put me down, you wild thing!"

Dark, dark was the lane outside, and the night an obsidian net, into which he walked carrying the girl. But her arms were looped around him; she discovered paths for him, clinging more tightly as he staggered against a wall, stumbled upon a gulley, or when her sweet hair was caught in the boughs of a little lime tree.

"Do not loose me, Filip, will you? Do not loose me," Cassia said, putting her lips against his temple.

His brain seemed bursting, his heart rocked within him, but he adored the rich grace of her limbs against his breast. "Here it is," she murmured, and he carried her into a path that led to her home in a little lawned garden where the smell of ripe apples upon the branches and the heavy lustre of roses stole upon the air. Roses and apples! Roses and apples! He carried her right into the porch before she slid down and stood close to him with her hands still upon his shoulders. He could breathe happily at the release, standing silent and looking round at the sky sprayed with wondrous stars but without a moon.

"You are stronger than I thought you, stronger than you look; you are really very strong," she whispered, nodding her head to him. Opening the buttons of his coat, she put her palm against his breast.

"Oh, how your heart does beat! Does it beat truly—and for whom?"

He had seized her wrists in a little fury of love, crying: "Little mother, little mother!"

"What are you saying?" asked the girl; but before he could continue there came a footstep sounding behind the door, and the clack of a bolt. . . .

What was that? Was that really a bolt or was it . . . was it . . . the snap of the trap? The man sat up in his room intently listening, with nerves quivering again, waiting for the trap to kill the little philosopher. When he felt it was all over he reached guardedly in the darkness for the lantern, turned on the beam, and opened the door of the cupboard. Focussing the light upon the trap, he was amazed to see the mouse sitting on its haunches before it, uncaught. Its head was bowed, but its bead-like eyes were full of brightness, and it sat blinking, it did not flee.

"Shoosh!" said the man, but the mouse did not move. "Why doesn't it go? Shoosh!" he said again, and suddenly the reason of the mouse's strange behaviour was made clear. The trap had not caught it completely, but it had broken off both its forefeet, and the thing crouched there holding out its two bleeding stumps humanly, too stricken to stir.

Horror flooded the man, and conquering his repugnance he plucked the mouse up quickly by the neck. Immediately the little thing fastened its teeth in his finger; the touch was no more than the slight prick of a pin. The man's impulse then exhausted itself. What should he do with it? He put his hand behind him, he dared not look, but there was nothing to be done except kill it at once, quickly, quickly. Oh, how should he do it? He bent towards the fire as if to drop the mouse into its quenching glow; but he paused and shuddered, he would hear its cries, he would have to listen. Should he crush it with finger and thumb? A glance towards the window decided him. He opened the sash with one hand and flung the wounded mouse far into the dark street. Closing the window with a crash, he sank into a chair, limp with pity too deep for tears.

So he sat for two minutes, five minutes, ten minutes. Anxiety and shame filled him with heat. He opened the window again, and the freezing air poured in and cooled him. Seizing his lantern, he ran down the echoing stairs, into the dark empty street, searching long and vainly for the little philosopher until he had to desist and return to his room, shivering, frozen to his very bones.

When he had recovered some warmth he took the trap from its shelf. The two feet dropped into his hand; he cast them into the fire. Then he once more set the trap and put it back carefully into the cupboard.

Dusky Ruth

BY

A. E. COPPARD

AT THE CLOSE of an April day, chilly and wet, the traveller came to a country town. In the Cotswolds, though the towns are small and sweet and the inns snug, the general habit of the land is bleak and bare. He had newly come upon upland roads so void of human affairs, so lonely, that they might have been made for some forgotten uses by departed men, and left to the unwitting passage of such strangers as himself. Even the unending walls, built of old rough laminated rock that detailed the far-spreading fields, had grown very old again in their courses; there were dabs of darkness, buttons of moss, and fossils on every stone. He had passed a few neighbourhoods, sometimes at the crook of a stream, or at the cross of debouching roads, where old habitations, their gangre-nated thatch riddled with bird-holes, had not been so much erected as just spattered about the places. Beyond these signs an odd lark or blackbird, the ruckle of partridges, or the nifty gallop of a hare, had been the only mitigation of the living loneliness that was almost as profound by day as by night. But the traveller had a care for such times and places. There are men who love to gaze with the mind at things that can never be seen, feel at least the throb of a beauty that will never be known, and hear over immense bleak reaches the echo of that which is no celestial music, but only their own hearts' vain cries; and though his garments clung to him like clay it was with deliberate questing step that the traveller trod the single street of the town, and at last entered the inn, shuffling his shoes in the doorway for a moment and striking the raindrops from his hat. Then he turned into a small smoking-room. Leather-lined benches, much worn, were fixed to the wall under the window and in other odd corners and nooks behind mahogany tables. One wall was furnished with all the congenial gear of a bar, but without any intervening counter. Opposite a bright fire was burning, and a neatly-dressed young woman sat before it in a Windsor chair, staring at the flames. There was no other inmate of the room, and as he entered, the girl rose up and greeted him. He found that he could be accommodated for the night, and in a few moments his hat and scarf were removed and placed inside the fender, his wet overcoat was taken to the kitchen, the landlord, an old fellow, was lending him a roomy pair of slippers, and a maid was setting supper in an adjoining room.

He sat while this was doing and talked to the barmaid. She had a beautiful, but rather mournful, face as it was lit by the firelight, and when her glance was turned away from it her eyes had a piercing brightness. Friendly and well-spoken as she was, the melancholy in her aspect was noticeable—perhaps it was the dim room, or the wet day, or the long hours ministering a multitude of cocktails to thirsty gallantry.

When he went to his supper he found cheering food and drink, with pleasant garniture of silver and mahogany. There were no other visitors, he was to be alone; blinds were drawn, lamps lit, and the fire at his back was comforting. So he sat long about his meal until a white-faced maid came to clear the table, discoursing to him of country things as she busied about the room. It was a long narrow room, with a sideboard and the door at one end and the fireplace at the other. A bookshelf, almost devoid of books, contained a number of plates; the long wall that faced the windows was almost destitute of pictures, but there were hung upon it, for some inscrutable but doubtless sufficient reason, many dish-covers, solidly shaped, of the kind held in such mysterious regard and known as "willow pattern"; one was even hung upon the face of a map. Two musty prints were mixed with them, presentments of horses having a stilted, extravagant physique and bestridden by images of inhuman and incommunicable dignity, clothed in whiskers, coloured jackets and tight white breeches.

He took down the books from the shelf, but his interest was speedily exhausted, and the almanacs, the county directory, and various guidebooks were exchanged for the *Cotswold Chronicle*. With this, having drawn the deep chair to the hearth, he whiled away the time. The newspaper amused him with its advertisements of stock shows, farm auctions, travelling quacks and conjurers, and there was a lengthy account of the execution of a local felon, one Timothy Bridger, who had murdered an infant in some shameful circumstances. This dazzling crescendo proved rather trying to the traveller; he threw down the paper.

The town was all quiet as the hills, and he could hear no sounds in the house. He got up and went across the hall to the smoke-room. The door was shut, but there was light within, and he entered. The girl sat there much as he had seen her on his arrival, still alone, with feet on fender. He shut the door behind him, sat down, and crossing his legs, puffed at his pipe, admired the snug little room and the pretty figure of the girl, which he could do without embarrassment as her meditative head, slightly bowed, was turned away from him. He could see something of her, too, in the mirror at the bar, which repeated also the agreeable contours of bottles of coloured wines and rich liqueurs— so entrancing in form and aspect that they seemed destined to charming histories, even in disuse—and those of familiar outline containing mere spirits or small beer, for which are reserved the harsher destinies of base oils, horse medicines, disinfectants, and cold tea. There were coloured glasses for bitter wines, white glasses for sweet, a tiny leaden sink beneath them, and the four black handles of the beer engine.

The girl wore a light blouse of silk, a short skirt of black velvet, and a pair of very thin silk stockings that showed the flesh of instep and shin so plainly that he could see they were reddened by the warmth of the fire. She had on a pair of dainty cloth shoes with high heels, but what was wonderful about her was the heap of rich black hair piled at the back of her head and shadowing the dusky neck. He sat puffing his pipe and letting the loud tick of the clock fill the quiet room. She did not stir and he could move no muscle. It was as if he had been willed to come there and wait silently. That, he felt now, had been his desire all the evening; and here, in her presence, he was more strangely stirred than by any event he could remember.

In youth he had viewed women as futile pitiable things that grew long hair, wore stays and garters, and prayed incomprehensible prayers. Viewing them in the stalls of the theatre from his vantage-point in the gallery, he always disliked the articulation of their naked shoulders. But still, there was a god in the sky, a god with flowing hair and exquisite eyes, whose one stride with an ardour grandly rendered took him across the whole round hemisphere to which his buoyant limbs were bound like spokes to the eternal rim and axle, his bright hair burning in the pity of the sunsets and tossing in the anger of the dawns.

Master traveller had indeed come into this room to be with this woman: she as surely desired him, and for all its accidental occasion it was as if he, walking the ways of the world, had suddenly come upon . . . what so imaginable with all permitted reverence as, well, just a shrine; and he, admirably humble, bowed the instant head.

Were there no other people within? The clock indicated a few minutes to nine. He sat on, still as stone, and the woman might have been of wax for all the movement or sound she made. There was allurement in the air between them; he had forborne his smoking, the pipe grew cold between his teeth. He waited for a look from her, a movement to break the trance of silence. No footfall in street or house, no voice in the inn, but the clock beating away as if pronouncing a doom. Suddenly it rasped out nine large notes, a bell in the town repeated them dolefully, and a cuckoo no further than the kitchen mocked them with three times three. After that came the weak steps of the old landlord along the hall, the slam of doors, the clatter of lock and bolt, and then the silence returning unendurably upon them.

He arose and stood behind her; he touched the black hair. She made no movement or sign. He pulled out two or three combs, and dropping them into her lap let the whole mass tumble about his hands. It had a curious harsh touch in the unravelling, but was so full and shining; black as a rook's wings it was. He slid his palms through it. His fingers searched it and fought with its fine strangeness; into his mind there travelled a serious thought, stilling his wayward fancy—this was no wayward fancy, but a rite accomplishing itself! *(Run, run, silly man, y'are lost!)* But having got so far he burnt his boats, leaned over, and drew her face back to him. And at that, seizing his wrists, she gave him back ardour for ardour, pressing his hands to her bosom, while the kiss was sealed and sealed again. Then she sprang up and picking his hat and scarf from the fender said:

"I have been drying them for you, but the hat has shrunk a bit, I'm sure—I tried it on."

He took them from her, and put them behind him; he leaned lightly back upon the table, holding it with both his hands behind him; he could not speak.

"Aren't you going to thank me for drying them?" she asked, picking her combs from the rug and repinning her hair.

"I wonder why we did that?" he asked shamedly.

"It is what I'm thinking too," she said.

"You were so beautiful about . . . about it, you know."

She made no rejoinder, but continued to bind her hair, looking brightly at him under her brows. When she had finished she went close to him.

"Will that do?"

"I'll take it down again."

"No, no, the old man or the old woman will be coming in."

"What of that?" he said, taking her into his arms. "Tell me your name."

She shook her head, but she returned his kisses and stroked his hair and shoulders with beautifully melting gestures.

"What is your name, I want to call you by your name?" he said. "I can't keep calling you Lovely Woman, Lovely Woman."

Again she shook her head and was dumb.

"I'll call you Ruth then, Dusky Ruth, Ruth of the black, beautiful hair."

"That is a nice-sounding name—I knew a deaf and dumb girl named Ruth; she went to Nottingham and married an organ-grinder—but I should like it for my name."

"Then I give it to you."

"Mine is so ugly."

"What is it?"

Again the shaken head and the burning caress.

"Then you shall be Ruth; will you keep that name?"

"Yes, if you give me the name I will keep it for you."

Time had indeed taken them by the forelock, and they looked upon a ruddled world.

"I stake my one talent," he said jestingly, "and behold it returns me fortyfold; I feel like the boy who catches three mice with one piece of cheese."

At ten o'clock the girl said:

"I must go and see how *they* are getting on," and she went to the door.

"Are we keeping them up?"

She nodded.

"Are you tired?"

"No, I am not tired."

She looked at him doubtfully.

"We ought not to stay in here; go into the coffee-room and I'll come there in a few minutes."

"Right," he whispered gaily, "we'll sit up all night."

She stood at the door for him to pass out, and he crossed the hall to the other room. It was in darkness except for the flash of the fire. Standing at the hearth he lit a match for the lamp, but paused at the globe; then he extinguished the match.

"No, it's better to sit in the firelight."

He heard voices at the other end of the house that seemed to have a chiding note in them.

"Lord," he thought, "she is getting into a row?"

Then her steps came echoing over the stone floors of the hall; she opened the door and stood there with a lighted candle in her hand; he stood at the other end of the room, smiling.

"Good night," she said.

"Oh no, no! come along," he protested, but not moving from the hearth.

"Got to go to bed," she answered.

"Are they angry with you?"

"No."

"Well, then, come over here and sit down."

"Got to go to bed," she said again, but she had meanwhile put her candlestick upon the little sideboard and was trimming the wick with a burnt match.

"Oh, come along, just half an hour," he protested. She did not answer but went on prodding the wick of the candle.

"Ten minutes, then," he said, still not going towards her.

"Five minutes," he begged.

She shook her head, and picking up the candlestick turned to the door. He did not move, he just called her name: "Ruth!"

She came back then, put down the candlestick and tiptoed across the room until he met her. The bliss of the embrace was so poignant that he was almost glad when she stood up again and said with affected steadiness, though he heard the tremor in her voice:

"I must get you your candle."

She brought one from the hall, set it on the table in front of him, and struck the match.

"What is my number?" he asked.

"Number six room," she answered, prodding the wick vaguely with her match, while a slip of white wax dropped over the shoulder of the new candle. "Number six . . . next to mine."

The match burnt out; she said abruptly "Good night," took up her own candle and left him there.

In a few moments he ascended the stairs and went into his room. He fastened the door, removed his coat, collar, and slippers, but the rack of passion had seized him and he moved about with no inclination to sleep. He sat down, but there was no medium of distraction. He tried to read the newspaper which he had carried up with him, and without realizing a single phrase, he forced himself to read again the whole account of the execution of the miscreant Bridger. When he had finished this he carefully folded the paper and stood up, listening. He went to the parting wall and tapped thereon with his finger-tips. He waited half a minute, one minute, two minutes; there was no answering sign. He tapped again, more loudly, with his knuckles, but there was no response, and he tapped many times. He opened his door as noiselessly as possible; along the dark passage there were slips of light under the other doors, the one next his own, and the one beyond that. He stood in the corridor listening to the rumble of old voices in the farther room, the old man and his wife going to their rest. Holding his breath fearfully, he stepped to *her* door and tapped gently upon it. There was no answer, but he could somehow divine her awareness of him; he tapped again; she moved to the door and whispered, "No, no, go away." He turned the handle, the door was locked.

"Let me in," he pleaded. He knew she was standing there an inch or two beyond him.

"Hush," she called softly. "Go away, the old woman has ears like a fox."

He stood silent for a moment.

"Unlock it," he urged; but he got no further reply, and feeling foolish and baffled he moved back to his own room, cast his clothes from him, doused the candle and crept into the bed with soul as wild as a storm-swept forest, his heart beating a vagrant summons. The room filled with strange heat, there was no composure for mind or limb, nothing but flaming visions and furious embraces.

"Morality . . . what is it but agreement with your own soul?"

So he lay for two hours—the clocks chimed twelve—listening with foolish persistency for *her* step along the corridor, fancying every light sound—and the night was full of them—was her hand upon the door.

Suddenly—and then it seemed as if his very heart would abash the house with its thunder—he could hear distinctly some one knocking on the wall. He got quickly from his bed and stood at the door, listening. Again the knocking was heard, and having half clothed himself he crept into the passage, which was now in utter darkness, trailing his hand along the wall until he felt her door; it was standing open. He entered her room and closed the door behind him. There was not the faintest gleam of light, he could see nothing. He whispered "Ruth!" and she was standing there. She touched him, but not speaking. He put out his hands, and they met round her neck; her hair was flowing in its great wave about her; he put his lips to her face and found that her eyes were streaming with tears, salt and strange and disturbing. In the close darkness he put his arms about her with no thought but to comfort her; one hand had plunged through the long harsh tresses and the other across her hips before he realized that she was ungowned; then he was aware of the softness of her breasts and the cold

naked sleekness of her shoulders. But she was crying there, crying silently with great tears, her strange sorrow stifling his desire.

"Ruth, Ruth, my beautiful dear!" he murmured soothingly. He felt
for the bed with one hand, and turning back the quilt and sheets he
lifted her in as easily as a mother does her child, replaced the bedding,
and, in his clothes, he lay stretched beside her comforting her. They
lay so, innocent as children, for an hour, when she seemed to have
gone to sleep. He rose then and went silently to his room, full of
weariness.

In the morning he breakfasted without seeing her, but as he had
business in the world that gave him just an hour longer at the inn
before he left it for good and all, he went into the smoke-room and
found her. She greeted him with curious gaze, but merrily enough, for
there were other men there now, farmers, a butcher, a registrar, an
old, old man. The hour passed, but not these men, and at length he
donned his coat, took up his stick, and said good-bye. Her shining
glances followed him to the door, and from the window as far as they
could view him.

W. F. HARVEY

The five stories that follow are grouped together because they illustrate as many different ways of manipulating outré themes.

The first of them is a horror story and I think a masterpiece of its kind.

When man is totally religionless such themes as Mr. Harvey's and the one you'll find in "Lord Mountdrago," a few pages further on, will disappear from literature, but not till then. Stories using them are as old as man's sense of wonder and fear. They emerge out of that sense even when they are playful, or mechanical, or vulgar. Every tribe, every race, every nation produces such stories and will continue to produce them until man either knows everything or has convinced himself that he does.

They appeal equally to the sophisticated mind—Henry James and Edith Wharton wrote superb horror stories—and to the naïf who revels in Superman. They have a double function. They give us a pleasurable shiver, for one thing. And they liberate us from our daily bondage to the probable.

W. F. Harvey's "August Heat" is what is known as a trick story. Its effect depends entirely on a completely impossible plot in which for ten minutes or so you are asked to believe. It differs from most other trick stories in that a second or third reading causes you to admire it more rather than less. You may not get from a rereading the cold, startled thrill that I think it gives you the first time, but you will get an extra pleasure from observing its flawless construction and the extraordinary economy of the style.

The excessive use of coincidence generally weakens a narrative. Here is one composed of nothing but coincidence, and how Mr. Harvey gets away with it!

Readers of Dunne's Experiment with Time or those who have come across his theories in J. B. Priestley's wonder-eyed popularizations will note how ingeniously Mr. Harvey uses the theme of pre-

cognition and plays upon that weird feeling we have all experienced
of something having happened to us before.

It is only honest to say that I discovered this story in Alexander
Laing's excellent collection of horror tales, The Haunted Omnibus.
For one anthologist to steal from another is at best a form of laziness.
I hope I will be forgiven simply on the ground that "August Heat" is
a whacking good story and should be introduced to as many readers
as possible.

August Heat

BY

W. F. HARVEY

PHENISTONE ROAD, CLAPHAM,
AUGUST 20TH, 19—. I have had what I believe to be the most remarkable day in my life, and while the events are still fresh in my mind, I wish to put them down on paper as clearly as possible.

Let me say at the outset that my name is James Clarence Withencroft.

I am forty years old, in perfect health, never having known a day's illness.

By profession I am an artist, not a very successful one, but I earn enough money by my black-and-white work to satisfy my necessary wants.

My only near relative, a sister, died five years ago, so that I am independent.

I breakfasted this morning at nine, and after glancing through the morning paper I lighted my pipe and proceeded to let my mind wander in the hope that I might chance upon some subject for my pencil.

The room, though door and windows were open, was oppressively hot, and I had just made up my mind that the coolest and most comfortable place in the neighbourhood would be the deep end of the public swimming bath, when the idea came.

I began to draw. So intent was I on my work that I left my lunch untouched, only stopping work when the clock of St. Jude's struck four.

The final result, for a hurried sketch, was, I felt sure, the best thing I had done.

It showed a criminal in the dock immediately after the judge had pronounced sentence. The man was fat—enormously fat. The flesh hung in rolls about his chin; it creased his huge, stumpy neck. He was clean shaven (perhaps I should say a few days before he must have been clean shaven) and almost bald. He stood in the dock, his short, clumsy fingers clasping the rail, looking straight in front of him. The feeling that his expression conveyed was not so much one of horror as of utter, absolute collapse.

There seemed nothing in the man strong enough to sustain that mountain of flesh.

I rolled up the sketch, and without quite knowing why, placed it in my pocket. Then with the rare sense of happiness which the knowledge of a good thing well done gives, I left the house.

I believe that I set out with the idea of calling upon Trenton, for I remember walking along Lytton Street and turning to the right along Gilchrist Road at the bottom of the hill where the men were at work on the new tram lines.

From there onwards I have only the vaguest recollections of where I went. The one thing of which I was fully conscious was the awful heat, that came up from the dusty asphalt pavement as an almost palpable wave. I longed for the thunder promised by the great banks of copper-coloured cloud that hung low over the western sky.

I must have walked five or six miles, when a small boy roused me from my reverie by asking the time.

It was twenty minutes to seven.

When he left me I began to take stock of my bearings. I found myself standing before a gate that led into a yard bordered by a strip of thirsty earth, where there were flowers, purple stock and scarlet geranium. Above the entrance was a board with the inscription—

CHS. ATKINSON   MONUMENTAL MASON
WORKER IN ENGLISH AND ITALIAN MARBLES

From the yard itself came a cheery whistle, the noise of hammer blows, and the cold sound of steel meeting stone.

A sudden impulse made me enter.

A man was sitting with his back towards me, busy at work on a slab of curiously veined marble. He turned round as he heard my steps and stopped short.

It was the man I had been drawing, whose portrait lay in my pocket.

He sat there, huge and elephantine, the sweat pouring from his scalp, which he wiped with a red silk handkerchief. But though the face was the same, the expression was absolutely different.

He greeted me smiling, as if we were old friends, and shook my hand.

I apologised for my intrusion.

"Everything is hot and glary outside," I said. "This seems an oasis in the wilderness."

"I don't know about the oasis," he replied, "but it certainly is hot, as hot as hell. Take a seat, sir!"

He pointed to the end of the gravestone on which he was at work, and I sat down.

"That's a beautiful piece of stone you've got hold of," I said.

He shook his head. "In a way it is," he answered; "the surface here is as fine as anything you could wish, but there's a big flaw at the back, though I don't expect you'd ever notice it. I could never make really a good job of a bit of marble like that. It would be all right in the summer like this; it wouldn't mind the blasted heat. But wait till the winter comes. There's nothing quite like frost to find out the weak points in stone."

"Then what's it for?" I asked.

The man burst out laughing.

"You'd hardly believe me if I was to tell you it's for an exhibition, but it's the truth. Artists have exhibitions: so do grocers and butchers; we have them too. All the latest little things in headstones, you know."

He went on to talk of marbles, which sort best withstood wind and rain, and which were easiest to work; then of his garden and a new sort of carnation he had bought. At the end of every other minute he would drop his tools, wipe his shining head, and curse the heat.

I said little, for I felt uneasy. There was something unnatural, uncanny, in meeting this man.

I tried at first to persuade myself that I had seen him before, that his face, unknown to me, had found a place in some out-of-the-way corner of my memory, but I knew that I was practicing little more than a plausible piece of self-deception.

Mr. Atkinson finished his work, spat on the ground, and got up with a sigh of relief.

"There! what do you think of that?" he said, with an air of evident pride.

The inscription which I read for the first time was this—

SACRED TO THE MEMORY
OF
JAMES CLARENCE WITHENCROFT.
BORN JAN. 18TH, 1860.
HE PASSED AWAY VERY SUDDENLY
ON AUGUST 20TH, 19—
"In the midst of life we are in death."

For some time I sat in silence. Then a cold shudder ran down my spine. I asked him where he had seen the name.

"Oh, I didn't see it anywhere," replied Mr. Atkinson. "I wanted some name, and I put down the first that came into my head. Why do you want to know?"

"It's a strange coincidence, but it happens to be mine."

He gave a long, low whistle.

"And the dates?"

"I can only answer for one of them, and that's correct."

"It's a rum go!" he said.

But he knew less than I did. I told him of my morning's work. I took the sketch from my pocket and showed it to him. As he looked, the expression of his face altered until it became more and more like that of the man I had drawn.

"And it was only the day before yesterday," he said, "that I told Maria there were no such things as ghosts!"

Neither of us had seen a ghost, but I knew what he meant.

"You probably heard my name," I said.

"And you must have seen me somewhere and have forgotten it! Were you at Clacton-on-Sea last July?"

I had never been to Clacton in my life. We were silent for some time. We were both looking at the same thing, the two dates on the gravestone, and one was right.

"Come inside and have some supper," said Mr. Atkinson.

His wife is a cheerful little woman, with the flaky red cheeks of the country-bred. Her husband introduced me as a friend of his who was an artist. The result was unfortunate, for after the sardines and water-cress had been removed, she brought me out a Doré Bible, and I had to sit and express my admiration for nearly half an hour.

I went outside, and found Atkinson sitting on the gravestone smoking.

We resumed the conversation at the point we had left off.

"You must excuse my asking," I said, "but do you know of anything you've done for which you could be put on trial?"

He shook his head.

"I'm not a bankrupt, the business is prosperous enough. Three years ago I gave turkeys to some of the guardians at Christmas, but that's all I can think of. And they were small ones, too," he added as an afterthought.

He got up, fetched a can from the porch, and began to water the flowers. "Twice a day regular in the hot weather," he said, "and then the heat sometimes gets the better of the delicate ones. And ferns, good Lord! they could never stand it. Where do you live?"

I told him my address. It would take an hour's quick walk to get back home.

"It's like this," he said. "We'll look at the matter straight. If you go back home to-night, you take your chance of accidents. A cart may run over you, and there's always banana skins and orange peel, to say nothing of fallen ladders."

He spoke of the improbable with an intense seriousness that would have been laughable six hours before. But I did not laugh.

"The best thing we can do," he continued, "is for you to stay here till twelve o'clock. We'll go upstairs and smoke; it may be cooler inside."

To my surprise I agreed.

We are sitting in a long, low room beneath the eaves. Atkinson has sent his wife to bed. He himself is busy sharpening some tools at a little oilstone, smoking one of my cigars the while.

The air seems charged with thunder. I am writing this at a shaky table before the open window. The leg is cracked, and Atkinson, who seems a handy man with his tools, is going to mend it as soon as he has finished putting an edge on his chisel.

It is after eleven now. I shall be gone in less than an hour.

But the heat is stifling.

It is enough to send a man mad.

MAX BEERBOHM

Max Beerbohm's "James Pethel" is not by any exact definition a horror story, nor does it make use of the supernatural. But it is so odd and chilling a tale, despite the elegant air with which it is told, that I include it here in my miniature collection of the literature of the outré. It employs, though in a very different way, the theme that lies back of "August Heat"—predestination. For Pethel is simply a man who gambles with destiny.

"James Pethel" is one of the tales to be found in Beerbohm's Seven Men. There are five tales in this book, about six men. The seventh is the narrator himself, the Incomparable Max. These stories have been severally reprinted by a generation of anthologists—Seven Men was published in 1919—but the volume itself, for some reason, masterpiece though it is, has not had a very wide circulation. I suppose this is because Beerbohm suffers from having identified himself too perfectly with the Yellow Book period. People think of him as sadly dated. Some of him is, but not Seven Men, and not this story of James Pethel.

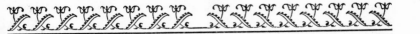

James Pethel

BY

MAX BEERBOHM

September 17, 1912

THOUGH SEVEN YEARS have gone by since the day when last I saw him, and though that day was but the morrow of my first meeting with him, I was shocked when I saw in my newspaper this morning the announcement of his sudden death.

I had formed, in the dim past, the habit of spending August in Dieppe. The place was less popular then than it is now. Some pleasant English people shared it with some pleasant French people. We used rather to resent the race-week—the third week of the month—as an intrusion on our privacy. We sneered as we read in the Paris edition of the *New York Herald* the names of the intruders. We disliked the nightly crush in the baccarat room of the Casino, and the croupiers' obvious excitement at the high play. I made a point of avoiding that room during that week, for the especial reason that the sight of serious, habitual gamblers has always filled me with a depression bordering on disgust. Most of the men, by some subtle stress of their ruling passion, have grown so monstrously fat, and most of the women so harrowingly thin. The rest of the women seem to be marked out for apoplexy, and the rest of the men to be wasting away. One feels that anything thrown at them would be either embedded or shattered, and looks vainly among them for a person furnished with the normal amount of flesh. Monsters they are, all of them, to the eye (though I believe that many of them have excellent moral qualities in private life); but, just as in an American town one goes sooner or later—goes against one's finer judgment, but somehow goes—into the dime-museums, so, year by year, in Dieppe's race-week, there would be always one evening when I drifted into the baccarat room. It was on such an evening that I first saw the man whose memory I here celebrate. My gaze was held by him for the very reason that he would have passed unnoticed elsewhere. He was conspicuous, not in virtue of the mere fact that he was taking the bank at the principal table, but because there was nothing at all odd about him.

Between his lips was a cigar of moderate size. Everything about him, except the amount of money he had been winning, seemed moderate. Just as he was neither fat nor thin, so had his face neither that extreme pallor nor that extreme redness which belongs to the faces of seasoned gamblers: it was just a clear pink. And his eyes had neither the unnatural brightness nor the unnatural dullness of the eyes around him: they were ordinarily clear eyes, of an ordinary grey. His very age was moderate: a putative thirty-six, not more ("Not less," I would have said in those days.) He assumed no air of nonchalance. He did not deal out the cards as though they bored him. But he had no look of grim concentration. I noticed that the removal of his cigar from his mouth made never the least difference to his face, for he kept his lips pursed out as steadily as ever when he was not smoking. And this constant pursing of his lips seemed to denote just a pensive interest.

His bank was nearly done now. There were but a few cards left. Opposite to him was a welter of parti-coloured counters which the croupier had not yet had time to sort out and add to the rouleaux already made; there were also a fair accumulation of notes and several little stacks of gold. In all, not less than five hundred pounds, certainly. Happy banker! How easily had he won in a few minutes more than I, with utmost pains, could earn in many months! I wished I were he. His lucre seemed to insult me personally. I disliked him. And yet I hoped he would not take another bank. I hoped he would have the good sense to pocket his winnings and go home. Deliberately to risk the loss of all those riches would intensify the insult to myself.

"Messieurs, la banque est aux enchères!" There was some brisk bidding, while the croupier tore open and shuffled the two packs. But it was as I feared: the gentleman whom I resented kept his place.

"Messieurs, la banque est faite. Quinze mille francs à la banque. Messieurs, les cartes passent! Messieurs, les cartes passent!"

Turning to go, I encountered a friend—one of the race-weekers, but in a sense a friend.

"Going to play?" I asked.

"Not while Jimmy Pethel's taking the bank," he answered, with a laugh.

"Is that the man's name?"

"Yes. Don't you know him? I thought every one knew old Jimmy Pethel."

I asked what there was so wonderful about "old Jimmy Pethel" that every one should be supposed to know him.

"Oh, he's a great character. Has extraordinary luck. Always."

I do not think my friend was versed in the pretty theory that good luck is the unconscious wisdom of them who in previous incarnations have been consciously wise. He was a member of the Stock Exchange, and I smiled as at a certain quaintness in his remark. I asked in what ways besides luck the "great character" was manifested. Oh, well, Pethel had made a huge "scoop" on the Stock Exchange when he was only twenty-three, and very soon doubled that, and doubled it again; then retired. He wasn't more than thirty-five now. And? Oh, well, he was a regular all-round sportsman—had gone after big game all over the world and had a good many narrow shaves. Great steeple-chaser, too. Rather settled down now. Lived in Leicestershire mostly. Had a big place there. Hunted five times a week. Still did an occasional flutter, though. Cleared eighty thousand in Mexicans last February. Wife had been a bar-maid at Cambridge. Married her when he was nineteen. Thing seemed to have turned out quite well. Altogether, a great character.

Possibly, thought I. But my cursory friend, accustomed to quick transactions and to things accepted "on the nod," had not proved his case to my slower, more literary intelligence. It was to him, however, that I owed, some minutes later, a chance of testing his opinion. At the cry of "Messieurs, la banque est aux enchères" we looked round and saw that the subject of our talk was preparing to rise from his place. "Now one can punt!" said Grierson (this was my friend's name), and turned to the bureau at which counters are for sale. "If old Jimmy Pethel punts," he added, "I shall just follow his luck." But this lodestar was not to be. While my friend was buying his counters, and I wondering whether I too would buy some, Pethel himself came up to the bureau. With his lips no longer pursed, he had lost his air of gravity, and looked younger. Behind him was an attendant bearing a big wooden bowl—that plain but romantic bowl supplied by the establishment to a banker whose gains are too great to be pocketed. He and Grierson greeted each other. He said he had arrived in Dieppe this afternoon—was here for a day or two. We were introduced. He spoke to me with some *empressement,* saying he was a "very great admirer" of my work. I no longer disliked him. Grierson, armed with counters, had now darted away to secure a place that had just been vacated. Pethel, with a wave of his hand towards the tables, said, "I suppose you never condescend to this sort of thing?"

"Well—" I smiled indulgently.

"Awful waste of time," he admitted.

I glanced down at the splendid mess of counters and gold and notes that were now becoming, under the swift fingers of the little man at the bureau, an orderly array. I did not say aloud that it pleased me to be, and to be seen, talking on terms of equality, to a man who had won so much. I did not say how wonderful it seemed to me that he, whom I had watched just now with awe and with aversion, had all the while been a great admirer of my work. I did but say (again indulgently) that I supposed baccarat to be as good a way of wasting time as another.

"Ah, but you despise us all the same!" He added that he always envied men who had resources within themselves. I laughed lightly, to imply that it *was* very pleasant to have such resources, but that I didn't want to boast. And indeed, I had never, I vow, felt flimsier than when the little man at the bureau, naming a fabulous sum, asked its owner whether he would take the main part in notes of mille francs? cinq mille? dix mille? quoi? Had it been mine, I should have asked to have it all in five-franc pieces. Pethel took it in the most compendious form and crumpled it into a pocket. I asked if he were going to play any more to-night.

"Oh, later on," he said. "I want to get a little sea-air into my lungs now"; and he asked with a sort of breezy diffidence if I would go with him. I was glad to do so. It flashed across my mind that yonder on the terrace he might suddenly blurt out, "I say, look here, don't think me awfully impertinent, but this money's no earthly use to me: I do wish you'd accept it, as a very small return for all the pleasure your work has given me, and . . . *There!* PLEASE! Not another word!" —all with such candour, delicacy, and genuine zeal that I should be unable to refuse. But I must not raise false hopes in my reader. Nothing of the sort happened. Nothing of that sort ever does happen.

We were not long on the terrace. It was not a night on which you could stroll and talk: there was a wind against which you had to stagger, holding your hat on tightly and shouting such remarks as might occur to you. Against that wind acquaintance could make no headway. Yet I see now that despite that wind—or rather because of it—I ought already to have known Pethel a little better than I did when we presently sat down together inside the café of the Casino. There had been a point in our walk, or our stagger, when we paused to lean over the parapet, looking down at the black and driven sea. And Pethel had shouted that it would be great fun to be out in a sailing-boat to-night and that at one time he had been very fond of sailing.

As we took our seats in the café, he looked around him with boyish interest and pleasure. Then, squaring his arms on the little table, he asked me what I would drink. I protested that I was the host—a position which he, with the quick courtesy of the very rich, yielded to me at once. I feared he would ask for champagne, and was gladdened by his demand for water. "Apollinaris? St. Galmier? Or what?" I asked. He preferred plain water. I felt bound to warn him that such water was never "safe" in these places. He said he had often heard that, but would risk it. I remonstrated, but he was firm. "Alors," I told the waiter, "pour Monsieur un verre d'eau fraîche, et pour moi un demi blonde." Pethel asked me to tell him who every one was. I told him no one was any one in particular, and suggested that we should talk about ourselves. "You mean," he laughed, "that you want to know who the devil I am?" I assured him that I had often heard of him. At this he was unaffectedly pleased. "But," I added, "it's always more interesting to hear a man talked about by himself." And indeed, since he had *not* handed his winnings over to me, I did hope he would at any rate give me some glimpses into that "great character" of his. Full though his life had been, he seemed but like a rather clever schoolboy out on a holiday. I wanted to know more.

"That beer does look good," he admitted when the waiter came back. I asked him to change his mind. But he shook his head, raised to his lips the tumbler of water that had been placed before him, and meditatively drank a deep draught. "I never," he then said, "touch alcohol of any sort." He looked solemn; but all men do look solemn when they speak of their own habits, whether positive or negative, and no matter how trivial; and so (though I had really no warrant for not supposing him a reclaimed drunkard) I dared ask him for what reason he abstained.

"When I say I *never* touch alcohol," he said hastily, in a tone as of self-defence, "I mean that I don't touch it often—or at any rate—well, I never touch it when I'm *gambling,* you know. It—it takes the edge off."

His tone did make me suspicious. For a moment I wondered whether he had married the barmaid rather for what she symbolised than for what in herself she was. But no, surely not: he had been only nineteen years old. Nor in any way had he now—this steady, brisk, clear-eyed fellow—the aspect of one who had since fallen. "The edge off the excitement?" I asked.

"Rather! Of course that sort of excitement seems awfully stupid to *you.* But—no use denying it—I do like a bit of a flutter—just occasionally, you know. And one has to be in trim for it. Suppose a man sat down dead drunk to a game of chance, what fun would it be for him? None. And it's only a question of degree. Soothe yourself ever so little with alcohol, and you don't get *quite* the full sensation of gambling. You do lose just a little something of the proper tremors before a coup, the proper throes during a coup, the proper thrill of joy or anguish after a coup. . . . You're bound to, you know," he added, purposely making this bathos when he saw me smiling at the heights to which he had risen.

"And to-night," I asked, remembering his prosaically pensive demeanour in taking the bank, "were you feeling these throes and thrills to the utmost?"

He nodded.

"And you'll feel them again to-night?"

"I hope so."

"I wonder you can stay away."

"Oh, one gets a bit deadened after an hour or so. One needs to be freshened up. So long as I don't bore you——"

I laughed, and held out my cigarette-case. "I rather wonder you smoke," I murmured, after giving him a light. "Nicotine's a sort of drug. Doesn't it soothe you? Don't you lose just a little something of the tremors and things?"

He looked at me gravely. "By Jove," he ejaculated, "I never thought of that. Perhaps you're right. 'Pon my word, I must think that over."

I wondered whether he were secretly laughing at me. Here was a man to whom (so I conceived, with an effort of the imagination) the loss or gain of a few hundred pounds could not matter. I told him I had spoken in jest. "To give up tobacco might," I said, "intensify the pleasant agonies of a gambler staking his little all. But in your case—well, frankly, I don't see where the pleasant agonies come in."

"You mean because I'm beastly rich?"

"Rich," I amended.

"All depends on what you call rich. Besides, I'm not the sort of fellow who's content with 3 per cent. A couple of months ago—I tell you this in confidence—I risked practically all I had, in an Argentine deal."

"And lost it?"

"No, as a matter of fact I made rather a good thing out of it. I did rather well last February, too. But there's no knowing the future. A few errors of judgment—a war here, a revolution there, a big strike somewhere else, and—" He blew a jet of smoke from his lips, and looked at me as at one whom he could trust to feel for him in a crash already come.

My sympathy lagged, and I stuck to the point of my inquiry. "Meanwhile," I suggested, "and all the more because you aren't merely a rich man, but also an active taker of big risks, how can these tiny little baccarat risks give you so much emotion?"

"There you rather have me," he laughed. "I've often wondered at that myself. I suppose," he puzzled it out, "I do a good lot of make-believe. While I'm playing a game like this game to-night, I *imagine* the stakes are huge, and I *imagine* I haven't another penny in the world."

"Ah! So that with you it's always a life-and-death affair?"

He looked away. "Oh, no, I don't say that."

"Stupid phrase," I admitted. "But," there was yet one point I would put to him, "if you have extraordinary luck—always——"

"There's no such thing as luck."

"No, strictly, I suppose, there isn't. But if in point of fact you always do win, then—well, surely, perfect luck driveth out fear?"

"Who ever said I always won?" he asked sharply.

I waved my hands and said, "Oh, you have the reputation, you know, for extraordinary luck."

"That isn't the same thing as always winning. Besides, I *haven't* extraordinary luck—never *have* had. Good heavens," he exclaimed, "if I thought I had any more chance of winning than of losing, I'd—I'd——"

"Never again set foot in that baccarat room to-night," I soothingly suggested.

"Oh, baccarat be blowed! I wasn't thinking of baccarat. I was thinking of—oh, lots of things; baccarat included, yes."

"What things?" I ventured to ask.

"What things?" He pushed back his chair, and "Look here," he said with a laugh, "don't pretend I haven't been boring your head off with all this talk about myself. You've been too patient. I'm off. Shall I see you to-morrow? Perhaps you'd lunch with us to-morrow? It would be a great pleasure for my wife. We're at the Hôtel Royal."

I said I should be most happy, and called the waiter; at sight of whom my friend said he had talked himself thirsty, and asked for another glass of water. He mentioned that he had brought his car over with him: his little daughter (by the news of whose existence I felt idiotically surprised) was very keen on motoring, and they were all three starting the day after to-morrow for "a spin through France." Afterwards, they were going on to Switzerland, "for some climbing." Did I care about motoring? If so, we might go for a spin after luncheon, to Rouen or somewhere? He drank his glass of water, and, linking a friendly arm in mine, passed out with me into the corridor. He asked what I was writing now, and said that he looked to me to "do something big, one of these days," and that he was sure I had it "in" me. This remark (though of course I pretended to be pleased by it) irritated me very much. It was destined, as you shall see, to irritate me very much more in recollection.

Yet was I glad he had asked me to luncheon. Glad because I liked him, glad because I dislike mysteries. Though you may think me very dense for not having thoroughly understood Pethel in the course of my first meeting with him, the fact is that I was only conscious, and that dimly, of something more in him than he had cared to reveal—some veil behind which perhaps lurked his right to the title so airily bestowed on him by Grierson. I assured myself, as I walked home, that if veil there were I should to-morrow find an eyelet.

But one's intuition when it is off duty seems always so much more powerful an engine than it does on active service; and next day, at sight of Pethel awaiting me outside his hotel, I became less confident. His, thought I, was a face which, for all its animation, would tell nothing—nothing, at any rate, that mattered. It expressed well enough that he was pleased to see me; but for the rest, I was reminded, it had a sort of frank inscrutability. Besides, it was at all points so very usual a face—a face that couldn't (so I then thought), even if it had leave to, betray connexion with a "great character." It was a strong face, certainly. But so are yours and mine.

And very fresh it looked, though, as he confessed, Pethel had sat up in "that beastly baccarat room" till 5 A.M. I asked, had he lost? Yes, he had lost steadily for four hours (proudly he laid stress on this), but in the end—well (he admitted), he had won it all back "and a bit more." "By the way," he murmured as we were about to enter the hall, "don't ever happen to mention to my wife what I told you about that Argentine deal. She's always rather nervous about—investments.

I don't tell her about them. She's rather a nervous woman altogether, I'm sorry to say."

This did not square with my preconception of her. Slave that I am to traditional imagery, I had figured her as "flaunting," as golden-haired, as haughty to most men but with a provocative smile across the shoulder for some. Nor indeed did her husband's words prevent me from the suspicion that my eyes deceived me when anon I was presented to a very pale small lady whose hair was rather white than grey. And the "little daughter"! This prodigy's hair was as yet "down," but looked as if it might be up at any moment: she was nearly as tall as her father, whom she very much resembled in face and figure and heartiness of hand-shake. Only after a rapid mental calculation could I account for her. "I must warn you, she's in a great rage this morning," said her father. "Do try to soothe her." She blushed, laughed, and bade her father not be so silly. I asked her the cause of her great rage. She said, "He only means I was disappointed. And he was just as disappointed as I was. Weren't you, now, Father?"

"I suppose they meant well, Peggy," he laughed.

"They were *quite* right," said Mrs. Pethel, evidently not for the first time.

"They," as I presently learned, were the authorities of the bathing establishment. Pethel had promised his daughter he would take her for a swim; but on their arrival at the bathing-cabins they were ruthlessly told that bathing was "défendu à cause du mauvais temps." This embargo was our theme as we sat down to luncheon. Miss Peggy was of opinion that the French were cowards. I pleaded for them that even in English watering-places bathing was forbidden when the sea was *very* rough. She did not admit that the sea was very rough to-day. Besides, she appealed to me, what was the fun of swimming in absolutely calm water? I dared not say that this was the only sort of water I liked to swim in. "They were *quite* right," said Mrs. Pethel yet again.

"Yes, but, darling Mother, you can't swim. Father and I are both splendid swimmers."

To gloze over the mother's disability, I looked brightly at Pethel, as though in ardent recognition of his prowess among waves. With a

movement of his head he indicated his daughter—indicated that there
was no one like her in the whole world. I beamed agreement. Indeed,
I did think her rather nice. If one liked the father (and I liked Pethel
all the more in that capacity), one couldn't help liking the daughter;
the two were so absurdly alike. Whenever he was looking at her (and
it was seldom that he looked away from her) the effect, if you cared
to be fantastic, was that of a very vain man before a mirror. It might
have occurred to me that, if there were any mystery in him, I could
solve it through her. But, in point of fact, I had forgotten all about
that possible mystery. The amateur detective was lost in the sympathetic observer of a father's love. That Pethel did love his daughter I
have never doubted. One passion is not less true because another pre-
dominates. No one who ever saw that father with that daughter could
doubt that he loved her intensely. And this intensity gauges for me
the strength of what else was in him.

Mrs. Pethel's love, though less explicit, was not less evidently profound. But the maternal instinct is less attractive to an onlooker, because he takes it more for granted, than the paternal. What endeared
poor Mrs. Pethel to me was—well, the inevitability of the epithet I
give her. She seemed, poor thing, so essentially out of it; and by "it"
is meant the glowing mutual affinity of husband and child. Not that
she didn't, in her little way, assert herself during the meal. But she
did so, I thought, with the knowledge that she didn't count, and never
would count. I wondered how it was that she had, in that Cambridge
bar-room long ago, counted for Pethel to the extent of matrimony.
But from any such room she seemed so utterly remote that she might
well be in all respects now an utterly changed woman. She did pre-
eminently look as if much had by some means been taken out of her,
with no compensatory process of putting in. Pethel looked so very
young for his age, whereas she would have had to be quite old to look
young for hers. I pitied her as one might a governess with two charges
who were hopelessly out of hand. But a governess, I reflected, can
always give notice. Love tied poor Mrs. Pethel fast to her present
situation.

As the three of them were to start next day on their tour through
France, and as the four of us were to make a tour to Rouen this after-

noon, the talk was much about motoring—a theme which Miss Peggy's enthusiasm made almost tolerable. I said to Mrs. Pethel, with more good-will than truth, that I supposed she was "very keen on it." She replied that she was.

"But darling Mother, you aren't. I believe you *hate* it. You're *always* asking Father to go slower. And what *is* the fun of just crawling along?"

"Oh, come, Peggy, we never crawl," said her father.

"No, indeed," said her mother, in a tone of which Pethel laughingly said it would put me off coming out with them this afternoon. I said, with an expert air to reassure Mrs. Pethel, that it wasn't fast driving, but only bad driving, that was a danger. "There, Mother!" cried Peggy. "Isn't that what we're always telling you?"

I felt that they were always either telling Mrs. Pethel something or, as in the matter of that intended bath, not telling her something. It seemed to me possible that Peggy advised her father about his "investments." I wondered whether they had yet told Mrs. Pethel of their intention to go on to Switzerland for some climbing.

Of his secretiveness for his wife's sake I had a touching little instance after luncheon. We had adjourned to have coffee in front of the hotel. The car was already in attendance, and Peggy had darted off to make her daily inspection of it. Pethel had given me a cigar, and his wife presently noticed that he himself was not smoking. He explained to her that he thought he had smoked too much lately, and that he was going to "knock it off" for a while. I would not have smiled if he had met my eye. But his avoidance of it made me quite sure that he really had been "thinking over" what I had said last night about nicotine and its possibly deleterious action on the gambling thrill.

Mrs. Pethel saw the smile that I could not repress. I explained that I was wishing *I* could knock off tobacco, and envying her husband's strength of character. She smiled too, but wanly, with her eyes on him. "Nobody has so much strength of character as he has," she said.

"Nonsense!" he laughed. "I'm the weakest of men."

"Yes," she said quietly. "That's true, too, James."

Again he laughed, but he flushed. I saw that Mrs. Pethel also had faintly flushed; and I became horribly conscious of following suit. In the sudden glow and silence created by Mrs. Pethel's paradox, I was grateful to the daughter for bouncing back into our midst and asking how soon we should be ready to start.

Pethel looked at his wife, who looked at me and rather strangely asked if I were sure I wanted to go with them. I protested that of course I did. Pethel asked her if *she* really wanted to come: "You see, dear, there was the run yesterday from Calais. And to-morrow you'll be on the road again, and all the days after."

"Yes," said Peggy, "I'm *sure* you'd much rather stay at home, darling Mother, and have a good rest."

"Shall we go and put on our things, Peggy?" replied Mrs. Pethel, rising from her chair. She asked her husband whether he were taking the chauffeur with him. He said he thought not.

"Oh, hurrah!" cried Peggy. "Then I can be on the front seat!"

"No, dear," said her mother. "I am sure Mr. Beerbohm would like to be on the front seat."

"You'd like to be with Mother, wouldn't you?" the girl appealed. I replied with all possible emphasis that I should like to be with Mrs. Pethel. But presently, when the mother and daughter reappeared in the guise of motorists, it became clear that my aspiration had been set aside. "I am to be with Mother," said Peggy.

I was inwardly glad that Mrs. Pethel could, after all, assert herself to some purpose. Had I thought she disliked me, I should have been hurt; but I was sure her desire that I should not sit with her was due merely to a belief that a person on the front seat was less safe in case of accidents than a person behind. And of course I did not expect her to prefer my life to her daughter's. Poor lady! My heart was with her. As the car glided along the sea-front and then under the Norman archway, through the town and past the environs, I wished that her husband inspired in her as much confidence as he did in me. For me the sight of his clear, firm profile (he did not wear motor-goggles) was an assurance in itself. From time to time (for I too was ungoggled) I looked round to nod and smile cheerfully at his wife. She always returned the nod, but left the smile to be returned by the daughter.

Pethel, like the good driver he was, did not talk: just drove. But he did, as we came out on to the Rouen road, say that in France he always rather missed the British police-traps. "Not," he added, "that I've ever fallen into one. But the chance that a policeman *may* at any moment dart out, and land you in a bit of a scrape, does rather add to the excitement, don't you think?" Though I answered in the tone of one to whom the chance of a police-trap is the very salt of life, I did not inwardly like the spirit of his remark. However, I dismissed it from my mind; and the sun was shining, and the wind had dropped: it was an ideal day for motoring; and the Norman landscape had never looked lovelier to me in its width of sober and silvery grace.

I presently felt that this landscape was not, after all, doing itself full justice. Was it not rushing rather too quickly past? "James!" said a shrill, faint voice from behind; and gradually—"Oh, darling Mother, really!" protested another voice—the landscape slackened pace. But after a while, little by little, the landscape lost patience, forgot its good manners, and flew faster, and faster than before. The road rushed furiously beneath us, like a river in spate. Avenues of poplars flashed past us, every tree of them on either side hissing and swishing angrily in the draught we made. Motors going Rouen-wards seemed to be past as quickly as motors that bore down on us. Hardly had I espied in the landscape ahead a château or other object of interest before I was craning my neck round for a final glimpse of it as it faded on the backward horizon. An endless up-hill road was breasted and crested in a twinkling and transformed into a decline near the end of which our car leapt straight across to the opposite ascent, and—"James!" again, and again by degrees the laws of Nature were re-established, but again by degrees revoked. I didn't doubt that speed in itself was no danger; but when the road was about to make a sharp curve why shouldn't Pethel, just as a matter of form, slow down slightly and sound a note or two of the hooter? Suppose another car were—well, that was all right: the road was clear. But at the next turning, when our car neither slackened nor hooted and *was,* for an instant, full on the wrong side of the road, I had within me a contraction which (at thought of what must have been if . . .) lasted though all was well. Loth to betray fear, I hadn't turned my face to Pethel. Eyes front!

And how about that wagon ahead, huge hay-wagon plodding with its back to us, seeming to occupy the whole road? Surely Pethel would slacken, hoot? No. Imagine a needle threaded with one swift gesture from afar. Even so was it that we shot, between wagon and road's edge, through; whereon, confronting us within a few yards—inches now, but we swerved—was a cart, a cart that incredibly we grazed not as we rushed on, on. Now indeed had I turned my eyes on Pethel's profile. And my eyes saw there that which stilled, with a greater emotion, all fear and wonder in me.

I think that for the first instant, oddly, what I felt was merely satisfaction, not hatred; for I all but asked him whether by not smoking to-day he had got a keener edge to his thrills. I understood him, and for an instant this sufficed me. Those pursed-out lips, so queerly different from the compressed lips of the normal motorist, and seeming, as elsewhere last night, to denote no more than pensive interest, had told me suddenly all that I needed to know about Pethel. Here, as there—and oh, ever so much better here than there!—he could gratify the passion that was in him. No need of any "make-believe" here! I remembered the strange look he had given when I asked if his gambling were always "a life-and-death affair." Here was the real thing —the authentic game, for the highest stakes! And here was I, a little extra-stake tossed on to the board. He had vowed I had it "in" me to do "something big." Perhaps, though, there had been a touch of his make-believe about that. . . . I am afraid it was not before my thought about myself that my moral sense began to operate and my hatred of Pethel set in. But I claim that I did see myself as no more than a mere detail in his villainy. Nor, in my just wrath for other sakes, was I without charity even for him. I gave him due credit for risking his own life—for having doubtless risked it, it and none other, again and again in the course of his adventurous—and abstemious—life by field and flood. I was even rather touched by memory of his insistence last night on another glass of that water which just *might* give him typhoid; rather touched by memory of his unsaying that he "never" touched alcohol—he who, in point of fact, had to be *always* gambling on something or other. I gave him due credit, too, for his devotion to his daughter. But his use of that devotion, his cold use of it to secure

for himself the utmost thrill of gambling, did seem utterly abominable
to me.

And it was even more for the mother than for the daughter that I
was incensed. That daughter did not know him, did but innocently
share his damnable love of chances. But that wife had for years known
him at least as well as I knew him now. Here again, I gave him credit
for wishing, though he didn't love her, to spare her what he could.
That he didn't love her I presumed from his indubitable willingness
not to stake her in this afternoon's game. That he never had loved her
—had taken her, in his precocious youth, simply as a gigantic chance
against him—was likely enough. So much the more credit to him for
such consideration as he showed her; but little enough this was. He
could wish to save her from being a looker-on at his game; but he
could, he couldn't not, go on playing. Assuredly she was right in
deeming him at once the strongest and the weakest of men. "Rather a
nervous woman"! I remembered an engraving that had hung in my
room at Oxford—and in scores of other rooms there: a presentment
by Sir Marcus (then Mr.) Stone of a very pretty young person in a
Gainsborough hat, seated beneath an ancestral elm, looking as though
she were about to cry, and entitled "A Gambler's Wife." Mrs. Pethel
was not like that. Of her there were no engravings for undergraduate
hearts to melt at. But there was one man, certainly, whose compassion was very much at her service. How was he going to help her?

I know not how many hair's-breadth escapes we may have had
while these thoughts passed through my brain. I had closed my eyes.
So preoccupied was I that, but for the constant rush of air against my
face, I might, for aught I knew, have been sitting ensconced in an
arm-chair at home. After a while, I was aware that this rush had
abated; I opened my eyes to the old familiar streets of Rouen. We
were to have tea at the Hôtel d'Angleterre. What was to be my line
of action? Should I take Pethel aside and say "Swear to me, on your
word of honour as a gentleman, that you will never again touch the
driving-gear (or whatever you call it) of a motor-car. Otherwise I
shall expose you to the world. Meanwhile, we shall return to Dieppe
by train"? He might flush—for I knew him capable of flushing—as he
asked me to explain. And after? He would laugh in my face. He

would advise me not to go motoring any more. He might even warn me not to go back to Dieppe in one of those dangerous railway-trains. He might even urge me to wait until a nice Bath chair had been sent out for me from England. . . .

I heard a voice (mine, alas) saying brightly, "Well, here we are!" I helped the ladies to descend. Tea was ordered. Pethel refused that stimulant and had a glass of water. I had a liqueur brandy. It was evident to me that tea meant much to Mrs. Pethel. She looked stronger after her second cup, and younger after her third. Still, it was my duty to help her, if I could. While I talked and laughed, I did not forget that. But—what on earth was I to do? I am no hero. I hate to be ridiculous. I am inveterately averse from any sort of fuss. Besides, how was I to be sure that my own personal dread of the return-journey hadn't something to do with my intention of tackling Pethel? I thought it had. What this woman would dare daily because she was a mother, could not I dare once? I reminded myself of Pethel's reputation for invariable luck. I reminded myself that he was an extraordinarily skilful driver. To that skill and luck I would pin my faith. . . .

What I seem to myself, do you ask of me?

But I answered your question a few lines back. Enough that my faith was rewarded. We did reach Dieppe safely. I still marvel that we did.

That evening, in the vestibule of the Casino, Grierson came up to me: "Seen Jimmy Pethel? He was asking for you. Wants to see you particularly. He's in the baccarat room, punting—winning hand over fist, *of* course. Said he'd seldom met a man he liked more than you. Great character, what?" One is always glad to be liked, and I plead guilty to a moment's gratification at the announcement that Pethel liked me. But I did not go and seek him in the baccarat room. A great character assuredly he was; but of a kind with which (very imperfect though I am, and no censor) I prefer not to associate.

Why he had particularly wanted to see me was made clear in a note sent by him to my room early next morning. He wondered if I could be induced to join them in their little tour. He hoped I wouldn't think it great cheek, his asking me. He thought it might rather amuse me to come. It would be a very great pleasure for his wife. He hoped I wouldn't say No. Would I send a line by bearer? They would be starting at 3 o'clock. He was mine sincerely.

It was not too late to tackle him, even now. Should I go round to his hotel? I hesitated and—well, I told you at the outset that my last meeting with him was on the morrow of my first. I forget what I wrote to him, but am sure that the excuse I made for myself was a good and graceful one, and that I sent my kindest regards to Mrs. Pethel. She had not (I am sure of that, too) authorised her husband to say she would like me to come with them. Else would not the thought of her have haunted me so poignantly as for a long time it did. I do not know whether she is still alive. No mention is made of her in the obituary notice which woke these memories in me. This notice I will, however, transcribe, because (for all its crudeness of phraseology) it is rather interesting both as an echo and as an amplification. Its title is—"Death of Wealthy Aviator." Its text is—"Widespread regret will be felt in Leicestershire at the tragic death of Mr. James Pethel, who had long resided there and was very popular as an all-round sportsman. In recent years he had been much interested in aviation, and had become one of the most enthusiastic of amateur airmen. Yesterday afternoon he fell down dead quite suddenly as he was returning to his house, apparently in his usual health and spirits, after descending from a short flight which despite an extremely high wind he had made on his new biplane and on which he was accompanied by his married daughter and her infant son. It is not expected that an inquest will be necessary, as his physician, Dr. Saunders, has certified death to be due to heart-disease, from which, it appears, the deceased gentleman had been suffering for some years. Dr. Saunders adds that he had repeatedly warned deceased that any strain on the nervous system might prove fatal."

Thus—for I presume that his ailment had its origin in his habits—James Pethel did not, despite that merely pensive look of his, live his life with impunity. And by reason of that life he died. As for the manner of his death, enough that he did die. Let not our hearts be vexed that his great luck was with him to the end.

W. SOMERSET MAUGHAM

COMMENTARY

Every reviewer, if you give him enough to drink, will break down and confess that there are certain passages, in the books he reads, that he does not read. The most conscientious of us skips at times, perhaps without quite knowing it. I, for example, am quite capable of skipping, in a kind of blank trance, entire novels about the American Revolution. But even in books that interest me, there are things my eye skates over with the agility of a Sonja Henie.

Dreams, for one. Now, most people who have any iron in their nature refuse to listen to accounts of other people's dreams. The weaker ones, who do listen, might as well have stopped their ears. A says to B, "I had the queerest dream the other night," and relates it. "Make any sense out of that?" inquires A. "No," replies honest B. "Neither can I," concludes A thoughtfully. It is of such stuff and nonsense that dreams are made on.

When I come to a description of a dream in a book, I by-pass it. I have never yet found that I missed much. But this excellent rule has its exceptions, and one of them has to do with Somerset Maugham's spooky story, "Lord Mountdrago." The story is about nothing but dreams, about two men, indeed, who inhabit each other's dreams, and in my literature of the outré it gets high marks. Like "August Heat," it works with coincidence, and only coincidence, and, like Mr. Harvey, Mr. Maugham gets away with it. It is unlike his usual work and that is why I have placed it apart from the other Maugham stories included in this book. It isn't, I suppose, even remotely a work of literary art, but it is so remarkable a work of literary artfulness that I predict for it a long anthological life.

Lord Mountdrago

BY

W. SOMERSET MAUGHAM

Dr. Audlin looked at the clock on his desk. It was twenty minutes to six. He was surprised that his patient was late, for Lord Mountdrago prided himself on his punctuality; he had a sententious way of expressing himself which gave the air of an epigram to a commonplace remark, and he was in the habit of saying that punctuality is a compliment you pay to the intelligent and a rebuke you administer to the stupid. Lord Mountdrago's appointment was for five-thirty.

There was in Dr. Audlin's appearance nothing to attract attention. He was tall and spare, with narrow shoulders and something of a stoop; his hair was grey and thin; his long, sallow face deeply lined. He was not more than fifty, but he looked older. His eyes, pale blue and rather large, were weary. When you had been with him for a while you noticed that they moved very little; they remained fixed on your face, but so empty of expression were they that it was no discomfort. They seldom lit up. They gave no clue to his thoughts nor changed with the words he spoke. If you were of an observant turn it might have struck you that he blinked much less often than most of us. His hands were on the large side, with long, tapering fingers; they were soft but firm, cool but not clammy. You could never have said what Dr. Audlin wore unless you had made a point of looking. His clothes were dark. His tie was black. His dress made his sallow lined face paler and his pale eyes more wan. He gave you the impression of a very sick man.

Dr. Audlin was a psychoanalyst. He had adopted the profession by accident and practised it with misgiving. When the war broke out he had not been long qualified and was getting experience at various hospitals; he offered his services to the authorities, and after a time was sent out to France. It was then that he discovered his singular gift. He could allay certain pains by the touch of his cool, firm hands, and by talking to them often induce sleep in men who were suffering from sleeplessness. He spoke slowly. His voice had no particular colour, and its tone did not alter with the words he uttered, but it was musical, soft and lulling. He told the men that they must rest, that they mustn't worry, that they must sleep; and rest stole into their jaded bones, tranquillity pushed their anxieties away, like a man finding a place for himself on a crowded bench, and slumber fell on their tired eyelids like the light rain of spring upon the fresh-turned earth. Dr. Audlin found that by speaking to men with that low, monotonous voice of his, by looking at them with his pale, quiet eyes, by stroking their weary foreheads with his long firm hands, he could soothe their perturbations, resolve the conflicts that distracted them and banish the phobias that made their lives a torment. Sometimes he effected cures that seemed miraculous. He restored speech to a man who, after being buried under the earth by a bursting shell, had been struck dumb, and he gave back the use of his limbs to another who had been paralyzed after a crash in a plane. He could not understand his powers; he was of a sceptical turn, and though they say that in circumstances of this kind the first thing is to believe in yourself, he never quite succeeded in doing that; and it was only the outcome of his activities, patent to the most incredulous observer, that obliged him to admit that he had some faculty, coming from he knew not where, obscure and uncertain, that enabled him to do things for which he could offer no explanation. When the war was over he went to Vienna and studied there, and afterwards to Zurich; and then settled down in London to practise the art he had so strongly acquired. He had been practising now for fifteen years, and had attained, in the specialty he followed, a distinguished reputation. People told one another of the amazing things he had done, and though his fees were high, he had as many patients as he had time to see. Dr. Audlin knew that he had achieved some very extraordinary results; he had saved men from suicide, others from the lunatic asylum, he had assuaged griefs that embittered useful lives, he had turned unhappy marriages into happy ones, he had eradicated

abnormal instincts and thus delivered not a few from a hateful bondage, he had given health to the sick in spirit; he had done all this, and
yet at the back of his mind remained the suspicion that he was little
more than a quack.

It went against his grain to exercise a power that he could not understand, and it offended his honesty to trade on the faith of the people
he treated when he had no faith in himself. He was rich enough now
to live without working, and the work exhausted him; a dozen times
he had been on the point of giving up practice. He knew all that
Freud and Jung and the rest of them had written. He was not satisfied; he had an intimate conviction that all their theory was hocus-
pocus, and yet there the results were, incomprehensible, but manifest.
And what had he not seen of human nature during the fifteen years
that patients had been coming to his dingy back room in Wimpole
Street? The revelations that had been poured into his ears, sometimes
only too willingly, sometimes with shame, with reservations, with
anger, had long ceased to surprise him. Nothing could shock him any
longer. He knew by now that men were liars, he knew how extravagant was their vanity; he knew far worse than that about them; but
he knew that it was not for him to judge or to condemn. But year by
year as these terrible confidences were imparted to him his face grew
a little greyer, its lines a little more marked and his pale eyes more
weary. He seldom laughed, but now and again when for relaxation he
read a novel he smiled. Did their authors really think the men and
women they wrote of were like that? If they only knew how much
more complicated they were, how much more unexpected, what ir-
reconcilable elements coexisted within their souls and what dark and
sinister contentions afflicted them!

It was a quarter to six. Of all the strange cases he had been called
upon to deal with, Dr. Audlin could remember none stranger than
that of Lord Mountdrago. For one thing the personality of his patient
made it singular. Lord Mountdrago was an able and a distinguished
man. Appointed Secretary for Foreign Affairs when still under forty,
now after three years in office he had seen his policy prevail. It was
generally acknowledged that he was the ablest politician in the Conservative Party, and only the fact that his father was a peer, on whose

death he would no longer be able to sit in the House of Commons, made it impossible for him to aim at the premiership. But if in these democratic times it is out of the question for a Prime Minister of England to be in the House of Lords, there was nothing to prevent Lord Mountdrago from continuing to be Secretary for Foreign Affairs in successive Conservative administrations and so for long directing the foreign policy of his country.

Lord Mountdrago had many good qualities. He had intelligence and industry. He was widely travelled and spoke several languages fluently. From early youth he had specialized in foreign affairs and had conscientiously made himself acquainted with the political and economic circumstances of other countries. He had courage, insight and determination. He was a good speaker, both on the platform and in the House, clear, precise and often witty. He was a brilliant debater and his gift of repartee was celebrated. He had a fine presence: he was a tall, handsome man, rather bald and somewhat too stout, but this gave him solidity and an air of maturity that were of service to him. As a young man he had been something of an athlete and had rowed in the Oxford boat, and he was known to be one of the best shots in England. At twenty-four he had married a girl of eighteen whose father was a duke and her mother a great American heiress, so that she had both position and wealth, and by her he had had two sons. For several years they had lived privately apart, but in public united, so that appearances were saved, and no other attachment on either side had given the gossips occasion to whisper. Lord Mountdrago indeed was too ambitious, too hard-working, and it must be added too patriotic, to be tempted by any pleasures that might interfere with his career. He had in short a great deal to make him a popular and successful figure. He had unfortunately great defects.

He was a fearful snob. You would not have been surprised at this if his father had been the first holder of the title. That the son of an ennobled lawyer, manufacturer or distiller should attach an inordinate importance to his rank is understandable. The earldom held by Lord Mountdrago's father was created by Charles II, and the barony held by the first earl dated from the Wars of the Roses. For three hundred years the successive holders of the title had allied themselves with the noblest families of England. But Lord Mountdrago was as conscious of his birth as a *nouveau riche* is conscious of his money. He never missed an opportunity of impressing it upon others. He had beautiful manners when he chose to display them, but this he did only with people whom he regarded as his equals. He was coldly insolent to those whom he looked upon as his social inferiors. He was rude to his servants and insulting to his secretaries. The subordinate officials in the government offices to which he had been successively attached feared and hated him. His arrogance was horrible. He knew that he was a great deal cleverer than most of the persons he had to do with, and never hesitated to apprise them of the fact. He had no patience with the infirmities of human nature. He felt himself born to command and was irritated with people who expected him to listen to their arguments or wished to hear the reasons for his decisions. He was immeasurably selfish. He looked upon any service that was rendered him as a right due to his rank and intelligence and therefore deserving of no gratitude. It never entered his head that he was called upon to do anything for others. He had many enemies: he despised them. He knew no one who merited his assistance, his sympathy or his compassion. He had no friends. He was distrusted by his chiefs, because they doubted his loyalty; he was unpopular with his party, because he was overbearing and discourteous; and yet his merit was so great, his patriotism so evident, his intelligence so solid and his management of affairs so brilliant, that they had to put up with him. And what made it possible to do this was that on occasion he could be enchanting: when he was with persons whom he considered his equals, or whom he wished to captivate, in the company of foreign dignitaries or women of distinction, he could be gay, witty and debonair; his manners then reminded you that in his veins ran the same blood as had run in the veins of Lord Chesterfield; he could tell a story with point, he could be natural, sensible and even profound. You were surprised at the extent of his knowledge and the sensitiveness of his taste. You thought him the best company in the world; you forgot that he had insulted you the day before and was quite capable of cutting you dead the next.

Lord Mountdrago almost failed to become Dr. Audlin's patient. A secretary rang up the doctor and told him that his lordship, wishing to consult him, would be glad if he would come to his house at ten o'clock on the following morning. Dr. Audlin answered that he was unable to go to Lord Mountdrago's house, but would be pleased to give him an appointment at his consulting room at five o'clock on the next day but one. The secretary took the message and presently rang back to say that Lord Mountdrago insisted on seeing Dr. Audlin in his own house and the doctor could fix his own fee. Dr. Audlin replied that he saw patients only in his consulting room and expressed his regret that unless Lord Mountdrago was prepared to come to him he could not give him his attention. In a quarter of an hour a brief message was delivered to him that his lordship would come not next day but one, but next day, at five.

When Lord Mountdrago was then shown in he did not come forward, but stood at the door and insolently looked the doctor up and down. Dr. Audlin perceived that he was in a rage; he gazed at him, silently, with still eyes. He saw a big heavy man, with greying hair, receding on the forehead so that it gave nobility to his brow, a puffy face with bold regular features and an expression of haughtiness. He had somewhat the look of one of the Bourbon sovereigns of the eighteenth century.

"It seems that it is as difficult to see you as a Prime Minister, Dr. Audlin. I'm an extremely busy man."

"Won't you sit down?" said the doctor.

His face showed no sign that Lord Mountdrago's speech in any way affected him. Dr. Audlin sat in his chair at the desk. Lord Mountdrago still stood, and his frown darkened.

"I think I should tell you that I am His Majesty's Secretary for Foreign Affairs," he said acidly.

"Won't you sit down?" the doctor repeated.

Lord Mountdrago made a gesture, which might have suggested that he was about to turn on his heel and stalk out of the room; but if that was his intention he apparently thought better of it. He seated himself. Dr. Audlin opened a large book and took up his pen. He wrote without looking at his patient.

"How old are you?"

"Forty-two."

"Are you married?"

"Yes."

"How long have you been married?"

"Eighteen years."

"Have you any children?"

"I have two sons."

Dr. Audlin noted down the facts as Lord Mountdrago abruptly answered his questions. Then he leaned back in his chair and looked at him. He did not speak; he just looked, gravely, with pale eyes that did not move.

"Why have you come to see me?" he asked at length.

"I've heard about you. Lady Canute is a patient of yours, I understand. She tells me you've done her a certain amount of good."

Dr. Audlin did not reply. His eyes remained fixed on the other's face, but they were so empty of expression that you might have thought he did not even see him.

"I can't do miracles," he said at length. Not a smile, but the shadow of a smile flickered in his eyes. "The Royal College of Physicians would not approve of it if I did."

Lord Mountdrago gave a brief chuckle. It seemed to lessen his hostility. He spoke more amiably.

"You have a very remarkable reputation. People seem to believe in you."

"Why have you come to me?" repeated Dr. Audlin.

Now it was Lord Mountdrago's turn to be silent. It looked as though he found it hard to answer. Dr. Audlin waited. At last Lord Mountdrago seemed to make an effort. He spoke.

"I'm in perfect health. Just as a matter of routine I had myself examined by my own doctor the other day, Sir Augustus Fitzherbert, I daresay you've heard of him, and he tells me I have the physique of a man of thirty. I work hard, but I'm never tired, and I enjoy my work. I smoke very little and I'm an extremely moderate drinker. I take a sufficiency of exercise and I lead a regular life. I am a perfectly sound, normal, healthy man. I quite expect you to think it very silly and childish of me to consult you."

Dr. Audlin saw that he must help him.

"I don't know if I can do anything to help you. I'll try. You're distressed?"

Lord Mountdrago frowned.

"The work that I'm engaged in is important. The decisions I am called upon to make can easily affect the welfare of the country and even the peace of the world. It is essential that my judgment should be balanced and my brain clear. I look upon it as my duty to eliminate any cause of worry that may interfere with my usefulness."

Dr. Audlin had never taken his eyes off him. He saw a great deal. He saw behind his patient's pompous manner and arrogant pride an anxiety that he could not dispel.

"I asked you to be good enough to come here because I know by experience that it's easier for someone to speak openly in the dingy surroundings of a doctor's consulting room than in his accustomed environment."

"They're certainly dingy," said Lord Mountdrago acidly. He paused. It was evident that this man who had so much self-assurance, so quick and decided a mind that he was never at a loss, at this moment was embarrassed. He smiled in order to show the doctor that he was at his ease, but his eyes betrayed his disquiet. When he spoke again it was with unnatural heartiness.

"The whole thing's so trivial that I can hardly bring myself to bother you with it. I'm afraid you'll just tell me not to be a fool and waste your valuable time."

"Even things that seem very trivial may have their importance. They can be a symptom of a deep-seated derangement. And my time is entirely at your disposal."

Dr. Audlin's voice was low and grave. The monotone in which he spoke was strangely soothing. Lord Mountdrago at length made up his mind to be frank.

"The fact is I've been having some very tiresome dreams lately. I know it's silly to pay any attention to them, but—well, the honest truth is that I'm afraid they've got on my nerves."

"Can you describe any of them to me?"

Lord Mountdrago smiled, but the smile that tried to be careless was only rueful.

"They're so idiotic, I can hardly bring myself to narrate them."

"Never mind."

"Well, the first I had was about a month ago. I dreamt that I was at a party at Connemara House. It was an official party. The King and Queen were to be there, and of course decorations were worn. I was wearing my ribbon and my star. I went into a sort of cloakroom they have to take off my coat. There was a little man there called Owen Griffiths, who's a Welsh member of Parliament, and to tell you the truth, I was surprised to see him. He's very common, and I said to myself: 'Really, Lydia Connemara is going too far, whom will she ask next?' I thought he looked at me rather curiously, but I didn't take any notice of him; in fact I cut the little bounder and walked upstairs. I suppose you've never been there?"

"Never."

"No, it's not the sort of house you'd ever be likely to go to. It's a rather vulgar house, but it's got a very fine marble staircase, and the Connemaras were at the top receiving their guests. Lady Connemara gave me a look of surprise when I shook hands with her, and began to giggle; I didn't pay much attention—she's a very silly, ill-bred woman, and her manners are no better than those of her ancestress whom King Charles II made a duchess. I must say the reception rooms at Connemara House are stately. I walked through, nodding to a number of people and shaking hands; then I saw the German Ambassador talking with one of the Austrian archdukes. I particularly wanted to have a word with him, so I went up and held out my hand. The moment the Archduke saw me he burst into a roar of laughter. I was deeply affronted. I looked him up and down sternly, but he only laughed the more. I was about to speak to him rather sharply, when there was a sudden hush, and I realized that the King and Queen had come. Turning my back on the Archduke, I stepped forward, and then, quite suddenly, I noticed that I hadn't got any trousers on. I was in short silk drawers, and I wore scarlet sock suspenders. No wonder Lady Connemara had giggled; no wonder the Archduke had laughed! I can't tell you what that moment was. An agony of shame. I awoke in a cold sweat. Oh, you don't know the relief I felt to find it was only a dream."

"It's the kind of dream that's not so very uncommon," said Dr. Audlin.

"I daresay not. But an odd thing happened next day. I was in the lobby of the House of Commons, when that fellow Griffiths walked slowly past me. He deliberately looked down at my legs, and then he looked me full in the face, and I was almost certain he winked. A ridiculous thought came to me. He'd been there the night before and seen me make that ghastly exhibition of myself and was enjoying the joke. But of course I knew that was impossible because it was only a dream. I gave him an icy glare, and he walked on. But he was grinning his head off."

Lord Mountdrago took his handkerchief out of his pocket and wiped the palms of his hands. He was making no attempt now to conceal his perturbation. Dr. Audlin never took his eyes off him.

"Tell me another dream."

"It was the night after, and it was even more absurd than the first one. I dreamt that I was in the House. There was a debate on foreign affairs which not only the country, but the world, had been looking forward to with the gravest concern. The government had decided on a change in their policy which vitally affected the future of the Empire. The occasion was historic. Of course the House was crowded. All the ambassadors were there. The galleries were packed. It fell to me to make the important speech of the evening. I had prepared it carefully. A man like me has enemies—there are a lot of people who resent my having achieved the position I have at an age when even the cleverest men are content with situations of relative obscurity—and I was determined that my speech should not only be worthy of the occasion, but should silence my detractors. It excited me to think that the whole world was hanging on my lips. I rose to my feet. If you've ever been in the House you'll know how members chat to one another during a debate, rustle papers and turn over reports. The silence was the silence of the grave when I began to speak. Suddenly I caught sight of that odious little bounder on one of the benches opposite, Griffiths, the Welsh member; he put out his tongue at me. I don't know if you've ever heard a vulgar music-hall song called 'A Bicycle Made for Two.' It was very popular a great many years ago. To show Griffiths how completely I despised him I began to sing it. I sang the first verse right through. There was a moment's surprise, and when I finished they cried 'Hear, hear,' on the opposite benches. I put up my hand to silence them and sang the second verse. The House listened to me in stony silence and I felt the song wasn't going down very well. I was vexed, for I have a good baritone voice, and I was determined that they should do me justice. When I started the third verse the members began to laugh; in an instant the laughter spread; the ambassadors, the strangers in the Distinguished Strangers' Gallery, the ladies in the Ladies' Gallery, the reporters, they shook, they bellowed, they held their sides, they rolled in their seats; everyone was overcome with laughter except the ministers on the Front Bench immediately behind me. In that incredible, in that unprecedented, uproar they sat petrified. I gave them a glance, and suddenly the enormity of what I had done fell upon me. I had made myself the laughing-stock of the whole world. With misery I realized that I should have to resign. I woke and knew it was only a dream."

Lord Mountdrago's grand manner had deserted him as he narrated this, and now having finished he was pale and trembling. But with an effort he pulled himself together. He forced a laugh to his shaking lips.

"The whole thing was so fantastic that I couldn't help being amused. I didn't give it another thought, and when I went into the House on the following afternoon I was feeling in very good form. The debate was dull, but I had to be there, and I read some documents that required my attention. For some reason I chanced to look up, and I saw that Griffiths was speaking. He has an unpleasant Welsh accent and an unprepossessing appearance. I couldn't imagine that he had anything to say that it was worth my while to listen to, and I was about to return to my papers when he quoted two lines from 'A Bicycle Made for Two.' I couldn't help glancing at him, and I saw that his eyes were fixed on me with a grin of bitter mockery. I faintly shrugged my shoulders. It was comic that a scrubby little Welsh member should look at me like that. It was an odd coincidence that he should quote two lines from that disastrous song that I'd sung all through in my dream. I began to read my papers again, but I don't mind telling you that I found it difficult to concentrate on them. I was a little puzzled. Owen Griffiths had been in my first dream, the one at Connemara House, and I'd received a very definite impression afterwards that he knew the sorry figure I'd cut. Was it a mere coincidence that he had just quoted those two lines? I asked myself if it was possible that he was dreaming the same dreams as I was. But of course the idea was preposterous, and I determined not to give it a second thought."

There was a silence. Dr. Audlin looked at Lord Mountdrago and Lord Mountdrago looked at Dr. Audlin.

"Other people's dreams are very boring. My wife used to dream occasionally and insist on telling me her dreams next day with circumstantial detail. I found it maddening."

Dr. Audlin faintly smiled.

"You're not boring me."

"I'll tell you one more dream I had a few days later. I dreamt that I went into a public house at Limehouse. I've never been to Limehouse in my life and I don't think I've ever been in a public house since I was at Oxford, and yet I saw the street and the place I went into as exactly as if I were at home there. I went into a room—I don't know whether they call it the saloon bar or the private bar; there was a fireplace and a large leather armchair on one side of it, and on the other a small sofa; a bar ran the whole length of the room, and over it you could see into the public bar. Near the door was a round marble-topped table and two armchairs beside it. It was a Saturday night, and the place was packed. It was brightly lit, but the smoke was so thick that it made my eyes smart. I was dressed like a rough, with a cap on my head and a handkerchief round my neck. It seemed to me that most of the people there were drunk. I thought it rather amusing. There was a gramophone going, or the radio, I don't know which, and in front of the fireplace two women were doing a grotesque dance. There was a little crowd round them, laughing, cheering and singing. I went up to have a look, and some man said to me: ' 'Ave a drink, Bill.' There were glasses on the table full of a dark liquid which I understand is called brown ale. He gave me a glass, and not wishing to be conspicuous I drank it. One of the women who were dancing broke away from the other and took hold of the glass. ' 'Ere, what's the idea?' she said. 'That's my beer you're putting away.' 'Oh, I'm so sorry,' I said, 'this gentleman offered it me, and I very naturally thought it was his to offer.' 'All right, mate,' she said, 'I don't mind. You come an' 'ave a dance with me.' Before I could protest she'd caught hold of me and we were dancing together. And then I found myself sitting in the armchair with the woman on my lap and we were sharing a glass of beer. I should tell you that sex has never played any great part in my life. I married young because in my position it was desirable that I should marry, but also in order to settle once for all the question of sex. I had the two sons I had made up my mind to have, and then I put the whole matter on one side. I've always been too busy to give much thought to that kind of thing, and living so much in the public eye as I do, it would have been madness to do anything that might give rise to scandal. The greatest asset a politician can have is a blameless record as far as women are concerned. I have no patience with the men who smash up their careers for women. I only despise them. The woman I had on my knees was drunk; she wasn't pretty and she wasn't young: in fact, she was just a blowsy old prostitute. She filled me with disgust, and yet when she put her mouth to mine and kissed me, though her breath stank of beer and her teeth were decayed, though I loathed myself, I wanted her—I wanted her with all my soul. Suddenly I heard a voice: 'That's right, old boy, have a good time.' I looked up, and there was Owen Griffiths. I tried to spring out of the chair, but that horrible woman wouldn't let me. 'Don't you pay no attention to 'im,' she said, ' 'e's only one of them nosy parkers.' 'You go to it,' he said. 'I know Moll. She'll give you your money's worth all right.' You know, I wasn't so much annoyed at his seeing me in that absurd situation as angry that he should address me as old boy. I pushed the woman aside and stood up and faced him. 'I don't know you, and I don't want to know you,' I said. 'I know you all right,' he said. 'And my advice to you, Molly, is, see that you get your money, he'll bilk you if he can.' There was a bottle of beer standing on the table close by. Without a word I seized it by the neck and hit him over the head with it as hard as I could. I made such a violent gesture that it woke me up."

"A dream of that sort is not incomprehensible," said Dr. Audlin. "It is the revenge nature takes on persons of unimpeachable character."

"The story's idiotic. I haven't told it you for its own sake. I've told it you for what happened next day. I wanted to look up something in a hurry, and I went into the library of the House. I got the book and began reading. I hadn't noticed when I sat down that Griffiths was sitting in a chair close by me. Another of the Labour Members came in and went up to him. 'Hullo, Owen,' he said to him, 'you're looking pretty dicky to-day.' 'I've got an awful headache,' he answered, 'I feel as if I'd been cracked over the head with a bottle.'"

Now Lord Mountdrago's face was grey with anguish.

"I knew then that the idea I'd had and dismissed as preposterous was true. I knew that Griffiths was dreaming my dreams and that he remembered them as well as I did."

"It may also have been a coincidence."

"When he spoke he didn't speak to his friend, he deliberately spoke to me. He looked at me with sullen resentment."

"Can you offer any suggestion why this same man should come into your dreams?"

"None."

Dr. Audlin's eyes had not left his patient's face and he saw that he lied. He had a pencil in his hand, and he drew a straggling line or two on his blotting paper. It often took a long time to get people to tell the truth, and yet they knew that unless they told it he could do nothing for them.

"The dream you've just described to me took place just over three weeks ago. Have you had any since?"

"Every night."

"And does this man Griffiths come into them all?"

"Yes."

The doctor drew more lines on his blotting paper. He wanted the silence, the drabness, the dull light of that little room to have its effect on Lord Mountdrago's sensibility. Lord Mountdrago threw himself back in his chair and turned his head away so that he should not see the other's grave eyes.

"Dr. Audlin, you must do something for me. I'm at the end of my tether. I shall go mad if this goes on. I'm afraid to go to sleep. Two or three nights I haven't. I've sat up reading and when I felt drowsy put on my coat and walked till I was exhausted. But I must have sleep. With all the work I have to do I must be at concert pitch; I must be in complete control of all my faculties. I need rest; sleep brings me none. I no sooner fall asleep than my dreams begin, and he's always there, that vulgar little cad, grinning at me, mocking me, despising me. It's a monstrous persecution. I tell you, Doctor, I'm not the man of my dreams; it's not fair to judge me by them. Ask anyone you like. I'm an honest, upright, decent man. No one can say anything against my moral character either private or public. My whole ambition is to serve my country and maintain its greatness. I have money, I have rank, I'm not exposed to many of the temptations of lesser men, so that it's no credit to me to be incorruptible; but this I can claim, that no honour, no personal advantage, no thought of self would induce me to swerve by a hairsbreadth from my duty. I've sacrificed everything to become the man I am. Greatness is my aim. Greatness is within my reach, and I'm losing my nerve. I'm not that mean, despicable, cowardly, lewd creature that horrible little man sees. I've told you three of my dreams; they're nothing; that man has seen me do things that are so beastly, so horrible, so shameful, that even if my life depended on it I wouldn't tell them. And he remembers them. I can hardly meet the derision and disgust I see in his eyes, and I even hesitate to speak because I know my words can seem to him nothing but utter humbug. He's seen me do things that no man with any self-respect would do, things for which men are driven out of the society of their fellows and sentenced to long terms of imprisonment; he's heard the foulness of my speech; he's seen me not only ridiculous, but revolting. He despises me and he no longer pretends to conceal it. I tell you that if you can't do something to help me I shall either kill myself or kill him."

"I wouldn't kill him if I were you," said Dr. Audlin coolly, in that soothing voice of his. "In this country the consequences of killing a fellow creature are awkward."

"I shouldn't be hanged for it, if that's what you mean. Who would know that I'd killed him? That dream of mine has shown me how. I told you, the day after I'd hit him over the head with a beer bottle he had such a headache that he couldn't see straight. He said so himself. That shows that he can feel with his waking body what happens to his body asleep. It's not with a bottle I shall hit him next time. One night, when I'm dreaming, I shall find myself with a knife in my hand or a revolver in my pocket—I must because I want to so intensely—and then I shall seize my opportunity. I'll stick him like a pig; I'll shoot him like a dog. In the heart. And then I shall be free of this fiendish persecution."

Some people might have thought that Lord Mountdrago was mad; after all the years during which Dr. Audlin had been treating the diseased souls of men he knew how thin a line divides those whom we call sane from those whom we call insane. He knew how often in men who to all appearance were healthy and normal, who were seemingly devoid of imagination, and who fulfilled the duties of common life with credit to themselves and with benefit to their fellows, when you gained their confidence, when you tore away the mask they wore to the world, you found not only hideous abnormality, but kinks so strange, mental extravagances so fantastic, that in that respect you could only call them lunatic. If you put them in an asylum, not all the asylums in the world would be large enough. Anyhow, a man was not certifiable because he had strange dreams and they had shattered his nerve. The case was singular, but it was only an exaggeration of others that had come under Dr. Audlin's observation; he was doubtful, however, whether the methods of treatment that he had so often found efficacious would here avail.

"Have you consulted any other member of my profession?" he asked.

"Only Sir Augustus. I merely told him that I suffered from nightmares. He said I was overworked and recommended me to go for a cruise. That's absurd. I can't leave the Foreign Office just now when the international situation needs constant attention. I'm indispensable, and I know it. On my conduct at the present juncture my whole future depends. He gave me sedatives. They had no effect. He gave me tonics. They were worse than useless. He's an old fool."

"Can you give any reason why it should be this particular man who persists in coming into your dreams?"

"You asked me that question before. I answered it."

That was true. But Dr. Audlin had not been satisfied with the answer.

"Just now you talked of persecution. Why should Owen Griffiths want to persecute you?"

"I don't know."

Lord Mountdrago's eyes shifted a little. Dr. Audlin was sure that he was not speaking the truth.

"Have you ever done him an injury?"

"Never."

Lord Mountdrago made no movement, but Dr. Audlin had a queer feeling that he shrank into his skin. He saw before him a large, proud man who gave the impression that the questions put to him were an insolence, and yet for all that, behind that façade, was something shifting and startled that made you think of a frightened animal in a trap. Dr. Audlin leaned forward and by the power of his eyes forced Lord Mountdrago to meet them.

"Are you quite sure?"

"Quite sure. You don't seem to understand that our ways lead along different paths. I don't wish to harp on it, but I must remind you that I am a Minister of the Crown and Griffiths is an obscure member of the Labour Party. Naturally there's no social connection between us; he's a man of very humble origin, he's not the sort of person I should be likely to meet at any of the houses I go to; and politically our respective stations are so far separated that we could not possibly have anything in common."

"I can do nothing for you unless you tell me the complete truth."

Lord Mountdrago raised his eyebrows. His voice was rasping.

"I'm not accustomed to having my word doubted, Dr. Audlin. If you're going to do that, I think to take up any more of your time can only be a waste of mine. If you will kindly let my secretary know what your fee is, he will see that a cheque is sent to you."

For all the expression that was to be seen on Dr. Audlin's face you might have thought that he simply had not heard what Lord Mountdrago said. He continued to look steadily into his eyes, and his voice was grave and low.

"Have you done anything to this man that *he* might look upon as an injury?"

Lord Mountdrago hesitated. He looked away, and then, as though there were in Dr. Audlin's eyes a compelling force that he could not resist, looked back. He answered sulkily:

"Only if he was a dirty, second-rate little cad."

"But that is exactly what you've described him to be."

Lord Mountdrago sighed. He was beaten. Dr. Audlin knew that the sigh meant he was going at last to say what he had till then held back. Now he had no longer to insist. He dropped his eyes and began again drawing vague geometrical figures on his blotting paper. The silence lasted two or three minutes.

"I'm anxious to tell you everything that can be of any use to you. If I didn't mention this before, it's only because it was so unimportant that I didn't see how it could possibly have anything to do with the case. Griffiths won a seat at the last election, and he began to make a nuisance of himself almost at once. His father's a miner, and he worked in a mine himself when he was a boy; he's been a schoolmaster in the board schools and a journalist. He's that half-baked, conceited intellectual, with inadequate knowledge, ill-considered ideas and impractical plans, that compulsory education has brought forth from the working classes. He's a scrawny, grey-faced man who looks half starved, and he's always very slovenly in appearance; heaven knows members nowadays don't bother much about their dress, but his clothes are an outrage to the dignity of the House. They're ostentatiously shabby, his collar's never clean, and his tie's never tied properly; he looks as if he hadn't had a bath for a month, and his hands are filthy. The Labour Party have two or three fellows on the Front Bench who've got a certain ability, but the rest of them don't amount to much. In the kingdom of the blind the one-eyed man is king: because Griffiths is glib and has a lot of superficial information on a number of subjects, the Whips on his side began to put him up to speak whenever there was a chance. It appeared that he fancied himself on foreign affairs, and he was continually asking me silly, tiresome questions. I don't mind telling you that I made a point of snubbing him as soundly as I thought he deserved. From the beginning I hated the way he

talked, his whining voice and his vulgar accent; he had nervous mannerisms that intensely irritated me. He talked rather shyly, hesitatingly,
as though it were torture to him to speak and yet he was forced to by
some inner passion, and often he used to say some very disconcerting
things. I'll admit that now and again he had a sort of tub-thumping
eloquence. It had a certain influence over the ill-regulated minds of the
members of his party. They were impressed by his earnestness, and
they weren't, as I was, nauseated by his sentimentality. A certain sentimentality is the common coin of political debate. Nations are governed by self-interest, but they prefer to believe that their aims are
altruistic, and the politician is justified if with fair words and fine
phrases he can persuade the electorate that the hard bargain he is
driving for his country's advantage tends to the good of humanity.
The mistake people like Griffiths make is to take these fair words and
fine phrases at their face value. He's a crank, and a noxious crank. He
calls himself an idealist. He has at his tongue's end all the tedious
blather that the intelligentsia have been boring us with for years. Non-
resistance. The brotherhood of man. You know the hopeless rubbish.
The worst of it was that it impressed not only his own party, it even
shook some of the sillier, more sloppy-minded members of ours. I
heard rumours that Griffiths was likely to get office when a Labour
Government came in; I even heard it suggested that he might get the
Foreign Office. The notion was grotesque but not impossible. One day
I had occasion to wind up a debate on foreign affairs which Griffiths
had opened. He'd spoken for an hour. I thought it a very good opportunity to cook his goose, and by God, sir, I cooked it. I tore his speech
to pieces. I pointed out the faultiness of his reasoning and emphasized
the deficiency of his knowledge. In the House of Commons the most
devastating weapon is ridicule: I mocked him; I bantered him; I was
in good form that day and the House rocked with laughter. Their
laughter excited me, and I excelled myself. The Opposition sat glum
and silent, but even some of them couldn't help laughing once or
twice; it's not intolerable, you know, to see a colleague, perhaps a rival,
made a fool of. And if ever a man was made a fool of, I made a fool
of Griffiths. He shrank down in his seat; I saw his face go white, and
presently he buried it in his hands. When I sat down I'd killed him.

I'd destroyed his prestige for ever; he had no more chance of getting office when a Labour Government came in than the policeman at the door. I heard afterwards that his father, the old miner, and his mother had come up from Wales, with various supporters of his in the constituency, to watch the triumph they expected him to have. They had seen only his utter humiliation. He'd won the constituency by the narrowest margin. An incident like that might very easily lose him his seat. But that was no business of mine."

"Should I be putting it too strongly if I said you had ruined his career?" asked Dr. Audlin.

"I don't suppose you would."

"That is a very serious injury you've done him."

"He brought it on himself."

"Have you never felt any qualms about it?"

"I think perhaps if I'd known that his father and mother were there I might have let him down a little more gently."

There was nothing further for Dr. Audlin to say, and he set about treating his patient in such a manner as he thought might avail. He sought by suggestion to make him forget his dreams when he awoke; he sought to make him sleep so deeply that he would not dream. He found Lord Mountdrago's resistance impossible to break down. At the end of an hour he dismissed him.

Since then he had seen Lord Mountdrago half a dozen times. He had done him no good. The frightful dreams continued every night to harass the unfortunate man, and it was clear that his general condition was growing rapidly worse. He was worn out. His irritability was uncontrollable. Lord Mountdrago was angry because he received no benefit from his treatment, and yet continued it, not only because it seemed his only hope, but because it was a relief to him to have someone with whom he could talk openly. Dr. Audlin came to the conclusion at last that there was only one way in which Lord Mountdrago could achieve deliverance, but he knew him well enough to be assured that of his own free will he would never, never take it. If Lord Mountdrago was to be saved from the breakdown that was threatening, he must be induced to take a step that must be abhorrent to his pride of birth and his self-complacency. Dr. Audlin was convinced that to delay was impossible. He was treating his patient by suggestion, and after several visits found him more susceptible to it. At length he managed to get him into a condition of somnolence. With his low, soft, monotonous voice he soothed his tortured nerves. He repeated the same words over and over again. Lord Mountdrago lay quite still, his eyes closed; his breathing was regular, and his limbs were relaxed. Then Dr. Audlin in the same quiet tone spoke the words he had prepared.

"You will go to Owen Griffiths and say that you are sorry that you caused him that great injury. You will say that you will do whatever lies in your power to undo the harm that you have done him."

The words acted on Lord Mountdrago like the blow of a whip across his face. He shook himself out of his hypnotic state and sprang to his feet. His eyes blazed with passion, and he poured forth upon Dr. Audlin a stream of angry vituperation such as even he had never heard. He swore at him. He cursed him. He used language of such obscenity that Dr. Audlin, who had heard every sort of foul word, sometimes from the lips of chaste and distinguished women, was surprised that he knew it.

"Apologize to that filthy little Welshman? I'd rather kill myself."

"I believe it to be the only way in which you can regain your balance."

Dr. Audlin had not often seen a man presumably sane in such a condition of uncontrollable fury. Lord Mountdrago grew red in the face, and his eyes bulged out of his head. He did really foam at the mouth. Dr. Audlin watched him coolly, waiting for the storm to wear itself out, and presently he saw that Lord Mountdrago, weakened by the strain to which he had been subjected for so many weeks, was exhausted.

"Sit down," he said then, sharply.

Lord Mountdrago crumpled up into a chair.

"Christ, I feel all in. I must rest a minute and then I'll go."

For five minutes perhaps they sat in complete silence. Lord Mountdrago was a gross, blustering bully, but he was also a gentleman. When he broke the silence he had recovered his self-control.

"I'm afraid I've been very rude to you. I'm ashamed of the things I've said to you, and I can only say you'd be justified if you refused to have anything more to do with me. I hope you won't do that. I feel that my visits to you do help me. I think you're my only chance."

"You mustn't give another thought to what you said. It was of no consequence."

"But there's one thing you mustn't ask me to do, and that is to make excuses to Griffiths."

"I've thought a great deal about your case. I don't pretend to understand it, but I believe that your only chance of release is to do what I proposed. I have a notion that we're none of us one self, but many, and one of the selves in you has risen up against the injury you did Griffiths and has taken on the form of Griffiths in your mind and is punishing you for what you cruelly did. If I were a priest I should tell you that it is your conscience that has adopted the shape and lineaments of this man to scourge you to repentance and persuade you to reparation."

"My conscience is clear. It's not my fault if I smashed the man's career. I crushed him like a slug in my garden. I regret nothing."

It was on these words that Lord Mountdrago had left him. Reading through his notes, while he waited, Dr. Audlin considered how best he could bring his patient to the state of mind that, now that his usual methods of treatment had failed, he thought alone could help him. He glanced at his clock. It was six. It was strange that Lord Mountdrago did not come. He knew he had intended to because a secretary had rung up that morning to say that he would be with him at the usual hour. He must have been detained by pressing work. This notion gave Dr. Audlin something else to think of: Lord Mountdrago was quite unfit to work and in no condition to deal with important matters of state. Dr. Audlin wondered whether it behooved him to get in touch with someone in authority, the Prime Minister or the Permanent Under Secretary for Foreign Affairs, and impart to him his conviction that Lord Mountdrago's mind was so unbalanced that it was dangerous to leave affairs of moment in his hands. It was a ticklish thing to do. He might cause needless trouble and get roundly snubbed for his pains. He shrugged his shoulders.

"After all," he reflected, "the politicians have made such a mess of the world during the last five-and-twenty years, I don't suppose it makes much odds if they're mad or sane."

He rang the bell.

"If Lord Mountdrago comes now, will you tell him that I have another appointment at six-fifteen and so I'm afraid I can't see him."

"Very good, sir."

"Has the evening paper come yet?"

"I'll go and see."

In a moment the servant brought it in. A huge headline ran across the front page: Tragic Death of Foreign Minister.

"My God!" cried Dr. Audlin.

For once he was wrenched out of his wonted calm. He was shocked, horribly shocked, and yet he was not altogether surprised. The possibility that Lord Mountdrago might commit suicide had occurred to him several times, for that it was suicide he could not doubt. The paper said that Lord Mountdrago had been waiting in a tube station, standing on the edge of the platform, and as the train came in was seen to fall on the rail. It was supposed that he had had a sudden attack of faintness. The paper went on to say that Lord Mountdrago had been suffering for some weeks from the effects of overwork, but had felt it impossible to absent himself while the foreign situation demanded his unremitting attention. Lord Mountdrago was another victim of the strain that modern politics placed upon those who played the more important parts in it. There was a neat little piece about the talents and industry, the patriotism and vision, of the deceased statesman, followed by various surmises upon the Prime Minister's choice of his successor. Dr. Audlin read all this. He had not liked Lord Mountdrago. The chief emotion that his death caused in him was dissatisfaction with himself because he had been able to do nothing for him.

Perhaps he had done wrong in not getting into touch with Lord Mountdrago's doctor. He was discouraged, as always when failure frustrated his conscientious efforts, and repulsion seized him for the theory and practice of this empiric doctrine by which he earned his living. He was dealing with dark and mysterious forces that it was perhaps beyond the powers of the human mind to understand. He was like a man blindfold trying to feel his way to he knew not whither. Listlessly he turned the pages of the paper. Suddenly he gave a great start, and an exclamation once more was forced from his lips. His eyes had fallen on a small paragraph near the bottom of a column. Sudden Death of an M.P., he read. Mr. Owen Griffiths, member for so-and-so, had been taken ill in Fleet Street that afternoon and when he was brought to Charing Cross Hospital life was found to be extinct. It was supposed that death was due to natural causes, but an inquest would be held. Dr. Audlin could hardly believe his eyes. Was it possible that the night before Lord Mountdrago had at last in his dream found himself possessed of the weapon, knife or gun, that he had wanted, and had killed his tormentor, and had that ghostly murder, in the same way as the blow with the bottle had given him a racking headache on the following day, taken effect a certain number of hours later on the waking man? Or was it, more mysterious and more frightful, that when Lord Mountdrago sought relief in death, the enemy he had so cruelly wronged, unappeased, escaping from his own mortality, had pursued him to some other sphere, there to torment him still? It was strange. The sensible thing was to look upon it merely as an odd coincidence. Dr. Audlin rang the bell.

"Tell Mrs. Milton that I'm sorry I can't see her this evening, I'm not well."

It was true; he shivered as though of an ague. With some kind of spiritual sense he seemed to envisage a bleak, a horrible void. The dark night of the soul engulfed him, and he felt a strange, primeval terror of he knew not what.

CONRAD AIKEN

COMMENTARY

Much pink-edged nonsense has been written by moony adults about the child's "dream world." Few of us actually remember our childhood visions. But how willing most of us are to think up the kind of visions it would be pleasant to remember having had! Such reconstructions are generally mere compliments paid to the imaginative, poetical children we would so like to have been. It would be a sad thing for sentiment if it were known how many of us pass through childhood in a vacant daze, minds half closed and mouths half open.

But not all. A certain number of children create intense imaginary worlds for themselves, worlds far superior in interest to anything reality has to offer. They do not tell us about this world, except by vague hints, for communication breaks the spell. Undersympathetic adults call these vague hints lies. Oversympathetic adults call them genius. Both kinds of adults are wrong.

The child generally "outgrows," as we say, his fantasies. "Outgrows" may be a poor word, for sometimes the fantasy is the largest thing the child will ever know during his entire life. Adjustment to reality is not always a process of development; it may involve diminution. The man who lives and dies a slave may have had his largest and most liberated moments during a brief period of childhood reverie.

But the fantasy may never be outgrown. It may become necessary to the child, a permanent door of escape from the outer world. It may, as in the Conrad Aiken story that follows, "take the place of everything." Then it assumes the form of hallucination; a compulsion neurosis is born; and mental derangement, temporary or permanent, may result. This is the situation treated in "Silent Snow, Secret Snow," one of the most haunting tales in our literature.

Note how unclinical it is, though it could never have been written before the birth of psychiatry or even, I should judge, before the advent of psychoanalysis. On the other hand, it is not oversimplified.

It is told not in the language of the twelve-year-old boy of the story but in that of a perceptive adult.

What makes "Silent Snow, Secret Snow" a masterly piece of writing is not that it is a successful study of the mechanism by which a mind fatally splits itself. The value of the tale lies in its human sympathy. Each of us has a secret place of his own into which, like a wounded animal, he crawls when things get too much for him. Paul Hasleman's place, his "secret screen of new snow between himself and the world," is merely our own private evasion magnified and intensified. Paul is not only a mental case. He is, so wise and true is this story, part of ourselves.

Silent Snow, Secret Snow

BY

CONRAD AIKEN

JUST WHY it should have happened, or why it should have happened just when it did, he could not, of course, possibly have said; nor perhaps could it even have occurred to him to ask. The thing was above all a secret, something to be preciously concealed from Mother and Father; and to that very fact it owed an enormous part of its deliciousness. It was like a peculiarly beautiful trinket to be carried unmentioned in one's trouser-pocket—a rare stamp, an old coin, a few tiny gold links found trodden out of shape on the path in the park, a pebble of carnelian, a sea shell distinguishable from all others by an unusual spot or stripe—and, as if it were anyone of these, he carried around with him everywhere a warm and persistent and increasingly beautiful sense of possession. Nor was it only a sense of possession—it was also a sense of protection. It was as if, in some delightful way, his secret gave him a fortress, a wall behind which he could retreat into heavenly seclusion. This was almost the first thing he had noticed about it—apart from the oddness of the thing itself—and it was this that now again, for the fiftieth time, occurred to him, as he sat in the little schoolroom. It was the half hour for geography. Miss Buell was revolving with one finger, slowly, a huge terrestrial globe which had been placed on her desk. The green and yellow continents passed and repassed, questions were asked and answered, and now the little girl in front of him, Deirdre, who had a funny little constellation of freckles on the back of her neck, exactly like the Big Dipper, was standing up and telling Miss Buell that the equator was the line that ran around the middle.

Miss Buell's face, which was old and grayish and kindly, with gray stiff curls beside the cheeks, and eyes that swam very brightly, like little minnows, behind thick glasses, wrinkled itself into a complication of amusements.

"Ah! I see. The earth is wearing a belt, or a sash. Or someone drew a line round it!"

"Oh, no—not that—I mean——"

In the general laughter, he did not share, or only a very little. He was thinking about the Arctic and Antarctic regions, which of course, on the globe, were white. Miss Buell was now telling them about the tropics, the jungles, the steamy heat of equatorial swamps, where the birds and butterflies, and even the snakes, were like living jewels. As he listened to these things, he was already, with a pleasant sense of half-effort, putting his secret between himself and the words. Was it really an effort at all? For effort implied something voluntary, and perhaps even something one did not especially want; whereas this was distinctly pleasant, and came almost of its own accord. All he needed to do was to think of that morning, the first one, and then of all the others——

But it was all so absurdly simple! It had amounted to so little. It was nothing, just an idea—and just why it should have become so wonderful, so permanent, was a mystery—a very pleasant one, to be sure, but also, in an amusing way, foolish. However, without ceasing to listen to Miss Buell, who had now moved up to the north temperate zone, he deliberately invited his memory of the first morning. It was only a moment or two after he had waked up—or perhaps the moment itself. But was there, to be exact, an exact moment? Was one awake all at once? or was it gradual? Anyway, it was after he had stretched a lazy hand up towards the headrail, and yawned, and then relaxed again among his warm covers, all the more grateful on a December morning, that the thing had happened. Suddenly, for no reason, he had thought of the postman, he remembered the postman. Perhaps there was nothing so odd in that. After all, he heard the postman almost every morning in his life—his heavy boots could be heard clumping round the corner at the top of the little cobbled hill-street, and then, progressively nearer, progressively louder, the double knock at each door, the crossings and re-crossings of the street, till finally the clumsy steps came stumbling across to the very door, and the tremendous knock came which shook the house itself.

(Miss Buell was saying "Vast wheat-growing areas in North America and Siberia."

Deirdre had for the moment placed her left hand across the back of her neck.)

But on this particular morning, the first morning, as he lay there with his eyes closed, he had for some reason *waited* for the postman. He wanted to hear him come round the corner. And that was precisely the joke—he never did. He never came. He never had come—*round the corner*—again. For when at last the steps *were* heard, they had already, he was quite sure, come a little down the hill, to the first house; and even so, the steps were curiously different—they were softer, they had a new secrecy about them, they were muffled and indistinct; and while the rhythm of them was the same, it now said a new thing —it said peace, it said remoteness, it said cold, it said sleep. And he had understood the situation at once—nothing could have seemed simpler—there had been snow in the night, such as all winter he had been longing for; and it was this which had rendered the postman's first footsteps inaudible, and the later ones faint. Of course! How lovely! And even now it must be snowing—it was going to be a snowy day— the long white ragged lines were drifting and sifting across the street, across the faces of the old houses, whispering and hushing, making little triangles of white in the corners between cobblestones, seething a little when the wind blew them over the ground to a drifted corner; and so it would be all day, getting deeper and deeper and silenter and silenter.

(Miss Buell was saying "Land of perpetual snow.")

All this time, of course (while he lay in bed), he had kept his eyes closed, listening to the nearer progress of the postman, the muffled footsteps thumping and slipping on the snow-sheathed cobbles; and all the other sounds—the double knocks, a frosty far-off voice or two, a bell ringing thinly and softly as if under a sheet of ice—had the same slightly abstracted quality, as if removed by one degree from actuality —as if everything in the world had been insulated by snow. But when at last, pleased, he opened his eyes, and turned them towards the window, to see for himself this long-desired and now so clearly imagined miracle—what he saw instead was brilliant sunlight on a roof; and when, astonished, he jumped out of bed and stared down into the street, expecting to see the cobbles obliterated by the snow, he saw nothing but the bare bright cobbles themselves.

Queer, the effect this extraordinary surprise had had upon him—all the following morning he had kept with him a sense as of snow falling about him, a secret screen of new snow between himself and the world. If he had not dreamed such a thing—and how could he have dreamed it while awake?—how else could one explain it? In any case, the delusion had been so vivid as to affect his entire behavior. He could not now remember whether it was on the first or the second morning—or was it even the third?—that his mother had drawn attention to some oddness in his manner.

"But my darling—" she had said at the breakfast table—"what has come over you? You don't seem to be listening. . . ."

And how often that very thing had happened since!

(Miss Buell was now asking if anyone knew the difference between the North Pole and the Magnetic Pole. Deirdre was holding up her flickering brown hand, and he could see the four white dimples that marked the knuckles.)

Perhaps it hadn't been either the second or third morning—or even the fourth or fifth. How could he be sure? How could he be sure just when the delicious *progress* had become clear? Just when it had really *begun?* The intervals weren't very precise. . . . All he now knew was, that at some point or other—perhaps the second day, perhaps the sixth —he had noticed that the presence of the snow was a little more insistent, the sound of it clearer; and, conversely, the sound of the postman's footsteps more indistinct. Not only could he not hear the steps come round the corner, he could not even hear them at the first house. It was below the first house that he heard them; and then, a few days later, it was below the second house that he heard them; and a few days later again, below the third. Gradually, gradually, the snow was becoming heavier, the sound of its seething louder, the cobblestones more and more muffled. When he found, each morning, on going to the window, after the ritual of listening, that the roofs and cobbles were as bare as ever, it made no difference. This was, after all, only what he had expected. It was even what pleased him, what rewarded him: the thing was his own, belonged to no one else. No one else knew about it, not even his mother and father. There, outside, were the bare cobbles; and here, inside, was the snow. Snow growing heavier each day, muffling the world, hiding the ugly, and deadening increasingly —above all—the steps of the postman.

"But my darling—" she had said at the luncheon table—"what has come over you? You don't seem to listen when people speak to you. That's the third time I've asked you to pass your plate. . . ."

How was one to explain this to Mother? or to Father? There was, of course, nothing to be done about it: nothing. All one could do was to laugh embarrassedly, pretend to be a little ashamed, apologize, and take a sudden and somewhat disingenuous interest in what was being done or said. The cat had stayed out all night. He had a curious swelling on his left cheek—perhaps somebody had kicked him, or a stone had struck him. Mrs. Kempton was or was not coming to tea. The house was going to be house cleaned, or "turned out," on Wednesday instead of Friday. A new lamp was provided, for his evening work— perhaps it was eye-strain which accounted for this new and so peculiar vagueness of his—Mother was looking at him with amusement as she said this, but with something else as well. A new lamp? A new lamp. Yes Mother, No Mother, Yes Mother. School is going very well. The geometry is very easy. The history is very dull. The geography is very interesting—particularly when it takes one to the North Pole. Why the North Pole? Oh, well, it would be fun to be an explorer. Another Peary or Scott or Shackleton. And then abruptly he found his interest in the talk at an end, stared at the pudding on his plate, listened, waited, and began once more—ah how heavenly, too, the first beginnings—to hear or feel—for could he actually hear it?—the silent snow, the secret snow.

(Miss Buell was telling them about the search for the Northwest Passage, about Hendrik Hudson, the Half Moon.)

This had been, indeed, the only distressing feature of the new experience: the fact that it so increasingly had brought him into a kind of mute misunderstanding, or even conflict, with his father and mother.

It was as if he were trying to lead a double life. On the one hand he had to be Paul Hasleman, and keep up the appearance of being that person—dress, wash, and answer intelligently when spoken to—; on the other, he had to explore this new world which had been opened to him. Nor could there be the slightest doubt—not the slightest—that the new world was the profounder and more wonderful of the two. It was irresistible. It was miraculous. Its beauty was simply beyond anything—beyond speech as beyond thought—utterly incommunicable. But how then, between the two worlds, of which he was thus constantly aware, was he to keep a balance? One must get up, one must go to breakfast, one must talk with Mother, go to school, do one's lessons—and, in all this, try not to appear too much of a fool. But if all the while one was also trying to extract the full deliciousness of another and quite separate existence, one which could not easily (if at all) be spoken of—how was one to manage? How was one to explain? Would it be safe to explain? Would it be absurd? Would it merely mean that he would get into some obscure kind of trouble?

These thoughts came and went, came and went, as softly and secretly as the snow; they were not precisely a disturbance, perhaps they were even a pleasure; he liked to have them; their presence was something almost palpable, something he could stroke with his hand, without closing his eyes, and without ceasing to see Miss Buell and the school-room and the globe and the freckles on Deirdre's neck; nevertheless he did in a sense cease to see, or to see the obvious external world, and substituted for this vision the vision of snow, the sound of snow, and the slow, almost soundless, approach of the postman. Yesterday, it had been only at the sixth house that the postman had become audible; the snow was much deeper now, it was falling more swiftly and heavily, the sound of its seething was more distinct, more soothing, more persistent. And this morning, it had been—as nearly as he could figure—just above the seventh house—perhaps only a step or two above: at most, he had heard two or three footsteps before the knock had sounded. . . . And with each such narrowing of the sphere, each nearer approach of the limit at which the postman was first audible, it was odd how sharply was increased the amount of illusion which had to be carried into the ordinary business of daily life. Each day, it

was harder to get out of bed, to go to the window, to look out at the
—as always—perfectly empty and snowless street. Each day it was more
difficult to go through the perfunctory motions of greeting Mother and
Father at breakfast, to reply to their questions, to put his books together and go to school. And at school, how extraordinarily hard to
conduct with success simultaneously the public life and the life that
was secret. There were times when he longed—positively ached—to
tell everyone about it—to burst out with it—only to be checked almost
at once by a far-off feeling as of some faint absurdity which was inherent in it—but *was* it absurd?—and more importantly by a sense
of mysterious power in his very secrecy. Yes: it must be kept secret.
That, more and more, became clear. At whatever cost to himself, whatever pain to others——

(Miss Buell looked straight at him, smiling, and said, "Perhaps we'll
ask Paul. I'm sure Paul will come out of his day-dream long enough
to be able to tell us. Won't you, Paul?" He rose slowly from his chair,
resting one hand on the brightly varnished desk, and deliberately stared
through the snow towards the blackboard. It was an effort, but it was
amusing to make it. "Yes," he said slowly, "it was what we now call
the Hudson River. This he thought to be the Northwest Passage. He
was disappointed." He sat down again, and as he did so Deirdre half
turned in her chair and gave him a shy smile, of approval and admiration.)

At whatever pain to others.

This part of it was very puzzling, very puzzling. Mother was very
nice, and so was Father. Yes, that was all true enough. He wanted to
be nice to them, to tell them everything—and yet, was it really wrong
of him to want to have a secret place of his own?

At bedtime, the night before, Mother had said, "If this goes on, my
lad, we'll have to see a doctor, we will! We can't have our boy—" But
what was it she had said? "Live in another world"? "Live so far
away"? The word "far" had been in it, he was sure, and then Mother
had taken up a magazine again and laughed a little, but with an expression which wasn't mirthful. He had felt sorry for her. . . .

The bell rang for dismissal. The sound came to him through long curved parallels of falling snow. He saw Deirdre rise, and had himself risen almost as soon—but not quite as soon—as she.

II

On the walk homeward, which was timeless, it pleased him to see through the accompaniment, or counterpoint, of snow, the items of mere externality on his way. There were many kinds of bricks in the sidewalks, and laid in many kinds of pattern. The garden walls too were various, some of wooden palings, some of plaster, some of stone. Twigs of bushes leaned over the walls; the little hard green winter-buds of lilac, on gray stems, sheathed and fat; other branches very thin and fine and black and desiccated. Dirty sparrows huddled in the bushes, as dull in color as dead fruit left in leafless trees. A single starling creaked on a weather vane. In the gutter, beside a drain, was a scrap of torn and dirty newspaper, caught in a little delta of filth: the word ECZEMA appeared in large capitals, and below it was a letter from Mrs. Amelia D. Cravath, 2100 Pine Street, Fort Worth, Texas, to the effect that after being a sufferer for years she had been cured by Caley's Ointment. In the little delta, beside the fan-shaped and deeply runneled continent of brown mud, were lost twigs, descended from their parent trees, dead matches, a rusty horse-chestnut burr, a small concentration of sparkling gravel on the lip of the sewer, a fragment of eggshell, a streak of yellow sawdust which had been wet and was now dry and congealed, a brown pebble, and a broken feather. Further on was a cement sidewalk, ruled into geometrical parallelograms, with a brass inlay at one end commemorating the contractors who had laid it, and, halfway across, an irregular and random series of dog-tracks, immortalized in synthetic stone. He knew these well, and always stepped on them; to cover the little hollows with his own foot had always been a queer pleasure; today he did it once more, but perfunctorily and detachedly, all the while thinking of something else. That was a dog, a long time ago, who had made a mistake and walked on the cement while it was still wet. He had probably wagged his tail, but that hadn't been recorded. Now, Paul Hasleman, aged twelve, on his way home from school, crossed the same river, which in the meantime had frozen into rock. Homeward through the snow, the snow falling in bright sunshine. Homeward?

Then came the gateway with the two posts surmounted by egg-shaped stones which had been cunningly balanced on their ends, as if by Columbus, and mortared in the very act of balance: a source of perpetual wonder. On the brick wall just beyond, the letter H had been stenciled, presumably for some purpose. H? H.

The green hydrant, with a little green-painted chain attached to the brass screw-cap.

The elm tree, with the great gray wound in the bark, kidney-shaped, into which he always put his hand—to feel the cold but living wood. The injury, he had been sure, was due to the gnawings of a tethered horse. But now it deserved only a passing palm, a merely tolerant eye. There were more important things. Miracles. Beyond the thoughts of trees, mere elms. Beyond the thoughts of sidewalks, mere stone, mere brick, mere cement. Beyond the thoughts even of his own shoes, which trod these sidewalks obediently, bearing a burden—far above—of elaborate mystery. He watched them. They were not very well polished; he had neglected them, for a very good reason: they were one of the many parts of the increasing difficulty of the daily return to daily life, the morning struggle. To get up, having at last opened one's eyes, to go to the window, and discover no snow, to wash, to dress, to descend the curving stairs to breakfast——

At whatever pain to others, nevertheless, one must persevere in severance, since the incommunicability of the experience demanded it. It was desirable of course to be kind to Mother and Father, especially as they seemed to be worried, but it was also desirable to be resolute. If they should decide—as appeared likely—to consult the doctor, Doctor Howells, and have Paul inspected, his heart listened to through a kind of dictaphone, his lungs, his stomach—well, that was all right. He would go through with it. He would give them answer for question, too—perhaps such answers as they hadn't expected? No. That would never do. For the secret world must, at all costs, be preserved.

The bird-house in the apple-tree was empty—it was the wrong time of year for wrens. The little round black door had lost its pleasure.

The wrens were enjoying other houses, other nests, remoter trees. But this too was a notion which he only vaguely and grazingly entertained —as if, for the moment, he merely touched an edge of it; there was something further on, which was already assuming a sharper importance; something which already teased at the corners of his eyes, teasing also at the corner of his mind. It was funny to think that he so wanted this, so awaited it—and yet found himself enjoying this momentary dalliance with the bird-house, as if for a quite deliberate postponement and enhancement of the approaching pleasure. He was aware of his delay, of his smiling and detached and now almost uncomprehending gaze at the little bird-house; he knew what he was going to look at next: it was his own little cobbled hill-street, his own house, the little river at the bottom of the hill, the grocer's shop with the cardboard man in the window—and now, thinking of all this, he turned his head, still smiling, and looking quickly right and left through the snow-laden sunlight.

And the mist of snow, as he had foreseen, was still on it—a ghost of snow falling in the bright sunlight, softly and steadily floating and turning and pausing, soundlessly meeting the snow that covered, as with a transparent mirage, the bare bright cobbles. He loved it—he stood still and loved it. Its beauty was paralyzing—beyond all words, all experience, all dream. No fairy-story he had ever read could be compared with it—none had ever given him this extraordinary combination of ethereal loveliness with a something else, unnameable, which was just faintly and deliciously terrifying. What was this thing? As he thought of it, he looked upward toward his own bedroom window, which was open—and it was as if he looked straight into the room and saw himself lying half awake in his bed. There he was—at this very instant he was still perhaps actually there—more truly there than standing here at the edge of the cobbled hill-street, with one hand lifted to shade his eyes against the snow-sun. Had he indeed ever left his room, in all this time? since that very first morning? Was the whole progress still being enacted there, was it still the same morning, and himself not yet wholly awake? And even now, had the postman not yet come round the corner? . . .

This idea amused him, and automatically, as he thought of it, he turned his head and looked toward the top of the hill. There was, of course, nothing there—nothing and no one. The street was empty and quiet. And all the more because of its emptiness it occurred to him to count the houses—a thing which, oddly enough, he hadn't before thought of doing. Of course, he had known there weren't many— many, that is, on his own side of the street, which were the ones that figured in the postman's progress—but nevertheless it came to him as something of a shock to find that there were precisely *six,* above his own house—his own house was the seventh.

Six!

Astonished, he looked at his own house—looked at the door, on which was the number thirteen—and then realized that the whole thing was exactly and logically and absurdly what he ought to have known. Just the same, the realization gave him abruptly, and even a little frighteningly, a sense of hurry. He was being hurried—he was being rushed. For—he knit his brows—he couldn't be mistaken—it was just above the *seventh* house, his *own* house, that the postman had first been audible this very morning. But in that case—in that case—did it mean that tomorrow he would hear nothing? The knock he had heard must have been the knock of their own door. Did it mean—and this was an idea which gave him a really extraordinary feeling of surprise —that he would never hear the postman again?—that tomorrow morn- ing the postman would already have passed the house, in a snow by then so deep as to render his footsteps completely inaudible? That he would have made his approach down the snow-filled street so sound- lessly, so secretly, that he, Paul Hasleman, there lying in bed, would not have waked in time, or, waking, would have heard nothing?

But how could that be? Unless even the knocker should be muffled in the snow—frozen tight, perhaps? . . . But in that case——

A vague feeling of disappointment came over him; a vague sadness, as if he felt himself deprived of something which he had long looked forward to, something much prized. After all this, all this beautiful progress, the slow delicious advance of the postman through the silent and secret snow, the knock creeping closer each day, and the footsteps nearer, the audible compass of the world thus daily narrowed, nar- rowed, narrowed, as the snow soothingly and beautifully encroached and deepened, after all this, was he to be defrauded of the one thing he had so wanted—to be able to count, as it were, the last two or three solemn footsteps, as they finally approached his own door? Was it all going to happen, at the end, so suddenly? or indeed, had it already happened? with no slow and subtle gradations of menace, in which he could luxuriate?

He gazed upward again, toward his own window which flashed in the sun: and this time almost with a feeling that it would be better if he *were* still in bed, in that room; for in that case this must still be the first morning, and there would be six more mornings to come—or, for that matter, seven or eight or nine—how could he be sure?—or even more.

III

After supper, the inquisition began. He stood before the doctor, under the lamp, and submitted silently to the usual thumpings and tappings.

"Now will you please say 'Ah!'?"

"Ah!"

"Now again please, if you don't mind."

"Ah."

"Say it slowly, and hold it if you can——"

"Ah-h-h-h-h-h——"

"Good."

How silly all this was. As if it had anything to do with his throat! Or his heart or lungs!

Relaxing his mouth, of which the corners, after all this absurd stretching, felt uncomfortable, he avoided the doctor's eyes, and stared towards the fireplace, past his mother's feet (in gray slippers) which projected from the green chair, and his father's feet (in brown slippers) which stood neatly side by side on the hearth rug.

"Hm. There is certainly nothing wrong there . . ."

He felt the doctor's eyes fixed upon him, and, as if merely to be polite, returned the look, but with a feeling of justifiable evasiveness.

"Now, young man, tell me—do you feel all right?"

"Yes, sir, quite all right."

"No headaches? no dizziness?"

"No, I don't think so."

"Let me see. Let's get a book, if you don't mind—yes, thank you, that will do splendidly—and now, Paul, if you'll just read it, holding it as you would normally hold it——"

He took the book and read:

"And another praise have I to tell for this the city our mother, the gift of a great god, a glory of the land most high; the might of horses, the might of young horses, the might of the sea. . . . For thou, son of Cronus, our lord Poseidon, hast throned herein this pride, since in these roads first thou didst show forth the curb that cures the rage of steeds. And the shapely oar, apt to men's hands, hath a wondrous speed on the brine, following the hundred-footed Nereids. . . . O land that art praised above all lands, now is it for thee to make those bright praises seen in deeds."

He stopped, tentatively, and lowered the heavy book.

"No—as I thought—there is certainly no superficial sign of eye-strain."

Silence thronged the room, and he was aware of the focused scrutiny of the three people who confronted him. . . .

"We could have his eyes examined—but I believe it is something else."

"What could it be?" This was his father's voice.

"It's only this curious absent-minded—" This was his mother's voice.

In the presence of the doctor, they both seemed irritatingly apologetic.

"I believe it is something else. Now Paul—I would like very much to ask you a question or two. You will answer them, won't you—you know I'm an old, old friend of yours, eh? That's right! . . ."

His back was thumped twice by the doctor's fat fist—then the doctor was grinning at him with false amiability, while with one fingernail he was scratching the top button of his waistcoat. Beyond the doctor's shoulder was the fire, the fingers of flame making light prestidigitation against the sooty fireback, the soft sound of their random flutter the only sound.

"I would like to know—is there anything that worries you?"

The doctor was again smiling, his eyelids low against the little black pupils, in each of which was a tiny white bead of light. Why answer him? why answer him at all? "At whatever pain to others"—but it was all a nuisance, this necessity for resistance, this necessity for attention: it was as if one had been stood up on a brilliantly lighted stage, under a great round blaze of spotlight; as if one were merely a trained seal, or a performing dog, or a fish, dipped out of an aquarium and held up by the tail. It would serve them right if he were merely to bark or growl. And meanwhile, to miss these last few precious hours, these hours of which every minute was more beautiful than the last, more menacing—? He still looked, as if from a great distance, at the beads of light in the doctor's eyes, at the fixed false smile, and then, beyond, once more at his mother's slippers, his father's slippers, the soft flutter of the fire. Even here, even amongst these hostile presences, and in this arranged light, he could see the snow, he could hear it—it was in the corners of the room, where the shadow was deepest, under the sofa, behind the half-opened door which led to the dining room. It was gentler here, softer, its seethe the quietest of whispers, as if, in defer-ence to a drawing room, it had quite deliberately put on its "manners"; it kept itself out of sight, obliterated itself, but distinctly with an air of saying, "Ah, but just wait! Wait till we are alone together! Then I will begin to tell you something new! Something white! something cold! something sleepy! something of cease, and peace, and the long bright curve of space! Tell them to go away. Banish them. Refuse to speak. Leave them, go upstairs to your room, turn out the light and get into bed—I will go with you, I will be waiting for you, I will tell you a better story than Little Kay of the Skates, or The Snow Ghost —I will surround your bed, I will close the windows, pile a deep drift against the door, so that none will ever again be able to enter. Speak to them! . . ." It seemed as if the little hissing voice came from a slow white spiral of falling flakes in the corner by the front window—but he could not be sure. He felt himself smiling, then, and said to the doctor, but without looking at him, looking beyond him still——

"Oh, no, I think not——"

"But are you sure, my boy?"

His father's voice came softly and coldly then—the familiar voice of silken warning. . . .

"You needn't answer at once, Paul—remember we're trying to help you—think it over and be quite sure, won't you?"

He felt himself smiling again, at the notion of being quite sure. What a joke! As if he weren't so sure that reassurance was no longer necessary, and all this cross-examination a ridiculous farce, a grotesque parody! What could they know about it? These gross intelligences, these humdrum minds so bound to the usual, the ordinary? Impossible to tell them about it! Why, even now, even now, with the proof so abundant, so formidable, so imminent, so appallingly present here in this very room, could they believe it?—could even his mother believe it? No—it was only too plain that if anything were said about it, the merest hint given, they would be incredulous—they would laugh—they would say "Absurd!" think things about him which weren't true. . . .

"Why no, I'm not worried—why should I be?"

He looked then straight at the doctor's low-lidded eyes, looked from one of them to the other, from one bead of light to the other, and gave a little laugh.

The doctor seemed to be disconcerted by this. He drew back in his chair, resting a fat white hand on either knee. The smile faded slowly from his face.

"Well, Paul!" he said, and paused gravely, "I'm afraid you don't take this quite seriously enough. I think you perhaps don't quite realize—don't quite realize—" He took a deep quick breath, and turned, as if helplessly, at a loss for words, to the others. But Mother and Father were both silent—no help was forthcoming.

"You must surely know, be aware, that you have not been quite yourself, of late? don't you know that? . . ."

It was amusing to watch the doctor's renewed attempt at a smile, a queer disorganized look, as of confidential embarrassment.

"I feel all right, sir," he said, and again gave the little laugh.

"And we're trying to help you." The doctor's tone sharpened.

"Yes sir, I know. But why? I'm all right. I'm just *thinking,* that's all."

His mother made a quick movement forward, resting a hand on the back of the doctor's chair.

"Thinking?" she said. "But my dear, about what?"

This was a direct challenge—and would have to be directly met. But before he met it, he looked again into the corner by the door, as if for reassurance. He smiled again at what he saw, at what he heard. The little spiral was still there, still softly whirling, like the ghost of a white kitten chasing the ghost of a white tail, and making as it did so the faintest of whispers. It was all right! If only he could remain firm, everything was going to be all right.

"Oh, about anything, about nothing—*you* know the way you do!"

"You mean—day-dreaming?"

"Oh, no—thinking!"

"But thinking about *what?*"

"Anything."

He laughed a third time—but this time, happening to glance upward towards his mother's face, he was appalled at the effect his laughter seemed to have upon her. Her mouth had opened in an expression of horror. . . . This was too bad! Unfortunate! He had known it would cause pain, of course—but he hadn't expected it to be quite so bad as this. Perhaps—perhaps if he just gave them a tiny gleaming hint——?

"About the snow," he said.

"What on earth!" This was his father's voice. The brown slippers came a step nearer on the hearth rug.

"But my dear, what do you mean?" This was his mother's voice.

The doctor merely stared.

"Just *snow,* that's all. I like to think about it."

"Tell us about it, my boy."

"But that's all it is. There's nothing to tell. *You* know what snow is?"

This he said almost angrily, for he felt they were trying to corner him. He turned sideways so as no longer to face the doctor, and the better to see the inch of blackness between the window-sill and the lowered curtain—the cold inch of beckoning and delicious night. At once he felt better, more assured.

"Mother—can I go to bed, now, please? I've got a headache."

"But I thought you said——"

"It's just come. It's all these questions—! Can I, Mother?"

"You can go as soon as the doctor has finished."

"Don't you think this thing ought to be gone into thoroughly, and *now?*" This was Father's voice. The brown slippers again came a step nearer, the voice was the well-known "punishment" voice, resonant and cruel.

"Oh, what's the use, Norman——"

Quite suddenly, everyone was silent. And without precisely facing them, nevertheless he was aware that all three of them were watching him with an extraordinary intensity—staring hard at him—as if he had done something monstrous, or was himself some kind of monster. He could hear the soft irregular flutter of the flames; the cluck-click-cluck-click of the clock; far and faint, two sudden spurts of laughter from the kitchen, as quickly cut off as begun; a murmur of water in the pipes; and then, the silence seemed to deepen, to spread out, to become worldlong and worldwide, to become timeless and shapeless, and to center inevitably and rightly, with a slow and sleepy but enormous concentration of all power, on the beginning of a new sound. What this new sound was going to be, he knew perfectly well. It might begin with a hiss, but it would end with a roar—there was no time to lose—he must escape. It mustn't happen here——

Without another word, he turned and ran up the stairs.

IV

Not a moment too soon. The darkness was coming in long white waves. A prolonged sibilance filled the night—a great seamless seethe of wild influence went abruptly across it—a cold low humming shook the windows. He shut the door and flung off his clothes in the dark. The bare black floor was like a little raft tossed in waves of snow, almost overwhelmed, washed under whitely, up again, smothered in curled billows of feather. The snow was laughing: it spoke from all sides at once: it pressed closer to him as he ran and jumped exulting into his bed.

"Listen to us!" it said. "Listen! We have come to tell you the story

we told you about. You remember? Lie down. Shut your eyes, now
—you will no longer see much—in this white darkness who could see,
or want to see? We will take the place of everything. . . . Listen——"

A beautiful varying dance of snow began at the front of the room,
came forward and then retreated, flattened out toward the floor, then
rose fountain-like to the ceiling, swayed, recruited itself from a new
stream of flakes which poured laughing in through the humming window, advanced again, lifted long white arms. It said peace, it said
remoteness, it said cold—it said——

But then a gash of horrible light fell brutally across the room from
the opening door—the snow drew back hissing—something alien had
come into the room—something hostile. This thing rushed at him,
clutched at him, shook him—and he was not merely horrified, he was
filled with such a loathing as he had never known. What was this?
this cruel disturbance? this act of anger and hate? It was as if he had
to reach up a hand toward another world for any understanding of it
—an effort of which he was only barely capable. But of that other
world he still remembered just enough to know the exorcising words.
They tore themselves from his other life suddenly——

"Mother! Mother! Go away! I hate you!"

And with that effort, everything was solved, everything became all
right: the seamless hiss advanced once more, the long white wavering
lines rose and fell like enormous whispering sea-waves, the whisper
becoming louder, the laughter more numerous.

"Listen!" it said. "We'll tell you the last, the most beautiful and
secret story—shut your eyes—it is a very small story—a story that gets
smaller and smaller—it comes inward instead of opening like a flower
—it is a flower becoming a seed—a little cold seed—do you hear? we
are leaning closer to you——"

The hiss was now becoming a roar—the whole world was a vast
moving screen of snow—but even now it said peace, it said remoteness,
it said cold, it said sleep.

E. B. WHITE

COMMENTARY

On March 6, 1939, Life published an illustrated account of some experiments on rats done by Professor Norman R. F. Maier of the University of Michigan. Professor Maier, by changing his stimuli in the middle of the experiment or by removing the expected satisfaction entirely, found that he could drive his rats crazy. Three weeks after this article appeared, E. B. White, an old Life reader, published "The Door" in the pages of The New Yorker. If I were asked to name the most brilliant piece of prose ever to appear in the columns of The New Yorker, I would propose "The Door," a freehand translation of Professor Maier's experiments into terms of modern living.

Readers may not find everything in this horrible, wonderful story entirely comprehensible, but what is frightening is that they will not find everything entirely incomprehensible either. It would be more comforting if "The Door" meant absolutely nothing to us but lunatic ravings. The trouble lies in the insidious sense it makes. For which of us, living as we do in a synthetic environment ("everything is something it isn't") and subjected to strains and pressures that modern man has not had time to get used to, does not feel a chilly sense of kinship with Mr. White's neurotic? Which of us does not recognize the truth of Mr. White's marvelous phrase, "the unspeakably bright imploring look of the frustrated"? We are all living in the Bomb Age, the Headline Age, the Speed Age, the Jitter Age, and who is there whose nerves are not touched or tortured by it?

It is this uneasy, cornered-rat mood of our period that Mr. White has, with extraordinary subtlety and ruthlessness, distilled in "The Door."

The Door

E. B. WHITE

EVERYTHING (he kept saying) is something it isn't. And everybody is always somewhere else. Maybe it was the city, being in the city, that made him feel how queer everything was and that it was something else. Maybe (he kept thinking) it was the names of the things. The names were tex and frequently koid. Or they were flex and oid or they were duroid (sani) or flexsan (duro), but everything was glass (but not quite glass) and the thing that you touched (the surface, washable, crease-resistant) was rubber, only it wasn't quite rubber and you didn't quite touch it but almost. The wall, which was glass but thrutex, turned out on being approached not to be a wall, it was something else, it was an opening or doorway—and the doorway (through which he saw himself approaching) turned out to be something else, it was a wall. And what he had eaten not having agreed with him.

He was in a washable house, but he wasn't sure. Now about those rats, he kept saying to himself. He meant the rats that the Professor had driven crazy by forcing them to deal with problems which were beyond the scope of rats, the insoluble problems. He meant the rats that had been trained to jump at the square card with the circle in the middle, and the card (because it was something it wasn't) would give way and let the rat into a place where the food was, but then one day it would be a trick played on the rat, and the card would be changed, and the rat would jump but the card wouldn't give way, and it was an impossible situation (for a rat) and the rat would go insane and into its eyes would come the unspeakably bright imploring look of the frustrated, and after the convulsions were over and the frantic racing

755

around, then the passive stage would set in and the willingness to let anything be done to it, even if it was something else.

He didn't know which door (or wall) or opening in the house to jump at, to get through, because one was an opening that wasn't a door (it was a void, or koid) and the other was a wall that wasn't an opening, it was a sanitary cupboard of the same color. He caught a glimpse of his eyes staring into his eyes, in the thrutex, and in them was the expression he had seen in the picture of the rats—weary after convulsions and the frantic racing around, when they were willing and did not mind having anything done to them. More and more (he kept saying) I am confronted by a problem which is incapable of solution (for this time even if he chose the right door, there would be no food behind it) and that is what madness is, and things seeming different from what they are. He heard, in the house, where he was, in the city to which he had gone (as toward a door which might, or might not, give way), a noise—not a loud noise but more of a low prefabricated humming. It came from a place in the base of the wall (or stat) where the flue carrying the filterable air was, and not far from the Minipiano, which was made of the same material nailbrushes are made of, and which was under the stairs. "This, too, has been tested," she said, pointing, but not at it, "and found viable." It wasn't a loud noise, he kept thinking, sorry that he had seen his eyes, even though it was through his own eyes that he had seen them.

First will come the convulsions (he said), then the exhaustion, then the willingness to let anything be done. "And you better believe it *will* be."

All his life he had been confronted by situations which were incapable of being solved, and there was a deliberateness behind all this, behind this changing of the card (or door), because they would always wait till you had learned to jump at the certain card (or door)—the one with the circle—and then they would change it on you. There have been so many doors changed on me, he said, in the last twenty years, but it is now becoming clear that it is an impossible situation, and the question is whether to jump again, even though they ruffle you in the rump with a blast of air—to make you jump. He wished he wasn't standing by the Minipiano. First they would teach you the prayers and the Psalms, and that would be the right door (the one with the circle), and the long sweet words with the holy sound, and that would be the one to jump at to get where the food was. Then one day you jumped and it didn't give way, so that all you got was the bump on the nose, and the first bewilderment, the first young bewilderment.

I don't know whether to tell her about the door they substituted or not, he said, the one with the equation on it and the picture of the amoeba reproducing itself by division. Or the one with the photostatic copy of the check for thirty-two dollars and fifty cents. But the jumping was so long ago, although the bump is . . . how those old wounds hurt! Being crazy this way wouldn't be so bad if only, if only. If only when you put your foot forward to take a step, the ground wouldn't come up to meet your foot the way it does. And the same way in the street (only I may never get back to the street unless I jump at the right door), the curb coming up to meet your foot, anticipating ever so delicately the weight of the body, which is somewhere else. "We could take your name," she said, "and send it to you." And it wouldn't be so bad if only you could read a sentence all the way through without jumping (your eye) to something else on the same page; and then (he kept thinking) there was that man out in Jersey, the one who started to chop his trees down, one by one, the man who began talking about how he would take his house to pieces, brick by brick, because he faced a problem incapable of solution, probably, so he began to hack at the trees in the yard, began to pluck with trembling fingers at the bricks in the house. Even if a house is not washable, it is worth taking down. It is not till later that the exhaustion sets in.

But it is inevitable that they will keep changing the doors on you, he said, because that is what they are for; and the thing is to get used to it and not let it unsettle the mind. But that would mean not jumping, and you can't. Nobody can not jump. There will be no not-jumping. Among rats, perhaps, but among people never. Everybody has to keep jumping at a door (the one with the circle on it) because that is the way everybody is, specially some people. You wouldn't want me, standing here, to tell you, would you, about my friend the poet (deceased) who said, "My heart has followed all my days something I cannot

name"? (It had the circle on it.) And like many poets, although few
so beloved, he is gone. It killed him, the jumping. First, of course
there were the preliminary bouts, the convulsions, and the calm and
the willingness.

I remember the door with the picture of the girl on it (only it was
spring), her arms outstretched in loveliness, her dress (it was the one
with the circle on it) uncaught, beginning the slow, clear, blinding cas-
cade—and I guess we would all like to try that door again, for it
seemed like the way and for a while it was the way, the door would
open and you would go through winged and exalted (like any rat
and the food would be there, the way the Professor had it arranged,
everything O.K., and you had chosen the right door for the world was
young. The time they changed that door on me, my nose bled for a
hundred hours—how do you like that, Madam? Or would you prefer
to show me further through this so strange house, or you could take
my name and send it to me, for although my heart has followed all
my days something I cannot name, I am tired of the jumping and
do not know which way to go, Madam, and I am not even sure that
I am not tried beyond the endurance of man (rat, if you will) and
have taken leave of sanity. What are you following these days, old
friend, after your recovery from the last bump? What is the name, or
is it something you cannot name? The rats have a name for it by this
time, perhaps, but I don't know what they call it. I call it plexikoid and
it comes in sheets, something like insulating board, unattainable and
ugli-proof.

And there was the man out in Jersey, because I keep thinking about
his terrible necessity and the passion and trouble he had gone to all
those years in the indescribable abundance of a householder's detail,
building the estate and the planting of the trees and in spring the lawn
dressing and in fall the bulbs for the spring burgeoning, and the watering of the grass on the long light evenings in summer and the gravel
for the driveway (all had to be thought out, planned) and the decorative borders, probably, the perennials and the bug spray, and the
building of the house from plans of the architect, first the sills, then the
studs, then the full corn in the ear, the floors laid on the floor timbers
smoothed, and then the carpets upon the smooth floors and the cur-

tains and the rods therefor. And then, almost without warning, he would be jumping at the same old door and it wouldn't give: they had changed it on him, making life no longer supportable under the elms in the elm shade, under the maples in the maple shade.

"Here you have the maximum of openness in a small room."

It was impossible to say (maybe it was the city) what made him feel the way he did, and I am not the only one either, he kept thinking—ask any doctor if I am. The doctors, they know how many there are, they even know where the trouble is only they don't like to tell you about the prefrontal lobe because that means making a hole in your skull and removing the work of centuries. It took so long coming, this lobe, so many, many years. (Is it something you read in the paper, perhaps?) And now, the strain being so great, the door having been changed by the Professor once too often . . . but it only means a whiff of ether, a few deft strokes, and the higher animal becomes a little easier in his mind and more like the lower one. From now on, you see, that's the way it will be, the ones with the small prefrontal lobes will win because the other ones are hurt too much by this incessant bumping. They can stand just so much, eh, Doctor? (And what is that, pray, that you have in your hand?) Still, you never can tell, eh, Madam?

He crossed (carefully) the room, the thick carpet under him softly, and went toward the door carefully, which was glass and he could see himself in it, and which, at his approach, opened to allow him to pass through; and beyond he half expected to find one of the old doors that he had known, perhaps the one with the circle, the one with the girl her arms outstretched in loveliness and beauty before him. But he saw instead a moving stairway, and descended in light (he kept thinking) to the street below and to the other people. As he stepped off, the ground came up slightly, to meet his foot.

S. J. PERELMAN

S. J. Perelman is a man who scorns wet hens, because he is so much madder than they are. He is the most precious lunatic in America and it is much more important to preserve him permanently than it is to keep that irritating old chicken's heart pulsating over at the Rockefeller Institute. Yet what is being done for Perelman, S. J.? Truly we are a nation that has not yet learned to honor its great men. Someday you'll be sorry, and it'll be too late.

Perelman is very, very funny but he is not so very, very funny as to obscure the fact that he is also an extraordinary prose writer. He's a good man from whom to learn the art of English. He has a masterly sense of cliché. Sometimes in the course of a single paragraph he will manipulate a number of different vintages of slang in such a manner as to make you perceive a good deal about the mutations of language. He handles a sentence as a good carpenter does a hammer and he is a master of that kind of comic effect which arises from a subtle use of the unexpected.

The Crazy School of American humor that flourished in the twenties is pretty nearly extinct. But Perelman persists. May he persist in persisting.

Is There an Osteosynchrondroitrician
in the House?

BY

S. J. PERELMAN

LOOKING BACK at it now, I see that every afternoon at 4:30 for the past five months I had fallen into an exact routine. First off, I'd tap the dottle from my pipe by knocking it against the hob. I never smoke a pipe, but I like to keep one with a little dottle in it, and an inexpensive hob to tap it against; when you're in the writing game, there are these little accessories you need. Then I'd slip off my worn old green smoking jacket, which I loathe, and start down Lexington Avenue for home. Sometimes, finding myself in my shirtsleeves, I'd have to run back to my atelier for my jacket and overcoat, but as I say, when you're in the writing game, it's strictly head-in-the-clouds. Now, Lexington Avenue is Lexington Avenue—when you've once seen Bloomingdale's and the Wil-Low Cafeteria, you don't go nostalgic all over as you might for the Avenue de l'Observatoire and the Closerie des Lilas.

Anyway, I'd be head down and scudding along under bare poles by the time I reached the block between Fifty-eighth and Fifty-seventh Streets, and my glance into those three shop windows would be purely automatic. First, the highly varnished *Schnecken* in the bakery; then the bones of a human foot shimmying slowly on a near-mahogany pedestal in the shoestore; and finally the clock set in the heel of a congress gaiter at the bootblack's. By now my shabby old reflexes would tell me it was time to buy an evening paper and bury my head in it. A little whim of my wife's; she liked to dig it up, as a puppy does a bone, while I was sipping my cocktail. Later on I taught her to frisk with a ball of yarn, but to get back to what happened Washington's Birthday.

I was hurrying homeward that holiday afternoon pretty much in the groove, humming an aria from "Till Tom Special" and wishing I could play the clarinet like a man named Goodman. Just as it occurred to me that I might drug this individual and torture his secret out of him, I came abreast the window of the shoestore containing the bones of the human foot. My mouth suddenly developed that curious dry feeling when I saw that they were vibrating, as usual, from north to south, every little metatarsal working with the blandest contempt for all I hold dear. I pressed my ear against the window and heard the faint clicking of the motor housed in the box beneath. A little scratch here and there on the shellac surface showed where one of the more enterprising toes had tried to do a solo but had quickly rejoined the band. Not only was the entire arch rolling forward and backward in an oily fashion, but it had evolved an obscene side sway at the same time, a good deal like the *danse à ventre*. Maybe the foot had belonged to an Ouled-Naïl girl, but I felt I didn't care to find out. I was aware immediately of an active desire to rush home and lie down attended by my loved ones. The only trouble was that when I started to leave that place, I could feel my arches acting according to all the proper orthopedic laws, and I swear people turned to look at me as if they heard a clicking sound.

The full deviltry of the thing only became apparent as I lay on my couch a bit later, a vinegar poultice on my forehead, drinking a cup of steaming tea. That little bevy of bones had been oscillating back and forth all through the Spanish Civil War, the agony of Czechoslovakia, and Danzig; this very minute it was undulating turgidly, heedless of the fact the store had been closed two hours. Furthermore, if its progress were not impeded by the two wires snaffled to the toes (I'll give you *that* thought to thrash around with some sleepless night), it might by now have encircled the world five times, with a stopover at the Eucharistic Congress in Manila. For a moment the implications were so surrealist that I started up alarmed. But since my loved ones had gone off to the movies and there was nobody to impress, I turned over and slept like a top, with no assistance except three and a half grains of barbital.

I could have reached my workshop the next morning by walking up Third Avenue, taking a cab up Lexington, or even crawling on my hands and knees past the shoestore to avoid that indecent window display, but my feet won their unequal struggle with my brain and carried me straight to the spot. Staring hypnotized at the macabre shuffle (halfway between a rhumba and a soft-shoe step), I realized that I was hearing a sign from above to take the matter in hand. I spent the morning shopping lower Third Avenue, and at noon, dressed as an attaché of the Department of Sanitation, began to lounge nonchalantly before the store. My broom was getting nearer and nearer the window when the manager came out noiselessly. My ducks must have been too snowy, for he gave one of his clerks a signal and a moment later a policeman turned the corner. Fortunately, I had stashed my civvies in the lobby of Proctor's Fifty-eighth Street Theatre, and by the time the breathless policeman rushed in, I had approached the wicket as cool as a cucumber, asked for two cucumbers in the balcony, and signed my name for Bank Nite. I flatter myself that I brought off the affair rather well.

My second attempt, however, was as fruitless as the first. I padded my stomach with a pillow, grayed my hair at the temples, and entered the shop fiercely. Pointing to the white piping on my vest, I represented myself as a portly banker from Portland, Maine, and asked the manager what he would take for the assets and good will, spot cash. I was about to make him a firm offer when I found myself being escorted out across the sidewalk, the manager's foot serving as fulcrum.

And there, precisely, the matter rests. I have given plenty of thought to the problem, and there is only one solution. Are there three young men in this city, with stout hearts and no dependents, who know what I mean? We can clean out that window with two well-directed grenades and get away over the rooftops. Given half a break, we'll stop that grisly *pas seul* ten seconds after we pull out the pins with our teeth. If we're caught, there's always the cyanide in our belts. First meeting tonight at nine in front of the Railroad Men's Y.M.C.A., and wear a blue cornflower. *Up the rebels!*

BERTRAND RUSSELL

COMMENTARY

Bertrand Russell wrote "A Free Man's Worship" in 1903, when he was only thirty-one. I understand that he does not think so highly of it now and perhaps does not entirely agree with the Russell of almost forty years ago. Possibly what he objects to is its note of stoical heroism which today he might smile at as romantic, since Lord Russell not only looks a little like Voltaire (which means nothing, for so does Henry Ford) but on occasion thinks like him. This grave and musical profession of faith in the unconquerable mind of man is somewhat removed from the skepticism, very likely a little weary, that has hallmarked Russell's thought for the last decade or so.

It may not be up-to-date Russell but much of its spirit remains pertinent today, when the choice between Force and Reason is presented to us not in Russell's abstract terms but in a manner that the simplest mind cannot help comprehending.

"A Free Man's Worship" is a religious essay; that is to say, an emotional expression of faith. It is a very old faith, never more movingly expressed than by the Emperor Marcus Aurelius (lords and emperors appear to have a special affinity for stoicism), though the dilemmas that Russell poses are those brought into relief by nineteenth-century science. Because it is an outburst of faith and not a reasoned argument, you are invited to read it more as poetry than as truth. Take a statement such as "Only within the scaffolding of these truths, only on the firm foundation of unyielding despair, can the soul's habitation henceforth be safely built." You cannot mark this true or false, but you may be moved by the emotion behind it.

"A Free Man's Worship," despite its gallant note of courage at the end, is one of the classic responses of pessimism called forth by the events of the nineteenth century. That century taught man he was a helpless atom in the grip of mechanical forces. The cries of despair that resounded produced some excellent literature: Stevenson's "Pulvis et Umbra" is one example, Russell's essay another.

764

Today, however, our pessimism is more deeply grounded or our faith more sorely tested, for not only is the universe against us (which might be borne, as Russell points out) but man is against himself, which is intolerable. It is the intense blackness of our position today that makes even this somber utterance seem haloed with idealism.

A Free Man's Worship

BY

BERTRAND RUSSELL

To Dr. Faustus in his study Mephistopheles told the history of the Creation, saying:

"The endless praises of the choirs of angels had begun to grow wearisome; for, after all, did he not deserve their praise? Had he not given them endless joy? Would it not be more amusing to obtain undeserved praise, to be worshipped by beings whom he tortured? He smiled inwardly, and resolved that the great drama should be performed.

"For countless ages the hot nebula whirled aimlessly through space. At length it began to take shape, the central mass threw off planets, the planets cooled, boiling seas and burning mountains heaved and tossed, from black masses of cloud hot sheets of rain deluged the barely solid crust. And now the first germ of life grew in the depths of the ocean, and developed rapidly in the fructifying warmth into vast forest trees, huge ferns springing from the damp mould, sea monsters breeding, fighting, devouring, and passing away. And from the monsters, as the play unfolded itself, Man was born, with the power of thought, the knowledge of good and evil and the cruel thirst for worship. And Man saw that all is passing in this mad, monstrous world, that all is struggling to snatch, at any cost, a few brief moments of life before Death's inexorable decree. And Man said: 'There is a hidden purpose, could we but fathom it, and the purpose is good; for we must reverence something, and in the visible world there is nothing worthy of reverence.' And Man stood aside from the struggle, resolving that God intended harmony to come out of chaos by human efforts. And when he followed the instincts which God had transmitted to him

766

from his ancestry of beasts of prey, he called it Sin, and asked God to forgive him. But he doubted whether he could be justly forgiven, until he invented a divine Plan by which God's wrath was to have been appeased. And seeing the present was bad, he made it yet worse, that thereby the future might be better. And he gave God thanks for the strength that enabled him to forgo even the joys that were possible. And God smiled; and when he saw that Man had become perfect in renunciation and worship, he sent another sun through the sky, which crashed into Man's sun; and all returned again to nebula.

" 'Yes,' he murmured, 'it was a good play; I will have it performed again.' "

Such, in outline, but even more purposeless, more void of meaning, is the world which Science presents for our belief. Amid such a world, if anywhere, our ideals henceforward must find a home. That Man is the product of causes which had no prevision of the end they were achieving; that his origin, his growth, his hopes and fears, his loves and his beliefs, are but the outcome of accidental collocations of atoms; that no fire, no heroism, no intensity of thought and feeling, can preserve an individual life beyond the grave; that all the labours of the ages, all the devotion, all the inspiration, all the noonday brightness of human genius, are destined to extinction in the vast death of the solar system, and that the whole temple of Man's achievement must inevitably be buried beneath the débris of a universe in ruins—all these things, if not quite beyond dispute, are yet so nearly certain, that no philosophy which rejects them can hope to stand. Only within the scaffolding of these truths, only on the firm foundation of unyielding despair, can the soul's habitation henceforth be safely built.

How, in such an alien and inhuman world, can so powerless a creature as Man preserve his aspirations untarnished? A strange mystery it is that Nature, omnipotent but blind, in the revolutions of her secular hurryings through the abysses of space, has brought forth at last a child, subject still to her power, but gifted with sight, with knowledge of good and evil, with the capacity of judging all the works of his unthinking Mother. In spite of Death, the mark and seal of the parental control, Man is yet free, during his brief years, to examine, to criticise, to know, and in imagination to create. To him alone, in the world with which he is acquainted, this freedom belongs; and in this lies his superiority to the resistless forces that control his outward life.

The savage, like ourselves, feels the oppression of his impotence before the powers of Nature; but having in himself nothing that he respects more than Power, he is willing to prostrate himself before his gods, without inquiring whether they are worthy of his worship. Pathetic and very terrible is the long history of cruelty and torture, of degradation and human sacrifice, endured in the hope of placating the jealous gods: surely, the trembling believer thinks, when what is most precious has been freely given, their lust for blood must be appeased, and more will not be required. The religion of Moloch—as such creeds may be generically called—is in essence the cringing submission of the slave, who dare not, even in his heart, allow the thought that his master deserves no adulation. Since the independence of ideals is not yet acknowledged, Power may be freely worshipped, and receive an unlimited respect, despite its wanton infliction of pain.

But gradually, as morality grows bolder, the claim of the ideal world begins to be felt; and worship, if it is not to cease, must be given to gods of another kind than those created by the savage. Some, though they feel the demands of the ideal, will still consciously reject them, still urging that naked Power is worthy of worship. Such is the attitude inculcated in God's answer to Job out of the whirlwind: the divine power and knowledge are paraded, but of the divine goodness there is no hint. Such also is the attitude of those who, in our own day, base their morality upon the struggle for survival, maintaining that the survivors are necessarily the fittest. But others, not content with an answer so repugnant to the moral sense, will adopt the position which we have become accustomed to regard as specially religious, maintaining that, in some hidden manner, the world of fact is really harmonious with the world of ideals. Thus Man creates God, all-powerful and all-good, the mystic unity of what is and what should be.

But the world of fact, after all, is not good; and, in submitting our judgment to it, there is an element of slavishness from which our thoughts must be purged. For in all things it is well to exalt the dignity of Man, by freeing him as far as possible from the tyranny of non-human Power. When we have realised that Power is largely bad, that man, with his knowledge of good and evil, is but a helpless atom in a world which has no such knowledge, the choice is again presented to us: Shall we worship Force, or shall we worship Goodness? Shall our God exist and be evil, or shall he be recognised as the creation of our own conscience?

The answer to this question is very momentous, and affects profoundly our whole morality. The worship of Force, to which Carlyle and Nietzsche and the creed of Militarism have accustomed us, is the result of failure to maintain our own ideals against a hostile universe: it is itself a prostrate submission to evil, a sacrifice of our best to Moloch. If strength indeed is to be respected, let us respect rather the strength of those who refuse that false "recognition of facts" which fails to recognise that facts are often bad. Let us admit that, in the world we know, there are many things that would be better otherwise, and that the ideals to which we do and must adhere are not realised in the realm of matter. Let us preserve our respect for truth, for beauty, for the ideal of perfection which life does not permit us to attain, though none of these things meet with the approval of the unconscious universe. If Power is bad, as it seems to be, let us reject it from our hearts. In this lies Man's true freedom: in determination to worship only the God created by our own love of the good, to respect only the heaven which inspires the insight of our best moments. In action, in desire, we must submit perpetually to the tyranny of outside forces; but in thought, in aspiration, we are free, free from our fellow-men, free from the petty planet on which our bodies impotently crawl, free even, while we live, from the tyranny of death. Let us learn, then, that energy of faith which enables us to live constantly in the vision of the good; and let us descend, in action, into the world of fact, with that vision always before us.

When first the opposition of fact and ideal grows fully visible, a spirit of fiery revolt, of fierce hatred of the gods, seems necessary to the assertion of freedom. To defy with Promethean constancy a hostile universe, to keep its evil always in view, always actively hated, to refuse no pain that the malice of Power can invent, appears to be the duty of all who will not bow before the inevitable. But indignation is still a bondage, for it compels our thoughts to be occupied with an evil world; and in the fierceness of desire from which rebellion springs there is a kind of self-assertion which it is necessary for the wise to overcome. Indignation is a submission of our thoughts, but not of our desires; the Stoic freedom in which wisdom consists is found in the submission of our desires, but not of our thoughts. From the submission of our desires springs the virtue of resignation; from the freedom of our thoughts springs the whole world of art and philosophy, and the vision of beauty by which, at last, we half reconquer the reluctant world. But the vision of beauty is possible only to unfettered contemplation, to thoughts not weighted by the load of eager wishes; and thus Freedom comes only to those who no longer ask of life that it shall yield them any of those personal goods that are subject to the mutations of Time.

Although the necessity of renunciation is evidence of the existence of evil, yet Christianity, in preaching it, has shown a wisdom exceeding that of the Promethean philosophy of rebellion. It must be admitted that, of the things we desire, some, though they prove impossible, are yet real goods; others, however, as ardently longed for, do not form part of a fully purified ideal. The belief that what must be renounced is bad, though sometimes false, is far less often false than untamed passion supposes; and the creed of religion, by providing a reason for proving that it is never false, has been the means of purifying our hopes by the discovery of many austere truths.

But there is in resignation a further good element: even real goods, when they are unattainable, ought not to be fretfully desired. To every man comes, sooner or later, the great renunciation. For the young, there is nothing unattainable; a good thing desired with the whole force of a passionate will, and yet impossible, is to them not credible. Yet, by death, by illness, by poverty, or by the voice of duty, we must learn, each one of us, that the world was not made for us and that, however beautiful may be the things we crave, Fate may nevertheless forbid them. It is the part of courage, when misfortune comes, to bear without repining the ruin of our hopes, to turn away our thoughts from vain regrets. This degree of submission to Power is not only just and right: it is the very gate of wisdom.

But passive renunciation is not the whole of wisdom; for not by renunciation alone can we build a temple for the worship of our own ideals. Haunting foreshadowings of the temple appear in the realm of imagination, in music, in architecture, in the untroubled kingdom of reason, and in the golden sunset magic of lyrics, where beauty shines and glows, remote from the touch of sorrow, remote from the fear of change, remote from the failures and disenchantments of the world of fact. In the contemplation of these things the vision of heaven will shape itself in our hearts, giving at once a touchstone to judge the world about us, and an inspiration by which to fashion to our needs whatever is not incapable of serving as a stone in the sacred temple.

Except for those rare spirits that are born without sin, there is a cavern of darkness to be traversed before that temple can be entered. The gate of the cavern is despair, and its floor is paved with the gravestones of abandoned hopes. There Self must die; there the eagerness, the greed of untamed desire must be slain, for only so can the soul be freed from the empire of Fate. But out of the cavern the Gate of Renunciation leads again to the daylight of wisdom, by whose radiance a new insight, a new joy, a new tenderness, shine forth to gladden the pilgrim's heart.

When, without the bitterness of impotent rebellion, we have learnt both to resign ourselves to the outward rule of Fate and to recognise that the non-human world is unworthy of our worship, it becomes possible at last so to transform and refashion the unconscious universe, so to transmute it in the crucible of imagination, that a new image of shining gold replaces the old idol of clay. In all the multiform facts of the world—in the visual shapes of trees and mountains and clouds, in the events of the life of Man, even in the very omnipotence of Death —the insight of creative idealism can find the reflection of a beauty which its own thoughts first made. In this way mind asserts its subtle mastery over the thoughtless forces of Nature. The more evil the material with which it deals, the more thwarting to untrained desire, the greater is its achievement in inducing the reluctant rock to yield up its hidden treasures, the prouder its victory in compelling the opposing forces to swell the pageant of its triumph. Of all the arts, Tragedy is the proudest, the most triumphant; for it builds its shining citadel in the very centre of the enemy's country, on the very summit of his highest mountain; from its impregnable watchtowers, his camps and arsenals, his columns and forts, are all revealed; within its walls the free life continues, while the legions of Death and Pain and Despair, and all the servile captains of tyrant Fate, afford the burghers of that dauntless city new spectacles of beauty. Happy those sacred ramparts, thrice happy the dwellers on that all-seeing eminence. Honour to those brave warriors who, through countless ages of warfare, have preserved for us the priceless heritage of liberty, and have kept undefiled by sacrilegious invaders the home of the unsubdued.

But the beauty of Tragedy does but make visible a quality which, in more or less obvious shapes, is present always and everywhere in life. In the spectacle of Death, in the endurance of intolerable pain, and in the irrevocableness of a vanished past, there is a sacredness, an overpowering awe, a feeling of the vastness, the depth, the inexhaustible mystery of existence, in which, as by some strange marriage of pain, the sufferer is bound to the world by bonds of sorrow. In these moments of insight, we lose all eagerness of temporary desire, all struggling and striving for petty ends, all care for the little trivial things that, to a superficial view, make up the common life of day by day; we see, surrounding the narrow raft illumined by the flickering light of human comradeship, the dark ocean on whose rolling waves we toss for a brief hour; from the great night without, a chill blast breaks in upon our refuge; all the loneliness of humanity amid hostile forces is concentrated upon the individual soul, which must struggle alone, with what of courage it can command, against the whole weight of a universe that cares nothing for its hopes and fears. Victory, in this struggle with the powers of darkness, is the true baptism into the glorious company of heroes, the true initiation into the overmastering beauty of human existence. From that awful encounter of the soul with the outer world, enunciation, wisdom, and charity are born; and with their birth a new life begins. To take into the inmost shrine of the soul the irresistible forces whose puppets we seem to be—Death and change, the irrevocableness of the past, and the powerlessness of Man before the blind hurry of the universe from vanity to vanity—to feel these things and know them is to conquer them.

This is the reason why the Past has such magical power. The

beauty of its motionless and silent pictures is like the enchanted purity of late autumn, when the leaves, though one breath would make them fall, still glow against the sky in golden glory. The Past does not change or strive; like Duncan, after life's fitful fever it sleeps well; what was eager and grasping, what was petty and transitory, has faded away, the things that were beautiful and eternal shine out of it like stars in the night. Its beauty, to a soul not worthy of it, is unendurable; but to a soul which has conquered Fate it is the key of religion.

The life of Man, viewed outwardly, is but a small thing in comparison with the forces of Nature. The slave is doomed to worship Time and Fate and Death, because they are greater than anything he finds in himself, and because all his thoughts are of things which they devour. But, great as they are, to think of them greatly, to feel their passionless splendour, is greater still. And such thought makes us free men; we no longer bow before the inevitable in Oriental subjection, but we absorb it, and make it a part of ourselves. To abandon the struggle for private happiness, to expel all eagerness of temporary desire, to burn with passion for eternal things—this is emancipation, and this is the free man's worship. And this liberation is effected by a contemplation of Fate; for Fate itself is subdued by the mind which leaves nothing to be purged by the purifying fire of Time.

United with his fellow-men by the strongest of all ties, the tie of a common doom, the free man finds that a new vision is with him always, shedding over every daily task the light of love. The life of Man is a long march through the night, surrounded by invisible foes, tortured by weariness and pain, towards a goal that few can hope to reach, and where none may tarry long. One by one, as they march, our comrades vanish from our sight, seized by the silent orders of omnipotent Death. Very brief is the time in which we can help them, in which their happiness or misery is decided. Be it ours to shed sunshine on their path, to lighten their sorrows by the balm of sympathy, to give them the pure joy of a never-tiring affection, to strengthen failing courage, to instil faith in hours of despair. Let us not weigh in grudging scales their merits and demerits, but let us think only of their need —of the sorrows, the difficulties, perhaps the blindnesses, that make the misery of their lives; let us remember that they are fellow-sufferers in the same darkness, actors in the same tragedy with ourselves. And so, when their day is over, when their good and their evil have become eternal by the immortality of the past, be it ours to feel that, where they suffered, where they failed, no deed of ours was the cause; but wherever a spark of the divine fire kindled in their hearts, we were ready with encouragement, with sympathy, with brave words in which high courage glowed.

Brief and powerless is Man's life; on him and all his race the slow, sure doom falls pitiless and dark. Blind to good and evil, reckless of destruction, omnipotent matter rolls on its relentless way; for Man, condemned to-day to lose his dearest, to-morrow himself to pass through the gate of darkness, it remains only to cherish, ere yet the blow falls, the lofty thoughts that ennoble his little day; disdaining the coward terrors of the slave of Fate, to worship at the shrine that his own hands have built; undismayed by the empire of chance, to preserve a mind free from the wanton tyranny that rules his outward life; proudly defiant of the irresistible forces that tolerate, for a moment, his knowledge and his condemnation, to sustain alone, a weary but unyielding Atlas, the world that his own ideals have fashioned despite the trampling march of unconscious power.

KATHERINE ANNE PORTER

COMMENTARY

Katherine Anne Porter does not write like Hemingway or feel things the way he does, but she shares with him and with a scattering of other American authors both the will and the ability to create by suggestion. She makes us sense more than she tells. The apparent content of her stories has less dimension than her real subject matter. Her very sentences and paragraphs, reverberating quietly in the mind, have a kind of echo value. Yet she never stoops to the easy devices of superficial symbolism but writes always with purity and directness.

Another quality distinguishing her short stories from the work of many of her fellows is that they have been thought out in advance. The remark is not quite as pointless as it sounds. So much contemporary American fiction bears the stamp of improvisation; the writer simply hasn't worked hard enough. Miss Porter calculates her effects, which is not to say that she gives the effect of calculation. She wastes not a word and each word has a purpose. James Joyce had a simple but profound way of saying of an author whose work he was unable to admire, "But it's not really written!" Miss Porter's stories seem to me in this sense written: you may not care for them, but you would be hard put to it to think of any other way in which they could be composed. They're final.

Her most finished work the curious reader will find in a collection of three long short stories, called Pale Horse, Pale Rider. They are all admirable. When I first read them I thought the title piece the best, but a rereading convinces me that "Noon Wine," here included, marks the high point of Miss Porter's superb art. "Noon Wine" is the kind of thing our earnest young Midwestern naturalists would give their right arm to be able to do as Miss Porter does. It is a story which, despite certain wry, humorous overtones, has violence and brutality as its base. Yet it is not the violence and brutality you remember but the characters, so simple, so perfectly understood and projected, so fatally linked by a destiny imposed upon them not by the patterning hand of Miss Porter but by the inarticulate, inchoate drives within their own hearts. I believe it to be a masterpiece.

Noon Wine

BY

KATHERINE ANNE PORTER

Time: 1896–1905
Place: Small South Texas Farm

THE TWO grubby small boys with tow-colored hair who were digging among the ragweed in the front yard sat back on their heels and said, "Hello," when the tall bony man with straw-colored hair turned in at their gate. He did not pause at the gate; it had swung back, conveniently half open, long ago, and was now sunk so firmly on its broken hinges no one thought of trying to close it. He did not even glance at the small boys, much less give them good-day. He just clumped down his big square dusty shoes one after the other steadily, like a man following a plow, as if he knew the place well and knew where he was going and what he would find there. Rounding the right-hand corner of the house under the row of chinaberry trees, he walked up to the side porch where Mr. Thompson was pushing a big swing churn back and forth.

Mr. Thompson was a tough weather-beaten man with stiff black hair and a week's growth of black whiskers. He was a noisy proud man who held his neck so straight his whole face stood level with his Adam's apple, and the whiskers continued down his neck and disappeared into a black thatch under his open collar. The churn rumbled and swished like the belly of a trotting horse, and Mr. Thompson seemed somehow to be driving a horse with one hand, reining it in and urging it forward; and every now and then he turned halfway around and squirted a tremendous spit of tobacco juice out over the steps. The door stones were brown and gleaming with fresh tobacco juice. Mr. Thompson had been churning quite a while and he was tired of it. He was just fetching a mouthful of juice to squirt again when the stranger came around the corner and stopped. Mr. Thompson saw a narrow-chested man with blue eyes so pale they were almost white, looking and not looking at him from a long gaunt face, under white eyebrows. Mr. Thompson judged him to be another of these Irishmen, by his long upper lip.

"Howdy do, sir," said Mr. Thompson politely, swinging his churn.

"I need work," said the man, clearly enough but with some kind of foreign accent Mr. Thompson couldn't place. It wasn't Cajun and it wasn't Nigger and it wasn't Dutch, so it had him stumped. "You need a man here?"

Mr. Thompson gave the churn a great shove and it swung back and forth several times on its own momentum. He sat on the steps, shot his quid into the grass, and said, "Set down. Maybe we can make a deal. I been kinda lookin' round for somebody. I had two niggers but they got into a cutting scrape up the creek last week, one of 'em dead now and the other in the hoosegow at Cold Springs. Neither one of 'em worth killing, come right down to it. So it looks like I'd better get somebody. Where'd you work last?"

"North Dakota," said the man, folding himself down on the other end of the steps, but not as if he were tired. He folded up and settled down as if it would be a long time before he got up again. He never had looked at Mr. Thompson, but there wasn't anything sneaking in his eye, either. He didn't seem to be looking anywhere else. His eyes sat in his head and let things pass by them. They didn't seem to be expecting to see anything worth looking at. Mr. Thompson waited a long time for the man to say something more, but he had gone into a brown study.

"North Dakota," said Mr. Thompson, trying to remember where that was. "That's a right smart distance off, seems to me."

"I can do everything on farm," said the man; "cheap. I need work."

Mr. Thompson settled himself to get down to business. "My name's Thompson, Mr. Royal Earle Thompson," he said.

"I'm Mr. Helton," said the man, "Mr. Olaf Helton." He did not move.

"Well, now," said Mr. Thompson in his most carrying voice, "I guess we'd better talk turkey."

When Mr. Thompson expected to drive a bargain he always grew very hearty and jovial. There was nothing wrong with him except that he hated like the devil to pay wages. He said so himself. "You furnish grub and a shack," he said, "and then you got to pay 'em besides. It ain't right. Besides the wear and tear on your implements," he said, "they just let everything go to rack and ruin." So he began to laugh and shout his way through the deal.

"Now, what I want to know is, how much you fixing to gouge outa me?" he brayed, slapping his knee. After he had kept it up as long as he could, he quieted down, feeling a little sheepish, and cut himself a chew. Mr. Helton was staring out somewhere between the barn and the orchard, and seemed to be sleeping with his eyes open.

"I'm good worker," said Mr. Helton as from the tomb. "I get dollar a day."

Mr. Thompson was so shocked he forgot to start laughing again at the top of his voice until it was nearly too late to do any good. "Haw, haw," he bawled. "Why, for a dollar a day I'd hire out myself. What kinda work is it where they pay you a dollar a day?"

"Wheatfields, North Dakota," said Mr. Helton, not even smiling.

Mr. Thompson stopped laughing. "Well, this ain't any wheatfield by a long shot. This is more of a dairy farm," he said, feeling apologetic. "My wife, she was set on a dairy, she seemed to like working around with cows and calves, so I humored her. But it was a mistake," he said. "I got nearly everything to do, anyhow. My wife ain't very strong. She's sick today, that's a fact. She's been porely for the last few days. We plant a little feed, and a corn patch, and there's the orchard, and a few pigs and chickens, but our main hold is the cows. Now just speakin' as one man to another, there ain't any money in it. Now I can't give you no dollar a day because ackshally I don't make that much out of it. No, sir, we get along on a lot less than a dollar a day, I'd say, if we figger up everything in the long run. Now, I paid seven dollars a month to the two niggers, three-fifty each, and grub, but what I say is, one middlin'-good white man ekals a whole passel of niggers any day in the week, so I'll give you seven dollars and you eat at the table with us, and you'll be treated like a white man, as the feller says——"

"That's all right," said Mr. Helton. "I take it."

"Well, now I guess we'll call it a deal, hey?" Mr. Thompson jumped up as if he had remembered important business. "Now, you just take hold of that churn and give it a few swings, will you, while I ride to town on a coupla little errands. I ain't been able to leave the place all week. I guess you know what to do with butter after you get it, don't you?"

"I know," said Mr. Helton without turning his head. "I know butter business." He had a strange drawling voice, and even when he spoke only two words his voice waved slowly up and down and the emphasis was in the wrong place. Mr. Thompson wondered what kind of foreigner Mr. Helton could be.

"Now just where did you say you worked last?" he asked, as if he expected Mr. Helton to contradict himself.

"North Dakota," said Mr. Helton.

"Well, one place is good as another once you get used to it," said Mr. Thompson, amply. "You're a forriner, ain't you?"

"I'm a Swede," said Mr. Helton, beginning to swing the churn.

Mr. Thompson let forth a booming laugh, as if this was the best joke on somebody he'd ever heard. "Well, I'll be damned," he said at the top of his voice. "A Swede: well, now, I'm afraid you'll get pretty lonesome around here. I never seen any Swedes in this neck of the woods."

"That's all right," said Mr. Helton. He went on swinging the churn as if he had been working on the place for years.

"In fact, I might as well tell you, you're practically the first Swede I ever laid eyes on."

"That's all right," said Mr. Helton.

Mr. Thompson went into the front room where Mrs. Thompson was lying down, with the green shades drawn. She had a bowl of water by her on the table and a wet cloth over her eyes. She took the cloth off at the sound of Mr. Thompson's boots and said, "What's all the noise out there? Who is it?"

"Got a feller out there says he's a Swede, Ellie," said Mr. Thompson; "says he knows how to make butter."

"I hope it turns out to be the truth," said Mrs. Thompson. "Looks like my head never will get any better."

"Don't you worry," said Mr. Thompson. "You fret too much. Now I'm gointa ride into town and get a little order of groceries."

"Don't you linger, now, Mr. Thompson," said Mrs. Thompson. "Don't go to the hotel." She meant the saloon; the proprietor also had rooms for rent upstairs.

"Just a coupla little toddies," said Mr. Thompson, laughing loudly, "never hurt anybody."

"I never took a dram in my life," said Mrs. Thompson, "and what's more I never will."

"I wasn't talking about the womenfolks," said Mr. Thompson.

The sound of the swinging churn rocked Mrs. Thompson first into a gentle doze, then a deep drowse from which she waked suddenly knowing that the swinging had stopped a good while ago. She sat up shading her weak eyes from the flat strips of late summer sunlight between the sill and the lowered shades. There she was, thank God, still alive, with supper to cook but no churning on hand, and her head still bewildered, but easy. Slowly she realized she had been hearing a new sound even in her sleep. Somebody was playing a tune on the harmonica, not merely shrilling up and down making a sickening noise, but really playing a pretty tune, merry and sad.

She went out through the kitchen, stepped off the porch, and stood facing the east, shading her eyes. When her vision cleared and settled, she saw a long, pale-haired man in blue jeans sitting in the doorway of the hired man's shack, tilted back in a kitchen chair, blowing away at the harmonica with his eyes shut. Mrs. Thompson's heart fluttered and sank. Heavens, he looked lazy and worthless, he did, now. First a lot of no-count fiddling darkies and then a no-count white man. It was just like Mr. Thompson to take on that kind. She did wish he would be more considerate, and take a little trouble with his business. She wanted to believe in her husband, and there were too many times when she couldn't. She wanted to believe that tomorrow, or at least the day after, life, such a battle at best, was going to be better.

She walked past the shack without glancing aside, stepping carefully, bent at the waist because of the nagging pain in her side, and went to the springhouse, trying to harden her mind to speak very plainly to that new hired man if he had not done his work.

The milk house was only another shack of weather-beaten boards nailed together hastily years before because they needed a milk house; it was meant to be temporary, and it was; already shapeless, leaning this way and that over a perpetual cool trickle of water that fell from a little grot, almost choked with pallid ferns. No one else in the whole countryside had such a spring on his land. Mr. and Mrs. Thompson felt they had a fortune in that spring, if ever they got around to doing anything with it.

Rickety wooden shelves clung at hazard in the square around the small pool where the larger pails of milk and butter stood, fresh and sweet in the cold water. One hand supporting her flat, pained side, the other shading her eyes, Mrs. Thompson leaned over and peered into the pails. The cream had been skimmed and set aside, there was a rich roll of butter, the wooden molds and shallow pans had been scrubbed and scalded for the first time in who knows when, the barrel was full of buttermilk ready for the pigs and the weanling calves, the hard packed-dirt floor had been swept smooth. Mrs. Thompson straightened up again, smiling tenderly. She had been ready to scold him, a poor man who needed a job, who had just come there and who might not have been expected to do things properly at first. There was nothing she could do to make up for the injustice she had done him in her thoughts but to tell him how she appreciated his good clean work, finished already, in no time at all. She ventured near the door of the shack with her careful steps; Mr. Helton opened his eyes, stopped playing, and brought his chair down straight, but did not look at her, or get up. She was a little frail woman with long thick brown hair in a braid, a suffering patient mouth and diseased eyes which cried easily. She wove her fingers into an eyeshade, thumbs on temples, and, winking her tearful lids, said with a polite little manner, "Howdy do, sir. I'm Miz Thompson, and I wanted to tell you I think you did real well in the milk house. It's always been a hard place to keep."

He said, "That's all right," in a slow voice, without moving.

Mrs. Thompson waited a moment. "That's a pretty tune you're playing. Most folks don't seem to get much music out of a harmonica."

Mr. Helton sat humped over, long legs sprawling, his spine in a bow, running his thumb over the square mouth-stops; except for his moving hand he might have been asleep. The harmonica was a big shiny new one, and Mrs. Thompson, her gaze wandering about, counted five others, all good and expensive, standing in a row on the shelf beside his cot. "He must carry them around in his jumper pocket," she thought, and noted there was not a sign of any other possession lying about. "I see you're mighty fond of music," she said. "We used to have an old accordion, and Mr. Thompson could play it right smart, but the little boys broke it up."

Mr. Helton stood up rather suddenly, the chair clattered under him, his knees straightened though his shoulders did not, and he looked at the floor as if he were listening carefully. "You know how little boys are," said Mrs. Thompson. "You'd better set them harmonicas on a high shelf or they'll be after them. They're great hands for getting into things. I try to learn 'em, but it don't do much good."

Mr. Helton, in one wide gesture of his long arms, swept his harmonicas up against his chest, and from there transferred them in a row to the ledge where the roof joined to the wall. He pushed them back almost out of sight.

"That'll do, maybe," said Mrs. Thompson. "Now I wonder," she said, turning and closing her eyes helplessly against the stronger western light, "I wonder what became of them little tads. I can't keep up with them." She had a way of speaking about her children as if they were rather troublesome nephews on a prolonged visit.

"Down by the creek," said Mr. Helton, in his hollow voice. Mrs. Thompson, pausing confusedly, decided he had answered her question. He stood in silent patience, not exactly waiting for her to go, perhaps, but pretty plainly not waiting for anything else. Mrs. Thompson was perfectly accustomed to all kinds of men full of all kinds of cranky ways. The point was, to find out just how Mr. Helton's crankiness was different from any other man's, and then get used to it, and let him feel at home. Her father had been cranky, her brothers and uncles had all been set in their ways and none of them alike; and every hired man she'd ever seen had quirks and crotchets of his own. Now here was Mr. Helton, who was a Swede, who wouldn't talk, and who played the harmonica besides.

"They'll be needing something to eat," said Mrs. Thompson in a vague friendly way, "pretty soon. Now I wonder what I ought to be thinking about for supper? Now what do you like to eat, Mr. Helton? We always have plenty of good butter and milk and cream, that's a blessing. Mr. Thompson says we ought to sell all of it, but I say my family comes first." Her little face went all out of shape in a pained blind smile.

"I eat anything," said Mr. Helton, his words wandering up and down.

He *can't* talk, for one thing, thought Mrs. Thompson; it's a shame to keep at him when he don't know the language good. She took a slow step away from the shack, looking back over her shoulder. "We usually have cornbread except on Sundays," she told him. "I suppose in your part of the country you don't get much good cornbread."

Not a word from Mr. Helton. She saw from her eye-corner that he had sat down again, looking at his harmonica, chair tilted. She hoped he would remember it was getting near milking time. As she moved away, he started playing again, the same tune.

Milking time came and went. Mrs. Thompson saw Mr. Helton going back and forth betwen the cow barn and the milk house. He swung along in an easy lope, shoulders bent, head hanging, the big buckets balancing like a pair of scales at the ends of his bony arms. Mr. Thompson rode in from town sitting straighter than usual, chin in, a towsack full of supplies swung behind the saddle. After a trip to the barn, he came into the kitchen full of good will, and gave Mrs. Thompson a hearty smack on the cheek after dusting her face off with his tough whiskers. He had been to the hotel, that was plain. "Took a look around the premises, Ellie," he shouted. "That Swede sure is grinding out the labor. But he is the closest mouthed feller I ever met up with in all my days. Looks like he's scared he'll crack his jaw if he opens his front teeth."

Mrs. Thompson was stirring up a big bowl of buttermilk cornbread. "You smell like a toper, Mr. Thompson," she said with perfect dignity. "I wish you'd get one of the little boys to bring me in an extra load of firewood. I'm thinking about baking a batch of cookies tomorrow."

Mr. Thompson, all at once smelling the liquor on his own breath, sneaked out, justly rebuked, and brought in the firewood himself. Arthur and Herbert, grubby from thatched head to toes, from skin to shirt, came stamping in yelling for supper. "Go wash your faces and comb your hair," said Mrs. Thompson, automatically. They retired to the porch. Each one put his hand under the pump and wet his forelock, combed it down with his fingers, and returned at once to the kitchen, where all the fair prospects of life were centered. Mrs. Thompson set an extra plate and commanded Arthur, the eldest, eight years old, to call Mr. Helton for supper.

Arthur, without moving from the spot, bawled like a bull calf, "Saaaaaay, Helllllton, suuuuuupper's ready!" and added in a lower voice, "You big Swede!"

"Listen to me," said Mrs. Thompson, "that's no way to act. Now you go out there and ask him decent, or I'll get your daddy to give you a good licking."

Mr. Helton loomed, long and gloomy, in the doorway. "Sit right there," boomed Mr. Thompson, waving his arm. Mr. Helton swung his square shoes across the kitchen in two steps, slumped onto the bench and sat. Mr. Thompson occupied his chair at the head of the table, the two boys scrambled into place opposite Mr. Helton, and Mrs. Thompson sat at the end nearest the stove. Mrs. Thompson clasped her hands, bowed her head and said aloud hastily, "Lord, for all these and Thy other blessings we thank Thee in Jesus' name, amen," trying to finish before Herbert's rusty little paw reached the nearest dish. Otherwise she would be duty-bound to send him away from the table, and growing children need their meals. Mr. Thompson and Arthur always waited, but Herbert, aged six, was too young to take training yet.

Mr. and Mrs. Thompson tried to engage Mr. Helton in conversation, but it was a failure. They tried first the weather, and then the crops, and then the cows, but Mr. Helton simply did not reply. Mr. Thompson then told something funny he had seen in town. It was about some of the other old grangers at the hotel, friends of his, giving beer to a goat, and the goat's subsequent behavior. Mr. Helton did not seem to hear. Mrs. Thompson laughed dutifully, but she didn't think it was very funny. She had heard it often before, though Mr. Thompson, each time he told it, pretended it had happened that self-same day. It must have happened years ago if it ever happened at all, and it had never been a story that Mrs. Thompson thought suitable for mixed company. The whole thing came of Mr. Thompson's weakness for a dram too much now and then, though he voted for local option at every election. She passed the food to Mr. Helton, who took a helping of everything, but not much, not enough to keep him up to his full powers if he expected to go on working the way he had started.

At last, he took a fair-sized piece of cornbread, wiped his plate up as clean as if it had been licked by a hound dog, stuffed his mouth full, and, still chewing, slid off the bench and started for the door.

"Good night, Mr. Helton," said Mrs. Thompson, and the other Thompsons took it up in a scattered chorus. "Good night, Mr. Helton!"

"Good night," said Mr. Helton's wavering voice grudgingly from the darkness.

"Gude not," said Arthur, imitating Mr. Helton.

"Gude not," said Herbert, the copy-cat.

"You don't do it right," said Arthur. "Now listen to me. Guuuuuude naht," and he ran a hollow scale in a luxury of successful impersonation. Herbert almost went into a fit with joy.

"Now you *stop* that," said Mrs. Thompson. "He can't help the way he talks. You ought to be ashamed of yourselves, both of you, making fun of a poor stranger like that. How'd you like to be a stranger in a strange land?"

"I'd like it," said Arthur. "I think it would be fun."

"They're both regular heathens, Ellie," said Mr. Thompson. "Just plain ignoramuses." He turned the face of awful fatherhood upon his young. "You're both going to get sent to school next year, and that'll knock some sense into you."

"I'm going to git sent to the 'formatory when I'm old enough," piped up Herbert. "That's where I'm goin'."

"Oh, you are, are you?" asked Mr. Thompson. "Who says so?"

"The Sunday School Superintendent," said Herbert, a bright boy showing off.

"You see?" said Mr. Thompson, staring at his wife. "What did I tell you?" He became a hurricane of wrath. "Get to bed, you two," he roared until his Adam's apple shuddered. "Get now before I take the hide off you!" They got, and shortly from their attic bedroom the sounds of scuffling and snoring and giggling and growling filled the house and shook the kitchen ceiling.

Mrs. Thompson held her head and said in a small uncertain voice, "It's no use picking on them when they're so young and tender. I can't stand it."

"My goodness, Ellie," said Mr. Thompson, "we've got to raise 'em. We can't just let 'em grow up hog wild."

She went on in another tone. "That Mr. Helton seems all right, even if he can't be made to talk. Wonder how he comes to be so far from home."

"Like I said, he isn't no whamper-jaw," said Mr. Thompson, "but he sure knows how to lay out the work. I guess that's the main thing around here. Country's full of fellers trampin' round looking for work."

Mrs. Thompson was gathering up the dishes. She now gathered up Mr. Thompson's plate from under his chin. "To tell you the honest truth," she remarked, "I think it's a mighty good change to have a man round the place who knows how to work and keep his mouth shut. Means he'll keep out of our business. Not that we've got anything to hide, but it's convenient."

"That's a fact," said Mr. Thompson. "Haw, haw," he shouted suddenly. "Means you can do all the talking, huh?"

"The only thing," went on Mrs. Thompson, "is this: he don't eat hearty enough to suit me. I like to see a man set down and relish a good meal. My granma used to say it was no use putting dependence on a man who won't set down and make out his dinner. I hope it won't be that way this time."

"Tell *you* the truth, Ellie," said Mr. Thompson, picking his teeth with a fork and leaning back in the best of good humors, "I always thought your granma was a ter'ble ole fool. She'd just say the first thing that popped into her head and call it God's wisdom."

"My granma wasn't anybody's fool. Nine times out of ten she knew what she was talking about. I always say, the first thing you think is the best thing you can say."

"Well," said Mr. Thompson, going into another shout, "you're so reefined about that goat story, you just try speaking out in mixed comp'ny sometime! You just try it. S'pose you happened to be thinking about a hen and a rooster, hey? I reckon you'd shock the Babtist preacher!" He gave her a good pinch on her thin little rump. "No more meat on you than a rabbit," he said, fondly. "Now I like 'em cornfed."

Mrs. Thompson looked at him open-eyed and blushed. She could see better by lamplight. "Why, Mr. Thompson, sometimes I think you're the evilest-minded man that ever lived." She took a handful of hair on the crown of his head and gave it a good, slow pull. "That's to show you how it feels, pinching so hard when you're supposed to be playing," she said, gently.

In spite of his situation in life, Mr. Thompson had never been able to outgrow his deep conviction that running a dairy and chasing after chickens was woman's work. He was fond of saying that he could plow a furrow, cut sorghum, shuck corn, handle a team, build a corn crib, as well as any man. Buying and selling, too, were man's work. Twice a week he drove the spring wagon to market with the fresh butter, a few eggs, fruits in their proper season, sold them, pocketed the change, and spent it as seemed best, being careful not to dig into Mrs. Thompson's pin money.

But from the first the cows worried him, coming up regularly twice a day to be milked, standing there reproaching him with their smug female faces. Calves worried him, fighting the rope and strangling themselves until their eyes bulged, trying to get at the teat. Wrestling with a calf unmanned him, like having to change a baby's diaper. Milk worried him, coming bitter sometimes, drying up, turning sour. Hens worried him, cackling, clucking, hatching out when you least expected it and leading their broods into the barnyard where the horses could

step on them, dying of roup and wryneck and getting plagues of
chicken lice; laying eggs all over God's creation so that half of them
were spoiled before a man could find them, in spite of a rack of nests
Mrs. Thompson had set out for them in the feed room. Hens were a
blasted nuisance.

Slopping hogs was hired man's work, in Mr. Thompson's opinion.
Killing hogs was a job for the boss, but scraping them and cutting
them up was for the hired man again; and again woman's proper
work was dressing meat, smoking, pickling, and making lard and sau-
sage. All his carefully limited fields of activity were related somehow
to Mr. Thompson's feeling for the appearance of things, his own appearance in the sight of God and man. "It don't *look* right," was his
final reason for not doing anything he did not wish to do.

It was his dignity and his reputation that he cared about, and there
were only a few kinds of work manly enough for Mr. Thompson to
undertake with his own hands. Mrs. Thompson, to whom so many
forms of work would have been becoming, had simply gone down on
him early. He saw, after a while, how short-sighted it had been of him
to expect much from Mrs. Thompson; he had fallen in love with her
delicate waist and lace-trimmed petticoats and big blue eyes, and,
though all those charms had disappeared, she had in the meantime
become Ellie to him, not at all the same person as Miss Ellen Bridges,
popular Sunday School teacher in the Mountain City First Baptist
Church, but his dear wife, Ellie, who was not strong. Deprived as he
was, however, of the main support in life which a man might expect
in marriage, he had almost without knowing it resigned himself to
failure. Head erect, a prompt payer of taxes, yearly subscriber to the
preacher's salary, land owner and father of a family, employer, a hearty
good fellow among men, Mr. Thompson knew, without putting it into
words, that he had been going steadily down hill. God amighty, it
did look like somebody around the place might take a rake in hand
now and then and clear up the clutter around the barn and the kitchen
steps. The wagon shed was so full of broken-down machinery and
ragged harness and old wagon wheels and battered milk pails and rotting lumber you could hardly drive in there any more. Not a soul on
the place would raise a hand to it, and as for him, he had all he could

do with his regular work. He would sometimes in the slack season sit for hours worrying about it, squirting tobacco on the ragweeds growing in a thicket against the wood pile, wondering what a fellow could do, handicapped as he was. He looked forward to the boys growing up soon; he was going to put them through the mill just as his own father had done with him when he was a boy; they were going to learn how to take hold and run the place right. He wasn't going to overdo it, but those two boys were going to earn their salt, or he'd know why. Great big lubbers sitting around whittling! Mr. Thompson sometimes grew quite enraged with them, when imagining their possible future, big lubbers sitting around whittling or thinking about fishing trips. Well, he'd put a stop to that, mighty damn quick.

As the seasons passed, and Mr. Helton took hold more and more, Mr. Thompson began to relax in his mind a little. There seemed to be nothing the fellow couldn't do, all in the day's work and as a matter of course. He got up at five o'clock in the morning, boiled his own coffee and fried his own bacon and was out in the cow lot before Mr. Thompson had even begun to yawn, stretch, groan, roar and thump around looking for his jeans. He milked the cows, kept the milk house, and churned the butter; rounded the hens up and somehow persuaded them to lay in the nests, not under the house and behind the haystacks; he fed them regularly and they hatched out until you couldn't set a foot down for them. Little by little the piles of trash around the barns and house disappeared. He carried buttermilk and corn to the hogs, and curried cockleburs out of the horses' manes. He was gentle with the calves, if a little grim with the cows and hens; judging by his conduct, Mr. Helton had never heard of the difference between man's and woman's work on a farm.

In the second year, he showed Mr. Thompson the picture of a cheese press in a mail order catalogue, and said, "This is a good thing. You buy this, I make cheese." The press was bought and Mr. Helton did make cheese, and it was sold, along with the increased butter and the crates of eggs. Sometimes Mr. Thompson felt a little contemptuous of Mr. Helton's ways. It did seem kind of picayune for a man to go around picking up half a dozen ears of corn that had fallen off the wagon on the way from the field, gathering up fallen fruit to feed to the pigs, storing up old nails and stray parts of machinery, spending good time stamping a fancy pattern on the butter before it went to market. Mr. Thompson, sitting up high on the spring-wagon seat, with the decorated butter in a five-gallon lard can wrapped in wet towsack, driving to town, chirruping to the horses and snapping the reins over their backs, sometimes thought that Mr. Helton was a pretty meeching sort of fellow; but he never gave way to these feelings, he knew a good thing when he had it. It was a fact the hogs were in better shape and sold for more money. It was a fact that Mr. Thompson stopped buying feed, Mr. Helton managed the crops so well. When beef- and hog-slaughtering time came, Mr. Helton knew how to save the scraps that Mr. Thompson had thrown away, and wasn't above scraping guts and filling them with sausages that he made by his own methods. In all, Mr. Thompson had no grounds for complaint. In the third year, he raised Mr. Helton's wages, though Mr. Helton had not asked for a raise. The fourth year, when Mr. Thompson was not only out of debt but had a little cash in the bank, he raised Mr. Helton's wages again, two dollars and a half a month each time.

"The man's worth it, Ellie," said Mr. Thompson, in a glow of self-justification for his extravagance. "He's made this place pay, and I want him to know I appreciate it."

Mr. Helton's silence, the pallor of his eyebrows and hair, his long, glum jaw and eyes that refused to see anything, even the work under his hands, had grown perfectly familiar to the Thompsons. At first, Mrs. Thompson complained a little. "It's like sitting down at the table with a disembodied spirit," she said. "You'd think he'd find something to say, sooner or later."

"Let him alone," said Mr. Thompson. "When he gets ready to talk, he'll talk."

The years passed, and Mr. Helton never got ready to talk. After his work was finished for the day, he would come up from the barn or the milk house or the chicken house, swinging his lantern, his big shoes clumping like pony hoofs on the hard path. They, sitting in the kitchen in the winter, or on the back porch in summer, would hear him drag out his wooden chair, hear the creak of it tilted back, and then for a little while he would play his single tune on one or another of his harmonicas. The harmonicas were in different keys, some lower and sweeter than the others, but the same changeless tune went on, a strange tune, with sudden turns in it, night after night, and sometimes even in the afternoons when Mr. Helton sat down to catch his breath. At first the Thompsons liked it very much, and always stopped to listen. Later there came a time when they were fairly sick of it, and began to wish to each other that he would learn a new one. At last they did not hear it any more, it was as natural as the sound of the wind rising in the evenings, or the cows lowing, or their own voices.

Mrs. Thompson pondered now and then over Mr. Helton's soul. He didn't seem to be a church-goer, and worked straight through Sunday as if it were any common day of the week. "I think we ought to invite him to go to hear Dr. Martin," she told Mr. Thompson. "It isn't very Christian of us not to ask him. He's not a forward kind of man. He'd wait to be asked."

"Let him alone," said Mr. Thompson. "The way I look at it, his religion is every man's own business. Besides, he ain't got any Sunday clothes. He wouldn't want to go to church in them jeans and jumpers of his. I don't know what he does with his money. He certainly don't spend it foolishly."

Still, once the notion got into her head, Mrs. Thompson could not rest until she invited Mr. Helton to go to church with the family next Sunday. He was pitching hay into neat little piles in the field back of the orchard. Mrs. Thompson put on smoked glasses and a sunbonnet and walked all the way down there to speak to him. He stopped and leaned on his pitchfork, listening, and for a moment Mrs. Thompson was almost frightened at his face. The pale eyes seemed to glare past her, the eyebrows frowned, the long jaw hardened. "I got work," he said bluntly, and lifting his pitchfork he turned from her and began to toss the hay. Mrs. Thompson, her feelings hurt, walked back thinking that by now she should be used to Mr. Helton's ways, but it did seem like a man, even a foreigner, could be just a little polite when you gave him a Christian invitation. "He's not polite, that's the only thing I've got against him," she said to Mr. Thompson. "He just can't seem to behave like other people. You'd think he had a grudge against the world," she said. "I sometimes don't know what to make of it."

In the second year something had happened that made Mrs. Thompson uneasy, the kind of thing she could not put into words, hardly into thoughts, and if she had tried to explain to Mr. Thompson it would have sounded worse than it was, or not bad enough. It was that kind of queer thing that seems to be giving a warning, and yet, nearly always nothing comes of it. It was on a hot, still spring day, and Mrs. Thompson had been down to the garden patch to pull some new carrots and green onions and string beans for dinner. As she worked, sunbonnet low over her eyes, putting each kind of vegetable in a pile by itself in her basket, she noticed how neatly Mr. Helton weeded, and how rich the soil was. He had spread it all over with manure from the barns, and worked it in, in the fall, and the vegetables were coming up fine and full. She walked back under the nubbly little fig trees where the unpruned branches leaned almost to the ground, and the thick leaves made a cool screen. Mrs. Thompson was always looking for shade to save her eyes. So she, looking idly about, saw through the screen a sight that struck her as very strange. If it had been a noisy spectacle, it would have been quite natural. It was the silence that struck her. Mr. Helton was shaking Arthur by the shoulders, ferociously, his face most terribly fixed and pale. Arthur's head snapped back and forth and he had not stiffened in resistance, as he did when Mrs. Thompson tried to shake him. His eyes were rather frightened, but surprised, too, probably more surprised than anything else. Herbert stood by meekly, watching. Mr. Helton dropped Arthur, and seized Herbert, and shook him with the same methodical ferocity, the same face of hatred. Herbert's mouth crumpled as if he would cry, but he made no sound. Mr. Helton let him go, turned and strode into the shack, and the little boys ran, as if for their lives, without a word. They disappeared around the corner to the front of the house.

Mrs. Thompson took time to set her basket on the kitchen table, to push her sunbonnet back on her head and draw it forward again, to look in the stove and make certain the fire was going, before she followed the boys. They were sitting huddled together under a clump of chinaberry trees in plain sight of her bedroom window, as if it were a safe place they had discovered.

"What are you doing?" asked Mrs. Thompson.

They looked hang-dog from under their foreheads and Arthur mumbled, "Nothin'."

"Nothing *now,* you mean," said Mrs. Thompson, severely. "Well, I have plenty for you to do. Come right in here this minute and help me fix vegetables. This minute."

They scrambled up very eagerly and followed her close. Mrs. Thompson tried to imagine what they had been up to; she did not like the notion of Mr. Helton taking it on himself to correct her little boys, but she was afraid to ask them for reasons. They might tell her a lie, and she would have to overtake them in it, and whip them. Or she would have to pretend to believe them, and they would get in the habit of lying. Or they might tell her the truth, and it would be something she would have to whip them for. The very thought of it gave her a headache. She supposed she might ask Mr. Helton, but it was not her place to ask. She would wait and tell Mr. Thompson, and let him get at the bottom of it. While her mind ran on, she kept the little boys hopping. "Cut those carrot tops closer, Herbert, you're just being careless. Arthur, stop breaking up the beans so little. They're little enough already. Herbert, you go get an armload of wood. Arthur, you take these onions and wash them under the pump. Herbert, as soon as you're done here, you get a broom and sweep out this kitchen. Arthur, you get a shovel and take up the ashes. Stop picking your nose, Herbert. How often must I tell you? Arthur, you go look in the top drawer of my bureau, left-hand side, and bring me the vaseline for Herbert's nose. Herbert, come here to me. . . ."

They galloped through their chores, their animal spirits rose with activity, and shortly they were out in the front yard again, engaged in a wrestling match. They sprawled and fought, scrambled, clutched, rose and fell shouting, as aimlessly, noisily, monotonously as two puppies. They imitated various animals, not a human sound from them, and their dirty faces were streaked with sweat. Mrs. Thompson, sitting at her window, watched them with baffled pride and tenderness, they were so sturdy and healthy and growing so fast; but uneasily, too, with her pained little smile and the tears rolling from her eyelids that clinched themselves against the sunlight. They were so idle and careless, as if they had no future in this world, and no immortal souls to save, and oh, what had they been up to that Mr. Helton had shaken them, with his face positively dangerous?

In the evening before supper, without a word to Mr. Thompson of the curious fear the sight had caused her, she told him that Mr. Helton had shaken the little boys for some reason. He stepped out to the shack and spoke to Mr. Helton. In five minutes he was back, glaring at his young. "He says them brats been fooling with his harmonicas, Ellie, blowing in them and getting them all dirty and full of spit and they don't play good."

"Did he say all that?" asked Mrs. Thompson. "It doesn't seem possible."

"Well, that's what he meant, anyhow," said Mr. Thompson. "He didn't say it just that way. But he acted pretty worked up about it."

"That's a shame," said Mrs. Thompson, "a perfect shame. Now we've got to do something so they'll remember they mustn't go into Mr. Helton's things."

"I'll tan their hides for them," said Mr. Thompson. "I'll take a calf rope to them if they don't look out."

"Maybe you'd better leave the whipping to me," said Mrs. Thompson. "You haven't got a light enough hand for children."

"That's just what's the matter with them now," shouted Mr. Thompson, "rotten spoiled and they'll wind up in the penitentiary. You don't half whip 'em. Just little love taps. My pa used to knock me down with a stick of stove wood or anything else that came handy."

"Well, that's not saying it's right," said Mrs. Thompson. "I don't hold with that way of raising children. It makes them run away from home. I've seen too much of it."

"I'll break every bone in 'em," said Mr. Thompson, simmering down, "if they don't mind you better and stop being so bull-headed."

"Leave the table and wash your face and hands," Mrs. Thompson commanded the boys, suddenly. They slunk out and dabbled at the pump and slunk in again, trying to make themselves small. They had learned long ago that their mother always made them wash when there was trouble ahead. They looked at their plates. Mr. Thompson opened up on them.

"Well, now, what you got to say for yourselves about going into Mr. Helton's shack and ruining his harmonicas?"

The two little boys wilted, their faces drooped into the grieved hopeless lines of children's faces when they are brought to the terrible bar of blind adult justice; their eyes telegraphed each other in panic, "Now we're really going to catch a licking"; in despair, they dropped their buttered cornbread on their plates, their hands lagged on the edge of the table.

"I ought to break your ribs," said Mr. Thompson, "and I'm a good mind to do it."

"Yes, sir," whispered Arthur, faintly.

"Yes, sir," said Herbert, his lip trembling.

"Now, papa," said Mrs. Thompson in a warning tone. The children did not glance at her. They had no faith in her good will. She had betrayed them in the first place. There was no trusting her. Now she might save them and she might not. No use depending on her.

"Well, you ought to get a good thrashing. You deserve it, don't you, Arthur?"

Arthur hung his head. "Yes, sir."

"And the next time I catch either of you hanging around Mr. Helton's shack, I'm going to take the hide off *both* of you, you hear me, Herbert?"

Herbert mumbled and choked, scattering his cornbread. "Yes, sir."

"Well, now sit up and eat your supper and not another word out of you," said Mr. Thompson, beginning on his own food. The little boys perked up somewhat and started chewing, but every time they looked around they met their parents' eyes, regarding them steadily. There was no telling when they would think of something new. The boys ate warily, trying not to be seen or heard, the cornbread sticking, the buttermilk gurgling, as it went down their gullets.

"And something else, Mr. Thompson," said Mrs. Thompson after a pause. "Tell Mr. Helton he's to come straight to us when they bother him, and not to trouble shaking them himself. Tell him we'll look after that."

"They're so mean," answered Mr. Thompson, staring at them. "It's a wonder he don't just kill 'em off and be done with it." But there was something in the tone that told Arthur and Herbert that nothing more worth worrying about was going to happen this time. Heaving deep sighs, they sat up, reaching for the food nearest them.

"Listen," said Mrs. Thompson, suddenly. The little boys stopped eating. "Mr. Helton hasn't come for his supper. Arthur, go and tell Mr. Helton he's late for supper. Tell him nice, now."

Arthur, miserably depressed, slid out of his place and made for the door, without a word.

There were no miracles of fortune to be brought to pass on a small dairy farm. The Thompsons did not grow rich, but they kept out of the poor house, as Mr. Thompson was fond of saying, meaning he had got a little foothold in spite of Ellie's poor health, and unexpected weather, and strange declines in market prices, and his own mysterious handicaps which weighed him down. Mr. Helton was the hope and the prop of the family, and all the Thompsons became fond of him, or at any rate they ceased to regard him as in any way peculiar, and looked upon him, from a distance they did not know how to bridge, as a good man and a good friend. Mr. Helton went his way, worked, played his tune. Nine years passed. The boys grew up and learned to work. They could not remember the time when Ole Helton hadn't been there: a grouchy cuss, Brother Bones; Mr. Helton, the dairymaid; that Big Swede. If he had heard them, he might have been annoyed at some of the names they called him. But he did not hear them, and besides they meant no harm—or at least such harm as existed was all there, in the names; the boys referred to their father as the Old Man, or the Old Geezer, but not to his face. They lived through by main strength all the grimy, secret, oblique phases of growing up and got past the crisis safely if anyone does. Their parents could see they were good solid boys with hearts of gold in spite of their rough ways. Mr. Thompson was relieved to find that, without knowing how he had done it, he had succeeded in raising a set of boys who were not trifling whittlers. They were such good boys Mr. Thompson began to believe they were born that way, and that he had never spoken a harsh word to them in their lives, much less thrashed them. Herbert and Arthur never disputed his word.

Mr. Helton, his hair wet with sweat, plastered to his dripping fore-head, his jumper streaked dark and light blue and clinging to his ribs, was chopping a little firewood. He chopped slowly, struck the ax into the end of the chopping log, and piled the wood up neatly. He then disappeared round the house into his shack, which shared with the wood pile a good shade from a row of mulberry trees. Mr. Thompson was lolling in a swing chair on the front porch, a place he had never liked. The chair was new, and Mrs. Thompson had wanted it on the front porch, though the side porch was the place for it, being cooler; and Mr. Thompson wanted to sit in the chair, so there he was. As soon as the new wore off of it, and Ellie's pride in it was exhausted, he would move it round to the side porch. Meantime the August heat was almost unbearable, the air so thick you could poke a hole in it. The dust was inches thick on everything, though Mr. Helton sprin-kled the whole yard regularly every night. He even shot the hose upward and washed the tree tops and the roof of the house. They had laid waterpipes to the kitchen and an outside faucet. Mr. Thompson must have dozed, for he opened his eyes and shut his mouth just in time to save his face before a stranger who had driven up to the front gate. Mr. Thompson stood up, put on his hat, pulled up his jeans, and watched while the stranger tied his team, attached to a light spring wagon, to the hitching post. Mr. Thompson recognized the team and wagon. They were from a livery stable in Buda. While the stranger was opening the gate, a strong gate that Mr. Helton had built and set firmly on its hinges several years back, Mr. Thompson strolled down the path to greet him and find out what in God's world a man's busi-ness might be that would bring him out at this time of day, in all this dust and welter.

He wasn't exactly a fat man. He was more like a man who had been fat recently. His skin was baggy and his clothes were too big for him, and he somehow looked like a man who should be fat, ordinarily, but who might have just got over a spell of sickness. Mr. Thompson didn't take to his looks at all, he couldn't say why.

The stranger took off his hat. He said in a loud hearty voice, "Is this Mr. Thompson, Mr. Royal Earle Thompson?"

"That's my name," said Mr. Thompson, almost quietly, he was so taken aback by the free manner of the stranger.

"My name is Hatch," said the stranger, "Mr. Homer T. Hatch, and I've come to see you about buying a horse."

"I reckon you've been misdirected," said Mr. Thompson. "I haven't got a horse for sale. Usually if I've got anything like that to sell," he said, "I tell the neighbors and tack up a little sign on the gate."

The fat man opened his mouth and roared with joy, showing rabbit teeth brown as shoeleather. Mr. Thompson saw nothing to laugh at, for once. The stranger shouted, "That's just an old joke of mine." He caught one of his hands in the other and shook hands with himself heartily. "I always say something like that when I'm calling on a stranger, because I've noticed that when a feller says he's come to buy something nobody takes him for a suspicious character. You see? Haw, haw, haw."

His joviality made Mr. Thompson nervous, because the expression in the man's eyes didn't match the sounds he was making. "Haw, haw," laughed Mr. Thompson obligingly, still not seeing the joke. "Well, that's all wasted on me because I never take any man for a suspicious character 'til he shows hisself to be one. Says or does something," he explained. "Until that happens, one man's as good as another, so far's *I'm* concerned."

"Well," said the stranger, suddenly very sober and sensible, "I ain't come neither to buy nor sell. Fact is, I want to see you about something that's of interest to us both. Yes, sir, I'd like to have a little talk with you, and it won't cost you a cent."

"I guess that's fair enough," said Mr. Thompson, reluctantly. "Come on around the house where there's a little shade."

They went round and seated themselves on two stumps under a chinaberry tree.

"Yes, sir, Homer T. Hatch is my name and America is my nation," said the stranger. "I reckon you must know the name? I used to have a cousin named Jameson Hatch lived up the country a ways."

"Don't think I know the name," said Mr. Thompson. "There's some Hatchers settled somewhere around Mountain City."

"Don't know the old Hatch family," cried the man in deep concern.

He seemed to be pitying Mr. Thompson's ignorance. "Why, we came over from Georgia fifty years ago. Been here long yourself?"

"Just all my whole life," said Mr. Thompson, beginning to feel peevish. "And my pa and my grampap before me. Yes, sir, we've been right here all along. Anybody wants to find a Thompson knows where to look for him. My grampap immigrated in 1836."

"From Ireland, I reckon?" said the stranger.

"From Pennsylvania," said Mr. Thompson. "Now what makes you think we came from Ireland?"

The stranger opened his mouth and began to shout with merriment, and he shook hands with himself as if he hadn't met himself for a long time. "Well, what I always says is, a feller's got to come from *somewhere,* ain't he?"

While they were talking, Mr. Thompson kept glancing at the face near him. He certainly did remind Mr. Thompson of somebody, or maybe he really had seen the man himself somewhere. He couldn't just place the features. Mr. Thompson finally decided it was just that all rabbit-teethed men looked alike.

"That's right," acknowledged Mr. Thompson, rather sourly, "but what I always say is, Thompsons have been settled here for so long it don't make much difference any more *where* they come from. Now a course, this is the slack season, and we're all just laying round a little, but nevertheless we've all got our chores to do, and I don't want to hurry you, and so if you've come to see me on business maybe we'd better get down to it."

"As I said, it's not in a way, and again in a way it is," said the fat man. "Now I'm looking for a man named Helton, Mr. Olaf Eric Helton, from North Dakota, and I was told up around the country a ways that I might find him here, and I wouldn't mind having a little talk with him. No, siree, I sure wouldn't mind, if it's all the same to you."

"I never knew his middle name," said Mr. Thompson, "but Mr. Helton is right here, and been here now for going on nine years. He's a mighty steady man, and you can tell anybody I said so."

"I'm glad to hear that," said Mr. Homer T. Hatch. "I like to hear of a feller mending his ways and settling down. Now when I knew Mr.

Helton he was pretty wild, yes, sir, wild is what he was, he didn't know his own mind atall. Well, now, it's going to be a great pleasure to me to meet up with an old friend and find him all settled down and doing well by hisself."

"We've all got to be young once," said Mr. Thompson. "It's like the measles, it breaks out all over you, and you're a nuisance to yourself and everybody else, but it don't last, and it usually don't leave no ill effects." He was so pleased with this notion he forgot and broke into a guffaw. The stranger folded his arms over his stomach and went into a kind of fit, roaring until he had tears in his eyes. Mr. Thompson stopped shouting and eyed the stranger uneasily. Now he liked a good laugh as well as any man, but there ought to be a little moderation. Now this feller laughed like a perfect lunatic, that was a fact. And he wasn't laughing because he really thought things were funny, either. He was laughing for reasons of his own. Mr. Thompson fell into a moody silence, and waited until Mr. Hatch settled down a little.

Mr. Hatch got out a very dirty blue cotton bandanna and wiped his eyes. "That joke just about caught me where I live," he said, almost apologetically. "Now I wish I could think up things as funny as that to say. It's a gift. It's . . ."

"If you want to speak to Mr. Helton, I'll go and round him up," said Mr. Thompson, making motions as if he might get up. "He may be in the milk house and he may be setting in his shack this time of day." It was drawing towards five o'clock. "It's right around the corner," he said.

"Oh, well, there ain't no special hurry," said Mr. Hatch. "I've been wanting to speak to him for a good long spell now and I guess a few minutes more won't make no difference. I just more wanted to locate him, like. That's all."

Mr. Thompson stopped beginning to stand up, and unbuttoned one more button of his shirt, and said, "Well, he's here, and he's this kind of man, that if he had any business with you he'd like to get it over. He don't dawdle, that's one thing you can say for him."

Mr. Hatch appeared to sulk a little at these words. He wiped his face with the bandanna and opened his mouth to speak, when round the house there came the music of Mr. Helton's harmonica. Mr. Thompson raised a finger. "There he is," said Mr. Thompson. "Now's your time."

Mr. Hatch cocked an ear towards the east side of the house and listened for a few seconds, a very strange expression on his face.

"I know that tune like I know the palm of my own hand," said Mr. Thompson, "but I never heard Mr. Helton say what it was."

"That's a kind of Scandahoovian song," said Mr. Hatch. "Where I come from they sing it a lot. In North Dakota, they sing it. It says something about starting out in the morning feeling so good you can't hardly stand it, so you drink up all your likker before noon. All the likker, y' understand, that you was saving for the noon lay-off. The words ain't much, but it's a pretty tune. It's a kind of drinking song." He sat there drooping a little, and Mr. Thompson didn't like his expression. It was a satisfied expression, but it was more like the cat that et the canary.

"So far as I know," said Mr. Thompson, "he ain't touched a drop since he's been on the place, and that's nine years this coming September. Yes, sir, nine years, so far as I know, he ain't wetted his whistle once. And that's more than I can say for myself," he said, meekly proud.

"Yes, that's a drinking song," said Mr. Hatch. "I used to play 'Little Brown Jug' on the fiddle when I was younger than I am now," he went on, "but this Helton, he just keeps it up. He just sits and plays it by himself."

"He's been playing it off and on for nine years right here on the place," said Mr. Thompson, feeling a little proprietary.

"And he was certainly singing it as well, fifteen years before that, in North Dakota," said Mr. Hatch. "He used to sit up in a straitjacket, practically, when he was in the asylum——"

"What's that you say?" said Mr. Thompson, "What's that?"

"Shucks, I didn't mean to tell you," said Mr. Hatch, a faint leer of regret in his drooping eyelids. "Shucks, that just slipped out. Funny, now I'd made up my mind I wouldn't say a word, because it would just make a lot of excitement, and what I say is, if a man has lived harmless and quiet for nine years it don't matter if he *is* loony, does it? So long's he keeps quiet and don't do nobody harm."

"You mean they had him in a straitjacket?" asked Mr. Thompson, uneasily. "In a lunatic asylum?"

"They sure did," said Mr. Hatch. "That's right where they had him, from time to time."

"They put my Aunt Ida in one of them things in the State asylum," said Mr. Thompson. "She got vi'lent, and they put her in one of these jackets with long sleeves and tied her to an iron ring in the wall, and Aunt Ida got so wild she broke a blood vessel and when they went to look after her she was dead. I'd think one of them things was dangerous."

"Mr. Helton used to sing his drinking song when he was in a straitjacket," said Mr. Hatch. "Nothing ever bothered him, except if you tried to make him talk. That bothered him, and he'd get vi'lent, like your Aunt Ida. He'd get vi'lent and then they'd put him in the jacket and go off and leave him, and he'd lay there perfickly contented, so far's you could see, singing his song. Then one night he just disappeared. Left, you might say, just went, and nobody ever saw hide or hair of him again. And then I come along and find him here," said Mr. Hatch, "all settled down and playing the same song."

"He never acted crazy to me," said Mr. Thompson. "He always acted like a sensible man, to me. He never got married, for one thing, and he works like a horse, and I bet he's got the first cent I paid him when he landed here, and he don't drink, and he never says a word, much less swear, and he don't waste time runnin' around Saturday nights, and if he's crazy," said Mr. Thompson, "why, I think I'll go crazy myself for a change."

"Haw, ha," said Mr. Hatch, "heh, he, that's good! Ha, ha, ha, I hadn't thought of it jes like that. Yeah, that's right! Let's all go crazy and get rid of our wives and save our money, hey?" He smiled unpleasantly, showing his little rabbit teeth.

Mr. Thompson felt he was being misunderstood. He turned around and motioned toward the open window back of the honeysuckle trellis. "Let's move off down here a little," he said. "I oughta thought of that before." His visitor bothered Mr. Thompson. He had a way of taking the words out of Mr. Thompson's mouth, turning them around and mixing them up until Mr. Thompson didn't know himself what he had said. "My wife's not very strong," said Mr. Thompson. "She's been kind of invalid now goin' on fourteen years. It's mighty tough on a poor man, havin' sickness in the family. She had four operations," he said proudly, "one right after the other, but they didn't do any good. For five years handrunnin', I just turned every nickel I made over to the doctors. Upshot is, she's a mighty delicate woman."

"My old woman," said Mr. Homer T. Hatch, "had a back like a mule, yes, sir. That woman could have moved the barn with her bare hands if she'd ever took the notion. I used to say, it was a good thing she didn't know her own stren'th. She's dead now, though. That kind wear out quicker than the puny ones. I never had much use for a woman always complainin'. I'd get rid of her mighty quick, yes, sir, mighty quick. It's just as you say: a dead loss, keepin' one of 'em up."

This was not at all what Mr. Thompson had heard himself say; he had been trying to explain that a wife as expensive as his was a credit to a man. "She's a mighty reasonable woman," said Mr. Thompson, feeling baffled, "but I wouldn't answer for what she'd say or do if she found out we'd had a lunatic on the place all this time." They had moved away from the window; Mr. Thompson took Mr. Hatch the front way, because if he went the back way they would have to pass Mr. Helton's shack. For some reason he didn't want the stranger to see or talk to Mr. Helton. It was strange, but that was the way Mr. Thompson felt.

Mr. Thompson sat down again, on the chopping log, offering his guest another tree stump. "Now, I mighta got upset myself at such a thing, once," said Mr. Thompson, "but now I *deefy* anything to get me lathered up." He cut himself an enormous plug of tobacco with his horn-handled pocketknife, and offered it to Mr. Hatch, who then produced his own plug and, opening a huge bowie knife with a long blade sharply whetted, cut off a large wad and put it in his mouth. They then compared plugs and both of them were astonished to see how different men's ideas of good chewing tobacco were.

"Now, for instance," said Mr. Hatch, "mine is lighter colored. That's because, for one thing, there ain't any sweetenin' in this plug. I like it dry, natural leaf, medium strong."

"A little sweetenin' don't do no harm so far as I'm concerned," said

Mr. Thompson, "but it's got to be mighty little. But with me, now, I want a strong leaf, I want it heavy-cured, as the feller says. There's a man near here, named Williams, Mr. John Morgan Williams, who chews a plug—well, sir, it's black as your hat and soft as melted tar. It fairly drips with molasses, jus' plain molasses, and it chews like licorice. Now, I don't call that a good chew."

"One man's meat," said Mr. Hatch, "is another man's poison. Now, such a chew would simply gag me. I couldn't begin to put it in my mouth."

"Well," said Mr. Thompson, a tinge of apology in his voice, "I jus' barely tasted it myself, you might say. Just took a little piece in my mouth and spit it out again."

"I'm dead sure I couldn't even get that far," said Mr. Hatch. "I like a dry natural chew without any artificial flavorin' of any kind."

Mr. Thompson began to feel that Mr. Hatch was trying to make out he had the best judgment in tobacco, and was going to keep up the argument until he proved it. He began to feel seriously annoyed with the fat man. After all, who was he and where did he come from? Who was he to go around telling other people what kind of tobacco to chew?

"Artificial flavorin'," Mr. Hatch went on, doggedly, "is jes put in to cover up a cheap leaf and make a man think he's gettin' somethin' more than he *is* gettin'. Even a little sweetenin' is a sign of a cheap leaf, you can mark my words."

"I've always paid a fair price for my plug," said Mr. Thompson, stiffly. "I'm not a rich man and I don't go round settin' myself up for one, but I'll say this, when it comes to such things as tobacco, I buy the best on the market."

"Sweetenin', even a little," began Mr. Hatch, shifting his plug and squirting tobacco juice at a dry-looking little rose bush that was having a hard enough time as it was, standing all day in the blazing sun, its roots clenched in the baked earth, "is the sign of——"

"About this Mr. Helton, now," said Mr. Thompson, determinedly, "I don't see no reason to hold it against a man because he went loony once or twice in his lifetime and so I don't expect to take no steps about it. Not a step. I've got nothin' against the man, he's always treated me fair. They's things and people," he went on, " 'nough to drive any man loony. The wonder to me is, more men don't wind up in straitjackets, the way things are going these days and times."

"That's right," said Mr. Hatch, promptly, entirely too promptly, as if he were turning Mr. Thompson's meaning back on him. "You took the words right out of my mouth. There ain't every man in a straitjacket that ought to be there. Ha, ha, you're right all right. You got the idea."

Mr. Thompson sat silent and chewed steadily and stared at a spot on the ground about six feet away and felt a slow muffled resentment climbing from somewhere deep down in him, climbing and spreading all through him. What was this fellow driving at? What was he trying to say? It wasn't so much his words, but his looks and his way of talking: that droopy look in the eye, that tone of voice, as if he was trying to mortify Mr. Thompson about something. Mr. Thompson didn't like it, but he couldn't get hold of it either. He wanted to turn around and shove the fellow off the stump, but it wouldn't look reasonable. Suppose something happened to the fellow when he fell off the stump, just for instance, if he fell on the ax and cut himself, and then someone should ask Mr. Thompson why he shoved him, and what could a man say? It would look mighty funny, it would sound mighty strange to say, Well, him and me fell out over a plug of tobacco. He might just shove him anyhow and then tell people he was a fat man not used to the heat and while he was talking he got dizzy and fell off by himself, or something like that, and it wouldn't be the truth either, because it wasn't the heat and it wasn't the tobacco. Mr. Thompson made up his mind to get the fellow off the place pretty quick, without seeming to be anxious, and watch him sharp till he was out of sight. It doesn't pay to be friendly with strangers from another part of the country. They're always up to something, or they'd stay at home where they belong.

"And they's some people," said Mr. Hatch, "would jus' as soon have a loonatic around their house as not, they can't see no difference between them and anybody else. I always say, if that's the way a man feels, don't care who he associates with, why, why, that's his business, not mine. I don't wanta have a thing to do with it. Now back home in North Dakota, we don't feel that way. I'd like to a seen anybody hiring a loonatic there, aspecially after what he done."

"I didn't understand your home was North Dakota," said Mr. Thompson. "I thought you said Georgia."

"I've got a married sister in North Dakota," said Mr. Hatch, "married a Swede, but a white man if ever I saw one. So I say *we* because we got into a little business together out that way. And it seems like home, kind of."

"What did he do?" asked Mr. Thompson, feeling very uneasy again.

"Oh, nothin' to speak of," said Mr. Hatch, jovially, "jus' went loony one day in the hayfield and shoved a pitchfork right square through his brother, when they was makin' hay. They was goin' to execute him, but they found out he had went crazy with the heat, as the feller says, and so they put him in the asylum. That's all he done. Nothin' to get lathered up about, ha, ha, ha!" he said, and taking out his sharp knife he began to slice off a chew as carefully as if he were cutting cake.

"Well," said Mr. Thompson, "I don't deny that's news. Yes, sir, news. But I still say somethin' must have drove him to it. Some men make you feel like giving 'em a good killing just by lookin' at you. His brother may a been a mean ornery cuss."

"Brother was going to get married," said Mr. Hatch; "used to go courtin' his girl nights. Borrowed Mr. Helton's harmonica to give her a serenade one evenin', and lost it. Brand new harmonica."

"He thinks a heap of his harmonicas," said Mr. Thompson. "Only money he ever spends, now and then he buys hisself a new one. Must have a dozen in that shack, all kinds and sizes."

"Brother wouldn't buy him a new one," said Mr. Hatch, "so Mr. Helton just ups, as I says, and runs his pitchfork through his brother. Now you know he musta been crazy to get all worked up over a little thing like that."

"Sounds like it," said Mr. Thompson, reluctant to agree in anything with this intrusive and disagreeable fellow. He kept thinking he couldn't remember when he had taken such a dislike to a man on first sight.

"Seems to me you'd get pretty sick of hearin' the same tune year in, year out," said Mr. Hatch.

"Well, sometimes I think it wouldn't do no harm if he learned a new one," said Mr. Thompson, "but he don't, so there's nothin' to be done about it. It's a pretty good tune, though."

"One of the Scandahoovians told me what it meant, that's how I come to know," said Mr. Hatch. "Especially that part about getting so gay you jus' go ahead and drink up all the likker you got on hand before noon. It seems like up in them Swede countries a man carries a bottle of wine around with him as a matter of course, at least that's the way I understood it. Those fellers will tell you anything, though—" He broke off and spat.

The idea of drinking any kind of liquor in this heat made Mr. Thompson dizzy. The idea of anybody feeling good on a day like this, for instance, made him tired. He felt he was really suffering from the heat. The fat man looked as if he had grown to the stump; he slumped there in his damp, dark clothes too big for him, his belly slack in his pants, his wide black felt hat pushed off his narrow forehead red with prickly heat. A bottle of good cold beer, now, would be a help, thought Mr. Thompson, remembering the four bottles sitting deep in the pool at the springhouse, and his dry tongue squirmed in his mouth. He wasn't going to offer this man anything, though, not even a drop of water. He wasn't even going to chew any more tobacco with him. He shot out his quid suddenly, and wiped his mouth on the back of his hand, and studied the head near him attentively. The man was no good, and he was there for no good, but what was he up to? Mr. Thompson made up his mind he'd give him a little more time to get his business, whatever it was, with Mr. Helton over, and then if he didn't get off the place he'd kick him off.

Mr. Hatch, as if he suspected Mr. Thompson's thoughts, turned his eyes, wicked and pig-like, on Mr. Thompson. "Fact is," he said, as if he had made up his mind about something, "I might need your help in the little matter I've got on hand, but it won't cost you any trouble. Now, this Mr. Helton here, like I tell you, he's a dangerous escaped loonatic, you might say. Now fact is, in the last twelve years or so I musta rounded up twenty-odd escaped loonatics, besides a couple of escaped convicts that I just run into by accident, like. I don't make a business of it, but if there's a reward, and there usually is a reward, of course, I get it. It amounts to a tidy little sum in the long run, but that ain't the main question. Fact is, I'm for law and order, I don't like to see lawbreakers and loonatics at large. It ain't the place for them. Now I reckon you're bound to agree with me on that, aren't you?"

Mr. Thompson said, "Well, circumstances alters cases, as the feller says. Now, what I know of Mr. Helton, he ain't dangerous, as I told you." Something serious was going to happen, Mr. Thompson could see that. He stopped thinking about it. He'd just let this fellow shoot off his head and then see what could be done about it. Without thinking he got out his knife and plug and started to cut a chew, then remembered himself and put them back in his pocket.

"The law," said Mr. Hatch, "is solidly behind me. Now this Mr. Helton, he's been one of my toughest cases. He's kept my record from being practically one hundred per cent. I knew him before he went loony, and I know the fam'ly, so I undertook to help out rounding him up. Well, sir, he was gone slick as a whistle, for all we knew the man was as good as dead long while ago. Now we never might have caught up with him, but do you know what he did? Well, sir, about two weeks ago his old mother gets a letter from him, and in that letter, what do you reckon she found? Well, it was a check on that little bank in town for eight hundred and fifty dollars, just like that; the letter wasn't nothing much, just said he was sending her a few little savings, she might need something, but there it was, name, postmark, date, everything. The old woman practically lost her mind with joy. She's gettin' childish, and it looked like she kinda forgot that her only living son killed his brother and went loony. Mr. Helton said he was getting along all right, and for her not to tell nobody. Well, natchally, she couldn't keep it to herself, with that check to cash and everything. So that's how I come to know." His feelings got the better of him. "You coulda knocked me down with a feather." He shook hands with himself and rocked, wagging his head, going "Heh, heh," in his throat. Mr. Thompson felt the corners of his mouth turning down. Why, the dirty low-down hound, sneaking around spying into other people's business like that. Collecting blood money, that's what it was! Let him talk!

"Yea, well, that musta been a surprise all right," he said, trying to hold his voice even. "I'd say a surprise."

"Well, siree," said Mr. Hatch, "the more I got to thinking about it, the more I just come to the conclusion that I'd better look into the matter a little, and so I talked to the old woman. She's pretty decrepit, now, half blind and all, but she was all for taking the first train out and going to see her son. I put it up to her square—how she was too feeble for the trip, and all. So, just as a favor to her, I told her for my expenses I'd come down and see Mr. Helton and bring her back all the news about him. She gave me a new shirt she made herself by hand, and a big Swedish kind of cake to bring to him, but I musta mislaid them along the road somewhere. It don't reely matter, though, he prob'ly ain't in any state of mind to appreciate 'em."

Mr. Thompson sat up and turning round on the log looked at Mr. Hatch and asked as quietly as he could, "And now what are you aiming to do? That's the question."

Mr. Hatch slouched up to his feet and shook himself. "Well, I come all prepared for a little scuffle," he said. "I got the handcuffs," he said, "but I don't want no violence if I can help it. I didn't want to say nothing around the countryside, making an uproar. I figured the two of us could overpower him." He reached into his big inside pocket and pulled them out. Handcuffs, for God's sake, thought Mr. Thompson. Coming round on a peaceable afternoon worrying a man, and making trouble, and fishing handcuffs out of his pocket on a decent family homestead, as if it was all in the day's work.

Mr. Thompson, his head buzzing, got up too. "Well," he said, roundly, "I want to tell you I think you've got a mighty sorry job on hand, you sure must be hard up for something to do, and now I want to give you a good piece of advice. You just drop the idea that you're going to come here and make trouble for Mr. Helton, and the quicker you drive that hired rig away from my front gate the better I'll be satisfied."

Mr. Hatch put one handcuff in his outside pocket, the other dangling down. He pulled his hat down over his eyes, and reminded Mr.

Thompson of a sheriff, somehow. He didn't seem in the least nervous, and didn't take up Mr. Thompson's words. He said, "Now listen just a minute, it ain't reasonable to suppose that a man like yourself is going to stand in the way of getting an escaped loonatic back to the asylum where he belongs. Now I know it's enough to throw you off, coming sudden like this, but fact is I counted on your being a respectable man and helping me out to see that justice is done. Now a course, if you won't help, I'll have to look around for help somewheres else. It won't look very good to your neighbors that you was harbring an escaped loonatic who killed his own brother, and then you refused to give him up. It will look mighty funny."

Mr. Thompson knew almost before he heard the words that it would look funny. It would put him in a mighty awkward position. He said, "But I've been trying to tell you all along that the man ain't loony now. He's been perfectly harmless for nine years. He's—he's——"

Mr. Thompson couldn't think how to describe how it was with Mr. Helton. "Why, he's been like one of the family," he said, "the best standby a man ever had." Mr. Thompson tried to see his way out. It was a fact Mr. Helton might go loony again any minute, and now this fellow talking around the country would put Mr. Thompson in a fix. It was a terrible position. He couldn't think of any way out. "You're crazy," Mr. Thompson roared suddenly, "you're the crazy one around here, you're crazier than he ever was! You get off this place or I'll handcuff you and turn you over to the law. You're trespassing," shouted Mr. Thompson. "Get out of here before I knock you down!"

He took a step towards the fat man, who backed off, shrinking, "Try it, try it, go ahead!" and then something happened that Mr. Thompson tried hard afterwards to piece together in his mind, and in fact it never did come straight. He saw the fat man with his long bowie knife in his hand, he saw Mr. Helton come round the corner on the run, his long jaw dropped, his arms swinging, his eyes wild. Mr. Helton came in between them, fists doubled up, then stopped short, glaring at the fat man, his big frame seemed to collapse, he trembled like a shied horse; and then the fat man drove at him, knife in one hand, handcuffs in the other. Mr. Thompson saw it coming, he saw the blade going into Mr. Helton's stomach, he knew he had the ax out of the log in his own hands, felt his arms go up over his head and bring the ax down on Mr. Hatch's head as if he were stunning a beef.

Mrs. Thompson had been listening uneasily for some time to the voices going on, one of them strange to her, but she was too tired at first to get up and come out to see what was going on. The confused shouting that rose so suddenly brought her up to her feet and out across the front porch without her slippers, hair half-braided. Shading her eyes, she saw first Mr. Helton, running all stooped over through the orchard, running like a man with dogs after him; and Mr. Thompson supporting himself on the ax handle was leaning over shaking by the shoulder a man Mrs. Thompson had never seen, who lay doubled up with the top of his head smashed and the blood running away in a greasy-looking puddle. Mr. Thompson, without taking his hand from the man's shoulder, said in a thick voice, "He killed Mr. Helton, he killed him, I saw him do it. I had to knock him out," he called loudly, "but he won't come to."

Mrs. Thompson said in a faint scream, "Why, yonder goes Mr. Helton," and she pointed. Mr. Thompson pulled himself up and looked where she pointed. Mrs. Thompson sat down slowly against the side of the house and began to slide forward on her face; she felt as if she were drowning, she couldn't rise to the top somehow, and her only thought was she was glad the boys were not there, they were out, fishing at Halifax, oh, God, she was glad the boys were not there.

Mr. and Mrs. Thompson drove up to their barn about sunset. Mr. Thompson handed the reins to his wife, got out to open the big door, and Mrs. Thompson guided old Jim in under the roof. The buggy was gray with dust and age, Mrs. Thompson's face was gray with dust and weariness, and Mr. Thompson's face, as he stood at the horse's head and began unhitching, was gray except for the dark blue of his freshly shaven jaws and chin, gray and blue and caved in, but patient, like a dead man's face.

Mrs. Thompson stepped down to the hard packed manure of the barn floor, and shook out her light flower-sprigged dress. She wore her smoked glasses, and her wide shady leghorn hat with the wreath of exhausted pink and blue forget-me-nots hid her forehead, fixed in a knot of distress.

The horse hung his head, raised a huge sigh and flexed his stiffened legs. Mr. Thompson's words came up muffled and hollow. "Poor ole Jim," he said, clearing his throat, "he looks pretty sunk in the ribs. I guess he's had a hard week." He lifted the harness up in one piece, slid it off and Jim walked out of the shafts halting a little. "Well, this is the last time," Mr. Thompson said, still talking to Jim. "Now you can get a good rest."

Mrs. Thompson closed her eyes behind her smoked glasses. The last time, and high time, and they should never have gone at all. She did not need her glasses any more, now the good darkness was coming down again, but her eyes ran full of tears steadily, though she was not crying, and she felt better with the glasses, safer, hidden away behind them. She took out her handkerchief with her hands shaking as they had been shaking ever since *that day,* and blew her nose. She said, "I see the boys have lighted the lamps. I hope they've started the stove going."

She stepped along the rough path holding her thin dress and starched petticoats around her, feeling her way between the sharp small stones, leaving the barn because she could hardly bear to be near Mr. Thompson, advancing slowly towards the house because she dreaded going there. Life was all one dread, the faces of her neighbors, of her boys, of her husband, the face of the whole world, the shape of her own house in the darkness, the very smell of the grass and the trees were horrible to her. There was no place to go, only one thing to do, bear it somehow —but how? She asked herself that question often. How was she going to keep on living now? Why had she lived at all? She wished now she had died one of those times when she had been so sick, instead of living on for this.

The boys were in the kitchen; Herbert was looking at the funny pictures from last Sunday's newspapers, the Katzenjammer Kids and Happy Hooligan. His chin was in his hands and his elbows on the table, and he was really reading and looking at the pictures, but his face was unhappy. Arthur was building the fire, adding kindling a stick at a time, watching it catch and blaze. His face was heavier and darker than Herbert's, but he was a little sullen by nature; Mrs. Thompson thought, he takes things harder, too. Arthur said, "Hello, Momma," and went on with his work. Herbert swept the papers together and moved over on the bench. They were big boys—fifteen and seventeen, and Arthur as tall as his father. Mrs. Thompson sat down beside Herbert, taking off her hat. She said, "I guess you're hungry. We were late today. We went the Log Hollow road, it's rougher than ever." Her pale mouth drooped with a sad fold on either side.

"I guess you saw the Mannings, then," said Herbert.

"Yes, and the Fergusons, and the Allbrights, and that new family McClellan."

"Anybody say anything?" asked Herbert.

"Nothing much, you know how it's been all along, some of them keeps saying, yes, they know it was a clear case and a fair trial and they say how glad they are your papa came out so well, and all that, some of 'em do, anyhow, but it looks like they don't really take sides with him. I'm about wore out," she said, the tears rolling again from under her dark glasses. "I don't know what good it does, but your papa can't seem to rest unless he's telling how it happened. I don't know."

"I don't think it does any good, not a speck," said Arthur, moving away from the stove. "It just keeps the whole question stirred up in people's minds. Everybody will go round telling what he heard, and the whole thing is going to get worse mixed up than ever. It just makes matters worse. I wish you could get Papa to stop driving round the country talking like that."

"Your papa knows best," said Mrs. Thompson. "You oughtn't to criticize him. He's got enough to put up with without that."

Arthur said nothing, his jaw stubborn. Mr. Thompson came in, his eyes hollowed out and dead-looking, his thick hands gray white and seamed from washing them clean every day before he started out to see the neighbors to tell them his side of the story. He was wearing his Sunday clothes, a thick pepper-and-salt-colored suit with a black string tie.

Mrs. Thompson stood up, her head swimming. "Now you-all get out of the kitchen, it's too hot in here and I need room. I'll get us a little bite of supper, if you'll just get out and give me some room."

They went as if they were glad to go, the boys outside, Mr. Thompson into his bedroom. She heard him groaning to himself as he took off his shoes, and heard the bed creak as he lay down. Mrs. Thompson opened the icebox and felt the sweet coldness flow out of it; she had never expected to have an icebox, much less did she hope to afford to keep it filled with ice. It still seemed like a miracle, after two or three years. There was the food, cold and clean, all ready to be warmed over. She would never have had that icebox if Mr. Helton hadn't happened along one day, just by the strangest luck; so saving, and so managing, so good, thought Mrs. Thompson, her heart swelling until she feared she would faint again, standing there with the door open and leaning her head upon it. She simply could not bear to remember Mr. Helton, with his long sad face and silent ways, who had always been so quiet and harmless, who had worked so hard and helped Mr. Thompson so much, running through the hot fields and woods, being hunted like a mad dog, everybody turning out with ropes and guns and sticks to catch and tie him. Oh, God, said Mrs. Thompson in a long dry moan, kneeling before the icebox and fumbling inside for the dishes, even if they did pile mattresses all over the jail floor and against the walls, and five men there to hold him to keep him from hurting himself any more, he was already hurt too badly, he couldn't have lived anyway. Mr. Barbee, the sheriff, told her about it. He said, well, they didn't aim to harm him but they had to catch him, he was crazy as a loon; he picked up rocks and tried to brain every man that got near him. He had two harmonicas in his jumper pocket, said the sheriff, but they fell out in the scuffle, and Mr. Helton tried to pick 'em up again, and that's when they finally got him. "They *had* to be rough, Miz Thompson, he fought like a wildcat." Yes, thought Mrs. Thompson again with the same bitterness, of course, they had to be rough. They always have to be rough. Mr. Thompson can't argue with a man and get him off the place peaceably; no, she thought, standing up and shutting the icebox, he has to kill somebody, he has to be a murderer and ruin his boys' lives and cause Mr. Helton to be killed like a mad dog.

Her thoughts stopped with a little soundless explosion, cleared and began again. The rest of Mr. Helton's harmonicas were still in the shack, his tune ran in Mrs. Thompson's head at certain times of the day. She missed it in the evenings. It seemed so strange she had never known the name of that song, nor what it meant, until after Mr. Helton was gone. Mrs. Thompson, trembling in the knees, took a drink of water at the sink and poured the red beans into the baking dish, and began to roll the pieces of chicken in flour to fry them. There was a time, she said to herself, when I thought I had neighbors and friends, there was a time when we could hold up our heads, there was a time when my husband hadn't killed a man and I could tell the truth to anybody about anything.

Mr. Thompson, turning on his bed, figured that he had done all he could, he'd just try to let the matter rest from now on. His lawyer, Mr. Burleigh, had told him right at the beginning, "Now you keep calm and collected. You've got a fine case, even if you haven't got witnesses. Your wife must sit in court, she'll be a powerful argument with the jury. You just plead not guilty and I'll do the rest. The trial is going to be a mere formality, you haven't got a thing to worry about. You'll be clean out of this before you know it." And to make talk Mr. Burleigh had got to telling about all the men he knew around the country who for one reason or another had been forced to kill somebody, always in self-defense, and there just wasn't anything to it at all. He even told about how his own father in the old days had shot and killed a man just for setting foot inside his gate when he told him not to. "Sure, I shot the scoundrel," said Mr. Burleigh's father, "in self-defense; I *told* him I'd shoot him if he set his foot in my yard, and he did, and I did." There had been bad blood between them for years, Mr. Burleigh said, and his father had waited a long time to catch the other fellow in the wrong, and when he did he certainly made the most of his opportunity.

"But Mr. Hatch, as I told you," Mr. Thompson had said, "made a pass at Mr. Helton with his bowie knife. That's why I took a hand."

"All the better," said Mr. Burleigh. "That stranger hadn't any right coming to your house on such an errand. Why, hell," said Mr. Burleigh, "that wasn't even manslaughter you committed. So now you just hold your horses and keep your shirt on. And don't say one word without I tell you."

Wasn't even manslaughter. Mr. Thompson had to cover Mr. Hatch
with a piece of wagon canvas and ride to town to tell the sheriff. It had
been hard on Ellie. When they got back, the sheriff and the coroner
and two deputies, they found her sitting beside the road, on a low
bridge over a gulley, about half a mile from the place. He had taken
her up behind his saddle and got her back to the house. He had already
told the sheriff that his wife had witnessed the whole business, and now
he had time, getting her to her room and in bed, to tell her what to say
if they asked anything. He had left out the part about Mr. Helton being crazy all along, but it came out at the trial. By Mr. Burleigh's advice Mr. Thompson had pretended to be perfectly ignorant; Mr. Hatch
hadn't said a word about that. Mr. Thompson pretended to believe
that Mr. Hatch had just come looking for Mr. Helton to settle old
scores, and the two members of Mr. Hatch's family who had come
down to try to get Mr. Thompson convicted didn't get anywhere at
all. It hadn't been much of a trial, Mr. Burleigh saw to that. He had
charged a reasonable fee, and Mr. Thompson had paid him and felt
grateful, but after it was over Mr. Burleigh didn't seem pleased to see
him when he got to dropping into the office to talk it over, telling him
things that had slipped his mind at first: trying to explain what an
ornery low hound Mr. Hatch had been, anyhow. Mr. Burleigh seemed
to have lost his interest; he looked sour and upset when he saw Mr.
Thompson at the door. Mr. Thompson kept saying to himself that
he'd got off, all right, just as Mr. Burleigh had predicted, but, but—
and it was right there that Mr. Thompson's mind struck, squirming
like an angleworm on a fishhook: he had killed Mr. Hatch, and he was
a murderer. That was the truth about himself that Mr. Thompson
couldn't grasp, even when he said the word to himself. Why, he had
not even once *thought* of killing anybody, much less Mr. Hatch, and
if Mr. Helton hadn't come out so unexpectedly, hearing the row, why,
then—but then, Mr. Helton had come on the run that way to help him.
What he couldn't understand was what happened next. He had seen
Mr. Hatch go after Mr. Helton with the knife, he had seen the point,
blade up, go into Mr. Helton's stomach and slice up like you slice a
hog, but when they finally caught Mr. Helton there wasn't a knife
scratch on him. Mr. Thompson knew he had the ax in his own hands

and felt himself lifting it, but he couldn't remember hitting Mr. Hatch. He couldn't remember it. He couldn't. He remembered only that he had been determined to stop Mr. Hatch from cutting Mr. Helton. If he was given a chance he could explain the whole matter. At the trial they hadn't let him talk. They just asked questions and he answered yes or no, and they never did get to the core of the matter. Since the trial, now, every day for a week he had washed and shaved and put on his best clothes and had taken Ellie with him to tell every neighbor he had that he never killed Mr. Hatch on purpose, and what good did it do? Nobody believed him. Even when he turned to Ellie and said, "You was there, you saw it, didn't you?" and Ellie spoke up, saying, "Yes, that's the truth. Mr. Thompson was trying to save Mr. Helton's life," and he added, "If you don't believe me, you can believe my wife. She won't lie," Mr. Thompson saw something in all their faces that disheartened him, made him feel empty and tired out. They didn't believe he was not a murderer.

Even Ellie never said anything to comfort him. He hoped she would say finally, "I remember now, Mr. Thompson, I really did come round the corner in time to see everything. It's not a lie, Mr. Thompson. Don't you worry." But as they drove together in silence, with the days still hot and dry, shortening for fall, day after day, the buggy jolting in the ruts, she said nothing; they grew to dread the sight of another house, and the people in it: all houses looked alike now, and the people— old neighbors or new—had the same expression when Mr. Thompson told them why he had come and began his story. Their eyes looked as if someone had pinched the eyeball at the back; they shriveled and the light went out of them. Some of them sat with fixed tight smiles trying to be friendly. "Yes, Mr. Thompson, we know how you must feel. It must be terrible for you, Mrs. Thompson. Yes, you know, I've about come to the point where I believe in such a thing as killing in self-defense. Why, certainly, we believe you, Mr. Thompson, why shouldn't we believe you? Didn't you have a perfectly fair and above-board trial? Well, now, natchally, Mr. Thompson, we think you done right."

Mr. Thompson was satisfied they didn't think so. Sometimes the air around him was so thick with their blame he fought and pushed with his fists, and the sweat broke out all over him, he shouted his story in a dust-choked voice, he would fairly bellow at last: "My wife, here, you know her, she was there, she saw and heard it all, if you don't believe me, ask her, she won't lie!" and Mrs. Thompson, with her hands knotted together, aching, her chin trembling, would never fail to say: "Yes, that's right, that's the truth——"

The last straw had been laid on today, Mr. Thompson decided. Tom Allbright, an old beau of Ellie's, why, he had squired Ellie around a whole summer, had come out to meet them when they drove up, and standing there bareheaded had stopped them from getting out. He had looked past them with an embarrassed frown on his face, telling them his wife's sister was there with a raft of young ones, and the house was pretty full and everything upset, or he'd ask them to come in. "We've been thinking of trying to get up to your place one of these days," said Mr. Allbright, moving away trying to look busy, "we've been mighty occupied up here of late." So they had to say, "Well, we just happened to be driving this way," and go on. "The Allbrights," said Mrs. Thompson, "always was fair-weather friends." "They look out for number one, that's a fact," said Mr. Thompson. But it was cold comfort to them both.

Finally Mrs. Thompson had given up. "Let's go home," she said. "Old Jim's tired and thirsty, and we've gone far enough."

Mr. Thompson said, "Well, while we're out this way, we might as well stop at the McClellans'." They drove in, and asked a little cotton-haired boy if his mamma and papa were at home. Mr. Thompson wanted to see them. The little boy stood gazing with his mouth open, then galloped into the house shouting. "Mommer, Popper, come out hyah. That man that kilt Mr. Hatch has come ter see yer!"

The man came out in his sock feet, with one gallus up, the other broken and dangling, and said, "Light down, Mr. Thompson, and come in. The ole woman's washing, but she'll git here." Mrs. Thompson, feeling her way, stepped down and sat in a broken rocking-chair on the porch that sagged under her feet. The woman of the house, barefooted, in a calico wrapper, sat on the edge of the porch, her fat sallow face full of curiosity. Mr. Thompson began, "Well, as I reckon you happen to know, I've had some strange troubles lately, and, as the feller says, it's not the kind of trouble that happens to a man every

day in the year, and there's some things I don't want no misunderstanding about in the neighbors' minds, so—" He halted and stumbled forward, and the two listening faces took on a mean look, a greedy,
despising look, a look that said plain as day, "My, you must be a purty
sorry feller to come round worrying about what *we* think, *we* know you
wouldn't be here if you had anybody else to turn to—my, I wouldn't
lower myself that much, myself." Mr. Thompson was ashamed of himself, he was suddenly in a rage, he'd like to knock their dirty skunk
heads together, the low-down white trash—but he held himself down
and went on to the end. "My wife will tell you," he said, and this was
the hardest place, because Ellie always without moving a muscle seemed
to stiffen as if somebody had threatened to hit her; "ask my wife, she
won't lie."

"It's true, I saw it——"

"Well, now," said the man, drily, scratching his ribs inside his shirt,
"that sholy is too bad. Well, now, I kaint see what we've got to do with
all this here however. I kaint see no good reason for us to git mixed up
in these murder matters, I shore kaint. Whichever way you look at it,
it ain't none of my business. However, it's mighty nice of you-all to
come around and give us the straight of it, fur we've heerd some
mighty queer yarns about it, mighty queer, I golly you couldn't hardly
make head ner tail of it."

"Evvybody goin' round shootin' they heads off," said the woman.
"Now we don't hold with killin'; the Bible says——"

"Shet yer trap," said the man, "and keep it shet 'r I'll shet it fer yer.
Now it shore looks like to me——"

"We mustn't linger," said Mrs. Thompson, unclasping her hands.
"We've lingered too long now. It's getting late, and we've far to go."
Mr. Thompson took the hint and followed her. The man and the
woman lolled against their rickety porch poles and watched them go.

Now lying on his bed, Mr. Thompson knew the end had come. Now,
this minute, lying in the bed where he had slept with Ellie for eighteen
years; under this roof where he had laid the shingles when he was
waiting to get married; there as he was with his whiskers already
sprouting since his shave that morning; with his fingers feeling his
bony chin, Mr. Thompson felt he was a dead man. He was dead to his

other life, he had got to the end of something without knowing why, and he had to make a fresh start, he did not know how. Something different was going to begin, he didn't know what. It was in some way not his business. He didn't feel he was going to have much to do with it. He got up, aching, hollow, and went out to the kitchen where Mrs. Thompson was just taking up the supper.

"Call the boys," said Mrs. Thompson. They had been down to the barn, and Arthur put out the lantern before hanging it on a nail near the door. Mr. Thompson didn't like their silence. They had hardly said a word about anything to him since that day. They seemed to avoid him, they ran the place together as if he wasn't there, and attended to everything without asking him for any advice. "What you boys been up to?" he asked, trying to be hearty. "Finishing your chores?"

"No, sir," said Arthur, "there ain't much to do. Just greasing some axles." Herbert said nothing. Mrs. Thompson bowed her head: "For these and all Thy blessings. . . . Amen," she whispered weakly, and the Thompsons sat there with their eyes down and their faces sorrowful, as if they were at a funeral.

Every time he shut his eyes, trying to sleep, Mr. Thompson's mind started up and began to run like a rabbit. It jumped from one thing to another, trying to pick up a trail here or there that would straighten out what had happened that day he killed Mr. Hatch. Try as he might, Mr. Thompson's mind would not go anywhere that it had not already been, he could not see anything but what he had seen once, and he knew that was not right. If he had not seen straight that first time, then everything about his killing Mr. Hatch was wrong from start to finish, and there was nothing more to be done about it, he might just as well give up. It still seemed to him that he had done, maybe not the right thing, but the only thing he could do, that day, but had he? *Did he have to kill Mr. Hatch?* He had never seen a man he hated more, the minute he laid eyes on him. He knew in his bones the fellow was there for trouble. What seemed so funny now was this: Why hadn't he just told Mr. Hatch to get out before he ever even got in?

Mrs. Thompson, her arms crossed on her breast, was lying beside him, perfectly still, but she seemed awake, somehow. "Asleep, Ellie?"

After all, he might have got rid of him peaceably, or maybe he might have had to overpower him and put those handcuffs on him and turn him over to the sheriff for disturbing the peace. The most they could have done was to lock Mr. Hatch up while he cooled off for a few days or fine him a little something. He would try to think of things he might have said to Mr. Hatch. Why, let's see, I could just have said, Now look here, Mr. Hatch, I want to talk to you as man to man. But his brain would go empty. What could he have said or done? But if he *could* have done anything else almost except kill Mr. Hatch, then nothing would have happened to Mr. Helton. Mr. Thompson hardly ever thought of Mr. Helton. His mind just skipped over him and went on. If he stopped to think about Mr. Helton he'd never in God's world get anywhere. He tried to imagine how it might all have been, this very night even, if Mr. Helton were still safe and sound out in his shack playing his tune about feeling so good in the morning, drinking up all the wine so you'd feel even better; and Mr. Hatch safe in jail somewhere, mad as hops, maybe, but out of harm's way and ready to listen to reason and to repent of his meanness, the dirty, yellow-livered hound coming around persecuting an innocent man and ruining a whole family that never harmed him! Mr. Thompson felt the veins of his forehead start up, his fists clutched as if they seized an ax handle, the sweat broke out on him, he bounded up from the bed with a yell smothered in his throat, and Ellie started up after him, crying out, "Oh, oh, don't! Don't! Don't!" as if she were having a nightmare. He stood shaking until his bones rattled in him, crying hoarsely, "Light the lamp, light the lamp, Ellie."

Instead, Mrs. Thompson gave a shrill weak scream, almost the same scream he had heard on that day she came around the house when he was standing there with the ax in his hand. He could not see her in the dark, but she was on the bed, rolling violently. He felt for her in horror, and his groping hands found her arms, up, and her own hands pulling her hair straight out from her head, her neck strained back, and the tight screams strangling her. He shouted out for Arthur, for Herbert. "Your mother!" he bawled, his voice cracking. As he held Mrs. Thompson's arms, the boys came tumbling in, Arthur with the lamp above his head. By this light Mr. Thompson saw Mrs. Thompson's eyes, wide open, staring dreadfully at him, the tears pouring. She sat up at sight of the boys, and held out one arm towards them, the hand wagging in a crazy circle, then dropped on her back again, and suddenly went limp. Arthur set the lamp on the table and turned on Mr. Thompson. "She's scared," he said, "she's scared to death." His face was in a knot of rage, his fists were doubled up, he faced his father as if he meant to strike him. Mr. Thompson's jaw fell, he was so surprised he stepped back from the bed. Herbert went to the other side. They stood on each side of Mrs. Thompson and watched Mr. Thompson as if he were a dangerous wild beast. "What did you do to her?" shouted Arthur, in a grown man's voice. "You touch her again and I'll blow your heart out!" Herbert was pale and his cheek twitched, but he was on Arthur's side; he would do what he could to help Arthur.

Mr. Thompson had no fight left in him. His knees bent as he stood, his chest collapsed. "Why, Arthur," he said, his words crumbling and his breath coming short. "She's fainted again. Get the ammonia." Arthur did not move. Herbert brought the bottle, and handed it, shrinking, to his father.

Mr. Thompson held it under Mrs. Thompson's nose. He poured a little in the palm of his hand and rubbed it on her forehead. She gasped and opened her eyes and turned her head away from him. Herbert began a doleful hopeless sniffling. "Mamma," he kept saying, "Mamma, don't die."

"I'm all right," Mrs. Thompson said. "Now don't you worry around. Now Herbert, you mustn't do that. I'm all right." She closed her eyes. Mr. Thompson began pulling on his best pants; he put on his socks and shoes. The boys sat on each side of the bed, watching Mrs. Thompson's face. Mr. Thompson put on his shirt and coat. He said, "I reckon I'll ride over and get the doctor. Don't look like all this fainting is a good sign. Now you just keep watch until I get back." They listened, but said nothing. He said, "Don't you get any notions in your head. I never did your mother any harm in my life, on purpose." He went out, and, looking back, saw Herbert staring at him from under his brows, like a stranger. "You'll know how to look after her," said Mr. Thompson.

Mr. Thompson went through the kitchen. There he lighted the lantern, took a thin pad of scratch paper and a stub pencil from the shelf where the boys kept their schoolbooks. He swung the lantern on his arm and reached into the cupboard where he kept the guns. The shotgun was there to his hand, primed and ready, a man never knows when he may need a shotgun. He went out of the house without looking around, or looking back when he had left it, passed his barn without seeing it, and struck out to the farthest end of his fields, which ran for half a mile to the east. So many blows had been struck at Mr. Thompson and from so many directions he couldn't stop any more to find out where he was hit. He walked on, over plowed ground and over meadow, going through barbed wire fences cautiously, putting his gun through first; he could almost see in the dark, now his eyes were used to it. Finally he came to the last fence; here he sat down, back against a post, lantern at his side, and, with the pad on his knee, moistened the stub pencil and began to write:

"Before Almighty God, the great judge of all before who I am about to appear, I do hereby solemnly swear that I did not take the life of Mr. Homer T. Hatch on purpose. It was done in defense of Mr. Helton. I did not aim to hit him with the ax but only to keep him off Mr. Helton. He aimed a blow at Mr. Helton who was not looking for it. It was my belief at the time that Mr. Hatch would of taken the life of Mr. Helton if I did not interfere. I have told all this to the judge and the jury and they let me off but nobody believes it. This is the only way I can prove I am not a cold blooded murderer like everybody seems to think. If I had been in Mr. Helton's place he would of done the same for me. I still think I done the only thing there was to do. My wife——"

Mr. Thompson stopped here to think a while. He wet the pencil point with the tip of his tongue and marked out the last two words. He sat a while blacking out the words until he had made a neat oblong patch where they had been, and started again:

"It was Mr. Homer T. Hatch who came to do wrong to a harmless man. He caused all this trouble and he deserved to die but I am sorry it was me who had to kill him."

He licked the point of his pencil again, and signed his full name carefully, folded the paper and put it in his outside pocket. Taking off his right shoe and sock, he set the butt of the shotgun along the ground with the twin barrels pointed towards his head. It was very awkward. He thought about this a little, leaning his head against the gun mouth. He was trembling and his head was drumming until he was deaf and blind, but he lay down flat on the earth on his side, drew the barrel under his chin and fumbled for the trigger with his great toe. That way he could work it.

KIN HUBBARD

COMMENTARY

Hoosiers, who never forget a native, of course know all about Frank McKinney Hubbard (1868–1930), but how many of the rest of us do? From 1901 to his death Kin Hubbard worked on the Indianapolis News and in its columns he created "The Sayings of Abe Martin." Newspapermen who know their business will tell you that technically Kin Hubbard was the greatest of American paragraphers. His paragraphs hardly ever ran above a sentence; some of them ("It's the good loser that finally loses out") are less than ten words long. I call them paragraphs because they are really telescoped anecdotes or arguments. Sometimes they are short stories: "Mr. and Mrs. Lettie Plum, married in June, couldn' git ther car out o' garage last evenin', so they had to go to bed hungry." Sometimes they are a fairly complex statement in which all the sentences between the first phrase and the last are omitted: "Miss Fawn Lippincut says she wouldn' marry th' best man on earth, but we supposed she wuz much younger."

It is concision that is Kin Hubbard's greatest quality. He has others, particularly an odd Yankee humor, compounded of horse sense and an almost poetical originality of observation: "Bees are not as busy as we think they are. They jest can't buzz any slower" or, quite as good, "We're all purty much alike when we git out o' town."

To my mind Kin Hubbard is the best of the cracker-barrel philosophers, better even than Mr. Dooley. His range is extremely narrow, as the samples here given indicate, but within it he is deadly accurate. You will find in his short, abrupt sentences the essence of that Middle West Lewis and Masters were later to convert into more complex satirical forms. He is a Hoosier Rochefoucauld.

The Sayings of Abe Martin

BY

KIN HUBBARD

Miss Fawn Lippincut went t' th' city t'day t' match a gold fish.

Miss Fawn Lippincut says she wouldn' marry th' best man on earth, but we supposed she wuz much younger.

Stew Nugent's mother has received word from th' authorities of an Illinoy city sayin' he is takin' th' winter short course in broom makin'.

Lafe Bud's uncle an' two cousins wuz killed in a auto, yisterday, by a train which refused t' change its course.

Mrs. Tipton Bud's uncle met with a serious auto accident t'day, owin' t' a near-sighted windshield.

Some people are so sensitive that they feel snubbed if an epidemic overlooks 'em.

It's th' good loser that finally loses out.

Miss Tawney Apple is confined t' her home by a swollen dresser drawer.

Mr. and Mrs. Tilford Moots an' niece, Miss Dody Moon, an' Mr. and Mrs. Fern Pash an' son Ratcliffe, attended a fire yisterday.

When a feller says, "It hain't th' money, but th' principle o' th' thing," it's th' money.

Mr. Lemmie Peters, whose graduation essay, "This Is Th' Age o' Opportunity," caused so much favorable comment a year ago, almost took th' agency fer th' Eclipse Fly Swatter yesterday.

It don't make no difference what it is, a woman'll buy anything she thinks a store is losin' money on.

I don't know o' nothin' that's as willin' an' seems to really enjoy its work like a revolvin' storm door.

Mr. an' Mrs. Lettie Plum, married in June, couldn' git ther car out o' garage last evenin', so they had to go to bed hungry.

Bees are not as busy as we think they are. They jest can't buzz any slower.

"I'm through with funerals," said Miss Pearl Purviance when she returned from the cemetery where not a soul mentioned her new hat.

One o' the finest accomplishments is makin' a long story short.

President Hoover hain't goin' to kiss no babies, an' accordin' to the newspaper pictures, those he picks up he holds like a Roman candle.

I kin allus tell a feller who has married a good housekeeper by the way he brightens up when I speak kindly to him.

Lile Tharp wuz held up an' robbed while exercisin' his police dog.

"Paw said if he wuzn' home by ten o'clock we'd know he'd been held up, so we might as well all go to bed," said Mrs. Leghorn Tharp, last night.

We're all purty much alike when we git out o' town.

Ther ought t' be some way t' eat celery so it wouldn' sound like you wuz steppin' on a basket.

Stew Nugent has decided t' go t' work till he kin find somethin' better.

Uncle Ike Weeks, our pop'lar an' accommodatin' saddler, took his first holiday in forty years yisterday an' picked out a cemetery lot.

Now an' then an innocent man is sent t' th' legislature.

Th' world gets better ever' day—then worse agin in th' evenin'.

Two homely people allus seem t' be so genuinely glad t' git t'gether.

The hardest thing is writin' a recommendation fer some one we know.

Lafe Bud found a quarter this mornin' jest as some young lady wuz goin' t' step on it.

Th' trouble with killin' somebuddy or stealin' somethin' is that we've got t' worry thro' a long, tiresome trial before we finally reach th' pardon board.

Oscar Sapp, who wuz buried under his car, t'day, died from th' loss o' blood while th' officers searched fer liquor.

Jake Bentley fell off a load o' hay t'day an' had t' crawl all th' way t' th' golf links t' have his leg set.

Carpenter Joe Moots dropped a hatchet on his toe when th' whistle blew t'day.

Mrs. Tilford Moots' gran'father, who has played golf fer th' past three years, died anyhow t'day.

While cuttin' a magazine in a hammock yisterday Miss Opal Moots severed a artery in her nose. Her mother, who wuz ironin' in th' cellar, escaped uninjured.

Miss Tawney Apple's niece wuz prematurely drowned yisterday while walkin' in a canoe.

Lafe Bud has lost his job at th' meat shop 'cause his thumb was too light.

Ike Lark stopped in th' Strictly Cash Grocery this mornin' t' light his pipe an' found th' proprietor leanin' o'er th' counter dead. Th' coroner says he's prob'ly been dead a week or ten days.

We like little children, 'cause they tear out as soon as they git what they want.

Mrs. Tipton Bud has sold her gold fish as they kept her tied down.

Tell Binkley says th' Tornado Insurance Agents' Union 'll hold an important business session here next month if they kin git an oriental dancer.

Mrs. Artie Small talks some o' movin' t' Niagary Falls, where she wuz so happy when first married.

Miss Eloise Moots has resigned from th' Monarch 5 & 10, and'll give her whole time t' her hair.

Th' little three-year-old son o' Landlord Gabe Craw got caught in th' continuous towel t'day, an' wuz thrown violently against th' ceilin'.

Joe Kite has quit his job at th' saw mill, but th' idea wuz not original with him.

Ez Pash says he allus hates t' break in a clean towel.

It's no disgrace t' be poor, but it might as well be.

Mr. an' Mrs. Tipton Bud, who have been quarantined fer two weeks, have both applied fer a divorce.

Hon. Ex-editur Cale Fluhart wuz a power politically fer years, but he never got prominent enough t' have his speeches garbled.

Some fellers pay a compliment like they expected a receipt.

Miss Fawn Lippincut took th' train at Morgantown fer Bloomin'ton t'day. She's gittin' t' be quite a traveler an' kin now ride without buyin' a orange.

DONALD CULROSS PEATTIE

COMMENTARY

Donald Culross Peattie's An Almanac for Moderns is already a classic, which does not in the least mean that a sufficient number of people have read it. I have selected from among its three hundred and sixty-five meditations a very large group, enough, I hope, to give you the quality of this lovely book.

I should say at once that I am not one of your bird-and-bee lovers. I turn the sour eye of an asphalt slave upon those hearty sons of Mother Nature who organize expeditions to the country, whip out pocket lenses, and challenge you to name the flowers growing along the road. Hence my deep gratitude to Mr. Peattie. He is a wide-visioned and catholic naturalist. He does not make me feel as if I were myself excluded from nature merely because I cannot list seven varieties of fern and have never gone wading in a swamp at five o'clock in the morning.

Though not of their stature, Mr. Peattie has in him the spirit of Thoreau and Huxley. He makes tadpoles and ants exciting, celebrates the charms of springhouses, pays judicious tributes to the great naturalists who have preceded him, comments upon the fact that Edward Lear at twenty was a perfect painter of parrots, ascends to poetry in his comparisons ("the warning cries of herons, like the drop of an old chain on its own coils"), and yet, with all this warmth, never departs from "the scientific frame of mind which does not humanize or sweeten what it must report."

I recommend his book for your spring reading, and, for that matter, for summer, autumn, and winter. An eye that, without losing its sense for the human and the transitory, trains itself on such constants as the nuclei of our cells, the death of stars, and the silent multiplication of bacteria can never record observations that are merely seasonable. It reveals, in this case, the very poetry of biology.

An Almanac for Moderns

(*Selections*)

BY

DONALD CULROSS PEATTIE

MARCH TWENTY-FIRST

ON THIS chill uncertain spring day, toward twilight, I have heard the first frog quaver from the marsh. That is a sound that Pharaoh listened to as it rose from the Nile, and it blended, I suppose, with his discontents and longings, as it does with ours. There is something lonely in that first shaken and uplifted trilling croak. And more than lonely, for I hear a warning in it, as Pharaoh heard the sound of plague. It speaks of the return of life, animal life, to the earth. It tells of all that is most unutterable in evolution—the terrible continuity and fluidity of protoplasm, the irrepressible forces of reproduction—not mystical human love, but the cold batrachian jelly by which we vertebrates are linked to the things that creep and writhe and are blind yet breed and have being. More than half it seems to threaten that when mankind has quite thoroughly shattered and eaten and debauched himself with his own follies, that voice may still be ringing out in the marshes of the Nile and the Thames and the Potomac, unconscious that Pharaoh wept for his son.

It always seems to me that no sooner do I hear the first frog trill than I find the first cloud of frog's eggs in a wayside pool, so swiftly does the emergent creature pour out the libation of its cool fertility. There is life where before there was none. It is as repulsive as it is beautiful, as silvery-black as it is slimy. Life, in short, raw and exciting, life almost in primordial form, irreducible element.

MARCH TWENTY-SECOND

FOR the ancients the world was a little place, bounded between Ind and Thule. The sky bent very low over Olympus, and astronomers had not yet taken the friendliness out of the stars. The shepherd kings of the desert called them by the names Job knew, Al-Debaran, Fomalhaut, Mizar, Al-Goth, Al-Tair, Deneb and Achernar. For the Greeks the glittering constellations made pictures of their heroes and heroines, and of beasts and birds. The heavenly truth of their Arcadian mythology blazed nightly in the skies for the simplest clod to read.

Through all this celestial splendor the sun plowed yearly in a broad track that they called the zodiac. As it entered each constellation a new month with fresh significances and consequences was marked down by a symbol. Lo, in the months when the rains descended, when the Nile and the Tigris and Yangtse rose, the sun entered the constellations that were like fishes, and like a water carrier! In the hot dry months it was in the constellation that is unmistakably a scorpion, bane of the desert. Who could say that the stars in their orderly procession did not sway a man's destiny?

Best of all, the year began with spring, with the vernal equinox. It was a natural, a pastoral, a homely sort of year, which a man could take to his heart and remember; he could tell the date by the feeling in his bones. It is the year which green things, and the beasts and birds in their migrations, all obey, a year like man's life, from his birth cry to the snows upon the philosopher's head.

MARCH TWENTY-THIRD

THE old almanacs have told off their years, and are dead with them. The weather-wisdom and the simple faith that cropped up through them as naturally as grass in an orchard are withered now, and their flowers of homely philosophy and seasonable prediction and reflection are dry, and only faintly, quaintly fragrant. The significance of the Bull and the Crab and the Lion are not more dead, for the modern mind, than the Nature philosophy of a generation ago. This age has seen the trees blasted to skeletons by the great guns, and the birds feeding on men's eyes. Pippa has passed.

It is not that man alone is vile. Man is a part of Nature. So is the atomic disassociation called high explosive. So are violent death, rape, agony, and rotting. They were all here, and quite natural, before our day, in the sweet sky and the blowing fields.

There is no philosophy with a shadow of realism about it, save a philosophy based upon Nature. It turns a smiling face, a surface easily conquered by the gun, the bridge, the dynamite stick. Yet there is no obedience but to its laws. Hammurabi spoke and Rameses commanded, and the rat gnawed and the sun shone and the hive followed its multiplex and golden order. Flowers pushed up their child faces in the spring, and the bacteria slowly took apart the stuff of life. Today the Kremlin commands, the Vatican speaks. And tomorrow the rat will still be fattening, the sun be a little older, and the bacteria remain lords of creation, whose subtraction would topple the rest of life.

Now how can a man base his way of thought on Nature and wear so happy a face? How can he take comfort from withering grass where he lays his head, from a dying sun to which he turns his face, from a mortal woman's head pressed on his shoulder? To say how that might be, well might he talk the year around.

APRIL FIRST

I SAY that it touches a man that his blood is sea water and his tears are salt, that the seed of his loins is scarcely different from the same cells in a seaweed, and that of stuff like his bones are coral made. I say that physical and biologic law lies down with him, and wakes when a child stirs in the womb, and that the sap in a tree, uprushing in the spring, and the smell of the loam, where the bacteria bestir themselves in darkness, and the path of the sun in the heaven, these are facts of first importance to his mental conclusions, and that a man who goes in no consciousness of them is a drifter and a dreamer, without a home or any contact with reality.

APRIL SECOND

EACH year, and above all, each spring, raises up for Nature a new generation of lovers—and this quite irrespective of the age of the new votary. As I write this a boy is going out to the marshes to watch with field glasses the mating of the red-winged blackbirds, rising up in airy swirls and clouds. Or perhaps he carries some manual to the field, and sits him down on an old log, to trace his way through Latin names, that seem at first so barbarous and stiff. There is no explaining why the boy has suddenly forsaken the ball and bat, or finds a kite less interesting in the spring skies than a bird. For a few weeks, or a few seasons, or perhaps for a lifetime, he will follow this bent with passion.

And at the same time there will be a man who all his life has put away this call, or never heard it before, who has come to the easier, latter end of life, when leisure is his own. And he goes out in the woods to collect his first botanical specimen and to learn that he has much to learn for all his years.

They are never to be forgotten—that first bird pursued through thicket and over field with serious intent, not to kill but to know it, or that first plant lifted reverently and excitedly from the earth. No spring returns but that I wish I might live again through the moment when I went out in the woods and sat down with a book in my hands, to learn not only the name, but the ways and the range and the charm of the windflower, *Anemone quinquefolia*.

APRIL SIXTH

THE last fling of winter is over, save for tingling nights and dawns rimed with a silver frost. Everywhere I hear the metallic clinking of the cricket frogs, the trilling of the toads, the gabble of the grackles. Today the first dragonflies have emerged to dart about in an afternoon sunshine that in the leafless thickets seemed as intense as a summer day, and over the swell of the fields, still high with their brown and yellow stands of grass and weeds, the heat waves shimmer. The earth, the soil itself, has a dreaming quality about it. It is warm now to the touch; it has come alive; it hides secrets that in a moment, in a little while, it will tell. Some of them are bursting out already—the first leaves of windflowers uncurling, the spears of mottled adder's tongue leaves and the furled up flags of bloodroot. Old earth is great with her children, the bulb and the grub, and the sleepy mammal and the seed.

APRIL SEVENTH

It was the way of seers of old to read in the flight of birds and the entrails of a ram destiny's intentions. Prophets there are today—economists, social theorists, iconoclasts and makers of new ikons for old—who read the doom of this and predict the rise of that, in the configuration of events as they fly overhead, or in the investigation of the past's cold carcass.

Man's ultimate fate is not written in the works of Spengler or Veblen or Marx, but in the nucleus of his own cells; his end, if it be predestined, is in the death of a star, or in a rising of the bacteria. He will do well to have a heed to the nature of life, for of life there is but one kind. Man shares it with the corn and the crow, the oak and the mayfly. Therefore in such natural things may he well search for auguries.

On any clear-skied day of the year I may be found engrossed in nothing weightier than watching an anthill or gathering inedible fungi, to all appearance strayed from the argument of my philosophy. But in truth it is philosophy that has a weakness toward straying; the facts upon which it is builded rest firm, and impel the philosopher to seek them, even aside, down the bypaths, under the bracken, in the small, anonymous places. Even here, escaped from all but a bright bird eye, all sound of traffic but the brook's over its stones, man is not rid of his crying inner query. And the smiling woodland silence falls knowledgeably upon his ears.

APRIL TWELFTH

THERE came a moment in this chill, palely green afternoon, as all the world was watery with running ponds, and the river boiling high and yellow, when I stood among the uncoiling fronds of the cinnamon ferns and listened to the first piping of the tree frog. I used not to distinguish him from the pond frogs, but my ear at last is attuned to the difference. A pond frog is a coarse and booming creature compared with the eery, contented and yet lonely little tree frog thrilling the light airs with its song.

It is strange how a note that must assuredly bespeak contentment, almost in this case a hymn of domestic felicity, can so trouble the heart of the listener. For the song rises over the creak-crack of the swamp frogs with an unearthly soaring wail, a note of keening that the country folk will say foretells a coming rain. And they are right in this. The tree frog never cries but a soft, oppressive dampness hangs upon the air, and spring thunder speaks in the western sky. Just so, in summer, do the cicadas, early in the morning, foretell a blazing day, and crickets in the autumn grass predict their deaths of frost.

APRIL EIGHTEENTH

THE ancient forms from which today's world evolved have not become impotent with age. From the old stumps new shoots spring up. Primitive as they are, those clouds of diatoms that fill the ponds in the first days of spring are new; these modern algæ are adapted to the cold seas and the frozen ponds of our barely post-glacial era, little hard infrangible atoms carven as it were out of silicon crystals. Those bacteria that prey exclusively upon men and the higher animals cannot be anything but recent developments. Everywhere is flow and flux.

So far from being a steady progress in our exalted direction, evolution for the most is tending quite otherwheres. It may troop joyfully backwards (or it looks backward from our view point) toward simplification, toward a successful laziness. Parasitism, for example, is a highly lucrative mode of life that has probably never been more abundant than in the present.

In short, evolution is not so much progress as it is simply change. It does not leave all its primitive forms behind. It carries them over from age to age, well knowing that they are the precious base of the pyramid on which the more fantastic and costly experiments must be carried.

APRIL NINETEENTH

If progress is an increasing power to master and mold environment, then there is a strong current of progress in evolution. A one-celled flagellate certainly has but the dullest awareness of its environment as it bumps aimlessly about, but the redwinged blackbird hanging its nest on the cattails and the muskrat digging crafty passages into and out of his home—these highly sentient, motile, instinctive and often intelligent creatures are a world and many ages beyond the blind and stupid flagellate. And last, in his majesty comes man, who if he does not like the marsh, will dig ditches and drain it off. In a year he will be turning a furrow there, sowing his domesticated crop, the obedient grain; he will drive out every animal and plant that does not bow down to him.

Man—man has the world in the hollow of his hand. He is a standing refutation of an old superstition like predestination—or a new one like determinism. His chances seem all but boundless, and boundless might be his optimism if he had not already thrown away so many of his opportunities. That very marsh was the home of waterfowl as valuable as they were beautiful. Now they must die, because in this world all breeding grounds are already crammed full. When he slays the birds, he lets loose their prey, and his worst enemy, the insects. He wastes his forests faster than he replaces them, and slaughters the mink and the beaver and the seal. He devours his limited coal supply ever faster; he fouls the rivers, invents poison gases and turns his destruction even on his own kind. And in the end he may present the spec-

tacle of some Brobdingnagian spoiled baby, gulping down his cake
and howling for it too.

APRIL TWENTY-EIGHTH

UNDER Audubon's brush, birds live as they live in the wild—forever
in motion, now teetering on a bough, now flinging themselves upon
the blue sea of air, now diving like the kingfisher or osprey, now snapping up an insect or standing almost on their feathered heads to reach
a pendent cherry. They come right off the page; they fly and swing,
they scream and sing and fight, they eat, court, preen, flutter, hunt lice
under their wings, or hide their little cold heads against the storm.

Nor are they merely bits of emotional impressionism, these bird
paintings; when Audubon was not pressed for time he rendered the
finest details of plumage, bent, it would seem, on not slurring one
barb on one pinion. His drawings thus became actually more valuable
to the scientist, who would not give a farthing for a bird by an impres-
sionist, than even museum specimens. For it was Audubon's way to
paint from creatures which had been dead only an hour or two; he
maintained that the luster of the living plumage flies before sundown.
He invented a unique method, too, of so wiring the little dead body
that it caught again the attributes of life.

And more. He painted the birds in their habitats. In the foregrounds
he would place the vegetation of his subject's haunt, and he seldom
fails to give us the food it eats, be it berry, insect or fish. And like an
Italian master of old, he delights in completing the environmental
study by little landscapes as background, perfect little glimpses of the
wilderness he knew. He gives us the dark cypress swamp, the dreamy
live-oaks hung with Spanish moss, the shining wood-ringed lakes and
the slow vast rivers. No greater technical demands were ever made
upon draughtsmanship than to represent these exquisite landscapes in
the background while keeping the proportion of microscopic attention
to detail in the bird of the foreground.

MAY FIRST

SPRING in any land has its special sweetnesses. Tulips and hyacinths, crocuses and narcissus that are wild flowers of the Mediterranean spring, are more familiar to the city dweller in the New World than the shy, frail spring flowers of his own country side. An English spring with the innocent faces of primroses looking up from their pale leaves, with celandine braving the winds of March, and bluebells in the woods when cuckoos call and nightingales return, is ours by right of poesy.

In this our western world, Thoreau has made New England springs immortal, and a host of lesser writers have followed him; indeed, most of the popular wildflower books emanate from the northeastern states where a rather bleak flora has been better loved, sung, and made decipherable than that of the richer lands to the south.

South of the Potomac spring comes on with balm and sweetness, with a peculiarly Appalachian fragrance, commingled of forests and mountains. It comes without treachery, without taking one step back, like the Sabine women, for every two steps forward. It sweeps up from Florida, past the sea islands of Georgia, through Hall and Habersham, through Charleston where the tea olive sheds its intense sweetness on the air, over the Carolinas, wakening the wild jasmine in the woods, filling the Blue Ridge with azalea and many kinds of trillium and the strange, earth-loving wild ginger, till it opens the bird-foot violet, and the redbud and dogwood of the two Virginias.

MAY TENTH

WAS it worth while for a mayfly to have been born, to have been a worm for weeks and a bride or a bridegroom for one day, only to perish? Such is not a question to which Nature will give the human mind an answer. She thrusts us all into life, and with her hand propels us like children through the rôle she has allotted us. You may weep about it or you may smile; that matters only to yourself. The trees that live five hundred years, or five thousand, see us human may-flies grow and mate and die while they are adding a foot to their girth. Well might they ask themselves if it be not a slavish and ephemeral soft thing to be born a man. *I wonder. LET US CLASP HANDS AND TURN OUR EYES TO THE HEAVENS = I.e. BUNK*

MAY TWELFTH

On this day I am pleased to mark down the most unexpected name upon the green calendar of naturalists. For it is the anniversary of the birth in 1812 of Edward Lear, whose nonsense and limericks are household words. No more puckish spirit ever lived, but few are the nature lovers today who remember that at twenty he had made himself celebrated by his painting of the Psittacidæ, the parrots. Artistic skill combined with extreme fidelity to nature in these paintings drew from Swainson the remark that Audubon could not have done better. The parrots drew the attention of the thirteenth Earl of Derby, who became practically his patron, and it was for the child Edward Stanley, later fifteenth earl, that the *Book of Nonsense* was composed. His non-sense botany, with its inimitable drawings, is one of the unappreciated items on the rare book list. Only a botanist with a sense of humor would understand how funny it is. And these are even rarer than the copies of that slim volume.

MAY FOURTEENTH

I love a brook far better than a river. If ever I buy a country tract it is going to have a brook on it. Indeed, I'm not sure that it will not be mostly brook—two long strips of land on each side of the watercourse. After all, Egypt was just such a shape. Or I shall buy two brooks where they run together—a Mesopotamia—and between them pitch the invisible Babylon of my heart. No house; no garden; not even a path. It shall be nothing but my domain, where I can, alone, explore the little wild strands, and mine my country for its smooth quartz stone and its fool's gold in the sands, and learn to know my subjects, the red triton, the wood frog, the water wren, and the caddis flies, water striders and Dytiscus beetles.

MAY EIGHTEENTH

THE number, variety and intricacy of the adaptation of bees to orchids is simply dazzling. There are bees with tongues which, when unrolled, are twice as long as the length of the whole animal; tropical bees exist that could tap a nectary if it were buried nearly a foot deep in the most complicated orchid. There are bees with special pouches for carrying pollen in their legs, and others with pollen-brushes on their feet, on their heads, on their abdomens, depending whether they seem intended by Nature for deep flowers, irregular two-lipped flowers, one-lipped flowers, composite flowers, or simple open flowers. The bees have invented more types of brushes with special uses than the eminent Mr. Fuller.

There are orchids that can only be fertilized by one particular type of bee, like the fit of a Yale lock to its particular key, and possibly there are bees that could satisfy their ethereal lust for nectar at only one orchid, I cannot say. But nothing would surprise me after reading Darwin and Müller and Kerner. Tropical bats also enter into nicely adjusted symbioses with white, night-blooming orchids that reserve their perfume until twilight falls.

The specializations in what must be regarded as the age of orchids are possibly reaching a stage so extreme that they will defeat their own ends. A very slight change in the climate or insect fauna—no more difference than would easily exterminate over-specialized man—might suffice to dethrone the orchid family, with its ten thousand species, from its leadership, just as the dinosaurs grew too great for the world and evolved to self-destruction.

MAY TWENTIETH

THE first night life of the year has begun for my brother animals. A few fireflies are to be seen, and the night moth, *Amphion nessus*, is abroad. And, as I strolled in this day's twilight, a night hawk swooped around my head as silently, and with as much boldness, as one of the bats which are now on the wing. His cousin the whippoorwill has already lifted his voice, just a few mysterious cries out of the depth of the wood.

In early spring, the dark hours are barren of life; each night is a little death, a return to winter. Now that the warm weather is assured, the woods and fields and even my garden are quite alive with nocturnal venturers. Small animal shapes move freely in the safety of the shadows. Sometimes I hear their faint footfalls on the leaves, sometimes I hear nothing, only know instinctively that some creature has passed by me, intent upon his private business in the kindly enveloping dark. Now against the screens the big May beetles bang, setting up an angry roaring with their harsh wings, and through the opened window breathes the perfume of night-flowering honeysuckle, the first of the year.

MAY TWENTY-THIRD

On this day in 1707, in southern Sweden, was born the man we know as Linnæus, Carolus Linnæus or Karl von Linné. His father had literally enjoyed no surname; he was Nils, the son of Bengt, for in old Sweden there were only patronymics. But he took a name unto himself from *Lin,* the linden. For two hundred years, in a corner of Jonsboda Parish, there had stood a mighty linden, sacred in family tradition, and from this totem Nils made himself a learned-sounding Latin name.

At Upsala, Linnæus passed the first year in dire want, putting paper in the soles of his worn shoes. The old botanical gardens, started by Rudbeck, had been allowed to fall into ruins, and the science of botany itself was then like a sleeping, dusty, dead-seeming garden in March, half full of lifeless brushwood—but for the rest secretly quick and budded and only awaiting a warming breath.

The only friend of Linnæus at this time was Artedi, who would have become the Linnæus of zoölogy but for falling into a canal and drowning. This lad was so poor that Linnæus and he loaned each other money, as only the destitute could do. These boys exchanged the usual wild ideas of young students—in this case nothing less than the principles of classification that ultimately brought order into the hopelessly muddled work of the herbalists struggling to find the plants of northern Europe in their Pliny and Theophrastus.

So like two winter birds, living on weed seeds, and sleeping in the lee of a tree trunk, the ragged hungry lads lived on till spring, when Dean Celsius, himself a naturalist, came to their aid with money, food, shelter, appointments, and gave them grace to think, without danger of turning into fasting visionaries.

MAY TWENTY-FOURTH

IN MAY, 1732 there rode out of the gates of gray old Upsala a thin young man in a light coat of West Gothland linsey without folds, lined with red shalloon, having small cuffs and a collar of shag; he wore leather breeches, and a round wig topped by a green leather cap, his feet in a pair of half-boots. On his saddle he carried a small leather bag containing two pairs of false sleeves, two half-shirts and one whole one, an inkstand, pencase, microscope, a gauze cap to protect him from gnats, a comb, drying papers for plants, and a few books. A fowling-piece hung at his side, and a graduated stick for measuring. In his pocket was a passport for Lapland from the governor of Upsala.

Linnæus was going into the field. In a sense that journey was the first of its kind ever made. It was the morning, the springtide of science, after the dark winter of the book-ridden Middle Ages, when men wrangled over Aristotle and quoted Pliny's authority. Linnæus was the first naturalist to whom it occurred to take a great trip to Nature itself. No wonder that as he rode north, the very larks burst into song.

"*Ecce suum* tirile, tirile, *suum* tirile *tractat!*" they sang, or so he records it with his quaint blend of Latin and fantasy. "The sky was clear and warm, while the west wind refreshed one with delicious

breath," he wrote. "The winter rye stood six inches high, and the barley was newly come into leaf. The birch was beginning to shoot and
all the trees leafing except the elm and aspen. Though only a few
spring flowers were in bloom it was obvious that the whole land was
smiling with the coming of spring."

MAY TWENTY-FIFTH

WHEN Linnæus published his great Lapland report, it was swiftly
translated into the languages of Europe. A door had been burst open,
and all men beheld that, outside, the fields were burning with flowers,
the sky ringing with bird song. Very disturbing, all that, to the
medieval-minded schoolmen, the obscurantists who would have kept
their science to themselves, like alchemists.

Dillenius of Oxford, looking out of his window at the young Swede
walking about in the botanical garden, cried: "There goes a man who
is bringing all botany into confusion!" He locked up the herbarium,
would not give Linnæus the books he wanted. But in the end, Linnæus, patient and tactful, persuaded him to look at his great system
of classification. Converted, the delighted Dillenius begged him to stay
forever and share his salary with him. Philip Miller, last of the herbalists, went over enthusiastically to him. The rich Clifford became his
patron. Gronovius published him at his own expense.

To understand Linnæus's "Sexual System" as he called it, we have
to cast an eye at the medieval confusion of the past, when a plant not
found in Theophrastus's two-thousand-year-old description of the
Greek flora might be thrown away as heretical. Classification was so
superficial that all prickly plants, for instance, were lumped together—
cacti and roses and thistles and even some poppies. What Linnæus did
was to classify by the number of stamens and pistils, every plant as a
species and assign it to a genus or clan of related species, and give it
two descriptive names in the universal language of Latin. Today all
this is a commonplace, the sure footing on which we rest—thanks to
the boy who would not become a tailor's apprentice.

MAY TWENTY-SIXTH

When once the new system of Linnæus had swept aside resistance, all Europe was ready to acknowledge him. The King of Spain offered him a princely salary and complete liberty. Clifford wanted never to part with him, and Boerhaave, the rich Dutch scholar, offered him travel in Africa and America.

But Linnæus was a young man, and a human one, and at heart a bit of a peasant. Sara Morœa was waiting for him, and like a bird that does its mating in the north, he flew back to his Sara and made her his wife. For a man of the world it was a great mistake, for the thrifty, cleanly, strapping Sara was no great lady. She thrashed her daughters, spoiled her son, urged her husband toward a lucrative practice as a physician at the cost of science, and told magnificent Gustavus Third to treat his servants better.

And there are other errors of Linnæus's judgment. To his weak boy he willed his collections and high position at Upsala, so that the vain young man attained to honors he had not earned and responsibilities he was not fitted for.

It must be admitted, too, that Linnæus's work was hasty; he was never quite a success as a zoölogist, and, owing partly to the state of knowledge at that time, he did not quite know what he was doing amongst the lower plants, the fungi, algæ, and ferns. His attempt to classify genera and species of metals is entirely untenable, and he was not the equal of Jussieu in grouping genera into natural families. But without his haste, without his lusty courage to undertake an outline of everything—hang the details!—science would have been delayed for decades. Even the faults of his character were human, natural and lovable.

MAY TWENTY-SEVENTH

At this season it used to be the custom, and I hope it still may be, for botanists everywhere to do honor to Linnæus by meeting together for a light-hearted trip afield in search of plants, in the good old style. Formidable has grown that once gentle science of botany—a thing of laboratories and test tubes, of the complex mathematics of the geneticist. For such is the way of a science. It begins in medieval wonder and magic; then a door opens to the fields, it goes forth to its Lapland, to delight and describe and classify. Next come the lens, the laboratory, the investigation of structure, the experiment with function, and at last the mechanical control of the life processes themselves. Sometimes the youngsters of today look back upon the descriptive era as dry, dilettante, unworthy of the name of science.

But more seasoned men, conscious of the history of their science, still hold the name of Linnæus in reverence. They remember that he did not foist Latin binomials on plants and animals, but pared the latinity down from some twenty words to two! To them the time of Linnæus is an age of innocence and the true beginnings of modernism. Who would not, if he could, go back today and join Linnæus and his pupils—so many of whom were to die for him at the ends of the earth —and march afield today to push the moss apart and find the little twin-flowers that he loved above all others, *Linnæa borealis?* Who would not be glad to come back with them, to the fluttering of banners and the piping of hautboys, and unslinging his heavy case of plants, stand with Thunberg and Peter Kalm and Fabricius and give the rousing *"Vivat Scientia! Vivat Linnæus!"*

JUNE FIRST

Now this is the best of life, that a man should have children who promise fair, and a loving wife, and that he should know what his work is, and own a sense of Nature. This sense is nothing less than a feeling for reality. I do not mean the reality intended by cantankerous and disagreeable people, who are so fond of calling upon *others* to face the unpleasant. They enjoy referring to the sores and cuts of life, to the power of evil, to their own disappointments and failures and the abysmal depths to which human nature can sink. But all these things—war and money and cruelty—are passing illu-

sions. These are the unquenchable realities—the power of the expanding seed to break a stone, the strength that sustains men to die for
others, the shortness of life that makes it so precious, all futurity hun-
gering in us, that makes woman taste so sweet.

JUNE SECOND

A man need not know how to name all the oaks or the moths, or be
able to recognize a synclinal fault, or tell time by the stars, in order to
possess Nature. He may have his mind solely on growing larkspurs, or
he may love a boat and a sail and a blue-eyed day at sea. He may have
a bent for making paths or banding birds, or he may be only an invet-
erate and curious walker.

But I contend that such a fellow has the best out of life—he and the
naturalists. You are ignorant of life if you do not love it or some portion of it, just as it is, a shaft of light from a nearby star, a flash of the
blue salt water that curls around the five upthrust rocks of the continents, a net of green leaves spread to catch the light and use it, and
you, walking under the trees. You, a handful of supple earth and long
white stones, with seawater running in your veins.

JUNE SIXTH

They came very secretly, in the night, perhaps; or it may have been
that for several days they had been assembling, emerging like bad,
buried deeds, out of the earth. I realize now that for several days I
had been seeing strange, transparent shards of insects upon the pavement, and on the steps down through the grass. But only today when
the children came in, bright-eyed with excitement, and interrupting
each other with a tale of enormous bugs everywhere, did I suspect of
what they spoke.

I found that the cicadas were thick even upon the steps of the porch,
huge, greenish and ruddy-brown heavy-bodied things with beautiful
great wings, two very long forewings and a shorter hind pair, through

which I could see the grass beneath as plainly as through a thin sheet
of mica. I only needed to reach down and pick one up to capture him;
he was so sluggish that he seemed like some sleeper awakened, dazed,
after having been lost to the world for many years.

Even then, so sluggish was I myself, I did not instantly understand
what an exciting discovery I had hit upon. The creature looked familiar, and yet I knew I had never seen him before. I thought of the
common dog-day locust with his loud crackling sizzling song, but it
was weeks before he would be due. No sound came from the creature
in my hand, and I went to explore the grounds for more.

I bagged a dozen, and went into the city with them. Delightful old
Dr. Howard was at his desk when I burst in. He opened the box and
one of my captives crawled out upon his hand. "Why, man," he cried,
"it's the seventeen-year cicada!" He seemed surprisingly pleased. "An
old entomologist can never tell," he explained, "whether he will live
to hear them again."

JUNE SEVENTEENTH

THE moon rose tonight at the full, and from its half of all the skies it
scatters away the stars; only the stabbing shafts of blue Vega pierce
through the fields of lunar radiance. The fainter stars are all put out
and heaven for once looks like the pictures in the star maps, with the
constellations bared to the bone. It would be a moment for learning
them as they are supposed to (and do not) look. But one peek at the
moon, even through the cheapest of lenses, is worth twenty Lions and
Virgins and Scorpions. That tombstone world! Those snowless alps
and frozen lava seas! The sense of its actual bulk, its spherical pon-
derability, when I first saw them through a telescope, were revolutionary to my feeling for all objects in heaven, and though I could not
see it move, I felt the swing of it in my bones, as of a great cold ball
hurled round upon an invisible leash by the earth's giant arm.

Not long ago the light from the moon was focused in a lens of a
special telescope at Staradale University in Czechoslovakia and transferred to a photo-electric cell. Translated into sound, these waves were

broadcast to London, and by report the noise was as the tolling of great bells deprived of resonance! Perfect symbol for a world that is dead. When Vega was heard, it was as the high pitched shouting of an angry crowd, but very far away; Vega, one hundred times the size of our sun, Vega, that incandescent blue giant, only twenty-six light years away, spoke to us with the voice of mass menace.

So after all there is music in the spheres, and though it is true that only light translated into sound may be heard, the sounds given out by an explosion or a nightingale are also but energy converted into waves that reach us through the ear.

JUNE TWENTY-FIRST

ON THIS day, on which I have such good reason to be grateful to my mother, I may perhaps be permitted to put down the profession of one naturalist's faith. Whatever rudiments of religion are innate in me are what ordinarily pass as pantheism, though I am not really prepared to worship everything. I could take oaks as seriously as a druid, but I draw the line at any Hindu idolatry of animals, so that I am not exactly an animist. On this, the summer solstice, I would enjoy lighting bonfires to the sun; I have ever loved the morning best. I could easily find it in me to worship some madonna or any symbol of woman and child, but I do not like symbols as well as I like the thing itself.

A man's real religion is that about which he becomes excited, the object or the cause he will defend, the point at which, spontaneously, he cries out in joy over a victory, or groans aloud from an injury. In France I once startled my wife by bursting into the house with a loud cry of joy. She hastened downstairs to learn what good fortune had befallen us in our old farmhouse above the Lake of Annecy. It was only that fresh snow had fallen on the Alps and sheeted their heads in pure glittering hoods. They looked to me like gods, standing just behind our house. If they were not gods to her, that is because her religion is several degrees less icy and remote. That morning happened to be memorable in the history of science because it was the day on which the discovery of a new planet was announced. This too wrung a cheer from me, and to the joy of my little son and with the tender indulgence of my wife, I declared a holiday, with a trip by steamer around the turquoise lake.

JUNE TWENTY-SIXTH

As LONG as one knows little of Nature save that which impinges upon one sensually, one is subject to the moods it throws, like a shadow, across the spirit. But as soon as one begins to search for knowledge in the thing that dims the light, the power of mood fades. A biologist confined to the prison isle of Ste. Marguerite would soon set up some equipment or technique for studying the swallows—the pulsation of their crowding population, the control of their behavior, their effect upon the rest of the animal life of the island, or something else from which significant conclusions could be drawn.

I accept the challenge of the artists that cool investigation may often be the death of poetry. As knowledge lessens the terror of plague, so it may take some of the soulfulness out of Nature. There is a sort of Wordsworthian sermonizing that shrinks before the biological frame of mind, just as the childish abhorrence of insects vanishes with familiarity. But not all poetry is really good poetry (however good it may sound). Good poetry is swift-winged, essential and truthful description—and so is good science.

JULY FIRST

THE bobolink is the only bird who never seems to know how to put a period to his musical sentence. All other Aves have a note, three notes, even a phrase that they utter; no matter how many times they may reiterate it, that is all they have to say. But I hear the bobolinks now in the orchard grass, spilling out a torrent of song. When we listen expecting soon to hear silence, he still has more to tell, and with an irrepressible invention he continues as if joy had no end in the telling, until perforce a smile spreads over our furrows and frowns, and we say, "Well, well, *well*, little fellow, is the world really as fine as all that?"

JULY SECOND

ON THIS day in Geneva was born François Huber, in 1750, whose father distinguished himself not only as a soldier and a member of the great coterie at Ferney, but as an authority on the flight of birds. François was only fifteen years old when he began to lose his sight, the most crushing blow which could befall one who had decided to devote himself to the study of ants. Total blindness finally fell upon him, but desperate handicaps are often the spur to triumph. With the aid of his wife, Marie Aimée Lullin, and his faithful servant François Burnens, who were his eyes for him, he continued his investigations, and laid down the very foundation stone of our scientific knowledge both of ants and honey bees. True, Réaumur had preceded him, but as it happened, Réaumur's work on ants was not published until modern times; it lay in a drawer, forgotten, so that it is from Huber that the great line of ant students stems—his son Pierre Huber, Auguste Forel, C. Emery, Sir John Lubbock, and William Morton Wheeler.

None of us could say that he would have liked to share the fate of François Huber, but there are few of us who would not have been proud to ride into immortality as did his servant or his faithful mate, to be remembered among those who, like the Cyrenian on the first Good Friday, served a great man in his hour of darkness.

JULY THIRD

IT WAS Huber, on a memorable summer day in 1804, who first discovered that some species of ants make slaves of others. But he made only a beginning in this study, and oddly enough it was another Swiss who was destined to carry the subject on. Auguste Forel was only seven years old when he observed one day that an army of big red ants with black bellies was fighting with a colony of black ants with which the child had long felt on terms of special friendliness. The boy tried to come to the aid of his friends, but the enemy were too many for him. The invaders were carrying off the little white eggs of the ants he liked. His mother took him off for a walk, so that when he returned he found, to his grief, all his black friends were dead.

The following year he was able to observe something still more astonishing. In the nest of the red-and-black ants he discovered many of his old black friends, living in a state of peaceful industry. He began to understand that the black ants were slaves, born in captivity.

When he was ten years old he was given a copy of Huber, and was enchanted to find his theory confirmed. But discovering that he already knew several things that were not found in Huber, he determined from that moment to become the historian of the ants, and, as I pen these words, he is still alive, Nestor of formicologists.

JULY SIXTH

On this day, in 1766, at Paisley, in Scotland, was born Alexander Wilson, the first great ornithologist of America, the rival of Audubon, scientist where Audubon was artist, luckless in love where Audubon was happy, retiring as an owl where Audubon was gay as a mockingbird, short-lived where Audubon lived long and reaped honors.

Wilson was bound out as a child to weavers, because as a herdboy he was too intent upon watching the birds. In the long years of slavery, humped like a crane over his loom, the iron entered into his soul. Wilson was ever a bitter man, where the world was concerned, but tender to the very few who were ever tender with him. Fleeing the loom room, he became a peddler, who sold stuffs and ribbons and laces for ladies, with ballads of his own composing. In Scottish vernacular, his ballads are often sincere, honest, fresh and genuine. But when he was forced to return to weaving, his libellous lampoons against the master weavers brought him a short prison term, and the humiliation of having to burn his shafts in public.

This was the turn of events which brought him to America, and tramping from Newcastle to Philadelphia he shot and examined his first American bird, a red-headed woodpecker, the most beautiful bird, as he said, that he had ever seen. Weaver, journeyman printer, and schoolmaster, he eked out his first American years amongst Pennsylvania Germans, rutabagas, hymn-howling Presbyterians, as he called them, and general penury.

His first encouragement came from William Bartram, with whose sister he fell vainly in love; Dr. Benjamin Barton, Bachman, Bonaparte, and George Ord, who made up the Athens of science for which Philadelphia then passed, aided him, and bit by bit, from this narrow, bitter breast where a poet had stifled, a great scientist was born.

JULY SEVENTH

It was to an America still partly wilderness, fresh with adventure, that the weary and driven little Scotsman came. You could expect in our woods then an ivory-billed woodpecker, the largest of all its tribe, a creature known to me only as a perfectly incredible specimen in museums. It has a glossy black body almost two feet long, a head crested with scarlet, and a great bill, ivory white. Once widespread in America, it is now all but extinct.

Not so in Wilson's time. He easily captured a specimen in the cypress swamps near Wilmington, North Carolina, and was conveying it, imprisoned under a blanket, in a large basket, to an inn, when it suddenly burst into the most ear-splitting and dismal sounds, like the voice of a baby in agony. Several women on the porch of the inn cast dark looks on the poor little man, as though he had been a kidnaper or an ogre. Marching proudly by them, Wilson conveyed the bird to his room to paint it. But it abruptly left off sitting for its portrait, and violently attacked Wilson about the face with the bill that is made to split oak. Fleeing the room, Wilson after an hour returned to hear the sound as of twenty wood choppers at work. He threw open the door, and discovered that his tropical carpenter had battered his way through the inner wall, and at that moment was engaged in enlarging an opening in the clapboards outside wide enough to admit his scarlet-crested head. Restrained in this, the proud spirited fowl moped and died, leaving Wilson his ivory bill and the innkeeper's bill for repairs.

JULY EIGHTH

WILSON proposed to become the biographer of all the birds of America. Governor Tompkins of New York told him that so far from paying $120 for a book about birds he would not give a hundred for all the birds in the country, if he had 'em alive! In Charleston Wilson wandered the streets looking for houses that would suggest that their owners might be persons of enough wealth and cultivation to subscribe to his book.

Up to his time nothing appreciable on American birds existed in writing, except some lists drawn up by Jefferson, Barton and Bartram, and some descriptions by Mark Catesby. When Wilson's volume containing the biographies of the hummingbird, catbird, mockingbird and kingbird appeared, he was—startling as it now seems—telling the world of science the first it had heard of them. If Wilson was no artist, if he lacked Audubon's power of dramatizing and englamoring each encounter with a new species, the little schoolmaster ("who didn't whip enough," as the parents complained) was at least a peerless observer, cautious, exact, conscientious, methodical—virtues, every one of them, which Audubon exhibited only exceptionally. Nature had not endowed him with the brush of an Audubon, yet he made a draughtsman of himself by dint of perseverance.

Whenever I hear the sweet, swinging *vree-hu, vree-heee* of the veery, called Wilson's thrush, I think of the lonely little weaver, the first bird lover to penetrate the desolate swamps, with only a little parrot on his shoulder for company.

JULY TWENTY-SECOND

THE summer world is the insect world. Like it or not, that is how it is. There are few insects that ever find the day too hot. The more relentlessly the sun beats down around my house, the faster whir the wings of the hovering wasp. Dragon flies are roused to a frenzy by the heat, dashing over the hot brown surface of the ponds with a metallic clicking of their wings that makes them seem like machines. The wasps grow ever more irritable with the heat, their bodies palpitating with alert life.

Just as many chemicals are inert at low temperatures, but rush together with explosive violence in a furnace, so the insects on a November day are easily captured, and seem bereft of their wits. In bleak weather I would pick up a wasp with only a slight wincing of my nerves. Now, when they come near me, limp with heat though I feel, I am galvanized with that tingling sensation of prickly fear such as stinging things inspire.

Of all the rivals of mankind for dominance on this earth no other creatures large enough to be seen with the naked eye have held out successfully save the insects. When we clear the forest, we rid ourselves of the forest insects, only to make way for the field insects. Man sows his crops—and what comes up? A host of long-faced, armorplated locusts who eat him out of house and home. We strike at them, but it is like striking at the sea. Whatever way we turn we find the insects there before us, in water, in air, on the earth and under it.

AUGUST THIRD

THOSE there are who are annoyed or repelled (or they affect to be), by what they call lush or extravagant beauty. They will enjoy nothing but the bleakest of New England scenery—a few hard-bitten pastures, a rocky wall, a moth-eaten hill that is neither a bold mountain nor a stirring plain, and a stern and paintless old house.

Of this company I do not make one. If it is shallow not to be able to see beauty in the austere, it is monkish, parsimonious and timid to despise the lavish and complex beauty of life reaching its full expression. I liked what little I ever saw of the tropics, and the fact that I was born in a region where Nature was economical of her colors and form begets in me no sentimental feelings about such scenes.

I love the southern landscape, and I love it in summer only a little less than in spring. The South, in winter, is mild enough, but it is little more; it is simply not itself. You probably do not know Labrador until you have lived a winter in it, and to taste the undiluted wine of a hot country, you should see it through a summer. I live in that intemperate zone that is icy in winter and flaming in summer; it blends the tastes of north and south.

And in summer the tropical element in it comes out. Now the heat shimmers above the marshes; it dances over the hills in a haze, engulfs the cool old houses as if they were islands on the landscape. Everywhere the deep blue green of heavy foliage is in full summer splendor; on all the pools the jade green sargassos of the duckweed stretch away across the stagnant water; in the breathless nights the whippoorwill complains, it has been said, that "It is so still, so still, so still!"

AUGUST FOURTH

Upon this day in 1849 was born William Henry Hudson. We loved him for something, either in his style or his viewpoint, that can only emerge from the soul of a loafer. Hudson was a loafer, it would seem, only partly from choice. Ill health and poverty in London are desperate shackles for a naturalist, and his marriage was unhappy. His wife long kept a boarding house in that city, and she need have been no termagant to find that a husband to whom sparrows and starlings were important, a husband who disappeared, to tramp the roads like a hobo, living on blackberries, was an exasperating mate.

The English readers love Hudson because he saw the poetry in the subtle charm of the English countryside, because he made even more intimate for them the already intimately known beauty of the downs and lanes. In London itself, in Richmond Park, on the housetops and in the gray streets, he looked where seven millions looked, and saw for them what they did not see.

But it is Hudson remembering his lost Argentine that I love to read. There is nothing like nostalgia for producing memorable writing; the poet must go unsatisfied. And Hudson, smoking in the back parlor of the London boarding house, and writing of the birds of La Plata, or the great thistle years upon the pampas, and all that he remembered of the purple lands and green mansions, becomes for me the Homer of nature lovers.

AUGUST ELEVENTH

TONIGHT the Perseids will be visible in all their glory—that swarm of meteors whose orbit we encounter tonight and through which we continue to move tomorrow night. Sixty-nine falling stars an hour is the average number that one can see, by keeping a sharp lookout at their central radiating point, the constellation of Perseus. This constellation does not rise until eleven, and is really not well placed for observation for another hour, but as nothing in Nature seems on this breathless night to have any intention of going to sleep before the witching hour, I shall stay up to watch.

A meteor is a meteor when it burns itself up in the sky; when it falls to earth, unconsumed by the heat of friction with our atmosphere, it is a meteorite. Of all the astronomical events, the fall of a meteorite is the most unnerving and yet the most reassuring. Reassuring because it proves to us that the depths of space are inhabited by bodies made of the same elements we have here on earth, that, at rock bottom, a man and a star are built of the same stuff. Alarming, in the thought that, were a meteor as large as some that have fallen in Arizona and Siberia, to crash upon New York or London, a million humans would instantly meet death.

AUGUST TWELFTH

THE best of summer star-gazing is that it is warm enough to fling yourself upon your back and gaze up at the stars without craning the neck. In a short time the sense of intimacy with the stars is established, as it never can be when a man stands erect. You may even lose the sense of gazing up, and enjoy the exciting sensation of gazing *down* into deep wells of space. Indeed, this is quite as correct as to say that we gaze upward at the stars. In reality there is no up and down in the universe. You are, in point of fact, a creature perpetually hung over the yawning abyss of Everywhere, suspended over it by our tiny terrestrial gravity which clamps you to the side of mother earth while you gaze down on Vega and Deneb and Arcturus and Altair whirling below you.

One can never look long in the August sky without beholding a shooting star, for the trail of the Perseids is spun fine at each end; only last night and tonight we pass through the thick node of them. If we ask ourselves what is a meteor—fragment of the lost planet between Mars and Jupiter, messenger from the farthest stars, or bit of a vanished comet—there seems no certain answer. The Perseids are thought to be traveling in the same orbit as that of Tuttle's comet of 1862, and to be a part of it. But what, after all, is a comet? Nothing more ghostly exists in time or space; it rushes at us out of a black hole of space, trails a fire that does not burn, a light that is no light, and looping close to the sun, vanishes again into space—to return at the appointed time when the sea of darkness again gives up its dead; or, more terrible still, never to return from its Avernus.

AUGUST NINETEENTH

THERE was once a poor young man in whose breast a scientist was stifling. He lived in the heart of a great city, far from tree and bird, unless it were a few desolate planes and some quarrelsome roof sparrows. This young man had not even a window to look upon the street, but, in his garret room, only a skylight. Without an overcoat, he was often in bad weather kept in his room for days together, with nothing to do but lie on his back and look out at the sky. As he gazed, the clouds in ever changing form drifted by; at first they seemed shapeless and fluid beyond all hope of grouping them into any types, but little by little he came to recognize the sorts you read about in books—the black threatening sheets of the nimbus clouds that bring snow, the cumulus, dream-castle clouds of a fine summer's afternoon, the high, immovable cirrus clouds, like feathers afloat in topmost heaven that promise fair weather.

As we can well believe, having nothing else to look at he soon had observed all the kinds of clouds you and I have ever noticed. And then, one day, he discovered a new kind, the mammato-cirrus, a formation so rare that it had never been observed before that time. Cut off from every other line of scientific investigation, this genius still found something new that a million other people in Paris could have seen that day if they had had the eyes of Jean-Baptiste-Pierre-Antoine de Monet de Lamarck.

AUGUST TWENTY-FIRST

Nor blood nor flesh nor hair nor feathers, not the chlorophyll or cellulose of the plants, is stranger than the stuff called chitin. Chitin is not only the hard shell of the dapper little beetles in their tail-coats; it is the glistening wing of the dragon fly, and his thousand faceted eye, the exquisite feathered antennæ of the moth by which it perceives the odor of its mate across miles of summer darkness, the feet of the laboring ant, the heavy armor of the lobster, the gossamer of the spider, the thread of the silkworm. There is very little about an insect, or for that matter any of its allies in the sea or upon the land, which is not chitinous. One moment the stuff is finer than the tresses of woman, and the next ponderous and stiff as the armor of a knight, and all without change in its chemical composition. As a bloom upon the wing of a luna moth fluttering across the moon, it is evanescent as snowflakes; encased in drops of amber where a Mesozoic beetle died, it has seen the ages pass without a change.

AUGUST TWENTY-SECOND

Something there is about a heron of wildwood nobility. That humped and stilted grace-and-awkwardness, that grand and pensive sorrowfulness that goes with marshes, that touches all marsh creatures, frogs and dragon flies and wild ducks, with the finger of tragedy laid on the tameless, the short of life. That leisurely taking off; that rushing sound in the pinions, that haughty, harsh, and yet haunting cry! Nobility that tempts the fowler's gun, not because the heron is fit to eat, but because he presents an easy mark against the sunset extinguishing its fire in the wild marsh water.

But come nearer to the herons, if only by the binoculars, and even a snowy egret reveals the unsavory ways of the stork family. That endless gormandizing after mud worms, that retching and regurgitating and liming; these things are disillusion itself, and when you actually attain their nests, in one of those heronries where there may be hundreds of families, all that can be inhuman and repugnant in a bird assails you. I would not tell myself the truth if I did not admit that birds can suddenly weary and repel me, just as ants and reptiles or mammals may. The animal lover (self-avowed) will reproach me in this. He *never*, he says, does anything but *love* birds at all times. I say he is a hypocrite; I say, too, that there are attitudes, emotions even, toward Nature, more real and vital and valuable than love.

There is a great deal more stingo, more savor and bite in Nature if you do not try to love everything you touch, smell, hear, see or step on. The disgust which a near encounter with a heronry awakens in me is part of heronness, an ingredient in the whole that, with trailing leg and probing bill, makes up the virtue and staying power of the idea of *Heron* in my mneme.

AUGUST THIRTY-FIRST

AUGUST, the aureate month, draws to its blazing close—a month of sun, if ever there was one. Gold in the grain on the round-backed hill fields. Gold in the wood sunflowers, and in the summer goldenrod waving plumes all through the woodlot, trooping down the meadow to the brookside, marching in the dust of the roadways. Gold in the wing of the wild canaries, dipping and twittering as they flit from weed to bush, as if invisible waves of air tossed them up and down. The orange and yellow clover butterflies seek out the thistle, and the

giant sulphur swallowtails are in their final brood. The amber, chaff-
filled dust gilds all the splendid sunsets in cloudless, burning skies.
Long, long after the sun has set, the sun-drenched earth gives back its
heat, radiates it to the dim stars; the moon gets up in gold; before it
lifts behind the black fields to the east I take it for a rick fire, till it
rises like an old gold coin, that thieves have clipped on one worn edge.

SEPTEMBER FIFTEENTH

AUTUMN at first is no more than a freshening of morning and evening,
a certain sweet and winy odor in the air that blows upon the cheek
as one steps out of doors in the morning, or opens the window at
night to lean out a moment and look at the stars, before turning at
last to sleep.

Autumn is the blooming of the goldenrod all through the oak woods
and across the fields. Autumn is the cricket's cry, the swarming of the
monarch and the storms of the Lisa butterfly. It is the odor of leaf
fires, the smell of crushed marigold leaves, of tansy leaves and the sharp
terebinthine scent of walnut husks that look so apple green and leave
so brown a stain.

Autumn is the end of vacation, the beginning of school, the gathering of grackles, the dropping of ripe plums, the swarming of yellow
hornets in the pear orchards. It is the ripening of the wild rice, the
meeting together of bobolink hordes, the first hint of scarlet in the
sumac leaf and the dewberry cane. It is the end of one more year's
experiment. Now Nature dismantles her instruments and lays them
away.

SEPTEMBER TWENTY-FOURTH

I TRY each year to disbelieve what my senses tell me, and to look at
the harvest moon in a cold and astronomical light. I know that it is
a small cold sphere of rock, airless, jagged and without activity. But
the harvest moon is not an astronomical fact. It is a knowing thing,
lifting its ruddy face above the rim of the world. Even to the thor-

oughly civilized mind, where caution for the future is supposed to rule all impulse, the orange moon of autumn invites the senses to some saturnalia, yet no festival of merriment. The harvest moon has no innocence, like the slim quarter moon of a spring twilight, nor has it the silver penny brilliance of the moon that looks down upon the resorts of summertime. Wise, ripe, and portly, like an old Bacchus, it waxes night after night.

SEPTEMBER TWENTY-FIFTH

Now is that opulent moment in the year, the harvest, a time of cream in old crocks in cool, newt-haunted spring-houses, of pears at the hour of perfection on old trees bent like women that, as the Bible says, bow down with child. In this field the grain stands, a harsh forest of golden straw nodding under the weight of the bearded spikes, and in that, it has been swept and all its fruitfulness carried off to fill the barns.

One will not see here, save in the steep tilted Blue Ridge farms, the man reaping by sickle in his solitary field, while his daughters bind the sheaves, nor the bouquet of wheat and pine boughs hung above the grange gable that is crammed to the doors. But we have our own sights and sounds at harvest time. There is the roar and the amber dust of the threshing machines, the laughter of the children riding home on the hayricks, the warfare of the crows and grackles in the painted woods, and the seething of juice in the apple presses. Then night falls and the workers sleep. The fields are stripped, and only the crickets chant in the midnight chill of the naked meadow.

SEPTEMBER TWENTY-SEVENTH

Now in the south the star Fomalhaut rises into view. The star maps, cast most of them for the latitude of London or New York, do not show this luminary as it shines for the better part of the world. They picture it as skimming low near the horizon, something that would be half lost in the glare of ground lights, or in evening damps and mists. In more fortunate latitudes it can be seen all through the autumn, rising at its highest full one third the way to the horizon. It shines, a zenith star, upon lands that I shall never see; it bears the name given it by the Arab shepherd astronomers of old, thousands of years ago when, by the shifting of the earth's axis, it was more readily visible in the northern hemisphere than now. To Romulus it rode for perhaps six months high in the heavens; for us it grazes the horizon for but three. It is a lost friend of our race, whose ghost returns to us. It is a glimpse into the past, a peek over the edge of things.

OCTOBER FIRST

Now the autumn colors march upon their triumphs. So still the woods stand, against the faultless blue of the sky, they seem like windows dyed with pigments meant to represent all the riches and display of history—pointed windows blazing with trumpeting angels, blazons and heraldic glitter, intricate, leaf-twined illumination, depths of holy gold within temporal scarlet, soft gleaming chalices encrusted with ruby and topaz, cloths of bronze and ells of green, embroideries of crimson, twist from the vats of saffron and Tyrian and fustian.

The north woods have somehow stolen the fame of autumnal glory from other quarters of the land. But what have they—maples and beeches and aspens and rowanberry—that we have not? Or their fiery viburnums or huckleberries or brambles? We have all their colors and more, and indeed it is the tropical element in our flora that imparts the most dazzling brilliance. The tupelo tree before my door and the persimmons across the valley glow with a somber anger, like leaves that would be evergreen if they might and turn to the color of smoldering charcoal only under compulsion. The sassafras and the sour gum shout with orange and scarlet, and the curious sweet gum, with its star-shaped leaves, exults in crimson and vermilions. Like the gold tulip tree leaf it has a look about it as of some vegetation that does not really belong in the flora of the world today.

And in truth they both, like so many of our trees, are sole survivors of once great families of ages past. In what autumns must the Tertiary have rejoiced, when leaves that are fossils now flamed with colors we can only imagine—flamed upon a world without men in it, to call it beautiful.

OCTOBER FOURTEENTH

IT LAY upon a rotting log—a delicate mass, intricate and yet without definite shape, like a bit of patternless lace dyed yellow. I picked it up in careful fingers, and the whole mass came lightly away from the log and lay firm as a fragment of fabric in my hand. Triumphantly I laid it in my vasculum which had only a few lichens and mosses in it, and proceeded on my way rejoicing. There is satisfaction for the student in finding a curiosity he has studied only in theory.

The Mycetoza—unpleasantly known as slime-molds or, sometimes, as flowers-of-tan—would seem upon first view to belong quite obviously to the fungi. They are flat, branched, irregular in form, without definite growth limit, and when they come to reproduce they form themselves into balls, into tiny chalices, feathery shoots, intricate ramified craniform masses like a morelle mushroom, or delicate knobbed forests like a bread mold, which release spores as any fungus will.

But, once liberated in a convenient film of moisture, these spores proceed to hatch out a blob of microscopic jelly like an amœba, which rolls and flows along, engulfing food in its streamers of protoplasm, or dancing along by its whip-like tail, for all the world like a flagellate or a male mammal's spermatozoön. When it meets another such creature it blends; a third is engulfed with total loss of identity into the shapeless mass, and the whole colony moves off, over logs or *through* them, inchin' along, avoiding light and useless obstructions, tracking down prey in the form of fungi and perhaps bacteria.

OCTOBER FIFTEENTH

WHEN I turn my lens on the slime-molds the whole intricate mass leaps to my eye as something more formless, less comprehensible, than it seemed to be when I saw it on the log. I would have supposed, from the brilliant ocher color, the appearance of threads and granulations, that some underlying plan or symmetry must be discovered upon closer examination. But in fact it seems now no more than a sheet of protoplasmic material, without muscles, nerves, or any organs of digestion, as formless as an amœba. More formless! For though I can make out an outer layer and an inner nuclear layer I cannot anywhere distinguish either the semblance of cells nor of individuals living colonially.

I might say it is an overgrown uni-cellular organism, but it would be as reasonable to say that it is a non-cellular organism. The unwalled protoplasm, with thousands of nuclei in it, is in a state of surge, a rhythmic flowing back and forth, that, I suppose, sets more strongly in one direction than the other when the creature is in motion. It is so far from being a single organism that, if made to pass through cotton wool, it will completely disperse into innumerable streams, as it must do when penetrating the log. Yet it is so little a random collection of individuals that on emerging on the other side of such a filter it will reassemble every particle of protoplasm and flow forward again—leaving behind its spores, as no doubt it will do in the log, thus sowing a fresh crop of itself.

The problem is not whether this raw plasmodium is a plant or an animal; it is whether we shall not have to admit that there are at least three kingdoms of living things—the plant, the animal, and the Mycetozoa. Are there perhaps other kingdoms that we wot not of?

OCTOBER NINETEENTH

EVERY sunny afternoon I hear the cricket still, sweetly chirruping, and as the nights grow frosty he often comes into my house. From the window he hops by preference into the waste-basket, there to tune his roundelay. He is fond of the bathtub, too, and he hides behind the wood where I stack it by the fireplace. But his favorite room in my house is the cellar.

Now a cricket out of doors is a pleasing sound. Some people fall asleep as soon as the rain begins to fall on the roof; some like the lap of a lake upon stones, or the boom of the ocean on an old sea-wall. I love to hear the crickets chanting when I drop toward sleep. But a cricket under the bed is quite another affair, and there is nothing to do but to get up, on chill feet, and hunt the serenader out, and tell him frankly, by throwing him out of the window, that he has entirely too much to say and says it too loudly.

Out in the night, his small skirl goes sweetly among his fellows'. They sing, I think, of orange moons and meadow mice, of the first hoar frost lying pure and cool as samite on the stubble fields, and of the falling of the dull gold globes from the persimmon tree, the ripening of the heavy pawpaws in the steep woods by the river. By the hearth they speak to my ears of firelight and books, of the cracking of nuts and tucking children into bed. To my cat, his eyes rolling with the fever of the chase, his hair rising with enjoyable terror, they are ghosts behind the book-cases.

OCTOBER TWENTY-SEVENTH

A TREE in its old age is like a bent but mellowed and wise old man; it inspires our respect and tender admiration; it is too noble to need our pity. We take the fading of flowers very lightly; it is regrettable to see them go, but we know they are not sentient beings; they cannot regret their fresh tints, nor know when the firm, fine form begins to droop.

But the old age of a butterfly, the fading of its colors, the dog-earing of its brave frail wings, is a pitiful thing, for if the butterfly does not know that it is beautiful, it certainly knows when it is buffeted by the winds, and weighted and abraded by the autumn rains. It is, after all, an animal, and akin to us; not even the most hard-shelled mechanists have ventured to deny that insects have nerves and emotions, though they may not have intelligence or will as we understand those words. And I for one am convinced, if birds feel the change of season, and little mammals creeping into their winter quarters, that butterflies in some lesser but not inconsiderable degree, are aware that for most of them the term of life is nearly done. Animals often show a sharper sense of the feeling and imminence of death than we.

NOVEMBER SIXTH

ON THIS day in 1848, in a fine old farmhouse near Swindon, was born Richard Jefferies, that naturalist and poet of nature whose works in influence and literary quality stand in English letters with those of Gilbert White and Hudson. Of the three he is the least known in America. Hudson was a cosmopolite, and Gilbert White almost universal—universally parochial. Jefferies stands deepest rooted in the soil; he melts into his scene and becomes its voice, speaking for it, as a dryad speaks for the oak she inhabits. He has the intense awareness of the genius of a spot that the classic nature lovers had, and in *Round About a Great Estate, Life of the Fields,* and *The Gamekeeper at Home,* he stems straight from Theocritus, the Sabine Farm and the *Bucolics.* He can make an acre of ground ring with lark song and glitter with dew. More than all other peoples, the English appreciate their nature; Jefferies is this love in its pure fonthead.

A failure as a novelist, Jefferies in his nature writing benefited by a novelist's powers of self-expression. He has that choice of the fresh word, that eye for the quietly dramatic, with which White was entirely unacquainted. Yet he wrote out of a conscientious naturalist's first-hand information, with religious fidelity to truth. If, through all his work, and most of all in his autobiography, *The Story of My Heart,* there is a strain of the melancholy, a way of narrating things as though he were remembering happy days, it is because much of his life he was writing of Nature from hospital beds, from poor city windows. Consumption, the malady of poets, slowly and very painfully destroyed this poet of the wild breeze on Beachy Head, of the hearty health of farm and soft-breathing beast, of granges packed to the door with sweetening hay.

NOVEMBER SEVENTH

THE saddest feelings evoked by musing over Richard Jefferies' tombstone are not that disease so crippled and embittered a life intended
for manly health and great fertility, but that his works have since been
buried with him. Yet the influence of Jefferies, not only as a nature
writer but as a novelist with a deep and exciting sense of the elemental,
is felt in modern literature. He had a way of peopling his Nature with
human figures that throws the scene into a most comprehensible relief
—the men, the children, the girls, just such as we would expect to
meet on a wild down in a copse roaring with the autumn wind, in a
poacher's cottage. Some of the ache of *A Shropshire Lad,* some of the
grand leisure of *Lavengro* and the imagination of *Wolf Solent* are in
Jefferies. The primal idea of *After London*—an England after the
cracking of western civilization, with London in ruins, and men fighting amidst the brambles and the forests returned—indicates a fine sense
of true time as Nature ticks it off. And *Bevis,* that small boy Crusoe,
that hobbledehoy Julius Cæsar of the Great Pond and the Down, just
too old to allow himself to be beaten and just too young to make im-
pudent compliments to lasses, stands out for me as a classic of a boy in
Nature and Nature in a boy.

NOVEMBER EIGHTH

Now to their long winter sleep retire the batrachians. A warm-blooded
animal, even one who purposes eventually to hibernate, may still keep
the field for a few weeks more. But the cool spring newts, the earthy
toad and the frog who looks like the lily pad he sits upon, make off
to their winter quarters.

The wood frog hides beneath old logs, and the others plunge under
the chill waters, there to burrow deep in the mud. But the toad begins
to delve under shrubbery or an old board or flagstone, and when I
catch him at the business he is usually working behind his back. For

his very tough hind feet, provided with conspicuous spurs, are his spades, and with these he digs his own burrow, almost his grave, and so, inch by inch, he backs into his house. When he has gone deep enough to escape the bitter surface frosts, he pulls his hole in after him, by drawing the earth down over his head.

Now with his toes curled up under him and his head bent down, he prepares to sleep. A great darkness comes over his jewel-like eyes, a numbness through his limbs. Like one dead, he lies with heart almost stopped, breath practically suspended, an earthy thing gone back to earth, a cold thing blended with the cold clod. Life flickers very low at this moment; it sinks into an icy torpor not readily distinguishable from decease; even a sort of *rigor mortis* sets in; the sleeping toad may be cut up in sections without arousing him to consciousness. So to preserve itself from death, life will feint with it, even lie down in its black arms, in order to rise in the morning the triumphant creatrix!

NOVEMBER FIFTEENTH

WE GROW a double larkspur in the garden, and exaggerated double dahlias so heavy that they cannot hold up their own heads. But these are like idle, childless women demanding to be young perpetually. In the marsh, on the steppe, in the crevices of cliffs, the purpose of life is fruition. I could never see why a man should rebel against this law, or imagine that the best of his dreams would be more precious than the children for whom he must compromise them.

Do you object that this is a weary round—soberly to beget, in debt and fear to house and raise, in order that my sober children, early yoked, shall continue dully to repeat my life, and work out for the benefit of some monarchical or socialistic society a gray and featureless Utopia? But I ask you, what is dull about the fulfillment of biological destiny? At every moment in that destiny the beauty and terror of life confront a man—still more a woman—and round the circle of the days the eyes of Death move watchfully, pondering on children running in the light, on woman in the night, on man at labor.

NOVEMBER TWENTY-FIRST

In a guest-thronged old Southern house, of a stormy November night, I was put as a child to sleep on a couch downstairs under the short blankets and old coats that make up an extra boy's bed on such occasions. At first it was very novel and pleasant to lie on the brocaded cushions in the fire-lit room. But I wakened, in a windy midnight, to a fire gone out. And somewhere there was a curious ticking sound as of a clock, but intermittent. I knew there was no clock about, and I tried hard not to recognize the sound.

But all the time I knew it well, for a young servant who liked to make children's eyes grow large had once told me what it meant. *Tick, tack, tack,* it came—that sound that the death-watch beetle makes in old woodwork, as he counts out the minutes that are left to some one who has not much longer to live. By day I knew that beetles do not occupy themselves with the span of human lives. But in the night I saw how logical it was that some one at this hour was living out his last minutes. With the first signs of dawn I gathered up my chill clothes and fled to the comfort of the old black cook just lighting a kitchen fire of fat pine. Does any one else, like me, feel again the eeriness of the beetle's pendulum when he listens to the stroke of the bedside watch in Strauss's *Death and Transfiguration?*

Sometimes I find the beetles still, up in my attic. The warmth that steals up to them from the heated house keeps them unseasonably alive, these hammer-headed Anobia. I know their presence by the telltale pile of sawdust on the floor though I never catch them in the open. But the uncanny associations with a creature which slowly devours my rooftree, while ever remaining invisible, have not faded; they tremble like an eidolon across my scientific knowledge.

NOVEMBER TWENTY-SIXTH

For days now the skies have let down torrents of rain upon the land. The fire logs have sung upon my hearth, and I have been house bound, deeply happy in the instincts that flower beneath a roof, content with a philosopher's existence. The sky is still heavy with unshed drops, but the human frame would stand no more confinement. I walked in the woods, with boot and stick, hunting that fresh surface of experience, that actual touch and smell of reality without which a philosophy soon becomes metaphysics.

Of birds there are very few about—not nearly so many as I see on a fine day in snowbound midwinter. Without snow, the tracks of little mammal neighbors are invisible, though my dog follows their eery trails upon the air, yelping and crashing through the thickets after every rabbit, warning the entire wood that I am coming and spreading silence and absence around me as a stone spreads ripples. If I shut the dog in, the crows from their signal lookouts forewarn the world of me as if I were a dangerous public enemy.

Everywhere now in the woods, the signs of sleep and death and decay abound. I break off the bark of an old stump and discover shiny beetle larvæ scurrying in embarrassment down the labyrinths they have made, small spiders tucking themselves into silk coverlets, a soft florescence of mold at work upon the wood. The wood itself is but a damp and rusty sawdust, reduced to that condition by innumerable insect carpenters, by the bills of woodpeckers, the teeth of little rodents, the dissolving power of the fungi and the final break-up wrought by those indefatigable little junkmen, the bacteria.

NOVEMBER TWENTY-SEVENTH

No PICTURE of life today is even worth a glance that does not show the bacteria as the foundation of life itself, the broad base of the pyramid on which all the rest is erected. We know them well enough as our most terrible enemies. But man's power over the pathogenic forms advances with a certainty of purpose, a display of courage and intelligence that heartens us back to a belief in ourselves. And in truth the deathy seeds that slay us still are the least significant of the whole lot; they are expensive hothouse parasites, so finicking in their requirements, so overspecialized in their adaptations, that they have written their own doom in time.

The bacteria which fire my imagination are those that I smell as I walk these days through the dripping woods, where the sodden leaves no longer rustle. I call it the smell of loam, but of a truth loam is no more than ordinary earth rich in soil bacteria. It is their gases which I scent, as it is the emanations from other sorts that generate the fetid odor of a bog, the stench of a carcass in the woods, the delectable reek of ferment in the hay-crammed barn.

It is among these harmless sorts that there flourish species which assist to break down the naked rock that once was the five continents thrust out of the seven seas; they have made them habitable for the rest of life. Green plants—the source directly or indirectly of all the food, fuel and apparel that we use—would find life unendurable but for the bacteria. And but for the kinds that inhabit symbiotically the digestive tracts of animals, the tough cellulose of plant food could never be dissolved and assimilated. Men, as well as insects and legumes, live out their days in an unconscious dependence upon organisms so minute that, like the angels of metaphysical monks, ten thousand may (and frequently do) stand on the point of a needle, and so numerous that they surpass all the stars in heaven.

NOVEMBER TWENTY-EIGHTH

We have the geologist's word for it that the oldest rocks that bear a fossil testimony to the existence of life show impresses of bacterial scars. The biologist is not soaring on reckless wax wings of fancy when he imagines that the bacteria may have rained upon earth from distant space. Germs, we call them when they invade our bodies; germs of life, too, primordial seeds, they may well have been. For harsh as the astronomer's outer realms may be, hostile to all delicate life forms like ourselves, the bacteria (some of which are anything but delicate) may well have been fitted to pass between the Scylla and Charybdis of the astronomer's ice and fire. These specks of dust, these particles fine as smoke, boast members which can endure prolonged subjection to the temperature of liquid hydrogen, that is, 260° below zero Centigrade. Most of them prefer to live in the total darkness that is the natural state of nothingness, in which the stars struggle like wavering candles, destined at length to burn up their tallow of allotted energy. Many are the bacteria which lead their darkling existence totally without air, and right here on earth there are still others that live in hot springs, or can, by walling themselves up in tough, dormant spore cells, resist repeated boilings. The only way in which the laboratory can rid itself of such stout foes it to incubate the spores until they are tricked into emerging as the vegetative, active and more delicate phase. As yet little is known of the longevity of such spores. Seeds of lotus, found in lakes dry two thousand years, have been made to sprout. But any seed is frail flesh indeed, compared to these pallid germs so fine that some will drain through a porcelain filter as wheat through a sieve, roll round the world as an invisible breath, spawn by the million in a few hours, or rest in dormancy no man knows how long.

NOVEMBER TWENTY-NINTH

Before a man has done with such a wild horde of rock-eating savages as the bacteria, all easy notions of what life is may break down as completely as the Newtonian physics before the onslaughts of the Einsteinian.

If I try to fix a vital temperature range between the freezing and the boiling points of water, the bacteria confound me. If I maintain that the very focus of vital forces is in the cell nucleus, there are certain bacteria that leap to my sight in the microscope, devoid of nuclei.

It is even a mystery in what kingdom to place them. The zoölogist will generally not admit them, the botanist is embarrassed to know what to do with them. He tucks them in somewhere near the fungi, because they are without green coloring, produce spores, and because so many are saprophytes or parasites. But the bacteria are without the double cell wall of plants, and whatever their cell wall may be composed of, it seems not to be cellulose, the very brick and mortar of plant life.

It is perhaps simplest to say that there are four kingdoms of living things, plant, animal, slime-mold and bacterial. How many more kingdoms may there be in this or other worlds? One of the startling discoveries of the modern age was that of the bacteriophages, organisms so small that they have never yet been seen, which disembowel bacteria and eat their vitals. They may be bacteria also, but just as possibly they are not, they may be something even stranger.

NOVEMBER THIRTIETH

THE end of the bacterial paradoxes is not yet. They have members of the guild which ply their trade without air, and others that take free nitrogen out of the atmosphere and utilize it. We think of the element carbon as the very stuff of organic tissue, blood of our blood and bone of our bone. But the bacteria might subsist in a world where the marvelously versatile element of carbon was extremely scarce. For some will ingest a diet of iron, or in default of it will substitute the element manganese.

There are not only sulphur bacteria, but certain ones of this persuasion have developed a pigmentation screen, absorbing and utilizing the sun's energy through it in the red and orange end of the spectrum, as green plants are able to do in their own color range. In this wise have these Lilliputian workers anticipated and rivaled chlorophyll, the green blood of the world.

No other organisms show so great a range of adaptability, from sun-utilizing species to others that live in total darkness, from aërobes or air-breathers to anaërobes. True, no one bacterium combines all these modes of living. But it is not necessary that any one species would be so versatile in order to imagine in them something very close to universal seeds of life.

The bacteria are only the most primitive, and adaptable-to-the-primitive beings that are at present known. They may have had—may still have—antecedents even more hardy and fitted to digest the raw stuff of the universe, perhaps even the interstellar calcium that is one of the recent discoveries of the watchers of the skies.

DECEMBER TWELFTH

I KEEP always on my desk a bit of an old olive root that I pulled out of the flames, one cold December evening on the Riviera. Intricate as a finger print, that root, in its fantastic whorls and devious involutions. Intricate as the history of Europe, which it very possibly witnessed, for the grove from which it came was planted by the Romans.

Between what the physicists call an organism, such as a fluorine atom, and what the biologists admit as an organism, there is this mighty difference, that a fluorine atom must ever remain the same and identically the same, lest it be fluorine no longer, while the root of an olive, and the finger tip of a man, are never twice the same. I do not say it is impossible to conceive in life the accidental occurrence of two perfect identities, but everything in our experience points in the other direction. Mendel showed once and for all that nothing is so unlike as two peas in a pod, and observation tends toward the belief that even one-celled animals have individualization.

In the bit of root nubble is written the history of the tree, the obstacles it met, the tropisms it followed, the lean years and the fat. So easy to touch a match to it; so forever out of reach to recreate a bit of wood like it!

As the fire glances from the burning log around the room it falls upon the faces of the people seated round the hearth with you. What do you really know of them, your own children, and the wife who bore them to you? All are locked mysteriously away in their individuality. So I guard the old olive root upon my desk, to keep myself humble as a scientist and, as a man, full of wonder.

DECEMBER THIRTEENTH

I STAND in the quiet woods, conscious that under my feet, in the soil, are millions of dead, millions of living things. That all around me are trees, half dead and half alive, and looking alike. I myself am perpetually dying. I do not mean that I am simply drifting ever nearer toward that right hand bracket that will ultimately close up the dates in my biography, but literally dying, cell by cell, artery by artery.

Scratch a live twig, and a bit of the green cambium layer will shine forth; scratch a live finger and blood will flow. These are cheery, colorful pennants of living things. But so much that is alive flies no flag, and wears the expressionless mask of the lifeless.

As I see it, the great and distinguishing feature of living things, however, is that they have needs—continual, and, incidentally, complex needs. I cannot conceive how even so organized a dead system as a crystal can be said to need anything. But a living creature, even when it sinks into that half-death of hibernation, even the seed in the bottom of the dried Mongolian marsh, awaiting rain through two thousand years, still has needs while there is life in it. The bacteria have needs, and it cannot be said too often that merely because a living creature is microscopic there is no justification for thinking that it brings us any nearer to the inanimate. The gulf between a bacterium and a carbon atom, even with all the latter's complexity, is greater than that between bacteria and men.

If you object that this criterion of life is chiefly a philosophical one, I reply that in the end the most absolute answers concerning every problem of matter, energy, time and life, will be found to be philosophical.

DECEMBER SEVENTEENTH

When I try to look at the sun my weak eyes flinch away before the light from our bright particular star, like an animal that cannot meet its master's gaze. But a man may look at Orion, and stare its brilliance down the sky, because, in truth, he need not see it as it is. One can recite the musical and ancient names of the gems that compose it—the three stars of the belt, Alnitak, Alnilam and Mintaka; Betelgeux is for the head, Rigel at the forward knee, and Saiph at the hinder foot, and in the outflung arm the glorious Bellatrix.

No constellation in all the sky is so vast, so dazzling, so heroic and exciting as this mighty hunter. The heart lifts up at the spectacle of those three perfectly matched jewels of the belt, at Rigel the color of glacial ice, and Betelgeux like some topaz flashing its splendor across the depths of space.

One of those strange variables that now is dim and then again is bright is Betelgeux, that in 1852 blazed out in such splendor it surpassed Capella, Vega and Arcturus, and was second only to that stabbing shaft of violet radiance, the dog star, Sirius, at the hunter's heels. The hue of Betelgeux appears to vary with its brightness, deepening to the color of embers as the star grows fainter, leaping to a blazing yellow as if it found fresh fuel—a sun that is flickering out, yet one still a thousand times as brilliant as our own.

But Rigel, in its youth, is ten thousand times as brilliant. And these intensities are not mere appearance, like that of Sirius, which is so bright largely because so near to us; they are the true measure of the size and heat of two great hells seething and pitching on through icy blackness.

DECEMBER EIGHTEENTH

THE mind of simple man, beholding Orion, conceived almost everything about that great configuration save the awful truth. The three belt stars are three steps cut in ice by the Great Eskimo, for little Eskimos to climb into heaven. To the Arab, Orion was a giant, to the Jews he was Nimrod, to the Egyptians Osiris. In Greece he was that hunter who dared boast that he could slay all the beasts, whereat a scorpion stung him in the heel.

But no sooner did the telescopes swing upon this giant, god, or brute, than thousands of thousands of stars sprang forth to the view of man—stars, and the Great Nebula, and the Horse's Head, that dark impenetrable mass behind which, as behind a hill, a blaze of brightness peeps. And between the stars were seen the looped festoons of light, like cirrus clouds upon a fair-weather sky, like spindrift brilliance washed up on the black shingle of nothingness.

Now indeed are we gazing at our own spiral nebula, the Milky Way, in one of its most terrifying and chaotic perspectives—black dust reefs of dead matter on which a sun might speed to ruin, streamers of incandescent gas, wandering fires of the air, and suns so vast that our own might drop into them and be lost as a stone is lost in a crater's pit. This is the inner circle of inferno in which our poor mortal planet spins about, bearing its freight, to us so precious, of life and hope.

DECEMBER NINETEENTH

MAN, that most inquisitive of mammals, has not stopped his searches within the Milky Way. He knows now that our sun is traveling in it, in a saraband, circling, maybe—but there has not yet been time to know it surely—round and round some core or nucleus whose awful heat and brilliance are mercifully hidden from us by a great cloud bank of inert matter somewhere in the constellation of Sagittarius.

But the telescope has revealed other nebulæ than ours, and there is one that even with the naked eye I just discern. To me it looks like a faint luminosity between the great W of Cassiopeia in the zenith and Andromeda at Cassiopeia's feet. Before me as I write I have a photograph of this other island universe in space, that shows me what astronomers see—a wild swirl of smoky light in which no individual stars appear but all seems like an act of creation coming out of chaos contorted with birth pangs. Only if the picture were enlarged to the size of this continent would a sun like ours be visible upon it, as a small speck.

Such is M 31, the great nebula of Andromeda. It is none other than a Milky Way, our nearest neighbor star city—so near that light, traveling from it at 186,000 miles a second, has only taken 900,000 years to reach us! Has it some destiny of its own? Are we, our Milky Way and M 31, two ships that pass in the night, who see each other, sides glittering with porthole lights, as they plow their way through space, turning a luminous furrow in the ultimate dark?

DECEMBER TWENTY-FIRST

On this day in 1823 was born Henri Fabre, the sage of Serignan, who entered the world of the insects like a transmogrified elf to spy upon them. The monstrous matings, the cannibalisms, the unnatural appetites, the hunts, the deaths, the smells, the fabulous eyes, the snatchings, gluttonies and rapes—he describes them, mildly scandalized but like a Christian, loving all. The drowsy corner of Provence where he had his roof and taught physics in a boy's school for him was a teeming jungle, a land of Lilliputian marvel and adventure, in which event was the trembling of a moth's feathered antenna, the knotting of a thread in a spider's web.

With all this wealth of observation, amassed over Fabre's very long life and flung before us in the most captivating, witty, readable style ever given to a reporter, the reader is surely carping to find a fault. Yet there were faults in Fabre's work. As an experimenter in animal psychology, behavior and mechanics, he was naïve and crude. His conclusions were too frequently *non sequiturs:* obstinate village piety made him forswear evolution and the door of interpretation that it would have opened for him.

But behind his words works the kindly spirit of Fabre himself, a valiant old man who for much of his life never owned a microscope and yet saw more than twenty microscopists, a man who lived, not the unnatural ascetic like Spinoza or the irresponsible wanderer like Audubon, but the whole man, taking a wife, keeping a rooftree, begetting children, and struggling to make their shirts meet their little breeches.

DECEMBER TWENTY-SECOND

Now is the darkest hour of all the year, the winter solstice. We are arrived at the antipodes of brave mid-summer, when it was once the custom for men to while away the few hours of the short night with bonfires and a blowing of conches and a making of wild young marriages, that men might hold the earth for the sun god during his brief descent beneath the horizon. But at this season of the year, when the sun was a pallid blur behind a junco-colored sky, a darkness fell upon the spirits of all men, and a splinter of ice was in their hearts. To some of us the winter solstice is an unimportant phase of terrestrial astronomy; of old it must have produced an emotional reaction which a Christian can only experience on Good Friday, and the breath-held Saturday that follows.

It is not the cold of far northern lands that drives the human animal to despair; cold is tingling, exciting, healthful, and it can, in a limited way, be overcome. It is the darkness that conquers the spirit, when the northern sun does not rise until late, only to skim low upon the horizon for an hour or two, and set. Now indeed is Balder slain of the mistletoe. Now life is at its lowest ebb, and the mind conceives a little what it will be like when the sun has burned to a red ember, its immense volume dissipated by constant radiation, and the earth drifted far out into space, the shrinking sun no longer able to hold her child upon a leash so close.

DECEMBER TWENTY-FIFTH

It was Francis of Assisi, I believe, the man who called the wind his brother and the birds his sisters, who gave the world the custom of exhibiting the crèche in church, where barn and hay, soft-breathing beasts, flowing breast and hungry babe, shepherd and star are elevated for delight. One who has spent a Christmas in some southern country, where an early Christianity still reigns, will understand how all else that to us means the holy festival is quite lacking there. It was originally, and still sometimes is, no more than a special Mass, scarcely as significant as Assumption, much less so than Easter. Out of the North the barbarian mind, forest born, brought tree worship, whether of fir or holly or yule log. It took mistletoe from the druids, stripped present-giving from New Year (where in Latin lands it still so largely stays) and made of Christmas a children's festival, set to the tune of the beloved joyful carols. It glorified woman and child and the brotherhood of men in a way that the Church in, let us say, the second century dreamed not on.

You will search the four Gospels in vain for a hint of the day or the month when Christ was born. December twenty-fifth was already being celebrated in the ancient world as the birthdate of the sun god Mithras, who came out of a rock three days after the darkest of the year. His birth was foretold of a star that shepherds and magi beheld. The ancient Angles had long been wont to hold this day sacred as Modranecht or Mother Night. Thus still do we flout old winter with green tree, and old mortality with child worship.

DECEMBER THIRTY-FIRST

EACH little year that passes is one more grain of sand slipped through the narrows of the hour glass of our universe. Physicists suppose that matter and energy in the universe are finite; I cannot imagine time in a cosmos that reached ultimate inertia and dissipation; the supply of time, too, then, may well be finite—particularly terrestrial time.

What did mankind do with the sand grain that is even now falling? He discovered new stars, and one more chemical element, the last with a chair reserved for it at the Round Table of the elements. He averted another great war—at least momentarily. He discovered several new methods of destroying his brothers with the utmost cruelty. He reëstablished in some countries tyranny, torture and religious intolerance; in others he toiled on, unencouraged but not discouraged, with the age-old problems like poverty, disease, prostitution and crime.

The best that we can say is that some of humanity shouldered the old loads; some hindered, hung back, even attacked the burden bearers. Most of us did nothing, neglected to raise a cheer for the struggling, passively permitted the wolves to go on devouring their hideous banquet of men and women, wolves of war and greed, vice and drugs.

Biologically considered, man is the sole being who has its destiny in its hands. And few of his species feel any sense of racial responsibility higher than the primitive one of begetting children. Yet now and then, as the years pass, comes a Noguchi, Pasteur, Beethoven,

Lincoln, Asoka, Marcus Aurelius or Plato. They are humanity as it might be.

JANUARY FOURTH

Now we are in the very lists of winter and what a winter, with the Atlantic coast lashed with storm on storm, with ships crying at sea through the lost staccato of their wireless. Cold blowing out of the Arctic, out of Keewatin, on the wings of cyclones that engulf a continent in a single maelstrom, vanish in the east to be followed by another. Frost reaching a finger to the tender tip of tropic Florida. And here, fresh ice thickening upon the unmelted old; ice on the loops of the country telegraph wires, every tree locked in a silver armor, a sort of a white Iron Maiden that breaks their bones and listens with glee to the cracking sound. Something there is in our North American winters peculiarly sadistic—with a pitiless love of inflicting suffering for its own sake wherever the poor are huddled in the smoky cities, wherever men, and women too, battle against the cold in lonely prairie houses. We have no Alps from west to east to block the way of roaring boreas, no southland protected against our north. Our mountains march with the north wind, and in the drafty gulfs between them, and along their outer flanks, raids the pack of the howling white-fanged days.

JANUARY SEVENTH

Fear rises out of all darkness, fear for us who are diurnal, not nocturnal animals. But I do not experience this sensation out of doors, as many people do. Night terrors are bred in closets, beds, cellars, attics, and all those traps and pits and sinks in which civilized man houses himself, blunts his senses and breeds his own ills. Out in the open night it may be cold, or windy, or rainy, but it is never anything in which a bogy could endure.

Indeed, if you think of night in the true, philosophical proportion, you must realize that it is the prevailing, the absolute thing. Light, day, burning suns and stars—all are the exception. They are but gleaming jewels spattered on the black cloth of darkness. Throughout the universe and eternity it is night that prevails. It is the mother of cosmos, capacious womb of light.

JANUARY TWELFTH

OUT of the southwest, a sluggish "low" has crept across the map of the land; the whistling "highs," with their peeled blue sky and icy breath, have shifted up, and in their place are gray skies again, heavy with snow. How kind is gray! Beautiful, delicate, elegant. And now, quite quietly it has begun to snow again. A new mask falling over the old one, a sense of deepening of mysterious winter, of an adventure in experience through which we shall not too swiftly see, as we see through the autumn's intentions from the first.

There is only one way to study snow crystals, and that is to take your microscope—or take a hand lens if nothing better offers—out of doors, or into some long-chilled room, as I did today, an attic where I opened a window to the damp drift, and caught the flakes upon a glass slide.

There is no telling of the beauty of snow crystals; one look is worth all words, and no comparisons are adequate—not even the tracery of a rose window, or altar lace on which old women have worn away needle-numbed fingers and a life-time of fading sight. But there is one charm which the snowflake possesses that is denied to most crystals, and above all to that emperor of them all, the carbon crystal or diamond, and that is that it is evanescent. Nothing in this world is really precious until we know that it will soon be gone. The lily, the starry daffodil, the regal iris (and these, too, are built upon a symmetry of six)—are the lovelier for their imminent vanishing. The snow crystal has but touched earth ere it begins to die.

JANUARY THIRTEENTH

THAT about snow crystals which confounds all understanding is how so many variations—millions perhaps—can be schemed upon the unvarying fundamental plan of six. Be it etched out to elaborations as fine feathered as a whole pane covered with frost designs, still there are always six rays to each delicate star, and one can still make out in the finest, the ultimate details of attenuated ornamentation, the same fundamental symmetry. There can be no chance about this; some cause underlies it, and I am no crystallographer to explain the details of a snowflake's fine-wrought surfaces, its internal tensions and stresses, its perfect equilibria and balanced strains that distend each fairy tracery and give to these flowers of the winter air their gossamer strength.

But one may hazard the guess that the six-sidedness of the snow crystal is in reality a doubling of three, just as the symmetry of the lily and the amaryllis is. Of all the magic numbers in old necromancy and modern science, three is the first. Three dimensions has matter; three is the least number of straight sides that will just inclose a space. Three legs is the smallest number that will just support the equilibrium and stresses of a stool. Two would not do; four are superfluous; and twice three points are required, and just required, to keep intact the frailest of all solids—a flake of snow.

JANUARY FOURTEENTH

CRYSTAL—the very word has a chime of delicate bells about it, a clash of shattering thin ice; it has a perishable sound, which enchants the poet, as its meaning does the mathematician. For the crystal is matter in its most organized form, wherein all the molecules are so disposed or polarized or deployed like a perfect regiment, that they stand equidistant from each other along planes of symmetry that may be simple or exquisitely complex. And the result is that, unlike the rest of inanimate matter, a crystal turns a definite face to the outside; it is discrete, organized, has a specific form. When you crack a crystal it does not break up in a jagged fracture like ordinary poured glass; it breaks along lines of its own symmetry; in effect, it merely becomes two or more crystals of smaller size; it can almost be said to reproduce, as the simplest organisms do, by fission. For given tne wherewithal, each fragment crystal will increase and grow, as the living cell will do.

Now frost is on the morning window panes, upstarting in intricate primal forests of moss form and fern form and tree and fungus. The growth of a forest of window frost is oddly like the growth of some fungus that springs up over night. If the temperature keep falling outside, and the relative amount of moisture increase on the inside, the frost flowers will continue to grow, and may be detected in their spread across the glass. Like living things, they branch like a tree, grow usually from the bottom upwards. If they cover the pane entirely they add thickness, as a tree does. But there is this vital difference, that the tree grows from the inside out, transforming its raw materials into something else, while the frost crystal can only add to its outside the chemically unaltered water vapor of the atmosphere.

JANUARY FIFTEENTH

WITH its internal stresses and specific properties of elasticity and cohesion, properties magnetic and electrical and optical, the crystal has elaborate organization. It seems but a slight step, then, to call it an organism, for indeed it is easy to see in what way the most complicated crystal is organized. But difficult, cantankerously difficult to analyze the organization of unicellular animals or plants. The crystal, with its elegant mathematics and its orderly molecules, is the mechanist's dream and ideal of organization. If only, if only living matter were so transparent! The mechanist cannot help feeling that somehow opaque, unpredictable protoplasm will yet give him a chance to see through it.

Haeckel, the great tower of mechanistic strength, did not hesitate to proclaim that the distinctive nature of life is due simply to its molecular and atomic structure, and needless to say all crystals threw him into an ecstasy. He firmly believed that the crystal and the living cell were in all ways comparable, both as to their chemical and physical makeup, their growth and their individuality. He practically classified crystals into genera and species, and then went on, with a mania like a numerologist's, to show a crystalline form in pollen grains, corals, infusorians and the arrangements of leaves and flowers around their axes of growth. The poor fellow—a man of the most romantic morality in private life—was faced, of course, with the old Aristotelian dilemma as to where spirit (or soul or God or vital force) dwells, when there is no difference save of degree (as he asserts) between living and non-living structure. He was in consequence driven further than was Aristotle who bestowed soul on a jellyfish; Haeckel had to assume that there is spirit and vital force in the inanimate rock, and he crowned his life work with a book entitled *The Souls of Crystals*.

JANUARY TWENTY-FOURTH

In the gray of the year, to our green-hungry eyes, the pines come into their greatness. The deciduous woods in winter have a steely and shelterless appearance, but even in a blinding snow storm pine woods have a look of warmth about them. Alone among trees, evergreens keep up their sap in the winter; the fires of life still burn in them.

I like our loblolly pines for their long glittering foliage, full of warmth and light at all seasons, bringing back to me the very smell of the South, the feeling of those grand sad lowlands of Georgia and the Carolinas. I like the yellow pine for its generous armored trunks built up of laminated plates like the leather shields of Homeric foot soldiers. But it is in the pitch pine that you have all that was ever embodied in the name of pine—the fondness for growing on craggy ledges, the wind-molded, storm-blasted shape, the dark and pungent foliage, the tears of silvery rosin bleeding from the rough male trunk, and the clusters of cones black against the sky. When it dies, it dies standing. And even as a skeleton, it has grandeur.

Its perfect complement is the white pine, a feminine tree with silky, silvery and perpetually talkative needles. Adorned by long shapely cones with delicate flexible pink scales, clad in a smooth and lustrous bark, it rises in a delicate pagoda-like shape. Instead of the bold ledge, the white pine loves the glen, and there it consorts, in the damp, shadowed air and the earth mold of the color of tanbark, with hemlocks in groves where the pine siskins unite in little flocks, conferring together in voices fine as the whisper of a small watch.

FEBRUARY FIRST

SCIENCE is a ship afloat upon a wide waste of waters. Less than Columbus does it know where the world is bound. It does not even know from what port we have set out.

These thoughts inspire the landlubber with terror. He begs to be allowed to dream that he knows what lies ahead. But for those whom William James called the "tough-minded," by which he really meant the stout-hearted, the search itself is the thing, the shore is perhaps but an illusion.

The beauty, the rightness, the excitement of the search are facts which even the humblest naturalist understands, though he has never done anything more than pursue an unknown bird in the woods for half a day, or climb an alp to find a saxifrage.

FEBRUARY NINETEENTH

Now is that strange hushed time of year when Nature seems to pause. The winds of winter are wearied. The weeds, once ranked high in the fields, are low and subject. The weathered leaves begin to fall from the oaks that have clutched them fiercely, as the old clutch at little comforts.

The moment is like a pause in a symphony, when the great composer brings the fury of his music to a stop, a rest so fateful and significant that in the silence the listener counts his own loud heartbeats as though they were his last—hoping for and almost dreading the beginning of the new theme in the next measures.

And what will it be, that melody, but the beginning of spring? The talk of thaw in many runnels, the sounds of birds finding again their voices, of tree toads trilling in chill twilights, of a spade that strikes a stone.

FEBRUARY TWENTIETH

PISCES follows Aquarius and between them they constitute what the astrologers call the watery signs. And now indeed the world brims over with "old February fill-dyke." The ancients knew it as "the time of rain and want." The snows have melted and the Tigris rises; the Nile and the Potomac fill as of old they did. Footing is treacherous; the winds are cold, and dampness hangs in all the airs; there is a feeling of wetness wiped upon the cheek and hands, and of small icy fingers laid upon the throat.

Before there can be spring there must be water, and water and more water; flowers appear when the rains are over and the floods gone down. But before flowering there must be growth, uprising of sap. Without water there can be no life; water is its very matrix; it is the medium in which the vital molecule exists, the fluid in which the colloid of protoplasm is suspended.

FEBRUARY TWENTY-FIRST

WATER is the one imaginable medium in which the ship of life could have been launched and expected to float.

All of the most vital processes take place in this great solvent. The absorption of nourishment is impossible either by a root in the soil, or in the body of man, save as the nutrient elements come dissolved in water. Only through a watery surface may the animal excrete its poisons—through the wall of the lungs, the kidneys and the sweat glands. So water is the seat of all our metabolism, constructive and destructive. The fires of life burn only in water.

Running, flowing, falling though we see it, it is in essence greatly conservative. You cannot easily cool it below the freezing point; so used is woman to the teakettle she does not think how, chemically, it is a hard task to boil water. This is because of its latent heat, and but for that a man's metabolism, the mere business of bodily living, would

soon bring on a temperature that would set fire to the carbon in his
bones.

Water everywhere, in the soil, in the air, in the seas and ponds, acts
as the world's great thermostat, preventing excessive upward march
of temperatures or great cold. Between the arctic ice fields and the
tropic seas a vast equalizing convection perpetually turns.

FEBRUARY TWENTY-SECOND

TOLERANT, capacious, water conveys and distributes the working material of the world. It is the incomparable solvent. It will hold intact the
salts dissolved in it, and at the same time constantly breaking them
down into their elements, constantly recombine those elements with
others. So for hungry protoplasm it performs a miracle; out of three
salts it can make nine. Undisturbed, it handles a great coming and
going of molecular traffic.

Water is abundant, willing, and quiet. It is not easily parted into
its two component elements, nor changed in temperature. There is
always the same unfailing amount of it in the world. It dissolves
without altering or being itself altered. Infinitely versatile, it is tranquilly stable. It does not, like helium, desert us for outer spaces, nor,
like oxygen, rush to combine with metal and so be lost to use.

FEBRUARY TWENTY-THIRD

IT IS the wetness of water with which a man has to deal these days;
wet feet, wet garden soil so heavy that the spade can scarcely turn it,
damp seeping into the depleted wood pile. When we say that water
is wet we mean that it climbs up things, against gravity, invades,
softens, dissolves or alters wherever it creeps. That creep the scientist
calls capillarity, and but for the capillarity of water how difficult it
were to do our business! We could not blot a page or wipe a surface
dry or wash dirt out of clothes. Water falling upon the earth would

never rise again; the garden would be thirsty a few moments after you had given it to drink.

But owing to capillarity it climbs, from grain of soil to grain, till it reaches the needy root, or flows out in springs. No other liquid will rise even half as high as water. And not only will it rise directly, but it spreads in every direction; without this, no irrigation would be possible.

The physics and mathematics of capillarity are complex beyond the understanding of such intellects as mine, but fundamentally it all rests upon a property of water more unique than all the rest, more vital to life, its strange surface tension.

FEBRUARY TWENTY-FOURTH

Down by the brook, in one of its quiet bays, the water striders are already out, skating over the calm pool as if it were ice, because the surface tension of the water just suffices to hold them up. If I push one of them through the surface, lo, they are not aquatic insects at all. They drown, like people who cannot swim and have fallen through the ice. Other insects there are in earliest spring that cling just under the surface, like balloons bumping the ceiling.

But this is merely the way in which a few living creatures may be said to have fun with the surface tension of water. This strangest of water's properties penetrates to the very structure of life itself. It goes straight to the colloidal nature of protoplasm, for nothing conceivable will present as much surface as a colloid or permanent suspension of particles in a liquid medium, and to that surface will adhere by surface tension the chemicals brought to the cell. Thus is explained the capacity of living matter to take up dyes; the chemistry of pigmentation hangs upon surface tension.

So water not only dissolves the rocks and by sheer plowing carries the soil down to make the valleys fertile; it is the basis of the beauty of the butterfly's wings, the colors in the crocus petal.

MARCH SECOND

HERE at the bottom of our sea of air a few creatures of frail flight are just emerged upon the spring. Like somber thoughts left over from the night, like lingering bits of winged sleep, the dark mourning cloaks flutter languidly in the sunlight, or cling on the twigs of the pussy willow, resembling last year's leaves. The midges swirl upon the air, not in the wild autumnal dance of their kind, but dreamily and without apparent purpose over the wood-brown pools of rain among the old leaves; they climb invisible spiral ladders tentatively toward the sun.

In the sky is a lightening, a heightening, after the close gray cap of winter. I notice the vulture there again, now that the winter hawks have gone; it reminds us of summer indolence and makes the day seem warmer than it is. Several airplanes too are out, and I take this for a sign of spring as valid as the first flight of the kildeer over the soppy, fire-browned river meadows. A youngster is stunting, perilously low, and another in his ebullience writes his name in smoke upon the heavens, and I shall be astonished if this is not part of a vernal male strut before a watching woman. I hear the drone of the planes released or suddenly cut off, and from the great hive across the river one after another takes the air in a proud conscious beauty.

MARCH ELEVENTH

I HAVE said that much of life and perhaps the best of it is not quite "nice." The business of early spring is not; it takes place in nakedness and candor, under high empty skies. Almost all the first buds to break their bonds send forth not leaves but frank catkins, or in the maple sheer pistil and stamen, devoid of the frilled trimmings of petals. The cedar sows the wind with its pollen now, because it is a relict of an age before bees, and it blooms in a month essentially barren of winged pollinators. The wood frogs, warmed like the spring flowers by the swift-heating earth, return to the primordial element of water for their spawning, and up from the oozy bottoms rise the pond frogs, to make of the half-world of the marges one breeding ground.

It is a fact that the philosopher afoot must not forget, that the astonishing embrace of the frog-kind, all in the eery green chill of earliest March, may be the attitude into which the tender passion throws these batrachians, but it is a world away from warm-blooded mating. It is a phlegmatic and persisting clasping, nothing more. It appears to be merely a reminder to the female that death brings up the rear of life's procession. When after patient hours he quits her, the female goes to the water to pour out her still unfertilized eggs. Only then are they baptized with the fecundating complement of the mate.

It is a startling bit of intelligence for the moralists, but the fact seems to be that sex is a force not necessarily concerned with reproduction; back in the primitive one-celled animals there are individuals that fuse without reproducing in consequence; the reproduction in those lowly states is but a simple fission of the cell, a self-division. It seems then that reproduction has, as it were, fastened itself on quite another force in the world; it has stolen a ride upon sex, which is a principle in its own right.

MARCH EIGHTEENTH

Now all life renews, in its hopes and in its threats, in its strict needs and in all that superabundance that we call by the name of beauty. In the same place where last I found them, the pale watery shoots of Equisetum rise; buds of flowers open, all crumpled like babies' hands; the phœbes have returned to the nests at the mouth of the cave, where before they bred and where poignant accidents befell them. With a touching hopefulness all things renew themselves, not undismayed, perhaps, by the terror and chanciness of fate, but because, God help them, they can do no other.

For life is a green cataract; it is an inundation, a march against the slings of death that counts no costs. Still it advances, waving its inquisitive antennæ, flaunting green banners. Life is adventure in experience, and when you are no longer greedy for the last drop of it, it means no more than that you have set your face, whether you know it or not, to the day when you shall depart without a backward look. Those who look backward longingly to the end die young, at whatever age.

MARCH NINETEENTH

I GO TO the cellar for the last logs in my woodpile, and disclose a family of mice who have trustingly taken up residence there. Their tiny young, all ears and belly, mere little sacks of milk in a furless skin, lie there blind and helpless, five little tangible, irrepressible evidences of some moment, not so many nights ago, when in between the walls of my house there took place an act to which I am not so egotistic as to deny the name of love.

But it is not this which moves me, but the look in the mother's eyes as she stares up at me, her tail to the wall, all power of decision fled from her. There I read, in her agonized glance, how precious is life even to her. She entreats me not to take it from her. She does not know of pity in the world, so has no hope of it. But life—no matter how one suffers in it, hungers, flees, and fights—life is her religion.

How can we ever hope, then, to commensurate this thing which we too share, when it is its own cause, its own reason for being, when, as soon as we are challenged to stand and deliver it, we tremble and beg, like the trapped mouse?

MARCH TWENTIETH

To THE terror that faces mice and men, a man at least can find an answer. This will be his religion.

Now how may a man base all his faith on Nature when in Nature there is no certain end awaiting the ambition of his race? When all is flux and fleet, the great flood tides of spring that are like to drown him, and the final neap tide of decease? How take comfort from the brave new greening of the grass, when grass must wither, or in the first eery whistle of the meadow larks, saying that life is "sweet-to-you, so sweet to you"? For life is not sweet to all men. It brings some blind into this world and of others requires blood and tears. The sun toward which man turns his face is a brief candle in the universe. His woman and his children are mortal as the flowers.

But it is not life's generosity, so capricious, that makes one man happy. It is rather the extent of his gratitude to life.

I say that it touches a man that his tears are only salt, and that the tides of youth rise, and, having fallen, rise again. Now he has lived to see another spring and to walk again beneath the faintly greening trees. So, having an ear for the uprising of sap, for the running of blood, having an eye for all things done most hiddenly, and a hand in the making of those small dear lives that are not built with hands, he lives at peace with great events.

THOMAS MANN

COMMENTARY

Early in 1937, Thomas Mann, exiled from Germany and temporarily domiciled in Zurich, received a brief communication, as follows:

To Herr Thomas Mann, writer: By the request of the Rector of the University of Bonn, I must inform you that as a consequence of your loss of citizenship the Philosophical Faculty finds itself obliged to strike your name off its roll of honorary doctors. Your right to use this title is canceled in accordance with Article VIII of the regulations concerning the conferring of degrees.

(signature illegible)

—DEAN

This letter was a tactical error on the part of the Nazis, for it drew from Thomas Mann a letter in reply. Somehow or other the reply found its way into the hands of many Germans (theoretically Nazis), particularly the young. It seems to have meant something to them. Some went so far as to memorize it, though it is very long. But perhaps their minds had plenty of room for it; their masters do not oversupply them with mental nourishment.

There is no need to comment on this letter. It is the expression of a great European and a great man. It will rank with Zola's J'accuse (it deals, of course, with a much greater subject than did Zola) as one of the classic responses of humanity to inhumanity.

A Letter to the Dean of the Philosophical Faculty of the University of Bonn

BY

THOMAS MANN

To THE Dean of the Philosophical Faculty of the University of Bonn:
I have received the melancholy communication which you addressed
to me on the nineteenth of December. Permit me to reply to it as
follows:

The German universities share a heavy responsibility for all the
present distresses which they called down upon their heads when they
tragically misunderstood their historic hour and allowed their soil to
nourish the ruthless forces which have devastated Germany morally,
politically, and economically.

This responsibility of theirs long ago destroyed my pleasure in my
academic honour and prevented me from making any use of it whatever. Moreover, I hold today an honorary degree of Doctor of Letters
conferred upon me more recently by Harvard University. I cannot
refrain from explaining to you the grounds upon which it was conferred. My diploma contains a sentence which, translated from the
Latin, runs as follows: ". . . we the President and Fellows with the
approval of the honourable Board of Overseers of the University in
solemn session have designated and appointed as honorary Doctor of
Letters Thomas Mann, famous author, who has interpreted life to
many of our fellow-citizens and together with a very few contemporaries sustains the high dignity of German culture; and we have
granted to him all the rights and privileges appertaining to this
degree."

In such terms, so curiously contradictory to the current German
view, do free and enlightened men across the ocean think of me—

and, I may add, not only there. It would never have occurred to me to boast of the words I have quoted; but here and today I may, nay, I must repeat them.

If you, Herr Dean (I am ignorant of the procedure involved), have posted a copy of your communication to me on the bulletin board of your university, it would gratify me to have this reply of mine receive the same honour. Perhaps some member of the university, some student or professor, may be visited by a sudden fear, a swiftly suppressed and dismaying presentiment, on reading a document which gives him in his disgracefully enforced isolation and ignorance a brief revealing glimpse of the free world of the intellect that still exists outside.

Here I might close. And yet at this moment certain further explanations seem to me desirable or at least permissible. I made no statement when my loss of civil rights was announced, though I was more than once asked to do so. But I regard the academic divestment as a suitable occasion for a brief personal declaration. I would beg you, Herr Dean (I have not even the honour of knowing your name), to regard yourself as merely the chance recipient of a communication not designed for you in a personal sense.

I have spent four years in an exile which it would be euphemistic to call voluntary since if I had remained in Germany or gone back there I should probably not be alive today. In these four years the odd blunder committed by fortune when she put me in this situation has never once ceased to trouble me. I could never have dreamed, it could never have been prophesied of me at my cradle, that I should spend my later years as an émigré, expropriated, outlawed, and committed to inevitable political protest.

From the beginning of my intellectual life I had felt myself in happiest accord with the temper of my nation and at home in its intellectual traditions. I am better suited to represent those traditions than to become a martyr for them; far more fitted to add a little to the gaiety of the world than to foster conflict and hatred in it. Something very wrong must have happened to make my life take so false and unnatural a turn. I tried to check it, this very wrong thing, so far as my weak powers were able—and in so doing I called down on myself the fate which I must now learn to reconcile with a nature essentially foreign to it.

Certainly I challenged the wrath of these despots by remaining away and giving evidence of my irrepressible disgust. But it is not merely in the last four years that I have done so. I felt thus long before, and was driven to it because I saw—earlier than my now desperate fellow-countrymen—who and what would emerge from all this. But when Germany had actually fallen into those hands I thought to keep silent. I believed that by the sacrifice I had made I had earned the right to silence; that it would enable me to preserve something dear to my heart—the contact with my public within Germany. My books, I said to myself, are written for Germans, for them above all; the outside world and its sympathy have always been for me only a happy accident. They are—these books of mine—the product of a mutually nourishing bond between nation and author, and depend on conditions which I myself have helped to create in Germany. Such bonds as these are delicate and of high importance; they ought not to be rudely sundered by politics. Though there might be impatient ones at home who, muzzled themselves, would take ill the silence of a free man, I was still able to hope that the great majority of Germans would understand my reserve, perhaps even thank me for it.

These were my assumptions. They could not be carried out. I could not have lived or worked, I should have suffocated, had I not been able now and again to cleanse my heart, so to speak, to give from time to time free vent to my abysmal disgust at what was happening at home—the contemptible words and still more contemptible deeds. Justly or not, my name had once and for all become connected for the world with the conception of a Germany which it loved and honoured. The disquieting challenge rang in my ears: that I and no other must in clear terms contradict the ugly falsification which this conception of Germany was now suffering. That challenge disturbed all the free-flowing creative fancies to which I would so gladly have yielded. It was a challenge hard to resist for one to whom it had always been given to express himself, to release himself through language, to whom experience had always been one with the purifying and preserving Word.

The mystery of the Word is great; the responsibility for it and its purity is of a symbolic and spiritual kind; it has not only an artistic but also a general ethical significance; it is responsibility itself, human responsibility quite simply, also the responsibility for one's own people, the duty of keeping pure its image in the sight of humanity. In the Word is involved the unity of humanity, the wholeness of the human problem, which permits nobody, today less than ever, to separate the intellectual and artistic from the political and social, and to isolate himself within the ivory tower of the "cultural" proper. This true totality is equated with humanity itself, and anyone—whoever he be— is making a criminal attack upon humanity when he undertakes to "totalize" a segment of human life—by which I mean politics, I mean the State.

A German author accustomed to this responsibility of the Word— a German whose patriotism, perhaps naively, expresses itself in a belief in the infinite moral significance of whatever happens in Germany— should he be silent, wholly silent, in the face of the inexpiable evil that is done daily in my country to bodies, souls, and minds, to right and truth, to men and mankind? And should he be silent in the face of the frightful danger to the whole continent presented by this soul-destroying regime, which exists in abysmal ignorance of the hour that has struck today in the world? It was not possible for me to be silent. And so, contrary to my intentions, came the utterances, the unavoidably compromising gestures which have now resulted in the absurd and deplorable business of my national excommunication. The mere knowledge of who these men are who happen to possess the pitiful outward power to deprive me of my German birthright is enough to make the act appear in all its absurdity. I, forsooth, am supposed to have dishonoured the Reich, Germany, in acknowledging that I am against *them*! They have the incredible effrontery to confuse themselves with Germany! When, after all, perhaps the moment is not far off when it will be of supreme importance to the German people not to be confused with them.

To what a pass, in less than four years, have they brought Germany! Ruined, sucked dry body and soul by armaments with which they threaten the whole world, holding up the whole world and hindering it in its real task of peace, loved by nobody, regarded with fear and cold aversion by all, it stands on the brink of economic disaster, while its "enemies" stretch out their hands in alarm to snatch back from the abyss so important a member of the future family of nations, to help it, if only it will come to its senses and try to understand the real needs of the world at this hour, instead of dreaming dreams about mythical "sacred necessities."

Yes, after all, it must be helped by those whom it hinders and menaces, in order that it may not drag down the rest of the continent with it and unleash the war upon which as the *ultima ratio* it keeps its eyes ever fixed. The mature and cultural states—by which I mean those which understand the fundamental fact that war is no longer permissible—treat this endangered and endangering country, or rather the impossible leaders into whose hands it has fallen, as doctors treat a sick man—with the utmost tact and caution, with inexhaustible if not very flattering patience. But it thinks it must play politics—the politics of power and hegemony—with the doctors. That is an unequal game. If one side plays politics when the other no longer thinks of politics but of peace, then for a time the first side reaps certain advantages. Anachronistic ignorance of the fact that war is no longer permissible results for a while of course in "successes" against those who are aware of the truth. But woe to the people which, not knowing what way to turn, at last actually seeks it way out through the abomination of war, hated of God and man! Such a people will be lost. It will be so vanquished that it will never rise again.

The meaning and purpose of the National Socialist state is this alone and can be only this: to put the German people in readiness for the "coming war" by ruthless repression, elimination, extirpation of every stirring of opposition; to make of them an instrument of war, infinitely compliant, without a single critical thought, driven by a blind and fanatical ignorance. Any other meaning and purpose, any other excuse this system cannot have; all the sacrifices of freedom, justice, human happiness, including the secret and open crimes for which it has blithely been responsible, can be justified only by the end—absolute fitness for war. If the idea of war as an aim in itself disappeared, the system would mean nothing but the exploitation of the people; it would be utterly senseless and superfluous.

Truth to tell, it *is* both of these, senseless and superfluous, not only because war will not be permitted it but also because its leading idea, the absolute readiness for war, will result precisely in the opposite of what it is striving for. No other people on earth is today so utterly incapable of war, so little in condition to endure one. That Germany would have no allies, not a single one in the world, is the first consideration but the smallest. Germany would be forsaken—terrible of course even in her isolation—but the really frightful thing would be the fact that she had forsaken herself. Intellectually reduced and humbled, morally gutted, inwardly torn apart by her deep mistrust of her leaders and the mischief they have done her in these years, profoundly uneasy herself, ignorant of the future, of course, but full of forebodings of evil, she would go into war not in the condition of 1914 but, even physically, of 1917 or 1918. The ten per cent of direct beneficiaries of the system—half even of them fallen away—would not be enough to win a war in which the majority of the rest would only see the opportunity of shaking off the shameful oppression that has weighed upon them so long—a war, that is, which after the first inevitable defeat would turn into a civil war.

No, this war is impossible; Germany cannot wage it; and if its dictators are in their senses, then their assurances of readiness for peace are not tactical lies repeated with a wink at their partisans; they spring from a faint-hearted perception of just this impossibility.

But if war cannot and shall not be—then why these robbers and murderers? Why isolation, world hostility, lawlessness, intellectual interdict, cultural darkness, and every other evil? Why not rather Germany's voluntary return to the European system, her reconciliation with Europe, with all the inward accompaniments of freedom, justice, well-being, and human decency, and a jubilant welcome from the rest of the world? Why not? Only because a regime which, in word and deed, denies the rights of man, which wants above all else to remain in power, would stultify itself and be abolished if, since it cannot make war, it actually made peace! But is that a reason?

I had forgotten, Herr Dean, that I was still addressing you. Certainly

I may console myself with the reflection that you long since ceased to read this letter, aghast at language which in Germany has long been unspoken, terrified because somebody dares use the German tongue with the ancient freedom. I have not spoken out of arrogant presumption, but out of a concern and a distress from which your usurpers did not release me when they decreed that I was no longer a German— a mental and spiritual distress from which for four years not an hour of my life has been free, and struggling with which I have had to accomplish my creative work day by day. The pressure was great. And as a man who out of diffidence in religious matters will seldom or never either by tongue or pen let the name of the Deity escape him, yet in moments of deep emotion cannot refrain, let me—since after all one cannot say everything—close this letter with the brief and fervent prayer: *God help our darkened and desecrated country and teach it to make its peace with the world and with itself!*

Thomas Mann

Küsnacht, Zurich, New Year's Day, 1937

And so we end with two paragraphs excerpted from a speech by one of the greatest of Americans, Justice Oliver Wendell Holmes. I have included these paragraphs first because they are so magnificently phrased and second because their prescience is almost terrifying. These words were delivered in 1913, some months before the First World War broke out. But they seem to tell, Nostradamus-like, of events just now coming to pass. What could Holmes have meant when he spoke of "competition from new races"? "Whether we can hang together and can fight" is at this moment the supreme question we Americans are asking ourselves. "Battling races and an impoverished earth"—it was a vision in 1913, a reality today. Even that fateful reference to Wagner is a precognition of the Nazi dream of world destruction, and "the new masters of the sky" might well be Stuka bombers. And, let us say it together, the stars that Holmes saw, though still to rise, will rise, and his prophecy be complete.

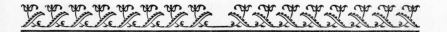

Excerpt from a Speech at a Dinner of the Harvard Law School Association of New York on February 15, 1913

BY

OLIVER WENDELL HOLMES

IF I AM right it will be a slow business for our people to reach rational views, assuming that we are allowed to work peaceably to that end. But as I grow older I grow calm. If I feel what are perhaps an old man's apprehensions, that competition from new races will cut deeper than working men's disputes and will test whether we can hang together and can fight; if I fear that we are running through the world's resources at a pace that we cannot keep; I do not lose my hopes. I do not pin my dreams for the future to my country or even to my race. I think it probable that civilization somehow will last as long as I care to look ahead—perhaps with smaller numbers, but perhaps also bred to greatness and splendor by science. I think it not improbable that man, like the grub that prepares a chamber for the winged thing it never has seen but is to be—that man may have cosmic destinies that he does not understand. And so beyond the vision of battling races and an impoverished earth I catch a dreaming glimpse of peace.

The other day my dream was pictured to my mind. It was evening. I was walking homeward on Pennsylvania Avenue near the Treasury, and as I looked beyond Sherman's Statue to the west the sky was aflame with scarlet and crimson from the setting sun. But, like the note of downfall in Wagner's opera, below the sky line there came from little globes the pallid discord of the electric lights. And I thought to myself the *Götterdämmerung* will end, and from those globes clustered like evil eggs will come the new masters of the sky.

It is like the time in which we live. But then I rememberd the faith
that I partly have expressed, faith in a universe not measured by our
fears, a universe that has thought and more than thought inside of it,
and as I gazed, after the sunset and above the electric lights, there
shone the stars.

CLIFTON FADIMAN *was born in New York City in 1904 and did not appear on the literary horizon until a full nineteen years later, at which time he wrote his first book review for* The Nation.

He was graduated from Columbia University in 1925 and for two years taught English at Ethical Culture High School. He was head editor of Simon and Schuster for six years and since 1933 has worked as book critic for The New Yorker.

The United States at large knows him as master of ceremonies for the radio program "Information, Please!"

Mr. Fadiman has been responsible for encouraging the work of many younger writers in his editorial and reviewing work. He has lectured extensively and is the editor of I Believe, *a book containing the personal philosophies of certain men and women of our times, which was published in 1939. He is one of the four members of the Selecting Committee of* The Readers Club.